THE FIRST AND LAST
KING OF HAITI

THE FIRST AND LAST KING OF HAITI

The Rise and Fall of
HENRY CHRISTOPHE

Marlene L. Daut

Alfred A. Knopf   New York 2025

Library of Congress Cataloging-in-Publication Data
Names: Daut, Marlene, author.
Title: The first and last king of Haiti: the rise and fall
of Henry Christophe / by Marlene L. Daut.
Description: First edition. | New York: Alfred A. Knopf, 2025.
| Includes bibliographical references and index.
Identifiers: LCCN 2024015051 | ISBN 9780593316160
(hardcover) | ISBN 9780593316177 (ebook)
Subjects: LCSH: Henri Christophe, King of Haiti, 1767–1820. | Haiti—Kings
and rulers—Biography. | Haiti—Politics and government—1804–1844.
Classification: LCC F1924.C47 D38 2025 | DDC
972.94/04092 [B]—dc23/eng/20240410
LC record available at https://lccn.loc.gov/2024015051

Jacket image: *His Majesty Henry Christophe, King of Haiti,* (detail), ca. 1816 by Richard Evans. Acervos Documentales de Puerto Rico y el Caribe, UPR–Río Piedras.
Jacket design by Linda Huang

Manufactured in the United States of America
First Edition
1st Printing

But what surprised Ti Noël most was the discovery that this marvelous world, the like of which the French governors of the Cap had never known, was a world of Negroes.

—Alejo Carpentier, *The Kingdom of This World*

They say in Haiti, atop the tall mountain, three-thousand feet above the sea, the ghost of King Henry Christophe, walks again in the lonely hills of his Citadelle like a distraught Hamlet, retracing the steps that took him from the stables of San Domingo to the top of the mountains as king . . . retracing his steps to find which mistake brought him death, which step in the long climb to the kingdom was unwise, miscalculated, misjudged . . .

—Richard Durham, *Black Hamlet*

CONTENTS

AUTHOR'S NOTE ON
TERMINOLOGY

King Henry spelled his name with a *y*. However, many Christophe chroniclers, both in Haiti and abroad, especially those who wrote in the twentieth century, use the more common French spelling "Henri." This biography uses the correct historical spelling of "Henry" when referring to the Haitian king, except for when directly quoting. In a less clear-cut vein, in the nineteenth century Haiti was frequently spelled both inside and outside the country with a *y*, as in "Hayti." While I have naturally reverted to the contemporary spelling, in direct quotations and titles I have made the decision to leave the historical spelling intact. I have adopted the same method for the colony of Saint-Domingue (French spelling), which was frequently called Santo Domingo or San Domingo or sometimes St. Domingo in both English- and Spanish-language sources and sometimes in German- and Italian-language texts as well. In the body of the text, I consistently refer to Saint-Domingue, but I have not changed source references or titles. Readers will also notice that I spell Toussaint Louverture's name the way he spelled it, without an apostrophe, but many eighteenth- and nineteenth-century chroniclers and writers spelled his name "L'Ouverture," a practice adopted by some twentieth-century and contemporary authors. I also spell the names of other revolutionary figures the way they signed their names, as in the cases of Jacques Morpas (written by others at times as "Maurepas"), Charles Belair (written also as "Bélair" with an accent), and Moyse (sometimes written as "Moïse"). Finally, more difficult was deciding what to do about the plethora of French titles, both for nobility (such as counts and dukes) and for published texts and other documents. For the former, I have decided to leave these words in their original format, that is, the Duc de la Marmelade or the Comte de Rosiers, instead of the Duke of Marmelade and the Count of Rosiers, because I find them close enough to English not to be distracting or confusing; while for the latter, I have opted for most titles to translate them into English in the body of the text, but in all cases to leave the source documents in their original French in the source notes.

This is a biography about a man who lived on at least two Caribbean islands, which themselves bounced back and forth between French, Spanish, and British control, who was transported in between to English-speaking Georgia during the American Revolutionary War, and whose wife lived in England and then Italy after his death. It is an appropriately polyglot story that spans from the Caribbean archipelago to British North America to the European continent. Encountering non-English-language words is thus a necessary part of the journey, just as it was part of King Henry's.

PROLOGUE:
KING HENRY'S DRAMA

On April 14, 1936, twenty-year-old Orson Welles directed his first major play. The production was an adaptation of William Shakespeare's *Macbeth* with an all-Black cast. Debuting in Harlem's storied Lafayette Theatre on Seventh Avenue at 132nd Street, the play sold out every one of its 1,223 seats. Ten blocks on either side of the theater had to be shut down due to the overwhelming crowds, and a police escort was required to lead the ticketed through the throng. The play went on to enjoy a sixty-four-performance run before touring the country with its astounding 110 cast members.[1] Though Welles is perhaps most remembered for directing and starring in the 1941 film *Citizen Kane,* which earned nine Academy Award nominations, it was his sensational—and Black—*Macbeth* that first made him a star.

In the original *Macbeth* the title character kills the king of Scotland so that he can become the reigning monarch. As king, Shakespeare's Macbeth meets a tragic end when civil war erupts and his rival Macduff beheads him. It was not the fictional Macbeth's death, however, that so attracted Harlem theatergoers. Inspired by the life of Haiti's first and only king, the formerly enslaved general Henry Christophe of Haitian revolutionary fame, Welles set his *Macbeth* in the early nineteenth-century Kingdom of Haiti rather than Shakespeare's original medieval Scotland, and most of the play's action took place within the backdrop of a large stone castle meant to replicate more King Henry's famous palace at Sans-Souci than Macbeth's royal Dunsinane.[2]

Erected in the early 1810s, Sans-Souci (meaning "without worry" in French) is located in the tiny hamlet of Milot, Haiti, just south of the northern coastal city of Cap-Haïtien. Partially destroyed by a magnitude 8.1 earthquake in 1842, today the palace doubles as a UNESCO World Heritage site, along with King Henry's enormous, fortified castle, the Citadelle Laferrière. Called the Citadelle Henry in the king's day, Christophe's famous fort, which survived the deadly quake, sits atop one of Haiti's highest mountain peaks peering all the way out to the Atlantic Ocean. Deemed the largest fortress in North America and widely hailed as the "eighth wonder of the world," the Citadelle is also the location of

King Henry's grave.[3] Like Macbeth, King Henry met his tragic end when a civil war broke out and the aristocracy turned against him. Yet unlike Macbeth, King Henry took his own life.

In many respects, Christophe lived more the life of a Shakespearean antihero than the Bard could ever have conjured. Born to an enslaved mother on the British-claimed island of Grenada, before his twelfth birthday Christophe found himself in North America participating in the American Revolutionary War. Trudging through the swamps of Georgia, he suffered a wound to the leg while French forces fought the British at the Battle of Savannah on October 9, 1779. By the 1780s, Christophe was still living a life of precarity, but now he was on the French-claimed island of Saint-Domingue, which had the reputation at the time of being the cruelest, and richest, slave colony in the Caribbean.

First visited by Christopher Columbus in 1492, the island was renamed La Isla Española (Hispaniola) by the Spanish who subsequently decimated the native population and instituted a plantation society based on enslaved African labor. The French formally took over the western side of the island in 1697 per the Treaty of Ryswick and renamed it Saint-Domingue. Saint-Domingue quickly became France's most prized overseas possession, producing more sugar, coffee, cotton, and indigo than any other colony in the world.[4] Employed at a hotel in the colony's most bustling city, Cap-Français (later Cap-Haïtien), young Christophe witnessed the constant comings and goings of the slave ships that by 1791 had transported more than 1.3 million Africans from the continent to toil in soul-crushing conditions.[5] He also had a front row seat to conversations about rights of citizenship for the colony's tens of thousands of free men of color, many of whom were also enslavers.

French slave codes initially allowed white men to marry African women after converting them to Catholicism, thereby granting the latter free status. The generations of children that resulted from these unions became known as the *gens de couleur libres,* or free people of color. Determined to preserve some semblance of division between the free people of color, descendants of enslaved African women and white male French colonists, the French passed a series of ordinances depriving free Black people and their mixed-race counterparts of equal rights, including access to the colony's schools and pensions. Some free Black families consequently sent their male children to France to be educated. In France, many of these free men of color witnessed the tumultuous storming of the Bastille prison in July 1789 and watched with hope as the revolutionary rhetoric of liberty, equality, and fraternity eventually led the French populace to overturn monarchical rule.

In August 1789, France's revolutionaries issued the Declaration of the Rights of Man and of the Citizen, in which they announced, "Men are born and remain free and equal in rights." While the emergence of this idea resulted in the creation of a National Assembly that was to initially govern alongside the king of France, this statement had implications back in Saint-Domingue as well. Armed with article 2's assertion that "liberty, property, safety, and resistance to oppression" were "natural and impre-scriptible," Saint-Domingue's *hommes de couleur,* or free men of color, insisted that the French government recognize them as equals.[6]

The idea of a revolution capable of producing equality for all lingered in Caribbean air for the next two years, but little did the white colonists suspect that when the revolution reached Saint-Domingue, it would be led not by free people of color but by the island's enslaved Black population.

Enslaved Africans (approx. 450,000) outnumbered both the white colo-nists (approx. 30,000) and the *gens de couleur libres* (approx. 28,000) by a ratio of nearly fifteen to one. The enslaved soon put this inequality to good use. The Black-led revolution burst forth on the night of August 22–23, 1791, in the northern plains of Saint-Domingue. By the middle of September, the island's Black freedom fighters had destroyed more than a thousand coffee and sugar plantations, and forty thousand of the enslaved were in open rebellion.[7] Eventually led by the famous general Toussaint Louverture, who, like Christophe, had previously been enslaved, the free-dom fighters demanded immediate liberation. Complicating matters for all the island's inhabitants, in January 1793 the French revolutionaries, who had abolished the monarchy to create a republic, executed King Louis XVI and then declared war on Great Britain and Spain. Subsequently, all three nations, England, France, and Spain—the foremost colonial powers in the Caribbean—wrestled for control over the most lucrative sugar colony in the Americas.

The situation took a dramatic and surprising turn in February 1794 when the French republican government, mired in war elsewhere in Europe as well, declared the abolition of slavery throughout all France's overseas possessions. Viewing this as a decisive victory, Louverture and his troops, among whom was eventually Christophe, joined forces with the French to defeat the armies of both England and Spain.

By 1801, Louverture sat at the head of the colony under the title of governor-general. His self-satisfaction is captured by the following state-ment: "I've been fighting for a long time, and if I must continue, I can. I have had to deal with three nations and I defeated all three."[8] The French, British, and Spanish were not Louverture's only rivals, however. In an extremely significant, but not often staged scene of his life, Christophe played an integral role—one he later came to fully regret—in the sequence of events that led to Louverture's capture, arrest, and deportation by the French.

Just as Louverture assumed near-complete control over Saint-Domingue, the Corsica-born French general Napoléon Bonaparte rose to power in France. In 1799, Bonaparte had helped to overthrow the existing government to become his country's first consul. Soon after taking over France, Bonaparte began plotting to defeat Louverture and reinstate slavery. In late 1801, Bonaparte sent his brother-in-law General Charles Victor Emmanuel Leclerc on an official expedition to Saint-Domingue. With thirty thousand French soldiers, Leclerc's mission faced many obstacles. The formerly enslaved population had been free from slavery for nearly a decade and vowed to fight the French if they tried to bring it back. Ever cautious of the optics of such an enormous armed flotilla, while hovering off the coast of Cap-Français, in February 1802, General Leclerc wrote to Christophe, commander over the city, who also held the rank of French general. In the letter Leclerc demanded to enter the port while denying that in sending these troops, part of the largest expedition to ever sail from France, the first consul intended to reinstate slavery. Christophe rightly suspected Bonaparte's deliberate display of military might. Unconvinced by French promises, he ordered Cap-Français burned to the ground after threatening Leclerc: "You will enter the town of Cap only once it has been reduced to ashes, and even on these ashes I will fight you."[9] Despite his overt obstinance, only a couple months later, in late April 1802, Christophe dealt a near-fatal blow to the revolution when he suddenly joined the very French forces he had previously and so ardently fought. His defection was followed by that of Jean-Jacques Dessalines, who later led the freedom fighters to victory against the French and declared Haiti's independence.

After he learned of Bonaparte's July 1802 reinstatement of slavery on the island of Guadeloupe, Christophe, like Dessalines, performed another about-face and reunited with the freedom fighters who transformed the revolution's mantra from "Liberty or Death!" to "Independence or Death!" The damage done by their previous defection was irrevocable, alas. Although Louverture had resigned from his position as governor-general of the colony in May, in June 1802 one of Leclerc's generals tricked Louverture into a meeting, summarily arrested him, along with his wife and children, and then forced them all onto a ship destined for France. The French subsequently imprisoned Louverture without a trial in the Fort de Joux in the Jura Mountains near Switzerland. Louverture's autopsy listed the date of his death as April 7, 1803. French doctors recorded the cause as starvation, pneumonia, and complications from an untreated stroke. Louverture thus never lived to see the hard-fought independence of the island he helped make free.

Christophe's trajectory, in contrast, floated ever upward. On January 1, 1804, after the freedom fighters, now calling themselves the *armée indigène*, or the indigenous army, definitively beat the French, Christophe signed his name, along with more than a dozen other Black generals, to the Haitian Declaration of Independence. Later that year, the Haitian army made Dessalines emperor Jacques I of the newly constituted Empire of Haiti.

Even with independence declared, Christophe's personal and political trials were just beginning. Shortly before he joined the *armée indigène*, Christophe sent his son, François Ferdinand, to Paris to be educated at the school Louverture's sons previously attended. Witnesses claimed that after France's embarrassing loss to Haiti, the French government retaliated by confiscating Ferdinand's belongings and abandoning the child to an orphanage. Christophe's son died penniless and alone on the streets of Paris in October 1805 at the age of only eleven.

One year later, another devastating loss visited the grieving father. On October 17, 1806, members of the emperor Dessalines's own military shot him off his horse on a bridge just outside Port-au-Prince. The emperor died immediately, and afterward his assassins dragged his tattered remains through the streets of Haiti's future capital. Two months later, the very conspirators who orchestrated the assassination ensured Christophe's election to president of a new Haitian state, proclaimed to be not an empire, after the fashion of Dessalines, but a republic, after the fashion of the United States. Worried that Dessalines's enemies might eventually force upon him the same fate suffered by his erstwhile friend and ally, Christophe refused to be sworn into office. Instead, he fled to the northern city of Cap-Haïtien and established a separate state, taking the ostentatious title of "President and Generalissimo of the Forces of the Earth and Seas of the State of Hayti." Another general from the Haitian Revolution, Alexandre Pétion, whom Christophe blamed for the assassination, became president over the republic seated in the southwestern city of Port-au-Prince. These moves effectively sparked a violent civil war between the northern state and the southern republic.

Then, on March 26, 1811, President Christophe radically changed the trajectory of his country when he announced that he would take the title of king; he was crowned in June 1811. By 1813 the Kingdom of Haiti boasted an entire system of nobility, with hundreds of dukes, counts, barons, and chevaliers, and the king began living with his wife and three remaining children in the richly adorned palace at Sans-Souci, whose complex architectural details—including its elegantly manicured gardens, elaborate fountains, sophisticated irrigation system, and unique, domed cathedral—rivaled the most opulent structures of old Europe. Yet the arduous labor it took to construct Sans-Souci and the Citadelle—with rumors circulated that more than twenty thousand laborers died—led to charges that the New World's first king merely brought to it old-world despotism.[10]

King Henry's reign came to a sudden and crashing end when he suffered a debilitating stroke that left an opening for the military and nobles to turn against him. Despondent, on October 8, 1820, the king shot himself in the heart. Ten days later, soldiers from the republic under the rule of Pétion's successor, Jean-Pierre Boyer, executed the king's youngest son and heir to the throne.

—

Since his death more than two hundred years ago, Christophe's tragic story has interested a broad array of playwrights, artists, novelists, and filmmakers across the world. In early 1821, the first work of theater devoted entirely to Christophe's rise and fall, *Christophe, King of Hayti,* was performed onstage at London's Royal Coburg Theatre. The second run of the play, written by the British playwright J. H. Amherst, had the famous Black actor Ira Aldridge playing the king in blackface.[11] But it was writers, readers, and performers from the early and mid-twentieth century who exhibited a near-continuous fascination with the story of the Haitian king and his short-lived kingdom.

The prolific Black playwright William Edgar Easton authored the first twentieth-century rendition of the king's life to make it to the stage, when in March 1912 the acclaimed Black actress Henrietta Vinton Davis directed and starred in Easton's *Christophe, a Tragedy in Prose of Imperial Haiti* at Lenox Casino in New York City. A famous white playwright, Eugene O'Neill, for his part, drew upon the lore of the Haitian king's death by silver bullet in his celebrated *Emperor Jones* (1920), whose title character, Brutus Jones, was played by the renowned Black actor Paul Robeson.[12]

In 1928, Christophe's life gained new appeal offstage with John W. Vandercook's *Black Majesty: The Slave Who Became a King.* Published by Harper & Brothers, *Black Majesty* was chosen as a "blue ribbon book" and introduced the Haitian king to thousands of international readers. Many were already primed with curiosity about Haiti's history due to the United States' ongoing occupation of the country, which began in 1915. Hardly devoid of 1920s-era racial stereotypes, Vandercook at least tried to humanize his subject. The foreword to *Black Majesty* plainly reads, "This is the life of a man. I have added nothing to the sparse records of old books and the fading memories that linger in the minds of men in his own country. Nor have I left anything out, except a few foolish, though extraordinarily common, legends that I found had no historical basis whatever."[13]

Another influential member of the public curious about the Haitian king was the Russian filmmaker Sergei Eisenstein, who purchased film rights to Vandercook's book in 1930. Although Eisenstein's movie was never made, he tapped Robeson, his chosen actor for the principal role in *Black Majesty,* to play Christophe in the second of his aspiring productions about the Haitian king, *The Black Consul.* During a public address in the Soviet Union after his final attempts to make that film failed, too, Eisenstein remarked that the story of the Haitian king was "like a Shakespearean tragedy," with Christophe's downfall occurring after a "breach between him and the Haitian revolutionary masses."[14]

Unable to quell his own enduring interest in formally playing Christophe after the failure of both Eisenstein's productions to reach the screen, Robeson brought the *Black Majesty* project to a different Hollywood director, James Whale, who had worked with Jerome Kern and Oscar Hammerstein of *Show Boat* fame. Whale, Kern, and Hammerstein in turn purchased the film rights to *Black Majesty* from Eisenstein. Robeson then told an interviewer from the *New York Herald Tribune*, "The most interesting thing I can see ahead for next season is the musical play that Jerome Kern and Oscar Hammerstein may do, based on *Black Majesty*, the story of Emperor Henri Christophe, who built his great citadel in Haiti and defeated Napoleon's troops. It sounds like great material, doesn't it?"[15] Unlike Welles's *Macbeth*, *Black Majesty* the musical was never made either.

Welles's success in bringing the tragedy of Christophe as the Haitian *Macbeth* to the stage was not without its own travails. During the four-month lead-up to opening night, there were many who doubted the feasibility of such a production. For one thing, Welles lacked experience. A white man from Wisconsin, Welles had primarily been a theater actor and had directed only a few smaller productions in England. That is, until his friend John Houseman (also white) of the Negro Theatre Unit of the WPA's Federal Theatre Project convinced the unit's co-director Rose McClendon, a distinguished Black actress, that Welles was the right man to bring *Macbeth*—the play that superstition says shall not be named in any theater—to Harlem. McClendon initially questioned whether the African American community would accept Welles as the rightful director of a Black Shakespearean production. However, McClendon relented after Welles's first wife, Virginia Nicolson, persuaded her husband to turn the "Scottish play" into a Haitian play.[16] Potential theatergoers were not so easily convinced. In the weeks before the debut, picketers repeatedly interrupted rehearsals. One overzealous protester attempted an unsuccessful knife attack on Welles himself. Yet opposition to the play seemed to evaporate just as quickly as it had materialized. Defying its many naysayers, the Haitian *Macbeth* became an overnight sensation.

Newspaper critics from across the United States generally extolled the adaptation. They expressed fascination for Welles's substitution of Haitian Vodou for the play's original and more nebulous witchcraft. This unheard-of transposition, with the attendant stereotypes about Haiti and Haitians that it brought to life, eventually earned the popular stage production the nickname "Voodoo *Macbeth*."[17] Welles's comments about why he set in the Caribbean what one critic called his "geographically irreverent *Macbeth*" were in large measure responsible for the exotic nickname and for its association with the rise and fall of Haiti's king.

When Bosley Crowther of *The New York Times* traveled to Harlem to interview Welles around ten days before the opening, Welles wryly remarked that the island setting of the play was not Haiti at all: "It's like the island that *The Tempest* was put on—just a mythical place which, because our company is composed of Negroes, may be anywhere in the West Indies." "As a matter of fact," the director continued with a smirk, "the only point in shifting the scene from Scotland was because the kilt is naturally not a particularly adaptable costume for Negro actors." Welles followed up this artful denial by explaining to Crowther, "The witch element in the play falls beautifully into the supernatural atmosphere of Haitian voodooism." Welles went on to concede that the historical period and figures of his *Macbeth* were drawn after the kingdom and king of Haiti. "The stormy history of Haiti during and subsequent to the French colonization in Napoleon's day—and the career of Henri Christophe, who became the 'Negro King of Haiti' . . . and ended by killing himself when his cruelty led to a revolt—form a striking parallel to *Macbeth*," Welles confirmed. "The costumes and settings of the production are therefore broadly in this period of Haiti's grimmest turbulence."[18] Given Welles's sources, these comments, particularly regarding the costumes, are not as innocent as they might seem.

Welles's biographer Simon Callow has revealed that with his wife's encouragement the *Macbeth* director "set to work with passion, researching the period and the curious figure of the gigantic Grenadian slave" and future king. The main source Welles relied upon was, in fact, a copy given to him by Nicolson of William Woodis Harvey's 1827 *Sketches of Hayti: From the Expulsion of the French to the Death of Christophe.*[19]

A Wesleyan preacher who missionized in Haiti from 1818 to 1824, Harvey had little sympathy, or respect, for King Henry and caricatured him and his nobility throughout the book. "All the officers, whatever their rank or character, were fond of dress to an extravagant degree," Harvey wrote. "But in the expence [*sic*] of their garments, and the ornaments with which they were decorated, they far exceeded the desire of their sovereign, and often rendered their appearance ridiculous" and "supremely fantastical." "Nor was it possible for an European to behold a negro thus arrayed without feeling amused," he said. Of the king's downfall, Harvey provided a résumé of Christophe's character flaws: "If his talents were great, his faults were numerous and glaring. His love of wealth could be exceeded only by his love of pomp and display. The violence of his temper could not always be checked, even by considerations of policy. His cruelty increased, as his ambitious views extended. And the unlimited power which he at length acquired, rendered him, as it has done many others, jealous, capricious, and tyrannical." Harvey concluded, therefore, "Though he was once numbered among the heroes of his country, and the benefactors of his race; the despotism of the latter part of his reign, unfortunately for his fame, has already ranked him among tyrants."[20] By drawing his understanding of the king principally from Harvey's travelogue, and likely a string of others produced in the English-speaking world, Welles ended up making his career promoting what was merely another caricature of an actual person, a historical figure, and an important one at that.

A more faithful retelling of King Henry's life would not emerge until the Haitian historian Vergniaud Leconte published the first substantial biography of Christophe, in French, in 1931. It was followed in 1967 by a mostly sympathetic English-language biography, *Christophe, King of Haiti,* loosely based on Leconte's account and written by the British author Hubert Cole. But the truth is that those who encountered King Henry's story in the twentieth century were more likely to be introduced to his life from fictional and dramatic portrayals.

The king of Haiti's tragic death is one of the most dramatized, and sensationalized, episodes in Haitian history. The Harlem Renaissance–era playwright May Miller, drawing on Vandercook's account, offered a romantic rendition of the king as a sympathetic family man outdone by his own ambitions in her 1935 never-staged one-act drama, *Christophe's Daughters,* originally published in the collection *Negro History in Thirteen Plays.* In the final scene of the play, Christophe's daughters, Améthyste and Athénaïs, and his wife, Queen Marie-Louise, are left to bear, with "half-choked sobs," the burden of the king's body and legacy.[21]

If Robeson never had the opportunity to play the Haitian king onstage, another famous Black actor of the early twentieth century, Rex Ingram, did. In February 1938, Ingram starred in the WPA production of William Du Bois's *Haiti,* subtitled *A Drama of the Black Napoleon,* based on the lives of Louverture and Christophe. Judging from reviews of the play, it was the story of Haiti's king that once more stole the spotlight. The *Amsterdam News* reported, "Rex Ingram's characterization of Christophe completely dominates the scene." Later, the paper noted that the first five days of the play's run surpassed the record set by Welles's *Macbeth* with attendance that reached 4,376 seats.[22]

The former director of the Haitian Centre d'Art and U.S. wartime spy, Selden Rodman, also put the tragedy of Christophe onto the stage in his three-act 1942 play, *The Revolutionists,* while in 1945 Dan Hammerman produced a highly political dramatization of the king's life in his *Henri Christophe* written for the American Negro Theatre in New York City. Just before he kills himself in Hammerman's production, the overwrought Haitian monarch reflects, "I don't know, maybe it's because a man has no right being a king in the first place."[23]

Yet it is Christophe's wife who offers the king a final insight in the host Richard Durham's 1949 two-part radio play about the king, *Black Hamlet,* which Durham wrote and produced for WMAQ out of Chicago. "You made your mistake in thinking your power came from yourself, and not the people," the queen counsels in the moments before King Henry takes his life. "Rebels who won their freedom from planters would not hesitate to take it back from you."[24] And in what is perhaps the most blatantly racist of all the stage productions, the Scottish author James Forsyth's 1975 play *Defiant Island: A Play Based on the Life of Henry Christophe of Haiti,* a character called only "Big Black" cries out just before Christophe shoots himself, with his head rolling to the ground, "I got chains, and you give me them." After this, another character called Dahomey shouts, "He shoot himself! Hisself shoot hisself," to which "Big Black" replies, as he seizes the fallen crown, "The man is dead! Ha!"[25] The tendency of historians, journalists, and artists alike to not just ridicule Christophe in this way but to portray his downfall as both righteous and inevitable has obscured the intricate personal and political events that led to the king's dramatic demise, making him one of the least understood heads of state in the history of the Americas.

For more than two hundred years some of the world's most famous writers have searched in vain for a lesson (or warning) in Christophe's reign. Christophe's life was performed onstage in three plays by the Nobel Prize–winning Saint Lucian author Derek Walcott, *Henri Christophe* (1948), *Drums and Colours* (1958), and *The Haitian Earth* (1984); in *Henri Christophe,* the priest who crowned Christophe cynically declares of the kingdom, "God, what a waste of blood, these cathedrals, castles, built; Bones in the masonry, skulls in the architrave, Tired masons falling from the chilly turrets." As for the king himself, Walcott referred to him in his book of essays, *What the Twilight Says,* as a "squalid fascist" who "chained [his] own people."[26] The Martinican writer Aimé Césaire, for his part, wrote in the prologue to the published version of his at times parodic dramatization of the king, *The Tragedy of King Christophe* (1963), "Sure Christophe was the King. King like Louis XIII, Louis XIV, Louis XV and some others. And like all kings, all real kings, *I mean to say all white kings,* he created a court and surrounded himself with nobility." In a much later interview about the play, Césaire explained that he "portrayed" Christophe "as a ridiculous man" because he "wanted to plunge through the grotesque to find the tragic."[27] Yet it was the Swiss-born Cuban novelist Alejo Carpentier's *The Kingdom of This World*—with its translations into English, French, German, Italian, Portuguese, Dutch, Russian, and Chinese—that has perhaps played the most influential role in promulgating the popular vision of Christophe as an uncommon tyrant.

Carpentier added spectacular lore to prior depictions of the king to explain why most of Christophe's men turned against him in the end. The king of Haiti was "a monarch of incredible exploits," Carpentier wrote, before adding that Christophe cut the throats of bulls every day "so that their blood could be added to the mortar to make [his] fortress impregnable." "The bulls' blood that those thick walls [of the Citadelle] had drunk was an infallible charm against the arms of the white men," Carpentier concluded. "But this blood had never been directed against Negroes, whose shouts, coming closer now, were invoking Powers to which they made blood sacrifice." Carpentier claimed in the prologue that his marvelous realist novel, first published in Spanish in 1949 and then in English translation in 1957, was "based on extremely rigorous documentation." However, judging from his almost entirely invented and historically inaccurate portrait of Christophe—among other obvious mistakes, Carpentier has the king's death occur on August 23, 1820, rather than October 8— it seems that the novelist drew less upon serious sources than on the kinds of runaway rumors about Christophe's reign that had been rampant in armchair sources for some time.[28]

In 1894, long before the dramatic scene of King Henry's death made it into twentieth-century plays and novels, a U.S. newspaperwoman, Fannie Brigham Ward of Michigan, having never traveled to Haiti, added a larger-than-life detail to Christophe's story that has become a myth all its own.[29] She said the king "shot himself with a silver bullet," as if he were a werewolf who could not be killed by lead. Referring to King Henry as a "cruel potentate," she finished her account by claiming that Christophe's Citadelle, which she said "took sixteen years to build," was undertaken with "such cruel treatment of the laborers employed upon it" that "30,000 persons perished in its construction." "There is no doubt that from the dizzy heights of its topmost towers thousands of people were thrown by order of the King," she concluded.[30] Ward's comments underscore that the most incredible and enduring mythology of King Henry's reign remains that of his putative tyranny.

A 1942 article titled "Henri Christophe: The Black Hitler," published in the *Pittsburgh Post-Gazette,* spared no hyperbole either. Elaborating upon a detail about the king's suicide originally included in Vandercook's book, Vincent Towne, the article's author, sinisterly insisted that the king shot himself not with silver but with a bullet made of "solid gold," after his "increasing beastliness and the avarice that had made him a multimillionaire led to an insurrection." Towne had no qualms about comparing King Henry to Adolf Hitler, that murderous German fascist, driving force of the Jewish Holocaust. "Like Hitler, he was cursed by a sadistic taint," Towne wrote. "One of his diversions was to watch several prisoners being flogged to death every morning while he ate a breakfast against a window overlooking the place of execution. Some say these executions were scheduled purely for his entertainment," he wrote.[31] Armed with such sensational journalistic and fictional sources, artists from across the world, one after the other, proclaimed in virtual artistic unison that King Henry had been nothing more than a despot who essentially re-enslaved his people.

A 1983 Spanish-language comic first published in Mexico and then in Bogotá, Colombia, called *Fuego: Majestad negra,* distributed all over the United States and Latin America (Ecuador, Venezuela, Puerto Rico, the Dominican Republic, Panama, Costa Rica, Honduras, El Salvador, and Guatemala), illustrated the king of Haiti's story over an astonishing 192 issues. In the final two issues of the comic, which took its title from Vandercook's *Black Majesty,* the Haitian people celebrate the king's suicide after they have ransacked and destroyed everything in the palace. "I hate everything that reminds me of the tyrant," one man exclaims. "With this, tyranny ends," another character remarks.[32]

In his widely read 1995 book on the history of Haiti, *Silencing the Past,* the famous Haitian historian Michel-Rolph Trouillot acknowledged both the seeming ubiquity of writing about the Haitian king and the world's somewhat uncanny fascination with him, dripping with simultaneous wonder and disdain. As he walked through Christophe's enormous stone Citadelle, Trouillot paused to run his fingers over the marble plaque that marks the spot where the king is buried. "Here lie the remains of King Henry Christophe, the Civilizer, who died October 8, 1820," reads the gravestone placed there in 1848. "I was as close as I would ever be to the body of Christophe—Henry I, King of Haiti," Trouillot thought while standing in front of the plaque. He then tried to explain the ambivalent place that Christophe occupies in the Caribbean literary imagination: "The Society of King Christophe's Friends, a small intellectual fraternity that included Aimé Césaire and Alejo Carpentier . . . were alchemists of memory, proud guardians of a past that they neither lived nor wished to have shared."[33] But just as with the other alchemists of his story, those Caribbean authors did not, with full justice, capture the richness of Christophe's life. Instead, like Welles and so many others, they paid into quasi-supernatural fabulations while turning King Henry's story into literary gold.

The prolific Haitian historian Hénock Trouillot, uncle of Michel-Rolph and fellow member of the Society of King Christophe's Friends, suggested a more practical reason for King Henry's illegibility, and infamy, in global political history. "At bottom, Christophe's greatest mistake," he said, "and that of his partisans, was to have disappeared too early from the scene, which is to say before the future historians of Pétion and Boyer's republic, who were his most pitiless adversaries." In suicide, Christophe could control his destiny, but he could not control his legacy. The British abolitionist William Wilberforce, friend and frequent correspondent of the king, acknowledged as much when he remarked, "Poor Christophe! I cannot help grieving at the idea of his character's being left to the dogs and vultures to be devoured." Vandercook concluded the same: "Christophe, as is often the fortune of great men, has been remembered chiefly by his enemies and the cruel and silly tales they told of him."[34] This is a problem of perspective that affects more than just the story of King Henry.

Despite its rich and full history, Haiti is often discussed by foreigners within a singular frame that revolves around poverty and violence, corruption and disaster—a point readily demonstrated by a 1994 article printed in *The Miami Herald* during the second U.S. occupation of Haiti: "World's Oldest Black Nation 'Ruthlessly Self-Destructive.'" The article's opening paragraph, skirting any historical reference to the United States' first occupation, from 1915 to 1934, insisted instead on an anachronistic parallel between King Henry's rule and that of Haiti's murderous twentieth-century dictator Jean-Claude Duvalier (called Baby Doc), whose henchmen, the Tonton Makouts, brutally executed more than thirty thousand Haitians. "In 1811, it was King Henri I. In 1849, it was Emperor Faustin I. A century or so later, it was Baby Doc who called himself 'President for Life.' Leaders in Haiti have a habit of declaring themselves firmly in control—and for life—only to be toppled by murder, coup or fateful circumstance."[35] After two centuries of almost consistently bad press for King Henry—in which Haitian leaders in general have been accused of "national incompetence," and the populace has been described as at once "progress resistant" and having "deep . . . in the psyche . . . a violence that goes beyond all violence"—telling fuller, more nuanced stories about Haitian historical figures remains an important challenge.[36] As it turns out, the reality of King Henry's life, as often happens, is far more complicated, and interesting, than the fiction.

In the early nineteenth century, Haiti was the only example in the Americas of a nation populated primarily by former enslaved Africans who had become free and independent. Other nations, including Haiti's trading partners, adopted a determined stance to prevent abolition and their colonies from becoming free and so refused to recognize Haitian sovereignty. When France finally agreed to do so in 1825, it demanded the astounding price of 150 million francs for the act. To preserve slavery in its territories, Britain failed to officially recognize Haitian independence until 1838, when slavery was fully abolished in its colonies. The United States refused recognition until after the start of the American Civil War, when most of the southern states had seceded from the Union. Nevertheless, Christophe published trade statistics, which showed that despite their fear of his country's influence on Atlantic world slave regimes, Haiti enjoyed thriving trade relations with plenty of nations, including Spain, Great Britain, Sweden, Denmark, the United States, the Netherlands, Prussia, and Bremen.[37] Writers from the kingdom claimed that any nation whose merchants traded with Haiti had de facto acknowledged Haitian liberty and independence from France. It is a daunting paradox to consider that when Haiti had sovereignty in the early nineteenth century, no other nation was willing to officially recognize it. In contrast, today's Haiti appears to be sovereign, but it remains under the colonial yoke in many ways.

While the contemporary media often portray today's Haiti as a land of perpetrators and victims ever in need of foreign occupation—portrayals that only increased following the deadly January 2010 earthquake in Port-au-Prince and again after the July 2021 assassination of Haiti's president, Jovenel Moïse—the story of King Henry reveals a proud, determined, and self-sufficient country whose culture was admired around the world, but one at the same time whose freedom many nations sought to strangle. Throughout King Henry's reign, France tried repeatedly to "restore Saint-Domingue," which meant to reinstate slavery and colonialism. Christophe insisted that every one of his labor reforms and all his laws, along with every physical structure he built, were meant to ensure that his country would never again fall under the yoke of French domination. King Henry's laws adamantly forbade chattel slavery, outlawed colonialism, and created an economically robust, financially solvent Black state, one not dependent on the transatlantic slave trade. At the same time, understanding the nation King Henry tried to create requires recognition that the world he lived in was one where Haiti's freedom was constantly under threat.

A caption under a photograph of one of the 365 bronze cannons located at the Citadelle displayed in a Colombian Cruises brochure from the 1930s, advertising a twenty-three-day cruise from New York to ten ports in Haiti, reads, "Waiting for an enemy that never came."[38] But come the enemies had, only their best weapon turned out to be imposing debt rather than firing cannons. Christophe was unequivocally against indemnifying France, and his death singularly opened the door for the French to force the Haitian government to pay for with money what they had already earned with their lives. In one of the most unfortunate episodes in Haitian history, France not only impoverished the Haitian people but got away with what may very well be the greatest heist in history. Even though in 1838 France reduced the indemnity it charged to Haiti to 90 million francs, a recent investigation by *The New York Times* confirmed that in the end Haiti paid France 112 million francs, or $560 million over more than a century (amounting to between $21 billion and $115 billion in total losses to the Haitian economy).[39]

Christophe's rise and fall thus tells not simply the tale of one man, and his personal journey from slave to king and the political turmoil that brought him down, but that of an entire nation still struggling to be free. Once one of the most popularly portrayed and well-known Haitian revolutionary figures in the world, King Henry remains as misunderstood now as in the past. Renewed attention to his reign might just restore him to his rightful place as one of the most important political figures of the nineteenth century whose downfall forever transformed Haiti's position in the world.

THE FIRST AND LAST
KING OF HAITI

INTRODUCTION: ON DOING JUSTICE TO CHRISTOPHE'S STORY

What does it mean to try to reconstruct the life of a man whose story has been largely chronicled by people who hated him or who were, at the very least, deeply ambivalent about him? There were times throughout the more than a decade of research that has gone into this book that I wanted to stand up in front of a crowd and repeat these lines from the white American abolitionist Wendell Phillips's famous 1861 speech about Christophe's rival Toussaint Louverture:

> If I stood here tonight to tell the story of Napoleon, I should take it from the lips of Frenchmen, who find no language rich enough to paint the great captain of the nineteenth century. Were I here to tell you the story of Washington, I should take it from your hearts—you, who think no marble white enough on which to carve the name of the Father of his Country. I am about to tell you the story of a negro who has left hardly one written line. I am to glean it from the reluctant testimony of Britons, Frenchmen, Spaniards—men who despised him as a negro and a slave, and hated him because he had beaten them in many a battle. All the materials for his biography are from the lips of his enemies.[1]

Phillips perhaps overstated the lack of first-person materials from Louverture, who was known to pen feisty letters and deliver passionate speeches in service of the freedom of his brethren. Still, his point stands. Almost all Louverture's nineteenth-century biographers, even those who claimed to revere him, reconstructed his life from the letters and papers of some of his most ardent detractors.[2]

As a Black man in a white world of slavery and empire, Christophe could hardly hope to have escaped this dynamic. With only a handful of exceptions, most of the key early chronicles of his life were recorded by his rivals, both Haitian and French, men who passionately hated him. One of Christophe's most fervent and long-standing supporters and his most prominent and prolific secretary, Jean-Louis, the Baron de Vastey, was executed by Jean-Pierre Boyer's army ten days after Christophe's demise. This left a narrative vacuum quickly filled by the king's enemies. Another of Christophe's erstwhile supporters, Juste Chanlatte, the Comte de Rosiers, for example, turned his back on the king almost immediately after his suicide.

A mere twenty days after the king's death, Chanlatte published a bitter missive using his new title, "General Chanlatte, the elder," in which he called Christophe "the scourge of Haiti." Filled with sensational language and imagery worthy of the most grotesque dramatist, the missive referred to the former king as a "big pig (such was the vulgar expression used to describe the rotundity and the ample capacity of his belly, where he put, it was said, the children he had massacred)." "To paint a detailed portrait of his enormous crimes," Chanlatte opined, would require "volume after volume," adding, "There is no language that contained expressions strong enough to fully render either the excesses of his barbarity nor the just horror that they must inspire."[3] Chanlatte's description of Haiti's deceased king soon circulated far beyond Haiti's borders, all the way to Bermuda, more than a thousand miles away. The *Bermuda Gazette* on March 10, 1821, referenced Chanlatte's "hideous portrait of the late Emperor of Hayti," whose "moral and physical features are represented equally horrible and disgusting. He is denominated the scourge of Hayti, and the disgrace of human nature." But the author of the article cynically pointed out that those who had once praised and devoted their lives to the king—after all, not a year before the king's death, Chanlatte staged an opera he wrote for Christophe in honor of Haitian independence—had, not without their own ambitions, very quickly turned against him. "Such, and much more so, is the fallen Henry described by those who have succeeded to his power," concluded the *Bermuda Gazette*.[4]

Chanlatte further defamed his former monarch when on November 5, 1820, a little under a month after the king's suicide, he published a poem in the anti-Christophe republican newspaper, *The Telegraph*. Titled "The First Twenty Days of the Month of October 1820: Is This a Dream?," the poem opens with a stanza that reads,

> Beneath the feet of a tyrant, crushed and withered,
> What had you become? O my dear fatherland!
> The fearful silence and sorrow of the tomb,
> Children, terror made mournful your cradle.
> Alas! where were those wives, those daughters,
> Those fathers and their sons, vain hope of families?
> Who were those beings slaughtered every night,
> Or in horrible irons by Christophe plunged! . . .
> Haiti! what an affront that I cannot understand!
> Put on the *cilice*, and cover yourself with ashes
> . . .

No, this is not a dream: delicious moments!
A bright future is unfolding before our eyes . . .
The throne is unsettled, it wobbles, it crumbles,
And already from the tyrant his soul to hell flies,
Sole refuge that remains for his myriad crimes.[5]

The poem's unambiguous theme is that Christophe was a merciless and debased killer, especially of women and children.

Posthumous defamation of Henry's character can be primarily traced to writers like Chanlatte working on behalf of the rival Republic of Haiti, those who "succeeded to his power," indeed. Charles Hérard-Dumesle (called Dumesle), a journalist, historian, politician, and poet who lived in the southern republic under Alexandre Pétion and then Boyer, admired Chanlatte's writing, repeating and extending the former Christophean nobleman's mostly ad hominem characterization of the king. In 1824, Dumesle published a long narrative—part epic poem, part historical treatise, and part political manifesto—*Voyage to the North of Haiti,* in which he said that Christophe possessed nothing resembling a "spirit of humanity," and that his "natural inclinations were more ferocious than that of a tiger or a panther." For this portrait, Dumesle claimed to have interviewed former subjects of Christophe, "that desolator of the north."[6]

During one of these sessions, an elderly man whom Dumesle referred to simply as "a guide," provided precious biographical information about Christophe, whom the guide claimed to have known, along with highly detailed descriptions of ordinary living conditions in the kingdom. The man accused the king in vivid terms of being an "unheard-of tyrant," one who set up an elaborate system of spying that turned neighbor against neighbor, broke up voluntary marriages to force new unions as a reward for noblemen who served his purposes, instituted a strict and repressive dress code, and frequently ordered corporal punishments for any nobles he determined to have disobeyed him. The guide also offered examples of the capricious executions he described as common in the kingdom.[7] All of this, Dumesle concluded, created a passive, fearful, and ultimately silenced society whose only goal was obedience in service of self-preservation.[8]

That Haitian writers publicly defamed a former hero of the Haitian Revolution opened the door for foreign authors to do so as well. Four years after Dumesle's book appeared, a British traveler named James Franklin, who spent considerable time in Haiti, but only after Christophe's death, published his own damning portrait of the king with his *The Present State of Hayti.* He charged that Christophe had forced women and children, the young and the old, the rich and the poor "to perform that labour which ought to have been performed by brutes."[9] The former British consul to Haiti, Charles Mackenzie, claiming to draw from Haitian accounts, wrote in his 1830 travel narrative that after his victory against Pétion in the battle over the port of Môle Saint-Nicolas, Christophe "butchered some of the survivors, razed the works and even cut down some of the trees that adorned the suburbs." Mackenzie called these acts "a melancholy monument of his vindictive fury."[10] A flood of narratives about the despotic king of Haiti subsequently flowed from the pens of writers around the world who claimed to have lived under his rule or to have interviewed people who did. There were accounts from the British explorer John Candler, the French traveler Gaspard Théodore Mollien, the Methodist preacher William Woodis Harvey, the famous German geographer Carl Ritter, and the Swedish artillery officer Johan Albrekt Abraham de Frese.[11] These alleged eyewitness accounts are remarkable in their repetitiveness: Christophe was a violent tyrant who tortured and virtually re-enslaved the populace.

It would be easy to conclude that Christophe must have been the despot that his enemies from the southern Republic of Haiti always claimed him to be, if it were not for many contrary accounts from seemingly disinterested foreigners who lived in the kingdom, too, like the British botanist William Hamilton, the Black American abolitionist Prince Saunders, and the British lieutenant George W. C. Courtenay.[12] These men spent years living under Christophe, some giving their accounts after his death, when they would have had little reason to fear speaking negatively about him, particularly given the dramatic change in the way that Christophe was being written about in the global public sphere.

Perhaps the account that most underscores how we must use caution in approaching sensational tales of the king's life, specifically those published after his death, is that of the renowned white British abolitionist Thomas Clarkson. In the famous letter he wrote to U.S. clergy denouncing ongoing slavery in the United States, Clarkson asked, "What shall I say of the talents of Henry Christophe, formerly king of a part of Hayti, the son of a slave, and of a complexion as black as jet?" "I corresponded with him for three years, and therefore knew him well. He devised when king, a noble plan for the education of every child," Clarkson explained. "He founded a university, and introduced into it the professors of Latin and Greek, and of mathematics, as well as of sculpture and painting. . . . He had devised also a liberal and well-digested plan of government for his people, but his premature death hindered it from being brought forward." Clarkson then concluded, "May I be permitted to say, without giving you the least offence, that you never had among *all your American presidents* a man of *greater genius* and *talents,* or of a *more acute, penetrating,* and *capacious mind* than the black man now mentioned, though undoubtedly these must have had a better knowledge of the world."[13] In Clarkson's eyes, Christophe's fight for the abolition of slavery and the freedom and independence of the Haitian people set him apart from other world leaders who had the power to eliminate slavery during the exact same time period in which Christophe lived, but chose otherwise.

So beloved was Christophe in certain abolitionist and antislavery circles that the French officer known as Colonel Vincent (Charles Humbert Marie) pleaded his love and admiration for Christophe in a letter to Thomas Clarkson dated October 17, 1820. Unaware that the king had committed suicide nine days earlier, Vincent wrote, "I spent, sir, fifteen years in Hayti in the midst of the revolutionary turmoil," where he saw "the severe and upright" Christophe regularly, and "receive[d] evidence of his affection and his esteem under his hospitable roof." Vincent described having been "pursued by the most duplicitous detention of General in Chief Toussaint, who would undoubtedly have killed me," only for Christophe to have saved him "with unparalleled zeal and activity." Vincent admitted his admiration for Christophe, "the one who reigns at this moment over the most beautiful part of Saint-Domingue, which he alone could pull from under from the chaos," and considered himself "indebted to the king of Hayti solely in relation to the services rendered to me and those quite otherwise important that he renders to the human species."[14]

Tout kòd gen de bout. Every rope has two ends. And every story has multiple sides.

This much was recognized by a British journalist who observed, "Since the downfall of Christophe, he has been represented, according to custom, as an assemblage of every bad quality: however, obvious facts speak in his favor: they can be opposed with advantage to the gratuitous or anonymous accusations directed against him."[15] Those who testified in favor of the king cited not only the schools, hospitals, and other infrastructure he created but his commitment to the fight against slavery. Christophe's military was known for confiscating the living human beings, shipped across the sea on slaving ships like cargo. If these ships entered Haitian waters, Christophe ordered his military to capture them and set the captive Africans free, after which the king granted them citizenship in Haiti.

In January 1811, the northern Haitian military captured a Portuguese slaver carrying two African children, who were as stunned to hear their native language, Hausa, spoken in Haiti as they were surprised to find some of their former compatriots already living there. At an official ceremony, Christophe asked one of the children to dance with him in the style of his former country, and "at the sound of the tambourine this young child performed this dance with astonishing truth, precision, and agility." Afterward, the child's former countrymen smothered him with kisses and caresses. "We might say that they saw in him the family members from whom they had been ripped away," the report concluded.[16] The northern state of Haiti interfered with the transatlantic slave trade again on February 2, 1811, when the Haitian military captured a Spanish ship, the *Santa Ana,* and liberated 205 Africans shackled in the hold.[17]

In October 1817, the *Royal Gazette of Hayti* reported that a Haitian warship had captured a Portuguese frigate near the port of the northern capital, Cap-Henry. The ship was on its way from Cape Verde, off the western coast of Africa, to Havana when officials from the Kingdom of Haiti took control of it and set free 145 Africans, "victims of cupidity and the odious traffic in human flesh." The captives were in a "horrible state," many of them having already perished and the survivors "resembled specters ready to die of misery and starvation." Once ashore in Haiti, a prodigious crowd greeted them with assurances that "they were free and among brothers and compatriots." The account continued, "It is impossible to imagine the joy that animated those unfortunate souls; they rushed to their knees to thank their brothers and their deliverers, shedding torrents of tears." Haitians who witnessed "that touching scene were crying as well." Only the slave traffickers could regard with disdain this scene of simultaneous tragedy and salvation: "The executioners alone were unable to be moved, and were only sorry to see their prey snatched away."[18]

The tendency of historians and artists alike to portray Christophe as an irredeemable monster has obscured the intricate personal and political events that shape even the most controversial life. King Henry's story, recorded in histories and plays, in poetry and novels, and in journalistic accounts, by his friends and his foes, is filled with enough legends and fables, ambiguities and silences, triumphs and failures to preclude anyone from claiming to set down the *true* version. The famous Citadelle completed under the king in 1813 and designed to protect Haiti from foreign invasion represents an unintentional symbol of the multiple possible interpretations of its creator's life. In Derek Walcott's estimation, even if King Henry's enormous fortress marked "the summit of the slave's emergence from bondage," while proving only that "the slave had surrendered one Egyptian darkness for another, that darkness was his will, that structure an image of the inaccessible achieved."[19]

In the early nineteenth century, Napoléon was forced to abdicate his throne twice, and following both occasions, King Henry successfully thwarted the efforts of his successor, Louis XVIII—reinstated as French king in 1814 and 1815—to "restore the French colony," which meant bringing back slavery.[20] Throughout the nineteenth century Haiti faced repeated existential threats to its sovereignty from the United States as well.[21] What nearly all previous chroniclers of Christophe's vexing reign share is failure to acknowledge that the Haitian king had created an independent and prosperous Black nation in a world hostile to the very existence of Black people.

Combing through pages and pages of correspondence, birth and death registers, newspapers published in multiple countries and multiple languages, I have become acutely aware that in my retelling of this life, my responsibility is more to my subjects, Henry Christophe and his family, than to any community. For, as the historian and memoirist Arlette Farge reminds us, "lives are not novels, and for those who have chosen to write history, the stakes are not fictional."[22] In telling the story of the very real life of Henry Christophe—father and son, brother and friend, husband and soldier, slave and king—I have tried to hew as closely as possible to narratives from the king himself, his family members, his allies, and those who personally knew him or claimed to have, regardless of their ultimate feelings and conclusions about him. At times, I felt forced to rely on the accounts of his enemies, but breaking with the ordinary tradition of the biographer who passes silent judgment on the reliability of sources, I also felt it necessary to use my voice to intervene, to provide context and background to help the reader understand the relationship between the chronicler and the subject of the chronicle. I have therefore approached understanding the king of Haiti's early life as a series of stories told about him, ones whose chains of recitation must be corroborated, verified, and counterbalanced against and alongside the new documentation unearthed here, oral and written, including enemy reports, as well as those that paint a more complicated but not necessarily more flattering portrait.

We shall begin, then, with the king's account of his life, or rather with the only account of his life that Christophe commissioned and would have read, the Baron de Vastey's *Essay on the Causes of the Revolution and Civil Wars of Haiti,* originally published in French in 1819, the year before the king's suicide.

1

A FUTURE KING IS BORN

A monument depicting Henry Christophe as one of Haiti's founders sits to this day on the Champ de Mars in Haiti's capital, Port-au-Prince, alongside statues of Generals Toussaint Louverture, Jean-Jacques Dessalines, and Alexandre Pétion. Unlike many other structures, these statues, including the one depicting Christophe as a soldier riding his horse into victory, survived the devastating earthquake that rocked the city in 2010, their immovable marble foundations a testament, perhaps, to the unshakable contributions of these men to Haitian freedom. However, there are stories these statues cannot ever tell, including why, at one time, Christophe turned his back on Louverture and, seemingly, the very revolution with which his name is so indelibly associated; or, how it came to pass that Christophe found himself accused of participating in the plot to assassinate Haiti's first ruler, Dessalines; or, what caused Haiti to eventually be split into two countries, with Christophe ruling in the north and Pétion in the south. Neither can these statues tell us what brought King Henry to believe on that dark October night in 1820 that the only way out of his mounting troubles was through the grave, or where and how his life began on another October day fifty-three years before that, but the voluminous print culture produced by the Kingdom of Haiti just might.

According to the *Royal Almanac of Haiti* for 1814, Christophe was born on October 6, 1767. Yearly publications that the bibliographer Ralph T. Esterquest has described as the "Burke's *Peerage* for Christophe's grandiose kingdom," the royal almanacs stand as the official record of every member of Christophe's family, court, and army.[1] Baron de Vastey seconded the birth date supplied by the almanac; and in his 1819 *Essay on the Causes of the Revolution and Civil Wars of Hayti*, a work commissioned by King Henry, Vastey added the important detail that Christophe was born on the Caribbean island of Grenada.[2]

While contemporary historians have tended to treat Vastey's writings as untrustworthy because he wrote on behalf of a king he loved, the king's own contemporaries viewed Vastey as the most authoritative and comprehensive source.

Thomas Clarkson was well acquainted with Vastey's works, not only because several of them were translated into English and circulated across Great Britain, even receiving reviews in prominent publications of the time, but also because in March 1819 Vastey sent him his 1817 *Political Reflections on Some French Books and Newspapers Concerning Hayti.* A few months later, Julien Prévost, the Comte de Limonade, sent Clarkson Vastey's newly published *Essay on the Causes of the Revolution and Civil Wars of Hayti.* Limonade noted that in Vastey's most recent publication Clarkson would find "a study of the character of the King . . . and discover new reasons for esteeming him ever more highly."[3] Clarkson's response underscores the famous British abolitionist's belief that Vastey, and uniquely Vastey—who called Christophe "the only sovereign, the only black prince, indeed, the only man of our color who can raise his voice effectively, to be heard and to plead . . . the cause of our oppressed brothers"[4]—could effectively communicate the facts of Christophe's life and other salient details of the kingdom to all friends of abolition.

On July 10, 1820, Clarkson penned a thirty-two-page letter to the Haitian king to say that writings like Vastey's were having a measurable effect. "When I was in France five years ago," Clarkson wrote, "I had the mortification to hear your Majesty's Government ridiculed, and your private character stigmatized. During my last journey, however, I had the satisfaction of observing that a considerable change had taken place in the public opinion on that subject, but particularly as to your character as an individual. You are now no longer the cruel monster which the ex-colonists represented you to be." "This happy change," Clarkson continued, "has been effected by your friends, who have circulated (both by means of Books and conversation) many facts relative to your political regulations, of which almost all had been before ignorant." Still, Clarkson thought that more could and should be done to reveal Christophe's "true character," "both as an individual and a legislator." "I would recommend it to your Majesty to avail yourself of the able and respectable talents of the Baron de Vastey by asking him to undertake a small literary work," Clarkson said. In the famous British abolitionist's estimation, familiarizing the French with the Haitian monarch's good character could melt away "those prejudices" that "have hitherto supposed people of colour to be incapable either of knowledge or virtue." Clarkson stressed that Vastey was best suited to undertake this endeavor. "I would advise, therefore, that the Baron de Vastey should directly compose a little work of about 40 or 50 pages only for this purpose; for the shorter the work, the better, provided it comprehended all the necessary facts," Clarkson insisted. But it "must be written by the Baron de Vastey," since "no one of your Majesty's friends in England could write it, because all the documents are in Hayti; and no person could write it who had not witnessed the whole process of the improvement which has taken place in your dominions."[5] While

Vastey's history of Haiti and his descriptions of Christophe's reign were considered definitive in the era, in the absence of government birth and death records later historians seemed unwilling to accept the birthplace and birth dates Vastey indicated.

Yet even if we inexplicably cast aside Christophe's own account of his birthplace and birth date (via Vastey and other works published by the royal press), nearly all those who knew Christophe—with the exception of Juste Chanlatte, the former Comte de Rosiers, who said Christophe was born in Saint-Kitts—state as a matter of fact that the future king was born on Grenada.[6] Hugh Cathcart, the British agent at Port-Républicain (today Port-au-Prince), mentioned that Christophe, with whom he was in frequent correspondence, was "a native of Grenada, and has been upwards of twenty years in this country."[7] The aforementioned Vincent, by way of the pro-Pétion Haitian historian Joseph Saint-Rémy, also confirmed Christophe's birthplace as Grenada and offered several key details about his life there.

Of all the Haitian historians of the nineteenth century, Saint-Rémy used methods—a mix of oral and documentary history—that most closely approximate modern historical methodologies. Unlike many of his counterparts, both domestic and foreign, Saint-Rémy usually sourced his claims, tracing them to archival documents or oral accounts from specific individuals. Before offering precious biographical details about Christophe, some of which could not be found in any other account at the time, Saint-Rémy informed his readers that his information was "almost all taken from a notice by M. de Vincent, director of fortifications in Saint-Domingue, and I owe the communication of these documents to his son, today one of the brightest lights of the Council of State in France."[8] Vincent's testimony allowed Saint-Rémy to write with confidence that Christophe was a "*griffe*, that is to say the son of a Negro and a mulatto, born in the quartier of *Sauteurs* on the island of Grenada on October 6, 1767." In a footnote, Saint-Rémy referenced the earlier mentioned *Royal Almanac* as a corroborating source and indicated that he sought to refute the misconception, repeated by Chanlatte and others, that Christophe was born on the island of Saint Kitts, officially known as Saint Christopher.[9] Saint-Rémy went on to stress that he drew his information from authoritative first-person testimonies, most of which came from the kingdom. The *Almanac* Saint-Rémy relied on was printed and produced in the Kingdom of Haiti for the king, amounting to a form of self-testimony, and Vincent knew Christophe personally. Vincent had worked with the future king in the colony while Christophe was commander over Cap-Français during the rebuilding efforts that followed the great fire of 1793.

One detail offered by Vincent, that Christophe was born in Sauteurs, a parish on northern Grenada,[10] strengthens the testimony of a far more unwitting Christophe chronicler, Philippe Rose Roume de Saint-Laurent, known as the agent Roume. Roume, the son of a white French plantation owner, was born in French-ruled Grenada in 1743.[11] The Roume plantations were located in Sauteurs,[12] where Vincent said that Christophe was born. In this light, Roume's reference to Christophe's birthplace takes on enormous significance.

In October 1799, Roume wrote to General Toussaint Louverture to complain about Christophe's leadership. Roume said his reluctance to punish Christophe came from his feelings of fraternity toward men who were, like him, from Grenada. "Citizen Christophe is a Creole from Grenada," Roume wrote, "and I am in the habit of regarding every person from that island as if they were my own brothers, even though I do not wish to spoil them when they engage in stupidity."[13] Did Roume know Christophe in Sauteurs? If so, what was the nature and duration of their acquaintance on the island they both previously called home?

—

Grenada sits in the eastern Caribbean Sea and is the southernmost island of the West Indian archipelago sometimes called the Windward Islands or the Lesser Antilles. The tiny island—about 345 square kilometers, or 133 square miles—is closer to Venezuela than it is to Martinique, the center of French commerce in the Caribbean for most of the seventeenth century.[14] Though not visible from the South American mainland, from Grenada on a clear day it might be possible to see several of the Grenadines stretching across the horizon.[15]

Grenada has an extremely mountainous terrain, except for the eastern section, Caps-Terre, which contains many fertile valleys and rivulets. These were useful for the construction of water mills on sugar plantations, sugar being Grenada's main export under both British and French rule.[16] In 1650, the French became the first Europeans to "settle" on the island, previously sighted by Christopher Columbus on his third voyage in 1498.[17] Before formal European colonization in the 1600s, the island was populated by various indigenous groups who lived on the land as early as 200–400 C.E.[18]

From the mid-seventeenth century until they ceded the island to the British in 1763, at the conclusion of the Seven Years' War, the French established a plantation society by engaging in violent warfare against native Grenadians and forcibly transporting and enslaving more than 4,000 captive Africans to work the land.[19] This number does not account for those of African descent born on the island whom the French subsequently enslaved, usually referred to as Creoles. In a 1766 census, there were 30,021 enslaved Africans across the island's sugar, cotton, and other plantations. After the Parish of Saint Andrew (Grand Marquis under the French), only the parish, Saint George, and its eponymous city, St. George's, contained more enslaved Africans than Sauteurs, or Saint Patrick, where Christophe was reportedly from, when the census was taken.[20]

Agent Roume's father, the elder Roume de Saint-Laurent, held more than 150 *carreaux de terre* on Grenada, or more than 550 acres of land, on some of which he grew sugar, coffee, and cacao, leaving also a large part uncultivated. While his son eventually became one of the highest-ranking French officials in Saint-Domingue, Roume de Saint-Laurent, the elder, had a prestigious reputation of his own in Grenada. He was reportedly the "first original French resident since 1763 to become a Naturalised British New Subject." As such, he was influential and "one of the few French residents to cooperate fully with the British." For this, Roume de Saint-Laurent *père* was knighted by the British monarchy in 1768. In the words of one scholar, "he received from the British many privileges" and "served as a bridge between the British and growth of isolated French communities."[21] These benefits also accrued to his son, though he, unlike his father, seemed to possess a great affinity for his French roots.

Although Roume de Saint-Laurent *fils* was deeply mired in the "ethnic tensions" between the French and the British that seemed only to increase with the change of imperial control after the Seven Years' War, he had an illustrious career even before his assignment to Saint-Domingue. In 1777, Roume migrated to Trinidad, which also briefly became a French colony from 1781 to 1793. As one of the first French planters to arrive, he helped transform the colony into a slave society while establishing himself as an important government official.[22] Roume then moved on to a position in Tobago and eventually to one in revolutionary Saint-Domingue.

Once on Saint-Domingue, named *agent particulier,* Roume consistently identified with his French identity and exalted French republicanism. This put him at odds with his fellow Grenadian Christophe. Roume was born under French rule, while Christophe was born four years after the British seized control. In his many complaints about Christophe during the latter's time as commander of Cap, Roume blamed the future king's British origins. In a letter to Louverture on November 25, 1799, Roume called Commander Christophe a "bad Frenchman" and an "anglo-maniac" (*anglomane*) who sought to collude with the U.S. and British governments to surrender Saint-Domingue to British control.[23]

Like Roume, some of Christophe's most ardent enemies and detractors referred to his *foreign* origins—his birth outside Saint-Domingue/Haiti— either to paint him as a threat to an established French order, to question his political loyalties, or to suggest his foreign birth was the source of his alleged despotism vis-à-vis the Haitian people. In one report published during Haiti's war of independence in *L'ambigu,* an anti-French newspaper in London, Christophe is described as "one of the principal leaders, who understands English. This has produced alarm, defiance, and an insurrection."[24] During the war of words that later accompanied the civil war between Pétion and Christophe, the authors of an anti-Christophe pamphlet wrote, "At least, Christophe is not Haitian. He is a foreigner; this is without a doubt the reason for which he plagues [Haiti] with death and destruction."[25] But one thing such accounts do not mention is that the man Roume described as an Anglophile soldier previously fought *on behalf* of the French government in service of *American* independence from England, the very country he was later described as seeking to collude with *against* the French.

To understand how Christophe left the land of his birth for French Saint-Domingue, we must look outward again to Vincent. Vincent offered the most suggestive account of Christophe's journey from enslaved Creole child on Grenada to embattled Black soldier participating in the Battle of Savannah in the American Revolutionary War. Vincent wrote that when the French general the Comte d'Estaing attacked Grenada in 1779, young Christophe was traveling between Sauteurs and the capital "with a commission from his master" and happened to be in the town of Gouyave when the French troops disembarked. "An officer, who liked his appearance, proposed that Christophe should follow him. He consented to it. This officer took him to Cap and then to the siege of Savannah."[26]

In 1763, Sauteurs had forty-eight plantations and nearly the same number of proprietors. By 1780, that number had shrunk to around twenty-five owners, many of whom were represented by their lawyers because they no longer lived on the island. Under French rule, the colony was mostly one of *settlers* who inhabited the land they owned. Under British rule of Grenada, as on many other British-controlled Caribbean islands, an absentee plantation society took root, except for the highly populated city of Saint George's (Basse-Terre). So, who was this "master," on behalf of whom young Christophe, only eleven years old, went to the populous capital on the coast with a mysterious commission that took him clear to the other side of the island and then up north to Gouyave on his way home?

Vastey remains one of the most important sources for the claim about Christophe's service at the Battle of Savannah. In his *Essay*, Vastey said Christophe had been wounded in the leg there. Yet Vastey did not offer any genealogical information about the king's parents or mention whether the king had been previously enslaved and by whom.[27] A detailed account of Christophe's parentage and early years in slavery can, in contrast, be found in Dumesle's *Voyage to the North of Hayti*. While getting Christophe's year of birth wrong (putting it in 1758, the year of Jean-Jacques Dessalines's presumed birth), Dumesle's source, the man he called his guide and who claimed to have known the king, offered an interesting explanation for the belief that Christophe was born on the island of Saint Kitts; at the same time Dumesle affirmed Vincent's claims about Christophe's origins in Grenada and parental genealogy. "Henry Christophe was born on Grenada, about the year 1758, even though many say that he was born on Saint Christopher and was taken while very young to the latter island." Christophe's mother was "a victim of the slave trade, she was sold to an American of African and European descent" who made her the governess of his children. She lived with this man "in intimate circumstances, which gave others and Christophe himself the idea that he was the son of this man." One distinct difference between Dumesle's account (as provided by the guide) and those of Roume and Vincent is that Dumesle's drips with the sensationalism that characterized southern and foreign Christophe biographies. "Be that as it may, from his earliest years he showed vicious inclinations, and that penchant for evil which never left him," Dumesle continued. "One day he was committing a theft when his alleged father caught him in the act and kicked him so hard that one of his legs was badly damaged. An unbridled passion for gambling often dragged him into the same fault; the man who had been his protector until then, but in whom the impure breath of the colonial system had corrupted all feeling, decided to sell him; this circumstance influenced the rest of his life." After this tragic abuse, Christophe was taken to the island of Saint-Thomas, "where his mother and his family had been living for some time." It was there that Christophe supposedly turned twenty-one and became the "confidant and companion in debauchery of his new master." The guide's account grew only more salacious and unbelievable after this recitation. "After he fell in love with a woman, his true character unfolded in all its hideousness," the guide said. "Jealous to the extreme, everything he saw aroused his suspicions." This mysterious woman who captured Christophe's heart was a prostitute. "An illicit commerce, which the colonists, in all their corruption, viewed as necessary for enslaving this new race of Americans, bound him to this woman and she became pregnant." The story then took an even more lurid turn. Christophe returned home at one point to find his female companion alone in the company of another man. "The Furies agitated his soul and he took a knife out and opened her breast with it." Authorities were set to punish Christophe when his "master" intervened to protect him by hiding him. After saving his life, the "master" sent Christophe clandestinely to Savannah to fight in the American War of Independence. Humanity had nothing to do with Christophe's salvation, Dumesle warned. The master's motives were mercenary: Christophe's enslaver "received an indemnity that was equivalent to his price, and Christophe, incorporated among the volunteers, was rightfully freed."[28]

The erroneous birth date in Dumesle's account underscores how easy it was, preying upon the voids created by lives not well documented, to invent the most fantastical tales of detraction. Christophe, born in 1767, not 1758, was too young to have committed many of the acts Dumesle described, especially impregnating a woman when he was only ten years old. Dumesle's account might be simple fabulation, but it might also represent the kind of mistaken identity common in southern writings about members of the northern kingdom.

Writers from the southern Republic of Haiti previously charged the Baron de Vastey with having slaughtered Frenchmen in Brittany during the French Reign of Terror. Confused with a family member with a similar name who did participate, Vastey, who was born in 1781 in Ennery, Saint-Domingue, had reached only his twelfth birthday by the time of the infamous 1793 *noyades de Nantes* (drownings in Nantes). Yet the rival Haitian journalist Noël Colombel claimed that Vastey had been in Nantes at the time with the notorious French revolutionary Jean-Baptiste Carrier, "that representative of barbarity, for whom he became a henchman and one of the most vile cronies."[29] The problem with this story, other than the unlikelihood that someone so young would be so important to someone like Carrier, is that Vastey was not in Nantes in 1793. He was in Rouen, at the home of his uncle Pierre Valentin Vastey, with whom he had resided since arriving in France in 1791 with his father, Jean Valentin Vastey, and his older brother. Letters between Jean Valentin Vastey, who eventually went back to Saint-Domingue, and his brother Pierre in Rouen suggest that the Vastey children, including the future baron, remained in Rouen for the duration of their stay. Both boys left France definitively to return to Saint-Domingue on March 8, 1796.[30]

In the southern republic, half-truths and no-truths alike were often exploited for political gain. In 1818, Colombel published another pamphlet taking aim at the king and his family. In his *Reflections on Some Facts Relating to Our Political Existence,* not only did Colombel repeat the rumor that Christophe ordered pregnant women murdered, but he said the king almost killed his own child simply because the baby was crying. "His own son, Monseigneur le Prince Victor, when he was only a few months old," Colombel writes, "was sleeping in the room where his father slept. The baby, experiencing some need, started to cry. Furious that the cries of his noble progeny had interrupted his slumber, [Christophe] rushed upon the poor royal offspring, like a madman, grabbed him by one leg, and was going to throw him out the window when his companion, who was right next to him, stopped his arm and prevented him from committing infanticide."[31]

When Christophe learned that the rumor that he tried to kill his son had circulated beyond Haiti, the king laughed heartily at both the absurdity and the implausibility. The British captain George W. C. Courtenay revealed that at one dinner Christophe mentioned the French "practice of inventing the most ridiculous stories about him." Referring to an even more exaggerated version of Colombel's tale, Courtenay wrote, "Amongst others, he mentioned one that lately appeared in their newspapers, of his having, in a paroxysm of rage, thrown the Prince Royal from a window of the palace for having disturbed his sleep." Christophe then pointed to the plump prince Victor, who was also at the dinner, while laughing. "These Frenchmen highly compliment my strength," Christophe remarked. "I fear that would require more than I am master of even to lift so stout a fellow."[32]

The French traveler Gaspard Théodore Mollien, who lived in Haiti for several years and claimed to have interviewed the king, offered a more plausible account of how Christophe went from being a child slave to a child soldier. Affirming once more the Haitian king's birth on Grenada, Mollien wrote, "His father was a mulatto, his mother, a negress slave, of the Ibo nation," an ethnic group in what is now Nigeria. "Christophe was therefore a *griffe*, even though he always tried to pass for black," Mollien explained, using the pseudoscientific racial terminology of the era. "His father, far from recognizing his son, did not buy him; it has even been asserted that he burdened him with more ill-treatment than anyone else; at least Christophe repeated this often, remembering it with bitterness." One day Christophe evidently brought up his father in Mollien's presence, remarking that "if ever chance brought him into his dominions, he would have his father dragged on the rack like the most odious of men." Christophe, on the contrary, spoke highly of one of his uncles, telling Mollien that it would have pleased him to see his uncle in Haiti and seat him "on his right hand, that was his expression." Mollien also explained how Christophe came into the orbit of the famous Comte d'Estaing, hero of the French siege of Grenada. "When d'Estaing seized Grenada in 1778 [*sic*], Christophe was taken with many other slaves and was saved from fate by several officers of the expeditionary army. He fell in with a Comte de Lauzun and followed him to Cap, and from there to the siege of Savannah, where he was wounded." Like Dumesle and his guide, Mollien got Christophe's birth date wrong, putting it at around 1760.[33] In addition, the siege of Grenada took place in July 1779, not 1778. Mollien's account, nevertheless, is the one whose order of events—whereby Christophe went from Grenada with d'Estaing's fleet after the French reconquest of the island, then briefly to Cap, and then on to Savannah—remains most logical.

—

The Comte d'Estaing left Toulon, France, with orders from King Louis XVI to fight with the American colonists in the American Revolutionary War on April 13, 1778. His fleet of seventeen vessels and frigates arrived in the southern United States on July 5 of the same year. Upon landfall, they captured a British privateer after five and a half hours of violent combat. After this, d'Estaing and his men, who did not include Armand-Louis de Gontaut, the Duc de Lauzun (mentioned in Mollien's account), set out for New York, where British forces had retreated following a major loss to General George Washington in Philadelphia and Delaware. The French fleet engaged in several successful but difficult military operations in Pennsylvania before they headed farther north to Rhode Island at the end of July. The squadron, lacking food and water, began to grow weary and, according to one French soldier, had grown even more distressed by the time they reached Boston in August. For nearly two months, they lived on a mere two ounces of rice and three cups of water per day.

When their new provisions arrived, d'Estaing's fleet did not return to France or head south to the Caribbean. Instead, they left Boston in early October and engaged in naval warfare in the Atlantic for two months. Their difficulties mounted. In addition to lacking provisions, they experienced equipment failures and damage to their ships. It was not until December 5 that d'Estaing, already in the South Atlantic, decided to change course and sail to Martinique to await new provisions. His fleet arrived on the ninth of that month.[34]

In contrast, de Lauzun, a French nobleman from Paris, served in the French marine, or navy, in Africa at the time. His detailed diary of his experiences and travels in the military reveals that he remained in Senegal after d'Estaing reached Martinique and never served in Grenada or Saint-Domingue, and therefore could not have been the one who took Christophe to Cap.[35] De Lauzun did, however, previously serve on a ship commanded by Louis-Philippe de Rigaud, the Marquis de Vaudreuil, who left him in Senegal to join d'Estaing's enormous fleet in Martinique in April 1779.[36] This fleet afterward made its way to Grenada, land of Christophe's birth.[37]

Before attempting to take away the Windward Islands, including Grenada, from King George III of England, d'Estaing's fleet needed to await provisions in Martinique. On June 27, the fleet, along with that of the Comte de Grasse (François Joseph Paul), saw arrive six more vessels and two frigates from the fleet of the famous general known as La Motte-Piquet (Count Toussaint-Guillaume Picquet de la Motte), after whom a street and a metro stop in contemporary Paris are named. La Motte-Piquet had among his troops eighteen hundred men originally destined for Saint-Domingue. With three massive fleets now ready to attack, d'Estaing ordered French forces to prepare to sail toward Grenada. On the morning of the thirtieth, twenty-five ships and ten frigates or privateers, with several boats and schooners, sailed from Fort Royal to lay siege to Grenada.

The impressive fleet arrived in sight of the island on the morning of July 2. By that evening, thirteen hundred French troops had landed, eventually joined by five hundred more. D'Estaing marched his troops toward Hospital Hill, overlooking the capital, where the English had concentrated their forces and all their hopes of success. On the night of July 3–4, the French, led by d'Estaing, the Vicomte de Noailles, and the Irish Comte de Dillon, attacked the British fortifications. Forcing through the entrenchments and batteries, they drove out the British troops in only one hour, according to d'Estaing's official report. As soon as the French troops seized Hospital Hill, they sought to ascend the Citadelle to proclaim their victory, but d'Estaing would not allow it. He gave an order instead to turn the cannon of the battery toward the Citadelle. At the first shot, the governor of Grenada, George Macartney, raised the parliamentary white flag and the firing ceased. Day had begun to break when the French squadron saw the flag appear on the battery of the hillcrest. But d'Estaing initially rejected Macartney's terms for a cease-fire, and the battle recommenced until three o'clock in the afternoon, when Macartney finally surrendered his colony, his troops, and his person. At the end of his report on the battle, the Comte d'Estaing concluded, "It would be difficult to find a post more inaccessible and more defended by nature than Hospital Hill, and it is impossible that any other troops could have shown more ardor and more valor than those who seized it." Still, d'Estaing lamented the loss of life that accompanied the victory. "The enemy's loss on this occasion was less considerable than our own," he concluded. "They had three officers killed and about thirty soldiers; the loss of the troops of the king amounted to thirty-nine men killed and sixty-seven wounded."[38] By July 5, French troops took possession of the fort, eventually capturing about seven hundred British prisoners. Was young Christophe among their number? Or perhaps Christophe was in the Saint George's port when the French took possession of twenty-one British merchant ships and thirty other boats. Or maybe he was on one of the nearby islands of Bequia or Carriacou, also part of Grenada, when they were subsequently captured by the French, along with all the British munitions there. Against all odds, the French won back the island they first claimed many decades earlier, with cries of "Vive le Roi" heard on all the vessels.[39] It was only then that d'Estaing prepared to sail toward Saint-Domingue.

Even if our young Christophe had already left Grenada at the time of the siege—as per Dumesle's account, which has him born in Grenada but taken to Saint Christopher and then Saint-Thomas—the sequence of events and the ships that d'Estaing had with him on his journey to Cap-Français are key to understanding how Christophe might have arrived in Saint-Domingue with d'Estaing's fleet by July 31, 1779, in time to join the same fleet when it set sail for Savannah, Georgia, in August.

On July 15, the French squadron left the Windward Islands after having embarked all the English prisoners. Five days later, an even larger fleet—having embarked hundreds of men and joined with additional ships, even as some of the frigates that fought at Grenada were dispatched elsewhere—arrived in Guadeloupe, where they repelled British forces again. The British were still anchored at Saint Christopher, and d'Estaing intended to meet them there. On the twenty-second, at daybreak, French troops arrived on Saint Christopher and encountered British gunfire. The French fleet attempted to circumnavigate the British vessels and sounded the cannon alarm. D'Estaing succeeded in losing the British ships and considered himself victorious.[40]

In a draft report meant for the government, d'Estaing explained the events that took his troops all over the Windward Islands after this, to all the places where Christophe was suspected of having been from or having lived prior to Saint-Domingue: Grenada, Saint Christopher, Saint Vincent, and the Grenadines. "His Majesty's squadron, after the naval combat and the taking of Grenada . . . received the oath of loyalty" from the islands of Carriacou and Bequia, "which led to the surrender of the other small Grenadine islands, which put the entire archipelago under the obedience of His Majesty [of France]." Afterwards, d'Estaing's fleet led the boats and merchant ships of the Windward Islands to Cap-Français, where they arrived on the last day of July.[41]

—

What we know for sure is that young Christophe somehow made his way from Grenada to Saint-Domingue. But did he watch the arrival of d'Estaing's enormous fleet from one of the boats, as most of the eyewitnesses say, or from the shore, as claimed Christophe's first biographer, the early twentieth-century Haitian historian Vergniaud Leconte?

According to Leconte, who offers an illuminating account of Christophe's early years—but one whose chain of recitation is not always clear—the future king of Haiti was "born free, having descended from a free father and mother." However, "he was so rebellious and disagreeable that his father placed him aboard a French *caboteur* whose captain he knew." The situation became precarious rather than protective for young Christophe when "the captain, for one reason or another, relieved himself of this duty, on one of his trips to Cap-Français, by entrusting the young child, not by selling him, as Carl Ritter says, to a Mr. Badèche, owner of a sugar factory in Petite-Anse, on the Portelance estate."[42] There was a sugar plantation owned by Madeline Portelance in Limonade, and another Portelance plantation was in Quartier-Morin in the environs of Cap-Français.[43] Yet a third plantation in Petite-Anse called Madeleine (sometimes spelled "Magdeleine") was owned by citizen Porte-lance. An extensive search, however, has not thus far produced any trace of young Christophe on these plantations. The Quartier-Morin Portelance plantation, nevertheless, was not far from the one called Saint-Michel, where a much older Christophe, then a commander in the French army, leased a plantation in the late 1790s.[44]

After working for several years for Badèche, Leconte claimed that when d'Estaing came to the island looking for recruits for his already immense army, "Christophe, who was only twelve years old, and in whom a bellicose and enterprising temperament had already manifested itself, went on his own initiative to be registered." Following closely the account given by Dumesle, Leconte wrote that Christophe subsequently became one of the *chasseurs-volontaires,* or the free men of color from Saint-Domingue who served as soldiers, alongside his fellow future revolutionaries André Rigaud, Jean-Baptiste Chavannes, and Louis Jacques Beauvais.[45] Although the Austrian naturalist Carl Ritter, whose account Leconte evoked, did live in the kingdom for a short time under Christophe (albeit, without ever meeting the king), and to whom the alleged error is attributed in other sources as well, the first known chronicler to claim that Christophe was previously enslaved was someone who, unlike Ritter, knew Christophe personally: Hugh Cathcart.[46] We also find this claim in the first-person testimonies of Vincent and the unnamed elderly guide, as recounted in the works of Saint-Rémy and Dumesle, respectively; and the British consul Mackenzie, in residence in Haiti from 1826 to 1827, claimed to have even met the daughter of the "French gentleman" who had enslaved Christophe.[47]

Although so many of those who knew Christophe during his life claimed he was once enslaved, borrowing almost verbatim the details in Leconte's account, in his 1967 biography of Christophe, the British historian Hubert Cole suggested that Christophe was deliberately circumspect about his early life. "For political reasons he was always imprecise about his family background," Cole claimed, "but it seems probable that one of his parents was not of pure Negro blood (his own complexion was not black but a deep red-brown) and that he was born free."[48] Ritter's much earlier claim that Christophe was not enslaved on Grenada—and which likely informed Leconte's and Cole's accounts—found echo in a newspaper article published in Port-au-Prince in 1842. "It is a generally known fact that this extraordinary man was born on the island of Saint Christopher, one of the West Indies: hence, the name of his country which has been added to his proper name." "The reason he had to go abroad," the article continued, is that Christophe "struck, it is said, a young white man of his own age, in a quarrel they were engaged in together, and according to the colonial laws of the time he was to be condemned to have his wrist slashed. His parents, to save him from this punishment, made him leave in secret, and he was taken to Saint-Domingue. Like so, a simple brawl of which no one has ever before heard, powerfully influenced the destiny of the island where he took refuge."[49] That Christophe's putatively free Black parents could consider Saint-Domingue, a land of terror and torture far more ensconced in slavery than any of the British Windward Islands, a possible asylum for their young Black child is difficult to conceive.

By the 1770s slavery in Saint-Domingue was already infamous. The French naturalist Michel-René Hilliard d'Auberteuil, sent by the French crown to Saint-Domingue to record the colony's natural history, lamented, "The majority of the negroes from Guinea ordinarily die after the first three years of being transported, and the laborious life of a negro born in the country does not usually surpass fifteen years." Although "since 1680 we have introduced more than 800,000 negroes into the colony," by the time of his writing, he said, "there existed only 290,000." Hilliard d'Auberteuil clarified, "It is not diseases that have weakened the black population to this extent; it is the tyranny of their masters."[50] None of the laws of France could prevent the colonists from killing the people they enslaved, who "perish daily *under chains or the whip*" and who were "knocked out, suffocated, [and] burned without any procedure."[51] Asking the people of France to hear these lamentations cost the naturalist: his book was pulled from circulation the year after its publication in 1776. The French Council of State decreed that "it contained otherwise reprehensible material; the author allowed himself by serious imputations, contrary to the truth, to attack the administration of the leaders of Saint-Domingue."[52] Still, the book circulated long enough and far enough for copies to reach England and the United States, as well as the colony of Saint-Domingue.

In 1814, the Baron de Vastey still had a copy of Hilliard d'Auberteuil's book to cite, including the above passage about enslaved Africans being daily assaulted. Noting the author's unabashed prejudices against Africans and people of African descent, Vastey found it strange that the government banned the book after having previously approved its publication. "What is more surprising is to see that a work like the one in question here, which could have saved those miserable colonists from themselves, by presenting them with methods of ameliorating and alleviating the lot of the unfortunate slaves and so-called free people," wrote Vastey, "that such a work, presented to the minister of the marine, approved by him, and printed with the approval and privilege of the king, was later suppressed as a dangerous book, by ordinance of the [same] king." Vastey knew that even a prejudice-filled book that dared to "show more humanity than the infamous colonists" was the problem. The government censored the book simply because its author "had reported to the French ministry merely a small fraction of the atrocities and abuses that then prevailed in Saint-Domingue." [53]

It is tempting to imagine Christophe somehow having escaped such abuses and terrors. The more likely scenario is that, like so many Black children living in the age of slavery, Christophe was forcibly separated from his parents and other kin.

An enslaved woman born on Bermuda, Mary Prince, offered a painstaking first-person account of the day she was separated from her family members at the age of twelve, before being forcibly moved around the Caribbean by various "masters." The "natal alienation" she describes stands as a monument to the enduring evils of slavery.[54] "Oh dear! I cannot bear to think of that day,—it is too much," Prince lamented. "It recalls the great grief that filled my heart, and the woeful thoughts that passed to and fro through my mind, whilst listening to the pitiful words of my poor mother, weeping for the loss of her children. I wish I could find words to tell you all I then felt and suffered." "The great God above alone knows the thoughts of the poor slave's heart, and the bitter pains which follow such separations as these," she continued. "All that we love taken away from us—Oh, it is sad, sad! and sore to be borne!" The sorrow of separation on the auction block had generational consequences. "I then saw my sisters led forth," she recalled, "and sold to different owners: so that we had not the sad satisfaction of being partners in bondage." "When the sale was over, my mother hugged and kissed us, and mourned over us, begging of us to keep up a good heart, and do our duty to our new masters. It was a sad parting; one went one way, one another, and our poor mammy went home with nothing." Prince had searing words for the theater-like atmosphere that accompanied the bondage and sale of her and her sisters: "Did one of the many by-standers, who were looking at us so carelessly, think of the pain that wrung the hearts of the negro woman and her young ones? No, no! . . . slavery hardens white people's hearts towards the blacks."[55]

Yes, it is tempting indeed to imagine a less traumatic origin for the future king of Haiti, a less dramatic separation from his parents. I, too, would prefer to believe that this child had agency and choice, like those Christophe chroniclers who paint him as an intrepid and determined youth, or that his parents were able to protect their Black child in a world that was all too accustomed to treating Black children as commodities to be bought and sold at auction.

In *Black Triumvirate,* a 1957 study of Louverture, Dessalines, and Christophe, Charles Moran concluded of the debate about whether the Haitian king was born with free or enslaved status, "His panegyrists have tried to prove that he was born of free parents. Fortunately, they have not succeeded. It is the fact that he was born a slave that makes his life so extraordinary."[56] In the absence of unimpeachable evidence, or chains of recitation (Moran offers none either), we shall consider all possibilities as we follow a young Christophe, not even twelve years old, to Saint-Domingue and then to Savannah, Georgia, to the American Revolutionary War. The fact that Christophe participated in the American fight for independence is one of the most remarkable parts of the future monarch's early life.

2

A CHILD IN A WORLD OF
SLAVERY AND REVOLUTION

By the time he reached his twelfth birthday, Christophe found himself participating in the American Revolutionary War at the Battle of Savannah, under the command of the famous French general Charles Henri Théodat, the Comte d'Estaing. Christophe was not the only Black soldier from the Caribbean to fight for U.S. freedom. Joining him was Louverture's storied rival André Rigaud and the fellow free men of color Vincent Ogé and Jean-Baptiste Chavannes. A monument to these fighters, called the Chasseurs-Volontaires, sits today in a shady square in Savannah, Georgia, depicting Christophe as a drummer boy. Although he caught a bullet in the leg, Christophe managed to survive the war. Many of those he fought alongside did not. The French spectacularly lost this campaign. We can only imagine the kinds of atrocities that Christophe witnessed before he was even thirteen years old. Haunting memories and psychologically catastrophic visions are the hallmarks of PTSD. While the deep and dark scars from multiple whippings etched into the back of Jean-Jacques Dessalines can be found in descriptions of him, much less discussed is Christophe's own tragic early history, and how the events of his most tender years might have emotionally and mentally, as well as physically, scarred him.

It would be hard to exaggerate how the arrival of the Comte d'Estaing's victorious fleet was anticipated and longed for in Saint-Domingue, where he previously ruled as governor-general. Even before the siege of Grenada, on January 26, 1779, the colony's official newspaper, the *Affiches américaines,* breathlessly reported d'Estaing's appearance in Martinique at the end of the year prior. "The arrival of the Comte d'Estaing in Martinique has been confirmed by the parliamentarians coming from Jamaica," the paper reported. "We have even been assured that it will not be long before we see him arrive here in Saint-Domingue."[1] A week later, on February 2, the *Affiches* carefully detailed the decorated war hero's movements: "Among the news extracted from Puerto Rico, by a Spanish ship, it was announced that Monsieur d'Estaing on his arrival in Martinique blocked Admiral Barrington, who was busy laying siege to Saint Lucia with seven ships of the line and seventy-six transport boats." Noting, however, that this prior information had been a false report (common at the time), the *Affiches* clarified, "The arrival in Port-au-Prince of the king's frigate, the *Andromaque*, commanded by the Chevalier de Buort, has contradicted all of this":

> The English are indeed in Saint Lucia, but they are in control of it, and our efforts to prevent them have so far been useless. The number of transport vessels that followed M. d'Estaing has increased to eighty. This vice admiral has been in Martinique for about a month and a half. It is said that he is waiting for the Comte de Grasse who will soon join him with six ships of the line. This report has been confirmed by a corsair from Antigua who arrived in Saint-Eustache on January 14.[2]

Such descriptions not only have much to tell us about d'Estaing's movements as he plotted the French reconquest of Grenada, Saint Vincent, and Saint Lucia but also demonstrate how seafarers ushered in an age of information highly dependent on vicissitudes of the sea and the goodwill and accuracy of those who sailed it.

Just a week after the *Andromaque* brought news of d'Estaing's actual whereabouts, an article in the *Affiches* lamented that this was the only news they had thus far been able to attain in Saint-Domingue about the French position in its battle with Great Britain over the Caribbean, a less well-trodden but vital part of the American Revolutionary War. "Everything is pretty calm here in Saint-Domingue," the writer explained. "The theater of hostilities is in the Windward Islands, where there is no doubt that the English, in control of Saint Lucia, will seek to extend their conquests." The safety of Caribbean waters and the successful siege of the Windward Islands all depended on d'Estaing. "Mr. d'Estaing, who observes them from Martinique, is surely in a position to oppose their slightest efforts," reported the *Affiches*. If he could only meet up with de Grasse, "whose arrival he awaits any day," d'Estaing "will be able to rush upon our enemies and will make them pay dearly for the moment of success from which they can derive no long-term advantage," the paper concluded.[3]

Jubilance practically jumped off the page when the *Affiches* eventually reported, via a Dutch ship, that the Comte de Grasse, accompanied by six vessels, four frigates, and a hundred transport boats, had finally arrived in Martinique, where d'Estaing awaited him. "We are awaiting the details with impatience," the paper noted, "and we will immediately hasten to communicate them to our readers."[4] By the time of the April 6, 1779, issue, the *Affiches* was still waiting for updates about d'Estaing and de Grasse's whereabouts and any information about the status of the war.[5] By July 20 the paper offered some tentative news: "M. the Comte d'Estaing has taken

Saint Vincent, and is currently engaged in the siege of Barbados." The paper cautioned, however, "We do not affirm this news as absolutely true, our correspondent in Port-au-Prince having derived it from a private individual who arrived in Jacmel from the Windward Islands."[6] The Saint-Dominguan press had to wait for the vice admiral to appear to gather definitive details of the famous siege that likely brought young Christophe to Saint-Domingue.

The ship carrying d'Estaing docked in the harbor of Cap-Français at four o'clock in the afternoon on July 31. In the days following his arrival, the inhabitants of the city treated d'Estaing to the fanfare and laurels of a celebrity. Saint-Dominguans expressed awe at the sight of the massive fleet.[7] They were proud of their former governor for reconquering Grenada, Saint Vincent, and the Grenadines. For this, d'Estaing's name would go down in French history. D'Estaing's celebrity endured on Saint-Domingue far longer than Grenada and Saint Vincent remained in France's possession. These Windward Islands were returned to British rule at the Treaty of Versailles in 1783, after which they did not gain their full independence from the British crown for nearly two hundred years.

Admiration for d'Estaing back in France was long and deep too. As early as 1766, there was a merchant ship from Bordeaux named the *Comte d'Estaing,* while d'Estaing's famous siege on Grenada was almost immediately transformed into an uncanny romantic play by Jean-Marie Collot d'Herbois titled *The French in Grenada; or, The Impromptus of War and Love.* First performed in Lille, France, in September 1779, the play went on to be staged throughout Provence the same year, and then in Cap-Français in September 1781. In the preface to the print edition, the author remarked that actors from Lille had learned to perform the play in less than four days. The Comte d'Estaing took less time to conquer Grenada and beat Admiral Byron, the playwright observed, and he hoped this play might be worthy recompense for the successes of the French army. "What wellborn Frenchman, living under Louis XVI, does not feel disposed, when he hears the story of such successes, to perform for the service of his king, something better than a piece of theater?" Collot d'Herbois asked. "For at least there is a bit of patriotism evident in performing such shows; and it is in their success that those who work for it find their reward." *The French in Grenada* was performed again in Saint-Domingue in 1784 after having been performed in Versailles for the honor of the king and the count himself.[8]

D'Estaing was no less loved or remembered in the eighteenth- and nineteenth-century United States, particularly in Georgia. In December 1785, the *Affiches* reported that d'Estaing had accepted twenty thousand acres of land from Georgia, "with the intention that he announced to found an establishment there, which will be devoted to public utility."[9] Yet in the mid-twentieth century the city of Savannah stopped just short of naming "a memorial battle park" after him. The president of the Georgia Historical Society condemned d'Estaing for failing to stop a mob from marching on Versailles in 1790: "There was no whiff of grape shot in 1790 that might have ended the French Revolution then and there." The count, for his part, told the revolutionary tribunal that eventually sentenced him to be executed by guillotine, "During the entire time I had command I took every precaution that was within my power in order to prevent any opposition being made to the intent of the people." This episode, coupled with complaints about d'Estaing's attitude during the Battle of Savannah—one French officer wrote that no soldier "dared open his mouth," since "no one was more fixed in his opinions or as stubborn [as the vice admiral] in his convictions"—disqualified him from this honor in Savannah. Still, the society acknowledged the count's bravery. "If there is question of the Count's judgment there is no question of his valor. During the attack there is a pathetic picture of him standing on the old road to Augusta below Springhill Redoubt, his wounded arm in a sling, trying to rally groups of soldiers and send them forward after one of the most disorganized attacks in military history."[10] Would young Christophe, reportedly fighting with the regiment of troops of color raised by d'Estaing, have had a chance to meet the famous and infamous vice admiral? Let us examine the latter's trajectory on Saint-Domingue to glimpse the way the old French count's destiny intersected with Haiti's future king.

—

The Comte d'Estaing's whiteness and uncontested free status endowed him with the privileges of a life well recorded. In contrast, as we saw in the previous chapter, Christophe's earliest years stand for the most part undocumented. Citing the birth date of October 6, 1767, given in the *Royal Almanac,* Moran concluded of this precious detail, "That so unimportant event as the birth of one more Negro child should have been so carefully recorded seems somewhat remarkable. It will take more than a Royal Almanac to satisfy the inhabitants of St. Kitts, who insist that he was a native of their island, and cite his name in support of their contention, slim evidence though this be."[11]

Meticulous documentation from the French national archives shows that Charles Henri Théodat, the Comte d'Estaing, was born on November 24, 1729, in Château de Ravel in Auvergne, France. According to his birth certificate, his parents were Charles François d'Estaing, the Marquis de Saillant and Vicomte de Ravel, and Marie Henriette Colbert de Maulevrier.[12] D'Estaing came from reportedly "illustrious origins." One of his ancestors had saved the life of Philippe Auguste at the Battle of Bouvines and, in so doing, "acquired the right to wear the full arms and livery of the king."[13] His noble birth undoubtedly helped d'Estaing to rise at a young age. The "Detail of Services" issued for him in 1792 by the French state notes that d'Estaing, a decorated military officer, served in the military for nearly all his adult life. He became a "musketeer" in 1745, and by the following year he had become a captain in Auvergne. From 1748 to 1763, d'Estaing rose through the ranks: regiment colonel, then brigadier, then camp marshal, then lieutenant, and eventually lieutenant general of the naval army. From 1764 to 1766, d'Estaing served as governor-general of Saint-Domingue and became vice admiral of the seas of Asia and America in 1777. In 1792, the French republic commended d'Estaing for his "navigation, valor, good conduct, zeal, patriotism, and former services as vice admiral" in promoting him for the final time to the rank of admiral.[14] While he was guillotined during the French Revolution, in 1794, the famous Comte d'Estaing went down in history as lieutenant general of the armies of the earth and admiral of the armies of the sea; until 1918, no other French officer had belonged at the same time to the army of the earth and that of the sea.[15]

Before being named governor-general of Saint-Domingue, d'Estaing had never visited the colony. Inexperience did not prevent him from quickly adapting to and adopting the ways of the white colonists, whose favor he sought to curry through benefactions. D'Estaing ordered regular feasts and elaborate celebrations, particularly in the port where "the harbors, dotted with ships, resounded with the noise of musical instruments." D'Estaing's goal was to create a rapprochement between the "traders who feed the colonists," the plantation owners, or enslavers of human beings, "and the colonists who supply materials for trade." This concurrence was supposed to spread joy and complement the frequent festivities held at the Government Palace. Yet while the white colonists and other people with free status "delivered themselves up to pleasure," d'Estaing alone "sometimes slipped away, followed by a single aide-de-camp," said the *Affiches*. During those parties, instead of taking part, the governor "rapidly transported himself a hundred leagues away, to the other extremity of the island, to survey the public prosperity from there." While Saint-Domingue offered a life of luxury, leisure, and pleasure to any colonist desiring it, d'Estaing supposedly preferred sleeping outdoors, "lying at the foot of a tree, with no other shelter, no bed other than his coat." This vision of d'Estaing, man of nature, sleeping soundly and safely outside, led the *Affiches* to conclude, "This man is not of this age, say his enemies; and too bad for this century!"[16] Enslaved Africans forcibly transported by the French to Saint-Domingue would not have experienced the island's wilderness as bucolic or its festivities as pleasurable. They endured a life of terror and torture.

The white French colonists of Saint-Domingue practiced some of the cruelest slave tortures in the entire Atlantic world. As slavery became more steadily ensconced on Saint-Domingue into the late eighteenth century, marronnage, or fugitivity, increased as well. French colonists exacted ret-ribution upon freedom-seeking enslaved Africans with cold recalcitrance. In a detailed exposé, Haiti's Baron de Vastey recorded the crimes against humanity and heinous tortures that more than a hundred French colonists inflicted on the people they enslaved. The colonist Corbierre liked to bleed his "blacks" and use their blood to clarify the sugar. For the slightest fault he ordered them burned alive. "One day one of his cows died from epi-zootic disease [*maladie épizootique*]," Vastey observed, "and wanting to avenge himself of this inevitable loss, he opened up a great pit, and both the cow and the guardian were buried inside it." Vosanges, planter in La Mine, "outdid" Corbierre, Vastey continued. He chained together two of the men he enslaved, and during their captivity one of them died, and the barbaric Vosanges buried the two victims in a single pit at the same time. The colonist Darech, on simple pretext, had his slaves burned alive, while Déville had them "broken with a bar." The colonist Voyare surpassed them in cruelty: "He had them broken [at the bar] and cut off their private parts." The authorities, far from intervening, were equally sadistic. Lom-bard, *conseiller,* or councilor, at the Conseil Supérieur (Supreme Court) of Cap-Français, amused himself by cutting the ears of the Black people he enslaved, and when he had rendered them into this "cruel state," he burst into "uncontrolled laughter." Courtin, seneschal judge, "had them flogged to death and hanged as a hobby."[17] Even without these cruel torments, life on Saint-Domingue was exceptionally brutal for the enslaved population.

From the late seventeenth to the late eighteenth century, enslavers forc-ibly brought over a million captive Africans to the colony. The tortur-ous labor conditions under French rule created an extraordinarily high death rate for enslaved people. When the revolution broke out in 1791, only around 450,000 enslaved Africans lived on the island, including those born there.[18] The Comte d'Estaing participated in all the monstrosities of slavery. He owned one small sugar plantation, the d'Estaing plantation in a hilly neighborhood above Cap-Français, where he enslaved more than a dozen Africans and their descendants. He purchased the property in 1764 and put it up for sale about fifteen years later.[19]

The 1778 for-sale advertisement for the d'Estaing plantation placed in the *Affiches* offers some information about the plantation and the people d'Estaing enslaved there. It was "a small plantation located in the hills of Cap, with sixteen heads of Negroes, both large and small, belonging to M. the Comte d'Estaing." Because the vice admiral was by that time an absentee owner, the advertisement instructed potential buyers to contact his proxy holder.[20] In November 1780, more than two years later, when the plantation had still not been sold, its dissolution was to be adjudicated to the "highest and last bidder, in cash," by the Barre du Siège Royal du Cap. This later notice tells us much about the opulence and wealth that even the most minimal holdings could produce in a slave colony. The plantation "consist[ed] of thirty-two *carreaux*[21] and six tenths of land, established as a garden, with a small mill and fruit trees." The property also featured

> a main house constructed with masonry, tiled and covered with shingles. . . . [O]n the two wings of this building are two cabinets, kitchen, oven, and vegetable garden, which forms a square closed off by a wooden skylight: another building 60 feet long, partly in masonry, forming a 36-foot-long-by-13-foot-wide hutch, and a 14-foot-long aviary enclosed in archal wire: in front of the large café is a terraced garden 160 feet long by 100 feet wide; at the support of the wall of the terrace, there are eleven huts for Negroes, the separations of which are composed of masonry: a barnyard of about 40 square feet, enclosed by walls, serving as a bullpen, and in which is a dovecote on polished masonry: two terraced gardens of 40 feet each in a square: another garden also on the terrace 150 feet long by 50 wide, and several other gardens. There are water sources on this plantation, which means it is easy and inexpensive to water the gardens.[22]

The history of the people d'Estaing enslaved on his seemingly idyllic plantation was also unwittingly recorded in the same pages as the sale of his land. Theirs is a very different story.

Nearly every issue of the *Affiches américaines* and the *Supplément aux Affiches américaines* contained ads and notices alerting the public about slave fugitivity (marronnage) and enslavers seeking the return of maroons, who freed themselves from the torturous conditions of plantation life. The section of the paper ordinarily called "Nègres marons" (sometimes spelled "marrons") listed fugitives who had been captured and were being held in jail until their so-called owners recovered their "property." The section called variations of "Esclaves en maronage," or "Slaves in marronnage," contained notices for fugitives who were still at large and whose enslavers hoped to make it impossible for them to enjoy free status in another city or parish, as in a fugitive notice for an enslaved woman accused of stealing money. Flore, listed as a "Négresse Congo," was about twenty-eight or twenty-nine years old when her "master" reported that she had gone maroon on April 11, 1766. He described her as having a "long nose, wide mouth, thick lips, mediocrely dressed, walking slowly, a bad-tempered look, not very talkative." According to him, Flore was a talented seamstress, but she was not branded, and therefore "she might be able to say she is free," and "she will perhaps also have a fake billet."[23]

The "Esclaves en maronage" tended to be more detailed than the "Nègres marons" section. Enslavers usually offered as much description as they could about "runaways" in the hopes they might be recognized. Still, the "Nègres marons" section in some ways reveals more than its more obviously granular counterpart because it relied on the captured Black subject for identifying details. Sometimes the incarcerated individuals refused to give any clues about their identity, including who previously enslaved them and could therefore claim ownership over them. The "Nègres marons" section remained one of the only places where enslaved people's own testimony about their identity was recorded. It is also where we learn about the terrible conditions inimical to plantation living.

An enslaved man named Joseph, from the d'Estaing plantation, shows up in the official record, having become visible in a new way upon his capture. During his incarceration at the Port-de-Paix jail, he told authorities that he belonged to the Comte d'Estaing, governor-general of the colony.[24] In 1766, another man d'Estaing enslaved, "a mulatto named Antoine, of a nice height, belonging to M. the Comte d'Estaing, has been maroon since July 9."[25] In November of the same year, Louis, a sixteen-year-old, described as a "very ugly mulatto," from the d'Estaing plantation, also became a maroon. The notice finished with the same instructions as those for Antoine: he was to be arrested on sight.[26]

The horrors of the slave market allowed details of the lives and identities of captive Africans to be recorded too. At the Barre du Siège Royal du Cap, we learn that an enslaved "Negress" named Pélagie, described as a "good laundress, belonging to M. the Comte d'Estaing," was to be sold alongside a schooner called the *Marianne*.[27] In August 1769, we learn what happened to the young Louis who earlier ran away from the d'Estaing plantation: authorities captured and returned him, after which d'Estaing had him sold, only for him to run away again.[28] An enslaved woman named Babet had details of her life recorded in the "Nègres marons" section, too, after authorities arrested and incarcerated her in the Fort-Dauphin jail on March 3, 1769. Described as "a Negress" from the "Fon nation," Babet had been branded on both breasts "with a great iron." She said she belonged to the Comte d'Estaing.[29]

Long after d'Estaing left the colony, long after he even owned a plantation there, the people he once enslaved continued to live with his name crudely stamped on their bodies—unfailing evidence of the tyranny of enslavers. "Perhaps the first letters learned by the unfortunate slaves . . . were the initials of the colonists," observed the eminent Haitian historian Jean Fouchard, "their black chests stamped with red iron thus becoming their first syllabary."[30] The initial sin of the first colonist to enslave a particular captive African had ricocheting consequences, recorded haphazardly through the brands on their body. These marks usually lasted the enslaved person's entire life. If an enslaved African had more than one "master," his or her body could be covered with names. This was the case with César, recorded as a "Negro" newly brought to the colony from the Gold Coast of Africa. He was stamped on one breast CASTRA and on the other with the family name of the governor-general of the colony who replaced d'Estaing, PR. DE ROHAN. This man's body, rather than any piece of paper, revealed that the Chevalier de Rohan's maternal grandfather, Prince de Rohan, enslaved him.[31] The body was simultaneously an enslaved person's archive and their enslavers' indictment.

So much information can be gleaned from descriptions of the so-called stamps. In May 1781, Drieau Lataille, owner of a hotel in Cap-Français, purchased a human being called Jean-Pierre who had at least two previous owners. Determined not to live under slavery, Jean-Pierre, listed as a "negro" who had previously escaped, took off again three days after Lataille bought him. A fugitive notice in the *Affiches* described him as from the "Congo nation," noting that he was stamped on one breast GAULON and on the other GARNIE, while above that was yet another stamp, LATAILLE AU CAP. Before entering the slave market once more, authorities arrested Jean-Pierre in Marmelade.[32] Not even the accumulated disfiguration of three separate stamps could discipline Jean-Pierre out of the inimitable freedom he enjoyed in Africa and into everyday terror and torture as a Saint-Dominguan slave.

Multiple stamps were common into the 1780s, as the enslaved population—those forcibly introduced from Africa and those born on the island—rose steadily. In January 1782 an ad appeared for Antoine, enslaved on the Bréda plantation, where Toussaint Louverture was born, enslaved, and later freed. Antoine, described as a Congo, was enslaved by M. Bayon de Libertat, for whom Louverture worked for several years after his emancipation. The stamps on Antoine's body revealed broad strokes of his life under slavery: the right breast read BREDA, while the left side was burnished with FRANCIOSY.[33] Another notice from August 14, 1781, described a "Creole from Grenada" in marronnage stamped J.B. & Ce and above that PAPCE. The man's name was Louis. He was five feet, three or four inches tall and could speak French, Spanish, and English. Louis, whose skin was "very black" and whose eyes were "small," knew how to read and had taken off in marronnage on July 30.[34] Of the many notices for enslaved people engaged in marronnage after 1779—when Christophe likely arrived in Saint-Domingue—it is this one that leads us back to the story of the Haitian king.

In the "Effects for Sale" section on August 24, 1779, a notice appeared for an upcoming auction for the "sale and adjudication to the highest and last bidder, of the quantity of twelve English Negroes taken in the port of Grenada on different boats and schooners, by the squadron of M. d'Estaing, during the conquest of that island."[35] After the siege, d'Estaing and his troops arrived at Saint-Domingue with at least twelve "English Negroes" whom they proceeded to sell.

We must pause to contemplate the possibility of young Christophe on *this* kind of auction block. Whether initially enslaved or enjoying free status on Grenada, if, as an eleven-year-old Black child, Christophe did find himself somehow on one of the many ships that made up d'Estaing's fleet from the Windward Islands, what protections might he have had once he arrived in Saint-Domingue? His freedom could have been imperiled in the Caribbean's most notorious colony in several ways, including being sold at auction to the highest bidder. So many vicissitudes of enslaved life are recorded in that wretched archive of the fugitive slave notice. The *Affiches* allows us to trace how some of the Grenadians sold in Saint-Domingue naturally rebelled, still dreaming of and striving for freedom.

Ships appearing in the port provided myriad opportunities for escape. A young enslaved man of about eighteen, described as a "Creole" named Jean-Pierre and "having a lock [*guigne*] on one of the toes of his left foot," ran away in July 1781. The notice advertising Jean-Pierre's *marronnage* observed that "he had previously escaped by way of the squadron of M. the Comte d'Estaing, in August 1779." Having unsuccessfully stowed away on one of the ships in d'Estaing's fleet, Jean-Pierre decided to try again. For a few days, "he took refuge on one of the king's vessels that are in the harbor." In the same issue, we find still more stowaways connected with d'Estaing's fleet:

> Two Negroes, one named Silvain, of the Congo nation, stamped GOUX ET MARIE-ROSE AU CAP, about nineteen years old, with a *nabot* on his foot and an iron collar on his neck; and the other named Michel, from the Dutch nation, without a stamp, saddle maker by profession, aged about forty-five, also having an iron collar with a chain that he broke to escape, left as maroons from the home of Sieur André, their master, on the twenty-fifth of this month. These Negroes had embarked with the squadron of M. the Comte d'Estaing, when it was in Cap; it is presumed that they were able to do the same: consequently, Sieur and Dame André request the captains of the vessels, as well as the merchant captains, to be kind enough to have inspections carried out on board their vessels and merchant ships and, in the event that they find foreign Negroes there, to have them arrested and taken to the jail.[36]

In the absence of clear information about how Christophe went from Grenada to Saint-Domingue to Savannah and back, what is important to understand is how it could have happened. Recall that the eyewitness Mollien, while mistaken about certain other details, claimed that after d'Estaing conquered Grenada, Christophe was captured with other enslaved individuals.[37] If Christophe sought to save himself from slavery, he might have run away from that Saint-Dominguan slave market or from a planter who purchased him. This allows us to imagine how he could have succeeded in finding refuge with the very fleet that likely brought him to Saint-Domingue in the first place.

It is painful to imagine our young Christophe, not yet having even celebrated his twelfth birthday, seeking to escape a carceral colony of terror
and misery by putting himself at the mercy of the French military as well
as the whims and winds of a merciless sea. Instead of reforming, or better yet eliminating, the system of terror and torture that was slavery, the
Comte d'Estaing, as governor-general, ingratiated himself with the colonists while enriching himself as a plantation owner and enslaver. D'Estaing
also strengthened the island's military by reforming the local militia, particularly the white troops, the Grenadiers, and the troops made up of free
men of color, the Chasseurs-Volontaires. It was with these troops that
Christophe found his way to Savannah, Georgia.

The Chasseurs-Volontaires corps was created by a 1762 ordinance of
the governor-general of Saint-Domingue: "This corps will be composed
of *free* Negroes and mulattoes, all of goodwill, serving without any other
commitment than that of performing more precisely the personal service to which they are already subject."[38] Even if Christophe had been a
stowaway on one of d'Estaing's ships, he ostensibly could have, through
maritime marronnage, gained freedom from slavery by enrolling in the
Chasseurs-Volontaires. In 1765, d'Estaing issued an ordinance regulating
these troops, reiterating that the Chasseurs-Volontaires were to be *gens
de couleur libres*: "All free people of color shall be required to serve in
the First Legion from the age of sixteen through nineteen"; "All newly
freedmen will only be able to enjoy their freedom after having served three
years in the First Legion or having found a replacement." The ordinance
also addressed how newly emancipated people of color could be replaced
by "non-free stand-ins," suggesting that it was theoretically possible for an
enslaved person to serve in a free person's stead, after which the enslaved
person would be freed. Free status would still therefore have been on the
horizon for an enslaved individual enrolled in the militia in lieu of his
"master." If an enslaved Christophe did join the militia in this way, perhaps it was in the hopes that this freedom would one day apply to him:
"The stand-ins who replace free people will be required to serve six years;
they will be treated as free and will obtain their freedom after this time."[39]

Might Christophe have seen or heard about a notice in the *Affiches* that
had appeared on April 6, 1779, recruiting both white and troops of color
to aid d'Estaing in his Caribbean conquests? It began with an appeal to
the French sense of honor—"Who is the Frenchman who does not feel the
courage and ardor within him at this moment reborn, the desire to go and
fight the enemies of the state?"—and goes on to describe the two categories of volunteers, the Grenadiers and the Chasseurs-Volontaires. Saint-
Domingue was a society dominated by color prejudice and segregation.
The military, too, was divided according to racist practices and beliefs.
"The first of this corps must be composed of whites and the second of
Negroes, mulattoes, and free people of color. . . . whole companies have

been formed, and all are burning to march with the expedition that is being prepared," read the notice.[40]

The 1779 ordinance regulating this corps stipulated once more, like its predecessors in 1762 and 1765, that the six hundred members of the Chasseurs-Volontaires were to be free subjects, *gens de couleur* from Saint-Domingue. The corps would comprise ten free companies consisting of a captain, a lieutenant, a sous-lieutenant, a quartermaster, four sergeants, eight corporals, sixty-four fusiliers, and two tambour players, or drummers.[41] The passing mention of the drummers is significant: a monument in downtown Savannah commemorating the troops of color from Saint-Domingue who fought for American liberty famously depicts Christophe as one of these drummer boys.

The monument, finished in 2007, displays several plaques explaining the statues as a "project of the Haitian American Historical Society": "The largest unit of soldiers of African descent who fought in the American Revolution was the brave 'les Chasseurs Volontaires de Saint-Domingue,' from Haiti. This regiment consisted of free men who volunteered for a campaign to capture Savannah from the British in 1779. Their sacrifice reminds us that men of African descent were also present on many other battlefields during the revolution." Young Christophe stands slightly apart from the other six soldiers, one of whom has fallen to the ground. A separate engraving explains, "This drummer represents young Henri Christophe, who participated in the October 9, 1779 Battle of Savannah. Christophe later became a leader in the struggle for Haitian independence from French colonial rule, ending in 1804. A commander of the Haitian army, he became king of Haiti, being among the first heads of state of African descent in the Western Hemisphere." D'Estaing's 1765 ordinance is the key to understanding how Christophe came to be characterized as a young drummer rather than as a young warrior, for it contained this clause: "Free Negroes over the age of twelve may be engaged as trumpeters or drummers."[42]

The creators of the monument enshrined the names of some of the other hundreds of Chasseurs-Volontaires who fought alongside Christophe too. "Although hundreds of other 'chasseurs volontaires' remain anonymous today," an engraving below the statues reads, "a number of them are documented and listed below":

Pierre Astrel
Louis Jacques Beauvais
Jean-Baptiste Mars Belley
Martial Besse
Guillaume Bleck
Pierre Cangé
Jean-Baptiste Chavannes

Henri Christophe
Pierre Faubert
Laurent Férou
Jean-Louise Froumentaine
Barthélemy-Médor Icard
Gédéon Jourdan
Jean-Pierre Lambert
Jean-Baptiste Léveillé
Christophe Mornet
Pierre Obas
Luc-Vincent Oliver
Pierre Pinchinat
Jean Piverger
André Rigaud[43]
Césaire Savary
Pierre Tessier
Jérome Thoby
Jean-Louis Villate

Saint-Rémy was among the first historians to provide a comprehensive list of the Haitians who fought in Savannah. His list is shorter and differs slightly from the one on the monument: "Rigaud, Beauvais, Lambert, Christophe Morney [sic], Villate, Bleck, Beauregard, Tourreaux, Féron, Cangé, Chavannes, Martial Besse, Léveillé, Mars Belley," and so on, but not Christophe.[44] The mid-nineteenth-century Haitian historian Thomas Madiou, in contrast, acknowledged Christophe to have been present; and the late nineteenth-century Haitian historian, Énélus Robin, repeating Saint-Rémy's list with Madiou's addition, added the name Jourdain.[45]

The late nineteenth-century African American historian T. G. Steward provided a list of the Chasseurs-Volontaires who fought at the Battle of Savannah that deviates slightly from the ones given by Haitian historians. "In an official record prepared in Paris, now before me, are these words," Steward wrote, " 'This legion saved the army at Savannah by bravely covering its retreat. Among the blacks who rendered signal services at that time were: Andre, Beauvais, Rigaud, Villatte, Beauregard, Lambert, who latterly became generals under the convention, including Henri Christophe, the future king of Haiti.' " Steward, unlike his predecessors, provided a documentary source, a chain of recitation, for his claim: "This quotation is taken from a paper secured by the Honorable Richard Rush, our minister to Paris in 1849, and is preserved in the Pennsylvania Historical Society. Henri Christophe received a dangerous gunshot wound in Savannah."[46] Like many historians before me, I attempted to track down the document Steward referenced.[47] I was not discouraged by the fact that George P. Clark concluded many decades ago, "after extensive search," the document could not "be located in the Society's collection, nor does the library have any record of its ever having been acquired." I sympathized with Clark's frustration when I also failed to locate the document in question, but I cannot agree with his conclusion that there is not "any original documentation to support Steward's Homeric list of Haitian heroes said to have been present at Savannah, not least among them Henri Christophe."[48] The most important document written about Christophe's life is the one he commissioned from Vastey who published his *Essay* in 1819, while the king was still living. Vastey wrote that Christophe was wounded at the Battle of Savannah. We can hardly dismiss this document in order to condone Clark's curious declaration that "what is missing, unfortunately, is primary documentation from the Haitian side—documentation which might offer on-the-scene reports from some of the Chasseurs Volontaires themselves."[49] Moreover, André Rigaud's official "État de service," or record of service, which bears his signature, also confirms his participation in the Chasseurs-Volontaires of Saint-Domingue who fought in Savannah, during which Rigaud suffered three small wounds, including one to his head.[50]

If Christophe confirmed his own participation in a roundabout but nonetheless public way, Rigaud confirmed his, as well as Beauvais's, in public ways too. After being released from prison in connection with a short-lived revolt of the free people of color against the white French colonists in October 1790, led by his fellow American Revolutionary War veterans Vincent Ogé and Jean-Baptiste Chavannes, Rigaud retired to Croix-des-Bouquets, where many *gens de couleur* and free Blacks had gathered to decide what to do next. They chose Louis Jacques Beauvais and Jean-Pierre Lambert as their leaders, and Rigaud to second them. Rigaud explained, "We were, Beauvais and I, among those who once on the plains of Savannah, fighting for the freedom of the peoples of America, had learned to fight for our own. Enthusiasts of the French Revolution, we had since then made the solemn oath to defend it until our last breath, and we have never wavered in our principles."[51] Historians have identified more than a dozen other men of color who also claimed in the eighteenth century that they served there.[52] Dumesle confirmed Chavannes' and Ogé's participation in the American War of Independence, too, though not necessarily at the Battle of Savannah. Dumesle wrote that Ogé "had been on the soil of the United States trying out for the first time his military talents, contributing to the conquest of American freedom."[53] Together, Rigaud's, Vastey's, and Dumesle's writings stand among the first publications to record the participation of Haiti's revolutionaries in the American War of Independence.

The self-styled spokesman of the free people of color, Julien Raimond, claimed that the *gens de couleur libres* found inspiration in their participation in the American Revolutionary War. Raimond wrote that the free men of color could easily assemble troops to fight the white colonists since "all those who were in Savannah are still offering themselves, and I am proud to believe that these three thousand men . . . would be a torrent against which Lucifer could oppose nothing." In a footnote, Raimond clarified, "In the war for America, a body of men of color was formed at Saint-Domingue who fought for freedom in America. These are the men we are talking about here."[54] Later documentary sources add less well-known names to the list of free men of color whose revolutionary careers began with the American War of Independence.[55]

One reason the identities of all the members of the Chasseurs-Volontaires do not come into the frame of the American Revolution more verifiably is that at the time of the Battle of Savannah in 1779, they were not yet *important*. Unlike most of the enslaved population, the births of individuals like Rigaud, Beauvais, and Chavannes were well recorded in the parish records of Saint-Domingue. Their military careers, however, were much less so. Researchers have therefore identified only a handful of service records for the other free men of color who served in Savannah.[56]

One such man was Jeanvier Dessalines, a plantation owner and enslaver from Cap-Français whose official record of service is held by the French Overseas Archives (Archives Nationales d'Outre-Mer) in Aix-en-Provence. Jeanvier Dessalines had married Toussaint Louverture's daughter Marie-Marthe, and according to some researchers he might have enslaved the future revolutionary turned emperor Jean-Jacques Dessalines. Jeanvier Dessalines began serving in the military in Saint-Domingue in 1767.[57] This Dessalines did not mention having fought in Savannah specifically, though he did note that he served as one of the Chasseurs-Volontaires for thirteen months during the "war in the United States."[58]

While men of color born with free status, like Jeanvier Dessalines, had many motivations for serving in the Chasseurs-Volontaires, a free man of color without official papers, possibly like our young Henry, might have had the extra motive of seeking once and for all the freedom dangled before his eyes. The 1779 reforms to the Chasseurs-Volontaires confirm that enslaved men could also join this body of "*gens de couleurs,* mulattoes, and free blacks": "As for the *chasseurs-volontaires* whose freedom is not ratified, they will obtain the ratification on their return from the campaign, on the certificate of good service, signed by the heads of the corps and their captain."[59]

In the late seventeenth century, some enslaved Africans had gained their freedom for serving in raids against the Spanish. A man called Captain Vincent gained both freedom and valor from serving in the French colonial militia.[60] In March 1780, the *Affiches* ran an obituary for Vincent Olivier, "known under the name of Captain Vincent," who had died at the age of 120 years old. Born in the colony in 1660 with enslaved status, Captain Vincent fought at the famous Battle of Carthage with the man who enslaved him. The governor of the colony named Vincent captain general of the colored militias in the dependency of Cap in 1716, and awarded him liberty for his service. Although too old to join the chasseurs in Savannah, Captain Vincent reportedly helped to recruit soldiers. A eulogy for him in the *Affiches* stated, "In the last years of his life he had lost none of his martial humor; he enjoyed hearing the story of heroic actions, and shortly before his death he spoke vibrantly of the services of MM. the Comte d'Estaing and de la Mothe-Piquet [*sic*]. This brave Negro will give those who need it new proof that a truly great soul, under whatever envelope it finds itself, imposes on all men, and silences before them even the prejudices that seem necessary." Due to his bravery, Captain Vincent, who reportedly left behind forty-nine children or grandchildren, received military honors at his death.[61] By the late 1770s, nevertheless, largely because of d'Estaing's reforms preventing free men of color from rising above the rank of sergeant, the Chasseurs-Volontaires who fought at the Battle of Savannah were ineligible for such accolades.[62]

While "mulattoes, *griffes,* and free blacks" could receive honors, they could not purchase exemptions from service, and the highest service they could perform was not to defeat enemy forces but to save the lives of white soldiers and officers, which could earn them a medal of valor. These medals of valor and the color of the buttonhole differed based on the person's perceived racial identity: a part white and part blue ribbon for the "mulattoes and *griffes,*" and one that was part black and part blue for the "Negroes."[63] That d'Estaing sought to segregate a military that, as Captain Vincent's career suggests, had been until then far more integrated shows that the famous count absorbed Saint-Domingue's most enduring and deadly export: color prejudice.

Julien Raimond (spelled "Raymond" on his baptismal certificate), a free man of color born in 1744 to a wealthy family of enslavers, narrated with distinct aplomb the growth and spread of the colony's prejudices. The colonists considered racism, called color prejudice at the time, the only way to sustain the system of slavery and preserve for enslavers and other property owners the enormous profits generated from the labor they forced Africans to perform using violence and torture. Raimond's parents, Pierre Raymond and Marie Begasse (sometimes spelled "Bagasse"), were plantation owners. This means their son had a material interest in the continuation of slavery, even though he also had a generational interest in blackness, and therefore in combating rising color prejudices.[64]

In his 1791 pamphlet, *Observations on the Origin and Progress of the Prejudices of the White Colonists Against the Men of Color,* Raimond explained the evolution of color prejudice on the island in social and political realms. At first, following Louis XIV's 1685 edict governing slavery (later called the *Code Noir*), white men were permitted to marry the African women they enslaved, if the women could be converted to Catholicism. As time went on, the white colonists began to increasingly disdain the mixed-race family formations that increased the free people of color to around thirty thousand, or about the same number as the white colonists. As the free population of color grew, so did the humiliations, slights, and insults to which the whites subjected them. The white colonial legislature passed oppressive laws. Before 1764, Raimond said that men of color "practiced the art of surgery." Afterward, "colored men were forbidden to practice this useful art; a monopoly was granted to whites. It was the same for the midwives of color. And as a result, concubinage rather than marriage was encouraged." Rather than completely abstaining from romantic relationships with women of color, white men simply refused to marry them. Some even took the children they had with women of color to the metropole and then married white women in France to give them legitimacy. "Can the jealousy of the whites be even imagined?" wrote an exasperated Raimond. "There was a decree . . . that forbade such marriages, even in France, and since then we have seen priests in Paris refuse to marry colored men here with white women." The laws created closer to the time the Haitian Revolution broke out were similarly oppressive and ridiculous. "We saw succeed these injustices other ordinances that increased the tyranny, as much as the absurdity. Some forbade people of color to use a wheeled car; another forbade them to dress in the manner of whites, and to don the same headdresses, or to wear jewelry." There were laws that "forbade the registration of the titles of nobility for whites who married women of color, others forbade people of color to go to France, or for their children to do so, even for the sake of education; others declared disqualified from the rank of whites those who married women of color." Other laws prohibited notaries and priests from using the word "free" on documents for people of color, and "others sought to force them to abandon the European name they had been given, to take one from the African idiom."[65]

By 1773, not only were free people of color barred from many professions, but many were forced to engage in corvées, or forced labor, particularly to recapture fugitives from slavery, or maroons.[66] The white colonists even sought to segregate churches and cemeteries. Vastey, himself a free man of color, born in 1781 to a white father and Black mother of mixed European and African ancestry, sharply rebuked the absurdity of white French colonial legislation. "What can I say?" he asked. "Oh, height of human vanity! Pride accompanied the whites into the beyond; they even needed to segregate the plots in the cemeteries." Vastey told the tale of white women who refused to share the pew with Black women in church. "In Jérémie one Maundy Thursday, Haitian women were chased out of the church at the instigation of white women," Vastey recalled.[67] Hilliard d'Auberteuil, author of that two-volume description of the colony eventually censored in France because it detailed the terrors and tortures of slavery, offered the free people of color and the slaves no favor when he justified colonial color prejudices. His book had not been censored because of the following passage, Vastey wryly remarked: "Self-interest and safety compel us to overwhelm the black race with such great contempt that anyone descending from it to the sixth generation is covered with an indelible stain."[68] Scorn was the mildest punishment that a free person of color could receive simply because they were of the "race of Blacks."

Vastey told the tale of a free man of color named Jean-Baptiste punished horribly for having not quickly enough obeyed an order from Barré de Saint-Venant, a white French colonist infamous for his prejudices and cruelty. The Conseil du Cap condemned Jean-Baptiste to be "put in a straightjacket for two hours, at the Clugny market in the same town, with this sign: 'Negro, insolent toward whites.'" The officials then sentenced him to be whipped, branded, and tied to the public chain gang as a convict, for three years. Something similar happened to a free Black man from Marmelade named Mongin, condemned by the instigation of Gauthier, a white planter, to be "put in a straitjacket, tied to a post, which will be for this purpose planted on the market place of this city, called Clugny, to stay there every day for seven hours starting at nine in the morning, having a sign in front and behind, bearing these words in large print: 'Free mulatto who raised his hand to a white man.'" After this, he was to be attached to the public chain gang to serve there as a convict, for three years.[69] Jean-Baptiste and Mongin were grown men, but still they found their freedom in peril.

Imagine what it would have been like for young Christophe, either striving for freedom or trying to maintain it in a place like Saint-Domingue. Men and boys who fought in Savannah did not always gain the freedom papers promised to them. And even if they did, liberty was often precarious. The July 30, 1783, issue of the *Affiches* revealed what happened to two "mulattoes" who claimed they were awarded freedom for their service in Savannah. Their brief self-testimony in the "Slaves in Marronnage" section of the paper shows they became *important* enough to enter the written archive only when they exercised an agency so dangerous it could lead to their incarceration, incapacitation, torture, or death:

Two mulattoes named Jean and Jean-Baptiste Lefevre, brothers, without stamps, claiming to be free on the pretext that they were part of the Savannah company under the orders of M. the Comte d'Estaing, have been maroons . . . for fifteen days. The first is twenty years old, five feet seven to eight inches tall, wig maker for men and women; and the second, twenty-four to twenty-five years old, five feet three to four inches tall, with an opaque spot over one eye and a suspicious look, postilion and knowing a little bit of masonry.[70]

This fugitive slave notice can help us to understand how Christophe's freedom, whether he came to Saint-Domingue with that status or not, could have been threatened at different turns, from Grenada to Cap-Français, to Savannah, and back to Cap. Christophe's biographer Hubert Cole agreed, "It is indeed likely that whether born free or not, so young a child would have had difficulty in retaining or proving his freedom."[71] But the Battle of Savannah was hell, too, and it would be hard to claim that his young life was any less precarious for having fought in another nation's violent war of independence. Our intrepid Christophe was still a child separated from his parents and likely all his kin. Christophe would have little to show for his travails except a wounded leg.

Perhaps the perils and possibilities of a soldier's life seemed thrilling to the young child. More likely, the whole enterprise filled him with terror and dread. An early life not well recorded leaves us only to imagine Christophe's thoughts and emotions as he watched the shores of Saint-Domingue disappear between August 17 and August 21, about three weeks after d'Estaing's fleet arrived. During that time, ship by ship, the famous fleet set sail once more, unbeknownst to most of the inhabitants of Saint-Domingue, for North America.

—

D'Estaing's fleet had arrived in Cap-Français on July 31 from the Windward Islands. There, most of the army was tasked with gathering up the volunteers from Saint-Domingue who were to join them. They also had to stock the ships with four months of food.[72] On August 10, the *Affiches américaines* reported that Spain had declared an alliance with France against Great Britain.[73] Two days later, the alliance was celebrated aboard d'Estaing's ship, the *Languedoc*,[74] and by the twenty-first a convoy of sixty ships, carrying about 6,000 men total, had set sail for North America from the Windward Islands and Saint-Domingue. Of those 6,000 men, between 700 and 750 were classified as Chasseurs-Volontaires.[75]

The sea was calm throughout most of their journey. Taking advantage of the nice weather and stagnant sea, d'Estaing ordered an officer from each vessel to board the *Languedoc* to receive instructions for disembarkation, and on September 1 the fleet of around twenty-two ships docked outside view of land, while four ships continued on to Charleston, South Carolina, to pick up escort ships. On the second, the first sign of trouble came when a violent burst of wind and rain pushed several of the anchored ships out to sea. They had to cut their cables to set sail, and the rudders of several ships were so damaged that they needed to be repaired before the convoy could continue. On the sixth, the vessels and frigates that had gone to Charleston returned and joined the army anchored at sea. On the seventh, after the rudders were repaired, the entire squadron approached Tybee Island outside Savannah.[76] They were about two leagues from shore when they perceived several British ships, which quickly fired on them from the river, before abandoning Tybee fort just before d'Estaing's fleet landed that night.[77] This was a harbinger of trouble to come. While d'Estaing enjoyed near immediate success in Grenada, the stage for his failure in Savannah was already being set.

Almost one year before, on November 12, 1778, Benjamin Franklin co-wrote a letter to the French minister of the marine, Antoine de Sartine (Comte d'Alby), to convince the French government of the benefits of joining the United States in its fight against England. The letter observed that France would be particularly useful to the American colonists because of its superior naval power. While extolling the superior condition of French ships, Franklin also warned de Sartine to account for the colder North American climate: "You will do well to embark on all the warships that you will send to America a lot of woolen stuffs for the sailors and particularly blankets and gloves or mittens, otherwise it will be extremely difficult for the sailors to fulfill their duty in the severe cold we experience on this coast."[78] On February 6, 1778, Louis XVI and Franklin had officially signed the Treaty of Commerce, complemented by the defensive and offensive Treaty of Alliance.[79]

D'Estaing had already experienced the North American continental climate and seemed undeterred. Preoccupied with gathering the troops to lead to Georgia, d'Estaing sent his major general, François Vicomte de Fontanges, to Charleston for an audience with General Benjamin Lincoln, Governor John Rutledge, and the consul of France. De Fontanges was supposed to provide details of d'Estaing's plans and gather the victuals that the U.S. government promised. However, the American troops, who needed victuals themselves, were unable to furnish the French troops with all that was promised. D'Estaing set sail anyway, without waiting for his envoy to return with this news.[80]

In July 1779, d'Estaing received a letter from the Marquis de Brétigny in South Carolina asking for his assistance. Brétigny warned that the province depended on d'Estaing to save it—that despite what the newspapers were reporting, the French were being beaten. De Brétigny pleaded, "If you were to arrive, monsieur, before the month of September, I dare to believe that you would take it without a problem," and he asked d'Estaing to disembark his troops between Port Royal and Savannah. "You will not find it wrong, sir, that I hazard my opinion on the kinds of troops you should send to this country. I believe that corps of Negroes and mulattoes are really the ones who will provide better service here. European troops would not easily endure the Carolina climate, and I would fear that disease would kill more soldiers than enemy fire." Reiterating that the French troops would not find anything that they were accustomed to, Brétigny said they lacked horses and carriages and had no basic necessities.[81]

Aboard the *Languedoc* on August 21, 1779, d'Estaing wrote to de Sartine informing him of his plan to aid the American revolutionaries.[82] Ten days later, the day before he entered Georgia waters, d'Estaing wrote to Governor Rutledge to declare his intention to assist American troops. "Monsieur, the letter which Your Excellency did me the honor of writing on July 20th last, caused me to take it upon myself to deviate from the path of the Windward Islands toward America to strike on our common enemy," the French count wrote. "I hope that the prompt success of the enterprise will justify my approach in the eyes of my Court." D'Estaing described how France could help the United States from the sea but noted that everything depended on American troops, their promptitude, and on Rutledge's orders: the movements of his army, the communication between the French and the American forces, the "secrecy of the directions that you are going to send to me," the trustworthiness and knowledge of the escorts and guides, and "the choice of the place where I will land." D'Estaing said that Brétigny, the former French nobleman now serving as a U.S. army officer, had told him that Rutledge changed his plans and positions. Frustrated, d'Estaing replied that he needed to know immediately what those plans were; otherwise, he said, "the war is thrown to the hazards of the wind, without them this war is just a game of chance." D'Estaing, who often wrote in code, urged the utmost discretion in any disclosure of the joint project. He wrote to the ambassador of France in Philadelphia to explain, "I am speaking to him, to avoid any inconvenience, of my arrival, only in coded numbers, and it is necessary that the couriers themselves do not understand it." D'Estaing wanted this mission to be completed quickly and with secrecy. "I would personally become criminal, and I would harm the general good of both Nations, if the troops that I will place on land in a suitable spot, were to stay there for more than eight days. I will lead them myself. You can count on their zeal, on mine, and on the extreme desire we have to be of use to you."[83] The stage was set for confusion. D'Estaing was not aware that the Americans could not provide the promised victuals and supplies until too late. Furthermore, attacks from the British as the French convoy entered the swampy marshes of Tybee Island, plus the weather, complicated the disembarkation. The lack of clear orders about which troops would do what also contributed to the eventual failure.

On September 23, Brétigny hastily wrote to d'Estaing, whose letter he received only the day before, even though it was dated from the ninth. Brétigny, tormented and fatigued by his perpetual worries, pleaded once more that he needed help in Charleston. Among other problems, an armed ship entered the river the day before. Brétigny did not have the men or weapons to repel it but managed to escape anyway. "Jean Barthe[84] couldn't have done better, especially since I never planned to be either a sailor or a supplier of food, two professions that are completely foreign to me." Brétigny apologized for his frankness, declaring that he wrote the same way he spoke. This statement seems to have been a pretext for another warning that foretold the troubles that eventually befell d'Estaing and his fleet. "Permit me, monsieur, to tell you, I don't believe your navy is accustomed to overcoming difficulties," Brétigny wrote. "Everything here is mountainous, everything monstrous, for these gentlemen. I tremble, when I see that, working according to the principle they seem to have adopted, I tremble, I say, that you will be poorly assisted." Brétigny knew that d'Estaing was worried too and hoped that he had not been misinformed about the number of American troops, which had not increased, and many of whom were very ill, in poor condition, or "people of bad will." Yet Brétigny still believed that the French-American alliance had the advantage.

Brétigny knew how to reassure the old count, promising d'Estaing that he would win the campaign despite the adversities they faced. "It will cost you some men, but after all our soldiers are not soldiers for nothing," Brétigny said. "Patience and cold blood, voilà, your motto, monsieur, the count, and come what may, the boat will survive." Appealing to d'Estaing's honor, pride, and desire for conquest and victory, Brétigny wrote that "this expedition . . . will always be perceived to have been a beautiful and just expedition. It will always do honor to your way of seeing things, and to the true and great ideas of a statesman. Small actions are made for ordinary men, and Monsieur the Comte d'Estaing was born for large endeavors, and large endeavors are only so in as much as they present us with difficulties to overcome."[85]

Let us now turn to the official write-up of the Battle of Savannah written by d'Estaing's scribe Antoine François Térence O'Connor to discover what befell d'Estaing and his troops, particularly the Chasseurs-Volontaires from Saint-Domingue.[86] Our young Christophe was about to find himself in the heart of a crushing and difficult battle.

On September 8, 1779, the Comte d'Estaing, commanding his massive fleet with three thousand landing troops, approached the shore of the Savannah River, about twenty miles from the city.[87] The next day, while French troops prepared to cross the river, British troops opened fire from Fort Tybee. The fort, located near a lighthouse on the northernmost tip of the island, was designed to prevent entrance into the river, though at this time it was only feebly defended.[88] The outnumbered and outgunned British quickly evacuated the fort, allowing d'Estaing to disembark his troops on Tybee Island. From the tenth to the eleventh, d'Estaing traveled with several of the ships nine leagues farther south, to the mouth of the Ossabaw River, followed by canoes and launches that carried the troops. The landing at Beaulieu (spelled in the manuscript "Biowlay," the way Georgians pronounced it), around twelve miles from Savannah, could not happen until the next day at nine o'clock in the evening. The weather eventually grew so severe that it was impossible to continue the disembarkation. The water at the mouth at the Ossabaw River had fallen so low that no further troops could be landed.[89] "Not even a canoe could be sent ashore," reported another eyewitness participant. "Nearly all the vessels, moored upon the open coast, were forced to set sail and go far out to sea to escape destruction."[90] The general had only twenty-four hundred men divided into three divisions, the first of which was commanded by the Comte d'Estaing.

The Chasseurs-Volontaires, composed of "mulattoes and free negroes from the island of Saint-Domingue," were commanded by Laurent-François Le Noir, the Marquis de Rouvray (often spelled "Rouvrai," or "Rouvré," as in the manuscript). The marquis was born in 1743 to a Normand family in France and served while still quite young in Canada, where he was severely wounded. De Rouvray was twice a prisoner of war, once in 1760 and again in 1763. Before and after Savannah he served in the military in Saint-Domingue. He later fled the Haitian Revolution and died in Philadelphia on July 18, 1798.[91] D'Estaing praised de Rouvray's heroism and valor despite the troubles that his chasseurs experienced during the battle. "During the time it lasted, he showed several marks of firmness and military intelligence: in charge of occupying a difficult and perhaps risky post. . . . This officer was in command of the trench the day the English were repulsed; his corps served with zeal and exactitude."[92] D'Estaing's instructions to de Rouvray on September 14 during the initial disembarkation allow us to imagine what our young Henry might have been doing while d'Estaing planned his attack. De Rouvray's men were to occupy the potentially vulnerable fork in the road in the woods between Savannah and Beaulieu, and, if possible, occupy the fort at Brewton Hill and seize everything they could, especially boats, cannons, or longboats. It was a long, swampy, perilous walk for de Rouvray's men. D'Estaing acknowledged as much: "The only observations that will be added to this are that it is five and a half miles from Orphan House plantation to the fork in the road that leads to Brewton's Hill and appears before you meet a road that should not be taken." He adopted the paternal tone he often took with officers under his command: "Monsieur de Rouvray will be careful after the fork in the road to take the one that leads to Costin and turn left to go on to the one leading to Brewton's Hill. If the galleys or armed crafts of the enemies should render the pier murderous to occupy, Monsieur de Rouvray will put his detachment under cover of their fire and will be content to occupy Brewton's Hill."[93]

At least one French officer disagreed with d'Estaing's praise for de Rouvray's military conduct, not because de Rouvray did not follow his superior officer's orders, but because of his inability to do so effectively. The officer Pechon, who described de Rouvray as commander of "two hundred mulattoes," wrote that the marquis failed during the battle because he did not have the qualities of a "good military man."[94] But if a good military man was meant to simply follow orders, then de Rouvray, like the Chasseurs-Volontaires he commanded, seems to have been fit for the task. On September 16, d'Estaing arrived at a camp near Savannah. He was joined by de Rouvray and the Chasseurs-Volontaires, who followed his instructions to the letter. General Lincoln, commanding a body of American troops, which had considerably increased but still numbered only about eighteen hundred men, set up camp nearby. Two days later, the Comte d'Estaing sent a missive asking General Augustine Prévost, "commander for his Britannic Majesty" in Savannah, to consider turning the city over to the Americans. Prévost asked for time—in effect, a cease-fire—to assemble a martial council to deliberate on such an important proposal, and he also announced his disposition to defend his post.

Granting the cease-fire allowed Prévost to gather the troops necessary for the eventual British victory and d'Estaing later recognized this as a colossal mistake on his part. His scribe O'Connor wrote, "Our generals were informed by the deserters that the garrisons of Bedford and Port Royal, containing about six hundred elite troops under the orders of Colonel Mitley, had joined that of Savannah and that the enemies had in place three regiments, effectively composing nineteen hundred men and two thousand men from the militia in various regiments, who were disciplined and hardened." If d'Estaing had known this when Prévost asked for a cease-fire, he might have paused to reflect before agreeing, or even ordered an immediate attack instead of waiting.

The approach to the city—bound by a river and an impassable marsh on one side, and British fortifications on the other—presented great difficulties for d'Estaing's army. Still, O'Connor wrote, d'Estaing "resolved to undertake everything rather than retreat."[95] On September 22, he ordered his army to leave their camp and encamp on a line half a mile from Savannah. De Rouvray's forces formed the right column of the army with General Lincoln, who needed to pass through the impenetrable swamp on the left. The hard work of digging trenches fell largely to the Chasseurs-Volontaires. On the night of September 23–24, the Comte d'Estaing led three hundred laborers, supported by four hundred grenadiers and chasseurs, to dig a trench at about 150 yards from the enemy line. They worked with so much order and silence that the British troops did not notice what the French side was doing until daybreak. Upon learning that the French were digging trenches, the British attacked. O'Connor said they made a sortie of three hundred men that reached the end of the gut of the trench, while one soldier claimed that it was more like six hundred men.[96] De Rouvray and his second-in-command, Colonel Thadée-Humphrey O'Dune, ordered the French troops to charge the enemy with bayonets, and the British fled back to their entrenchments.

Forcing the British to retreat was far more deadly for the French side. Those attacks took out twelve officers and eighty-eight grenadiers or chasseurs who were killed or wounded. Losses from the British side were less severe because of the short distance to return to their trenches. "The large quantity of cannonballs and shells that they kept firing at our soldiers did not slow down their activity or the work of the siege," O'Connor reported.[97]

According to the officer Pechon, on the evening of the twenty-third, "the general having decided to besiege three thousand well-entrenched men with twenty-five hundred very tired and half-naked men . . . the opening of the trench was made at 150 fathoms from the works of our enemies. The grenadiers and chasseurs were placed belly to earth in front, still having small posts in front of them up to thirty paces from the enemy sentries who fortunately did not patrol during the night." But, according to Pechon, the next day, when the British attacked their trenches, de Rouvray and O'Dune committed the fatal error that resulted in four officers being killed and nine wounded, with 101 grenadiers and Chasseurs-Volontaires losing their lives. "If we hadn't come out of the trench, we wouldn't have lost a single man," Pechon lamented.[98] Another French officer agreed: "Our imprudence in leaving our trench to pursue them exposed us to the artillery fire of their redoubts and batteries, and caused the loss of seventy men killed and wounded; among whom were several officers."[99] Was it in this attack that our young Henry was wounded in the leg?

It is hard to imagine an eleven-year-old boy fighting in combat, and the French troops would have had little use for a drummer during this operation, given the secrecy and silence it required. Perhaps Henry participated in the treacherous work of digging the trench that night and early the next morning. Had he been wounded when the British attacked the trenches, he would have been transported to the hospital with the other French casualties. According to Pechon, this hospital was hardly adequate. Due to lack of "linen" and surgeons, only those who were lightly wounded were able to be saved. The others were abandoned and died, he said, "in horrific pain."[100]

Several smaller operations occurred from the time the trench digging finished until the early days of October. On October 2, French troops unsuccessfully bombarded Savannah with heavy cannonade. On the third the French tried and failed again.[101] Then, during the night of the fourth to the fifth, the French troops bombed British works, and by daybreak the gunners and bombers were firing with such great activity that General d'Estaing ordered them to fire less often and with more discretion. All the same, the British worked hard to dig more trenches while defending themselves from French fire, which had reached Savannah and caused several houses to burst into flames.[102]

By that time, d'Estaing had grown eager for the campaign to end. It was fall, hurricane season in the southeastern United States, and rough weather imminently approached. Still, the French general persuaded himself that the American troops could adequately defend or at least fend off any British attack that might come by land. Having been informed by several deserters from the British side that the right side of the enemy encampment was guarded by only a few militias, d'Estaing, in concert with General Lincoln, decided to attack this location.

D'Estaing tried once more to warn General Prévost of the imminent arrival of the allied troops and offered him time to prepare for evacuation. D'Estaing and Lincoln wrote a joint letter to Prévost on October 6 calling his rejection of this offer "conduct, monsieur, sufficient to prohibit between us all that could be the cause of the slightest loss of time."[103] All the arrangements for the siege were made with the greatest secrecy, and on October 8, the troops were warned to be ready to march at the first order.

The other soldiers and the Chasseurs-Volontaires, where Henry would have been if he was not already wounded and at the hospital, had very specific orders: to carry out a false attack and guard the trenches. A second column also had orders to carry out a divergence attack meant to distract the enemy from the real attack. General Lincoln was to lead a third column of the elite American infantry, preceded by the cavalry of General Casimir Pulaski, known and beloved in Europe for striving for the freedom of his birthland, Poland. D'Estaing furnished the head of each division with a copy of his detailed instructions, which were read out loud to every officer.[104]

On the ninth, at half past three in the morning, the troops set out. The fire of the false attacks was a signal for the real one. This began at daybreak. "Our vanguard then moved quickly," O'Connor said, but the enemy fought them off. The British struck the French, who "approached rapidly with cries of *Vive le Roi*," amid grapeshot and musket fire. "The number of dead and wounded put disorder in the columns," and the Americans were "forced to fall back."[105] The fearless, or foolhardy, d'Estaing, nevertheless, wanted to start the attack again. The sun had not yet risen when the Chasseurs-Volontaires of Saint-Domingue began their false attack, with the other troops rapidly advancing. The British were not fooled.[106] Well-directed grapeshot and musket fire struck French troops, crisscrossing the French ranks from the land batteries and the boats anchored in the river. The dead and wounded began falling. D'Estaing, struck by a bullet, fell to the ground too. Yet he persisted, staying on the battlefield and continuing to give orders. He knew the French needed to retreat, but he was stubborn. For this obstinacy, he received two more shots, one in the right arm and the other in the left leg. His troops urged him to withdraw, to no avail. He only allowed himself to be transported to his tent after all the troops had returned to their camp.

Ten officers lay dead on the battlefield. Thirty-three others were injured. A hundred and forty soldiers were dead, and 339 wounded. The Americans lost a few soldiers as well. General Pulaski saw his thigh pierced clean through, which led to his death two days later. The British losses were minimal since they were never forced to fully emerge from their entrenchments.[107] Christophe would have celebrated his twelfth birthday either on this bloody battlefield or in the hospital.

The British and French commanders agreed upon a truce until the morning to bury the dead and remove the wounded. "One cannot praise enough the manner in which the British treated the wounded French officers and soldiers, who remained prisoners of war, by giving them all the help and care they could need," O'Connor wrote. "On the same day, the Comte d'Estaing and all the wounded officers and soldiers were transported to Thunderbluff [hospital], where the ambulance was stationed." D'Estaing left the command to the Comte de Dillon, to whom he passed on his instructions for the retreat, "which was executed with so much order and activity that all the artillery and the patients were re-embarked within the space of eight days," O'Connor said. By the afternoon of October 20, the troops had re-embarked and boarded their ships. O'Connor finished the official account with praise for several military officers: "The wise and truly military precautions and arrangements that the Comte de Dillon and the Vicomte de Noailles employed in the execution of the orders of the Comte d'Estaing in all circumstances give the highest praise to their zeal and their talents. General [d'Estaing] only arrived on board a day before the troops; a few days later the wind became so violent and the sea so furious that the ships were forced to sail successively."[108]

Despite his injuries, d'Estaing gave minute instructions to each ship commander about their destination. Among other directives, he ordered "two hundred chasseurs-volontaires to assemble at Grenada. . . . Food, money, and effects intended for this colony will also be delivered on the spot." However, "if unforeseen events have caused Grenada to fall into the power of the enemy," the food, troops, and money would be returned to Martinique, he directed.[109] D'Estaing's directives, coupled with O'Connor's narrative of the re-embarkation, are not insignificant to our interest in Christophe's return to Saint-Domingue. Despite d'Estaing's very specific directions, three ships carrying the Chasseurs-Volontaires from Saint-Domingue reached Cap-Français in November 1779. Another returned in December of the same year. One of them possibly carried Christophe.

De Rouvray, "forced by a very serious inconvenience to return to Europe," did not travel with the Chasseurs-Volontaires back to Saint-Domingue. He later praised the men under his command and provided important information about their destinies after the failed siege. He reported to the French minister of the marine, "I will confine myself, monsignor, to telling you that the corps of chasseurs-volontaires that I commanded served there with the greatest distinction and the greatest valor. I hope, monsignor, that the Comte de Dillon will have said the same to you about it, as well as the Comte d'Estaing, who never ceased to praise them. . . . The awful damage to every part of the corps, which was the result of the end of the campaign, the most tiring that these troops were ever made to endure, forced me to quit the army three days after the attack on the entrenchments." De Rouvray remained upset because, while he was incapacitated from a fever after the campaign, he learned that d'Estaing dispatched 150 to 200 men from his corps to "reinforce the garrison in Grenada." "The situation in which I found myself then did not allow me to make representations on this subject to M. the Comte d'Estaing," de Rouvray lamented to the minister of the marine. "But, monsignor, I cannot prevent myself from observing to you that the *chasseurs-volontaires* are almost all landowners who have abandoned their fortunes to serve the king and that there was no humanity in sending them to a colony that is foreign to them to serve as a garrison there. I have no doubt, monsignor, that this has produced the worst effect among the people of color in Saint-Domingue, and I would not be surprised if it resulted in the entire dissolution of the corps, due to a general desertion of their comrades to the Spaniards. Rejoicing in your justice and your humanity, you will kindly give your orders for these unfortunate men to be sent back to their homeland."[110]

D'Estaing must have had his reasons for sending the Chasseurs-Volontaires on for more service rather than home to rest. While the count basically agreed with O'Connor's account, though it was "perhaps lacking a bit of accuracy and contained some exaggerated details, or some that I seem to have perceived differently from what he said they were," d'Estaing offered several reasons of his own for the failure. The first of which was that the enemy was not surprised, and surprise was the capital aim of the campaign, for "everything depended upon it." Nevertheless, d'Estaing reported that all the officers fought with bravery. He ended his addendum to O'Connor's write-up by attaching the surgeon's report on the wounded soldiers. He also mentioned the mortal wound suffered by Pulaski, before reiterating that his troops had been expected to accomplish a victory on land, rather than by sea, without shoes, provisions, equipage, or any transportation.[111] After all this, d'Estaing still ordered many of the troops, including many men of color from the Chasseurs-Volontaires of Saint-Domingue, sent to the Windward Islands to assist with France's other campaigns. Yet bad weather caused the failure of this plan, and at least three of these ships were forced to divert to Saint-Domingue. This is most likely how Christophe found himself once more in France's richest and most torturous slave colony.

—

If the re-embarkation of the troops went off with the utmost order, the departure out to sea could not have gone less smoothly. Within three months of the battle, the Chasseurs-Volontaires were dispersed over three thousand miles. Many of them did not return home for three more years. "One Chasseur company of 62 [men] escorted casualties to Charleston, South Carolina, after the Battle of Savannah, and was the sole French troop serving during the siege of that city in the spring of 1780," the historian John Garrigus has written. "More than one-third of the entire Volontaire force, 150 to 200 men, was sent by d'Estaing's orders to Grenada in the eastern Caribbean. Two and one-half years later over one hundred members of this detachment were still serving there."[112] The siege's failure did not tarnish d'Estaing's reputation, either in France or in Saint-Domingue.

D'Estaing was honored at Versailles multiple times, along with many of his troops, including de Rouvray, for his command of the Chasseurs-Volontaires.[113] Even some of the "mulattoes" who made their way to Paris were honored. The May 2, 1780, issue of the *Affiches* reflected, "It must have seemed extraordinary to see armed, disciplined, and seasoned people of color in Europe. . . . moreover, it is assured that this corps served very well, and it seems that all the officers who were a part of the last campaign agree in praising it." The article concluded, "We learn with pleasure that the king gave marks of his satisfaction to the officers of the troops currently in the colony who were part of the Georgia expedition."[114] It is extremely unlikely, though not impossible, that Christophe was among those Chasseurs-Volontaires who traveled to France and then back to Saint-Domingue. The members of the Chasseurs-Volontaires were supposed to be either men of color with free status or those whose liberty would be ratified upon the completion of their service. In theory, Christophe could therefore not have been forced into slavery in the France of the late eighteenth century, but he would have been too young to fend for himself in a European country whose customs and ways were unknown to him.

In the interim between when the Chasseurs-Volontaires honored in Paris left Savannah and returned to Saint-Domingue, misinformation abounded. Saint-Dominguans had not been informed either of the day that d'Estaing and his fleet left Saint-Domingue or of his destination once he departed. Judging from its reporting, the editors of the *Affiches* were under the impression that d'Estaing and his squadron were returning to France. The Spanish insisted he had set sail for the American continent.[115] Later, the *Affiches* reported more accurate information, even if still laden with speculation about the mission. In the absence of official information, conjecture continued to fill the void and satisfy the public desire to follow the movements of their beloved former governor-general. Once it learned of the Battle of Savannah, the *Affiches* initially reported that d'Estaing's troops had been victorious. "A letter from Charles-Town informs us that the Comte d'Estaing, on his arrival in Georgia, immediately disembarked a corps of troops and caused the English to attack at the posts of Beaufort and Port Royal, from which they had been driven out with a loss of nine hundred men taken or killed," stated the November 9, 1779, issue. "At the news of this advantage of our allies, all the troops and militia of South Carolina assembled to join the French and cooperate with them in the total expulsion of the enemies from this part of the continent."[116]

The next week, the *Affiches* published a sober update, after the three ships dispatched to the Windward Islands arrived bearing the news that the siege had colossally failed. "We then learned of the poor success of the Georgia expedition, which several combined circumstances caused to fail. The small French army, after a siege as long as it was murderous, was obliged to withdraw from Savannah, where the besieged were, so to speak, in greater number than the besiegers." Never missing a chance to take a dig at the British, the *Affiches* concluded, "We do not doubt that the English will trumpet their advantage very loudly. They will take great care to exaggerate our losses and diminish theirs." The paper saluted the "impetuous courage" of French troops, gave a rough tally of the casualties, and ended, "General [d'Estaing] himself is among the wounded; it is to be hoped that his wound is not dangerous and will not suspend his activities for long and, despite the blows of misfortune, will make him always formidable to enemies and precious to the nation."[117]

As 1779 ended, news continued to trickle in about the various fleets that fought at Savannah. On December 14, 1779, the paper still expressed uncertainty about the whereabouts of much of d'Estaing's fleet, and therefore "all that one could say on this subject is reduced to more or less risky conjectures." The paper did reveal the arrival of several more officers from the Chasseurs-Volontaires on a ship recently arrived from Martinique, noting, "It has been rumored since their arrival that a detachment of this corps and two officers perished while embarking on one of the king's vessels."[118] However, the *Affiches,* contrary to its usual practice, did not reveal which ship landed on Saint-Domingue with the Chasseurs-Volontaires that December, but it is possible that Christophe was on it.

The scattered arrival of these ships suggests how Christophe could have gone from the battlefield of Savannah back to Saint-Domingue. Although we cannot entirely dismiss the possibility that Christophe returned with much later ships, strong circumstantial evidence suggests that he arrived with one of the earlier ships. Documents produced both by the Kingdom of Haiti and other chroniclers who knew the king consistently report his participation at the Battle of Savannah, but not elsewhere in the Windward Islands or in Charleston afterward. Since Christophe did eventually make his way back to Saint-Domingue, perhaps the question is more what he did once there and what avenues were open to him in a slave colony as a Black child who had fought for freedom in another land.

The Battle of Savannah was an utter disaster. And the glory showered on d'Estaing because of his previous successful siege of Grenada did not necessarily redound to the Chasseurs-Volontaires. De Rouvray, who, as the head of the Chasseurs-Volontaires, would have known Christophe, was not yet back from France and could have offered little protection. From Savannah, de Rouvray went home to Tours and then to Paris, though he remained interested in returning to Saint-Domingue and reprising his role as commander of the Chasseurs-Volontaires.[119] In July 1780, the French government belatedly paid de Rouvray for his service in Savannah and named him "inspector of the mulatto and colored militia," the body that

Saint-Domingue's governor-general established to replace the Chasseurs-Volontaires.[120] On the same day that de Rouvray received his orders to return to Saint-Domingue, the French minister of the marine announced that "the corps of Chasseurs-Volontaires, the men of color . . . of which M. de Rouvray was colonel, has been dissolved." Its replacement, the Chasseurs-Royaux, was likewise dissolved. Moving forward, "militias made up of the *gens de couleurs* will not involve the existence of a colonel *en pied*. M. de Rouvray can therefore only be appointed as an inspector under the orders of the governor-general." De Rouvray, while preserving his rank as colonel, was to thus be "inspector of all the militias of mulattoes and free negroes of this colony."[121] Given de Rouvray's trajectory as commander of these troops, it is possible that he crossed paths with young Henry again. That is, of course, if Christophe remained with the Chasseurs-Volontaires after the return of these troops to the island. Barely older than he was at the time of the Battle of Savannah, Christophe might have found favor at this time with his former commander, if his commander had not been a white colonist with a reputation for cruelty. It is quite possible that de Rouvray's return only imperiled young Christophe, who was already susceptible due to his age.

De Rouvray was a hardened enslaver who owned a plantation in Terrier-Rouge, in the dependency of Cap-Français. A notice he placed in the *Affiches* on January 12, 1779, leaves no doubt that for de Rouvray the freedom he fought for on the North American continent did not extend to "negroes." In the ad, de Rouvray "gives notice that one of his negroes, named Stanislaus, carpenter and coachman, has gone maroon." The Chevalier de Rohan had previously enslaved Stanislaus, and de Rouvray had "lent him" since acquiring him to the Comte d'Ennery. This meant that Stanislaus likely had "acquaintances in almost every workhouse in the colony," de Rouvray's ad stated, before adding, "He left wearing a gray frock coat, and he must have also had on a green jacket from the livery of M. de Rouvray." De Rouvray plainly spelled out his thoughts to authorities about the man he had forced into bondage: "We would do well to warn again that this Negro is a very dangerous scoundrel, to whom M. de Rouvray has the most serious crimes to impute." De Rouvray offered "50 piastres in compensation to anyone who might bring him back."[122]

We know that de Rouvray returned to Saint-Domingue shortly after his military reappointment in July 1781, whereas Christophe could have arrived in any number of different ways and at any number of different moments. None of the eyewitnesses nor Vastey in his official account mentions any service in the army between the end of the Savannah expedition and the start of the Haitian Revolution in 1791. But it is clear that although he found himself on Saint-Domingue, those with whom he served on the battlefields of Savannah continued to help shape his destiny.

3

TRACING GENEALOGIES
TO THE FUTURE KING

Poor, wounded child. What did you do when you returned to Saint-Domingue, the home that was not your home? Nearly every white Frenchman, down to the least of them, no matter their eventual destiny, enjoyed a life recorded in parish and civil registers, courts of law, and state archives. Black life under French colonial rule was so dispensable, in contrast, as to make recording even the barest facts of existence—life and death—exceedingly rare. Thus, the particulars of Christophe's early life live in infinite contestation. But recovering lives not well documented means resisting the colonial drive to cast the details of Black subjects into oblivion. Hoping to present the story of a full life, I have found it necessary to pull every thread, in some cases so far as to land only in a pile of shreds. Yet maybe weaving together the fabric of Christophe's early years should be more like looking for patches to quilt rather than searching endlessly for the most perfect yarns to knit. A dizzying multitude of names and stories, some known and others quite unknown, surged forth in the barest as in the most voluminous of previously unearthed documentary traces; there are Coidavids and Dureaus, Badêches and Pétignys, Monjeons and Gayes. One unlikely name the grand riddle of young Christophe has quite newly brought forth is that of Faxardo. Originally from Spain, members of this family of Jewish converts to Catholicism were the owners of one of Christophe's most well-known but least chronicled early locales: La Couronne Hotel. Yet perhaps the most surprising surname that has risen here to the surface is Marie-Louise's own. For our future queen was born with the last name not of Coidavid but of Malgrin. We might not have yet determined the precise contours of their world in Saint-Domingue before the revolution that made Haiti free, but it is certain that the interacting destinies of our subject with his and his wife's known relatives and associates hold the key to one day unfolding the full family history of the king and queen of Haiti.

An 1807 French encyclopedia of noteworthy individuals called the *Biographie moderne* (Modern biography) appears to be the first source to have connected Henry Christophe to the "trader [*négociant*]named Badêche," to whom he was reportedly sold in Cap after serving in the Battle of Savannah.[1] The competing *Biographie des hommes vivants* (Biography of living men), published in 1816, further complicated this story by adding a conflicting detail. The later *Biographie* acknowledged the existence of the tale about Badèche having purchased Christophe to be his "slave" while also averring, "There is no agreement about Christophe's origins." Citing the beliefs of some (though the entry does not say precisely whom), the writer continued by suggesting that Christophe was actually born in the colony of Saint-Domingue on a plantation in Limonade owned by Laurent Dureau de la Malle and later his son, the celebrated French translator Jean-Baptiste Dureau de la Malle.[2] An even later 1833 entry in the multivolume encyclopedia, rebranded as the *Biographie universelle* (Universal biography), somewhat cleared up its 1816 story by clarifying that Christophe had been born on the island of Grenada and that it was only after having fought in the American War of Independence that he "was employed as a commander or overseer of negroes at a plantation in Limonade, which belonged at the time to Dureau de la Malle."[3]

Though stories linking Christophe's birth to the Dureau (de la Malle) plantation in the Bois-de-Lance quartier of Limonade continued to be published, an extensive search through the plantation records for the Dureau family's eight separate plantations in Saint-Domingue has not turned up any trace of Christophe.[4] Perhaps this makes sense since Mollien, who said he derived the details of Christophe's biography from the king himself, offered proof that he claimed definitively linked Christophe to Badèche (spelled "Badèche" in Mollien's account), while not mentioning at all Dureau de la Malle. Mollien wrote that after the Battle of Savannah, Christophe was taken to Cap-Français, where he was "bought by M. Badèche, who lived with Mlle Maujon [*sic*] [usually spelled "Monjeon" or "Mongeon"], owner of the Auberge de la Couronne."[5] Nearly all Christophe's twentieth-century biographers repeat some version of this story: Badèche enslaved Christophe upon his return to Saint-Domingue, and Christophe later worked for or was enslaved by a Mademoiselle Monjeon at a hotel called La Couronne on rue Espagnole in Cap-Français.[6] But Dumesle's guide and Mollien remain the only *first-person* testimonies to link Christophe with Badèche *and* with the hotel. "At the end of the [Savannah] campaign, Colonel Pétigny's uncle, also a volunteer, urged [Christophe] to come to Cap, where he could practice his preferred trade as a mason," the guide said. "But having arrived in this town, [Christophe] preferred to attach himself to a superior officer of the garrison from Cap, named Badèche, who had since retired from service and was exercising the art of [sugar] refinery." Freedom remained precarious for people of color in the colony. The guide's account suggests this fact had the direst of consequences for Christophe. "This colonial officer," the guide said, "having lost everything he owned in gambling, had no scruples in exposing Christophe's fate to the hazards of gaming; the winner, to whose discretion he fell, sold him to the owner of the Hôtel de la Couronne, and no law protected him against this, the greatest of attacks."[7] The name Badêche does not appear in documentation of the king's life produced by nineteenth-century writers from the kingdom. However, the other name, only incidentally uttered by the guide, Pétigny, has resurfaced again and again in connection with the king, in a way that lends strong credence to the idea that at some point he aided young Christophe.

Recorded on a December 1780 baptismal record from the parish registers of Cap-Français for a "Jean-Baptiste, *quarteron*, aged two months old, *fils naturel*, or child out of wedlock, of Adélaïde, *mulatresse libre*," is the name Jean-Baptiste Pétigny. Pétigny, described as a "free mulatto," acted as the child's godfather.[8] The same name also appeared in a 1776 registry of landowners in Cap-Français. Listed as "Jean-Baptiste Petigni [*sic*] free mulatto," he owned "one-fourth of a building" in the city, which included "two wooden and masonry barracks." In 1787, Pétigny still owned the property, according to the land register for that year, which also revealed that Pétigny's house stood at number 916 and sat at the intersection between rue des Trois Chandeliers and rue Saint-Jacques (later rue Jean-Jacques), only a few blocks from La Couronne hotel.[9]

There were other free Black and white colonial families called Pétigny in colonial Saint-Domingue, but Jean-Baptiste Pétigny is the most likely candidate to have been the Chasseur-Volontaire who participated in the Battle of Savannah alongside Christophe.[10] Members of this Jean-Baptiste Pétigny's family populate dozens of pages in the nineteenth-century civil records of Haiti, called the État Civil. These records directly tie the individual destinies of multiple people bearing the name Pétigny, immediate descendants of Jean-Baptiste, to Christophe.[11] In 1811, for instance, King Henry made Célestin Pétigny (called Pétigny fils), son of Jean-Baptiste Pétigny and a woman named Anne Léveillé, a chevalier.[12] Célestin, born in either 1771 or 1772, had previously stood among the illustrious signers of the 1806 constitution who created the Republic of Haiti. During the great schism, Célestin clearly chose to tie his fate to Christophe's, and his eventual kingdom, rather than to Pétion's, and the republic. Célestin's importance to the king only grew from there. By 1814 he held the position of "crown prosecutor" in the kingdom, and he was also a singer, actor, and director at the royal theater. The younger Pétigny was clearly some kind of jack-of-all-trades. By December 1818, Christophe employed him as a "monitor," or teacher, in the kingdom's royal academy;[13] and Célestin Pétigny was important enough to Christophe to have his own coat of arms in the armorial of Haiti, which consisted of "two silver sparrowhawks with beaks of sable," bearing a black shield with a painted rooster. Below was a ribbon with his motto, "Glory is my guide."[14] Later, Christophe assigned Célestin control over the Dustout sugar plantation in Sans-Souci as part of the redistribution of former French plantations.[15]

The successes enjoyed by Célestin trickled down to his children as well. Christophe appointed Célestin's son Bellonière (also spelled "Bélonière"), who held the rank of sous-lieutenant, and *commissaire,* or commissioner, in his special police force called the *gardes du corps;* while another of Célestin's sons, Joseph, held an important post in the admiralty of the northern city of Port-de-Paix.[16] Perhaps Christophe elevated this family in his kingdom because their grandfather Jean-Baptiste had protected him in those vulnerable years after the Battle of Savannah.

Jean-Baptiste Pétigny lived a long and evidently quite prosperous life in the kingdom as well. Pétigny, the elder, died in Cap, four years after Christophe's death, in 1824, at the age of eighty-four. His death certificate listed his father and mother only as Pétigny and Babé, respectively, with his profession listed as simply "property owner."[17]

Colonial records for another member of a free Black Pétigny family, likely related to Jean-Baptiste Pétigny, provide further clues about how Christophe might have been able to make his extraordinary rise in Saint-Domingue in connection with the Pétignys and other fighters from the Savannah expedition. In the 1770s and 1780s a free man of color named Jean-Pierre Pétigny worked in the building trade in Cap-Français, but this Pétigny was an enslaver. In 1781, he purchased a twenty-six-year-old woman stamped L. SUSON on her right breast, B.SC. on her shoulder, and I.S. on her left breast. She was reportedly from the Fon nation of Dahomey and had been "sold" to him for 1,800 colonial livres. In 1784, this same Jean-Pierre Pétigny "bought" another twenty-five-year-old "Creole" for 3,000 livres.[18] Colonial records also confirm that Jean-Pierre Pétigny had commercial dealings with Jean François Édouard Léveillé, a sergeant in the Chasseurs-Volontaires who also served in Savannah, possibly related to Jean-Baptiste Pétigny's wife, Anne Léveillé.[19] It would make sense that Christophe's intimate circle at this time would have included mostly fellow members of the Chasseurs-Volontaires, since as a newcomer to the island, and still practically a child, the chasseurs were likely the only people he knew. A yet more detailed colonial record ties Jean-Pierre Pétigny, the builder, to the kind of apprenticeship that could have brought young Christophe, alone and without any kin, into this Pétigny family member's particular orbit.

In August 1783, Jean-Pierre Pétigny signed a contract to employ in a five-year apprenticeship a free child of color named Jean Germain, son of Mathieu Moreau, "a sailor and free mulatto." The contract said that Pétigny, then living on the rue des Religieuses, "took and retained the said Jean Germain as his apprentice." Pétigny's contract further stated that he "promises to show and teach his status as a carpenter [to Germain] and all that he is engaged with," and it indicated that Pétigny would also "feed, lodge, provide him with a bed, and treat him humanely and as a good master." Germain, in return, was required to "learn as best he was able all that would be shown to him by the said Pétigny and to obey him in all that he would command him to do that was lawful and honest."[20] These details are important since multiple Christophe chroniclers describe the future king as a mason who learned his trade under either a Pétigny or a Badèche.

Documentary evidence tying the future Haitian king to Badèche/ Badèche remains far more circumstantial. But a highly suggestive mention in the *Affiches* did refer to a man named Badèche whose life intertwined with a Black man named Henry whose identifying details closely match the biographical information about Christophe introduced in other sources. Recall that the first published text to link Christophe to a Mr. Badèche came to us from the 1807 *Biographie moderne,* which identified the latter as a "trader in Cap." The December 26, 1772, issue of the *Supplément aux Affiches américaines* confirms that there was in Saint-Domingue a "M. Badèche, trader in Cap," deeply involved in the slave trade. This "Badèche" can be found on a notice listed in the "Esclaves en maronage" section as the contact person for anyone with information about a fugitive from slavery described as a "nègre Congo" named Paul, stamped HEULANT DONDON, aged about twenty-five years old, and claimed as the property of a M. Heulant, planter in Haut du Trou in Dondon.[21]

According to Dumesle's guide, Badèche was a retired military officer whose gambling problem eventually led him to sell Christophe. The guide's Badèche owned a sugar refinery, though he did not reveal the location of the plantation. The *Affiches,* in contrast, listed a plantation owner and enslaver named "Badèche" as a "planter in Maribaroux," near the border of the Spanish side of the island. Then, in March 1789, a fugitive from slavery named Jean-Louis, described as a "mulatto" "without a visible stamp, eighteen years old, height of five feet, one inch tall," showed up in the "État des nègres épaves," or unclaimed slaves, section of the *Affiches.* Jean-Louis had reportedly been "saying that he belonged to M. Badèche, planter in Maribaroux."[22] Yet it is a different mention of Badèche, the planter, in the *Affiches* that has been considered by some more recent Christophe chroniclers to constitute near-explosive confirmation of Mollien's and Dumesle's accounts. On April 25, 1789, the *Supplément aux Affiches américaines* printed an ad for a fugitive from slavery that read,

Henry, mulatto, mason by trade, about twenty-two years old, five feet, two inches tall, fairly handsome in figure, strong in feet and legs, having always his mouth agape, has been maroon for about four months; he has been seen in the Acul, Périgourdins, and Grande-Ravine districts of Limbé; it is in this last district where he learned his trade of mason, at the residence of Pierre-Paul, n.l. [*nègre libre*/free negro];

it is believed that he is saying he is free, and that he calls himself Badêche: anyone who encounters him should have him arrested, and to give notice of it to Mr. Paquot, former receiver of the abandoned [slaves] in Cap, rue Bourbon. There will be a 2 *portugaises* reward.[23]

The age essentially fits, because Henry would have been nearly twenty-two years old, and according to Colonel Vincent, when he returned from Savannah, Christophe "practiced the profession of masonry." With this ad, therefore, we have a name match, an age match, and a profession match, plus the connection to Badêche, along with the story about Christophe having gained liberty or at least having claimed it at some point, only to be perilously pursued as a slave.

Drawing on the notice communicated to him by Vincent's son, Saint-Rémy added more details that would seem to confirm the prior accounts. Saint-Rémy said that after having been incorporated into the Chasseurs-Volontaires, Christophe had at first gained his freedom. Afterward "another French officer, to whom Christophe attached himself," and whom Saint-Rémy did not name, "brought him back to Cap, where he worked as a mason." Even without naming Pétigny as the one who might have trained him in such a profession, nor Badêche as Christophe's eventual enslaver, in Saint-Rémy/Vincent's account "that officer, who had a passion for gambling, lost everything he owned, and had no qualms about using his protégé as collateral, whom he also lost." As a result, "Christophe was sold in Cap as an abandoned slave to Miss Minjon [Monjeon], mistress of the Hôtel de la Couronne."[24]

The interlocking stories of Christophe's freedom being taken away, along with the ad linking the enslaved man Henry, "saying he is free," to Badêche, encapsulate the precarities of Black freedom in Saint-Domingue. The *Affiches* was filled with notices of Black people insisting they were free but who were subjected to slavery or incarceration anyway. An ad for "Joseph, Mulatto, stamped CHERRUELLE & J. MASSE, maroon since August 20 last," "saying he is free," underscores the disturbing plausibility of the alleged circumstances multiple Christophe chroniclers aver forced the future king into enslaved status. This same Joseph argued for his liberty by "claiming to be a *chasseur-volontaire* currently on leave." After being held in captivity on the suspicion of being a fugitive, Joseph evidently "escaped from the dungeon of Mr. Gautier, planter in Dondon, on the night of December 28 last, where he was detained at the request of Mr. Laferrière, planter in said place, who had him arrested on the denunciation of Mr. Lavalière, captain of the regiment in Cap, as a maroon." Anyone who recognized Joseph was encouraged to arrest him or have him arrested and alert Mr. Masse, "procurer in Fort Dauphin," who would provide compensation.[25] Apart from stating their names, an enslaved person "saying he is free" remained one of the most consistently recorded utterances

from the thousands of Black people at large in the colony due to marronnage or incarcerated for having previously engaged in it. The ads in the
Affiches thus cataloged a remarkable record of the specific instabilities of
freedom that cohered to former Chasseurs-Volontaires, like Christophe,
many of whom returned home to Saint-Domingue saying they were free
but found themselves subjected to slavery anyway.

Christophe's best-known twentieth-century biographer, Vergniaud
Leconte, put the sugar planter named Badêche on the Portelance plantation in the district of Petite-Anse, where there is a plantation today called
Madeline. Though neither confirms the chain of recitation—either written or oral—both Cole and a later biographer, Louis-Émile Élie, gave the
same trajectory to Christophe, clearly drawing from Leconte's account.[26]
Leconte said that Badêche had made Christophe "a student of cooking"
and that Christophe so excelled in this art that he eventually became
"lead chef" on Badêche's plantation in Petite-Anse, adding that at the
time Badêche "had formed a partnership with Miss Monjeon," who ran
"a hotel, under the ensign of La Couronne, located in Cap, at rue Espagnole," today called rue Henri-Christophe. Claiming that Christophe
was "a dozen years old" at that moment, Leconte further put him with
the Chasseurs-Volontaires, but only *after* Christophe allegedly began his
apprenticeship at the hotel. In other words, in Leconte's account, Christophe somehow ended up living in Saint-Domingue *before* the Battle of
Savannah. Upon his return from Savannah, in Leconte's retelling, Badêche
reemployed Christophe at the hotel "as supervisor and butler." The hotel
reportedly thrived under Christophe's direction. So much so that Leconte
claimed the future king eventually took over management of the hotel
from Badêche and Monjeon entirely. "The Revolution of 1789 saw him
become an innkeeper," Leconte concluded. "He was twenty-two years old
at the time."[27]

Christophe did, in fact, work at the La Couronne hotel in some capacity,
but my precise documentation of the hotel's various owners and managers
from the 1760s until Haitian independence contradicts Leconte's account.

Multiple men from the era who knew Christophe personally put him
at the Couronne hotel, starting with Cathcart. Cathcart may be the earliest source, in fact, to have connected Christophe to the lucrative and
fancy inn. But perhaps most important, Cathcart appears to be the only
one of his acquaintances who wrote this information down while Christophe was still alive. "He was formerly maître d'Hotel, at the Couronne,"
Cathcart wrote to General Maitland in 1799.[28] A white French lawyer
who served as the chief clerk for the admiralty of Port-au-Prince in the
late eighteenth century, Alfred de Laujon, wrote in his 1835 memoir that
he personally saw Christophe working at the hotel: "It would be a great
omission on my part to fail to disclose that dining one day at the Hôtel
de la Couronne, which was the most renowned in Cap, I had the honor of

being served there by a man whose head was to be crowned one day. That famous Christophe, that northern tyrant, that monster of nature, was a slave in this hotel."[29] Colonel Vincent also placed Christophe at the Couronne but Saint-Rémy added the detail that Christophe "soon became, by the spirit of leading with which he was endowed and due to the affection of his mistress, the butler of the establishment." "It was in this job that he learned," Saint-Rémy continued, "having been in regular contact with foreigners, to judge men and things, to speak a quite pure French, and to read and write."[30] In yet another chronicler's recollection, Christophe had charge of the hotel's stables, "and the voyagers never had anything but praise to offer him concerning the exercise of his functions." One voyager, whose account was published in 1815, while he did not name the Couronne specifically, claimed that in his profession as a waiter Christophe had the occasion to often serve none other than the Marquis de Rouvray, head of the Chasseurs-Volontaires during the Savannah expedition.[31]

In keeping with his usual style of narration, Dumesle's guide offered a highly editorialized, even sensational account of Christophe's time at the hotel. The guide claimed that forced into slavery there, but "skillful in the art of flattering the passions, [Christophe] soon performed with his new boss the role he had played with his first master." Having acquired "the stewardship of his house," Christophe "became so insinuating" with his new enslaver's wife "that she was reproached for having shown him too much kindness." The guide's story then grew fantastic. The enslaver's "suspicions, which would have been fatal to anyone but Christophe, were useful to him," the guide continued. Christophe became "more and more necessary to his master, who, either concerned with his wife's reputation, and wanting to ward off odious suspicions about her, or because her absence seemed necessary to him so he could indulge in debauchery without reservation, for which he had a decided taste, sent her to France where she remained until 1790." Once the revolution broke out, the wife evidently returned to Cap, and at the announcement of the slave rebellion Christophe "was freed again with the intention of ensuring his attachment to the colonists, and there is also reason to believe that it is at this point that his patron had the desire to remove him from his house," ostensibly to prevent further fraternizing with his wife.[32]

Mollien, who reported that Christophe spoke to him intimately of this part of his early life, recalled that Christophe worked at the hotel, too, after having been "purchased" by Badêche, who lived with a "Mlle Maujon [sic], of the inn called La Couronne." Though slightly less sensational than Dumesle's account, Mollien's is still filled with salacious tidbits worthy of any daytime drama. "He distinguished himself at her home by his intelligence, his honesty, his cleanliness, a certain refinement in his dress, and above all his lack of socializing with the other slaves," Mollien wrote. "By grace of his good conduct, he became her confidant and the butler of the inn; he was noticed there by the regulars who were happy to show him their satisfaction with frequent gratuities." Christophe allegedly used the money he earned at the hotel to buy his own domestic slave with the consent of his "mistress" as well as a "little negro slave to serve him whom he made a martyr." "The character of Christophe, the slave, already showed what he was later to become for so many people, cruel, vindictive," Mollien claimed. In a fit of rage, Mollien alleged, Christophe set the enslaved child's clothing on fire. Christophe's hatred for the child grew every day, Mollien said, and Christophe resolved to get rid of him, to sell him, or to use the enslaved child's value in exchange for his own freedom vis-à-vis Monjeon. Christophe supposedly proposed this very exchange to Monjeon, who rejected it outright. It is not clear from Mollien's account how he arrived at these details, but we must assume they came from one of the king's enemies. We can hardly imagine Christophe admitting to having enslaved someone, and especially to having treated a young child so cruelly. Nevertheless, Christophe's plan supposedly worked. Monjeon eventually relented on the condition that he pay her 150 louis and agree to manage large dinners at the hotel. The "sale" would have been complete, but Christophe did not have the sum that Monjeon demanded. Therefore, "his friends lent it to him, and Christophe took his rank among the free," Mollien wrote.[33]

Although many Christophe chroniclers have claimed that the hotel on rue Espagnole called La Couronne belonged to or was managed by Badêche and/or a woman named Monjeon (sometimes spelled "Mongeon"), documentary evidence does not at this time indicate that Badêche had anything to do with the hotel, and he certainly does not appear to have been an official owner or manager. However, a woman named Luce Monjeon did become co-manager of the hotel in the late spring of 1787.[34]

The earliest records for the Hôtel de la Couronne de France (also known as the Auberge la Couronne), one of the oldest inns in Cap-Français, date from the late 1760s. Situated at the intersection of rue Canard and rue Espagnole, one of the longest streets in Cap, the hotel that eventually became known as La Couronne was initially established under the name of L'Auberge du Dauphin Couronné by a free man of color known as Toussaint Morepas (sometimes spelled "Maurepas"), also known as "Toussaint, the Mulatto." Management of the hotel, under the new name of La Couronne de France, was eventually transferred to a widow named Husard and her associate, a man named Briot, who later moved the hotel slightly down the street to rue Espagnole and rue des Trois Visages.[35] The pair faced much competition, not only in Cap-Français in general, but on the rue Espagnole in particular.

By the 1760s, rue Espagnole already bustled with activity. The boulevard was home to a nunnery, several pensions, schools, shops, and restaurants, as well as other inns and hotels.[36] One such inn, owned by Drieau

Lataille, whom we earlier met, was far more vast and more luxurious than Morepas's had been. "All the possible conveniences and amenities can be found here, such as single- and two-bedroom accommodations, separate rooms and apartments for those who do not want to share, and where they will be, if they want, served separately and with the utmost delicacy, having in his home a very good white cook," read an ad for Lataille's hotel in the *Affiches*. The hotel also offered "large and beautiful sheds for horses and carriages" as well as "horses and carriages for hire which he purposely keeps in a separate yard, opposite his house, where he has very large sheds, with coachmen and postilions, and Negroes to run errands throughout the dependency."[37]

By February 1781, Husard and Briot were ready to compete with Lataille. In the notice the pair issued to announce the relocation of the Couronne hotel, Husard and Briot said they had "acquired a larger and more convenient one under the same ensign, on the same street, next to Sieur Lataille." "This house offers all kinds of amenities for carriages, horses, and animals of every nature," their ad read. "There are sheds, stables in the French style, a very large courtyard that can be locked, ten apartments, and twenty master bedrooms." In this new locale, "Dame Husard and her associate will neglect nothing to satisfy the inhabitants who will do them the honor of staying at their residence."[38] From this time forward, the Couronne de France was considered one of the most luxurious hotels for Saint-Dominguan planters, as well as for newly arrived travelers and transplants from across the world. One such visitor, Sieur Michel, arrived at the hotel in late January 1783. Not long after, he took out an ad in the *Affiches* notifying the public that at his store, located at the Couronne hotel, customers could find "cotton fabrics of all qualities, loincloths from Madagascar for men's clothes and women's negligees, Chinese bed mats, and so on."[39] Christophe might have had the opportunity to watch La Couronne's transformation from simple inn to luxurious hotel, but probably not to enjoy its many delights.

Husard and Briot quit the hotel in May 1783. On the fourteenth, an announcement in the *Affiches* noted that "Sirs Meyer and Monier, the first previously a chef, and head butler of the Prince-de-Broglie, give notice that they have acquired everything that was a part of the Auberge de la Couronne, rue Espagnole." Meyer and Monier announced they would continue to receive guests and "offer to the public their services in all kinds of cuisine; they will also be responsible for training students. They will provide at home, or prepare to send to people who want it, all kinds of meals."[40] This ad reveals more than a simple change in management for the very hotel where, according to numerous eyewitnesses, Christophe worked in the decade before the Haitian Revolution began. Meyer, a chef of some renown, offered to share his skills with students. In many accounts, Christophe acquired his culinary proficiency at this very hotel, which doubled as a culinary school (most cooks in the colony were people of color, enslaved or free), eventually taking over the management of the large dinners for which the Couronne became famous.

While Meyer and Monier were busy selling off their properties elsewhere in the colony and cementing the Couronne as the most popular and frequented hotel in Cap,[41] another eventual Christophe associate was moving into the neighborhood too: the oft-evoked woman named Monjeon. On March 31, 1784, a detailed notice stated that "Mademoiselle Mongeon" wished to alert the public that "Sieur Étienne Flury, formerly residing at her home at the Caffé [sic] de la Bourse, left it on the twenty-fifth of this month, that he does not have any engagements in any business concerning the said café and in the event that he represents himself as having any, those charges will be of his own account, and not related to that of the said café."[42] Not long after breaking her connection with Flury, Monjeon followed the custom of the colony and informed the public of her plan to return to France. She sought to sell her café, which was "well furnished, with all the advantages one could wish for in a house like this." Along with the building and its contents, she planned to sell the "Negroes" enslaved by her therein.[43]

Yet it appears that Monjeon did not leave the colony after selling her café. Only a few weeks after the above notice appeared, Monjeon entered into a partnership with a man named Jean-Pierre Gaye (sometimes spelled "Gay") and Félix Doubrere, the latter the owner of the Hôtel du Bon-Chasseur on rue Espagnole and rue de la Vielle Jouaillerie. The agreement spelled out that for a period of two years Monjeon and Gaye, known for their "hard work and industriousness," would run the hotel. As a pair they were entitled to one-third of the hotel's profits, while Doubrere, as the owner of the building, would keep the other two-thirds. The agreement included a list of people enslaved by the hotelier, though none match the name, age, or nation of Christophe. As its caretakers, Monjeon and Gaye did not drag their feet to advertise the Bon Chasseur, which they described as "well furnished and with twelve bedrooms to let," including baths and "all the amenities necessary for MM. the Voyagers, as well as a very fine stable to lodge their horses." The ad also boasted that the hotel met standards of "the greatest cleanliness." The Bon Chasseur, like the Couronne, could also accommodate residents, not simply short-term guests: "Mademoiselle Monjeon and Gaye take boarders at full board and half board."[44] Doubrere's vast hotel, under the direction of Monjeon and Gaye, provided yet more competition for the Couronne.

Capitalizing on the apparent popularity and allure of baths among inn guests in Cap-Français, Meyer and Monier took out their own ad in September 1784 to differentiate their hotel from the competition: "Meyer and Monier, owners of the Auberge de la Couronne de France, rue Espagnole, have the honor to inform the public, and particularly the residents, that they have just made improvements to their residence, for the convenience of those who will do them the honor of staying with them."[45] Although the ad referred to the pair as the owners, notarial records and other documents from the time show them, like Monjeon and Gaye of the Bon Chasseur, to have been merely La Couronne's managers.

The Saint-Domingue government's 1776 survey of owners and renters on every street in Saint-Domingue shows that a property owner named Alexandre Faxardo (under one of his known transcriptions, Fessard) had acquired numerous properties in Cap through inheritance, including two flanking rue des Trois Visages, which the hotel bordered. A 1787 government report listing the owner of every house in Cap-Français by address number offered yet more specific and confirmatory information, listing a property owner named "Fexardo" (yet another known transcription for Faxardo) as the owner of four emplacements on rue Espagnole, numbers 714, a portion of 786, 787, and 788, the latter (number 788) the site of the famous Hôtel de la Couronne de France on rue Espagnole.

The elaborate maps the French government produced for the reconstruction of Cap-Français after the 1793 fire show a city organized by continuous plot or building address, starting with the number 1 on the edge of the rue du Conseil (later rue de la Convention) and winding continuously from north to south and then back up and down again, ending with building number 1011 on rue Sainte-Avoie (later rue Militaire), near the Grande Casernes and the Hôpital de la Providence. The hotel stood at the corner of rue Espagnole and rue des Trois Visages (previously rue Vierges) just north of the Place Royale (Place Nationale) at the other end of the street from Cap's famous theater house, the Salle de Spectacle.[46]

The owner of the building housing the hotel was a French colonist of Spanish descent named Alexandre Abraham Faxardo (occasionally spelled "Fexardo" as in the 1787 cadastre, or Fessard, as in the earlier 1776 version). He inherited the property along with a considerable sum of money after a successful lawsuit in 1781 that allowed him to claim a large portion of his uncle Salomon Pierre Faxardo's enormous estate amounting to more than 400,000 colonial livres following the latter's death in 1773. The lawsuit was complicated and involved France's laws of *aubaine* that precluded foreigners from certain countries, such as Portugal, along with Jewish people, from inheriting property in the colony. Due to a clerical error, some family members in the colony were listed as Portuguese Jews upon their deaths. It took the Faxardo heirs born in Saint-Domingue, whose origins were demonstrably in seventeenth-century Spain but whose family members had been naturalized French citizens since the early eighteenth century, several years to successfully contest the claim and become the rightful inheritors of the Faxardo estate. The naturalized family members and their heirs born in France and Saint-Domingue claimed they had long since converted to Catholicism and presented evidence, such as lack of male circumcision, by which they successfully proved they were not barred from inheriting property in the colony.[47]

Alexandre Faxardo leased the building where the hotel had been established to Monier (first name unknown) and Charles Meyer beginning on July 17, 1784, according to an agreement signed before the notary in Cap on that day.[48] By June 1786, Alexandre Faxardo was conducting his business out of the hotel, too, under the ensign of MM. Faxardo frères.[49] The partnership must have been a fruitful one. In September, Meyer and Monier announced they had completed the construction of "very spacious and very airy" open stables, along with other amenities, promising that "anyone will feel at home in all the elegance and cleanliness here so as to leave nothing to be desired." They also ensured they would "continue to provide meals of any variety for those in town."[50] Still, it was hard to stay in business. Competitors likewise added amenities regularly, and new hotels seemed constantly to crop up on the bustling rue Espagnole.

Before long, Monier desired to exit the hotel business. A notice from January 1785 informed the public that Meyer and Monier had dissolved their "society," or company, and that Meyer would now "solely manage the Hôtel de la Couronne de France."[51] The renamed and now solely managed Hôtel de la Couronne de France faced still more competition. Just one month later, a woman named Cécile LaRue, owner of the Hôtel des Habitants on rue Espagnole and rue du Canard, the former site of the Couronne under the ownership of Morepas, placed an ad in the *Affiches* noting that she was opening her house with baths and stables to guests too.[52]

As a lone innkeeper, Meyer made constant adjustments to his offerings at the Couronne to keep up with the competition. On January 25, 1786, he placed an ad to "alert Messieurs the Planters that he will take possession on February 2 next of a newly built hotel adjoining the one he occupies, consisting of thirty-two upper and lower rooms, very well furnished, with a large courtyard, French-style stables, able to house forty horses, sheds, and other amenities."[53] By mid-April, the expansion of the Couronne was complete.[54] The announcement for the hotel's newly expanded amenities and services provides a detailed and instructive description of Henry's potential surroundings. The announcement said that Meyer, "having spared nothing for the embellishment of his furniture, has made arrangements for several rooms with one or two twin beds, very well furnished, to receive ladies here who will be good enough to give him the pleasure and honor of staying in his home." Meyer would take in boarders and planned to have apprentices and grass available year-round for cattle and for guests' horses. This greatly expanded hotel boasted that in addition to "ordinary amenities" it could offer "more sumptuous meals."[55] Just before the expansion was complete, to replace Monier, whose cooking was renowned in the colony, Meyer placed an ad that said he sought to "take on or lease a Negro who is a good cook and a wig maker who is able to do the hair of men and women, and twelve to fifteen Negroes born in this country, able to work in a garden."[56] If Henry was not already at the hotel, perhaps he ended up there because of this ad.

Throughout Monier's management the luxurious hotel continued to be a lively place where white visitors could hawk their wares, sell their services, and enjoy the life of luxury and leisure denied to those enslaved on the premises. Perhaps the enslaved Black laborers of the Couronne de France watched as Gérard, a painter newly arrived from Paris, drew portraits in miniature of the colony's inhabitants for 3 *portugaises* per bust, also giving drawing lessons at the hotel.[57] Likewise they might have witnessed a Mr. Dumas selling "two superb repeater watches, adorned with diamonds."[58] Perhaps it was on these premises and dreaming of one day owning these very things that our Henry Christophe motivated himself to learn business strategies and developed the acumen that led him later to become one of the colony's most successful businessmen.

Running a large establishment in the colony, such as a hotel, was a serious undertaking, which perhaps accounts for the number of times the Couronne changed management since Toussaint Morepas—who was still alive and managing a plantation in Grande-Rivière on the eve of the French Revolution—first established the Auberge du Dauphin Couronné on rue Espagnole and rue Canard.[59] On May 24, 1787, the Couronne's management changed once again and seemingly for the final time. According to a rental agreement issued by the notary of Saint-Domingue three days before Gaye and Monjeon took over, on May 24, Faxardo had newly leased the building housing the hotel to the duo, who were now its managers, as Monier and Meyer had been. On June 2, 1787, the *Affiches* printed an ad formally announcing that Monjeon and Gaye, now under the title of MM. Gaye & Compagnie, had acquired the famous Hôtel de la Couronne de France, which the ad called "well known enough that it is not necessary to describe it."[60]

Monjeon and Gaye had not evidently experienced success in their first attempt to partner with one of Cap's prominent hoteliers. The pair dissolved their partnership with Doubrere and relinquished all interest in the Bon Chasseur hotel long before their lease was set to expire, but just two months after they signed it. On November 27, 1784, a notary officially dissolved the "society" between Doubrere and Monjeon and Gaye,[61] and subsequently an ad in the *Affiches* featured Monjeon and Gaye's previous property, as now managed by a man named Chévrier. Alongside the ad there was an announcement that Jean-Baptiste, Congo, "a cook, previously belonging to the late Mr. Bernard Longueville, about thirty years old, stamped on the right breast with different stamps, and only a few days ago newly stamped on the same breast, Villevaleix," left as a maroon. "Anyone who arrests him and brings him back to Mr. Chévrier managing the Hôtel du Bon-Chasseur and public baths, rue Espagnole, will be rewarded." What a juxtaposition. No luxury was spared for the white planters, especially as regarded the cuisine, despite the enslaved Black cook Jean-Baptiste's self-liberation. "A proper table and good food will be the care and the occupations of the said sir Chévrier," the ad concluded, "and will show him to be of a most honest character deserving their esteem and benevolence."[62] There would have been ample opportunity for Christophe to escape, too, like Jean-Baptiste, if indeed any of the Couronne hotel's various managers held him in torturous bondage, rather than employed him in freedom, on the premises.

Urban hoteliers and other city dwellers experienced the same difficulties forcing captive Africans to remain enslaved on their properties as plantation owners in the plains and mountains, and they subjected enslaved men, women, and children to similar tortures. The fugitive slave notices printed in the *Affiches* provide crucial, if elusive, information about how hoteliers treated the people they enslaved at their fancy establishments. As with Chévrier and Doubrere, Meyer and the previous co-manager Monier enslaved Africans and their descendants at the Couronne hotel. A particularly telling ad for a fugitive from slavery appeared in the *Affiches* in July 1787, just one month after Gaye and Monjeon took over the hotel's management. The enslaved man in question, "having marks of his country on his chest and being thin, was arrested in Marmelade" and "did not know how to say his name nor that of his master." Yet the marks on his body could do some talking. The notice revealed that he had stamps that read "MEYER" and "DEMONEEU," "as far as we can tell," the ad clarified. The latter stamp is a phonetic way of pronouncing "de Monier," or "belonging to Monier." Slave trafficking had also occurred at the hotel. On December 14, 1785, in the "For Sale" section, a M. Deméoque, residing at the "Hôtel de la Couronne de France," sought to sell "six beautiful Negroes and Negresses, including two Creoles, from a newly sold café." The ad guaranteed them as "good subjects, who would be worth the cash."[63] It is not terribly out of the realm of possibility to imagine that Christophe encountered these people sold under the same roof where he lived and where he was perhaps enslaved.

Slavery continued at the hotel, as elsewhere in the colony, even after the enormous freedom uprising began in August 1791. In the December 24, 1792, issue of the *General Monitor of the French Part of Saint-Domingue,* another fugitive slave ad appeared indicating the enslaved man in marronnage "belonged" to someone living at the Couronne hotel. "On the thirteenth of the current month, a negro left as a maroon belonging to citizen Chauvet Dubreuil, named Antoine, of the Congo nation, aged about twenty-eight, stocky, well-made legs, skin a little reddish, marked with smallpox, and stamped on the right breast, Ve. Constant, almost illegibly. Those who have information about him are requested to give notice at the Maison de la Couronne, or to the citizens Demouhaison and Lelong, traders in Cap."[64] While we have now been able to confirm that the hotel still operated on the eve of general emancipation of the colony's enslaved population in 1793, the fate of the hotel following the famous June 1793, burning of Cap, which precipitated general emancipation of the enslaved population, can now also be determined using notarial documents.

In July 1793, around ten days after the great fire in Cap, Alexandre Faxardo announced his intention to leave the colony for New England.[65] His will reveals that he resided in the United States for about a year before returning to Saint-Domingue to take up residence on the Île de la Tortue. In July 1794, Faxardo traveled from his home on the island of La Tortue to appear before a notary in the northern coastal city of Port-de-Paix with the singular goal of providing the terms of his last wishes. In the will he dictated before the justice of the peace, Faxardo left to his sister, Rachel Roze Faxardo (married name Pereire), then living in Bordeaux, homes at 786, 787, and 788 rue Espagnole. In 1799, Rachel Roze submitted a petition to the government seeking permission to allow "citizen Grenier," another businessman in Cap, to rehabilitate the properties on her behalf. The petition Rachel Roze submitted confirms not only the precise location of the hotel at number 788 but that Monjeon and Gaye remained the Couronne's managers at the time of the 1793 fire that destroyed nearly the entire street.[66]

Aside from revealing the hotel's precise location and its status after the fire, the documents submitted by Rachel Roze, along with her brother's will, contained a precise survey of the hotel's actual state in 1799 when she petitioned for its reconstruction. The residence directly next door to the hotel, number 787, also owned by Faxardo, somehow survived the fire and the revolution intact. Rachel Roze's petition reveals that in 1799 house number 787 on rue Française (formerly Espagnole), "forming the corner of the said rue and rue du Chantier occupying the site of approximately half an islet, is intact on the ground floor and first floor and built of masonry covered in *thuiles* [dry stones]." Although the house was "presently in need of repair, being absolutely degraded in various rooms and even totally as to floors and roof tiles," it was nevertheless habitable, "furnished still with its iron bars as well as its windows." Remarkably, there were people living on the property, and some of them were running businesses. "It is observed moreover that the part of the ground floor overlooking rue Française is occupied by citizen Auzou, elementary school teacher to whom the administration has provided housing," the surveyor noted. The home at 787 still had bedrooms, offices, a kitchen, a well, and a courtyard, in which the French government allowed its musicians and police officers to reside.

As for house number 788, the former site of the hotel, it remained in shambles. The surveyors who submitted their report with Rachel Roze's petition observed, "Next to the said house rue Française [number 787] is a space of approximately a quarter of an islet on which is built a house on the ground floor forming the corner of the said street and the rue des Trois Visages, which was set on fire, and at number 788, there being only the walls in fairly good condition, in the courtyard of which it seems that there existed various high rooms forming a floor, folded into the walls which still exist and which by means of some repairs have been brought to support the structure and that previously served as an auberge under the name of the Couronne occupied by the *citoyen* Mayere [*sic*] and the *cito-yenne* Mongeon." The French government, under Louverture's authority, granted Grenier, last known caretaker of the hotel, and possibly the same Jean-Pierre Grenier who was a known associate of Christophe's, as we shall later see, possession of both properties. He also acquired the lease for the entirely burned property next door, save the walls, at number 786, part of which had previously been occupied by the late hotelier Drieau Lataille.[67]

If number 787 survived the 1793 fire, it was not so lucky in the one ordered by Christophe in February 1802. In early March of that year, Jean-Baptiste LeGrand, a harquebusier, or gunner, submitted an application to lease house number 787, listed as belonging to a planter named Dumont Lagrange. LeGrand's application stated, "There is a burned-down house on rues Sautier [Chantier] and Espagnole under number 787 belonging to citizen Dumont Lagrange, resident on the American continent." Lagrange owned many plantations in Saint-Domingue, but until this time he was not associated with house number 787 in Cap.[68] This strongly indicates fraud or a mistake. If Rachel Roze sold the property to Lagrange some time before Christophe ordered the city set aflame, the French government did not recognize the sale. French government records from 1803 list the owner of the emplacement at 787 rue Espagnole (along with those at 786 and 788) as "Fexardo." Rachel Roze later claimed and was awarded an indemnity for the same house in 1828 in the amount of 10,000 francs.[69] Although LeGrand's application to rehabilitate number 787 did not reveal what happened to number 788, site of the former hotel, it did provide an imperfect clue. A later notation dated March 28, 1802, scribbled by a French official down the side of LeGrand's original application, stated that the two closest neighbors to number 787 on rue Espagnole had received permission to rebuild their properties.[70] Those reconstructions likely never occurred either. Rachel Roze claimed and was awarded an indemnity of 10,800 francs in 1828 for building number 788, the former hotel.[71] And with that document, revealing the final (official) owner of the Hôtel de la Couronne to have been Alexandre Faxardo's sister, Rachel Roze, so vanishes the immediate trace of an establishment that was once the crossroads of colonial Cap-Français and home to Henry Christophe, the future king of Haiti.

While these documents reveal what happened to the owners of the hotel, they tell us little about what happened to its managers, and nothing about Christophe's trajectory in the years leading up to and immediately following the start of the Black freedom struggle in August 1791. For both, we can look back to Saint-Domingue's newspapers.

When Monjeon and Gaye took over management of the hotel in 1787, they were clearly worried that the loss of Meyer, the hotel's famous chef, would affect the Couronne's reputation. They took out an additional ad just a few weeks after their acquisition to inform the public that the hotel had a new chef, famous in his own right, who would be taking on "apprentice cooks and pastry chefs." Not only did they make this chef, Sieur Riefau, the "manager of their hotel," but they also emphasized that he had been "engaged at the hotel for several years, and was well known to Messieurs the Inhabitants due to his talents, since he had already worked for some time with Mr. Meyer." With Riefau running the show, Monjeon and Gaye confidently announced, "They will provide meals in town at various prices."[72] Importantly, since this ad announces Riefau as the manager and head chef of the hotel at the time that Gaye and Monjeon took on its direction, it suggests that if Christophe did ascend to a management position, it was likely some time after 1787.

Although Gaye and Monjeon remained the managers or directors of the hotel in the wake of the French Revolution and on the eve of the wide-scale slave revolt that led to the Haitian Revolution and, eventually, independence, the hotel might have had its own troubles unrelated to those already brewing in the colony. On January 27, 1790, Monjeon and Gaye placed an ad in the *Affiches* to reassure the public that while the hotel continued to smoothly operate, they were implementing changes to better accommodate their guests: "Gaye & compagnie, managers of the Hôtel de la Couronne de France, rue Espagnole, give notice to the residents that far from having given up their eagerness to procure everything that their guests may need, they have just on the contrary increased the number of their servants, their furniture and lodgings." "They will never cease to redouble their efforts and their attention so as to be deserving of the confidence and esteem of those who will do them the honor of staying at their residence," the ad continued.[73] Yet by the spring of 1792, after the Black freedom struggle had begun in earnest, notices for the hotel in the colony's newspapers, suggestively, no longer mentioned Monjeon.[74]

It is perhaps too much to hope that a Black man, without his own fortune, like young Henry, might appear by name as one of the "slaves" or "servants," in any of the Couronne hotel's many ads, except perhaps in the sections reserved for the sale of "negroes," or announcing their incarceration. Yet perusing the *Affiches* does permit us to further imagine the world that young Henry might have inhabited on the rue Espagnole, specifically at the Couronne hotel, under its many managers.

Among the many visitors who resided at or lived near the hotel were clothing makers, priests, businessmen, sailors and ship captains, human traffickers, apothecaries, and saddle and carriage makers.[75] The rue Espagnole was also home to the Salle de Spectacle, where Henry, who grew to love theater and the opera, might have caught a glimpse of Collot d'Herbois's play about the French siege of Grenada being performed by the Comedians of Cap in 1781. A site of segregation, the "rear of the amphitheater" was reserved for "mulattoes and mulattas," which is to say free people of color, men and women. Enslaved Africans sometimes accompanied their enslavers to the segregated theater house as well.[76]

If, as our eyewitnesses have it, Christophe still lived on rue Espagnole and worked at the Couronne the year before the Haitian Revolution began in 1791, he might have, on the afternoon of July 11, 1790, witnessed something to rival Saint-Domingue's many works of theater. A few weeks prior, Hibert, a long-standing resident and "saddle and carriage maker," announced his plan to hold a lottery at the hotel for a "superb car in the form of a stagecoach, mounted on two wheels and four springs, very soft and light." The bottom of the carriage was cherry colored, the train was painted green with harnesses for five horses, "enriched with a quantity of ornaments, as well as buckles and bits of the bridles, and boots for the coachmen, all fur gilded." At Hibert's residence located in the Couronne hotel, those seeking to acquire the elaborate carriage could purchase one of ninety lottery tickets for 1 *portugaise* apiece. Hibert estimated the worth of the carriage at approximately 6,000 colonial livres. The public would be notified of the winner in about fifteen days, once the lottery was complete.[77]

Years later, as king, Christophe deeply admired the kind of luxurious carriage that he might have first witnessed being offered to the lucky winner of Hibert's lottery. In July 1815, the American press reported that the king of Haiti "had a state carriage made in London," the likes of which had never been seen, having been constructed specifically for use in Haiti. "The shape being entirely novel" with "the front projecting outward for the purpose of shade, which is exceedingly pleasing to the eye, the lining [was] of the richest velvet, embroidered with the star of the order of St. Henry," while the "drapery was fringed with gold of immense richness." "The seat and forepart, resembling the lions' standards, are solidly gilt," the description continued. "The braces and every ornament correspond with equal grandeur." All told, Christophe had twenty-two other such elaborate carriages made for the royal family and other members of his nobility.[78]

Carriages and lavish dinners, dangled before his eyes but just out of reach, must have nourished some ambition in Christophe's adolescent soul. At the hotel, Christophe would have been surrounded by opportunities and fineries of which he and the colony's enslaved population could only dream. By 1790, rue Espagnole remained Cap's busiest and most expensive avenue. Previously home to a nunnery and to dentists and goldsmiths, there was by then a dye factory and a veterinary school, as well as several boarding schools, including one specifically for girls.[79] Yet these schools were for little white children, not girls of color born into free Black families, like Christophe's future wife, Marie-Louise. If young Marie-Louise, eleven years his junior, could not have run into him while attending a nearby school, how did the future king and queen of Haiti meet?

—

The future queen of Haiti was born on May 8, 1778, according to the only known official record of her birth date in the *Royal Almanac of Haiti*. Marie-Louise's biographer, Marceau Louis, without revealing the chain of recitation, claimed that she was born Marie-Louise Coidavid on the Bedou plantation in the commune of Ouanaminthe to Black parents with free status. Noting that Henry and Marie-Louise married in 1793—the date can be independently confirmed by the *Royal Almanac* as having occurred on July 15—Louis owned that he could not be sure how the pair might have met. "Did the two young people meet one day during a patrol made by Christophe through Ouanaminthe," Louis asked, "or was Marie-Louise more likely to have been in Cap?" "We do not know anything about it at all," Louis concluded. "But what is certain is a very sweet sentiment must have arisen between them and that in 1793 they married."[80]

Although there was a free Black family in Ouanaminthe by the name of Bédou (sometimes spelled "Bedout" and with or without an accent), records from that plantation have not yet produced any documentary traces connecting Marie-Louise or any Coidavids to the family.[81] Mollien and the guide from Dumesle's *Voyage* once again provide the most detailed accounts of what Christophe was doing just before the eruption of the large-scale Black freedom struggle in August 1791 and how he met Marie-Louise, whom he wed on the eve of general emancipation. "Once freed, he had to provide for his subsistence," Mollien wrote. "He soon found the means; he became a *courtier* [a broker]: he went aboard American ships to buy poultry and resold it at the market for small profits. In a short time, he had enough to take an interest in the butchery run by Désormes, whose good faith he easily betrayed, and whom he later compensated by admitting him into his intimacy and showering him with favors." Mollien further claimed that Christophe frequently needed money because of his gambling habit. In vain, he would one day win a fortune, only to lose it the next, Mollien said. The French traveler also alleged that in gambling Christophe frequently engaged in quarrels that he almost always won.

In Mollien's recollection, Christophe met Marie-Louise amid these troubles and scams. "Christophe's resources were increasingly exhausted every day; he did not know how to procure more: love got him out of this trouble. Marie-Louise Cosavit [*sic*], a free negress, aged twenty-eight [the age, based on her date of birth, is wrong], wise and beautiful, caught the eye of the former butler of La Couronne." Mollien further claimed that the future queen had been an herb and vegetable market woman, and that she had amassed a small fortune that Christophe coveted. Christophe had also caught Marie-Louise's eye, Mollien claimed, but she was constrained by prejudice from pursuing her love for him. "Indeed, a woman free from birth marrying an *affranchi*," or a former enslaved person, "was considered a social taboo," he wrote. Yet Christophe insisted he could win over Marie-Louise despite the social prejudices of the colony. "Her lover only became more determined since this union would ennoble him and exempt him from paying into the colonial fund the sum of 3,000 francs, which the law obliged him to pay to be considered free and no longer simply *freed*," Mollien continued. Christophe's persistence evidently paid off. Marie-Louise, despite her family's opposition, chose the man she loved, and the two future monarchs married. Thanks to this marriage, Christophe, Mollien concluded, "reached the highest ambitions for a black man," wealth, in the French traveler's eye.[82]

Mollien might have drawn his account from the one recited to the Martinican jurist and enslaver Moreau de Saint-Méry by a free woman of color named Praxelles, godmother to one of Christophe's daughters. Repeating the error that Christophe was a "Creole" from "Saint Christopher," she said that he had been taken to the colony by his "British master," who ran the "Café de la Couronne on rue Espagnole." In her account, Christophe remained enslaved at the Couronne throughout the early years of the Black freedom struggle. It was only after the 1793 fire in Cap that he gained his freedom and sought to marry Marie-Louise, Praxelles said, "daughter of a free, rich and respected negro residing in Cap," in the "Petite Guinée" neighborhood, in the vicinity of what Praxelles called the "café de la Couronne." According to Praxelles, Marie-Louise's father initially refused the union, and the two only wed after his death.[83]

Dumesle's guide offered a much more sensational story about the events that led to the marriage of the future king and queen of Haiti. After gaining his freedom by working at the hotel, Christophe "either remained indolent, or sided with the colonists, by joining the gendarmerie that they formed" in response to the Black freedom struggle. With the arrival of French commissioners, in 1792, Christophe enrolled in the "*troupes franches*, where he served as an officer." In this account, Christophe eventually became "a corsair, exposing himself at sea to the hazards of fortune, and in his adventurous journeys formed the project of going to kidnap a golden virgin owned by a church in Rio-de-la Hacha on the Côte-Ferme." Dumesle would then have Christophe serving in a Black regiment that contained "Commander Codavid [*sic*], father of Madame Christophe." Like Mollien, Dumesle claimed that "this marriage was one of the principal causes of [Christophe's] rapid and astonishing fortune; he was given command of Petite-Anse and then became regiment colonel."[84]

Many of Christophe's twentieth-century chroniclers claimed that a free Black man named Coidavid owned the Couronne hotel to explain how Henry met Marie-Louise.[85] However, as we have seen, Coidavid did not own the hotel on the eve of the Haitian Revolution, when Marie-Louise was just thirteen years old. At that time, the hotel was owned by Alexandre Faxardo and managed by Gaye, and possibly still Monjeon. Alongside the repeated and inaccurate speculation about Coidavid's ownership of the hotel exists another, perhaps graver error that has prevented previous chroniclers from accurately unfolding the family relations of the king and queen of Haiti. Marie-Louise, who did go on to use the last name Coidavid after Christophe's death, seems to have been born with an altogether different last name: Malgrin.

After an extensive search through the parish records of Saint-Domingue, I have been unable to locate either a definitive baptismal record for Marie-Louise or a marriage record for her and Christophe. Records such as these would be critical in establishing their parentage and dates of birth with more certainty, because such entries usually contained genealogical notes about the subject's parents and any witnesses present. The *Royal Almanac,* recall, listed Marie-Louise's birth date as May 8, 1778, but did not say where she had been born. Yet Marie-Louise, who died in Italy in 1851, told the recorder of her will that she was born in Cap, not Ouanaminthe, as her biographer Louis wrote.[86]

Nevertheless, real estate documents from Saint-Domingue under French republican rule do reveal some crucial details about the elusive Marie-Louise's family background. A lease from December 1794 shows that in the year after their marriage Christophe and Marie-Louise, with their infant son, Ferdinand, rented and lived in a property owned by the wealthy French colonist Léonard Picard, at 326 rue Dauphine and des Trois Chandeliers.[87] Perhaps Christophe met or crossed paths there with the future Baron de Vastey's cousin Pierre Louis Vastey, who lived in a home at the same intersection.[88] A series of additional lease, sale, and construction agreements from 1801 to 1802 authorized Christophe and his wife, Marie-Louise *Malgrin,* to buy and renovate a property in the heart of Cap-Français that previously belonged to the same planter and proprietor Picard. The home, for which they paid 30,000 colonial livres in 1801, was near the church of Notre Dame de l'Assomption at number 312 rue Dauphine and the Place d'Armes. This property, which had burned in June 1793 during the fires that ravished Cap, unlike the home at number 326, included a house and part of a factory, the latter facing the church's burned-out bell tower, also owned by Picard, and for which Christophe and Marie-Louise paid an additional 6,600 colonial livres.[89]

In 1801, at the time that Picard, who also owned a plantation in Plaisance and multiple properties in Cap, initially sold the house and the factory across from the church to Christophe, the future king of Haiti held the rank of brigadier general and was commander in chief of the arrondissement of Cap. The sale agreement, like the document authorizing the property's reconstruction, listed his wife and co-owner as "Dame Marie-Louise *Malgrin,* wife of Citizen Henry Christophe."[90] Other documents concerning the sale and renovation of the Picard-owned property list Christophe's wife as Marie-Louise Malgrin, too, not Coidavid.[91] Among these important documents is an additional bill of sale for the same house on rue Dauphine (later renamed rue d'Égalité) issued specifically to "Marie-Louise Malgrin," "wife of Citizen Henry Christophe, brigadier general, commander in chief of the arrondissement of Cap." This agreement was issued to Marie-Louise in her name specifically because she was to oversee the extensive renovations on the property.[92]

It was not unusual for the wives of prominent generals to hold properties in their names. Suzanne Louverture, wife of Toussaint Louverture, held one such property in the commune of Ennery (renamed Louverture at the time) in her own name, too. Yet the French government later confiscated all the properties owned by the ex-generals, or their wives, who defected from the French republican army after Louverture's arrest and deportation in June 1802.[93]

After Christophe joined the *armée indigène* to defeat French troops and prevent the reinstatement of slavery by Napoléon Bonaparte, the French republic confiscated the house he purchased from Picard and all others held by Christophe and "his wife in common property . . . who is also among the rebels."[94] On June 29, 1803, the French republic listed for sale the house in Marie-Louise Malgrin's name. The announcement described the unfinished property as "having a facade of sixty-two feet on the Place d'Armes and sixty-one feet, six inches on rue Dauphine." "There is to be found the beginnings of a building constructed in masonry about six feet high, not including the foundations, forming a division of four stores, including two on the Place d'Armes and two on rue Dauphine, two stores in the back, two cabinets, two kitchens with a courtyard and a well."[95] The property had been legally and officially sold to Marie-Louise, yet the Picard inheritors later applied for and received an indemnity for this house and twelve others in Cap, in the amount of 51,816 francs, as if these properties had been lost to their family because of Haitian independence.[96] This sort of indemnity scheme became common in 1820s and 1830s France.[97]

While they waited for the elaborate home they were reconstructing to be built by Alexandre Faraud, who later oversaw the construction of the Citadelle, Marie-Louise and Christophe likely spent most of their time at Saint-Michel, the plantation they leased in Quartier-Morin.[98] By the time of these leases, bills of sale, and their confiscations, the Christophes—Marie-Louise is referred to later in these documents as Madame

Christophe—had already welcomed three children into their family. François Ferdinand Henry was born the year after their marriage on May 15, 1794; Améthyste-Henry, called Première by her father, was born four years later, on May 9, 1798; and her sister, Anne Athénaïs-Henry (sometimes spelled "Athénaïre"), came into the world on July 7, 1800. The family was eventually complete with the birth of another son, Jacques Victor-Henry, born shortly after Haitian independence on March 3, 1804.[99]

Even though Marie-Louise, whom Vastey described as "of average height," with "expressive eyes" and "a beautiful figure," and of a kind and sweet disposition, seems to have been born not a Coidavid but a Malgrin, there was a free Black family called Coidavid (sometimes spelled "Coidavis," "Coidavie," "Quoidavie," and even "Codavy") living in colonial and then revolutionary Saint-Domingue.[100] There were also free Black Malgrins living in the colony. Marie-Louise can now be connected to both clans.

The French Overseas Archives are housed in a brutalist building not far from the center of Aix-en-Provence, France. These archives contain a folder that has seemingly gone unperused by previous Christophe chroniclers. It is marked "Coidavis (Nadine)/Coidavis (Vincent)." Nadine and Vincent Coidavis were the children of a Black military officer, "Citoyen Coidavis," chef de brigade and military commander of Fort Bélair and its dependencies.[101] Coidavis's military record, housed in the same archive, bears the following heading: "Coidavie (Jacques) . . . militia sergeant who became brigade leader of the Second Regiment of *troupes franches*, in Saint-Domingue, an VI." The details on his record of service allow us to confirm that this Jacques Coidavie was the same Citoyen Coidavis granted ownership in October 1796 over a piece of land behind a house called Bélair, bordered on one side by the ravine of La Fossette. Jacques Coidavie, who signed the deed with the more common spelling "Coidavid" (which is how we shall refer to him hereafter), was born in Cap-Français in 1737 and started his military career as a tambour player, or drummer. Later, he became sergeant major in a battalion of Chasseurs-Volontaires. Coidavid finished his military career as chef de brigade of the battalion of Fort Bélair, after having been promoted on April 3, 1796.[102] Also in 1796, Coidavid requested and received a "provisional concession" for the property in La Fossette, described as "a plot of uncultivated land about five or six *carreaux*," containing "no establishment [except] a few huts belonging to the state, in which some citizens have taken refuge."[103] This same Jacques Coidavid, it turns out, had been married to Marie-Louise's mother.

On October 30, 1783, Jacques Coidavid, described as a "free Negro, native of Cap," married a Black woman named Marie-Jeanne, "called Zulica," described as a "free Negress from Petite-Anse, Parish of Quartier-Morin." The witness to their marriage, which took place in Cap-Français, was none other than Jean-Baptiste Belley, a formerly enslaved man from

Senegal, who, in 1776, lived just south of the Couronne hotel on the rue des Trois Visages, which abutted the fancy inn to the east. Belley later served as the first Black deputy at the French National Convention when it abolished slavery in all French overseas territories in 1794.[104] Just a couple months after they wed, on Christmas Day 1783, the Coidavid couple welcomed a son, described as a "negro" on his baptismal certificate, whom they named Noël, most likely after the religious holiday. His parents are listed as "Jacques Codavy [sic]" and "Marie-Jeanne, Negress, his wife." Noël's godfather was once again Belley while his godmother was "Marie-Louise, free negress," very likely his older sister, the future queen of Haiti.[105] Aside from showing that the free Black Coidavid family circulated in prominent circles with other free Black inhabitants of the colony, this document implies that Jacques Coidavid was likely Marie-Louise's stepfather, since Noël Coidavid was her brother.

All kingdom records list Marie-Louise's brother as a man named Noël Coidavid. According to the *Royal Almanac,* Prince Noël Coidavid (spelled "Noele" in this instance) was the "brother of the queen." Born on September 10, 1784, he is listed in the almanac as husband to Célestine Joseph since September 14, 1809.[106] Although the birth date in the almanac conflicts with the one on Noël's baptismal certificate (such discrepancies were not uncommon in the era), more important than the specific day of his birth is that the almanac connects the Noël "Codavy," whose parents were Jacques and Marie-Jeanne Coidavid, to Marie-Louise *Malgrin.*

We can be reasonably certain that since Noël Coidavid was her brother, and Marie-Louise used the name Malgrin at the time of her marriage to Christophe, she was likely the child of Noël's mother, Marie-Jeanne, the woman called Zulica, who later married Jacques Coidavid, who was Noël's, but likely not Marie-Louise's, father. If Marie-Louise were Marie-Jeanne's child born out of wedlock, and not Coidavid's biological child, following the custom of the colony she would have used her mother's name, which seems quite likely to have been Malgrin. The fact that Christophe and Marie-Louise raised Noël strengthens the idea that Marie-Louise was his godmother and thus responsible for his upbringing in the event of his parents' demise.

Christophe made Noël Coidavid a prince in 1811 and bestowed on him the title of the Duc de Port-de-Paix in the edict of April 8, 1811, which created the nobility. Noël's coat of arms featured two silver-crowned ostriches bearing the black and red flag of the kingdom, which was painted on a shield with three-winged insects flying above. The shield said, "It is beautiful to die for your king."[107] "Lieutenant Noël Coidavid," a grenadier in the Third Battalion of the Second Regiment of the royal army, later served as "grand marshal of Haiti, colonel general of the Haitian Guard," and he was present at the king and his sister's coronation in June 1811.[108]

Christophe and Marie-Louise were devastated when Prince Noël died in a terrible accident at the Citadelle on August 25, 1818, after lightning hit the building and caused a huge explosion followed by a fire. A hundred and fifty-nine inhabitants of the kingdom died. The eulogy in the September 27, 1818, edition of the *Royal Gazette,* entirely dedicated to the deceased prince, offers precious information about Christophe's relationship to his wife's younger brother. "Raised under the eyes of King Henry I from his earliest youth, he learned, under this great captain, the noble profession of arms," the eulogy read. "He fought valiantly for the freedom and independence of his country. It was during this combat, raised in the life of military camps, that he acquired that calm, that cold blood, that uncommon bravery which distinguished him in danger." With Noël it seems that Christophe first experienced the paternal love that he later showered upon his own children. Noël reportedly loved his brother-in-law too, having for the king, according to the eulogy, "a filial attachment, unfailing fidelity, and boundless obedience; [he was] always ready to carry out his orders in the most difficult undertakings." Owing to the distinct trust he placed in his brother-in-law, the king, "who honored him with a truly paternal friendship, entrusted to his zeal, his assiduity, and his devotion the care of the Citadelle Henry, that Symbol of Liberty and Independence." Unfortunately, that monument to liberty and independence became the prince's tomb.

The blaze that turned the Citadelle into a fiery fortress struck at around five o'clock in the afternoon on that fateful August day and "plunged into mourning and consternation all the friends of the fatherland." "That unfortunate prince," the eulogy continued, "worthy of a better fate, perished in a fatal and forever regrettable manner, in a deplorable event, in the flower of his life." The prince, "after having spent thirty-three years, eleven months, and fifteen days in this world, bears away with him the tears and the regrets of his king, his family, and his fellow citizens." Afterward, the king had Noël interred at the Citadelle Henry, "in a monument that His Majesty, our august and beloved sovereign, has erected there, to perpetuate the memory of the prince, object of his affection."[109]

According to Marie-Louise's will, her brother Noël had at least two children, to whom she sought to bequeath some of her money after her own death in 1851. Marie-Louise left "to Signor Pietro Hardy Son of Noel [*sic*] Coidavid, Nephew of the Testatrix, one hundred Spanish Pillar dollars. To Signora [Mamita], another daughter of the said Signor Noel Coidavid, one hundred Spanish Pillar dollars."[110] Prince Noël's wife, Célestine Joseph Coidavid, does not seem to have ever remarried, though she did give birth to another daughter in 1827. A death certificate dated March 1, 1850, for a Marie Rose Cléomène, "fille naturelle," noted that she had been a seamstress by profession, born in Cap-Haïtien to the "widow Noël Coidavid," a *marchande,* or marketwoman. A man named Ménard was listed as the girl's father.[111]

Though she had not used her stepfather Jacques Coidavid's last name at the time she married Christophe, Marie-Louise must have thought highly enough of him to begin using the name later. During her husband's life, Marie-Louise signed her name as "Femme Christophe." By the time she made her will, while living in exile in Italy, she definitively used the name Coidavid.[112]

Jacques Coidavid passed away sometime in 1799 or early 1800. Following his death, Nadine and Vincent Coidavid sought co-ownership of their father's house in La Fossette. Their petition to the government described the property in some detail. "The said house is located at the end of La Fosette near a property named La Borry; near the Champs Elissés [sic]; there is on this land a house composed of three bedrooms and a cabinet and gallery and a dovecote and a small hut containing two cabinets in poor condition." The children offered 200 livres per year for the farm, "as this plot has never been leased." Before signing off as Nadine Coidavis and Vincent Coidavis—whose signatures, the document said, were written with a "borrowed hand"—the petitioners wrote that they would naturally conform to all the clauses and conditions to which the property would be subjected. It is not clear whether the Coidavid children ever received authorization to take over the property, but with their petition they laid out their plan to prove that they could maintain the land and produce revenue on it at the annual price of 200 colonial livres.[113]

After his death, Nadine and Vincent also sought to take possession of some of their father's other properties. Jacques Coidavid had leased many properties in Saint-Domingue, including the Clérisse sugar plantation in Quartier-Morin, where his wife, Marie-Jeanne, was from and where he intersected often with Christophe. In 1759, the property belonged to Pierre Barthélémy Clérisse, "member of the Chambre of Agriculture of Cap."[114] At the start of the rebellion, the Clérisse plantation produced annually 46,158 livres of sugar, and the plantation had twenty-five plots for growing sugarcane, along with sixty "cultivators," or laborers, "twenty-seven mules, twenty-seven oxen, four cows, two *bouvards* [baby cows], one gazelle, three *cabrouets* [wheeled carts], and one animal mill [*moulin à bêtes*]." The owner of the Clérisse plantation had evidently abandoned it, leaving it vulnerable to being confiscated by the French government as a part of the large-scale affermage system put into place by the French commissioner Léger-Félicité Sonthonax and Julien Raimond, also a French commissioner at the time. A man named Jean Louis Narcisse oversaw the day-to-day operations. After Jacques Coidavid's death, Narcisse, along with the children's guardian at that time, a man listed only as "Citizen Colas," petitioned the French government for authorization to continue to manage and lease the plantation on the Coidavid children's behalf.[115]

Plantations subjected to affermage had been seized by the government and assigned to various military officers to run them and produce profit for the French republic, a portion of which the officer would share. Coidavid's three-year lease of the Clérisse plantation, signed by Sonthonax and Raimond, detailed how Coidavid was to care for and augment the land to encourage sugar cultivation and mandated how he should compensate the free laborers—referred to as *citoyens* and *citoyennes*—the formerly enslaved people, now citizens of France.[116] To acquire the property in La Fossette, Coidavid agreed to "have it surveyed at his expense" and to present to the French government a "certificate of *arpentage*."[117]

Christophe likewise participated intimately in affermage. In the 1790s, post-emancipation, he leased the plantation Saint-Michel in Quartier-Morin, the neighborhood where Coidavid lived with Marie-Louise's mother.[118] The sum required to lease the property was 70,000 livres of sugar "en nature," the annual amount of raw sugar Christophe needed to produce for the French government.[119] Such an extensive and lucrative property required many hands. At the time of general emancipation in 1793, the Saint-Michel plantation had 122 Africans cultivating sugar on its land.[120] When Christophe gained control, around the end of 1794, the land was supposed to be worked by free cultivators, called *cultivateurs* and *cultivatrices*, rather than *nègres* and *négresses*. They were supposed to share in the profits of the plantation, which remained considerable.[121]

Records show that Christophe and Coidavid crossed paths in Quartier-Morin. The Saint-Michel sugar plantation was near the edge of Petite-Anse, only slightly north of the Clérisse and Mazères plantations overseen by Coidavid. The French government's affermage documentation reveals that the Clérisse plantation in the quartier of Grande-Rivière was leased to Coidavid for 400 livres per year and had been established as a "place à vivres," a plantation growing everyday foodstuffs for the colony's stores. These records also show that in April 1798, Coidavid had been, for at least three years, leasing Charrier, a high-revenue plantation in the banlieue du Cap that produced a stunning 96,000 livres of raw sugar per year.[122] Coidavid also leased the Mazères plantation in Quartier-Morin, right next to the Clérisse farm, where Coidavid and Christophe interacted directly. Some time before August 2, 1797, Coidavid and Jean Louis Narcisse, who listed themselves as "farmers" on the Mazères plantation, stated in a report to Raimond, detailing the state of the plantation, that they had received a "letter of invitation" to do this "from Citizen Henry Christophe, chef de brigade and inspector."[123]

Combining information found in Marie-Louise's will with French colonial documentation yields other pertinent information about how the Coidavid strand of the family intersected with the Christophes. It is quite likely that Marie-Louise did not remain close with Jacques Coidavid's other children, Vincent and Nadine, who might have been older children from a previous marriage or, more likely, younger children from a subsequent marriage. The official request that Vincent and Nadine Coida-vid submitted to the French government to acquire their father Jacques's property after his death does not mention anything about these children's mother or any other siblings or claimants.[124] The request did reveal that Vincent and Nadine Coidavid were minors, a detail that suggests they had not been taken under the wing of Christophe and Marie-Louise as Noël had been. The dossier submitted on behalf of Nadine and Vincent Coida-vid by their "guardian" Colas in June 1800 stated directly that the claim-ants were minors, and on other property claims submitted by Nadine and Vincent, under their signatures read the words "par main d'emprunt," or by a borrowed hand, indicating the two could not sign the documents themselves, perhaps because they were too young.[125] One such document in the affermage dossier for the Coidavid family, signed only "Gast," reads, "I, the undersigned, declare that I wish to farm the dwelling known as Coidavid, established for gardening, located in La Fossette, for the annual price of 300 francs."[126] Was Gast yet another or a subsequent guardian, and did his application supersede or complement the Coidavid children's own? Unlike many other properties, the French government did not know the status of the owner of La Fossette (had he abandoned the property or could he still make a rightful claim?). This ambiguity initially allowed Jacques Coidavid to lease it and kept that door open for his children.[127]

As for Marie-Louise, she spoke vaguely of other siblings to the recorder of her will. The will states that other than nephews, Ferdinand and Victor, children "of a brother or sister of hers, whom she does not well remember from having been for a long time absent from her country," Marie-Louise had one living sister, "Geneviève Coidavid." Louise-Geneviève Coidavid had married Jean-Louis Michel Pierrot (sometimes spelled "Pierrault"), a nobleman in Christophe's kingdom and briefly the president of Haiti (1845–46).[128] Louise-Geneviève's sons André Coidavid and Joseph Coi-david had been members of the royal prince's staff and they and their families remained in the country after the king's death.[129] There are, in fact, dozens of records for Coidavids in nineteenth-century Haiti's civil register, including several men named Joseph. One such Joseph Coidavid was a "baron" and "imperial prosecutor at the imperial court of justice" under Haiti's second emperor, Faustin Soulouque.[130] It was likely this same Joseph Coidavid with whom the Haitian author Demesvar Delorme recalled sharing a "panic-stricken moment" during the deadly 1842 quake that struck Cap when Delorme was just eleven years old.[131]

With a fuller picture of the Coidavid clan's relationship to the future queen coming into focus, there yet remain many questions about Marie-Louise's lineage vis-à-vis the Malgrins. A free Black family or families called Malgrin lived in Saint-Domingue as early as the 1750s. The *Affiches* and the parish registers tell an intriguing story about the entanglements of freedom and slavery in the eighteenth-century colonial world of Saint-Domingue while providing potential clues about Marie-Louise's mother's origins.

On July 29, 1767, a notice for a "slave in marronnage" stamped MAL-GRIN appeared in the *Affiches*. The man's enslaver, not a Malgrin, searched in earnest for "a Thiamba Negro, named Alexis, stamped MAL-GRIN, height five feet, two to three inches, aged twenty-eight to thirty, maroon since the nineteenth of this month."[132] The branding on the bodies of the enslaved continued to tell a partial story of their lives. While Alexis's current "owner" pursued him as the legal claimant, the stamp reading Malgrin suggested that he had a prior enslaver whose name had been burned in iron on his body to serve as a permanent record. The *Affiches* provided another clue about where the Malgrin family member who previously enslaved Alexis lived. In the Ouanaminthe jail, the city where some Christophe chroniclers locate Marie-Louise's birth, can be found mention of "a Fon Negro, named Louis, claiming to belong to Sr. Margrin, residing in this town."[133] The *Affiches* regularly contained typos of this sort and variously or alternatively spelled names; and another notice from the *Affiches* provides tantalizing room for speculation about the trajectory of Louis and his potential connection to the Malgrin family of Saint-Domingue. Under "Enslaved Maroons Brought to the Jail" in the city of Cap two decades later, on June 21, 1787, there is a notice for "two new Negroes, about twenty-four years old, small in stature, stamped on the chest J. Berteau, arrested at the *coupe de Gonaïves* by a detachment, according to the report of Louis Malgrin, cavalier in the *maréchaussée* from Plaisance."[134] Might this Louis Malgrin be the same enslaved individual who ran away from the planter "Margrin" so many years before? Plaisance, in the northwest of the colony, is far from Ouanaminthe, in the northeast, on the border of the Spanish side. But enslaved Black people in Saint-Domingue, especially if related to white French colonists, gained their freedom in many ways in the colonial era, including using mobility and fugitivity.

In the parish registers, there exist numerous records for members of the same or a related free Black family who variously spelled their last name as "Malgraine," "Malgrain," and "Malgrin." Among these records emerge multiple women named Marie-Jeanne Malgrin, but the advanced or young age and/or early deaths of these women rule them out as being Marie-Louise's mother. Yet it is highly likely that these women, nevertheless, were some of Marie-Louise's family members, necessitating a closer look at their trajectories. On December 30, 1755, a child named Joseph Malgrain, referred to as a "negrillon," was baptized in the parish of Gros-Morne, in the Plaine du Nord. Joseph, a *fils légitime*, had been born to Pierre Malgrain, "nègre libre," and his wife, Marie-Jeanne.[135] Two and a half years later, Pierre and Marie-Jeanne welcomed another child, a daughter, whom they named Françoise.[136] The death register for a much older child of Pierre and Marie-Jeanne Malgrain's adds more information about this free Black family, including suggesting that this Marie-Jean Malgrain was of advanced age, and therefore could not have been the Marie-Jeanne who married Jacques Coidavid and bore a child in 1783. Their much older daughter Suzanne Malgrain, called Suzon, "négresse libre," was buried on July 19, 1760, at the age of twenty years old. The detailed notation on this record lists Pierre Malgrain as an "inhabitant of Boucand Richard," a rural section just outside Gros-Morne in the Plaine du Nord.[137]

The Malgrains of Gros-Morne were an extensive family with many offshoots. In 1781, three years after our Marie-Louise's birth, the parish recorded a baptism for a Françoise Hortense Malgrain, "négresse."[138] The large family continued to branch. While most of the Malgrins lived in the north, an outlying notice for a Malgrin family member was recorded in the parish register for Petit Saint-Louis du Sud, way down in southern Saint-Domingue, in the arrondissement of Aquin.[139] In Plaisance, back in northwest Saint-Domingue, a Marie-Jeanne Malgrin passed away in 1786, but being only fourteen years old at the time of her death, she was neither the Marie-Jeanne married to Pierre Malgrain and mother to many children in Gros-Morne nor our Marie-Louise's mother. Outside the parish registers, there is also a trace of a Charles Malgrin, captain of the gendarmerie in Limbé during the Haitian Revolution.[140]

Though I hoped to find definitive evidence of Christophe's and Marie-Louise's parentage and other relations in the parish registers, through either their marriage or the baptism of their children, other genealogies for the Christophes emerged in the documentation produced by the Kingdom of Haiti.

The *Royal Almanac* reveals that the king had a nephew, Prince Jean, born on October 17, 1780. Jean Christophe had initially married a white British woman named Sarah Lassen. When Sarah died in October 1812, Prince Jean married Marie-Augustine Chancy, who, according to the kingdom's records, was Marie-Louise's niece (and Toussaint Louverture's). Chancy was also the widow of André Vernet, a former general from the Haitian Revolution and the late minister of finance for the kingdom.[141]

Prince Jean, whom Christophe gave the title of the Duc du Port-Margot, died in Port-à-Piment at the age of thirty-six on July 4, 1817, after suffering from a long illness. Christophe loved his nephew dearly and considered him a cherished friend. "He bears the regrets of our august sovereign, who honored him with a special friendship, and of the army and the navy, of which he was one of the greatest strengths, of his family, his friends, and his fellow citizens," said his eulogy. Saddened that illness prevented him from attending to his duties as "Grand Marshall, Grand Admiral of Haiti, Grand Cross of the Royal and Military Order of Saint Henry, Grand *Panetier* of the King," Prince Jean revealed himself, through his last words, to be an eminent patriot. He urged his fellow Haitians to "fight until the last breath for their freedom and independence and prefer rather to be exterminated to the last of them, than to return under the yoke of our oppressors." The prince's remains were buried in the vault of the Royal Church of Sans-Souci.[142]

Prince Jean's status as the king's nephew suggests that Christophe had a brother or sister. Although the chain of recitation is unclear, some chroniclers claim that Prince Jean was born on the island of Saint Lucia to Christophe's sister, Marie.[143] A search through the parish records of colonial Saint-Domingue has not at this point produced any trace for either of these family members, but there was a free Black Christophe family in the colony. Although there was an ostensibly white Christophe family too— a M. Christophe was director of a "depot" at the Port-au-Prince post office and remained in that position until as late as April 1790—the surname Christophe was not common in the colony.[144] Examining the sparse mentions of the Black Christophes may therefore one day yield more precise connections.

In the parish of Cavaillon, a death record exists from 1774 for one Jean Christophe, a "free negro" who died at the age of fifty.[145] In 1794, the same parish recorded the death of forty-one-year-old Anne Devesus, "*fille naturelle* of Devesus and Anne Christophe"; another Anne Christophe, or perhaps the same woman, lived in Cap in 1803, according to a government survey produced that year.[146] The parish register of nearby Croix-des-Bouquets yields a much more substantial mention of a Christophe family member: another Henry Christophe born in 1755 to a free Black mother listed as a quadroon named Olive. The child's father was not listed, but Olive evidently lived in the home of a Monsieur Henry, "cavalry captain and inhabitant of la Boulle, quartier of Port-au-Prince." The child's godparents are named as Monsieur Christophe, commandant in Grand-Goâve, and Madame Anne Paschal, his wife. The fact that Paschal, Christophe, and Henry were all listed by their last names and as "Monsieur" and "Madame" stands as evidence of their whiteness, along with the lack of any mention of their color.[147] Perhaps this baby Henry Christophe was then the same "free negro" listed in the July 19, 1788, issue of the *Affiches* as the "owner" of "Adelaide, Congo, stamped on the right side of the breast CB CAP, on the left, in reverse, G. DAUMAS AU CAP, bearing the marks of smallpox, with a scar on her right temple, about twenty-four years old, height five feet, one inch, saying she belongs to one named Christophe, n.l. [*nègre libre*]."[148]

The *Royal Almanac* for 1814 also listed multiple members of the kingdom bearing the last name Christophe. However, in contrast with the king's nephew Jean, their precise connection to the king remains unclear.[149] Among those many members of the military and aristocracy bearing the name Christophe, the case of Jean Christophe (not the same as the king's nephew, the Duc du Port-Margot, born in 1780 and died in 1817) stands out. This sous-lieutenant very well might have been the same Jean Christophe, "fils naturel" of Dorothée, two months old on February 21, 1785, when he was baptized in Cap. Strengthening the probability of a genealogical connection to the king, this Jean Christophe's baptismal certificate lists the Christophe and Coidavid family friend Jean-Baptiste Belley as the child's godfather while a woman named Petronille, "free negress," acted as his godmother.[150]

Whatever and wherever his initial origins, what we know for certain is that by 1792 Henry Christophe had gone from being an enslaved child to a military officer participating in one of the most momentous struggles for freedom the world has ever seen. His wife, though she appears to have been born with free status, had clearly been inclined, like her husband, to throw her lot in with the formerly enslaved population rebelling against French torture and terror. The British ship captain, George W. C. Courtenay, who lived in the kingdom for some time, recalled that Marie-Louise, whom he described as a "very amiable and charitable woman," was "fond of relating her adventures during the revolution, the whole of which time she accompanied her husband, with her children on her back, often without any other food than wild fruit and berries, and generally exposed to the weather, sometimes half clothed."[151] While Courtenay revealed this anecdote in a playful way, to amuse his readers with tales of the Haitian king and his royal family, one can only imagine that Marie-Louise related this story to him, if in fact it is true, with a far more serious tone.

Marie-Louise's brother Noël's death had not marked the first time that she mourned the loss of a sibling. Marie-Louise had another sister, known as Tante Marie. In 1802, this sister accompanied François Ferdinand, the firstborn child of Marie-Louise and Henry, to France; picture the boy earlier, if you will, traveling proudly on his mother's back during the revolution, unaware of the many existing dangers in the colony and the ones yet to come on the Continent. The nephew and aunt never saw their homeland again. The fateful voyage across the Atlantic precipitated both Ferdinand's and Tante Marie's deaths in Paris in 1805, just one year after Christophe helped ensure Haitian independence.[152]

To get to the stories of romance and tragedy, heroism and strife, that cost the Christophe family not just their friends but their children and other relatives, too, we must now walk through the revolution with them.

4

RISING AND FALLING
WITH REVOLUTION

An enslaved person sometimes bore the external marks of bondage: chains and balls on their feet, thumb clamps on their fingers, a chain around their neck. These instruments of physical and psychological terror and torture were meant to prevent marronnage, or fugitivity, while also maintaining slavery's status quo. The colonists implemented chattel slavery with the goal of making the condition virtually inalienable. The balls and chains, like the iron brands on African skin, were the outward accoutrements of ownership. Such objects were designed to perform African slavery into material and inalienable existence for white European enslavers. But rampant marronnage laid bare the greatest fiction of the white colonists' terrible artifices. Resistance could not be contained by chaining the person. The trappings of revolution were in the slave's soul. Any honest enslaver, a contradiction in terms, knew that the slavery he imposed on another could only ever be a temporary condition, one any enslaved person with enough courage, wherewithal, or physical ability could at any moment breach. Caught up in the revolutionary whirl for freedom swirling around Cap from 1791 to 1793, Christophe found himself by turns free and then unfree, jailed and then released. Given his difficult beginnings in the early days of Haiti's revolution to end slavery, who could have predicted that by the end of the decade not only would the colony see general emancipation but Christophe would play the role of one of the most valued and respected military officers of the famous general Toussaint Louverture while transforming himself into one of the colony's most successful Black businessmen.

On October 5, 1779, a fugitive slave notice appeared in the *Affiches américaines* for "three Negroes" identified as "Bouqueman, hunter; Jean-Jacques, Creole, coachman, without a stamp, and David, stamped X, a Negro from Guinea." The three had reportedly "left as maroons from the plantation of Mr. Cailleau, the elder, and of the widow Madame Dorlic, in Maribaroux." "The first two, aged forty to forty-two, are two of the most dangerous subjects, whom it is important to arrest, one is five feet, three inches tall, with a round face, small eyes, and a fierce look," the ad continued. "The coachman, five feet, four inches tall, has sunken eyes, open nostrils, a large mouth with missing front teeth, and arched legs that throw him to the left side as he walks." While not described with such ferocious language, the final fugitive, David, was of particular concern to Dorlic, his enslaver. David had escaped with "a *nabot* [on his foot], a chain, and thumb clamps." A *nabot* was a cast-iron ball that usually weighed about twenty-five pounds but could weigh as much as thirty pounds in Saint-Domingue. It was difficult to walk with such an apparatus, which was the point. David managed to escape anyway. Anyone who recognized the three maroons from Maribaroux was to have them arrested and transported to the nearest jail, "with the greatest possible security."[1]

Enslaved people were far more likely to engage in group marronnage, like Bouqueman, Jean-Jacques, and David, rather than solo fugitivity. Maroons found some measure of safety, security, kinship, and community in numbers.[2] Wherever communities of maroons formed on Saint-Domingue, the possibility of rebellion existed. The fear and reality of enslaved Africans engaging in group revolt was the reason for Saint-Domingue's infamous *maréchaussées,* or slave patrols. Little did the planters know that these communities of maroons would one day take marronnage from seemingly simple group rebellion to deliberately organized revolution. One group of maroons in particular, led by a man named Boukman Dutty (sometimes called Dutty Boukman), opened the age of the Haitian Revolution. If the three maroons from Maribaroux managed to escape recapture and remain in marronnage, they might have lived to see the beginnings of, and perhaps help to plan—in the case of Bouqueman, whose name is pronounced phonetically the same as Boukman—the world's largest and most sustained armed revolt against slavery.

Most historical accounts of the Haitian Revolution begin by evoking the gathering of enslaved people in a mid-August religious ceremony in a northern part of the colony called Morne-Rouge. In what has been labeled the Bois Caïman ceremony, Boukman and a Black female religious leader (later identified by her grandson and granddaughter as Cécile Fatiman, a "green-eyed mulatto woman with long silken black hair, the daughter of a Corsican prince and an African woman" who was herself a *mambo,* or a "Vodou high priestess") addressed the crowd with words to inspire rebellion against slavery.[3] First, Fatiman killed a sacrificial pig and subsequently offered the blood of the animal to the adherents to seal the pact of resistance. Boukman then reportedly delivered the call to rebel in Haitian Creole: "The god of the white man calls him to commit crimes; our god asks only good works of us. But this god who is so good orders revenge! He will direct our hands; he will aid us. Throw away the image of the god of the whites who thirsts for our tears and listen to the voice of liberty which speaks in the hearts of all of us."[4]

The story of Bois Caïman expanded throughout the eighteenth and nineteenth centuries with each new chronicler adding details not mentioned in previous accounts.[5] But Dumesle's *Voyage to the North of Hayti* from 1824 is the first known written source to document the contents of Boukman's speech and contains the transcription still referenced by most scholars today. Dumesle's narration has also helped to differentiate the later August Bois Caïman ceremony from the earlier one in Morne-Rouge. Dumesle recalled that toward the middle of the month of August 1791 cultivators, manufacturers, and artisans from northern Saint-Domingue gathered in the middle of the night in the thick forest that covers the summit of Morne-Rouge. Amid a violent storm, they formed the plan for a vast insurrection, which they sanctioned a week later, in Bois Caïman, with a religious ceremony.[6]

Previous historians have determined that the plan for insurrection was likely first pronounced at the assembly in Morne-Rouge, which occurred on Sunday, August 14, with the religious ceremony at Bois Caïman taking place about a week later in a spot not far from Morne-Rouge, on the twenty-first.[7] This chronology squares with Dumesle's account, which is the most complete, even if patently poetic and literary. Dumesle understood there to have been two distinct events, one where the planning took place on the fourteenth, and a second one, most likely on the twenty-first at Bois Caïman, sanctifying the earlier tactical plans for war while seeking protection from "the God of the Black man."[8]

The second gathering bore fruit immediately. Near midnight on August 22, Black freedom fighters set ablaze several plantations in the northern plain. "We hasten to inform you of the cruel and disastrous events that have happened to us here over the past few days," wrote the General Assembly of Saint-Domingue seated in Cap-Français to the municipality of Les Cayes, located way down in the south, on August 23. "The Negro slaves have been gathering in considerable numbers; for the past few days, wherever they go, they have been setting fire to everything, and cutting the throats of all the whites they meet. They seize every weapon and use them for this purpose," the letter continued. "From the various steps they have taken, it appears that the conspiracy must be general throughout the colony." The authorities then described their attempts to curb "the scourge that is afflicting us," including the description of "an attack in which a hundred Negroes have been killed, the rest are on the run," saying, "we continue to pursue them vigorously."[9]

Records from Saint-Michel, the white-colonist-owned sugar plantation in Quartier-Morin that Christophe eventually leased, provide a play-by-play account of the spread of these fires throughout the northern plain and the colonial government's initial response. It took two days for the insurrection to spread from the northern plain to Quartier-Morin, southeast of Cap. On Thursday, August 25, the bursar of the Saint-Michel plantation, which remarkably never burned, revealed in his daily account that thirty-five dragoons arrived in the quartier between 5:00 in the morning and 12:30 in the afternoon. Their presence could not stop the progression of the rebellion. By one o'clock, the freedom fighters had set fire to the neighboring huts where enslaved people usually slept. The burning of the entire quartier followed that afternoon and continued for the next two days.

Eventually, plantations east and south of Saint-Michel blazed with fire as well, along with everything in between. By Saturday, the twenty-seventh, the fires had spread to Limonade, where the bursar reported that several white colonists had died at the hands of Black freedom fighters. By the twenty-eighth, it seemed that the white colonists' efforts to use the colonial dragoons to quell the growing rebellion would not succeed. Not long after, the freedom uprising became "general" in the plain of Cap.

Some of the colonists did persistently try to halt the progress of the Black freedom struggle. The Chevalier de Loze, for his part, established a six-bullet cannon on the hill of one plantation. Yet the swift march of the freedom fighters was not so easily thwarted. The Black revolutionaries burned the Limonade pier on the twenty-ninth, while the "murder" of several white men was reported in the city on the same day. Monsieur de Rouvray, under whom Christophe previously served at the Battle of Savannah, tried to use his militia to stop the freedom struggle too.[10]

A white French eyewitness, stationed near Haut-du-Cap, whose unsigned, handwritten letters were found in the archives of Charles Boutin, treasurer general to the French minister of the marine, reported that the same day, August 29, de Rouvray arrived in Caracol, in the savannas of Limonade. De Rouvray's troops consisted largely of free men of color from Sainte-Suzanne and Trou, in the parish of Ouanaminthe. De Rouvray planned to march on Limonade and surround the northern plain. Suggesting that he received this information from de Rouvray himself, the unnamed soldier insisted, "He will burn the sugarcane and have them all cut down to find those brigands. This is the first news that has come to us from M. de Rouvray." De Rouvray had with him two hundred men of color who sought, the soldier added, to help him to prevent the freedom struggle from spreading to Jacquezy, east of Cap near the Bay of Caracol.[11]

Although the freedom struggle seemed to be sparing Saint-Domingue's most important city, Cap-Français, the colonists believed that many of the enslaved in Cap had participated in the "plot to burn everything." The white colonists alleged the Black freedom fighters had plans to "slit the throats of all the whites." As a result, the white colonists and enslavers arrested and jailed many of their "domestics," or enslaved people who worked inside the homes of their enslavers, adding only more fuel to the flames of the rebellion. Several white men accused of aiding the freedom fighters, some wearing blackface, were also killed in battle or executed after their capture.[12]

By Wednesday, August 31, enslaved freedom fighters had gathered once more at the Saint-Michel plantation and thereafter attacked the city of Haut-du-Cap. That same day, de Rouvray, now with eight hundred well-armed men by his side, after having secured Jacquezy, marched toward the Quartier-Morin, the location of the Saint-Michel plantation. His aim was nothing less than to perform a "proud butchery," in the words of the unnamed soldier, who insisted that "God wants it to be this way." Once the promised battalions from Artois and Normandy have arrived, he insisted, "we will be able to set out on our campaign and exterminate these scoundrels."[13] A "butchery" aimed at extermination quickly emerged as the only goal of the anti-freedom and enslaving French colonists and their allies in the French army. Some of the colony's white inhabitants, however, reportedly fought for Black freedom too.

The unnamed soldier reported on September 1 that the Black freedom fighters successfully "enlisted" L. Noël, a white man, "drum major of the patriot grenadiers in Cap," "to set fire to the city." Not long after, the French colonial army captured him, the soldier wrote. French officials sentenced Noël to be hanged the same afternoon, along with six Black freedom fighters. Later the same day de Rouvray reported that perfect calm reigned in Jacquezy, after his troops executed "five negroes" fighting for freedom. French tactics to stop the course of the freedom struggle only grew more murderous under de Rouvray's continued efforts. "Le Trou, Fort-Dauphin, Maribaroux, are now calm," the eyewitness soldier averred. At least for the white planters. The soldier also wrote that "workers in the atelier where Monsieur Baron is located in Fort-Dauphin, having set fire to two large plots of land for growing sugarcane, were entirely sabered by order of the general, with the exception of small children." "The atelier workers at the Varennes plantation in Trou suffered the same fate," he continued, before bragging, "M. de Rouvray killed nearly three hundred that he encountered on his way there." The soldier finished with an even more lugubrious boast: "M. de Rouvray set up camp yesterday at Roucou, spreading terror everywhere he went along the way."[14] And terror was entirely the point. After reporting the arrests of one white man and three Spanish *griffes*[15] suspected of colluding with the Black freedom fighters, the unnamed soldier coolly observed, "They will be tortured before being broken on the wheel." The soldier also reported that the French lieutenant colonel Anne-Louis Touzard (sometimes spelled "Tousard"), commander of the dragoons in Cap, had been given the right by the colony's governing body in the assembly to "shoot all white people who leave their posts."[16]

What these early accounts suggest is that both the white enslavers who took up arms and the French military trying to stop the freedom struggle killed in much higher numbers than the Black freedom fighters, particularly in the early days of the Black armed resistance for liberty. The first week of December, de Rouvray told his daughter, the Comtesse de Lostanges, for example, that he had killed more than three thousand "brigands" in eight separate battles since the beginning of the freedom struggle.[17] The unnamed eyewitness offered an arrogant reason for the disparity in white and Black death rates. "I reckon we're a hundred times stronger," he said.[18] As usual, enslaved Black people striving for freedom suffered the greatest consequences.[19]

On September 1, Pierre Cap, one of the Black leaders of the freedom fighters, who already had free status at the time of the uprising, arrived at Morne du Cap. Considered by the white colonists a "very dangerous negro," according to a white planter and enslaver from the Briard plantation, Pierre Cap soon had by his side fifty other freedom fighters occupying an outpost on the Daux (sometimes spelled "Daut" or "Deaux") plantation in neighboring Haut-du-Cap. For his efforts to fight for freedom, French colonial officials arrested Pierre Cap on September 2 and reportedly tortured him that afternoon until he provided his punishers the names of several other white men allegedly aiding and abetting the freedom fighters. On the fifth, the soldier reported that "the negro [Pierre] Cap was broken alive yesterday afternoon."[20] The unnamed soldier also reported that in Port-Margot, on September 3, "more than 4,000 rebels and two whites who were at their head were killed," after the white colonists inhabiting the city took up arms to try to stop the freedom struggle. The soldier admitted of the Black freedom fighters, "All they asked for was freedom . . . and for the inhabitants to lay down their arms." Later in the same letter, he averred, "The rebels are always asking for liberty, which they believe the king has accorded them." The same soldier reported that on September 4, once more in Haut-du-Cap, the French army killed more than 150 Black freedom fighters, while de Rouvray recalled having killed at least 220 in the parish of Limonade on the same day.[21] As for the bursar from the Saint-Michel plantation, he reported that on November 9 the French hanged a Black man named Clou working as a carpenter there for participating in the freedom struggle. He was fifty-four years old. His hard-fought taste of freedom, earned only in the twilight of his life, was short-lived and marred by war.

Along with the blazing plantations, death, and despair all around, there were desertions. Enslaved people's refusal to work brought the colony's famously wealthy and bustling economy to an abrupt standstill. Records from the Saint-Michel plantation show that enslaved resistance spanned all ages. Those who did not overtly participate in the freedom struggle essentially came and went at will, sometimes working to plant *vivres,* or everyday foodstuffs, like potatoes, manioc, and bananas, and other times absconding for days on end.[22] Not participating in the armed rebellion for liberty hardly provided protection from the anti-freedom white colonists. On September 6, the unnamed soldier reported, "This morning one of our porters encountered a detachment of 180 negroes collecting food near Morne-Rouge, and we attacked them." The majority of the Black gatherers fled, he continued, abandoning their horses "and climbing the steepest hillsides on all fours." "We were able to kill only about twenty of them," he lamented.[23] The most remarkable part of this soldier's report, and what makes it an outlier, is that he consistently acknowledged that the white colonists killed in far greater numbers than the Black freedom fighters.

The French media usually reported only that the white colonists were under siege while conveniently failing to characterize as armed resistance to slavery the relatively meager personal violence the white enslavers faced during the first weeks of the Black freedom strike. "The news from Saint-Domingue is horrifying," reported the Paris-based *Le courrier extraordinaire* at the top of its October 30, 1791, issue, after news of the colony's troubles reached France later that fall. "Two hundred plantations on fire; three hundred whites massacred."[24]

Although white women participated in the horrors of torturing the people they enslaved like white men, white female victimhood at the hands of Black "villains" soon became one of the most common justifications for the massive, genocidal operation the French used to try to stop the freedom struggle. In the anonymously published French-language *History of the Disasters of Saint-Domingue* (1795), when the revolutionaries happen upon a pregnant white woman, they are described as having "attached her to a tree, opened up her belly, and fed her baby to the pigs, right before the eyes of the unfortunate dying woman."[25] Portraying Black people as perpetrators of violence rather than its victims served as justification for the greatest violence against them and functioned as a deliberate distraction from the everyday depredations of slavery. De Rouvray's wife later wrote a letter to her daughter in which she insisted that to save Saint-Domingue, all people of color in the colony had to be "crush[ed]" either by sterilization or deportation.[26]

Although it took a while for the Black freedom struggle to reach Cap, news of the uprising arrived there almost immediately and had a deleterious effect on the Colonial Assembly of Saint-Domingue. Composed of white enslavers and other colonists, the Colonial Assembly had been created in the wake of the ratification of the Declaration of the Rights of Man back in France. This assembly tasked itself with responding to ardent demands from the free people of color for equal rights of representation vis-à-vis the law. But as the French Revolution wore on, the free men of color accused the Colonial Assembly of striving for independence from France and attempting to separate the colony from the metropole. The situation escalated when the Colonial Assembly pronounced that it, not the National Assembly back in metropolitan France, would make laws concerning the free people of color in Saint-Domingue.[27] This was problematic since the rebellion of free people of color—particularly the one that led to the short-lived October 1790 revolt and February 1791 execution of two prominent free men of color, Vincent Ogé and Jean-Baptiste Chavannes, and around twenty of their allies—represented primarily a conflict about whether colonial laws or metropolitan laws would reign in the colony.

On March 28, 1790, the National Assembly in France had ratified a law declaring that "all free persons, property-owning or established for two years and paying taxes, will enjoy the voting rights that constitute active citizenship." But the white colonists opposed any legislation that would give even meager rights of citizenship to people of color. Even though free people of color had been barred from participation in the Estates General back in France, too, both Julien Raimond and Vincent Ogé, a wealthy merchant of color from Dondon, began to organize in Paris anyway. Raimond, who viewed himself as a spokesperson for free people of color, met with the National Assembly at Versailles and appeared at the Club Massiac, a pro-slavery organization, where his pleas for the rights of free people of color did little to change the minds of the conservative absentee planters he found there. Ogé, in contrast, visited both the Club Massiac and the Société des Amis des Noirs (Society of the Friends of the Blacks), a famous abolitionist society, and proposed to them his policy of gradual emancipation, which would have incrementally freed the enslaved while compensating enslavers. Ogé claimed this method would avoid bloody conflict. Yet the white planters "coldly" received Ogé at the Club Massiac and prevented him from fully espousing his plan. Even though the absentee planters of France, like those living in Saint-Domingue, seemed ill-inclined to consider the requests of free people of color for civic equality, on March 28, 1790, the National Assembly declared that all free people in the colony should have equal rights. Ogé rushed home to see the effects of the decree upon life in Saint-Domingue. When he learned that the white planters still refused to acknowledge the orders of the National Assembly, he wrote a letter in which he declared that if the decree were not upheld, he would "not answer for those disorders which may arise from merited revenge." Ogé also demanded that the governor of Saint-Domingue, Philibert François Rouxel de Blanchelande, immediately extend voting rights to Saint-Domingue's free population of color. Seeing that his remonstrations and warnings went largely unheeded, in October 1790, Ogé along with Jean-Baptiste Chavannes, of Grande-Rivière, and around 250 free men of color, decided to use force to achieve political rights. Ogé's revolt famously failed, causing him to flee to the Spanish side of the island. Upon his successful extradition back to French Saint-Domingue, in February 1791, Ogé, Chavannes, and about twenty others were publicly "broken on the wheel" by the French government in a square in Cap-Français. Afterward, the colonists stuck both leaders' heads on pikes to serve as a warning for anyone else who might try to obtain rights equal to those of the white colonists.

After the executions, the white colonists continued to challenge the National Assembly's authority to make laws for Saint-Domingue. After several additional violent conflicts with the free men of color, the National Assembly clarified the meaning of the law of March 28. All too belatedly, on May 15, 1791, the National Assembly decreed that "the legislature will never deliberate on the political status of people of color who were not born of free fathers and mothers without the previous, free, and unprompted request of the colonies; that the presently existing Colonial Assemblies will remain in place, but that the Parish Assemblies and future Colonial Assemblies will admit the people of color born of free fathers and mothers if they otherwise have the required status." Although landowning free men of color viewed this law as merely a compromise—since it set up only conditional citizenship for free men of color by requiring them to be property owners born of free parents—many were willing to accept it. The white French colonists, however, remained opposed. As a result, the National Assembly included much stronger language in the May 29, 1791, instructions specifically related to "the status of persons in the colonies." "The National Assembly could not refuse to render this March 28 decree," the instructions read. "It cannot grant one part of the empire the ability to exclude men from active citizenship when the constitutional laws guarantee those rights in the entire empire."[28] In other words, separate laws could not be made for people of color since the laws of French citizenship required that the National Assembly not distinguish among "free" people. Yet denying those rights was exactly what the Colonial Assembly intended. The vagaries of the National Assembly's language strengthened their case. The law and its instructions stopped just short of proclaiming the free men of color, specifically, to be active citizens. Instead, the lawmakers insisted the matter had been settled since the term "all free persons" necessarily applied to the free men of color.

While the Colonial Assembly debated the meaning of the word "person" with the colony's free population of color, the enslaved of Saint-Domingue had their own preoccupations. Instead of petitions and speeches, they used well-worn revolutionary tactics to take their freedom. Boukman began by killing the man who had enslaved him, at least according to one alleged eyewitness. An enslaver named Clémont owned a plantation in Limbé where he had forced Boukman to serve as his coachman. With his "master" gone, Boukman led the enslaved of the atelier to set fire to the plantation. Two other enslaved men immediately joined Boukman: Jean-François, a coachman on the Bullet plantation, and Georges Biassou, a sugar refiner on the Biassou plantation after which he was named. Armed with "hoes, spears, pruning hooks, and marching to the lugubrious sound of the conch," the freedom fighters under their leadership reportedly set fire to the entire northern plain in less than seventeen days. After this, all that could evidently be heard was the "ringing of funeral bells coming from the dwellings."[29]

The Colonial Assembly responded with incredulity, issuing threats to Boukman, Jean-François, and Biassou while demanding that France send military reinforcements. The French colonists even put a bounty on Boukman's head. The offer worked. In November 1791, a white colonist known as Mr. Michel received 6,000 livres for assassinating Boukman, the architect of the Haitian Revolution who had for two months bravely led the freedom struggle.[30] The French colonists then decapitated and burned his body. With their veritable mania for heads on pikes, the colonists afterward exposed Boukman's in the middle of the Place d'Armes in Cap with a sign that read, "Head of Boukman, leader of the rebels." The white French colonists desired only to see vengeful massacre, not freedom's dawn, in the dead leader's eyes. "Never did a severed head conserve so much expression: the open and still glistening eyes seemed to send his troops the signal to massacre," wrote one nineteenth-century chronicler.[31]

The colonists, meanwhile, desperately waited for reinforcements. Troops finally arrived in late November 1791, around the same time as three commissioners, Roume, Frédéric de Mirbeck, and Edmond de Saint-Léger. It is perhaps at this moment that Christophe would have met for the first time or have been reunited with Roume de Saint-Laurent, that native of Grenada, who later became Christophe's reluctant ally.

The French colonists greeted the three commissioners in Cap as saviors. Upon arrival, Mirbeck addressed the crowd that had gathered to meet them, followed by Roume. The latter told the white colonists, "It is no longer pashas surrounded by Janissaries[32] that France sends to you; we are three of your brothers, all citizens who come without ostentation." Saint-Léger also gave a speech to reaffirm that the National Assembly sent the three commissioners to establish peace. "Saint-Domingue is too important a part of the French Empire, and the French people of the metropole and the colonies are now linked by all too indissoluble ties," Saint-Léger declared.[33] Despite these hints that the commissioners represented the interests of the National Assembly and were there to further disempower the colonial assemblies, the colonists expressed distinct joy to see the French commissioners and military officers arrive on the island for their putative protection.

If Christophe remained at the Couronne hotel after the start of the freedom uprising, he might have crossed paths with the first officers and soldiers to arrive. Some French troops had arrived in Cap-Français just before the commissioners, but to deleterious rather than salutary effect. On November 21, a Mr. Berault appeared before the Colonial Assembly to complain that thirty of the newly arrived officers had spread themselves throughout the city and proceeded to engage in "indecent and reprehensible conduct in every respect; several among others, at the Café de la Comédie and at the Hôtel de la Couronne, dared to make the most unconstitutional and incendiary remarks. . . . A crowd of citizens soon surrounded them; they were driven back to the seaside."[34] Over several days additional testimony emerged about the conduct of these troops. On the twenty-third, a Mr. Jouette appeared on the podium before the Colonial Assembly and declared, "It is important for the assembly that the behavior of the officers of the royal marine at the Auberge de la Couronne be noted . . . we are attached to the constitution, and the officers of the royal marine have made very unconstitutional remarks in this inn and elsewhere." He asked that anyone with "knowledge of it, on their conscience and their honor, make the most exact declaration before your auditor-commissioners to this effect."[35] Additional testimony clarified that the officers had professed royalist devotion, instead of fealty to the National Assembly and the constitution the French revolutionaries had created. "One of the guests of the Auberge de la Couronne had to be saved from the effects of the indignation of the citizens, who, having retired to a café, affected to flout their civic-mindedness there with the most unconstitutional remarks," the account continued. Eventually the authorities sent back to France around a dozen officers who had lunched at the Couronne hotel.[36] These mentions of the hotel—variously called the "Hotel de la Couronne," "Auberge de la Couronne," and "Maison de la Couronne"—offer a brief glimpse into its history during the earliest days of the revolution.[37] If Christophe remained employed at the hotel in the early days of the freedom struggle, he might have had a front row seat to this flurry of revolutionary activity and the controversy taking place within its walls and throughout the city of Cap.

After Boukman's death at the hands of the white French colonists, Jean-François, Biassou, and Toussaint (not yet going by Louverture) became the leaders of the freedom struggle. Initially, they tried to negotiate a peaceful return to order. Their letters from the fall and winter of 1791 highlight the conciliatory attitude of the Black freedom fighters during the earliest days of the liberty struggle and the stubborn racism of the white colonists unwilling to make any concessions. The freedom leaders hardly asked for general or outright emancipation. Instead, they insisted on better working conditions, including the elimination of whipping, and on the dissolution of existing distinctions, from the standpoint of citizenship, between the free people of color, called the *nouveaux libres,* or newly freed, and those designated *ancien libres,* or who had free Black or mixed-race parents. If French officials granted them the "first principles of their demands," including the emancipation of and amnesty for the generals and commanders, the leaders insisted that "public prosperity will be reborn from its ashes," a resonant phrase that later became a part of Christophe's motto as king of Haiti.[38]

The obstinance of the white French colonists remained impressive. In addition to suggesting that the enslaved freedom fighters did not and could not write these negotiating missives, the pro-slavery colonists implied that the ideas found in the letters were not those of the freedom fighters either, and even that the letters might be entirely fake—that is, written, conceived of, and sent by people other than the *Black* leaders of the freedom struggle. "We must therefore see [in person] Jean-François and Biassou, or one of the two," the assembly officially responded. "Let the rebels think about the fact that we are expecting from France forces that will overthrow all who oppose the righteous vengeance of the nation and the king," the assembly threatened. As the Spanish king reinforced his troops in Santo Domingo, the eastern and Spanish-claimed side of Saint-Domingue, the national civil commissioners of France planned a meeting with the leaders of the freedom struggle. They initially asked the Colonial Assembly for four members to accompany them to a spot in Marie-Louise's neighborhood, the Saint-Michel plantation in Quartier-Morin. Yet the assembly changed course and declined, saying that it already gave its response to the "revoltees."[39] The three French commissioners therefore went on their own. The leaders on the side of the freedom struggle decided that Jean François would meet the French commissioners on the Saint-Michel plantation in mid-December. Although the meeting resulted in the successful release of several white prisoners, no cease-fire could be agreed upon, partly because the enslaved freedom fighters were unwilling to put down their arms, aware that their self-proclaimed leaders were negotiating more for their own freedoms than for those of the masses.[40]

In their December 12 letter, Biassou and company rather surprisingly offered to help the French combat the African masses, if their other demands were granted. However, the Black leaders acknowledged how difficult such a task would be. The leaders of the freedom fighters knew that quelling the uprising would be more easily ordered than done. "We cannot hide from you the fact that we will have to camp out across the different parishes for a very long time," Biassou and company warned. "Many Negroes will contaminate the forests, where they will hide out, and constant pursuit of them will be necessary, braving danger and fatigue."[41] This was de facto recognition that their leadership of the Black masses was deeply contingent.

Meanwhile, the commissioners Saint-Léger and Mirbeck returned to France as the entire western portion of the colony sank into open rebellion, from enslaved freedom fighters to free people of color striving for equal rights. Then came the law of April 4, 1792, which proclaimed that free people of color, provided they had been born to parents with free status, had the same rights as free whites. But it was too late. The previous month more plantations had been set ablaze and enslaved freedom fighters in the western province were almost universally in arms. Led by an enslaved chief named Hyacinthe from the Ducoudray plantation, the freedom fighters set fire to the plain of Cul-de-Sac, eventually also attacking Port-au-Prince and Croix-des-Bouquets, as they forced white French troops to flee.[42]

With the whole colony, from north to south, east to west, fully engaged in the freedom uprising, the French government knew it had to do something drastic and fast. Along with the law of April 4, the French government sent three new commissioners to the island to enforce it. Léger-Félicité Sonthonax, Étienne Polverel, and Jean-Antoine Ailhaud arrived in Cap on September 18, 1792.[43] Only a few days later the National Assembly abolished the French monarchy and declared France a republic.

Just one year later Sonthonax and Polverel declared emancipation from slavery on the island. This was a dramatic and, to some, a confusing reversal. Both men had loudly announced upon their arrival their intention to protect slavery. Sonthonax even admitted this in a roundabout way in the preamble to his August 1793 emancipation decree, when he acknowledged that he had previously announced slavery was "necessary for agriculture." Sonthonax tried to make an excuse for this when he confessed, "If, by the greatest of imprudence, we had, at that time, broken the bonds which chained the slaves to their masters, no doubt their first movement would have been to pounce on their executioners, and in their all too righteous fury, they would easily have confused the innocent with the guilty." "Our powers, moreover, did not extend so far as to be able to pronounce on the fate of the Africans, and we would have been perjurers and criminals if the law had been violated by us," he continued. Suggesting that the abolition of the monarchy and creation of the republic had opened the door for abolition—rather than the constant rebellion of the enslaved population—the commissioner declared, "Today's circumstances are very different," before he insisted, "The French republic wants liberty and equality for every man."[44] Yet the colonists had already seized upon Sonthonax's seemingly pro-slavery declarations of September 1792 as evidence of his duplicity and had committed to publicizing the commissioners' pro-slavery stance in the most visible way.

The March 28, 1793, issue of the *Revolutionary Newspaper of the French Part of the Colony of Saint-Domingue* professed to be "dedicated to the republic of September 20, 1792," the day the National Assembly abolished the monarchy. The journal's epigraph, however, came not from any of the documents that made France a republic rather than a monarchy the day afterward. Instead, the epigraph was taken from the *"Proclamations of September 24 and December 30, 1792,"* described as an *"oath solemnly pronounced in the church of Cap, by the civil commissioners"* who had declared, "The colonies are part of the French Empire.—We declare in its name that SLAVERY is necessary to the culture and prosperity of the colonies, that it is neither in the principles nor in the will of the nation to touch in this respect the properties of the colonists.—We shall die rather than suffer the execution of an antipopular plot."[45]

Christophe, whether having enslaved or free status when the second set of commissioners arrived, would have doubtless been affected by the incoherence between the National Assembly (on whose behalf the commissioners served), the white planters (who wanted both slavery to continue and for the free people of color to be denied rights of citizenship), and many free people of color (who wanted equal rights with whites, but for slavery to be maintained). Just before Sonthonax and Polverel determined they had little choice but to decree general emancipation (Ailhaud, for his part, abandoned his post shortly after arrival), Christophe and Marie-Louise wed. Perhaps taking advantage of the commissioners' July 11 law newly allowing marriage between Black people of different social classes with payment of a fee, their official wedding date was July 15, 1793.[46] Yet something quite arresting and unforgettable had happened just the month before.

On June 21, 1793, Christophe's home city of Cap nearly burned to the ground. The circumstances surrounding this fire have much to tell about how Christophe, whose participation in the freedom struggle is about to come more fully into view, gained, preserved, and cemented his own liberty during the first few years of the Haitian Revolution.

—

Complicated events led to the burning of Cap. They revolved primarily around the actions of the French general François-Thomas Galbaud du Fort, or simply Galbaud. By the early spring of 1793, Sonthonax and Polverel had, with some success, forced compliance with the law of April 4, 1792. Nearly the entire northern province had acceded to the rule of law handed down by the National Assembly, and the white colonists were almost universally subdued into agreement in Port-au-Prince and Jacmel. The two commissioners next set their sights on the city of Jérémie, down in the southwestern peninsula of the colony. There, however, white independence strivers, who reared their heads once more in the wake of the January 1793 execution of France's king Louis XVI, continuously tried to thwart their efforts.[47] And so the infighting and power struggles between the white colonists and the French metropolitan government continued amid the armed Black freedom struggle. Galbaud soon became a lasting symbol of this chaos.

General Galbaud, a decorated French military officer and the man designated by the National Assembly to become the new governor-general of the island, arrived in Cap on May 6, 1793. But in the interim between his appointment and his arrival on Saint-Domingue, his eligibility for the position had technically become null. The law of April 4, according to the commissioners, excluded Galbaud from the colony's highest office. To prevent the white French colonists from placing their own interests above that of the French metropolitan government, the law specifically barred property owners in Saint-Domingue from becoming governor. Almost as soon as he was named governor, Galbaud's mother died, and he consequently inherited her property in Saint-Domingue. This was the first strike against him. The second was that even though his instructions from the French government stated that he could assume his office as governor-general only after having been instated by the French commissioners, Galbaud appeared before the municipality of Cap immediately after his arrival and began giving orders.[48]

Sonthonax and Polverel could hardly hide their disapproval. The colonists, in contrast, exploded with glee to see Galbaud assume office. They believed he would advocate to keep the free people of color from obtaining equal rights, especially the rights of citizenship and representation. It turns out that Galbaud had no problem stoking the figurative flames between the free people of color and the white colonists until Cap was consumed by literal flames. Aware of the opposition of the commissioners, Galbaud began his questionable tenure by claiming they had no authority over him and that he could even have them deported.

On June 10, Sonthonax and Polverel arrived in Cap to ward off Galbaud and the men he recruited to his cause. Galbaud continued to undermine the commissioners, doing nothing to quell rumors he started that he was not subject to their authority or that he was vested with the power to deport the commissioners. In a tense meeting with the commissioners Galbaud essentially acceded to the nullification of his appointment, but not before averring that he preferred to return to France, "because besides, he would never agree to be the passive instrument of the commission's requisitions." The commissioners refused to tolerate any more of his harangues, and on June 14, they deposed Galbaud and sent him aboard the ship *Normande* with instructions for his deportation.[49]

So much damage had already been done, but there was still more to come. More than a hundred merchant ships dotted the harbor in Cap, some of which carried white colonists from Jacmel and Port-au-Prince scheduled for deportation for having opposed the April 4 law and the authority of the civil commissioners. Several prominent deportees encouraged Galbaud to revolt against the commissioners. On the twentieth, Galbaud essentially took over the *Normande* by recruiting its sailors to his side, doing the same with another ship called the *Amérique*. Galbaud harangued the soldiers on board both ships, drumming up further ire against the commissioners while proclaiming himself to be invested with the powers over the earth and the sea. He went on to declare the commissioners "traitors to their country" and invited the sailors and other men on board to follow him to the shore to dispute the commissioners' authority. These already disillusioned and armed men appeared all too ready to follow Galbaud's orders. "Citizens of the vessels of the republic are advised that the signal to descend will be a cannon blast from under the blue flag at the mizzenmast head," Galbaud ordered, and the sailors complied.[50]

In response, the commissioners tasked a white French general, Étienne Laveaux, commander of the National Guard in Cap, though ill, with opposing this new rebellion using "force for force." Laveaux ordered his more than two hundred men, most of whom were free people of color, to shoot down anyone who attempted to come ashore, and the commander of the Fort du Gris-Gris, who had six mortars, was ordered to "bombard any rowboats heading toward land." Galbaud made his way to shore, nonetheless, where dozens of white colonists greeted his arrival with enthusiasm, reportedly shouting, "To the Government [House]!" One of the bloodiest battles of the revolution thereafter ensued, with more than two thousand people losing their lives over three days, as the Government House saw continuous battery with cannon shot. Then, on June 21, 1793, Black freedom fighters—urged on by Sonthonax, some said, while others blamed Galbaud—set fire to the city of Cap, burning nearly every structure in the center of the city to the ground, with damage estimated into the billions.[51]

With the city on fire, the commissioners fled to Camp Bréda accompanied by General Antoine Chanlatte (brother of Juste Chanlatte) and his legionnaires of free men of color, among whom were Christophe and Jean-Baptiste Belley.[52] Unlike Toussaint, Biassou, and Jean-François, who had joined the Spanish army following the breakdown in their negotiations with the commissioners, Saint-Rémy claimed that by 1793 Christophe served with French artillery, after having been enrolled in the maréchaussée.[53] Dispatches from the French commissioners confirm his enrollment in the French military as early as June 1793. The circumstances of how this came about, however, are nothing short of remarkable and have not thus far been related in any other account of Christophe's life. It turns out that the days leading up to the June 21 fire are key to understanding Christophe's involvement in that momentous event.

Just two days before the fire, Christophe wrote a letter to the commissioners. Christophe, this letter reveals, was not at liberty in June 1793, only two months prior to Sonthonax's August decree. His lack of freedom was not because of slavery, per se. Instead, Christophe found himself incarcerated in one of the carceral colony's many jails, for an offense unrelated to the revolution, in his words.

At eight o'clock in the morning on June 19, 1793, Christophe addressed a letter to the civil commissioners, written from the prison in Cap. He began less with an assertion of his innocence, although he did imply it, than by imploring the commissioners to heed his advice about a conspiracy afoot. "As the affair for which I am detained has nothing to do with the revolution," Christophe began his letter, "I am too much attached to my fatherland and to the wise constitution to believe myself guilty, and I really would be, if I did not warn you of a criminal plot that is being concocted before me." Christophe went on to note that for several days an aide-de-camp repeatedly visited a newly arrived prisoner by the name of Denard. These visits aroused Christophe's suspicion. The civil commissioners had ordered Denard's arrest on June 13, 1793, condemning him to be held indefinitely. Christophe was already in the jail when Denard arrived, and Christophe disclosed to the commissioners that the visits from an aide-de-camp began immediately after the new prisoner's arrival. Christophe could not confirm the reason for these visits until two hours before he penned the letter to the commissioners. At six o'clock in the morning on June 19, Christophe said, the aide-de-camp arrived as usual, but this time he wore a white jacket and revealed his name to be "Cresser or Cressoire." Denard asked Christophe to step aside into a separate part of the prison so he could speak to the aide-de-camp in private. Christophe overheard the conversation anyway. The aide-de-camp said to Denard, "The crew of the *Concorde* runs to Galbaud incessantly telling him that since they were the ones who brought him to Saint-Domingue, they will never let him leave. This crew is entirely on his side and is sure of all the others, and they want to take Galbaud ashore, but he replied that they had to wait and that he was going to inquire about the disposition of the people in town." "He dispatched me for this reason," the aide continued, "and I went to four or five houses, whose inhabitants assured me that at the first movement in the harbor, the whole town would rise for him. By ending my tour at the prison, it will be easy for you all to get out, and I'm counting on you, Denard." Denard listened attentively to the aide's speech and then gave him a letter "written in circles," or code, meant for Galbaud. Denard also reassured the aide that everything would turn out just as planned.

Christophe claimed that he had deciphered the coded letter and revealed to the commissioners that in it Denard had reassured Galbaud that "the two chiefs of the harbor are of the same mind, that discontent in town is at its height, that the prisoners are devoted to [Galbaud], calling him a god and beseeching him to save the colony." The aide planned to return at noon, ostensibly to provide Denard with Galbaud's reply. Denard, clearly believing that Christophe also supported Galbaud, consequently asked him to take dictation on "a slip of paper" intended for Galbaud. "I didn't think I should forgo the opportunity, since it provided me with the means to warn you of the plots hatched by the wicked who want to take away the peace we are about to enjoy," Christophe explained to the commissioners. Christophe finished the letter by observing that the porter did not know the contents of his missive, which Christophe did not at first sign, out of precaution. "I believe my handwriting and name are known to you, but I'll sign if you demand it," Christophe concluded. The commissioners evidently did want Christophe to sign the letter. In a note from Cap dated

August 1, 1793, and scribbled on the bottom of a handwritten copy of the letter, Christophe wrote before signing his name, "On the orders of the civil commissioner of the republic, who represented the above letter to me, I have hastened to sign it, and to attest to its sincerity once more."[54] Christophe's information must have checked out. The same day, the nineteenth, the commissioners hastily sent an order commanding the head of the city's police department "to transport himself at once to the jail of this city, to seize all papers he finds, either on Denard or in the room occupied by the said Denard."[55] The information also compelled the commissioners to liberate Christophe.

The very next day, June 20, Christophe found himself released from the jail, but now beholden to the commissioners and required to serve their goals. The commissioners had liberated several other prisoners from the jail in Cap too, although without mentioning them by name. Christophe, in contrast, was mentioned specifically. The commissioners had expressly forbidden the commander "to hand over to any individual the negroes released from the jail on this day." Written just below these orders stood the civil commissioners' directive for the commandant of Haut-du-Cap to "put at Henry Christophe's disposition two 8-pounder cannons."[56] In one way or another, then, Christophe found freedom in connection with the Galbaud affair.

In the meantime, back at the camp that bore the name of Toussaint Louverture's enslaver, Bréda, the commissioners swore the solemn resolution to give liberty to any of the enslaved who enrolled in the French army under the banner of the republic. This law was in effect the first abolition by the French government.[57] It was not a benevolent move to erase prejudices and establish equality, however, but a pragmatic one designed to stop the rebellion.

Galbaud commanded more than six thousand sailors and five battalions of the National Guard. Many white colonists had also volunteered to assist him on foot and on horse. The commissioners, on the contrary, had only three hundred free people of color and two hundred line troops. Galbaud therefore considered victory only a matter of time as he issued an order to have the commissioners arrested on sight.[58]

Although the promises of freedom and amnesty were not enough to persuade Jean-François and Biassou, fighting at the time, like Toussaint, on behalf of the Spanish *against* France, several other prominent freedom fighters did respond to the call.[59] Pierrot, commander over Port-Français, joined French forces in Haut-du-Cap, while Pierre Baptiste Léveillé and Martial Besse, the latter a free man of color born in Terrier-Rouge and raised in France, took over in Cap from the increasingly ill Laveaux.[60]

The city of Cap set aflame must have been a frightful sight by the time Besse arrived with 180 dragoons. He and his men, along with Pierrot and his band, successfully penetrated the city and took over Fort Bélair and several other key positions, which allowed them to establish a cannon and bombard the arsenal where Galbaud had hidden. Pierrot and Besse pursued the sailors relentlessly, forcing them to reembark by five o'clock in the evening on the twenty-third. Galbaud, on the verge of capture, escaped from the arsenal and nearly drowned as he tried to reach his boat. By seven o'clock on the evening of the twenty-third, Besse and Pierrot had achieved an unlikely victory in ridding Cap of the white French counterrevolutionaries. Still, the fires continued to rage for days, and the once opulent colonial city was strewn with cadavers.[61]

For Besse's efforts, Sonthonax promoted him to commander of Terrier-Rouge.[62] As for Christophe, who reportedly fought "valiantly" on behalf of the French commissioners, who had given him charge of the two cannons, he likely already had free status vis-à-vis slavery. Christophe's direct correspondence with Sonthonax, his ability to read and write, and the familiarity with which he addressed the commissioners (for example, "I believe my handwriting and name are known to you") make it unlikely he would have had enslaved status at the time of his incarceration.[63] However, many other Black inhabitants directly acquired freedom papers for fighting for the republic during Galbaud's insurrection.

On June 24, the commissioners issued an order to André Vernet, saying that driven by the "counterrevolutionary" events into which "Galbaud has plunged the colony," and encouraged by the necessity to fly to France's defense, they authorized Vernet, later minister of finance under King Henry, but at this time commander of the second division of the National Guard in Marmelade, to provide liberty to any enslaved man willing to fight on the side of the republic.[64] Additional orders soon followed declaring, in the cities of Port-au-Prince, Plaisance, and Gonaïves, the emancipation of dozens of "negroes" who fought in defense of the colony "or on behalf of their masters," including some who fought against "negroes in rebellion."[65] What these freedom papers inadvertently show is that the "counterrevolution" the civil commissioners accused Galbaud of having led was complicated by the armed resistance of enslaved Africans, some of whom were fighting against both Galbaud's faction and that of the civil commissioners. By dangling formalized freedom before the eyes of Black freedom fighters already in open rebellion against slavery, the commissioners redoubled their military power. They also unwittingly revealed cracks in their own authority.

The French general César Galbaud, brother of the infamous French general François-Thomas Galbaud du Fort (whose governorship of the colony the commissioners contested), reported that on June 25, four days after the fire began, ten thousand "negroes in revolt" came down from the mountains into the charred city to present a motion to Sonthonax demanding he "proclaim general liberty for all the slaves in the colony." "That idea was well received, and we expect very soon to see this proclamation," César Galbaud reported to his brother from his jail cell in Cap, where he had been detained for seventy days at the time he wrote this letter.[66] Perhaps it is for this reason that on June 25 the commissioners issued an order permitting Lieutenant Colonel Pacot, commander of the western department, to "arm, if he deems it necessary for the interests of the republic, all the slaves he judges worthy of being [armed]."[67] Just a week later, on July 2, Sonthonax and Polverel issued a second proclamation, extending the one from June 21, in order to grant "amnesty" and "liberty" to all the "slaves in rebellion," from any part of the colony, who had taken or who would agree in the future to take up arms to "defend the colony."[68]

The social and political circumstances of enslaved individuals and free people of color in the wake of Galbaud's insurrection and on the eve of general emancipation evolved quickly. Galbaud's insurrection, the destruction of Cap, and the invasion of the British and Spanish—along with the fact that Jean-François, Biassou, and Toussaint had recently joined the latter—essentially forced Sonthonax and Polverel to take any measures conceivable to strengthen their authority.

Desperate to see the war on the island come to an end, on August 29, 1793, Sonthonax stunned the colony's white inhabitants when he addressed the enslaved men and women of Saint-Domingue with words of official emancipation. "The French republic wants liberty and equality to exist for all men, without distinction of color," Sonthonax's decree read.

Thirty-three articles announcing the formal abolition of slavery in the northern plain followed the fiery preamble. Proclaiming "men are born free and equal in rights," the first article mandated that the "Declaration of the Rights of Man and the Citizen" should be "printed, published, and posted everywhere"; while the second observed, "All Negroes and people of mixed blood currently enslaved are declared free to enjoy all rights pertaining to French citizenship." A series of complicated provisions followed. Article 9 mandated, "Slaves currently attached to the plantations of their former masters will be obliged to remain there and work the land." Articles 11 and 12 then laid out a system of compensation for such "laborers" who were to share a third of the plantation's revenues, equal thirds belonging to the planter and to the French government, respectively.[69] Echoes of these labor laws later stamped policy under Toussaint Louverture's rule, as well as those of Dessalines, Christophe, and eventually Boyer.

A little less than a month after Sonthonax shook the island with this decree, his fellow French commissioner Polverel followed Sonthonax's lead by formally abolishing slavery in the sections of the colony under his authority, first in the western part of the colony and then in the south. Combined, Sonthonax's and Polverel's decrees effectively meant general emancipation.[70] Yet, coincidentally, on August 29, 1793—the same day Sonthonax declared the enslaved of the north emancipated—Louverture gave his equally famous speech to his "Brothers and Friends" at Camp

Turel. "You have perhaps heard my name. You are aware, brothers, that I have undertaken vengeance, and that I want freedom and equality to reign in Saint Domingue. I have been working since the beginning to bring it into existence. . . . Equality cannot exist without liberty, and for liberty to exist we need unity."[71] Following this speech, Louverture united several factions together and later proclaimed himself the "founder of liberty" in the colony.[72]

The truth is that the formerly enslaved masses had already brought the plantation economy to a distinct halt, and it was their freedom struggle that ended the ability of the French colonial merchants of legalized human trafficking to profit from slavery. The *Affiches américaines* acknowledged as much all the way back in July 1793, just a few weeks after the great fires in Cap and more than a month before either Sonthonax's emancipation proclamation or Louverture's speech. Even though the *Affiches* remained perhaps Saint-Domingue's greatest and certainly most read pro-slavery publication, on July 11 the newspaper performed somewhat of an about-face. "Events succeed one another with such rapidity and in forms so various, so unforeseen, so little pre-calculated," the opening sentence of an article in that issue stated, "that it is as impossible to foretell what Saint-Domingue will be like in a month, as it would have been a month ago to predict Galbaud's burning of the town of Cap and the massacre of more than three thousand individuals." The writer went on to argue for general emancipation as the only way to save the colony. First, he decried the existence of enslaved children in the colony "in whose veins free or French blood already circulates," "because their fathers chose the mold of a slave negress to deposit the material of a child who should have been born free." The mothers of these children should also be free "as a reparation due to nature and liberty so cruelly outraged in Saint-Domingue." This first step, the paper averred, "will lead us gradually to general emancipation, which is becoming every day of the most urgent necessity." Going on to use a number of justifications, the author finally admitted that slavery existed only in name at that point because of "the insurrection, which for three years has resulted in a state of affairs where the slaves no longer follow any laws other than that of their own wills, and which has so familiarized them with murder, arson, and plunder that they cannot even be persuaded that they are committing crimes, removing forever the hope of subjecting them again to the yoke of slavery."[73] The writer, in a roundabout way, and clearly unintentionally, recognized not only that the enslaved had already liberated themselves in a very material sense but that the "crimes" the white colonists charged them with were open to interpretation. The Black freedom fighters, determined never to be subjected to slavery again, and to use any means available to ensure their freedom, viewed what the French colonists called their "crimes" as wholly righteous and fully justified acts of freedom.

Although Sonthonax and Polverel merely made official the material liberties enslaved Africans had already conjured into reality, leaders like Louverture, and less visible actors like Christophe, benefited from general emancipation enormously. In the post-emancipation period both men advanced their military careers in new ways and formed free Black families. Yet while Louverture's rise was largely only upward, Christophe continued to experience problems integrating himself into the French republic's colony.

In October 1793, with formal emancipation in the air, Christophe further ingratiated himself with the commissioners. On October 10, Sonthonax wrote that Christophe, a "citizen of Petite-Rivière," had assisted the civil commissioners by delivering to them letters he found at "Camp Prunier," in the same parish, written by Biassou and Jean-François.[74] Just two months later, Christophe appeared yet again in trouble. A letter he wrote to a magistrate in December 1793, and signed with an original signature matching Christophe's, reveals he was being held in custody by the French government once more, but this time far from his home, way down in the city Polverel renamed Port-Républicain (Port-au-Prince). Because the letter has only recently been recovered, it is worth including in its entirety for what it tells us about the ongoing precarities of Black freedom in the then slavery-free colony of Saint-Domingue:

The Barracks of Port-Républicain,
December 4, 1793, Year 2 of the Republic.

Citizen Magistrate,

An illness caused by the grief of my imprisonment, from which I have barely recovered, has deprived me of the honor of remembering to write you sooner. I shall never forget that it is to you that I owe the little comfort I enjoy in the barracks, where I am much better off than in prison, thanks to your kindness. Please accept my sincere thanks, but I am no less a captive for it. You know what my crime is: I only dared to call myself one of Commissioner Sonthonax's secretaries to prevent myself from starving to death on the road, as the 2 *portugaises* he had given me in Cap were not enough for such a long and arduous journey. I must beg for mercy before you and the commissioner. I therefore beg you in mercy to remind him that I had the good fortune to prove my patriotism to him in Cap, since this is what his kindness deserved. Since then, my behavior has remained the same, and I groan in captivity and in the most terrible misery. I must confess that I have received nothing but kindness from citizens Domergue and Boyé,[75] local commanders, and to whom I owe my existence. Since I no longer wish to bother them, I am reduced to despair. If I were free, I'd procure for myself some work, because I love work, and I'd get myself a livelihood. Citizen Magistrate, I am at your knees, I implore your support, you have a sensitive heart, and you would be truly affected by my state if you understood its horror. You promised to get me out. The commissioner won't refuse you, and I owe my freedom to you, the greatest of good deeds. I beg you, at least grant me freedom to the city, given my poor health, on pain of presenting myself every day. This will at least give me the means to procure the necessities of life by working. If they prefer to give me a job in equal measure, where I am desired by all the officers whose esteem I have earned through my conduct, this would put me in a position to give further proof of the patriotism that has always animated me and for which I will spill every last drop of my blood to defend, the most beautiful cause in the universe! I am placing all my hope and all my confidence in you, take pity on the deplorable state to which I am reduced, you have already deigned to take an interest in my misfortune, complete my happiness by according me the city for a prison under penalty of presenting myself every day to the commander, or by obtaining a sub-lieutenancy for me in the legion. I await this grace from you, please let me know if I can expect it. My life will be consecrated to you, and it will never be at peace until I am able to thank you for such a blessing. Your answer will put an end to my misfortune, by rendering me the happiest of men.

Regards,
Christophe[76]

Unlike his earlier letter to the commissioners, this one revealed the reason for Christophe's incarceration. Although he had clearly been providing services to Sonthonax in Cap (for which he received some compensation), somewhere along the way he stood accused of having "misrepresented" his connection to the civil commissioner, landing him in custody. Languishing in the barracks of the southwestern city of Port-au-Prince for an indeterminate amount of time, Christophe—who appears to refer to his prior enslavement or incarceration in the letter—seemed lonely and miserable. He must have been missing his wife too.

By December 1793, Christophe and Marie-Louise were already expecting their first baby. It must have wrenched the soon-to-be father's heart to find himself so far away from his new wife and future child.

Although we cannot say for sure how Christophe's release from the barracks came about, what comes clearly into focus is that from December 1793, when he found himself in an unfree state, to December 1794, when he enjoyed life as a rich, successful, and respected businessman and new father in Cap, his life underwent a remarkable and unlikely transformation.

—

The freedom struggle in Saint-Domingue that crushed the plantation economy, forcing Sonthonax and Polverel to formally abolish slavery, had repercussions across the Atlantic Ocean. In February 1794, the French National Convention followed in the wake of Saint-Domingue's Black freedom fighters by universally abolishing slavery across all French overseas territories: "The National Convention declares that the enslavement of negroes in all the colonies is abolished; as a result, it is decreed that all men, without distinction of color, living in the colonies are French citizens."[77] By the time news of the decree reached Saint-Domingue, Toussaint had already joined the French military. Biassou, in contrast, remained with the Spanish until their defeat by French forces in 1795, which resulted in the signing of the Treaty of Basel, by which Spain ceded the eastern part of the island to France. After this, Biassou emigrated to Florida.[78] As for Jean-François, he faced a more fraught trajectory. Initially arrested by the French, he was eventually deported to Havana and from there went to Spain. Jean-François is believed to have died destitute in western Europe sometime in the early nineteenth century.[79]

The revolution took on a different tenor from the moment the Black soldiers and officers led by Toussaint became not just citizens but an integral part of the French military. The governor of Saint-Domingue had tasked Toussaint, who later rose to the rank of French general, with getting rid of the Spanish and then the British. New opportunities for Black men, as French citizens, pushed Christophe more prominently into the world of the colony in this period too, but not at first as a military man. Although he had been incarcerated by the French just one year earlier, by December 1794 he had clearly been free long enough to gain the money necessary to rent a house in Cap at number 326 rue Dauphine and des Trois Chandeliers, owned by Léonard Picard, for 1,010 colonial livres per year, to be paid in four equal terms every three months, with one month in advance.

Christophe's new home was expansive. According to the lease, it consisted of "a ground floor with four bedrooms, a hall, a courtyard, two cabinets, three kitchens, and a well, and upstairs, forming a pavilion into two large bedrooms." There were also "four cabinets and two kitchens." This lease is key for many reasons. It affirms that Christophe lived in Cap at the time the contract was signed, having ostensibly moved there from Petite-Rivière, where he was previously stationed, sometime between December 1793, when he was imprisoned way down in the south, and December 1794, when he was already living in Cap, according to the lease.[80] The lease also mentions a citizen Faraud (spelled "Fareau" on the lease), who later became a key member of the king's administration and whom Christophe made a baron in 1811.[81]

Faraud, appointed the colony's chief engineer for Cap's reconstruction, would also eventually be appointed chief architect of King Henry's famous Citadelle. This same Faraud (first name Alexandre)—whose coat of arms under King Henry was flanked by two silver rabbits, tellingly containing the words "Citadelle Henry"—had been a Christophe associate since at least December 1794, when the future king signed the lease for the apartment adjoining the home on rue Dauphine and des Trois Chandeliers.[82] While evincing a clear, and swift, reversal in Christophe's circumstances, the lease contained a clause that spelled out Faraud's responsibilities and obligations and Christophe's obligations to him: "It is further agreed that will be yielded to Citizen Fareau, engineer in this department, an apartment dependent on the house and consisting of a small hall on the ground floor with a courtyard, kitchen, study, and two bedrooms with three studies forming the pavilion." Faraud and Christophe essentially lived in the same building, if not the same dwelling. This made sense because like Christophe, Faraud worked on behalf of the French government to rebuild, restore, and repair the devastated city of Cap. For his efforts, Faraud received the sum of 505 colonial livres paid every three months. Christophe, according to the lease, remained responsible for providing "guarantee of the above." The agreement was signed with what is perhaps the earliest known full signature of the future king of Haiti.[83]

Though not as fancy as the signature he later adopted as king, the signed lease suggests that Christophe had emerged as a well-respected and trusted member of the community, as well as a man of means. The house in Cap was large and its rent not inexpensive. Christophe made his living not only by helping with the reconstruction efforts in Cap, as revealed by the lease, but by running several state-owned plantations under Sonthonax's affermage system.

The June 1793 fire in Cap had caused extensive damage. The French initially appointed Colonel Vincent, the same one whose son transmitted his father's precious biographical notes about Christophe to Saint-Rémy, as the director of fortifications to oversee reconstruction of the city. This was how he first crossed paths with Christophe. Nearly the entire rue Espagnole, renamed rue Française, frightfully bore the remnants of the fires that charred it. Of the more prominent structures, the Salle de Spectacle, at the other end of the street from the Couronne hotel, suffered such damage that it had not yet been rebuilt in 1800, even though it had been leased since 1798 to a citizen Val.[84] Still ostensibly managed at the time of the fire by Gaye, and possibly also Monjeon, the Couronne, as we have seen, did not survive unscathed either.[85]

By January 1801, reconstruction on the Salle de Spectacle, like the reconstruction of the Couronne, seems not to have even begun. In fact, the first indications that the Couronne might ever be rehabilitated appeared belatedly in 1802, when Rachel Roze Faxardo, who inherited the former hotel from her brother, sought to claim it. Recall that the colonist Legrand officially applied to reconstruct the bottom portion of building number 787, the property next door to the hotel. In his petition, he noted that everything neighboring the building he wanted to reconstruct had been burned and stood in total shambles, but that the other owners had already received permission to proceed. By 1803, the government had finally approved a request for the hotel's reconstruction, as the survey of the city listed the property as occupied by an "architect" named Griveause.[86]

Documentary evidence of the Couronne's ownership, management, and reconstruction do not associate Christophe, who many chroniclers claimed owned the hotel following emancipation, with the Couronne in the period following the fire. However, Christophe did hold extensive leases in the city, including some designated for reconstruction. Beginning on December 27, 1794, the French government granted Christophe a lease over a home at 273 rue Dauphine and des Trois Chandeliers. The home, which had not burned, sat directly across the street from the one Christophe lived in at 326 rue Dauphine and for which he signed the lease only a few days later. Just a week later, Christophe entered a partnership to lease yet a third home on the outskirts of Cap, near the Place Royale (Place Nationale), which had not yet been rebuilt.[87]

These leases explain not only Christophe's occupation before he assumed his post in the military as commander of Quartier-Morin and Petite-Anse in 1796 but how he enriched himself in the colony post-emancipation. From 1795 to late 1802, when he defected from the French military definitively, Christophe oversaw extensive plantations on behalf of the French republic. By 1799, he had amassed quite a fortune. That year, he reportedly told the British agent Hugh Cathcart that he possessed about 2 million colonial livres, equivalent at the time to around $250,000.[88]

The city of Cap and its suburbs were the first of the Saint-Dominguan regions to undergo wide-scale sequester and affermage. In the wake of the disastrous Galbaud affair, the civil commissioners issued a proclamation that declared all "movable and immovable property of all the citizens who have fled from the colony without permission or authorization, and who have no representatives will be seized, sequestered, and placed in the hands of the French republic." In October 1793, the French government created an extensive table of the abandoned plantations near Cap-Français and its environs, including the parishes of Trou, Jacquezy, Limonade, Quartier-Morin, and Petite-Anse. The Saint-Michel plantation in Quartier-Morin and the Chabanon plantation in Limonade, two of Christophe's first properties under affermage, are both listed as abandoned on the register, which left them open to sequester.[89]

In concert with the commission's orders, several government officials, including the Baron de Vastey's cousin Pierre Louis Vastey, traveled to the town of Petite-Anse to take stock of the abandoned plantations. The government proceeded to seize, sequester, and put under government control all the furniture and buildings of abandoned plantations and other properties. The first plantation listed in the officials' report to the commissioners was, in fact, the Saint-Michel plantation and a large "emplacement," a "guildive," or distillery, that neighbored it to the east; the owner of both stood accused of having fled the colony without authorization as an "émigré" with Galbaud's convoy, consequently losing all claim to his property in Saint-Domingue.[90]

Aside from providing new and previously unrecovered information about one of the plantations where Christophe spent much of his time and resources before 1802, the document reveals that Christophe was not yet commander of Petite-Anse. It is not until December 16, 1796, that official documents list Christophe as commander over Petite-Anse and Quartier-Morin. In the interim, he continued to enlarge his network of commercial partnerships, along with the number of plantations he leased.

Christophe had various successful partnerships during this time, which may explain how affermage became so lucrative for him.[91] On January 1, 1797, a man called Prioleau, a U.S. merchant, partnered with Christophe to lease the Chabanon plantation in Limonade for 6,000 colonial livres per year.[92] But it is his partnership with his friend Granier on the Destruilles (sometimes spelled "Détreilles") plantation, whose owners were listed as absentee on the October 1793 register, that may hold the key to Christophe's early wealth.

Located in the northern part of Quartier-Morin, near the sea, the Destruilles plantation bordered Chatenoye plantation to the north and the much larger Charittes plantation to the south, east, and west. Consisting of approximately four *carreaux* of cultivated land in sugar and foodstuffs, the Destruilles plantation also contained a vast savanna of ten *carreaux* with two barriers, north and south, constructed in masonry. In addition to the large sugar factory, the property contained eleven straw huts for the cultivators still living on the land and a working hospital with a covered gallery. Importantly, both Granier and Christophe signed the lease with their original signatures, suggesting they had an equal partnership.[93]

On December 31, 1796, the commissioners approved Christophe and Granier's lease over the Destruilles sugar plantation. Christophe and Granier subsequently farmed the property together under the name "Citizen Granier, Henry Christophe and Company."[94] Granier also solely oversaw several plantations leased under his name, Granier and Company.[95] The Destruilles plantation appears to be the only one that the two leased together. The partnership lasted until 1798, when the property's owner, Pierre Jean Marie Meneust, submitted a formal petition to lift the sequester. Meneust claimed that he had not illegally abandoned the colony, and therefore that Christophe and Granier's claim should be nullified. Meneust hired Jean-Pierre Grenier, an older *négociant,* or businessman, from Cap-Français—he was seventy-five in 1801—who later represented Christophe on several unrelated commercial deals. The government eventually granted Meneust's request because he could prove that he resided in France since 1782. Meneust had insisted, as a result, that he should never have been on the list of émigrés and that his plantation should not have been consequently subjected to sequester. French authorities agreed. On September 8, 1798, the government lifted the sequester. With Meneust's rights of ownership restored, the French government nullified Christophe and Granier's lease.[96]

Although their commercial partnership seems to have been dissolved along with their claim to the Destruilles plantation, Granier and Christophe remained intimate associates and friends. So close were the two men that in February 1802 Christophe sent Granier, referred to as his "homme d'affaires," who was also "commander of a section of the National Guard," to deliver his famous letter to Leclerc, whereby Christophe denied the French general entry into Cap-Français. After Christophe had the city of Cap burned during Leclerc's 1802 military invasion, Leclerc bragged that he had Granier arrested along with several other known Christophe associates.[97]

Christophe's long-standing regard for his former business associate, who at least one chronicler claims served as godfather to Christophe's son Ferdinand, is clear from his response to Granier's detention.[98] Reacting with a mix of anger, alarm, and despondency, Christophe asked General Jean-Louis Vilton, the godfather to at least one of Christophe's daughters, and previously the commander of the arrondissement of Quartier-Morin, "What is his crime?" "What harm has he done? Is it only to have been my friend?"[99] Vilton denied that Leclerc arrested Granier simply because of his connection to Christophe. "With regard to Granier, your friend, he is detained," Vilton confirmed before claiming this was "not because of his connection to you; it is because he has many enemies here who have no doubt slandered him." Vilton then claimed that Granier, who was according to one chronicler, married to Vilton's sister, would without a doubt soon be released, once "the government is able to obtain better information about his case."[100]

Their friendship was evidently deep enough for Christophe to plead on Granier's behalf while also pointing out the French government's duplicity and Leclerc's flouting of the law. "The unfortunate Granier is detained, and no doubt, you say, because of some calumnies launched against him by his enemies," Christophe replied to Vilton. "Should such a detention take place without evidence?" he asked. "And does a just and impartial government postpone with such a long delay the administration of the proofs necessary for a deserved condemnation or a just absolution?"

Christophe reminded Vilton that his argument on Granier's behalf was not solely based on their friendship but had an even stronger basis in the law. "But does it fall to me, in the situation I find myself, to plead the cause of friendship? Do not forget, my dear friend, the laws of which I have just spoken."[101] Christophe had earlier told Vilton that he feared not only for his own life but for that of his intimate associate. "I await every day the blow that must annihilate me," Christophe wrote, before wondering aloud if Granier "has perhaps already ceased to exist."[102]

Granier lived at least until February 1802, when he helped deliver Christophe's fateful letter to Leclerc, but unlike many of Christophe's early associates he does not appear in any of the newspapers and other documentation about officials from the State of Haiti or the Kingdom of Haiti under Christophe's rule from 1807 to 1820. If Granier did survive the revolution and the Leclerc expedition, his close association with Christophe would have presumably continued.

Yet before Christophe got himself (and Granier) tangled up in Leclerc's treachery, they were both deeply mired in, and profiting from, the French colonial affermage system. Leasing sequestered plantations could be quite lucrative. But many factors could threaten a "farmer's" ability to make profits. Aside from the colonists and their heirs who might contest the legitimacy and legality of any sequester, as Christophe and Granier experienced with Meneust, many of the plantations had been burned and needed to be completely rehabilitated. Finding enough laborers to cultivate and rejuvenate these lands was not always easy either.

While only 44 "cultivators" worked the Chabanon plantation in April 1795, two years before Christophe began a new lease, 122 ostensibly free laborers still worked on the Saint-Michel plantation. Pierre Louis Vastey and his associates named all of the laborers in the August 1, 1793, inventory they collected for the municipality of Cap at the time of the plantation's sequestration, among whom remained dozens of Black men, women, and children.[103] The colony's laws around affermage made it difficult for citizen-cultivators to leave the plantations, such that these 122 laborers likely still lived and worked on the property when Christophe took over the lease in June 1797.[104]

Christophe experienced distinct problems on the other plantations that he leased while trying to have them cultivated by "free hands" so he could meet his expansive fiduciary obligations to the French government. In August 1797, the same year he took over the Saint-Michel plantation, Christophe began leasing the Butler (sometimes written "Buclair") sugar plantation in Limonade. The terrain was large, with about 120 *carreaux* of land. However, unlike those on the Saint-Michel plantation, the buildings on Butler had been entirely burned. Christophe therefore had to exert more time and energy to make this plantation profitable, even buying a replacement mill from the government. Complicating the situation, Christophe's profile as a farmer expanded just as his military responsibilities grew. Noël, the *gérant,* or manager,[105] ran the day-to-day operations of the Butler plantation, while Grenier, listed as a "fermier" from the Brémont plantation, also in Limonade, handled the financial affairs. Grenier put in a request on Christophe's behalf to the administrators of the National Domains to have the soldiers garrisoned on both plantations removed. The administrators agreed and asked Brigadier General Hyacinthe Moyse, nephew of Toussaint Louverture and friend to Christophe, "to give his orders to have the garrison withdrawn from the Brémont and Butler plantations, whose farmers have fulfilled their commitments to the republic."[106]

Some of Christophe's newfound military responsibilities also related to the new labor system he profited from as a businessman and farmer. In June 1797, Christophe had been promoted to inspector of the quartier of Petite-Anse and of the Plaine du Nord. Within four months, Christophe was fully exercising his duties as both chef de brigade and inspector, which is why Jacques Coidavid, married to Christophe's wife's mother, submitted his affermage request to Christophe directly before addressing Raimond.[107] It was under the title of inspector that Christophe also addressed Raimond, then a civil commissioner and his direct superior, with a request to lease the Butler plantation. "I request that the Butler plantation, located in the Bois de Lance district, be leased to me for the space of three years," stated Christophe in an original handwritten letter signed by him. "I am making an offer for it at 5,000 per year," he continued. He explained how he had arrived at this amount by noting that the plantation had been entirely "ruined" by the fires, adding, "There are no buildings whatsoever, not even any *cannes à rouler.*"[108] Christophe tried to improve the Butler plantation by securing tools and apparatuses to run it more effectively, including a scow (large flat-bottomed boat used for transporting goods) and "a watermill, a large roller, and other pieces of wood that I am offering to buy for the watermill of the Bucler [*sic*] estate that I have leased, wanting to put this plantation in good condition to roll [sugar]." Of the watermill and other equipment, he added in his formal request to Raimond, "The objects that I am asking for are indispensable to me."[109] Raimond recognized Christophe's "superior industriousness," according to one nineteenth-century Christophe chronicler, who perhaps exaggerated a bit when he claimed that Christophe, "a money man, above all else," leased some thirty sequestered plantations under Raimond's watch.[110]

Despite the shabby conditions of the property and land, Christophe managed to meet his obligation of 5,000 livres in raw sugar and continued to lease the Butler plantation even as warfare and other troubles on the island increased his military responsibilities.[111] As brigadier general, Christophe wrote a letter to Louverture in August 1801 asking for a seven-year lease over the Butler plantation. Using his own printed letterhead—which speaks to his growing importance, influence, and stature—Christophe explained to the governor-general why the Butler sugar plantation had not been profitable to him and how he planned to rectify the situation by "rebuild[ing] the sugar factory and the other buildings needed for it, repair[ing] the canal that conducts the water there, [and] redo[ing] the water mill and all that is necessary to activate and facilitate its operation." Christophe knew his proposition would be both expensive and time-consuming. "I will not conceal from you that these repairs will take up a considerable amount of time and will require very large advances for which I will only be able to compensate myself at the end of the duration of my seven-year lease," he told Louverture. Christophe hoped that after seven years he would be "reimbursed by the owners of this plantation for the expenses that I will have made here for the reconstructions and repairs, by such means as will suit us legitimately and mutually, by him or his authorized representative." Louverture approved Christophe's request on August 22, 1801.[112]

The Butler plantation documents not only reveal the inner workings of affermage—the dossier contains a detailed leasing agreement that spelled out Christophe's obligations toward the French government and toward the cultivators working the land—but also mark his trajectory from chef de brigade, or colonel, and commander over Petite-Anse to brigadier general and commander of Cap-Français. The renewed and revised lease for the Butler plantation, formally issued to Christophe by Raimond on August 26, 1801, listed the former chef de brigade under his new title and gave him control over the plantation for the seven years he requested.[113]

It is the dossier for the Saint-Michel plantation that provides a fuller picture of Christophe's trajectory from businessman, head of "Christophe et Cie," or Christophe and Company, to highly ranked military officer, to rebel of the French republic. The earliest mention of Christophe as a military officer in the affermage documents—as commander of Petite-Anse and Quartier-Morin—is in a document dated December 1796, but Christophe's promotion from commander to chef de bataillon (major) occurred on June 8, 1796, according to French military records.[114] Four months later, in October 1796, Christophe no longer held the position of commander of Quartier-Morin, but had been promoted from chef de bataillon to chef de brigade.[115] At the same time, he continued as the top military officer in Petite-Anse.[116] By the end of November 1797, Christophe had been catapulted to the fore of the colony's military hierarchy, donning the title of chef de brigade and commander of Petite-Anse and Cap-Français.[117] By March 1799, Louverture had increased Christophe's military responsibilities even more. To fill the vacancy left by the departure of Brigadier General Léveillé, Louverture appointed Christophe commander in chief of the arrondissement of Cap. That same year, Louverture formally requested from the French government Christophe's promotion to brigadier general.[118]

In the meantime, Christophe continued to farm. In 1797, the French government had approved yet another of his petitions to lease a separate home attached to the Saint-Michel property. This property was quite substantial. It consisted of "a large house constructed in masonry between two posts covered in *essentes* [wooden chestnut shingles used for roofing], about fifty feet long by eighteen wide with a gallery and peristyle in front, divided into a hall, two bedrooms, two cabinets with a skylight forming a forecourt and a small divided building in two rooms covered in *thuiles*." Christophe had to promise to keep the property in good shape, as a "good father of the family," until the end of the lease.[119]

Judging from the receipts that Christophe submitted to the French government, the Saint-Michel sugar plantation was not nearly as disastrous as the Butler plantation. After only one year, Christophe easily met his obligation to provide the government with 70,000 livres of raw sugar. Christophe continued to lease the Saint-Michel plantation for almost his entire French military career. Granier continued to represent his interests vis-à-vis the plantation as Christophe's military responsibilities grew. On Christophe's behalf, Granier signed the lease renewal for the Saint-Michel plantation in 1799—when Christophe was engaged in fervent battle against General André Rigaud in the south—and had the sugar stores due to the government deposited.[120]

Christophe remained in control until General Louverture released the sequester of the Saint-Michel sugar plantation on July 8, 1801. By that time, Christophe had officially ascended to the rank of brigadier general, as had Dessalines a couple years before.[121] As a powerful military man Christophe did not easily relinquish Saint-Michel, where he lived at the time with his family. However, the heirs to the plantation, the Harouards, living in La Rochelle, France, when the French government nullified Christophe's lease, had been trying to regain control of the plantation for a year and a half.[122] Their ultimately successful petition reveals intricate details about Christophe's life during this time. When Pierre Henri DuPont de Gault, who had the Harouards' power of attorney, arrived at the Saint-Michel plantation after the government had lifted the sequester, to his "great astonishment," he said, "he found General Christophe [still] in possession of it." DuPont de Gault reported this to Jean Madelmond, the director of the National Domains, who succeeded Raimond after he died. According to DuPont de Gault, Christophe had been improperly awarded the lease for this plantation and another owned by the Harouard heirs, "against the expectations of the owners, who were aware of the lifting of the sequester but who had never given power to award it." DuPont de Gault deeply feared interfering on a plantation claimed by Christophe, which is why, according to Madelmond, DuPont de Gault did not at first try to disrupt Christophe's claim to the property.

Upon further study, Madelmond determined that the late Raimond, who previously acted as the Harouard heirs' power of attorney, had in fact consented to lease the two Saint-Michel plantations to Christophe, unbeknownst to his clients, supposedly at a price far below the plantation's worth—60,000 livres of raw sugar for seven years for both plantations, even though Christophe previously leased the two plantations for 70,000 and 21,000 livres, respectively. The heirs therefore sought to "request the annulment of these farming leases on their plantations," and the French government granted their petition, "owing to the rebellion of ex-general Christophe, [whose] properties are subject to sequestration and given that the aforementioned farms are part of it and that these properties remain inactive."[123] Although Madelmond's report had a rather staid tone, DuPont de Gault's October 25, 1802, letter to the colonial prefect in Saint-Domingue about the situation with the Harouard heirs was anything but dry. DuPont de Gault revealed that about three months earlier, while Christophe still held the rank of French general under Leclerc, in the wake of Louverture's arrest, DuPont de Gault arrived at the Saint-Michel plantation to find "the rebel Christophe." DuPont de Gault claimed he had not established the claim of the Harouard heirs at that time due to fear. "I was surely endowed with the power to nullify the lease, but fearing to thwart the wishes of the government, I did not exercise actions to militate in favor of the Harouard family." However, once Christophe defected to the *armée indigène,* DuPont de Gault felt that he could safely act in the best interest of his clients. "Today these motives no longer exist. The traitor Christophe is on the run, he has joined the rebels, due to this fact, the property he enjoyed, either legally or illegally, is abandoned and the Saint-Michel plantations of which he was unjustly named the farmer can only be handed over to the owners." DuPont de Gault then complained that Raimond had no authority to lease the plantations to Christophe without the a priori consent of the Harouard heirs, in the first place. "Citizen Raimond abused his power of attorney by leasing the Saint-Michel plantations to his former partner and close friend Christophe for seven years at the modest price of sixty thousand in sugar per year for the two plantations," DuPont de Gault charged. "Raimond absolutely abused the trust of the Citizens Harouard," he continued, "but also his place as administrator of the National Domains to which he had been elevated by Toussaint Louverture." "Such was the conduct of Raimond, and that of Christophe, under the aegis of Toussaint's constitution proclaimed on July 6, 1801, in which Raimond was one of the collaborators," DuPont de Gault continued, before calling Raimond the "instigator" of the famous constitution. The lawyer concluded that even though Raimond had died, the colony still suffered the effects of his presence, to the detriment of the

French republic. "But this man, whose legacy will long be felt in Saint-Domingue, is no longer among the mortals, and his worthy friend Christophe, with his assistance, has proved that he was merely a traitor."[124] The plantations were subsequently returned to the Harouard heirs, allowing them to later make a lucrative claim to the infamous indemnity.

The French government released the sequester over the Butler plantation in Limonade, also leased by Christophe, in a much less dramatic way, but only after most of the Black generals had either been deported like Louverture, died like Moyse, or joined Dessalines's *armée indigène* like Christophe. The heirs of the Butler plantation also claimed two of the Bréda plantations in the Plaine du Nord, including one in Haut-du-Cap where Toussaint Louverture was born, enslaved, and emancipated, along with a brickworks in Cap, also called Bréda.[125]

Importantly, the French government had leased the Bréda sugar plantation in Haut-du-Cap, where Louverture had been enslaved, to General Moyse, about whom we are to learn more in the next chapter, including how he died at the hands of his own adopted uncle, Louverture. Moyse began leasing the lucrative plantation on May 5, 1797. According to a letter he wrote three years later to the administrators of the National Domains, he did not intend to continue leasing the plantation after his three-year lease expired.[126] Moyse did continue to lease numerous other plantations throughout the colony, as far east as Maribaroux and as far south as Saint-Marc. Yet it was Christophe's residence in Cap that likely brought Moyse and Christophe into each other's social orbit, with Christophe even becoming the guardian of Moyse's child after the latter's execution in November 1802.[127]

Affermage introduced Christophe to some of the highest-ranking members of the colonial French government like Raimond and Sonthonax. Yet it was his military prowess that brought him into the inner circle of Toussaint Louverture and General Moyse, whom Christophe considered not merely his superiors but also his friends. It was at Christophe's residence in Cap-Français that a home purchase for General Louverture's wife, Suzanne, was ultimately ratified in March 1799. Like the home that Christophe later purchased for Marie-Louise, the home Louverture bought for Suzanne was expansive and expensive.

The opulent home for Suzanne cost 99,000 francs or 1,500 *portugaises*. The property was enormous. Constructed in masonry, it was divided on the first floor into "five bedrooms and a shop, two corridors with two staircases that each had a *caravane* [pulley] to arrive at the second floor, three cabinets, three kitchens with a gallery, a courtyard in the center of which is a well, the courtyard and the well divided by a tiled wall." The upstairs featured "five double-framed bedrooms, two half-framed closets, also overlooking the street; plus five cabinets and a kitchen with a gallery on masonry pillars, and at the height of the cabinets and kitchen is a wooden gallery, the whole covered in *thuiles* with slabs to collect the rain-water and channel it into the courtyard, the said apartments at the top are tiled in marble and small Provençal tiles adorned on the two doors opening to the streets, with latticework on the windows; three striking iron balconies, one of which is in a light tower at the corner of the two streets; the windows lined with iron banquettes; all well enclosed with locks, clamps, hooks, and bolts; finally, there is an attic overlooking the two streets." Neither Suzanne Louverture nor her husband was present at Christophe's home for the sale. Instead, they were represented by Marie-Thérèse Coyotte, referred to in later documents as "a close confidante of the ex-general Toussaint." Described on the bill of sale as Suzanne Louverture's "commère," a term meaning here a good friend of the family, the couple had vested Coyotte with the right "to sign in [Suzanne's] name and as [her] power of attorney" on March 20, 1799, in the canton of Ennery, where Suzanne lived with Louverture at the time. Three days later, Coyotte traveled to Christophe's home to sign the papers.[128]

General Louverture likely entrusted this task to Christophe's particular oversight in the intimate space of the latter's home because of their growing fondness for each other. This fondness had both social and economic implications. Louverture had to personally sign off on many of the farm leases that Christophe sought, as well as on properties in Cap that Christophe later purchased. The leasing system offered Christophe a way to provide for his family and to enrich himself in a colony where wealth had primarily been reserved for white Europeans and their descendants, to the detriment of Black and Creole Africans. Although money could not solve all Christophe's problems, it did facilitate his extraordinarily swift rise. Yet no amount of money could erase the difficult past Christophe had already lived through, nor could it prevent the worst difficulties of his future.

COMPLICATED VICTORIES

By the time Christophe was sworn in as brigadier general, he had already been involved in some of the most momentous affairs of the colony, from Louverture's expulsion of Commissioner Sonthonax in 1797, to the departure of the agent Théodore Hédouville in 1798, to helping Louverture defeat his rival General André Rigaud in 1800. Soon thereafter Christophe played his part in the 1801 deportation of the agent Roume and the tragic death of his dear friend General Moyse, ordered shockingly later that year by Moyse's uncle Toussaint Louverture. Christophe's life during this time was also marked by many personal milestones. His first child, François Ferdinand, had been born in May 1794, and his second child, a daughter named Améthyste, was born nearly four years later to the day, with yet another daughter, Athénaïs, joining the family two years after that. The four-year gap between when Marie-Louise bore their first child and their second might be explained by the fact that her husband was occupied during this time not just with affermage but with climbing the ranks of the military. Christophe's swift post-emancipation ascent—his rapid transformation from enslaved child in Grenada to wealthy French general in Saint-Domingue—was nothing less than extraordinary. With a mere six years having passed since general emancipation, Christophe had gone from being a nonfactor in French colonial affairs to one of the most important generals in France's army. But Christophe's prosperity and prominence did not always extend to his family and friends. His success as a farmer, businessman, and military officer coincided with a fraught period in his life, one that tested his mettle as a man, a soldier, and a republican, as much as it exposed his limitations as a husband, a father, and a friend.

"Do you swear to the general in chief to always be subordinate to your leaders, to obey them in everything they command of you for the greatest interest of the colony?" read the oath that the military officer Jacques Scipion Morpas (sometimes spelled "Maurepas") swore at the time of his promotion to brigadier general on June 8, 1801. Christophe, officially confirmed in that rank that year, too, and possibly sworn in on the same day, would have likely repeated the same or a similar oath. "Do you swear to the general in chief to defend your country, the island of Saint-Domingue, against all odds, if some enemies still desire to put you back in irons? Do you swear to the general in chief to defend at the peril of your life the freedom, the equality of the republic?" The only acceptable response was, "I swear."[1] Although colonial documentation has not thus far yielded the exact date upon which Christophe became a Black *French* general, precise records of his involvement in affermage have produced for the first time an intricate chronology of his military rise.

In the years following the great fire of 1793, Christophe worked closely with Colonel Vincent, France's director of fortifications, and Faraud, the chief engineer and architect of Cap, the latter of whom Vincent reported to the French government had been "infinitely useful to this city in the civil engineering sector, which he manages perfectly," saying, "we owe him, for the most part, all that has been best rebuilt in Cap."[2] Their mission was simple: rebuild the scorched, war-torn city from its ashes. When he was not in Cap-Français, Christophe followed the orders of his direct superiors, Louverture, as general in chief, and Division General Moyse, commander over the northern division, which included the city of Cap-Français. Christophe's growing prominence also put him into the sights— and then the crosshairs—of the French commissioners and other official agents of the French republic sent to strengthen metropolitan France's control over the colony.

In 1794, at the urging of angry white colonists, the French government recalled Sonthonax and Polverel to France to account for their conduct. Polverel died in 1795 just after pleading his case. The French government exonerated Sonthonax, for his part, and he returned to the colony two years later, this time as one of five commissioners.[3] When the new civil commission—consisting of Marc Antoine Giraud, Pierre Leblanc, Julien Raimond, Sonthonax, and Roume—landed in Saint-Domingue on May 11, 1796, the revolutionary government in France was undergoing massive changes. The National Convention resigned their authority in October 1796, and an entity called the Executive Directory began governing the republic. The new civil commission, led by Sonthonax, elevated Louverture to the grade of division general. The Executive Directory confirmed this promotion a few months afterward.[4]

In only a few years, Louverture had become one of the most important Black military figures in the world, and one of only a handful of Black men, including the famous novelist Alexandre Dumas's father, General Thomas-Alexandre Dumas, to attain the rank of general in the French military.[5] As division general, Louverture commanded the entire western part of the colony, and a short time afterward he became head of the whole military. Not everyone greeted his rise with approval. In July 1795, the French government had also promoted Louverture's rivals André Rigaud and Jacques Beauvais, but while Louverture achieved further promotion, they remained in the rank of brigadier generals, and therefore the two stood unhappily ranked below Louverture.[6] Moreover, although the white French general Étienne Laveaux, of the Galbaud opposition, has been credited with giving Toussaint the moniker Louverture to replace Bréda, the name of his enslaver, Louverture also reportedly viewed Laveaux as a rival.

In December 1795, following their involvement in the colony's war against Spain that led to the Treaty of Basel, which ceded the eastern (Spanish) side of the island to France, Louverture, Christophe, Dessalines, Moyse, and dozens of other important military officers signed a letter professing gratitude to General Laveaux for his leadership and swore fealty to and willingness to fight for the French republic in its ongoing war with Great Britain.[7] Yet by the fall of 1796, Louverture, with Christophe's help, maneuvered to get Laveaux, then the governor of Saint-Domingue, recalled to France by the Executive Directory. Laveaux, who had made Louverture his lieutenant governor while dubbing him the liberator of the colony, left Saint-Domingue on October 19, 1796. This left Sonthonax, for the moment, as Louverture's greatest rival on the French side.[8]

While it may seem that Sonthonax and Louverture should have been allies—both considered themselves the emancipators of the colony, after all—Louverture believed that Sonthonax wanted independence from France, something Louverture claimed not to desire. While Louverture easily convinced both Christophe and Moyse, his key allies in the north, to view Sonthonax as a dangerous enemy, Louverture also needed to convince Commissioner Raimond. Christophe played a principal role in this process and ultimately in Louverture's mission to send Sonthonax back to France, helping Louverture to establish himself as the highest authority in the colony.

Ever since their return to the colony, Raimond had entertained his own suspicions about Sonthonax. He had received numerous reports that Sonthonax not only harbored ardent prejudices against the so-called men of color but often disparaged Raimond as "that mulatto Raimond." At the time, free people of color in the colony considered the word "mulatto" a racial epithet. Raimond was not a military man, though, and he had long professed an abhorrence for revolutionary violence, even though he watched it work in favor of the enslaved population. In a report to the Executive Directory, Raimond averred, "No one has more horror than me for revolt, massacre, and assassination." His avowed hatred of violence aside, Raimond declared complete loyalty to the French republic and to his mission as a French commissioner. Therefore, even after he received complaint after complaint about Sonthonax's violent machinations in the south against the *hommes de couleur,* Raimond believed that any sanction of Sonthonax's conduct needed to come from the French government back in France, not from him or from any other official in the colony.

While Raimond grew weary and wary of Sonthonax, he distracted himself with his duties overseeing the colony's vast affermage system. This was in many respects the perfect job for Raimond. Born into a family of landholding enslavers, Raimond excelled in administration, not military operations. He believed that farming was the only way to stop and destroy "brigandage and to bring back to a regular life men brutalized by long enslavement and still demoralized by the habit of a wandering and vagabond lifestyle and by the excesses of all kinds that, in Saint-Domingue even more than in Europe, had bloodied the revolution." But Sonthonax angered Raimond when he tried to convince Louverture to oppose Raimond's agrarian reforms designed to bring about the "restoration of vibrant farming." Raimond characterized Sonthonax's opposition as part of a plan to achieve the island's independence. In his handwritten account to the Directory, later printed as a pamphlet, Raimond tried to convince the French government that he and Louverture had no choice but to send Sonthonax back to France. Raimond's account contained a play-by-play narration of how and why they felt forced to adopt this drastic measure. It also detailed Christophe's role in the affair.[9]

Raimond believed that his first task was to gain Louverture's support, not with the aim of eliminating Sonthonax, but to affirm the affermage system that Raimond helped conceive and manage. He therefore invited Louverture for a meeting at his home. When Louverture arrived, Raimond asked him to take a seat next to him. He took the general's hands in his and said, "You see, General, that you don't have to go before the commissioners to arrive at an agreement; know that we love you, and that we have no other desire than to do good for the colony." "You speak in the plural," Louverture responded. Commissioner Raimond, surprised by this reply, found Louverture cold and wondered if the general's demeanor spoke of some deeper calculation taking place. Rather than enumerating his many complaints against Sonthonax, Raimond saw this as an opportunity to win Louverture over on the matter closest to Raimond's heart: affermage.

Certain reforms were necessary to the success of affermage, Raimond told Louverture, but some of the other commissioners were putting obstacles in Raimond's way. Affermage required paying the cultivators, Raimond said, which Commissioner Leblanc opposed, for example. Sonthonax, in great contrast, wanted nothing to do with the system at all, preferring that the government recruit and train former cultivators for the army instead. "But without farming," Raimond said to Louverture, "how will we produce income? And without income, how will we pay the troops? How will we feed and dress them?" Louverture had little reason to oppose Raimond's reforms. He had benefited from affermage immensely, holding in lease more than a dozen plantations all over the colony. After the adoption of Raimond's system, key officials and soldiers, like Christophe and Coidavid, Dessalines and Rigaud, along with Louverture, leased even more plantations, sometimes numbering into the dozens for single officers.[10]

Yet the affermage system, which purportedly relied on the labor of free citizens compensated for their work based on the profits of the plantation, did not always run smoothly. Questions about adequate compensation for the workers and the French government provided fodder for the ongoing squabbles among the commissioners.[11] Sonthonax criticized affermage as a grand scheme for the commissioners to enrich themselves by exploiting the colony's Black laborers and coercing the Black military officers to assist them. Raimond defended himself by pointing out that he no longer leased any plantations, precisely to avoid the accusation that he benefited from the affermage system he designed. While Sonthonax and Raimond reached some manner of détente after four days of debate, Sonthonax continued to undermine affermage behind Raimond's back. "Sonthonax wanted to reign; my plan was to bring order, and it was only through anarchy that he could achieve the dominance he longed for," Raimond complained.

While working to undermine affermage, Sonthonax took steps to shore up his political power. He invited leaders from different parts of the colony—including General Moyse and Christophe, then commander in Petite-Anse—to request elections in their cantons, provided, Raimond said, that they allowed Sonthonax and his allies to guide their choices. "In a word," wrote Raimond, "all those whom [Sonthonax] knew to have some influence on the people in their respective townships received the request or the order to support with their authority those whom Sonthonax was appointing or would appoint." Sonthonax was not above doling out gifts and "gratifications" to the officers, said Raimond: "Everything is done to buy votes, and it cost the colony 100,000 francs to have Sonthonax's deputies named." Raimond's list of accusations against Sonthonax, a roundabout justification for having him recalled, was long and detailed. Their insistence that Sonthonax wanted independence eventually united Raimond and Louverture. Raimond averred that Sonthonax had, on multiple occasions, told him directly that the colony had no business being controlled by France or any other European power. "From that moment forward," Raimond concluded, "we resolved to sound out General Toussaint, and above all to open his eyes to the perfidious projects that the conduct of Sonthonax caused us to suspect."

Raimond's ire for Sonthonax only grew after the latter started to publicly slander Louverture. Raimond tried to warn Louverture, who had become increasingly plagued with his own worries about Sonthonax. Although Raimond had trouble maintaining contact with Louverture during this period, suddenly Louverture reported to Raimond that he had just told Sonthonax that the salvation of the colony required the latter's departure within four days. Raimond professed astonishment. He had not intended a coup, but something more like a recall. Raimond worried not only about the implications of this move on the spirits and minds of the cultivators, who, in his view, saw Sonthonax as a liberator, but also about the personal consequences of such a move, particularly for Louverture. He reminded Louverture, therefore, that Sonthonax had been the first to proclaim general liberty. He told the general to think of his two children in France, "as if hostages to your loyalty."

Raimond knew of what he spoke. In 1796, he had helped conceive the plan to send the Black children of prominent officers to France to be educated at the government's cost, stressing the importance of "public instruction." But a report from the Directory issued in September–October 1799 shows that the French government's goal was not entirely philanthropic. The report stated, "In bringing to France the children of Toussaint and Rigaud, and of their principal lieutenants, in order to give them a free education, the Directory's aim had been not only to consolidate the work of Liberty through enlightenment and instruction but also to secure in the person of these children hostages to the loyalty of their fathers, who have become, by force of circumstance, the absolute masters of the colony."[12] Louverture, not fully aware of this political manipulation on the part of France and thus unable to fully conceive the threat, insisted that Sonthonax had to go. Incapable of changing Louverture's mind, the next day Raimond went to Louverture's house once more to try to move the general. Raimond's efforts were to no avail.

Louverture, meanwhile, developed his own plan to win over Raimond. The day after his last meeting with Raimond, at seven o'clock in the evening, General Moyse, Charles Chevalier, and Christophe visited Raimond's home, where they declared, "In the name of the general [Louverture] . . . Sonthonax has to leave within three days, otherwise the colony will be lost." Raimond continued to express surprise and disbelief at this attempted coup. "I represented the consequences to them, with all the warmth and energy of which I am capable," Raimond wrote. The three men listened to Raimond's protests in silence, until Christophe glanced over at the other officers, as if to get the signal to proceed. He then told Raimond coolly, "Commissioner, your good faith abuses you. Sonthonax is a true villain who wants to destroy the colony." "He offered me ten times to get you on board," Christophe said. "He even outlined the steps I was to take." Christophe then said that Sonthonax encouraged him to raise up the cultivators in the plain against Raimond. "He told me to tell them that they should not want to farm, because that was the method you would use to put them back into slavery. If I did not tell you all this before, it is because I did not want to afflict your heart, and to introduce, between your colleague and you, a disunity, which could only be fatal to us all." Christophe continued by confessing, "But today you must know everything; above all, the commissioner must leave in three days, otherwise the colony is lost." Christophe's speech achieved the desired effect. "I knew Sonthonax had intended to get me on board," Raimond told Christophe. "I had no idea it was by such treacherous means." "As for the rest," Raimond continued, "it is not my position that is in question here, but about the respect due to the national representatives; it's not about me; it is the safety of the colony that we must concern ourselves with; tell the general that I beg him to take no side before I have spoken to him."

Raimond did not wait long. At five o'clock the next morning, he arrived at the home of Louverture, who seemed hardly thrilled to see the commissioner at that hour. The general in chief seemed even more irritated by Raimond's lingering hesitation to take the final step to banish Sonthonax. "Sonthonax is still trying to trick you and set the colony on fire," Louverture warned.

Did Raimond change course because he feared Louverture more than Sonthonax? Raimond denied that he acted out of fear, and instead said he came to agree with Louverture's plan because he was convinced that Sonthonax would rather irrevocably destroy the colony than see it flourish under Louverture. After Raimond traveled to Sonthonax's home to force his resignation, Sonthonax ultimately agreed to leave on the condition that the inhabitants be told that it was his choice and that he be furnished with a letter attesting to his "honorable conduct."[13]

On August 20, 1797, General Louverture along with several other key military officers provided "Citizen Representative and Commissioner" Sonthonax with a letter attesting to his honorable service in Saint-Domingue.[14] Louverture's letter to the municipal administrators two days later explained that Sonthonax's departure for France involved a mission to report on the affairs of the colony.[15] Naturally, Louverture maintained his own version of what happened in the months, weeks, and days leading up to Sonthonax's departure. While some of the details and accusations differ from Raimond's account, Louverture affirmed Raimond's most important charge when he told the French Directory that Sonthonax had been vying to make the colony independent from France, necessitating the commissioner's immediate departure.[16]

In late October 1797, Louverture reported to Colonel Vincent that with Sonthonax gone, his ongoing conflict with General André Rigaud had virtually dissipated.[17] However, another agent of the French government was on the way to sow seeds of discord between these two generals: Gabriel-Marie-Théodore-Joseph d'Hédouville. The conflict among the three men also involved Christophe, who played a far more public role in this affair than he did in the Sonthonax case. Yet when Christophe sided with the eventual victor, Louverture, he was temporarily relieved of his duties as commander of Cap-Français and put into service for Louverture's war against not the French agent but General Rigaud.

—

Back in France, the Directory watched with disquietude as Louverture became a singular figure of authority in Saint-Domingue. Though Sonthonax returned home in disgrace, his report to the Directory harmed Louverture's reputation, particularly the claim that Louverture sought to rid Saint-Domingue not only of French authority but of the French altogether.[18]

To underscore its own authority, the Directory named Hédouville as French *agent particulier* to the colony. Hédouville arrived in April 1798, nearly eight months after Sonthonax's departure. Raimond welcomed the new French agent while also making sure to praise the conduct of his ally Louverture. Hédouville's response to Raimond's lauding of Louverture unwittingly foreshadowed the ensuing political struggle. Hédouville wrote that he looked forward to having Louverture as his "second."[19]

Although Hédouville also professed his delight at how farming flourished under Louverture, the French agent quickly began to insert himself into the colony's affairs in a way that suggested disapproval to Louverture and Raimond and evoked slavery to the cultivators. Given that affermage relied on the laborers' willingness to work, any unrest or dissatisfaction on their part threatened the authority of division generals and municipal commanders like Christophe.

When Hédouville issued a proclamation directed at the cultivators in early August, he knew that he had first to convince high-ranking officers and commanders like Christophe, who at that time held the position of interim commander of the eastern arrondissement, of not just the goal of his reforms but how each commander would personally benefit from the new rules he sought to implement.[20] Hédouville told the commanders to explain to the cultivators, "really well" and in Creole, the purpose of the new labor laws. He spoke of those he said had "brought trouble to the colony": "anarchists and royalists," "attempting every means to harm agriculture and prevent prosperity." Hédouville accused such troublemakers of trying to "persuade the cultivators that freedom consists in not working." He further charged this crowd of putative agitators with attempting to manipulate the citizen-cultivators to quit laboring altogether and with having an independence project that would force "the metropole to abandon" the colony if it could no longer "produce income." "But no, the friends of liberty," Hédouville insisted, "true Republicans will make the cultivators feel that labor alone can afford them happiness by providing them with plenty of means to support their families and by raising the colony to the degree of splendor that it must attain." Following this directive, Hédouville enclosed the decree that eventually compelled Louverture, Moyse, and Christophe to desire his departure for France.[21]

The preamble to Hédouville's decree stated that any man who did not engage in labor would be declared a "vagabond" and condemned to "a detention more or less long according to the requirements of the case." Hédouville then quoted from the Declaration of the Rights of Man before declaring, "Every man can pledge his time and services, but he cannot sell himself or be sold: his person is not alienable property." This was clearly meant to allay fears that the French agent sought to bring back slavery. The subsequent articles of the decree, which described harsh changes compared with Louverture and Raimond's system, were to be implemented under the watchful eyes of commanders like Christophe and Moyse.

Hédouville's rules, though they fixed the hours of work, provided fodder for the brewing controversy and consternation among the cultivators who now had to be "engaged for a minimum of three years" on specific plantations without the right to leave. The decree forbade the farmer or property owner to allow any cultivator to quit the property or farm where they had contracted an "engagement." The punishment for any cultivator moving about without permission was imprisonment, "the first time for one month, the second for six months, and the third for one year." The carceral colony was back, which could only have reminded those previously engaged in marronnage, and then jailed by the state, of their previous captivity. Cultivators could likewise be fined for not working under the "pretext of illness," while "any vagabond who is arrested and who has not contracted an engagement will be put in prison for six months." Engagements, in other words, like indentured servitude, were not especially voluntary. Any member of the public who was not a property owner, in the military, or otherwise employed in a profession authorized by the French government was required to "engage" in the work of farming too. Finally, there would be consequences for "movements," or rebellions, on the plantations, with punishments for those who participated in or caused them.[22]

These marked changes to affermage were not the French agent's sole attempt to shore up his authority and impose his will on the colony. After Louverture made an autonomous agreement with General Thomas Maitland of England for trade and the evacuation of British troops who occupied the southern part of the colony, Hédouville published a separate decree to reorganize the military. Louverture remained the highest military officer as general in chief. However, the decree made it clear that Louverture reported directly to Hédouville.[23]

The final conflict between the two men, and what ultimately led to Hédouville's departure, arose when, in response to the cultivators' protests against his "engagements" system, Hédouville ordered General Moyse stripped of his military titles. Part of Hédouville's problem was that he failed to visit the places in the colony where conflicts occurred. It was almost as if he were afraid to leave Cap-Français.[24] He only learned of problems in other locales by messenger. By the time he learned of the protests, it was already too late for Hédouville to stop the opposition of the cultivators in Fort-Liberté (previously Fort-Dauphin), upset about Hédouville's farming reforms. In petition after petition, the cultivators registered their complaints against the idea that they had to be yoked to particular plantations, like slaves. They were also upset that one of Hédouville's officers declared General Moyse, commander of Fort-Liberté, an "outlaw," "destitute" of his military rank and duties.

On October 13, 1798, in Moyse's absence from Fort-Liberté, his brother took up arms and led the Fifth Demi-brigade to the streets to protest what they viewed as General Hédouville's threat to the cultivators' freedom. Hédouville ordered an armed response to this rebellion and contacted Louverture to demand that the general in chief quell this "insurrection." Meanwhile, according to Hédouville's report to the Directory, "Moyse's wives" distributed cartridges to the Fifth Regiment, under Moyse's direct command. Moyse did not reportedly return to Fort-Liberté until two days later, on the morning of the twenty-fourth, after the French killed his brother, the captain of the grenadiers, along with five or six others, and took ten officers and 125 other men prisoners. Moyse, fearing his own capture, eventually abandoned his horse and fled to a nearby marsh until he reached the city of Vallières.[25]

Hédouville's recollection of Christophe's involvement, though prejudiced and biased—he once wrote that Christophe "manages to be as deceitful as he is ambitious"—is the most complete account we have of the future king's participation in this consequential revolutionary event. Hédouville said he made it clear to Louverture, who was on his way to Cap, that he wanted the general in chief to do everything in his power "to quash Moyse's rebellion." Yet the same morning that Moyse fled, Louverture dispatched Christophe and Chef de Brigade Robert, commander over a Black regiment in garrison in Cap. Hédouville claimed that instead of preventing the rebellion, the two men allowed it to happen.

In Hédouville's account, it was Vincent, newly returned from France, who denounced Louverture to the French agent and suggested that Louverture was aware of and involved in the insurrection himself. Vincent reported that Louverture slept the night before at the Héricourt plantation, in the commune of Limonade, and subsequently refused to travel to Cap to meet with Hédouville, saying that he feared being assassinated or sent back to France. Moreover, when Vincent delivered the message from Hédouville, Louverture had Vincent arrested. Recall that Vincent later claimed it was Christophe who rescued him from imprisonment and ultimately saved his life.[26]

While Vincent remained an often-ambivalent, fair-weather Christophe supporter, Hédouville was an outright enemy. "Based on the violent suspicions that Chef de Brigade Christophe inspired in all the friends of the republic," Hédouville wrote, "I engaged Citizen Télémaque, a black justice of the peace of the commune of Cap, who had the ability to sound out his dispositions." According to Cézar Télémaque, Christophe reassured him of his devotion to the republic but made it no secret that he trusted and supported Louverture too. Christophe also revealed to Télémaque that he had visited Louverture the day before at the Héricourt plantation in Limonade.

Guillaume Manigat, a Black justice of the peace in Fort-Liberté and one of Hédouville's most trusted officers, led the French strike against the regiment from Fort-Liberté. Manigat eventually sent Hédouville eleven officers from Moyse's regiment whom he had arrested after the revolt and whom Hédouville subsequently detained on board three frigates in the port. The French agent did not express satisfaction once the alleged rebellion was quashed. He charged that the raising of the Fifth Regiment in Fort-Liberté was evidence that Louverture and company, including Christophe, were promoting a "system of independence."

After this violent clash, Louverture invited Hédouville to tour the colony to see the immensity of his work with the army. Hédouville remained highly suspicious, though, because he had heard that Louverture had taken a meeting on the Flaville plantation, "occupied by a (black) brigade leader of that name," whom Hédouville considered "a very bad subject," as well as General Moyse and Chef de Brigade Christophe.[27] Hédouville had many reasons for seeking to avoid Moyse and Louverture. Hédouville's man Manigat had just stripped the "outlaw" Moyse of his military rank and duties, after which Moyse fled to the Héricourt plantation, where Louverture greeted his nephew, "covered in dust," "his hat in hand," and "almost nude"[28]; moreover, Manigat had just sent Moyse's other brother, along with 125 men of the Fifth Regiment, to Hédouville, who ordered their "dismissal and return to the plantation of their choice." Convinced that the whole affair was a conspiracy from the start, Hédouville accused Augustin Clervaux, commander over Môle Saint-Nicolas, of having tried to cut off all communication with Cap, by way of the sea and land.

In response to what he believed constituted a vast conspiracy against him, Hédouville sought reinforcements from the French military as he prepared for an attack from Louverture, who he claimed was trying to have him poisoned. Chef de Brigade Robert, commander of the National Guard in Cap, the source of this poisoning accusation, continued to be a key conduit of information for Hédouville. According to Robert, Louverture's troops in Cap would have been ill-disposed to defend the city on Hédouville's orders, while Citizen Coidavid, Christophe's father-in-law and commander over Fort-Bélair, was already "weak." This information, Hédouville reported, "robbed me of all hope of being able to defend it successfully." Shortly thereafter, Christophe delivered his troops from

Petite-Anse and Fort Saint-Michel to Louverture for reinforcement. Meanwhile, Hédouville issued a proclamation to the citizens of Fort-Liberté, condemning the revolt and the "disorder" of the Fifth Demi-brigade.

Ultimately, Hédouville blamed the entire affair on General Moyse, saying that instead of going to find Manigat or Hédouville, Moyse fled from his house and sought refuge in the fort.[29] Hédouville then explained that even though he ordered the disarmament to avoid bloodshed, "Blood has flown!" "But rest assured, citizens," he wrote. "There are only two men among the republicans who are injured and whose deaths we will not have to mourn."[30]

News of this conflict spread quickly. The cultivators and farmers of the north reacted with outrage at the killing and arrests of the Fifth Demi-brigade, particularly the destitution and outlaw status of Moyse. Immediately after the conflict, administrators around the northern part of the colony received a series of petitions, all demanding Hédouville's unequivocal deportation. A week after Moyse's arrest, the administrators of several municipalities, citing the petitions issued by cultivators in their locales, demanded Hédouville's immediate departure. They also asked Louverture to use all means at his disposal to maintain order and tranquility. On the same day, the citizens of Marmelade issued a decree defending Moyse, praising Louverture, and demanding the suspension of both Hédouville and Manigat. The next day, the administrators of the municipality of Toussaint Louverture (previously Ennery), having received a damning petition from the citizen-cultivators of that region, issued a more forceful statement against the French agent. The petitioners were upset not only by what happened to the Fifth Demi-brigade but also by the fact that Hédouville and Manigat ordered Moyse to be captured "dead or alive." The cultivators remonstrated against Hédouville by claiming that he wanted to bring back slavery, and they asked for General Moyse to "stay to defend us against those who want to enslave us." "We would rather die than suffer that General Hédouville would harm him," the petition read. "He is a leader who has always bravely fought against the enemies of the republic." The cultivators of Louverture assembled for the municipality and the justice of the peace to hear their complaints from their own mouths. "We don't want to work anymore," they told the administrators. "We prefer to die if General Hédouville does not leave the colony. We no longer want to be engaged; we'd rather remain in the woods forever if he doesn't leave," said the petition signed "the *culivateurs* and *cultivatrices* of Louverture." In response, the administrators declared their ongoing loyalty to Louverture while essentially voting no confidence in the French agent whose conduct they condemned in the strongest of terms.[31]

The citizen-cultivators of Louverture were not the only ones to register such a damning petition with authorities in order to condemn Hédouville. The "citizen-inhabitants" of Gonaïves registered their complaints to the municipality on October 27, 1798.[32] Dozens of citizens in the commune of Port-à-Piment and Terre-Neuve also appeared before authorities of their municipality to assert their will. One of those citizen-cultivators, a man named Mayombé, conveyed his chagrin, along with that of his fellow cultivators, "about the engagements we were forced to commit to under the law of Agent Hédouville." "We reject the said proclamation since it violates our rights to liberty," the cultivators said. "We don't need engagements to work. Our good general Toussaint Louverture, who rescued us from the hands of the Spanish and the English, has repeated to us that the free man must work." Like those from other sections of the colony, they also demanded Hédouville's recall to France and that "the brave general Moyse, whom Hédouville made an outlaw, be restored to his rights and duties." The postscript to this letter, signed by several of the cultivators, read, "P.S. We forgot to tell you that if Agent Hédouville does not leave, our resolution has been made, we will no longer work." Another petition, this one from the cultivators in Petite-Rivière, was read aloud, partially in Creole, to a crowd gathered before the justice of the peace and the commandant de la place (local commander in charge of a jurisdiction). "He wants to bring war again to our country" (*Li vlé faire encore la guerre dans pays-ci avec nous*), they said of Hédouville. The cultivators then told the entire story from their perspective, in Creole:

> To take away our freedom, we have also learned that they arrested two hundred of our brothers, that they took them to Cap, Citizen Hédouville disarmed them, and told them that they were going to be taken to the plantations of other masters. That is why we think that the same thing is going to happen to us since we have demanded that the brave general Moyse remain our leader and continue to fight for our rights as he has always done. His compensation for having so well defended us against the enemies of the French republic is that today Agent Hédouville has given an order to have him arrested and killed. We have learned that they have killed twenty-two of our brave officers who fought for our liberty and preserved this country for France. They arrested them and took them to Cap. Citizen Hédouville had them embarked, along with two of Moyse's brothers; they shipped one off and killed the other. We understand that this is the compensation that will be delivered to us as well. As such we are warning you, since General Moyse is condemned to death, that we will refuse to work, preferring to die, since that is the fate that awaits us. We demand action from the municipality. Hail the French republic!

> —Signed on behalf of the people, Jean-Pierre, Paul-Augustin, Dominque[33]

A nonviolent protest against the French agent took place out in the open with the approval of colonial administrators. Following the signed petitions from the northern plain, the managers and *cultivateurs* and *cultivatrices* of Gros-Morne appeared before their municipality to protest Hédouville's engagements system and Moyse's treatment. They similarly requested Hédouville's departure and Moyse's reinstatement.[34]

At the time of the first petitions against Hédouville, the troops stationed near the post of Haut-du-Cap had, in Hédouville's recollection, taken over Fort-Bélair with no resistance. The troops opened the gates of Haut-du-Cap for Louverture at the same time. Hédouville continued to try to prevent the "rebels" from breaching the city of Cap. "Moyse and General Dessalines . . . are advancing on the road to Haut-du-Cap with their troops and the armed cultivators," he said. "They are insulting our grenadiers," Hédouville continued, "and threatening to have the soldiers in the forts fire on the frigates." But with the military largely siding with Louverture, Moyse, Dessalines, and Christophe, Hédouville claimed he had no choice but to leave. However, he also claimed he decided to depart the colony on October 22, before the first petitions were presented, although he did not actually leave until the twenty-seventh.[35]

While Hédouville traveled by ship to Brest, France, more than six hundred white colonists were leaving Saint-Domingue too. Before his escape, Hédouville engaged in one last back-and-forth with Louverture over the eleven prisoners. Hédouville admitted that he threatened to have them all hanged upon the "least movement."[36] Yet according to Louverture's report to the Directory, the Black troops writ large had expressed anger toward Hédouville, who, per the so-called engagements system, sought to remove them from the military and send them to be employed in agriculture. Louverture also explained that he had traveled to the Héricourt plantation not to foment revolt but to prevent it. A quickly spreading uprising had evidently occurred on that plantation and had the possibility of becoming general rather than regional. Instead of being praised for his swift ability to quell that conflict by reassuring the cultivators that France would not reinstate slavery, Louverture said Hédouville accused him of betraying the republic, calling him responsible for the Fort-Liberté revolt and for General Moyse's destitution.

Louverture also knew that Hédouville had charged him, as the colony's general in chief, with desiring independence from France. Yet Louverture had some charges of his own to make. He accused Hédouville of having led the "first colony" of France to the verge of ruin because of his perfidy toward the people of color of Saint-Domingue, whom Hédouville encouraged to commit "arbitrary and liberticidal acts, to revolt against his authority," in the hopes of "forging the irons of a new slavery." Louverture finished his report by reminding the Directory of all he had done for the "triumph of liberty," saying his only "crime" was to have taken away

Hédouville's chance to be the one who chased away the English. "After all this, General Hédouville will not claim in France, as he dared to say here, before his departure, that it was I who made him embark," Louverture wrote. "I declare that I had never thought of it, and never was there a greater false claim. Besides, everyone knows well enough that he had been planning his departure for more than a month, and that if he kept the three frigates in the harbor, it was because he had some hidden motives that we did not know about."[37]

The French agent's departure did little to keep him from slandering Louverture after his ship arrived in Brest after thirty-nine days at sea. In his report to the French government, Hédouville said the republic needed to sow division in the colony to save it, and the best way to achieve this was "to maintain the hatred that exists between mulattoes and blacks and to oppose Rigaud and Toussaint." "I would not, however, venture to answer for the purity of intentions of the first, but I must do him justice by assuring you that I have nothing but praise for his conduct," Hédouville continued. Claiming that he could have sought refuge in the south with Rigaud, he justified abandoning the colony entirely by saying he thought it more prudent and important to return to France to give his account to the Directory.[38]

While in the colony, nevertheless, Hédouville had covertly worked to undermine Louverture by stoking discord between the general in chief and Rigaud. Hédouville believed that of all the generals of color, Rigaud, commander of the southern division, could most effectively mount a challenge to Louverture and had the most reason to do so.

Not long after Hédouville's departure Louverture and Rigaud became embroiled in a war of words that rapidly turned into a war of guns. Louverture claimed that Rigaud had expressed prejudices against him for being "Black." Rigaud, for his part, said that Louverture trumped up the charge of racism to turn the other generals, military officers, and cultivators against him. Rigaud insisted that Louverture invented these accusations merely to get rid of him, since Rigaud presented the clearest challenge to Louverture's authority. Yet Rigaud's biggest complaint was more political than personal: Louverture's agreements with Americans and the British, outside the bounds of French authority.[39] Rigaud referred to Louverture's treaty with Great Britain and autonomous trade agreements with the United States, without consulting the metropolitan French government, as betrayals of the French republic. In Rigaud's words, Louverture had violated the French constitution "with an act of sovereignty and of scission with France," which, in Rigaud's mind, amounted to proclaiming de facto independence.[40] Rigaud vigorously charged that Louverture's treaty with Maitland, in particular, was both "liberticidal and anti-republican."[41] "Perhaps it is in his new capacity as an independent leader, the sovereign of Saint-Domingue," Rigaud concluded, "that he proclaims me to be insubordinate, a traitor, and a rebel, and so on."[42] It is clear from this letter that Rigaud read his conflict with Louverture to be not one of color, although he argued that Louverture tried to make it one when Louverture accused Rigaud of being prejudiced, but one of principle.

Hédouville had sought to exploit existing tensions of color and race between the *ancien libre* people of color and the formerly enslaved population. But the conflict between Rigaud and Louverture should be understood as fundamentally about power.[43] Christophe soon found himself embroiled in not just Rigaud and Louverture's war of words but the actual civil war that erupted between these two French generals. In the wake of Hédouville's departure, Louverture appealed to Christophe's fellow Grenadian the agent Roume, Hédouville's designated successor in case of emergency, to come to Cap-Français from Santo Domingo to take Hédouville's place.[44]

Roume did not alone benefit from Hédouville's departure. On March 24, 1799, Louverture wrote to the French minister of the marine to request a promotion for Christophe, from chef de brigade to brigadier general. Louverture credited Christophe with having secured and "restored tranquility" to the famous port city of Cap-Français over which Louverture had newly given him command. Louverture also praised Christophe as responsible for "the order that reigns in the countryside [and] the progress of farming," which he called the "happy results of [Christophe's] wisdom, prudence, and love for his country."[45] Now Christophe's devotion to and willingness to serve France would experience another test and earn him new enemies.

Christophe's role in Louverture's conflict with Rigaud transformed Roume's previously positive opinion of the Grenadian native, because the French agent suddenly, and dangerously, went from being a Christophe ally to a Christophe detractor.

———

The tangled roots undergirding Rigaud and Louverture's war against each other are numerous and strand in many directions. The two disagreed about the treatment of the French émigrés, or French colonists who fled the revolution, taking refuge in enemy territory such as England or colonies controlled by Great Britain. Rigaud wanted to adhere to French laws requiring sequestration and confiscation of their properties, while Louverture wanted to welcome a limited number of them back. The two French generals also disagreed over trade with England and the United States, with Rigaud insisting the colony needed to remain deferential to the French republic and avoid any actions that smelled of an independence project. And Rigaud, who believed that Hédouville wanted to make him general in chief of the colony, watched his chance to rule slip away as Louverture ingratiated himself with the new French agent.

When conflict arose between Louverture and Rigaud once more, Roume sided with Louverture and took command of nearly the entire southern division—Léogâne, Jacmel, Miragoâne, Petit- and Grand-Goâve—away from Rigaud. In response, both Rigaud and Beauvais submitted their resignations from the French army. Yet Roume immediately rejected Rigaud's resignation while Louverture rejected Beauvais's.[46] Afterward, Louverture, who would have been all too happy to accept Rigaud's resignation, penned a famous diatribe against the former commander of the south, accusing Rigaud of being prejudiced against him because of the color of his skin and his African origins. Louverture also called Rigaud a "slanderer, liar, schemer, shrewd, haughty, ambitious, jealous, despotic, wicked, artful, vindictive, cruel, tyrannical, homicidal, factious, murderer, insubordinate." Finally, and most offensively for Rigaud, who loved to tout his loyalty to the French republic, Louverture called him a "traitor."[47] At this point, the civil war seemed almost inevitable, and Roume found himself embroiled in the conflict from the start. Roume had taken Louverture's side, which meant that the French republic had sided with Louverture, at least theoretically.

When actual fighting broke out in the so-called War of the South between Rigaud and Louverture—with Louverture establishing his headquarters in Port-au-Prince and Rigaud in Miragoâne—Christophe had been commander of the arrondissement of Cap for about a year. Roume, who previously approved this, soon grew distraught about it. Although Louverture had repaired the colony's relationship with England through his secret treaty with Maitland, Roume claimed that during Hédouville's tenure Christophe had plotted with the British to orchestrate Roume's departure.[48]

In late November 1799, Roume wrote that damning letter to Louverture in which he referred to Christophe as an "anglo-maniac." Roume went further in accusing Christophe of wanting to make Saint-Domingue a British colony. "The American government, in concert with that of England, has agreed to many things on the belief that it would be possible for them to render Saint-Domingue independent," Roume told Louverture, before charging that "Commander Cristophe [sic] and a few others" had colluded with both British "spies" and the American consul "to put [Louverture] at odds with the agent [Roume], to make it seem necessary to send him away, such that you would lose all confidence in the French Directory." "And it was citizen Vincent, director of fortifications, who most pressed for the agent's departure, since he dared not to take on his responsibility to save the country," Roume wrote, saying that Vincent had urged " 'ridding it of a monster such as Roume.' " Roume was therefore overjoyed to have learned from Louverture that General Moyse had replaced Christophe as commander of Cap. "It is fortunate, Citizen General, that you sent that same Vincent to France and that you withdrew Commander Cristophe [*sic*], it is again fortunate that you replaced that *anglo-mane* with the Republican Moyse, and this is what has foiled all the plots that they had directed against you rather than against me."[49]

Roume might have simply been paranoid. The former chef de brigade Grandet had openly accused Christophe of plotting Hédouville's departure from the very beginning of the latter's arrival in the colony. Grandet, who served for twenty-three years in Saint-Domingue, was deported from the colony after being kept in jail for six months, according to his report to the French minister of the marine, dating from mid-1799. Claiming that he had been "deprived of all assistance, even of that which humankind has never refused to villains," Grandet identified General Moyse and Chef de Brigade Christophe as the authors of his misfortune. He claimed that Moyse and Christophe "vied to have [Hédouville] embarked" as soon as Hédouville set foot on the island, and that the two of them together—one as the commander in chief over the department of the north and the other as commander in Cap—had spread the rumor among the cultivators that Hédouville sought to bring back slavery.

According to Grandet, when Christophe spied Hédouville's convoy off the coast of Cap, he told Grandet, "Here comes that agent, if he doesn't do what we want, we'll get him sent back soon." Grandet did not indicate whether or how he responded to Christophe. Instead, Grandet said that he returned to his post and went to see General Moyse, who received him in a friendly manner. "You are very pleased that the agent has arrived," Moyse reportedly said, laughing. "All decent people should be," Grandet replied. Grandet then claimed that Moyse revealed a conspiracy to him whereby all the Black leaders would gather in the mountains to plot the re-embarkment of the French agent Hédouville and the destitution of all the white French generals with whom they were at odds. Grandet claimed that the Black generals conceived the plan to deploy the Fifth Demi-brigade led by Moyse against the French agent only when they could not find fault with Hédouville. Because Grandet fought against them, Louverture's soldiers sent him to jail in Petite-Anse, which pleased Louverture, whom Grandet labeled "the veritable author of this rebellion."

The day after Grandet's arrest, Louverture allegedly went to the prison to personally interrogate him. "He said to me, first, according to his usual hypocrisy, that he was very upset to see me in this position," Grandet recalled. Louverture then supposedly told Grandet he believed him to be a "good officer," but that Grandet was "wrong to take this side." The general in chief had not decided whether Grandet's involvement constituted a capital crime and said he would perhaps spare the officer's life. Moyse and Christophe, in contrast, voted for him to be executed. Instead of being executed, Grandet said he remained incarcerated in the humid prison for forty days, with both his feet in irons and without anyone to speak to. Later he was transferred to a jail in Cap, where he stayed for only one day before being taken to Port-de-Paix, "where I was put in irons on a camp bed between two posts where I remained until March 25," after which he said he was taken barefoot back to Cap and then deported to France.[50] Roume was not partial to Grandet, however, and therefore not predisposed to hold a negative opinion of Christophe due solely to the latter's account of him.

Quite the contrary, Roume previously held Christophe in high regard and frequently received visits and updates from him in the wake of Hédouville's departure and Louverture's elevation of Christophe to commander of Cap. In a letter he wrote to Louverture on April 6, 1799, Roume mentioned that Christophe had visited him that morning, making sure to note that he (Roume) remained "very satisfied" with Christophe's military conduct.[51] Roume frequently visited Christophe on the Saint-Michel plantation, too, where the commander of Cap lived with his family. On one such visit, Roume grew so impressed with the makeshift school that Christophe operated on the plantation that he wrote about it to Étienne Eustache Bruix, the French minister of the marine. Roume told the minister what Christophe explained to him: most of the plantations were being farmed by "black citizens" who could not read but who wanted their children to be able to do so. To facilitate this learning, Black farmers employed white teachers who brought books and all the accoutrements for writing. Usually, it was only necessary for one plantation in a single locality to employ such an individual. Children from neighboring plantations were then encouraged to attend provided their parents could pay a half or three-quarters of a gourde every month to the schoolteacher. "Fathers and mothers, despite their lack of means, are saving up," Roume concluded, to offer even the most rudimentary education for their children.[52] Yes, before they were enemies, Roume and Christophe were friends. Their friendship changed rapidly over the course of 1799.

Only a few months after penning that letter to the French minister, Roume, suspecting Christophe of wanting to have him deported, suddenly had nothing good to say about the commander of Cap. Just two months after Grandet's deportation, Roume said he received a vicious complaint against Christophe from an elderly woman. Roume, seemingly without reserve, gave the utmost credence to the woman's account. At one o'clock in the afternoon on August 21, 1799, Roume recalled that a distressed woman appeared before him to protest what she called Christophe's wrongful imprisonment of her son. She said that Christophe arrested, detained, and jailed her son, a regiment captain, without having any crime against him recorded and without any judgment about his fate determined by French authorities.

The woman pleaded with Roume to prevent her son's execution and asked for him to be granted a trial. Moved, Roume wrote to Christophe immediately. Using his characteristic style of reprimand masked as rhetorical innocence, Roume began, "This request, based on our republican laws, which are known to be based on nature's eternal code, seemed to me too just and too simple for it to experience the slightest difficulty." He continued, "Consequently, I have returned it to you for accommodation." Yet even though Roume reacted immediately to the woman's request, he said that forty-five minutes later she reappeared before him. "She told me, looking very distressed," Roume wrote to Christophe, "that you received her petition without saying anything consoling to her. She asked me to tell you about her son. I promised to do it the next morning, and she left with tears in her eyes, begging me to see you this very evening and not to wait until tomorrow morning, because it might be too late."

Roume claimed that his mind simmered with worry after the woman's second departure. The French agent's disquietude only increased when he recalled that he previously overheard from many different people that "on several occasions in Cap nocturnal executions without trial had been carried out and that, among other things, the late general Pierre Michel had often performed these during the tenure of the previous agents." Roume dropped all pretense of an innocent inquiry in the paragraphs that followed. Claiming to have a "soul too torn" and a "grieving heart," Roume wrote that he could hardly believe the charges constituted anything other than "calumny," given that "the situation is so contrary to all the principles accepted in France and among all nations." "If I dared to take it upon myself to come to the traditionally French part of Saint-Domingue, it was only due to the highest opinion I have of the virtues of the general in chief," he continued. "If I dared to entrust the fate of the agency to the discretion of the city of Cap, it was only after the praise that I intended to give to the general in chief and to everyone under the commander Henry Christophe. Since my stay in Cap, I have had a thousand occasions to admire your wise impartiality, your energetic republicanism, and your good heart." "I am therefore persuaded to tell you, Citizen Commander, that I have never ordered or tolerated arbitrary executions," he said. "You have carried these out only from the examples you have seen under the earlier agents." Although this might have been a fitting conclusion, Roume had more to say to the commander he claimed to admire and respect. The final paragraphs illustrate the difficult relationship emerging between the two men: one of mutual disapprobation. "But now that you have here an agent who is a friend of the colony, who never fears anything when it comes to defending your just rights, who knows no friends except those of the good cause, from now on, say I, Citizen Commander, you are to view arbitrary acts only with the eyes of indignation."

Roume found the woman's claims of arbitrary justice so alarming that he informed Christophe that he had already written to Louverture, "to ask him to give the most affirmative orders to prevent the accomplices of any revolts from being taken to courts other than legally constituted councils of war." Roume made his motive clear, saying he had no doubt that Louverture would "satisfy my just request." He told Christophe, therefore, "I would not have spoken to you about this thing without the circumstances of today." Roume concluded with a threat and a remonstrance: "What might have been done is without remedy, and I see it only as a continuation of the unfortunate state in which the colony has remained for a long time." Roume did not mind the execution of criminals, he said, but protested against doing so outside proper procedure. As a stickler for rules and order, Roume claimed to merely want to ensure French republican principles of justice.[53]

By that time, Christophe knew of Roume's disinclination to trust him, but Christophe also knew the kind of evidence French administrators appreciated. In his detailed response to the French agent, Christophe did not indicate which of the prisoners was the complaining woman's son. But he defended himself by implying that her son was one of many who had recently engaged in violent rebellions against the French republic, and he provided numerous documents to support his account. Adopting a more detached rhetorical tone than the French agent, Christophe wrote,

Citizen Agent,

I have the honor to send you herewith (1) a copy of the declaration of citizen Louis Labeliné, chef de brigade, commander in chief of the National Guard of Limonade, against Moline and his consorts; (2) a copy of the order I gave to citizen Charles of the First Regiment to go to Gonaïves to receive the prisoners who had been engaged in the conspiracy, as well as the report that testifies to the revolt of the said prisoners against the detachment; (3) a copy of the order given to Citizen Raymond, captain, commanding the company of gunners of the Second Demi-brigade, to go to Borgne to get the prisoners who had conspired against the republic, and the report made on this subject by citizen Raymond of the various measures which these citizens, commanders of said detachments, were obliged to take against the prisoners and rebels, and which provide strong evidence of their liberticidal projects. My emotions were greatly affected when I became aware of these events, and one might say a state of affairs like this, in which extreme measures had to be taken, can only be appreciated by understanding the circumstances.

Salut and Respect. Signed: Henry Christophe[54]

One can almost feel his exasperation. It must have been strange to have recently seen promotion by Louverture, along with increasing responsibility, only to have to constantly address complaints about his conduct. Roume hardly stood in a position to understand or appreciate the difficulties that military officers like Christophe endured because of the colony's warring factions.

According to the officers and soldiers who signed the deposition Christophe included with his missive to Roume, the case in question involved Louis Nicolas Moline, Joseph Pirouneau, and Jean Édouard Viaud, as well as six others, who had been "condemned to death on the sixteenth of the current month, for the crime of conspiracy against the internal security of the northern department of Saint-Domingue." When the captured men appeared before the municipality to answer for their actions, some of them refused to accept judgment against them. Pirouneau, called Garçon, "at the time of the execution reportedly approached the commander in chief of the district, telling him that 'it was not he who should be put to death, but that there were many others and that he would denounce them if we wanted to give him the time.'" Following this outburst, Viaud cried out with indignation, "Oh! what a coward"; while Moline shouted to him in a loud and clear voice, "Pirouneau, you are a coward to denounce your comrades like so; let me teach you how to die. As for me, I will die with satisfaction," after which, according to the deposition, "he exhaled his insults against the commander in chief of the borough," which is to say Christophe.

The captured men continued to heap opprobrium on Christophe and his soldiers. They also tried to escape: "We affirm that in this interval, several of the condemned, having fled, were recaptured a few moments later and that the said Pirouneau, the last to remain alive, stood alone to undergo his judgment." Pirouneau remained obstinate and determined to escape with his life. He approached Christophe and promised to reveal the entire plot while imploring, "Remember that you have always looked upon me as your child." Such manipulation, coming from a man in open rebellion only moments earlier, did not move Commander Christophe. As soon as Pirouneau spoke, Christophe cut him off to ask "why he had not come to instruct him of the conspiracy when there was still time." Pirouneau had an excuse ready: "I didn't, because you always refused me your confidence and you never look kindly on me."

Christophe wanted to know who led the conspiracy. Pirouneau, as the last man standing, had no one to dispute his account and could therefore blame whomever he wanted. Pirouneau pointed to Moline, saying he was the leader, along with all the other dead men, whose bodies remained strewn about the room. "They were supposed to start by cutting off your head . . . and of many other leaders who are under the orders of General Toussaint, and there are still many of them out there," Pirouneau admitted. "I know where the list is; I will expose them, if you bring them here." Claiming "all the youth of Cap were involved in this conspiracy,"

Pirouneau specifically implicated "Citizens Dupont, ex-commander of the northern band, Robert, chef de brigade and local commander of Fort-Liberté; Jean Pellet and Fify." After this desperate testimony, Pirouneau was immediately executed.[55]

The other documents that Christophe sent to Roume told the tale of yet more conspiracies and rebellion. Christophe sent direct testimony from officers under his command to the French agent to justify the deadly force sometimes used by his soldiers when circumstances prevented them from delivering accused men to the appropriate officials for judgment. On August 10, 1799, Christophe ordered a soldier named Charles, captain of the First Regiment, to take command of a detachment and then travel to Gonaïves to conduct some prisoners to Cap. "The commander of the said detachment is ordered not to let escape any of the said prisoners, to take the necessary precautions and all the means that are at his disposal to prevent anyone from freeing them, and to fire against those who would present themselves for this purpose, and even to fire on those from among the prisoners who would attempt to use force or engage in rebellion against their leaders."[56] The subsequent death of all sixty-eight of the prisoners still required an urgent explanation and a patent justification. Charles submitted an official statement to Christophe on August 17, 1799, to explain why not a single prisoner survived. Charles wrote, "Having arrived between the Chabaud and the Delord plantations, the prisoners revolted against us, which forced me, not being able to conduct them anymore in this state, to order them to be fired upon, after which none of them remained. We threw them on the ground." After having "put the prisoners out of a position to harm us," Charles concluded, "we found two packs of cartridges, which we took with us. We went to the Alquier camp, where we drew up this report."[57]

Raymond experienced similar difficulties when Christophe ordered him "to go with his detachment to Borgne to transfer the prisoners from Port-de-Paix to Cap." Though Christophe gave these orders, they came from Louverture. Christophe counseled Raymond to avoid letting the prisoners escape with the same instructions that he gave to Charles: to use any means necessary, even death.[58] Raymond's mission also ended in bloodshed.

When Raymond arrived at the prison, he received the twenty-eight "prisoner-conspirators," accused of having "sown discord and encouraged the peaceful cultivators to rebel against the republic." It was not until Raymond and the prisoners were en route that trouble began once more. "I set out with the said prisoners to take them to Cap," Raymond wrote. "Out of humanity, I let them free so that they could walk more easily, and when I least expected it, they surprised my troops and disarmed some of them and revolted against me and my detachment." The soldiers under Raymond's command did not escape without wounds. "Several of the soldiers were grabbed by the collar, in hand-to-hand combat with the prisoners, several of whom received minor injuries," he wrote. These prisoners remained determined, perhaps encouraged by having succeeded in surprising the captors sent to transfer them. The "prisoner-conspirators" began screaming wildly and called out to the so-called *hommes de couleur,* "the friends of Rigaud," to assist them. In detecting some movement in the countryside around him, Raymond understood he was about to be assaulted again, the victim of yet another plot. "I saw myself in danger, as well as my detachment. Having uselessly employed the voice of gentleness to attempt to restore order," Raymond continued, "I was forced to use the weapons I had at my disposal against the said prisoners who fell under our blows and remained on the ground." Raymond expressed more contrition than Charles. He concluded, "I then made my way to Cap, forced to have taken actions that are repugnant to my character." "Public security, that of my detachment, required this measure," he wrote in prose dripping with simultaneous grief and effective pride. "And it was only with great courage and valor that I remained master of the battlefield, without which our prisoners would have been taken from us at the expense of our lives."[59]

Though Christophe patiently justified his actions in the Moline/Pirouneau affair and that of his soldiers in each of these instances, Roume had clearly tired of dealing with him. At the height of the War of the South, Louverture ordered Christophe to travel to the western department to aid in the fight. Even with Christophe gone from Cap, Roume's complaints about his conduct continued. In Christophe's place, Louverture installed Moyse, brigadier general and commander in chief of the northern department.[60] Dessalines, who commanded the western department, was seated in Léogâne, where he met his future wife, Marie-Claire Heureuse, while Christophe, Clervaux, and another officer named Laplume sat at the head of their respective divisions. Louverture gave each the directive to follow the orders of Dessalines, whom he made commander in chief of the War of the South. Christophe, for his part, commanded the second division of the army operating against Rigaud.[61]

While Roume could hardly hide his joy that Christophe no longer commanded in Cap, complaints against the commander soon began to accumulate once more, increasing Roume's irritation against his fellow Grenadian. On October 24, 1799, Roume wrote to Louverture that he had watched "with satisfaction" as the latter executed the Directory's decree concerning the reorganization of the colony's troops. "My satisfaction is further increased by the goal that you have in mind of bringing the European troops together under the orders of Chef de Brigade Henry Christophe for the glorious expedition we have just agreed upon, because although I am very unhappy with Commander Christophe in his capacity as commander of Cap, where he is constantly surrounded by a procession of sycophants and vile usurpers who make him commit all sorts of indecency and villainies, I am convinced that when you have rid him of this ugly entourage, he will resume all the energy befitting a republican warrior and will justify not only your confidence but mine as well." Roume reminded Louverture that "it was I who first proposed to employ him in this memorable enterprise," and "moreover, Citizen Christophe is a Creole from Grenada and I have the way of looking at all the people of this island as if they were my own brothers."[62] Although Roume professed reluctance to punish Christophe due to feelings of Grenadian fraternity, it was not enough to prevent him from denouncing Christophe soon after.

Louverture had ordered Christophe to organize his troops for the strike against the south. Christophe's ability to carry out these orders was at times tested by the insubordination of the men under his command. Louverture charged the commander of the artillery, a man named Fousenqui, with insubordination on October 20, 1799. Louverture claimed that the artillery commander had gathered men working on various plantations and forced them to join the army without having an order from his superiors to do so. When Fousenqui was questioned, he blamed Christophe. Fousenqui then also reported this to Roume. Louverture expressed surprise that Roume had been willing to take Fousenqui's word over Christophe's and his own. "According to military hierarchy, Citizen Fousenqui should have had nothing to say, or to undertake, except to execute the orders of his leaders," Louverture reminded the French agent. "I am all the angrier with him, since he has pushed his insubordination to the point of making you angry with Commander Christophe, on whom I rely a great deal for the execution of my planned operations." "I assure you that if Citizen Fousenqui persists in his misconduct, I will remove his command. I am writing accordingly to Brigadier General Martial Besse and will have him replaced," Louverture said. Before closing, Louverture issued a final defense of Christophe. "What surprised me most, Citizen Agent, I cannot conceal from you," Toussaint wrote, "is that you gave more credence to Citizen Fousenqui than to Commander Christophe."[63]

Four days later Roume responded with more accusations against the commander. Though he approved of Christophe's release of several prisoners held aboard ships in the harbor, Roume had little else positive to say. Claiming that Christophe repeatedly abused his authority under the guise of the approbation of the agency, Roume wrote, "Suffice it for me to make this observation to you, such that you might feel all the indecency of this process, and such that you will send orders to Commander Christophe to no longer play games with the agency in the way in which I realize that he endeavors to do. I could have made similar denunciations to you a long time ago if I had not had hope that by dint of gentleness and patience I would end up making him perceive his errors, but there are incorrigible beings and my experiences prove to me that this commander is one of them." As for Louverture's defense of Christophe in the Fousenqui scandal, Roume made it no secret that he did not trust Christophe's version of events. Roume then implored Louverture to take Fousenqui's side of the story seriously regardless of his lower rank. "I hope, therefore, Citizen General, that according to the explanations that Citizen Fousenquy [*sic*] will have given you that you will send orders for the very prompt organization of the artillery," Roume concluded.[64]

Despite Roume's numerous complaints—and the fact that Louverture previously found occasion to rebuke Christophe over his handling of administrative matters after Louverture's appointment of Christophe to interim commander over the east—what Louverture most needed were allies and capable military officers.[65] Louverture trusted Christophe despite his sometimes inconsistent leadership. On November 19, 1799, with more than a hint of triumph, Louverture wrote to Roume to explain that the "European troops" that he had "organized into a batallion" in the west to fight against Rigaud were now being prepared for combat by Clervaux and Christophe.[66]

Being embroiled in the War of the South was still not enough to keep Christophe from being one of the French agent's targets. On December 25, 1799, Roume wrote to Louverture with yet another grievance. Earlier that month, a man named Thomas appeared before Roume to complain about Christophe's conduct. Thomas referred to an incriminating letter he said Christophe sent him from Jacmel. Before describing the letter, Roume made it no secret that he had already taken Thomas's side. Thomas had been employed at drafting affermage and sequestration documents, and Roume planned to promote him to an administrator position at the National Domains. Christophe thwarted this plan with his accusation that Thomas accepted "presents given to him by those who obtained in-person release from sequestration." "Citizen Thomas, as soon as he received the letter from Commander Christophe, brought it to me, although I am very convinced that this letter is only further proof of the deceitfulness and the wickedness of Commander Christophe," Roume wrote, "[and] despite the good opinion I have of Citizen Thomas, I have judged that the employees of the agency should not even be suspected of prevarication."

Roume judged that if inhabitants of the colony paid for or offered gifts to have their properties released from sequester, they were crazier than Christophe and "deserve to lose their money." On the flip side, if Thomas were "guilty of the prevarication of which he is accused by Commander Christophe, not only would I dismiss him from the offices of the agency, but I would condemn him in person to pay into the coffers of the republic . . . all the sums that he would have received." Roume did not actually believe these measures would be necessary. Yet he subsequently counseled Louverture to ask Christophe for proof, ordering that Christophe "categorically name the people he says have paid in person for the lifting of sequesters to citizen Thomas." Roume clearly did not believe that these names would be forthcoming. "If Commander Christophe does not name anyone, I would see in his denunciation [of Thomas] only a filth worthy of him and finally quite similar to the rest of his conduct," Roume wrote.[67] Although Roume wanted Louverture to reprimand Christophe, it was Roume who soon found himself in the general in chief's bad graces.

While Louverture was deeply involved in the fight against Rigaud, Hugh Cathcart, who claimed to have been in daily contact with Louverture, wrote a letter to General Maitland in late November 1799. According to Cathcart, Louverture told him that "in the future he would never receive any chief from France. He said that he had a vessel at the Cape for the purpose of embarking Roume (the agent) and that he should have done it long before this time, if he was not afraid that he might find his way to Rigaud, and turn the tables upon him." Cathcart mentioned that Christophe had been recently promoted to the rank of colonel (equivalent to chef de brigade in the French army) and that he had made himself indispensable to Louverture.

That month, Louverture organized his army in the west to strike Jacmel in the hopes of finally bringing the war with Rigaud to an end. Christophe was about to enter Jacmel with several thousand troops at his command. "The whole of his army is now below Légoâne, about 1,000 cavalry and 18,000 infantry," Cathcart wrote. "He has brought his whole force from the north. These troops were well cloathed [sic] and Armed, considering his resources, and in much better discipline than the other Troops that I had before seen." Cathcart, in seeing how well organized and outfitted Louverture's army was (thanks to Christophe), now believed that the general in chief stood to be the victor. "Toussaint has certainly now got the Military ascendancy over Rigaud. He will however find much difficulty in completely overcoming [Rigaud], and it will take him a longer time to accomplish the task than he seems at the outset to have been aware of." The extra support, in terms of both soldiers and money, that Christophe provided was integral to Louverture's eventual success.

Christophe's lower rank did not mean that he was less capable than Dessalines, Cathcart further explained. "Henry Christophe, whom I have mentioned in a former part of the letter, appears to possess fully as much influence and power as either Dessalines or Moyse (although he ranks only a chef de brigade)," Cathcart wrote. "He is equally as ambitious and far superior to either of them in abilities, knowledge of the world (if I may be allowed to use the expression) and in his resources." Noting that Christophe "brought with him from the Cape, one hundred and fifty cavalry—Fifty of whom were dressed as Hussards, and 2,600 Infantry, by far the best dressed and Armed of Toussaint's Troops (they went by the name of Colonel Christophe's Army)," Cathcart explained that Christophe "also brought with him Provisions and Ammunition, sufficient for three months for them alone and 1800 Doubloons in Gold to pay them in a Brig named the *Rebecca* . . . The cargo consisted of Five hundred barrels of flour and one hundred and twenty barrels of Pork, besides cloathing [*sic*]—one Brass 12 Pounder, and one ditto & ditto, and Two hundred balls for each, with Ammunition & c. He told me that he had not troubled Toussaint for any of the above mentioned articles, but had furnished them at his own Expense." "He is now supposed to have amassed a fortune of two millions of livres of this colony, very near Two hundred and fifty thousand dollars," Cathcart concluded.

Despite Cathcart's high opinion of Christophe, he did have some words of criticism for the colonel. Punishing people for insubordination remained an accusation that followed Christophe from his time as a soldier in the French military to his eventual kingship. Cathcart told Maitland that three British vessels traveling between Cap and Gonaïves to load supplies met with difficulty owing to Christophe's behavior upon their return to Cap. "The Master of one of them having displeased Henry Christophe—he made his soldiers beat him," Cathcart claimed. "Upon my complaining to Toussaint, Christophe was ordered to make an apology. When he had done so he added, had the Master been a Frenchman and conducted himself in such a manner, he would have ordered him to have been shot upon the spot." Cathcart concluded, "He seems much surprised that I should have received the business in such a serious light as to have complained to Toussaint of his conduct."[68]

Christophe's involvement in the War of the South reached its height when Louverture forced capture of Jacmel, an important position in the west. In November 1799, Toussaint's army assembled before Jacmel. The city lacked a leader. Pétion offered himself to Rigaud and was given command. Afterward, Pétion vigorously repelled Christophe's assault against Grand-Fort. This may have been the first time the two men fought each other in battle. Christophe then assaulted Fort-Pavillon, initially achieving the position, only to be later chased away once more. "The women and children who came out [of the city during the evacuation] were, say some historians, well received on Dessalines's side, but pursued on Christophe's," wrote Vergniaud Leconte. According to the pro-Pétion Haitian historian Saint-Rémy, "Those whom instinct had led to Dessalines were received with that humanity that we owe to women and to the unfortunate. But those who had the misfortune of fate to exit on Christophe's side were first repelled with cannon shots," and were afterward "precipitated with their children into the well of the Ogé dwelling." Louverture eventually won the city in April 1800.[69]

After his victory, Louverture gave a speech to the citizens of the southern department, both rebuking and welcoming them back to his rule. Louverture sought to convince his audience that his war against Rigaud was about preserving equality. "If one carefully examines his artful, but largely impolitic conduct, one could not help but to say that Rigaud did not like his color, and that he preferred to sacrifice it to his pride, to his ambition, than to work for its happiness," Louverture declared. "Indeed, citizens, the majority of those he misled perished, either in combat or on the scaffold; the others are still dying in this rebellion." Louverture reiterated his intention to welcome the people of the south with open arms—rhetoric Christophe would become familiar with in his own civil war with Pétion. But if, on the contrary, the people of the south decided to fight him, "in vain, the army of General Toussaint Louverture led by the generals and other commanders and members of the army whose bravery you already know, will fight you, and you will be defeated," Louverture told the crowd. Louverture would even accept Rigaud, if the latter were to return in good faith and admit his faults. "But if Rigaud persists, and if he refuses to take advantage of such a great offer, come to me, all of you, fathers and mothers of families, I will receive you with open arms, as the father of the prodigal son received his son after his repentance."[70]

At the same time, just outside Jacmel, Dessalines pressed forward with his army. Resistance by Rigaud no longer seemed possible. Thus it was that Rigaud embarked from Tiburon in the last days of July 1800 with his wife, children, brother, and several of his key officers. Rigaud, however, later found himself detained first by the French on the island of Guadeloupe and then by the British, some say on the island of Saint Christopher, others on the island of Dominica, in the far eastern Antilles.[71]

Louverture definitively declared victory in the War of the South the same month Rigaud fled. Louverture stayed for three weeks in Port-au-Prince afterward to reorganize his administration, before going on to Léogâne to celebrate the success. A Te Deum Catholic hymn of gratitude was sung and congratulations were addressed to the army. Louverture promoted Dessalines to division general, while Christophe continued to await official sanction of Louverture's request for his promotion to brigadier general. All military promotions in the colony were subject to the sanction of the metropolitan government, which Louverture hastened to request from the first consul, Napoléon Bonaparte, now ruling France in the wake of the overthrow of the Executive Directory in 1799. Christophe, for his part, subsequently returned to the north and became once more commander over Cap.[72]

Amid the fighting with Rigaud, Louverture had called on Christophe to take charge of a critical mission to establish French authority over the eastern part of the island, or Santo Domingo. Just prior to Louverture's calling him into service, Christophe had been so ill as to remain out of service entirely. His absence distressed Louverture greatly, and he expressed satisfaction upon learning from Dessalines that Christophe had recovered. In his letter of May 13, 1800, Louverture told Christophe, whom he addressed with the title of "Chef de brigade . . . Commanding a column of the army on the march against the southern rebels," "The great interests of our country require that I send to Santo Domingo a superior officer worthy of the greatest trust due to his zeal and love of our freedom." "Generals Moyse and Dessalines, as well as you, are the only ones in whom I can place confidence to serve our common interests, with the assurance that they will be well defended and supported," Louverture continued. "After careful consideration, I decided to choose you to fulfill this important mission," Louverture concluded.[73] Christophe accepted the call.

But while in in the east, he missed an important family event. Christophe's wife, Marie-Louise, gave birth to their third child, Anne Athénaïs-Henry, on July 7, 1800, about three weeks before Rigaud fled the colony.[74]

Yet it seemed that every time Louverture overcame a challenge, a new one surged up. This time the standoff would take a familiar cast as Louverture went toe to toe, in large part due to the mission in Santo Domingo, with yet another French agent, Roume. Christophe involved himself in his quest to rid the colony of Roume, but with much more equivocation, or so it seems, than he had assisted Louverture with Sonthonax, Hédouville, Rigaud, and Santo Domingo.

Though the Spanish ceded the eastern part of Santo Domingo to France in 1795, the abolition of slavery was not being enforced on that side of the island. In January 1801, Louverture proclaimed an end to slavery in the east when he triumphantly captured the capital, Santo Domingo, and declared his intention to enforce French republican laws per the Treaty of Basel and the law of February 1794.[75] However, neither the consuls in the metropole nor the French agent in Saint-Domingue, which is to say Roume, had authorized this siege. The consuls and the French agent, in fact, viewed Louverture's autonomous strike in the east as another sign of his growing power and as a distinct threat to their authority.

Louverture opened several ports on the eastern side of the island to foreign commerce, just as he had on the western side.[76] And a few days after the successful January 1801 siege of the east, Louverture went to Cap and discussed the creation of Saint-Domingue's constitution with the Central Assembly, composed of ten members, with two representatives for each region.[77] Six departments in all were formed, including one called Toussaint Louverture, whose principal city was in Gonaïves.[78]

To prepare for the mission in the east, Louverture needed to do more than to simply press the recovering Christophe back into service. He first had to either neutralize or remove his greatest obstacle, the agent Roume. Louverture's prior threats to Roume had not been idle. On April 11, 1800, Louverture had Roume arrested in Haut-du-Cap.[79] What a vast change in the circumstances of their previously close relationship. Just a little over a year earlier, on February 19, 1799, Louverture appeared as a witness to Roume's marriage to his longtime partner, a free woman of color also from Grenada, Marianne Elizabeth Rochard, with whom he had a ten-year-old daughter.[80] Now, as with Laveaux, Sonthonax, and Hédouville, Louverture wanted the agent Roume gone. In response to his change of fortune,

Roume tried to revoke Louverture's authorization to extend his authority to the Spanish side of the island. It is clear, however, that Roume's decrees, as much as his wishes, were null at that point. On November 26, several months after Louverture definitively defeated Rigaud, he had Moyse take Roume from Haut-du-Cap to Dondon, where Roume remained detained, according to Louverture's orders, "until the French government recalled him to give his report."[81]

Roume told the story of his downfall in a roundabout fashion in a letter to the French abolitionist the abbé Grégoire written from Philadelphia on October 18, 1801, and later published in the French journal *La décade philosophique* (The Philosophical Decade). According to Roume, Louverture held him for "about eighteen months in captivity, both at the Maison Nationale of Cap-Français and in the town of Haut-du-Cap, and lastly for nine months on the summit of one of the mountains of Dondon, where I almost perished of misery and disease, with my wife and my daughter." In the end, Louverture did not wait for the government's instructions. "Toussaint," Roume continued, "had me transported to the United States of America, doubtless persuaded that the power of a sovereign was too well assured for him to have anything left to fear from the part of a national authority figure so conveniently placed to watch over his inconsistencies and direct them in the manner most appropriate to the interests of France."[82] It is true that Louverture did not allow Roume to embark for the United States until August 1801, and only after he wrote to Bonaparte to say that he believed Roume was too old to serve any longer.[83] In Philadelphia, Roume wrote to the French minister of the marine to further explain his perspective. He implicated Christophe in his arrest and revealed that he had been incarcerated at the home of General Vilton, commander of Petite-Anse, just before his "deportation."[84] Roume only returned to Paris in early September 1802, where he died three years later at the age of eighty.[85]

Just before Louverture sent Roume packing to the United States, Bonaparte, following his ascendance to first consul, created a new constitution that paved the way for the reinstatement of slavery in France's colonies. The new constitution allowed one set of laws to apply in metropolitan France and another in the overseas territories.[86]

Louverture had no intention to wait for the Consulate to make those new laws. Instead, he directed the Central Assembly of Saint-Domingue to create a new constitution specifically for the island. Nothing marked Louverture's awesome power more than the July 1801 constitution that made him governor-general for life with the right to name his successor. Not everyone in his administration agreed that Louverture's new constitution was the best way of keeping peace between the colony and the Consulate. Both Christophe and Vincent reportedly disagreed with the idea of a constitution. Yet Louverture tasked Vincent all the same with taking the constitution and a packet of letters to Bonaparte to explain the governor-general's logic. Before he left, Vincent had an audience with Christophe. In his narration of that meeting, Vincent claimed that Christophe declared, "The constitution is Toussaint's crime," and said, "I will never sign it." "It is folly of us to think that we can govern ourselves; we are only too happy if we are granted a few positions," Christophe concluded. "I will fight against Toussaint rather than support such an ambition." In Vincent's not at all disinterested recollection, Christophe grew so distressed over this constitution that he "distanced his heart from the men apparently responsible for writing it," which included his dear friend Raimond.[87]

Vincent then gave Christophe an unsealed letter for Louverture, to which the brigadier general replied, "Commander Vincent, you are the only European who really loves the men of Saint-Domingue; you have always told us the truth. The draft constitution was written by our most dangerous enemies; we will be taking a power that cannot be ours. If the government would only give us one part of the powers by which we should be governed, we will be very happy." Vincent had a long list of complaints to reveal to Christophe before the latter retired to his home. That the self-proclaimed governor-general was fairly obsessed with Bonaparte not responding to his letters, bringing it up often enough to annoy the director of fortifications, was high on Vincent's list of complaints against Louverture.

Christophe had high rank at this point, but Moyse, Louverture's nephew, remained Christophe's direct superior. Perhaps this is why Christophe confided in him about the meeting he had with Vincent, including the latter's remarks and criticisms of the constitution. Christophe's disclosure to Moyse hastened Vincent's departure from the colony, or so Vincent said. Vincent embarked for France in July 1801 and arrived in September. Though he criticized Louverture while still in the colony, in France, Vincent seemingly in good faith presented the constitution and other documents that Louverture sent to Bonaparte and the consuls.[88] Among these were several missives from Louverture addressed directly to Bonaparte. Bonaparte's initial silence when presented with this new constitution only gave Louverture more reason to complain about the cold treatment.[89]

Four months earlier, Louverture had appeared to be in the good graces of Bonaparte, who praised Louverture as he promoted him. "I am ordering the minister of the marine to send you the *brevet* of captain general of the French part of Saint-Domingue," the handwritten decree read. "The government could not provide you with a greater mark of confidence." Bonaparte signed off with his own signature and a warm attempt at reassurance, "I greet you affectionately."[90] Yet by the time Louverture followed up his July 16 letter, he seemed increasingly exasperated by Bonaparte's silence. The following month, Louverture sent a letter to the French minister of the marine asking him to transmit yet another missive to the first consul, in which Louverture sought to provide "all the details you could desire" about the situation in Saint-Domingue, "as well as to destroy in your mind all the calumnies of my enemies who are jealous of the tranquility enjoyed in the colony and the rapid steps toward prosperity it is making under the administration of a black man, and who would like to persuade the French government to undertake measures that would introduce disorder into the order of things that I have established there."[91]

Though Louverture might not have yet fully understood, he had a new rival in France: Napoléon Bonaparte. Louverture knew of his many rivals in Saint-Domingue, but those he had consistently defeated. He must have known, too, or at least suspected, that others could and would take their place if they had the chance.

When did Christophe, who witnessed Louverture dismiss, deport, or arrest previous rivals, begin to worry over his own status in the military and his relationship with the general in chief turned governor-general? Did the dismissals and arrests of the French commissioners, agents, and military officers, much of which he participated in, cause Christophe to suspect Louverture's ability to lead? Or did Christophe on the contrary see Louverture's wins as opportunities to bolster his own position? If he hoped to get closer to Louverture, Christophe would have to be careful and strategic.

One of Louverture's conflicts was about to put all his most trusted confidants on edge. Louverture, after having Roume arrested and deported, ordered the execution of his own adopted nephew, General Moyse, who had fought bravely by his side since the beginning of the revolution.

—

Following the eastern siege, Louverture promised Moyse a promotion to division general. Paul Louverture, Toussaint's much younger brother, became brigadier general with command over the department of Engaño, and General Clervaux was given command over Samaná. When he returned from the victorious campaign in the east, Moyse, also inspector of agriculture, had orders to execute Louverture's October 1800 farming regulations. However, Louverture's new regulations reportedly appeared to Moyse to infringe on the cultivators' freedom.[92]

Louverture decreed that moving forward the cultivators would be subject to the same laws as the military. These laws not only spelled out how insubordination would be punished but also regulated the farmers' movements and terms of service. "It must also be forbidden for cultivators to leave their plantations to reside on another, without legal permission." The preamble was even more severe and pedantic: "Since the revolution, male and female cultivators, who, because they were young at the time, had not yet engaged in farming, do not want to engage in it today, because, they say, they are free, and pass their days only in running about and wandering, becoming a very bad example to the other cultivators, whereas every day, in contrast, the generals, officers, noncommissioned officers, and soldiers are in permanent activity, to ensure the sacred rights of all." For Louverture, a lack of discipline in labor meant a lack of respect for the principles of liberty, as he explained in article 2: "All the managers, drivers, and cultivators who do not fulfill with diligence the duties that farming imposes on them will be arrested and punished with the same severity as the soldiers who deviate from theirs," after which "if he is a manager, he will be placed in one of the corps constituting the army of Saint-Domingue; if he is a driver, he will be fired from his job, relegated to a simple farmer to engage in farming, and will no longer be able to claim the job of driver; if he is a farmer or a cultivator, he will be punished with the same severity as a simple soldier."

Article 3 essentially outlawed idleness, a law that resurfaced under King Henry in 1812 with his famous *Code Henry*. Louverture's version stipulated, "All the male and female cultivators who remain idle . . . will be required to return immediately to their respective plantations." If they could not prove themselves "engaged in a useful enterprise, which provides for their existence (understand that the state of domesticity is not considered useful)," they would be "required to return to their plantations, under the personal responsibility of the people whom they serve." Many of these articles resembled the "engagement" system, which had led to the rebellion against Hédouville in Fort-Liberté. "Any individual, male or female, whosoever, who is not a cultivator, must prove immediately that he is engaged in a useful state that provides for his subsistence and that allows him to pay taxes to the republic," another article stated. Failure to do so would result in arrest, and if found guilty, the person would be either incorporated into the army or forced to farm: "This measure, which must be strictly enforced, will prevent vagrancy, since it will require everyone to usefully occupy themselves."[93]

In an attempt to simplify the colony's financial administration, Louverture abolished the rule requiring farmers to pay one-quarter of the revenue to the state, but also declared that anything exported from the colony required a payment of 20 percent. The system favored the proprietors, many of whom were white French colonists—former enslavers—while limiting the freedom and opportunities of the laborers, the previously enslaved.[94] King Henry's state-run newspaper, the *Royal Gazette,* later drew a damning conclusion about Louverture's system, calling it a "state close to that of the prejudices and slavery we suffered under the ignominious yoke of the French." "Under Toussaint," the paper continued, "everything tended to resemble the old order of things; financial and civil administration was entirely in the hands of the ex-colonists under regulations almost as harsh as those of the ancien régime; agriculture flourished; and the ex-colonists were masters of all their property."[95] There was someone who criticized Louverture's labor policies in the era too.

Louverture's nephew Moyse rebelled against his uncle, many said over these labor decrees, beginning the night of October 21, 1801. Although the various reports that poured in somewhat differ, Louverture came to believe that on that night Moyse hastened to the northern plain, where he incited the farmers to take up arms against white French property owners, the former colonists, whom Moyse considered the "fatal protégés of the Governor." Before Christophe could react, as the highest-ranking officer overseeing that area after Moyse, 317 people had already been killed. As the commandant of Cap, Brigadier General Christophe was nonetheless still technically under Division General Moyse in the military hierarchy. Yet Christophe reportedly did not share his superior officer's opinion of Louverture's laws. On the evening of the twenty-second, Christophe received word that a crowd of rowdy people with ill intentions had gathered. Christophe wasted no time reacting. He broke up the gathering and interrogated the participants about any possible conspiracy against the government and demanded to know the identities of its organizers. Christophe and his soldiers made more than thirty arrests that night, with one anonymous eyewitness recalling, "General Henry Christophe's vigor saved Cap from the disaster that threatened it."

In this same account, Moyse waited outside the city to ascertain the results of the disorder he had encouraged. Finding that his plot had not succeeded, Moyse fled to the Plaine du Nord, raising rebellions there and throughout northern Haiti. Upon learning that his superior, General Moyse, had engaged in outright massacres, Christophe set out to the north on October 24 to order the cultivators to return to their plantations, in accordance with Louverture's directives. Once in Port-Margot, Christophe ordered some executions of his own and instructed any captured rebels to shoot the leaders of the rebellion. By the twenty-fifth, Dessalines had arrived in Plaisance and allegedly killed all who had participated in the rebellion. Astonishingly, Moyse obeyed when Louverture ordered him to appear and answer for his conduct. Louverture said to his nephew, "Everything suggests that you are behind this revolt," the eyewitness reported. "You must justify yourself as a matter of honor," Louverture continued. He then ordered Moyse to return to Dondon, another of the towns in rebellion, and "arrest those who are guilty, but above all don't have them shot," Louverture warned. "Bring them back to me alive under secure guard." Moyse evidently obeyed the order and even agreed to quash the rebellion he allegedly started. "On the face of it, everything pointed to him as the organizer of this mayhem," the eyewitness judged. "It was therefore decided to arrest him and have him tried." Louverture had everyone connected to or suspected of having aided and abetted Moyse, to the tune of forty prisoners, executed that November.[96]

Yet it was Christophe who provided Louverture with the intelligence he needed to understand how the rebellion broke out and whose testimony in a roundabout way confirmed other reports Louverture had received alleging that Moyse had instigated the troubles. In fact, until Christophe wrote to Louverture on October 26, the governor-general did not have a clear timeline of the events that had led to the "disorders" in the north. It turns out that it all started in Cap under Christophe's watchful eyes. Writing from a plantation in Limbé, Christophe told Louverture that on the evening of October 21, the commander of the National Guard in Cap reported to him several "threats to public tranquility" taking place in the city. Christophe immediately mounted his horse, accompanied by his guards, and rode to the area known as the *carénage*, on the northern edge of the city, near the port, where Christophe had been told the gatherings continued. At first, he tried to disperse the assembled, but one of those present had a haughty attitude and seemed ill-inclined to follow the brigadier general's directives. Christophe, never one to suffer insubordination, swiftly charged at the man with his horse and pushed him against the wall, which caused the man to fall to the ground. Then, drawing his saber, as if to strike him, instead Christophe ordered his guards to arrest the man. Christophe had the captive taken to the arsenal, the building next door, and left the battalion chief Aurange in charge of him. Aurange subsequently put the man in prison to await further instructions, while Christophe returned to the *carénage* to disperse any ongoing gatherings.

Once he returned to the arsenal, Christophe learned that the man who he ordered arrested was called Trois Balles (Three Balls), known to be one of the city's "most daring troublemakers." After a lengthy interrogation Trois Balles revealed the whole plot, naming the other "conspirators" and specifically designating a man named Saintonge as the leader of the plotted uprising in Cap. Trois Balles also identified as leaders two additional men, Jean Baptiste Lebon and Bonhomme, both of the Bailly plantation just south of Cap in the parish of Marmelade.[97] This information provided Christophe with what he needed to stop the so-called rebellion. Christophe employed dozens of patrol officers and battalions at his disposal. They ultimately succeeded in arresting Lebon, Saintonge, and Bonhomme. Yet the troubles were hardly over.

Christophe had barely returned home when the sound of rifle shots surprised him. Speeding out the door once more, he mounted his horse and headed for the spot where he heard the gunfire. En route, Christophe encountered Louis Gabart, commander of the gendarmerie, who told him that he had been shot at and that a man had been killed. The "rebels" soon thereafter attacked Christophe, who, outmaneuvering them, forced them to abandon their weapons. Afterward the men fled to the mountains. At least one of them was bayoneted to death, however, while another received a slash wound to the face and was transported to the hospital. Brigadier General Christophe spent the next two days successfully restoring "order" to the city, which meant arresting or eliminating those identified as troublemakers. Just when he thought things might quiet down, he received reports of "uprisings" in neighboring Acul, Limbé, Port-Margot, Marmelade, Plaisance, and Dondon and that the "rebels" had cried out, "Death to all the whites!" Having now a clearer sense of the severity and potential cause of the situation, Christophe took several demi-brigades, squadrons, and other military detachments with him and set out for the city of Acul. Passing along the way the city of Limbé, where he wrote Louverture from Madame Fage's plantation, Christophe found the whole town in general rebellion. The commander of the city, Joseph Flaville, threw his hands up as he told Christophe that he had not been able to stop the people from engaging in insurrection. Christophe, though angry, ordered Commander Flaville to immediately quash the rebellion.

Christophe, for his part, did not have time to lose. Rushing over to Port-Margot, he found many cultivators in arms. Feigning to have more troops with him than he had, the brigadier general threatened the cultivators and ordered them to lay down their weapons. He also commanded them to reveal the name of the leader of their rebellion. Christophe told Louverture that all named were "immediately shot by the rebels themselves, who after this execution, surrendered their weapons and withdrew to their homes." With "order" having been restored to Port-Margot, Christophe returned to Limbé, only to find that yet another insurrection had broken out in his absence. This time, Commander Flaville refused to appear before him. Christophe therefore ordered Flaville's arrest and had him taken to Acul and from there on to Cap to be imprisoned.

Somewhat remarkably, given the generalized turmoil, during Christophe's absence from Cap, the situation in that city remained calm. And Christophe reported that Dessalines had succeeded in stopping rebellions in Louverture (formerly Ennery) and Marmelade, as well as other smaller cities. But Christophe finished his report to Louverture with a highly suggestive observation about the cause of the whole affair: "General Moïse [sic], who had been absent since October 17, reappeared [in Cap] on October 26, but stayed only two hours. His presence produced such terror that when a spontaneously gathered group announced his arrival, every door closed."[98]

All subsequent information Louverture received seemed to confirm the inference that Louverture read into Christophe's official account. Immediately after receiving this report, following Moyse's return to Cap on October 26, Louverture met with Dessalines and Christophe on the Héricourt plantation. Given the serious accusations contained in his report, Louverture ordered Christophe to return to Cap and watch over the city, and ostensibly, the movements of his nephew. Although Louverture seemed pained in the official report he wrote for the French government about this affair, he admitted that after receiving Christophe's account, he could no longer deny "the unanimous reports of military commanders, the cries of the rebels, the interrogations of those who had been arrested, all of whom agreed that General Moyse authored this conspiracy." Worse still, Louverture claimed to have learned that "this conspiracy" was hardly one led by cultivators in protest over Louverture's agricultural policies. Instead, he said, "hatched by the deepest perversity," the rebellion appeared to be aimed at the government and the white colonists living in the northern division. "The rebels have pointed out the author enough," Louverture reported. "The leaders tried to convince the people, in order to push them to commit these atrocities, that I had sold the blacks to the whites and that General Moyse alone had refused to sign this supposed contract, but that Generals Dessalines and Christophe had agreed to subscribe to it." "In Limbé, the authors of this infamy even had chains made so that, on the day of the revolt, they could be shown to the blacks as proof of our absurd plan to sell them," Louverture wrote. Louverture finished his report with his characteristic pathos tinged with bravado: "The wounds from this event are great, without a doubt; the recollection of it will never fade from my memory." "My heart is broken with grief," he continued, "but if the hand of God had not restrained the rage of the monsters who wanted to dishonor us, we would have much more to mourn still."[99] Louverture, despite his confession of grief, remained convinced that he had convicted the right man and labored to prove this to the colony's inhabitants as much as to the French government.

What Louverture did not confess, at least not in his printed accounts, was that he had received information indicating that "France had instigated the revolt of Moyse, and that the British Government had engaged to join with the republic in offensive measures against the country." Louverture reportedly told precisely this to the British agent W. L. Whitefield (or Whitfield) in a meeting that took place between the two men in December 1801, in the presence of Dessalines, shortly after news of the impending Peace of Amiens reached the island.[100]

General Moyse's death meant that the French state confiscated all the properties he either leased or bought. Moyse's affermage dossier is extensive and speaks not just to his high standing in the colony but to the highly lucrative nature of the colony's labor system, one that allowed him to purchase a second home in Cap-Français and to ostensibly acquire the 7 million livres in gold stores French officials allegedly found there after his arrest.[101] The French colonial government confiscated and sequestered Moyse's home in Cap, like all others owned or leased by the late general. The sequester documents reveal information about a woman named Poignon (sometimes spelled "Pognon"), who might have been one of Moyse's mysterious "wives." It explains that the property was occupied by "Pognon, negress, who obtained it from the ex-general Moyse, who had previously acquired it." Colonial officials determined the property eligible for sequester, "whether it belonged to the Negro Moyse, rightfully; or if it is the property of the named Pognon, who is among the rebels." General Leclerc later ordered the property transformed into the Bureau de Poste, which is the function it served at the time of the sequester.[102] In addition to revealing that Christophe helped Poignon acquire a mule from Moyse's plantations, the affermage documents also indicate that Christophe obtained guardianship over at least one of Moyse's children following the latter's death.[103] The two generals had worked together both in affermage and in the military, but Moyse's strife with his uncle put distinct strain on his previously close working relationship with Christophe.

Christophe could have had Moyse arrested when the latter returned to Cap, but as one Christophe chronicler has asked, would Christophe have had an excuse sufficient enough to explain why he arrested the governor-general's nephew without an order to do so?[104] Or maybe Christophe did not have Moyse arrested because of their personal relationship. After all the two were close enough for Moyse to entrust his child to Christophe, and so close were Christophe and Moyse that in July 1801 Louverture only learned of the death of one of his nephew's infant sons from Christophe.[105] No, the task of arresting Moyse was Louverture's alone. Louverture arrested his nephew on the Héricourt plantation. A commission later found Moyse guilty, and Louverture had him executed by fusillade in Port-de-Paix's Grand-Fort.[106]

Still, Christophe's positive opinion of his former superior persisted long after Moyse's death. As king, in his 1814 *Manifeste du roi* (King's manifesto), Christophe blamed Louverture for the "sacrifice" of his own nephew, who "had deviated from the orders [Louverture] gave for the protection of the colonists." Christophe also suggested that Moyse's execution was the principal cause for "the weak resistance experienced by the French" during the Leclerc expedition, which had ultimately proved the governor-general's downfall.[107]

Louverture clearly had enemies among the French colonists and the *hommes de couleur,* many of whom believed that Louverture favored the white French colonists. He also had enemies among the citizen-cultivators, or the formerly enslaved Africans, who largely supported General Moyse. After he ordered his ever-popular nephew's execution, Louverture's popularity further waned.

After Moyse's death, as commander of Cap, Christophe would have been present at the proclamation of November 25 where Louverture tried to justify his nephew's execution to the military. "Since the Revolution, I have done everything in my power to bring back happiness to my country and ensure the freedom of my fellow citizens," Toussaint said. "I have always and energetically urged upon all our soldiers subordination, discipline, and obedience, without which there can be no army." For years, Louverture said, he had likewise compelled Moyse to observe these obligations: "These are the principles and feelings that I put into a thousand of my letters. At every opportunity, I sought to explain to him the holy maxims of our faith. However, instead of listening to the advice of a father, and obeying the orders of a leader devoted to the well-being of the colony, he only wanted to be ruled by his passions and follow his fatal inclinations." For this, the governor-general averred, "he has met with a wretched end." "The cruel experience that I have just had will not be useless for me," Louverture concluded, "and after the misconduct of General Moyse, no one will be named division general until further orders from the French government." Dessalines, the only division general at this moment, remained the head of the western department.[108]

Louverture had managed to eliminate every rival who had challenged his authority. In the wake of the death of Moyse, who Roume once said possessed fully enough power with the cultivators in the north to raise the colony against Louverture, the question on everyone's mind must have been, who's next? After all, before Sonthonax, Hédouville, Rigaud, Roume, and Moyse, there had been Laveaux, whom Rigaud credited with providing Toussaint with the moniker Louverture.[109]

Now there was Bonaparte and, in the most unexpected of ways, Christophe.

With Bonaparte's ascent to first consul of France in 1799, Louverture had to confront a new enemy, one who refused to meet him face-to-face and who intended to exploit the existing fissures and cracks in the colony. It is clear that Christophe became a key element of the French plot to neutralize if not altogether eliminate Louverture. What is less clear is if he understood his role in the plot.

Perhaps it was having watched Louverture defeat so many of his previous allies or maybe it was Christophe's lifelong instinct of self-preservation and self-defense that caused him to give up on Louverture. Alternatively, it is possible Christophe envisioned seizing power with Louverture gone. More likely, given the way events unfolded and how the French spoke of the plan to arrest Louverture and all the Black generals, Christophe really could not see through French treachery. No matter, the effect was the same. Christophe's actions helped bring the governor-general to his knees.

Yet it must be acknowledged that some Christophe associates reported the brigadier general's changing opinion of Louverture long before Bonaparte ordered his brother-in-law Leclerc to the island. Roume claimed that during his imprisonment at the home of General Vilton, who considered Christophe a "dear friend" and was godfather to one of Christophe's daughters, Vilton told Roume that "Christophe was ashamed of having been duped by Toussaint for so long and of having blindly obeyed him." Vilton believed that in the months before the Leclerc expedition, Christophe had finally "opened his eyes" to the truth about the man Roume called the "supposed governor" of the island. Roume continued to believe the governor-general, "that political Tartuff [*sic*],"[110] wanted independence, and said that according to Vilton, Christophe soon came to the same conclusion. Stunningly, Roume said that in hindsight he should have "destituted" Louverture at the time of his treaty with General Maitland and replaced him as commander in chief with "Chef de Brigade Christophe, idol of this army." Such a move, Roume believed, would have immediately ended the War of the South. "I would have ordered Christophe to force Rigaud, Laplume, Dessalines, and Moyse to cease the hostilities that had only just begun." "Christophe was very aware how advantageous this arrangement would have been to him, but he was so sure of the purity of Louverture's intentions that he even persuaded me of it," Roume admitted. This newfound confidence in Christophe would have surprised Louverture. Louverture had been intimately privy to the French agent's endless complaints about the commander of Cap only the year before. Roume claimed further still that Christophe had major complaints of his own against Louverture. "Not only did Christophe tell me that the general in chief would have to be an atrocious villain, but he would also have to be stupid or insane, if he wanted to betray France and to bind himself with England and make the colony independent." Roume's duplicity shines through: earlier he accused Christophe of having tried to have him deported to France so that he could push the colony into deeper political and commercial relations with England and the United States. Now Roume threw this same charge against Louverture. The best way to defame an enemy in colonial Saint-Domingue remained to accuse them by turns of colluding with England to make the colony independent or of plotting with the French colonists to bring back slavery.

Roume's sudden, and suspicious, clairvoyance about Christophe's leadership skills was only encouraged by the intriguing conversation he claimed to have had with Vilton. "Commander Vilton further told me," Roume continued, "that Christophe only accepted Toussaint's *brevet* of brigadier general so as not to be shot on the suspicion that a refusal would have aroused." Roume also agreed that the salvation of Cap in the face of Moyse's rebellion—which he now charged Louverture with having orchestrated—was due entirely to Christophe's conduct. Roume believed that Louverture was the true author of this "crime." He also insisted that Louverture had not yet had Christophe executed only because Louverture knew of Christophe's popularity with the cultivators, the Black military officers, and many French soldiers alike, in addition to the white proprietors whom Roume claimed Christophe supported in affermage in his position as inspector. Roume believed that Christophe's influence with the latter stood as the principal reason that Louverture knew he could not yet eliminate the commander of Cap, whom he promoted to brigadier general but refused to give any new responsibilities, such as division general over the north in the wake of Moyse's death. Perhaps to cover up his contradictory statements about Christophe, Roume claimed that during his imprisonment he had been passing clandestine letters to both Christophe and Vilton through the British consul Edward Stevens to prepare for a French expedition's arrival, in the hopes of finally getting rid of Louverture.[111]

Roume's sudden confidence in Christophe was more surprising than the longtime Christophe supporter Vincent's. Just before the Leclerc expedition set sail, Vincent wrote a series of reports advising the French government how Leclerc and Rochambeau could best rid the colony of the Black freedom fighters, city by city, morne by morne. Noting that Moyse controlled the northwestern mountain range called La Mine and Dessalines had control of the Montagne Noire in central Saint-Domingue, Vincent averred, "that is the spot in fact, where the blacks have established their hopes of resistance and their blue mountain project," a reference to the Blue Mountain maroons of Jamaica. Counseling that "Rochambeau, can more than anyone else, annihilate this project," Vincent asserted that Christophe, "an excellent man," in contrast, had made it known that "we can count greatly on him."[112]

On November 20, 1801, Vincent wrote directly to Leclerc, who already had orders to go to Saint-Domingue, to say that Christophe was the most important general to win to the French side and turn against Louverture. Revealing that the French government planned to use Louverture's sons against him, Vincent counseled that the children's teacher, the abbé Jean-Baptiste Coisnon, would be instrumental to the plot of ascertaining which Black generals might be open to the consulate's goal of ridding the colony of Louverture. [113] "It will only take a little time for Citizen Coesnon [sic] to know whom he can count on; he will probably be unhappy with General Moyse," Vincent wrote, unaware that the general had already been put to death. "He will only gain an interview with the general in chief with great difficulty, but I hope he will be able to meet General Christophe, who will seem unremarkable in Moyse's presence, but to whom he can speak with confidence." If the French could not "contain Generals Toussaint and Moyse," then at least they could "count on" Christophe and Granier, along with some other officials and "all the whites" to "save Cap." Vincent advised Coisnon first to "try all means of conciliation," but if that failed, he should attempt to "divide the leaders; he could even powerfully join these two means together by announcing only to Christophe how high public opinion and the esteem of the government are of him, and to hope for it to always see him as a good Frenchman." The French republican project of sowing division in Saint-Domingue/Haiti, as these missives clearly show, was of long duration and immediate consequence.

Vincent concluded, "If the primary black leaders can be disunited, they will rather be submissive, that is obvious."[114]

Sadly, the French government fulfilled its divide-and-conquer strategy all too well. Our future king's journey will bring us next to the events that led to Christophe's defection from Louverture's army, and ultimately to the governor-general's arrest, deportation, and death in a cold prison in the Jura Mountains of France. Although the French designated Christophe "the Arsonist of Cap," after he ordered the city burned to the ground upon the Leclerc expedition's arrival in February 1802, one high-ranking officer said he was not at all surprised when Christophe defected to the French side only two months later.

General Dessalines viewed such an about-face as not at all out of character, implying that something similar had happened in the War of the South when Rigaud, he said, had almost persuaded Christophe to fight on his side. "My dear governor, I have just received your letter dated the twelfth of this month, where you express to me the embarrassing position you are in due to the betrayal of General Christophe surrendering to the enemy," Dessalines wrote on May 5, 1802. "What did you expect, my dear governor, this is what we have been expecting from the cowards for a long time. You know Christophe, and he was incapable of resisting with us and continuing to wage war." Dessalines finished by averring, "Remember that when you let Christophe correspond with Rigaud, he dragged him into his party. The same ill [consequence] occurred this time by letting him correspond with General Leclerc. As for me, it is repugnant to my heart to enter into any conference with the enemy, so long as you are here; for that right belongs to you alone."[115] Despite this declaration, within a few days of having written this letter, Dessalines also surrendered to the French, joining Louverture who had already done so. While Dessalines labored to paint Christophe as the ultimate traitor, Christophe's betrayal paled in comparison to the one Dessalines committed just a month later. If Christophe were responsible for the defection of much of Louverture's forces, Dessalines—whose wedding celebration in Saint-Marc Louverture attended on the eve of Moyse's "rebellion"[116]—played an even more distinct role in the eventual arrest of the former governor-general of Saint-Domingue.

6

LOVE, LOSS, AND BETRAYAL
UNDER UNCERTAIN SKIES

By his thirty-fifth birthday, Christophe's life had been transformed to an extent he probably could never have preconceived. From an enslaved child he had grown into an embattled hero of not one but two New World revolutions. Now he is about to make two tragic mistakes. The first, seemingly the result of professional ambition, led him to turn away from his friend and commander, the famous revolutionary general Toussaint Louverture. The second, no doubt an impulse of unbridled fatherly love, occasioned the sad and lonely death of Christophe and Marie-Louise's firstborn son, Ferdinand. Henry was only twelve years old when he participated in the American War of Independence. Ferdinand will have barely reached the age of eight when his father sends him to France to be educated in the middle of Haiti's violent struggle to be free. The child will have just attained his eleventh birthday when the world's greatest war for Black humanity triumphed. But the fortunes of freedom wrought by the armée indigène were not to redound to young Ferdinand. His future resided only in relegation to the streets of Paris, where the neglect of the French government, not unlike in the case of Toussaint Louverture, occasioned a terrible and singular death in July 1805. It would be easy to paint the father's maneuvers resulting in these outcomes as by turns perfidy or folly, but as these momentous revolutionary events unfolded, Christophe had no idea of the colossal consequence of yoking his fate to the whims and vicissitudes of the treacherous and duplicitous slavery-striving Napoléon Bonaparte. Only later, when the blood of Haiti's thirteen-year struggle for freedom was set to cool, could Christophe look back and see that the two mistakes—turning away from Louverture and sending his son to France—were perhaps only one. Toussaint's death merely foreshadowed Ferdinand's. And Christophe's profound lack of foresight—coupled with an equally deep unawareness of the potential significance of his actions—meant that it would be a long time before the future king could begin to fathom this new destiny.

On the morning of April 7, 1803, a guard found Toussaint Louverture dead in the Fort de Joux prison in France, where the French had held him captive for nearly eight months. This death was hardly an accident. In the final weeks and days of his life, Louverture's French jailers denied him medical care for his fevers, stomachaches, and cough, and they neglected to provide wood to burn for his freezing cell. That January, in fact, Louverture's guard, Chef de Bataillon F. Amiot, had written to Denis Decrès, the French minister of the marine, to inform him of the increasing gravity of Louverture's condition: the captive suffered from constant fevers, severe stomachaches, loss of appetite, vomiting, and whole-body inflammation. Although Amiot's predecessor—Commander Louis Philibert Baille de Beauregard—reported similar medical problems to French officials in the fall of 1802, no doctor visited Louverture during his incarceration in the Fort de Joux. Baille justified this by saying "the prisoner" was likely faking his symptoms, more proof of "that destroyer of humankind's" "aggregate[d] monstrosity."[1]

Only after Amiot found Louverture's cold and lifeless body—his head resting upon the woodless chimney in his cell, as if he were in gentle slumber rather than in rigor mortis—did a surgeon named Gresset and the medical doctor Tavernier arrive to assess Louverture's condition. The case must have been immediately obvious. The official autopsy described Louverture's mouth as filled with blood.[2]

Seven months before his death, in September 1802, Louverture, assisted by his domestic, Mars Plaisir, also imprisoned, had given a written memoir to General Marie-François Auguste de Caffarelli, whom Bonaparte sent to interrogate him. In the memoir, Louverture defended his conduct as a French general and complained about the treatment he received despite his title and rank. Louverture said everything that had led up to and befallen him since his arrest in June 1802 was due to the color of his skin. "Without a doubt I owe this treatment to my color," Toussaint wrote, "but my color, my color, has it ever prevented me from serving my country with diligence and devotion?":

Arbitrarily arrested without anyone explaining or telling me why, all of my assets seized, my entire family ravished, my papers confiscated and kept from me, shipped out and sent over here, nude like an earthworm, with the most atrocious of calumnies having been spread about me. . . . All because I am black.[3]

Baille confirmed in a letter to Decrès that he denied medical care to Louverture because of the color of his skin: "The composition of negroes being nothing at all resembling that of Europeans, I am ill-inclined to provide him with a doctor or a surgeon, which would be useless in his case."[4] The meticulous records kept by the French government suggest that Amiot, for his part, was dangerously obtuse, at best, or criminally disingenuous, at worst. When questioned about how Louverture's condition became fatal under his later surveillance, Amiot claimed that Louverture "never asked for any doctors."[5]

There are painfully relevant lessons in the story of Louverture's death about the disproportionate and wrongful incarceration of Black men, the relationship between denial of care and prison neglect and the deadliness of racism. But to understand how the murder of the once exalted and celebrated Toussaint Louverture would subsequently have an enormous impact on the trajectory of the Haitian Revolution, and more specifically on Christophe's role within it, it is necessary to understand who Louverture was as a father, friend, and French general.

Some say Louverture was born in May 1743 on the Bréda plantation in Haut-du-Cap in Saint-Domingue.[6] Others say Louverture was born in the colony in 1746. According to Louverture's son Isaac, a key source of information, his father had been the grandson of an Allada prince named Gaou-Guinou.[7] Although Toussaint, called Toussaint Bréda at the time, was previously enslaved, by 1776 he had free status and worked for Louis Pantaléon de Noé, a white Creole. Close to the end of the decade Toussaint partnered with an enslaved woman named Suzanne Simon Baptiste, who had had at least one child, Placide, from a previous relationship with a free man of color.[8] Louverture and Suzanne went on to have two children together, Isaac and Saint-Jean, the latter of whom was born in 1791, the year the revolution formally began.

Like many important free men of color, in 1796 Louverture sent his two older sons, Placide and Isaac, to Paris to receive a French education.[9] While Isaac insisted that the Black children were treated like quasi-royalty at the Collège de la Marche in France, Napoléon's first wife, Joséphine de Beauharnais (née Tascher de La Pagerie), a white Creole from Martinique, confessed that the French government viewed these children as hostages. In her posthumously published memoirs, Joséphine wrote that she had urged her husband not to send an expedition to Saint-Domingue since such a decision, she said, would be a "fatal move" that "would forever take this beautiful colony away from France." She counseled Bonaparte to instead "keep Toussaint Louverture there. That is the man required to govern the blacks." She subsequently asked her husband, "What complaints could you have against this leader of the blacks? He has always maintained a correspondence with you. He has done even more: he has given you, in some sense, his children for hostages."[10] Though he later claimed he regretted this decision, Bonaparte did not heed his wife's warnings. Instead, he directed his brother-in-law, General Charles Victor Emmanuel Leclerc, to head to Saint-Domingue to crush Louverture.

Recall that in February 1801, Louverture called forth an assembly to create a constitution for Saint-Domingue. Completed in May, the constitution was formally signed by Louverture two months later and sent to Bonaparte.[11] Although the constitution declared that the inhabitants of Saint-Domingue were henceforth "free and French," Bonaparte interpreted the constitution's nomination of Louverture as "governor-general for life" as a declaration of war. In his own memoirs, written during his second exile on the island of Saint-Helena, Napoléon explained this constitution as the final impetus for the expedition: "Toussaint knew very well that in proclaiming his constitution, he had thrown away his mask and had drawn his sword out of its sheath forever."[12] In the moment, however, it seemed that Bonaparte simply seized the opportunity he long awaited: to restore slavery.

On November 19, 1801, Bonaparte wrote to Leclerc, whom he had already given official orders to lead the expedition, and whom he addressed with the title of "commander in chief of the expeditionary corps of Saint-Domingue." Clearly influenced by Vincent, Bonaparte said he had recently learned of "a great opposition brewing in Saint-Domingue against Toussaint." "At the head appears to be General Christophe," Bonaparte continued. "It is believed that it was as a result of this opposition that Toussaint suspended the implementation of the constitution until the response of the metropole." Bonaparte went on to say that as a result of the putative conflict between Louverture and Christophe any obstacles Leclerc might encounter were likely to be "far less ardent" than he previously believed. Encouraging his brother-in-law to not delay his departure for any reason, Bonaparte finished by reminding him to provide periodic news about his sister Pauline Bonaparte, Leclerc's wife. "I like to think that she will also share a little of the glory of your expedition," the first consul added.[13]

Louverture was in Santo Domingo, on the eastern side of the island, ceded to France by Spain in 1795, when Leclerc arrived off the coast of Cap at the start of February 1802 with around thirty thousand French troops. Having been appointed brigadier general in the French army, Christophe, as commander over the city, and contrary to Bonaparte's supposition, adhered to Louverture's standing order to not allow any military fleets to dock without prior approval. Christophe therefore denied entry to Bonaparte's forces. Leclerc responded with disbelief and fury. "I have learned with indignation, Citizen General," Leclerc wrote to Christophe on February 3, 1802, "that you are refusing to receive the French squadron and the army I command, under the pretext that you have not received an order to do so from the general government." Leclerc then threatened to send fifteen thousand men the next day at daybreak to Fort Picolet and Fort Bélair, with another four thousand to be sent to Fort-Liberté, and yet another eight thousand to go to Port-Républicain. Leclerc made sure to note that these were "forces capable of subduing rebels, should we find any there."[14]

Christophe took on a similarly menacing tone in his response. "General," he said, "I have the honor of informing you that I cannot deliver these forts and posts, over which I have been given command, before having received an order from Governor-General Toussaint-Louverture, from whom I derive my authority." Christophe did send his aide-de-camp to tell Louverture about Leclerc's arrival, but in the meantime Christophe issued his own warning: "You say that the French government has sent forces to Saint-Domingue that are capable of subduing the rebels, if any are to be found here, but it is you who come to create them among a people who are peaceful subjects of France, and the hostile intentions that you have just shown have provided us with reasons to fight you." "If you realize these threats," Christophe continued, "I will resist as an officer general must; and . . . please understand that you will only enter the city of Cap after having watched it be reduced to ashes. And even upon these ashes, I will fight you." Christophe ended his missive with a punishing metaphor: "As for the troops who you claim are disembarking at this very moment, I can only consider them a house of cards that the slightest wind will topple."[15]

Behind the scenes, Christophe entered a different battle. Administrators in Cap urged him to let the fleet land. These municipal authorities later reported to the French minister of the marine that Christophe said he denied entry to the troops because Louverture had not authorized him to allow in more than two or three ships at a time and he had been "forbidden to allow any more." Some members of the French National Guard did not agree with Christophe's decision and submitted a formal petition to him at his home at midnight on February 3. Attempting to convince him that he did not have the power to refuse to "obey the Mother Country," they tried to "move his soul by offering a harrowing picture of the misfortunes of which Cap was to become the theater if he persisted in his refusal." Citing irregularities about the way Leclerc and his fleet of soldiers behaved since their arrival and casting doubt on Leclerc's authority as "captain general," Christophe remained unmoved. He reportedly repeated to the guards that if Leclerc persisted, "the earth will burn before the fleet has time to dock in the port." The next day, the mayor of Cap and other citizens, growing desperate in the face of Christophe's obstinance, brought in several of Christophe's friends whom they asked to persuade him to stand down. Instead, Christophe and his associates came up with a plan to request a forty-eight-hour delay from Leclerc, which they argued would give Christophe time to seek authorization from Louverture. Among those sent on board Leclerc's ship the *Océan* for this mission were Father Corneille Brelle (né Corneille de Douai), previously a priest in Cap and later apostolic prefect and then archbishop under King Henry;[16] Tobias Lear, consul from the United States; and Christophe's friend and business partner in affermage, the unfortunate Granier, whom the French arrested, as we earlier saw, therefore preventing him from returning with the deputation that gave Christophe the news that Leclerc planned to imminently enter the port.

Before Leclerc landed, administrators tried once more to convince the commander of Cap, even parading women, children, and old men before Christophe on the Champ de Mars. A prodigious crowd showed up to "represent to him the extent of the evil of which they were to become victims," if he continued to refuse. Christophe did not intend to yield. The administrators reported, "We then saw that all was lost, and that the threats he had made were soon to come true." Only strong winds prevented Leclerc's ships from gaining port half an hour after Christophe's deputies returned from the *Océan*.

While the French flotilla waited for favorable winds, Christophe prepared for war. Repeating famous words from one of Louverture's proclamations, he told his soldiers to get ready to "vanquish or die." He evacuated the city of women and children, distributed firebrands to his troops standing guard at multiple posts, and ordered his men to set fire to Cap at the first sound of the cannons. The next day, however, the winds increased, and Christophe initially told the troops to stand down. When a French ship was spied gaining the coastline anyway, Christophe gave the fatal signal, and his beloved city was set aflame once more. By eleven o'clock on the night of February 4 all Cap-Français seemingly blazed with fire. Residents fled in every direction. The cries and groans of women and children reportedly floated like embers through the air.[17]

In a letter to Leclerc, written ten days later, Louverture defended Christophe's actions and suggested that the brigadier general had only followed his orders. In the February 14 missive written from the city of Verrettes, Louverture first acknowledged having received a letter from Leclerc in the interim by way of his children Isaac and Placide. Louverture then brought up the arrival of French troops. "I have been informed by the account given to me by General Christophe, and by the letter you wrote to him, of which he sent me a copy, and by what I saw with my own eyes, and by the little common sense I have of the way things happened at the arrival of your squadron, and of the means it used to enter Cap." Louverture then explained why he gave Christophe and the other generals a standing order to refuse entry to large military squadrons:

I must observe that at all times when a squadron appears, it is customary to send an *aviso* [dispatch boat] ahead to warn of its arrival; this is what was not done. Second, as the news coming from abroad spoke of peace [with England], but since no notice of it had reached me from the French government, I thought then that it was our enemies who could be spreading these rumors with the intention of coming to attack us. Consequently, I ordered all the generals and commanders of districts under my orders to take their precautions and to make sure that if there were any vessels of war, if they were French, and in this case, if it was a vessel or two with or without troops, to admit them, but that if there was a squadron, they had to give me an account of it before allowing entrance to the port.

"You will agree, Citizen General, that if General Christophe refused entry into the port to your squadron, it was not his fault, he was only executing the orders he received, and you will agree that per military order and hierarchy, superior chiefs should not address subordinates but the chief who commands, because that kind of inversion of military discipline can cause insubordination, from which result endless misfortunes," Louverture concluded.[18]

Louverture later denied that his standing order would have authorized Christophe to burn the city. Indeed, Isaac later said his father first learned of the fire when he saw from a distance an orange-red sky filled with clouds of smoke. In Isaac Louverture's retelling, "The flames of the fire were glimpsed almost at the same time by the French fleet and by Toussaint-Louverture, who was arriving from Santo-Domingo from the heights of Grand-Boucan."[19] In the memoirs he gave to Caffarelli to defend his conduct, Louverture also insisted that he first spied smoke off in the distance on his way back from Santo Domingo. Riding his horse at full speed, Louverture said he tried to enter the city, but colonists fleeing the destruction obstructed his route. Obligated to turn around, Louverture soon ran into General Christophe and questioned him immediately. Louverture asked him who gave "orders to set fire to the city." Christophe replied that "he took it upon himself to do so." "I very vigorously rebuked him for having resorted to such dire means. Why did you not instead use the troops to defend the city until my arrival?" Louverture asked. "What do you want from me, General?" Christophe reportedly replied. "My duty, necessity, the circumstances, the constantly reiterated threats from the commander of the squadron, forced me into it." Christophe then stoked Louverture's suspicions about the goal of Leclerc's expedition. Christophe noted that if Leclerc really had peaceful intentions, he would have awaited Louverture's arrival, he would not have killed half the garrison guarding Fort-Liberté or caused the city of Acul to fall; in Christophe's words, "he would never have engaged in the kinds of hostilities of which he is guilty."[20]

Caffarelli did not believe a word of Louverture's account. When he returned to the prison, he handed the pages of the memoir back to Louverture, telling him coldly, "I have read nothing of interest here." However, in the report he submitted to the French government, Caffarelli claimed Louverture admitted to issuing the order for Christophe to burn down Cap. According to Caffarelli, Louverture said, "Everything I did, I did for the good of the Colony, for the freedom of those of my color. If Leclerc had not announced his arrival in Cap by way of shooting cannons, all these ills would have been prevented. Henri Christophe, in burning down Cap, as a response to Leclerc's threat to force entry into that city, obeyed the orders that I had given to him,—it was the same with General Maurepas in Port-de-Paix,—Dessalines in Saint-Marc. I was exasperated by his imprudent and impolitic attacks. I felt obliged to defend myself."[21]

Whether or not Caffarelli's account is to be believed, in his February 14 letter to Leclerc, Louverture insisted that more blame rested with Leclerc than with Christophe. "I believe I have earned the title of the peacemaker of Saint-Domingue, since I brought peace, abundance, happiness, and prosperity to an island that was torn by internal factions and whose external enemies were fighting over its tatters," he wrote. "On your arrival the greatest of order had been established; farming had made astonishing progress." "My conscience is pure, and I do not have the slightest reproach to make of myself, if the haste with which you wanted to enter Cap caused the devastation of this city and its surroundings," Louverture concluded. "I have never been foolish enough to think of fighting against France, the colony does not need to be conquered by its own arms, since we are and have never ceased to be French."[22]

According to Boisrond-Tonnerre, writing in 1804, Louverture did give secret directives to his generals to oppose the disembarkation of any military squadrons *and* to set fire to the cities, in case it was not possible to resist them.[23] In one eyewitness account of the landing of the Leclerc expedition furnished to the governor of Jamaica, George Nugent, dated February 13, 1802, from Cuba, the anonymous writer, who had since fled the colony, disclosed that Christophe sent a missive to Leclerc averring that he did not have permission, "under the orders of the governor," to allow any military fleets to enter the port. Acknowledging that Christophe sent a letter right away to inform Louverture of the French squadron's arrival, the witness continued, "The impatient French landed troops, under General Defourneaux, at Limbé, and Caracol, who marched to attack Cap by land, while the ships attacked by sea." The writer went on to presume that Christophe only burned the city after Louverture arrived at the Héricourt plantation to give the "signal to set fire to the city," believing that it was "impossible to resist the maneuvers of the French."[24] In his letter of April 10, 1802, to his friend Commander Vilton, Christophe seemed to confirm that he burned the city in concert with what he understood as Louverture's order. Whether the order directly, rather than indirectly, related to the arrival of French troops or if it was a standing order against any military squadrons, Christophe did not say. Christophe merely claimed that by ordering Cap set ablaze, he had followed a command of Louverture's that could "only have been lifted by him."[25] The eyewitness who wrote to Governor Nugent further reported that on February 9, a week after the fire in Cap, General Dessalines set fire to the city of Saint-Marc, on the direct orders of Louverture, before fleeing to Gonaïves. Yet in this case, the putative eyewitness claimed to have seen the directive with his own eyes, insisting that "General Toussaint's order was to burn everything as soon as the French appear." General Pierre Agé, as narrated in the same account, likewise followed in Christophe's footsteps by denying Leclerc's troops entry into Port-Républicain, saying that he did not have permission from Louverture to allow them to land.[26]

Whatever the actual orders from Louverture were, or were not, the boldness of being the first to set fire to any of the colony's cities, and the fact that higher-ranking generals followed his lead, suggest that Christophe was at that point nearly as powerful a player in the war for the island's freedom as Louverture himself.

—

The French punished both Louverture and Christophe for the fires, but it was Louverture who paid most immediately for Christophe's opposition to Leclerc, both personally and politically. Louverture said that when he returned to his plantation in Ennery to greet his newly returned children, he found another letter from Leclerc dated February 17, as well as a proclamation signed by the French commander that made both him and Christophe "outlaws."[27] "Every citizen is ordered to treat them as follows: rebels of the French republic," the declaration read.[28] Louverture remained obstinate in the face of the charge that he was no longer a general but a "rebel." He immediately wrote to Bonaparte, "I refute [Leclerc's] proclamation, and I declare him to be an outlaw."[29] Louverture also took this opportunity to complain to the first consul that Leclerc treated him dishonorably, "because I am black," and he demanded that Bonaparte send another commander to the colony to replace Leclerc. Otherwise, he wrote, "I will aid General Leclerc in occasioning the greatest of evils to befall the colony by way of the resistance that I will use in opposing him."[30]

On February 24, Louverture sent Christophe a copy of his proclamation making Leclerc an outlaw. Christophe subsequently circulated copies in all the military camps, in concert with Louverture's orders.[31] Leclerc circulated his proclamation, too, not only in the colony but across the Atlantic in France and for a time seemed to gain the upper hand in the information war.

By late spring, the republic's official newspaper, *Le moniteur universel*, had printed articles describing both Louverture and Christophe as "outlaws." One declared that "the cruelty and barbarity of Toussaint are without example"; another claimed that Louverture intended to slaughter the entire white population of the colony's major cities.[32] Other French newspapers joined the fray. One referred to the recent burning of Cap as evidence of the many "furies" delivered up by the "ferocious Christophe," whom the paper also described as hell-bent on assassinating every white Frenchman.[33]

Negative media attention, it turns out, did not pose the greatest threat to Louverture and Christophe's security. Leclerc had also conceived a plot to use Louverture's children as pawns, a situation with which Christophe unfortunately became familiar only a short time later. When Louverture rebuked Leclerc's letter—the one that gave him only four days to surrender[34]—Leclerc directed Coisnon, the children's teacher, to take Isaac and Placide to the Louverture plantation in Ennery to pressure their father. Louverture observed that while the letter his children brought from Bonaparte ordered him to submit to Leclerc's authority, still averring that the French battalion had come "in peace," all Leclerc's actions since his arrival "amounted to war." Louverture told Coisnon, "In the midst of such violence and destruction, I must not forget that I am carrying a sword. . . . As such, if, as you have said, General Leclerc sincerely desires peace, let him stop the advance of his troops."[35]

However, in the time between their arrival in France and their return with Coisnon, the situation with Louverture's sons had become unknowably treacherous. Having been invited to dine at the home of the Bonapartes just before their departure from France, Isaac remained dazzled by the royal treatment both boys experienced in Parisian society, especially from Joséphine. In Leclerc's presence, Bonaparte told Isaac that his father was "a great man, he has rendered eminent services to France," insisting that Bonaparte promised him "glory and honor." "Do not believe for a moment that France intends to bring war to Saint-Domingue," Bonaparte told the teenager. "The army that we are sending there is intended not to fight the country's troops but to increase their forces." Bonaparte then introduced Leclerc as his "brother-in-law, whom I am appointing captain general and who will command this army."[36]

Bonaparte's reassuring words initially compelled Isaac to try to persuade his father to submit to Leclerc's authority. But almost all the revolution's first historians—most of whom participated in the revolution—considered Bonaparte's words coercion and manipulation. Vastey concluded of this, "The French tried to use the general's children as instruments to separate the father from the cause of his countrymen." The French had sought to pit "national love . . . against paternal love," Vastey opined. "This unfortunate father was placed by the barbaric French in the cruel position of having to choose between the salvation of his brothers and his country, on the one hand, and the life of his own children, on the other," Vastey said.[37] A French historian and former military officer who served under Leclerc described Louverture as having fully understood the ultimatum. Louverture reportedly told "his children that he left them free to choose between their country and their father; that he did not blame them for their attachment to France, which was responsible for their education." However, "there were the men of his color, whose future he could not compromise by placing them at the mercy" of an expedition comprised of "all of his personal enemies." France "puts more confidence in its weapons than in rights," Louverture said, and "if [the French] did not know how to coexist with the blacks while [the blacks] still had some power, what would it be like when he and his men did not any longer have any?" Hearing these words, both Isaac and Placide threw themselves into their father's arms, but they reportedly found his countenance cold. All he could say to them was, "My children, pick your side, whichever it is, I will always cherish you." Isaac offered only a tepid and ambiguous reaction to his father's decision. Twenty-two-year-old Placide, in contrast, was decisive. "I am yours, my father," he said, sobbing. "I fear the future, I fear slavery; I am ready to fight alongside you to oppose it; I no longer know France."[38]

Despite having to choose between the safety of his children and the righteousness of the revolution—and having effectively forced his sons to do so as well—Louverture quickly saw things unravel. No stranger to betrayal—having fought and defeated his fellow general André Rigaud over control of the southern part of the colony and having had his own nephew General Moyse executed as a traitor in November 1801—Louverture considered the loss of one of his greatest allies in Christophe particularly shocking.

Most accounts of the Haitian Revolution, past and present, skip over the intricate exchanges among Christophe, Leclerc, and several of the latter's key military officers. However, this correspondence, which Christophe ordered to be published in 1810 and again in 1814, is key to understanding the future king's seeming betrayal of General Louverture and how he defended himself against that charge.[39] Chanlatte, a key eyewitness and veteran of the revolution, published the entirety of Christophe's correspondence with French officials immediately preceding and then following the fire in his 1810 pamphlet *The Cry of Nature*. To contextualize Christophe's defection to the French, Chanlatte first insisted that Christophe had no knowledge of Leclerc's or Bonaparte's intention to reinstate slavery. Chanlatte wrote in fact that at the outset of his negotiations with the French, Christophe "positively declared that before putting down his weapons, he needed the sweet certitude that the liberty for which he had so ardently fought would be preserved intact."[40]

The letters clearly show that before he agreed to rejoin the French army, Christophe sought confirmation that the French government did not intend to reinstate slavery. Leclerc earlier attempted to provide such reassurance, by circulating a proclamation in both French and Creole from the consuls of France to the inhabitants of Saint-Domingue, which stated that "the blacks were assured of the liberty they had fought for." It also stated that Leclerc had come to "protect with his great forces" everyone in the colony "from the enemy," "regardless of your origins and your color." "If anyone tells you these forces have come to take your liberty," the proclamation read, "tell them that France gave us our liberty." "Whoever dares to separate themselves from the captain general will be a traitor to the country, and the fury of the republic will devour him like fire devours dried sugarcane."[41] France's putative assurances of Black liberty were always laden with threats of white violence. Perhaps this is what initially led Christophe and Louverture to mistrust Leclerc. They wanted proof from the French government in the form of an official decree signed by the consuls of France and ratified by its legislative body and National Assembly. Leclerc's actions up to that point, as Christophe repeatedly noted, did not bring portents of peace, but only more proof of war.

Leclerc's February 17, 1802, proclamation declaring Louverture and Christophe outlaws had been posted throughout the colony in both French and Creole too. Filled with disingenuous self-defense and clearly duplicitous statements, Leclerc's proclamation stated, "I have come here, on behalf of the French government, to bring you peace and happiness. I feared I would encounter obstacles by way of the ambitious leaders of the colony: I was not mistaken." "General Toussaint Louverture sent his children back to me with a letter in which he assured me that he desired nothing more than the happiness of the colony and that he was ready to obey the orders that I had given to him," Leclerc said. However, Leclerc charged that Louverture continued to oppose and deny his authority, so now Leclerc would "teach that rebel all there is to know about the strength of the French government." He declared, "From this moment forward, [Louverture] can only be seen in the eyes of every good Frenchman who lives in Saint-Domingue as an insensible monster."[42] Yet following advice he received from Colonel Vincent, a quite fairweather ally, Leclerc looked for an opportunity to turn Louverture's most important generals against him. Vincent had also singled out Dessalines or Moyse, but Leclerc went for Christophe.[43]

After declaring him an "outlaw," Leclerc repeatedly pressed Christophe, whom he claimed to admire, for a meeting. Eventually, Christophe agreed to meet Leclerc, but on one condition: Leclerc needed to publicize laws ratified in France stating that slavery would remain abolished in Saint-Domingue. In his letter of April 24, 1802, Leclerc promised Christophe that he would do exactly this.[44] Two days earlier, Christophe had written Leclerc to promise that after the laws were made public, he would submit immediately to French authority: "Exhibiting these laws before the eyes of the people will stop the shedding of French blood by the French, will give the republic back its children who are still prepared to serve it, and will ensure that the horrors of civil war will be succeeded by tranquility, peace, and prosperity for this unhappy colony." Christophe further declared, "It would be to perpetuate these evils until the destruction of an entire people was accomplished to deny them access to these laws, which are necessary for the salvation of this land."[45] That same day Christophe reiterated his demand to General Vilton. "If these laws are in your possession, let me know," Christophe wrote. "If they exist, and you are not in possession of them, please try to get access to them for me."[46]

Christophe's insistence did bear fruit, although it was not precisely what he wanted. On April 25, Leclerc issued a decree offering to make public "the basis for the provisional structure that I will provide to the colony; but that will not be definitive until it will have been approved by the French government, and which will have as its base the liberty and equality of all the inhabitants of Saint-Domingue, without distinction of color."[47]

Although some accounts place Christophe's final meeting with Leclerc, in which the former provisionally defected to the French side, in Haut-du-Cap as early as April 6,[48] it is clear from his correspondence that he first agreed to rejoin the French colonial army on April 26, the day after the formal publication of Leclerc's promise that French laws would treat all people in the colony equally, regardless of skin color.[49] Christophe seemed convinced, at least on the surface, by Leclerc's promises that the French had no plan to reinstate slavery, and he negotiated his surrender on condition that he retain his rank of general in the French army. That same day, which is to say April 26, Leclerc issued a decree to revoke the one he previously issued where he decreed Christophe "hors la loi," or outside the law.[50] The next morning Christophe met with Leclerc in Haut-du-Cap to officially surrender, per the account of Charles Magon, the commander at Fort-Liberté, who wrote to inform General Rochambeau of Christophe's reintegration.[51]

In a letter to the minister of the marine, Leclerc offered his own perspective of the events that led to Christophe's submission, eventually printed in *Le moniteur universel* for all to see: "Christophe told me that he had always been a friend to white people, whose social qualities and education he appreciated more than any other man of color, that all the Europeans who visited Saint-Domingue could attest to his principles and his conduct, but that the urgent circumstances . . . had not left him able to behave as he would have wanted to." According to Leclerc, Christophe then supposedly asked the captain general, "if there could still be any salvation for him." "I answered him that with French people the door is always open for repentance," Leclerc explained, since "a single bad decision, whatever its consequences, could never erase for [the republic] the memory of the services that a man had already rendered." Because Leclerc had received only "personally favorable" information about Christophe, Leclerc said he told the commander of Cap, "as long as he is willing to put himself at my service, his situation would be resolved." After several additional meetings, "Christophe finally told me that I only had to send him my orders," Leclerc concluded.[52]

After this final encounter, Christophe traveled to Marmelade to await Louverture's arrival from Ennery. When Louverture arrived, much to everyone's surprise, Christophe told him that Leclerc seemed to regret having caused violence in Saint-Domingue and stood prepared to negotiate a peace treaty. Although Christophe admitted that he urged Leclerc to take a similar meeting with Louverture, Christophe did not reveal that he had already entered into an agreement that amounted to his defection from the side of the "rebels" to the French side, nor did he mention Isaac's later accusation that Leclerc asked Christophe to assassinate Louverture.[53]

According to the letters that Chanlatte printed in 1810, Leclerc never asked him to kill the governor-general, but he did ask Christophe to persuade Louverture to stand down, and failing that, to "furnish us with the means to capture Toussaint Louverture."[54] Christophe did not mention this to Louverture either. And he certainly did not reveal that he had agreed to follow orders from the French captain general, or that he had every intention of carrying them out. At their final meeting, Leclerc had given Christophe an order to "go alone to the borough of Cap, to send back all the cultivators he still had with him, to assemble all the troops who were under his orders." Following Christophe's submission to French forces, Leclerc reported, "more than two thousand residents of Cap, who were at that time hiding in the most distant mountains, came back. The ammunition and artillery that [Christophe] had in his possession came under [French] control, and about twelve hundred men from his remaining troops were reunited with ours."[55] Louverture knew nothing of these orders or Leclerc's agreement with Christophe, but he still reacted coldly to Christophe's half revelations. First, he rebuked Christophe for breaching the chain of command by meeting with Leclerc without his superior officer's permission. Louverture then expressly forbade Christophe to meet with Leclerc again, lest he be formally charged with insubordination. Amid all this ire, Christophe did manage to get Louverture to accept a letter from Leclerc.

After this meeting with Christophe, according to Dessalines's secretary Boisrond-Tonnerre, Louverture complained to Dessalines that he had been "abandoned by General Christophe." "I know this general far too well," Dessalines replied in Boisrond-Tonnerre's recollection, "to believe for even an instant that he would have gone to Cap without your orders." Dessalines at first rebuked Louverture for giving credibility to this tale, a sign, perhaps, of the ultimately fatal fracturing of their already fragile friendship. "Comport yourself without artifice in front of me and tell me at once if you have already submitted to the French government," Dessalines insisted. "Toussaint then gave him the letter from Leclerc, which he claimed not to have read." "Impossible!" Dessalines told him. "You must know its contents. Who gave you this letter?" "Christophe," Louverture replied. Dessalines wanted to know why Louverture allowed Christophe to return to Cap instead of arresting him on the spot for disobeying the chain of command. Dessalines then read the letter in front of Louverture, and becoming increasingly indignant, he finished by protesting that Louverture would be responsible for all the evils that were about to befall his compatriots due to "his softness." Although Louverture subsequently quit Dessalines under pretext of going to arrest Christophe, in Boisrond-Tonnerre's retelling the governor-general went to meet with Leclerc instead.[56]

Isaac believed his father when he said he had not yet read the letter Christophe gave him before his meeting with Dessalines. For Isaac, this was one of the greatest errors his father ever committed. If Louverture had read the letter, "he would have known everything that had come to pass between Leclerc and Christophe." When Louverture finally did discover the contents of the letter the next day, his disappointment turned to indignation, Isaac revealed. Instead of going to Leclerc, Isaac said his father immediately ordered his adjutant general to find Christophe and tell him to report back to Marmelade. But it was too late. Christophe had already followed Leclerc's order to deliver the city of Cap and the corresponding troops to the French expeditionary army.[57] Not only did Christophe's move augment the French colonial army by the requested twelve hundred men, but he also surrendered a hundred cannons and a huge quantity of weapons and ammunition.[58]

Aware of Louverture's displeasure, Christophe understandably refused to return to Marmelade, sealing not only his defection but, unbeknownst to anyone at the time, Louverture's as well. Even though Christophe was hardly the first defector—he was preceded by Generals Clervaux, Morpas, Laplume, and Louverture's own brother, Paul—his was in many ways the most confusing and vexing. Isaac reported that the men under Christophe's direct command remained perplexed because Christophe initially resisted Leclerc with more ardent opposition than almost anyone else involved. "The conduct of General Christophe," Isaac wrote, "seemed incomprehensible to these officers, especially when they considered that General Christophe, having been attacked unnecessarily by General Leclerc, made the desperate decision to burn down the capital of Saint-Domingue, which was just rebuilt at a huge cost."[59]

Dessalines did not express surprise, however, or at least that is what he told Louverture in his letter of May 5, 1802. Contrary to Boisrond-Tonnerre's rendition, in this missive Dessalines claimed that Christophe did not have the fortitude to withstand French entreaties. Dessalines also brought up a new concern about another key officer whom Dessalines claimed Christophe might be able to persuade to submit to the French. "My dear governor," Dessalines wrote, "I cannot remain silent with respect to you about the fact that Brigadier General Charles Belair is very close to Christophe. Once he has arrived, I urge you not to leave him in any command that is not near you, for I would think it more prudent to keep him close. Upon receipt of your letter, I sent an officer to him to accelerate his march to reach you as quickly as possible without alerting him on the subject." This was surprising information. While Moyse was Louverture's nephew by choice, Belair was his nephew through blood relation. So many betrayals of men once close to Louverture encouraged Dessalines to reiterate his loyalty. He professed eagerness to continue combating the French, and he outlined the steps he planned to take to resist them, starting with gathering hundreds of reinforcements. "My dear governor, as for me," he continued, "at the slightest attack I am determined to use my dagger. The first one who wavers, or merits reprimands, will serve as an example in my army."[60]

Such protestations of loyalty might not have meant much to the war-weary Louverture by then. In the months prior to his defection, Christophe had also expressed his willingness to resist the French at any cost, and he peppered his missives to the governor-general with unequivocal declarations of affection and loyalty.[61] By mid-March, Christophe had become so key to Louverture's resistance to the French that the governor-general gave him a new title. Instead of simple commander of the arrondissement of Cap, by March 8, 1802, Christophe was signing his letters as "commandant en chef le cordon du Nord" (commander in chief of the northern cordon).[62] Two weeks later, the newly promoted Christophe expressed his joy at receiving news from Louverture detailing several of their army's victories, including during the weeks-long March 1802 Battle of Crête-à-Pierrot. Louverture's troops initially gained a fleeting win over the fort, led by General Louis-Daure Lamartinière and his wife Marie-Jeanne, the latter of whom supplied the Black troops with ammunition and gunpowder and even took her own shots at French troops, all while dressed in a "Mamluk outfit." "The news contained in this letter of the victory won over our enemies at Crête-à-Pierrot and which I shared with all our brothers-in-arms has caused the truest pleasure to all," Christophe said in reply to Louverture:

> I congratulate those who, animated by the powerful zeal of liberty, have known so completely how to make their enemies bite the dust. Ah, without a doubt, my dear governor, God, in testing us, will always find us worthy of our freedom; he will not allow our enemies, covetous of our rights, to take it away from us. We are his children; he will deign to direct and make triumph our efforts and the cause of justice and liberty.

Christophe also expressed approval that Louverture ordered more cities burned to combat the enemy French. "Your second letter bears praise for the brave men who repelled the enemy at Vallières and carried out the burning of establishments in the districts of Limonade, Petite-Anse, and Quartier-Morin," Christophe said. "These praises, my dear governor, are for each of those who cooperated in these actions, a stimulus to new successes. . . . Each of us feels that we must, on every occasion, prove to our enemies that they must atone for the crime of having dared to attack liberty and the imprescriptible rights of nature."[63] Christophe's letters to Louverture also tell the story of the ambiguities of warfare. Many battles were beset with frustrating difficulties, including betrayals by men supposedly fighting with those resisting invading French troops.

On April 2, 1802, Christophe wrote to Louverture to inform him that the day before "the enemy" had attacked Sainte-Suzanne, located to the southeast of Cap. Enemy troops now marched toward Camp Poulard while being "repulsed by our brave soldiers." After two months of near-constant warfare of this kind, sometimes against men like Jacques Vincent, whom the Black officers had previously fought with, Christophe's soldiers felt exhausted and exasperated. In one day's battle alone, Christophe reported, "the firing lasted from six o'clock in the morning until four o'clock in the afternoon."[64] One of Christophe's final missives to Louverture before he defected to the French further bespeaks the outsized difficulties facing the men fighting under Louverture's command. On April 14, 1802, Christophe wrote the governor-general to tell him of yet more important posts besieged by Leclerc's troops. Great loss of life accompanied one battle. "My dear general, I am reporting to you that on [April 12] Port-Français was attacked by our enemies," Christophe began. "After a six-hour battle, our brave soldiers repulsed the enemy, despite their great numbers, and forced them to retreat. Their losses were numerous, and Dupont, who commanded this landing, is among the dead. The enemies took the corpses with them, but our brothers-in-arms recognized them. On our side, the loss was reduced to five men killed and ten wounded."[65] As Christophe intimated, those designated enemy troops by this time included some men who previously fought with Louverture and Christophe, complicating every new victory.

The fact that after April 27, Christophe, with his military prowess, sharp intelligence, and keen verbal and tactical skills, had joined those fighting on the side of the French against Louverture's troops had far more serious implications than Dessalines's lighthearted dismissal might suggest. Instead of continuing to provide Louverture with needed intelligence and military support, Christophe now worked for Louverture's most dangerous rival on the island, General Leclerc.

—

On May 1, 1802, Christophe wrote to Leclerc to send him a copy of two letters written by Louverture, as well as a copy of his not yet sent reply. Effectively asking the captain general for permission to respond, Christophe wrote, "If you approve of it, Citizen General, I will pass it on to him. I will wait to do so until you tell me if I can send it to him."[66] The letter that Christophe wrote to Louverture that same day reflects the lingering intimacy of their previous relationship. "You promised me . . . that you would make the sacrifices that the public interest required of you when liberty and independence were assured for all our brothers," Christophe insisted. He then implored Louverture to meet with Leclerc and to "recognize the authority of the representative of France and submit to him." "Return to the republic's arms," Christophe counseled. "Her representative is stretching his arms out towards you."[67] With Christophe firmly under the command of the republic, Louverture watched the possibility of preserving his authority over the colony evaporate before his eyes as more and more men who earlier and bravely fought by his side defected. Eventually, Louverture saw no choice but to enter negotiations with Leclerc. In Vastey's account, Louverture chose Christophe as his representative, in recognition of his "long-standing and signal service."[68]

Had Louverture been persuaded by Christophe's missive? Or was he simply tired of a war that had started to seem eternal, with no end in sight? Accounts differ as to when precisely Louverture agreed to recognize Leclerc's authority. Yet on May 1—the same day that Christophe sent his letter—Leclerc issued a decree nullifying his proclamation of February 17, by which he had rendered "Toussaint Louverture an outlaw." "In consequence," the decree stated, "it is ordered for all citizens and soldiers to regard as null and void that article."[69]

Dessalines seemed unaware of this decree. On May 4, 1802, he wrote to Louverture to offer some advice. The originally signed letter, which is held by the Moorland-Spingarn Research Center at Howard University in an unprocessed collection unavailable to the public is worth quoting at length for several reasons. First, it shows that Louverture did not make the decision to resign his position and lay down his arms before April 29, which is when he ordered his nephew Brigadier General Charles Belair to appear before him with all the troops under his command; on the same day Louverture wrote to Leclerc to request a meeting where he would be given formal assurance of "the general Liberty and Equality of all my Concitoyens on solid and unshakeable bases."[70] Second, it demonstrates that Dessalines had now firmly placed himself in the role of principal supporter, confidant, and ally, once occupied by Christophe. Third, it speaks to the difficult conditions of combat experienced by those still under Louverture's command and the perils and promises of recruiting to Louverture's side the inhabitants of the mountains, who refused to recognize French authority but remained wary of Louverture. Fourth, and finally, it gives a hint of Dessalines's own military prowess and propensity for leadership:

My dear Governor, I have just received a letter from Brigadier
General Charles Belair, writing from the Lagourgue plantation, as
well as a copy of your letter from [April 29], which orders him to

come before you with all the forces under his command, with the exception of two companies, which you told him to leave with Chef de Brigade Montanban. . . . Although I am a soldier and ready to obey all your orders, allow me to tell you that it is impossible that two companies can remain encamped in this place before the Artibonite has taken on water. Brigadier General Charles Belair tells me that he would expect my new orders before leaving the Lagourgue plantation, and that he has also written to you to get your new orders. I warn you, my governor, that in order not to delay him from meeting up with you, I have ordered him to continue his march with the four hundred men under his orders.

I have taken the liberty of making some observations to you, when you think about them, if you find them good, you will leave things as they are, or you will send me your new orders.

. . . As for the post where I am, I dare to hope that the [additional forces] will be there if the enemy comes to attack me.

Salut and Respect, Division General Dessalines

In a postscript, Dessalines detailed the possibility of augmenting the army with new recruits from the mountains, a tactic he used during the later stages of the revolution. "P.S. My governor, two young men just arrived who say they are from the parish of Verrettes and who tell us that we have many soldiers of different corps in the mountains of that region, and that they do not know how to join up with us," Dessalines wrote. While the French sought in earnest to recruit those very soldiers to their side, Dessalines revealed that, according to the two young men, they had not yet been successful. "I want to let you know that I am taking advantage of the fact that the Artibonite has not yet taken on water, to send an officer from this quartier to fetch and cross them over to this side."[71]

By this time, most of the prominent Black generals in the colony had abandoned Louverture. Therefore, even if Christophe's May 1 letter reached him the same day, Louverture might have seen no other option but to try to save his own life and that of his family by admitting defeat. The once haughty and proud general, previously so obstinate in the face of violent French attempts to cow him into submission, was now required to apologize and essentially prostrate himself before the very French military he recently opposed. "Toussaint, with his hard and proud manner . . . announced, at last, under these circumstances, his regret over the approach that he had adopted and remorse over his crimes," wrote one observer of the meeting. "This haughty and ferocious chief remained filled with embarrassment over being criticized in front of men in whose eyes he had lost the air of superiority that he had clung to for so long and for whom he had become an object of horror and contempt. He therefore concealed nothing of his feelings, announcing his submission as an imposition, in fact refusing both power and the offer made to him that he could retain his authority, reserving the right to decide upon the terms of his own treaty in common with Dessalines."[72] Even while agreeing to submit to Leclerc's authority, Louverture defended his conduct with a final rebuke for the captain general. He told Leclerc that when the French fleet arrived off the coast of Cap, "You knew very well that I was in Santo Domingo; there was still time to warn me." As for Christophe, Louverture reminded Leclerc once more that the commander of Cap "asked you to allow him sufficient time to inform me of the appearance of a French squadron on our coasts," but instead "you reduc[ed] the people to despair with your threats and exposed your army to the crater of a volcano."[73]

Louverture's defection was just as consequential as Christophe's. Dessalines's almost immediately followed. While Caffarelli reported that Dessalines defected four days after Christophe,[74] Saint-Rémy claimed that Generals Dessalines and Belair only reluctantly submitted to the French, with tears in their eyes, on May 12, after the above-described meeting took place.[75] Dessalines's secretary Boisrond-Tonnerre, however, characterized Dessalines's alleged defection as merely a ruse. Acknowledging also that it was unclear whether Leclerc was really "duped," Boisrond-Tonnerre recalled, "Dessalines, swallowing his wrath for the time being, made a virtue out of necessity and went to lead the army at Saint-Marc. It was therefore for his troops, or rather the desire to preserve them from the horrors he foresaw, that Dessalines appeared to submit, but he nonetheless kept in his heart the project of raising the flag of rebellion as soon as the French gave him a pretext."[76] Although the kingdom's official historian, the Baron de Vastey, did not mention Christophe's own defection to the French, even while inserting passages from Boisrond-Tonnerre's text about Dessalines into his own, Vastey also asserted that Dessalines had merely faked his loyalty to Leclerc and the French army.[77]

Having only begrudgingly accepted Leclerc's authority, Louverture declined the offer to remain a French general, opting to retire instead.[78] Leclerc accepted Louverture's resignation and reassured the frustrated and disappointed Louverture that he could fully "retire to [his] home with every assurance of safety."[79] But Louverture did not find safety at home. Although he officially retired from the French army and went home to his wife and children, French officers repeatedly accused him of inciting ongoing insurrection among the "blacks." French newspapers, as well as Leclerc's letters, referred to secret missives supposedly exchanged between Louverture and commanders over regions of the colony still in open rebellion.[80] With these alleged letters, and with intelligence allegedly gathered from Dessalines, Leclerc told Bonaparte he had no choice but to issue another warrant for Louverture's arrest.[81] In the letter he sent to the French minister of the marine four days after Louverture's arrest,

Leclerc claimed, "Toussaint sought to organize, among the cultivators, an insurrection to have them rise up en masse." "Reports that have reached me . . . from General Dessalines himself," Leclerc continued, "revealing the conduct he has engaged in since his submission, leave me no doubt in this regard." "I am sending to France, with his entire family, this undoubtedly perfidious man, who, with so much hypocrisy, has done us so much harm," Leclerc announced.[82]

Before defending the conduct of both Dessalines and Christophe, Chanlatte, for his part, observed that during this doleful period the French government sought to persuade each of the Haitian generals to arrest the others.[83] Chanlatte knew of what he spoke. The day before Louverture's arrest, Leclerc bragged in a letter to Bonaparte that in forcing Louverture's submission, he had achieved a crucial goal, "which was to separate him from Dessalines and Christophe and their troops." "I'm going to order [Louverture's] arrest, and I think I can count on Dessalines enough for this," Leclerc continued. "I don't think he'll escape, but if he does, I'll have Christophe and Dessalines pursue him," he wrote.[84] Such a climate of betrayal, uncertainty, ambiguity, and outright perfidy did lead to cracks among the Haitian generals. Christophe remarked in a letter to Commander Vilton in April 1802 that he no longer had many friends he believed he could trust. Christophe said he felt "like Diogenes, with a lantern in hand at high noon . . . searching in vain for an honest man."[85]

Christophe had every reason to suspect the intentions of some of the other Black revolutionaries, as much as the officers from the French military. Boisrond-Tonnerre testified that contrary to Leclerc's claim Dessalines never intended to aid the French in arresting Louverture but that he did seek to have his own men arrest the retired governor-general. Dessalines, according to Boisrond-Tonnerre, had disagreed with Louverture's desire to submit to the French. Fearing that Louverture might give up too much in any negotiations, Dessalines addressed a small number of soldiers in his inner circle and described his plan "to invite Louverture to a meeting, under the pretext of making arrangements to ensure his safety, and then to arrest and confine him to the mountains, under the surveillance of a guard, only until the fate of war decided if the country was to remain French." Evidently, the men in Dessalines's confidence agreed to this plot, but the French got to Louverture first.[86]

On June 3, 1802, a French general named Jean-Baptiste Brunet, right-hand man to Leclerc, wrote Louverture a letter that gives hints of the explosive role potentially played by Dessalines in Louverture's arrest. Brunet began, sympathetically, "It is all too common for men in high positions to be deceived by those closest to them." "Have you not had the disastrous experience yourself?" he asked. Brunet then refuted the idea that he might be one of Louverture's deceivers. "I never wrote to him [Leclerc] that there were armed gatherings at Dennery [Ennery]," Brunet continued. "Come to see me with your concerns, and I will furnish you with the proof. I will show you my correspondence before and since the pacification. You will see if after having been an enemy, but a loyal one, I know how, when all is said and done, to cast a veil over the past and become a frank and sincere friend." Brunet then unwittingly portended the role that Dessalines, perhaps unintentionally, played in Louverture's arrest and demise. "If your domestic occupations do not allow you to do me the same honor of a visit that I expect today from General Dessalines, I will return to Dennery, and I will put before your eyes the letters that the general in chief wrote to me and my answers to him." Brunet concluded with more talk of Dessalines: "General, consider me a neighbor and consequently a friend. Since General Dessalines is coming to dine here today, I did not deem it appropriate to send the officer you sent me to Saint-Marc; [the officer] will give [Dessalines] your letter while drinking to your health."[87] Brunet sent this letter four days before Louverture's arrest, and it turns out that Dessalines did visit Brunet. In a letter he penned to General Rochambeau seven days after Louverture's arrest, Dessalines also mentioned having met with Leclerc, who gave him the important commission of traveling to Plaisance to convince to "return to order" the "leaders" whom the "ex-general Louverture" had "excited into rebellion." "General Brunet and I have succeeded in this," Dessalines announced.[88]

In his own account of how the arrest unfolded, General Brunet expressed more than a little partiality to Dessalines and admitted using him and his wife to lure Louverture into a trap. On May 23, Brunet intimated to Rochambeau that Dessalines had animosity for the retired governor-general Louverture because he had not allowed Dessalines to participate in the making of the 1801 constitution. "He was not even allowed to sign it," Brunet wrote. "Toussaint used him as an instrument to achieve his goals, without ever telling him anything about the reasons why he ordered this or that measure: in the end, they feared each other without liking or esteeming each other in any way."[89] The same day that he arrested Louverture, but before it took place, Brunet informed Leclerc that he was frustrated because he could not figure out where Louverture slept at night and had been unable to persuade the retired general to meet him in person. Exasperated by his own inability to even locate Louverture at that point, Brunet hatched the plot to meet with Dessalines later that day, as soon as the latter returned to Cap. "I'll take a chance on him," Brunet told his superior. What transpired at the meeting is only known to us through the account that Brunet gave to Leclerc about two weeks after he arrested Louverture. "It wasn't just with fine promises that I managed to make Toussaint and his main acolytes fall into my nets," Brunet stated. "It took something more powerful," he continued. "That is to say money and gifts." Enclosed with this letter was a statement listing the money Brunet allegedly spent to "bribe" Dessalines and his wife. Bribe them to do exactly what, the letter does not say. However, the letter does say that the captain of the ship where Louverture was captive, along with riflemen from the Fifth Demi-brigade, were promised sums of money for "binding Toussaint and taking him on board the frigate that was to convey him to France."[90]

Examining together Brunet's and Louverture's missives gives some sense of the intriciate plot the French used to ensnare Louverture. Two days after Brunet wrote his obsequious letter to Louverture, and two days before Brunet arrested him, Louverture requested that General Brunet meet with him on his own territory in Ennery. Louverture expressed concern about circulating lies that put into question his honor and devotion to France. "I have always served the republic with honor and glory; I believe I deserve the esteem of the French government," Louverture wrote. Noting he suffered from unwellness because a tree branch had fallen on him, Louverture said he remained interested in meeting with Brunet and invited the French general to visit him in Ennery, adding that it would give him great pleasure. "I am bringing my wife to my plantations," Louverture said, perhaps to entice Brunet to show up, since Suzanne Louverture was renowned for her kindness. "You will have the satisfaction of seeing her and I may receive you," Louverture concluded.[91] Brunet seemed not at all inclined to meet Louverture on his own territory, nevertheless, and declined this request.

Two days after this, on June 7, 1802, Brunet summoned Louverture to a meeting once more. Brunet used as a pretext the deaths of three French soldiers who had their throats slit the day before, he said, by "about fifty brigands" along the route to Cap. Claiming he had too much work to do to travel to meet with Louverture at his plantation, Brunet implored Louverture to come to him. "We have, my dear general," Brunet wrote, "arrangements to make together which it is impossible to deal with in letters but which a one-hour conference will suffice to complete."[92] Having denied Brunet's previous requests to meet in person on Brunet's territory, Louverture showed similar disinclination to accede to this new demand. However, at the unfortunate urgings of his children, Louverture belatedly agreed, later admitting that he left in the middle of the night with only two officers by his side. When he arrived in Cap after the approximately seventy-kilometer journey, Brunet denied having orders to meet with him. "He then apologized to me, saying that he needed to leave the room for a moment, and while he was leaving, he called an officer to keep me company. No sooner had he left than an aide-de-camp to General Leclerc entered, accompanied by a very large number of grenadiers, who surrounded me, took possession of me, tied me up like a criminal, and led me on board the frigate the *Créole*," Louverture later recalled.[93]

Brunet's account of that night also exists and differs in tone and purpose from Louverture's recollection. At about ten o'clock on the seventh, Brunet wrote to Leclerc to confirm that an hour earlier he succeeded in arresting Louverture, who had arrived at his home with only a single aide-de-camp and one "domestic." "I had the patience to listen for an hour to his customary jeremiads," Brunet complained. "Meanwhile, his two companions were being invited to eat and drink," he continued. "All of a sudden entered Deputy Haque, my chief of staff. . . . [F]eigning some obligation, I left him alone with Haque. A few minutes later entered Captain Duingle of the Carabiniers of the brave Fifth [Demi-brigade], along with Captain Heuman, my aide-de-camp, with two others, and our villain was taken without putting up any resistance."[94]

Brunet could not help but brag about the success of the ruse he used to capture the great general Toussaint Louverture. "My dear general," Brunet wrote to Leclerc on June 9, 1802. "The end of the expedition has been as successful as the beginning: everywhere the most complete victory has crowned my designs." "The ex-governor, his wife, his two sons, . . . and his most intimate and avowed supporters are in our power. The arrests took place in various spots, far away from one another, and yet not a single target was missed. So much celerity and secrecy was put into the execution of this. I remain quite happy that everything went off without bloodshed." Brunet then gave a detailed report to Leclerc about the identities of the prisoners, including Louverture's wife and children, as well as a summary of Louverture's papers. "No less important is the seizure of the correspondence and all the papers of Toussaint. I have only hastily gone through a few pieces, but I was easily convinced of their importance. I invite you to have them scrupulously examined. You will find in them valuable information about everything that is important for you to know," he continued. "There are still a few villains to be arrested, but I am on their heels, and they will soon share the fate of their worthy patron," Brunet boasted.[95]

Just before he was taken on board the *Créole*, Louverture uttered what were to be his last words of protest on the island: "You dare to arrest me; you are dishonoring an honorable officer. . . . Is this how you demonstrate faith in treaties; you are traitors and perjurers. But God is just, and I will be avenged."[96] After the French embarked Louverture, they sent soldiers to arrest his entire family—including his 105-year-old blind godfather—and forced them onto a ship waiting in the port of Gonaïves. Louverture's testimony about the way the French treated his family during their captivity is as heart wrenching as it is horrifying. At the sight of the French troops, the women and children on the plantation ran half naked into the woods. "These horrors were committed in my home," Louverture recalled: "The commander of Ennery was at the head of a hundred men who descended upon the dwelling where my wife and my nieces could be found. They were arrested, without even having been given time to get dressed, or gather any of their effects, nor any of my things that were in their possession; they were taken away like criminals." The two different ships carrying Louverture and his family members eventually reunited about four leagues from the port at Cap-Français, where the French forced the entire brood aboard a third ship, the now infamous *Héros,* which carried them as prisoners to France. Like his wife and children, Louverture never saw the island again.[97]

Upon their arrival in Brest, the French immediately and for the last time separated Louverture from his wife and sons. His final letter to Suzanne, dictated to his domestic, Mars Plaisir, dated September 16, 1802, began, "My dear wife, I am taking advantage of this moment to give you an update. I was very sick upon arriving here . . . but thanks be to God, I am now feeling much better. You know of my love for my family and my attachment to a cherished wife." Louverture told Suzanne that he had no news about her and the children, other than about Placide, who he thought might be with her. He implored his wife to "tenderly embrace" his son, before signing off, "I am for life, your faithful husband. Toussaint Louverture."[98] Placide, incarcerated on a ship separately from both his parents, similarly wrote to them:

My dearest mother and father,

I am first of all on the brig the *Noyade.* I do not know yet my fate, maybe I will never see you again. Given that, know that whatever my fate, no matter where I will be, I will survive, I beg of you, to keep your courage, to think of me sometimes. I will give you my news. I am not dead. Give me yours, if you have the opportunity. I am very well. I am with people who have shown a lot of kindness to me. . . .

I embrace you as I love you.
Your son, Placide Louverture[99]

In September, after the French transferred Louverture to the Fort de Joux prison in the Jura Mountains of France, with orders directly from Bonaparte requiring him to be held "incommunicado," Caffarelli arrived to question him. Bonaparte had instructed Caffarelli to "make Toussaint understand the enormity of the crime of which he is guilty of committing in taking up arms against the republic; that we viewed him as a rebel from the moment he published his constitution." "You must try to record everything he says about his different plans, likewise about the existence of his treasures," Bonaparte insisted.[100]

Louverture continued to ardently deny the French government's accusations against him. He told Caffarelli, "Your claim that I shot six black men charged with burying my treasures—that I sent ships laden with gold to England and the United States are slanderous fables." Regarding the charge that Louverture raided French coffers, Louverture responded by telling Caffarelli, "As for the treasures of mine of which you speak with so much insistence, they do not exist." It was Christophe, Louverture said, who was "responsible for depositing 900,000 francs from Cap, but kept most of it for himself!" Caffarelli remained unconvinced and continued to paint Louverture as a scoundrel and a liar.[101]

The official report of Louverture's death, dated April 7, 1803, confirmed that he died from a combination of pneumonia and a stroke. The autopsy also recorded that both his lungs were filled with blood—his heart no doubt also filled with the most bitter regrets.[102]

Preventing news of Louverture's death from reaching Saint-Domingue became of paramount importance to the French government. Common sense suggested to French leaders that news of the neglect and torture that Louverture endured would only feed into the ire of those still in open rebellion. These included many formerly enslaved Africans living in the mountains, such as Christophe's rival Colonel Jean-Baptiste Sans-Souci. Would knowing of France's treatment of Louverture only further encourage the independent army in the mountains to fight until the death? The arrest had already been "a stroke of lightning for Dessalines," according to Boisrond-Tonnerre, one that foretold the spreading of general unrest among the formerly enslaved population, from one end of the island to the other.[103]

The French government's official newspaper, *Le moniteur universel,* was not only circumspect about Louverture's status at the prison, and later his death, but completely silent. On April 25, 1803, about two weeks after Louverture's death, the minister of the marine published a letter about ongoing affairs in Saint-Domingue in which he made no mention of the fate of the revolutionary leader who recently died in French captivity.[104] No French newspaper appears to have reported the former French general's death until April 28, when the *Journal des débats* printed a pithy notice containing multiple errors. "It was reported from Besançon, on the second of this month," the article said, "that Toussaint Louverture, who was detained at Fort de Joux, has died there eight days earlier."[105] Another newspaper repeated this stunning information on April 29, before the news disappeared from French papers.[106]

Even though the most prominent newspaper in Saint-Domingue, *Les Affiches américaines,* did not report Toussaint's death, this information made its way back to the war-torn colony anyway. This was at least in part thanks to an exiled French journalist named Jean-Gabriel Peltier, whose anti-Napoleonic screeds put him in the crosshairs of the French consul. While living in exile in England, Peltier became editor of *L'ambigu,* a literary and political journal he founded in 1802. The publication appeared three times per month and circulated heavily in Saint-Domingue and continued to do so in Christophe's Haiti. Peltier even became one of Christophe's most trusted confidants, whom Christophe, as president of Haiti, later made his "chargé d'affaires."[107] A painfully detailed diatribe about Toussaint's arrest—the memory of which the French tried to cast into oblivion—appeared in *L'ambigu* in mid-1803, concluding, "Toussaint Louverture was arrested in opposition to the good faith of the treaty, and the deception used to capture him necessarily aroused discontent." News of the arrest, the issue acknowledged, caused further conflagrations to erupt in the colony, making it even more crucial for the French to keep knowledge of Louverture's death out of the opposition's eyesight or earshot.[108] Leclerc had warned the minister of the marine, Decrès, that any attempt to condemn or execute Louverture must not occur until after the French had reestablished their control over the colony. When the proper moment arrived, Leclerc offered to furnish the French minister with "documents to put [Louverture] on trial, if you want to have recourse to what was done before the armistice I granted him." However, he cautioned that "where things presently stand, his trial and execution would only embitter the spirits of the blacks."[109] This letter, perhaps unwittingly, reveals the motive behind the French neglect that led to the wrongful death of the never convicted *French* general Toussaint Louverture.

Despite continuous attempts by many powerful people in France to cover up the seriousness of their crime against the man they had held prisoner without any trial or formal charges, Louverture's death knell was heard around the Atlantic world. We read in *The Times* of London on May 3, 1803, "Toussaint Louverture is dead. He died, according to letters from Besançon, in prison, a few days ago. The fate of this man has been singularly unfortunate, and his treatment most cruel. He died, we believe, without a friend to close his eyes. We have never heard that his wife and children, though they were brought over from St. Domingo with him, have ever been permitted to see him during his imprisonment."[110] By June, the news reached the United States with New York papers reporting, "Toussaint Louverture, the celebrated African Chief, is dead."[111] The news likely reached Haiti around the same time through the newspaper channels that functioned as an information superhighway.

News of Louverture's terrible fate taught the other revolutionary leaders that there could no longer be any meaningful negotiations for peace. In 1807, as president of Haiti, Christophe issued a proclamation to the people of the north to explain that they had a national duty to always mistrust the French: "I have already pointed out to you the treacherous conspiracies that a handful of villains dared to plot against your freedom.

194

These men, strangers to all human feelings, forced me, in spite of myself, to wage war upon them."[112] Later, we find the following description of Louverture's capture and arrest in the *Royal Gazette of Hayti:*

> Toussaint Louverture voluntarily gave up his authority and laid down his arms: withdrawn to his home, stripped of all his grandeur, like that famous Roman [Spartacus], he had cultivated with his own hands that same land that he had defended with his weapons; he urged us, through his words and example, to imitate him, to work and live peacefully with our families. Against the good faith of the treaties, the French lured him into a trap: he was arrested, loaded with irons; his wife, his children, his family, his officers, experienced the same fatal destiny. Thrown aboard French vessels, they were taken to Europe to end their unhappy days, with poison, in dungeons and in irons![113]

The effect of Louverture's arrest emerged more immediately in some parts of the colony. Several generals from the opposition—namely, Sylla, Candi, Makaya, and Christophe's rival Sans-Souci—continued to lead independent bands of armed Black troops determined never to be enslaved again. France's treatment of Louverture only made these freedom fighters more ardent in their conviction that Dessalines and Christophe had committed a grave error. "The arrest of General Toussaint has produced some riots," we read in Leclerc's letter to the minister of the marine. "Two rebel chiefs have already been arrested. I have ordered them to be shot."[114] Instead of lessening the violence, Louverture's deportation only increased it. Because of Bonaparte's May 1802 decree, which allowed for the continuation of slavery in Martinique, and a yellow fever outbreak ravaging French troops, the one that took Leclerc's life that November, the colony stood in deeper trouble than ever before.

The French military had met serious opposition when they effectively reinstated slavery in the French colony of Guadeloupe in July 1802. Although French troops there engaged in a fierce battle against thousands of men of color, General Antoine Richepanse, who oversaw the mission, declared victory to the French minister of the marine that August. His letter to that effect was printed in *Le moniteur universel:* "Now that security and tranquility are fully established . . . fifteen thousand [Negroes from the plantations] have been returned to their dwellings, where they will be contained by severe discipline."[115] Despite knowing of this decree, Christophe did not officially join the independent freedom fighters until October 1802, according to French military reports. Was it the situation in Martinique and Guadeloupe or was it news of Louverture's treatment in France that had more immediate bearing on Christophe's change of heart? Or perhaps, it was something far more personally alarming. Did

Christophe—who had already mistakenly confided his child to duplicitous French arms—somehow get word of Leclerc and Bonaparte's plot to
have him arrested?

—

The key to understanding Christophe's about-face, like Louverture's own,
lies less in his rank as a general than in his role as a father. To understand
the accidental importance of Ferdinand Christophe in the events of the
Haitian Revolution, we must start with the fateful decision Christophe
made to send his son with his wife's sister Marie to France.[116]

In May 1802, just after he agreed to return to the French army, Christophe decided to send his son Ferdinand to the same school where Louverture's children had been pupils, the Collège de la Marche. There, Ferdinand
would be under the tutelage of the same teacher who taught Louverture's
boys, Coisnon. Previously, the school operated as an exclusive haven
for "American blacks" from the French colonies. Louverture's children,
as well as those of his rival Rigaud and those of Dessalines's secretary
Boisrond-Tonnerre, had all attended, along with children of color from
other prominent and wealthy Saint-Domingue families. Christophe likely
knew that the agent Roume, who had so admired his makeshift school
at Saint-Michel, had already sent the fourteen-year-old mixed-race son
of his second wife, Maurice, called Jaquin, to the Collège.[117] Christophe
likewise sought to position his son to pursue a life of letters rather than
the life of war he had known as a young boy.

Ferdinand Christophe came into the world alongside Black freedom on
May 15, 1794, just three months after the French National Convention
declared the abolition of slavery in all French overseas territories. Yet his
light left the world just as Black freedom in the Americas took another
gigantic leap forward. As punishment for his father's revolutionary acts,
the French government left Ferdinand to die in the streets of Paris, after
they locked up his aunt and guardian in the infamous Pitié-Salpêtrière
mental institution.[118]

Was it naïveté or ambition that led Christophe to believe that his son
would be safe in French arms? Or perhaps behind Christophe's decision
lies a more painful truth. From late April to late September 1802, Christophe, at least on the surface, aided the French military in disarming the
Black cultivators and other independents fighting the French army. If Christophe's submission was a ruse, Leclerc was entirely fooled. The captain
general expressed repeated satisfaction with the conduct of Christophe,
Dessalines, and Morpas during the French military's efforts to subdue the
"rebels." Leclerc even told Bonaparte that both Christophe and Dessalines
implored him to take them to France at the end of the expedition when
Leclerc would ostensibly depart.[119] Although by the end of September
1802 he came to rightly suspect that Dessalines was assisting the "rebels,"

Leclerc claimed that Christophe still filled him with "confidence," noting in the same breath, "I'm sending his eldest son to France to be educated." Leclerc still said he would arrest Morpas first and then Christophe.[120]

Christophe's choice to entrust his son to the care of the French only makes sense within the larger context of his role as a French general serving the interests of the French republic. When the French lieutenant Pamphile de Lacroix, in another French general named Boudet's presence, asked Christophe at a September meeting why the rebellion grew day after day, even after almost all the most prominent Black generals had returned to the French side, Christophe reportedly replied, "If you were of the same skin color as us, would you be as confident as I am, who has just handed over my only son Ferdinand to General Boudet, to have him raised in France?" In Christophe's opinion, the so-called brigands were not the real cause of the continuing violence in the colony. Instead, the actual danger lay "in the general sentiments of the blacks; those from Saint-Domingue are frightened, because they know about the decree of May 20, 1802, which maintains slavery and the slave trade in the colonies returned to France," Christophe said. He referred to Bonaparte's infamous decree that allowed for slavery in all reacquired territories, following the March 1802 Treaty of Amiens, which officially ended the war between England and France and restored Martinique and other previously lost dependencies to the French republic. That July, two months after the May decree, Bonaparte officially reinstated slavery in the entire French Empire, with the exception of Saint-Domingue, but including Guadeloupe, where it had been abolished since 1794. Although Christophe clearly understood the implications of the maintenance of slavery and the slave trade in Martinique, which he referenced at the meeting, and its relationship to the growing opposition in Saint-Domingue, he reportedly reiterated his belief in the "sincerity of General Leclerc," saying that he would not have reunited with the French military if he really believed France intended to bring back slavery in Saint-Domingue.[121]

What Christophe did not know was that Bonaparte had already issued explicit instructions to General Leclerc to rid the colony of "all the black generals," including him. "Without this, we will have done nothing, and an immense and beautiful colony will still be on a volcano, and will inspire confidence in neither capitalists, colonists, nor commerce," Bonaparte counseled his brother-in-law. In his original instructions to Leclerc concerning the reestablishment of slavery in Saint-Domingue the first consul specifically singled out for deportation Christophe, along with Louverture and Dessalines. The detailed missive laid out a plan for first "seducing" Toussaint Louverture, before arresting and deporting him in the second phase. "Win over Christophe, Clairveaux [sic], Maurepas, Félix, Romain, Jasmin, and so on, and all other blacks favorable to the whites," Bonaparte advised. Afterward, he told Leclerc to snare them too. "In the first phase, confirm their ranks and positions," Bonaparte directed. "In the third phase, send them all to France with their ranks if they served well during the second phase." The third phase was to be unmistakably violent and had only one true goal: "If Toussaint, Dessalines, or Moyse have been captured under arms, they will be judged by a military commission within twenty-four hours and shot as rebels. Whatever happens, during the third phase you should disarm all negroes, regardless of the party to which they belong, and return them to field work."[122] In mid-March 1802, more than a month into the expedition, Bonaparte wrote to Leclerc to remind him of its goal: "Follow exactly the instructions, and as soon as you have defeated Toussaint, Christophe, Dessalines, and the principal brigands, and the black masses have been disarmed, send back to the continent all the blacks and men of color who played a role in these troubles."[123]

Even though Christophe rejoined the French army in late April 1802, and nearly all the Black French generals had done so by May, the directive coming from the French government did not change. The French minister of the marine, while he could not have been aware of Louverture's arrest at the time, wrote a letter to Leclerc on June 14, 1802, ostensibly congratulating him on Louverture's submission and reiterating France's ultimate goal. Louverture's capture did not mean the "bloody war" waged to restore slavery was over, Minister Decrès cautioned, however: "As far as concerns the return to the ancien régime with respect to the blacks . . . for some time to come, vigilance, order, and a discipline that is both rural and military must replace the absolute and unyielding enslavement of your colony's people of color." "When they have felt by comparison the difference between a usurping and tyrannical yoke and that of the legitimate owner, interested in their preservation, the time will have come to return them to their original condition, from which it has been so disastrous to have withdrawn them," Decrès sinisterly concluded.[124] The first consul, for his part, wrote to Leclerc on July 22, 1802, more than a month after Louverture's arrest and deportation, "We look forward to the arrival of Christophe and Dessalines in France. Toussaint's arrival has been extremely honorable for you and is a subject of tranquility and hope for our commerce."[125] Two months later, and in the same letter to Bonaparte where he discussed sending Christophe's son to France, Leclerc revealed to Bonaparte the plan he developed to arrest Christophe as well as Dessalines and Morpas. "Not being strong enough to entirely fight off Dessalines, Morpas, Christophe, and the others, I am using them against one another," Leclerc wrote. All three of the men, he said, could be the leader of the colony, but since Dessalines had recently fallen out with Morpas, according to the captain general, Leclerc planned to arrest Morpas first. He observed, however, that for the rest of the plot to work, he needed to arrest Christophe and Dessalines on the same day.[126] Such duplicity wholly characterized the French government's relationship to its Black generals since Bonaparte's rise to power.

On November 18, 1801, Bonaparte had belatedly responded to Governor-General Louverture in a letter dripping with obsequious prose. Bonaparte implored Louverture to "assist with your advice, influence, and talents the captain general [Leclerc]," whom Bonaparte revealed to be en route to the colony. "What more can you desire? The freedom of the blacks?" Bonaparte rhetorically asked. "You know that in every country we enter, we've given it to people who didn't have it."[127] This was a blatant lie. One month earlier, on October 7, 1801, amid the preliminary peace talks with Great Britain that eventually returned Martinique, Saint Lucia, and other overseas colonies previously lost to the British to French rule, Bonaparte insisted that slavery would prevail on those islands. He told Decrès to order all French officials in those territories "to make known to the inhabitants of Martinique and Saint Lucia, in the name of the government, that they will have nothing to fear concerning the freedom of the negroes, who will be maintained in their present state."[128] Even though on November 18 Bonaparte praised Louverture, averring that "if France's flag flies over Saint-Domingue today, it is owing to you and the brave blacks," just five days earlier Bonaparte wrote to his chief diplomat, Charles-Maurice de Talleyrand-Périgord (called Talleyrand), to explain the paramount importance of getting rid of Louverture: "In the decision I made to annihilate the government of the blacks in Saint-Domingue, I was guided less by considerations of trade and finance than by the need to stifle in all parts of the world every germ of worry and unrest." He further explained that if he did not remove Louverture, sooner or later, the "scepter of the New World" would "fall into the hands of the blacks."[129] Yet it is the letter Bonaparte penned to General Leclerc on November 19, the day after he wrote to praise Louverture, that truly reveals the manipulative character of the man to whom Christophe had entrusted his son.

First referencing his letter to Louverture, Bonaparte boasted that Great Britain would assist France, having "given Jamaica orders to help us and provide us with everything they can." Bonaparte finished the letter to his brother-in-law with the euphemism of "restoring the colony" that the French continued to use during their decades-long quest to reinstate slavery on the island: "I look forward to learning that you have rendered the republic the greatest service its commerce and navigation have to hope for, and that we can proclaim you the restorer of our great colony."[130] Even though Christophe could hardly have been aware of these machinations, by September 1802 he knew that Leclerc had summarily arrested and deported Louverture, maintained slavery in Martinique, and likely also that he had reinstated it in Guadeloupe. What we do not know is whether Christophe knew that the same day of his submission to France in April 1802, Bonaparte had taken the bold step to reinstate the slave trade entirely, and had nullifed Louverture's 1801 constitution.[131]

Their eventual rivalry notwithstanding, General Alexandre Pétion, future president of Haiti, questioned Christophe's decision. When Christophe stopped by Pétion's house in Haut-du-Cap in late September, Pétion allegedly told him, "You are making a mistake by sending your son to France; take him back, there is still time. A great commotion is afoot." Before thanking Pétion and even shaking his hand, Christophe evidently replied, "The atmosphere is dripping with blood; sorrow marks every face; I told General Boudet some hard truths. If the whites persist in their ways, everything will be lost to them."[132] Even if Christophe wanted to change his mind, it was already too late. On September 28, Ferdinand set sail for France, with his mother's sister Tante Marie as his guardian.

Tante Marie, called Mademoiselle Marie by those who knew her in Paris, was raised in a convent in France, along with her brother Bonnaire. When Ferdinand and his aunt reached France, they gave the letters of introduction furnished to them by a French priest and friend of the family's, the abbé Collin, to a Monsieur Lambert, clerk for a justice of the peace, who was to house them until Ferdinand could be enrolled in school. Ferdinand entered the Collège de la Marche in mid-fall 1802, just as Bonaparte ordered it shuttered. The eight-year-old child would then find himself on the streets of Paris, where he died a penniless orphan, without a friend to his name. As for his aunt, the prim and proper middle-aged woman found herself committed to a mental asylum.[133] The outcome of the revolution in Saint-Domingue had direct bearing on both their fates.

After Leclerc's death by yellow fever on November 2, 1802, France's possibility of defeating the growing opposition in Saint-Domingue quickly evaporated. Leclerc's successor, General Rochambeau, took desperate measures in a last-ditch attempt to retain French authority and restore slavery. A French military officer reported that in late 1802, Rochambeau, following a policy previously outlined by Leclerc, directed French troops to throw into the sea more than fifteen hundred Black people and other people of color.[134] In an 1803 article for the Philadelphia-based *Literary Magazine and American Register*, a U.S. merchant, an eyewitness, recounted that in November 1802 he observed "scenes that bear the deepest tinge of barbarous atrocity." "Seven or eight hundred blacks, and men of colour, were seized upon in the streets, in the public places, in the very houses, and for the moment confined within the walls of a prison. Thence they were hurried on board the national vessels lying in the harbor, from whence they were plunged into eternity." This mass murder was no isolated incident: "These horrid scenes were repeated at Leogane [*sic*], at Petit-Guave [*sic*], and in the whole circuit of Jeremie [*sic*]." Later, in L'Anse-à-Veau, "several blacks and one white from Nantes, whose name I well remember was Billiard, were all carried on board the [ship] *Adelaide* for the purpose of being sunk in a watery grave." After this "premeditated barbarity," the merchant concluded, "the billows now washed these unfortunate victims to the shore, floating with their eyes, as it were, turned

Map of the island of Grenada,
birthplace of Henry Christophe.

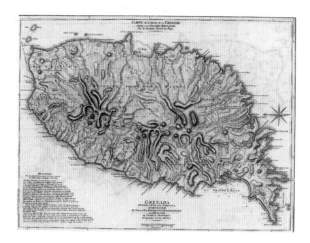

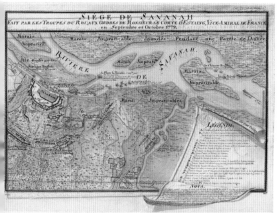

Map of the French siege at the
Battle of Savannah in Georgia.

color-coded map of the island of Saint-Domingue from 1825, showing, in lime
green, the former French part of the colony that formed the Kingdom of Haiti under
Christophe; in darker green, the former French part of the colony that comprised the
Republic of Haiti under Pétion; in bright yellow, the part of the island ruled by the
French from 1697 to 1776, and then ruled by the Spanish from 1776 to 1800; and in
beige, the former Spanish part of the island, incorporated into the Republic of Haiti
under President Jean-Pierre Boyer in 1822.

Map of the city of Cap-Français and its surroundings on the island of St. Domingue, 1786.

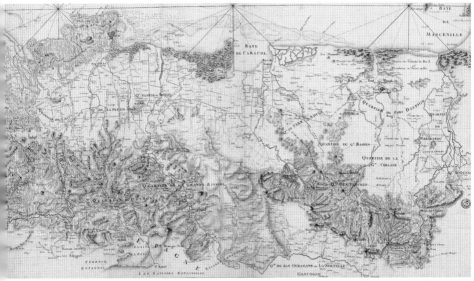

Topographical map, from 1760, of the regions of Cap-Français and Fort-Dauphin, in the northeast of the French colony of St. Domingue. This map shows the names and borders of plantations in the north, where Christophe and the other Black revolutionaries leased many farms following the 1794 French abolition of slavery in all France's overseas territories.

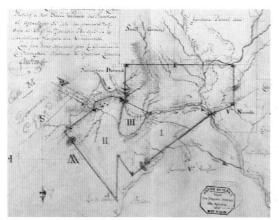

Map showing the boundaries of several plantations in the western department of the colony, specifically one owned by Suzanne Louverture, wife of Toussaint Louverture, General-in-Chief of the Army of Saint-Domingue, ca. 1799.

Façade of the side of Christophe's proposed house in Cap-Français at number 312 rue de l'Égalité, near the Place d'Armes, 1802.

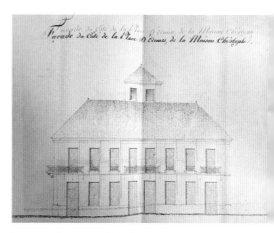

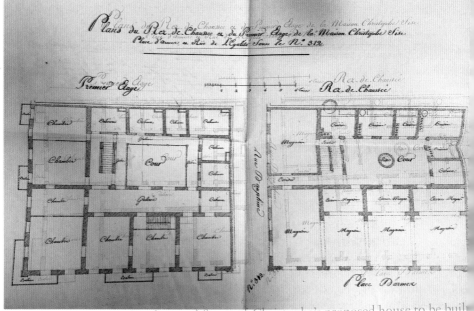

Plans for the ground and second floors of Christophe's proposed house to be built at number 312 rue de l'Égalité in Cap-Français, next to the Place d'Armes, 1802.

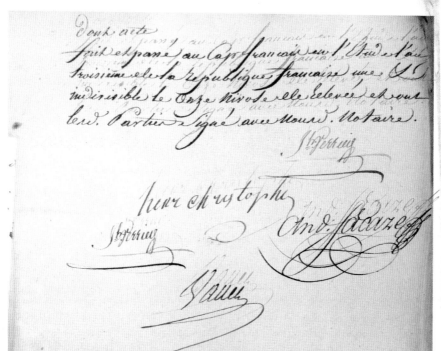

Earliest known full signature of Henry Christophe on the lease for house number 326, owned by Léonard Picard, on the rue de l'Égalité in Cap-Français. December 1794.

Signature of Christophe on a letter he wrote to French colonial authorities seeking release while detained in the Port-au-Prince barracks, dated December 1793.

Signature of Henry Christophe as chef de brigade on a letter he wrote to Commissioner Julien Raimond in August 1797, showing the evolution of Christophe's signature as he gained more authority and responsibility in Saint-Domingue.

The fancy signature adopted by Henry Christophe, general in chief of the Haitian army, at the time (and later as king), as shown on a letter he wrote to the emperor Jean-Jacques Dessalines on July 13, 1806.

French-government-commissioned map of the city of Cap-Français on which are marked in black the ravages of the June 1793 fire and, in red, the islets, parts of islets, buildings, and other structures that still existed after the fire that occurred on June 21, 1793, and in which most of the city suffered damage. Published around 1793.

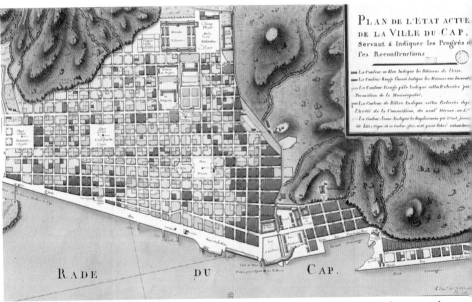

French-government-commissioned map of the city of Cap-Français, indicating the progress of its reconstruction in 1800, following the June 1793 fire that destroyed most of the city's buildings. The color blue shows buildings owned by the French government; buildings marked in dark red indicate structures that did not burn in the fire; buildings appearing in pink and beige mark those sites the government authorize for reconstruction; those buildings colored yellow indicate plots of land that containe no structure at the time of the fire; those in gray indicate buildings not authorized for reconstruction that remained in a burned-down state.

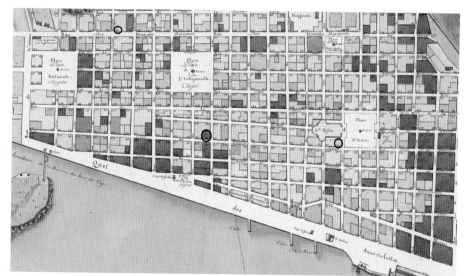

Portion of the French government's 1800 map of the reconstruction of Cap-Français, showing with black circles the home that Christophe leased at number 326 rue de l'Égalité, the home he proposed to build on the same street at number 312, and, farther south, the site of the not yet authorized for reconstruction La Couronne hotel at number 788 rue Espagnole/Française, where Christophe previously worked and which had burned almost entirely.

CHRISTOPHE
Incendiaire de la ville du Cap,
dont il était commandant en chef.

Paris chez l'Éditeur rue St Jacques N 198.

King Henry's coat of arms, bearing his famous mottoes, above which is a description written in cursive handwriting: "Azure gate leading to the Golden Phoenix, the background of the shield dotted with stars; for supports, two ermine lions armed with golden crowns." The ribbon below the phoenix reads, "I am reborn from my ashes." The pink ribbon under the lions says, "God is my cause, and my sword."

towards heaven, they seemed to demand vengeance on the author of their untimely death."[135]

Around this time, Minister Decrès—the same official who ordered the torture of Louverture—arrived at the Collège de la Marche and openly rebuked the students of color. Among them were not only Christophe's son Ferdinand but Louis-Rémy Clervaux, the son of General Augustin Clervaux. Clervaux, along with Christophe and Dessalines, signed a preliminary Declaration of Independence on November 29, 1803, and like Christophe and Dessalines, Clervaux had abandoned the Black army in the spring of 1802, only to later reunite with it in the fall. During the period of reunification with France, both Christophe and Clervaux confided their children to Leclerc to be sent to Paris, via General Boudet. By November, the man who promised the children's safe passage and protection no longer lived, and the French government considered their parents rebels of the republic.

Because this was the case with many others in the school, Decrès told the children the French government no longer intended to provide student pensions and that any pupils who did not have the means to pay would be sent into the army. Both Louis-Rémy and Ferdinand were in that category. While the French government determined an appropriate destination for their military service, the boys were placed in La Maison des Orphelins in Paris, along with the youngest student at the school, six-and-a-half-year-old Valère Morrisseau.[136] Neither Christophe nor Clervaux is ever known to have seen his child again.[137]

Revenge against the children of the revolutionaries was clearly one of the goals. In an April 1803 letter, written a week before Louverture's death, Decrès outlined his ultimate plan for Ferdinand: "The financial state in which his parents have left him and the education that they have proposed for him suit him perhaps less than any other individual of color; the safety and future of the colonies require perhaps that he should be reminded of this and limited to agricultural and mechanical work." Rather ironically, Decrès proposed Bonaparte's home island of Corsica as the best place for young Ferdinand to learn the "mechanical" and "agricultural" trades.[138]

A letter from Blaise Le Chat, another pupil, dated from Marseille on July 10, 1814, gives some inkling of what happened at the school just before the Haitian army defeated the French in Saint-Domingue. In late 1802, Le Chat wrote, "Decrès came to the college and gathered all the Americans together in the courtyard, and after speaking to us in the harshest of terms, he at last told us that the government no longer desired to take responsibility for our education, that he felt it had already done too much for people like us, and that, from that moment forward, the school of the colonies had ceased to exist."[139] Ferdinand initially went back to Lambert's to join his aunt. Then, in December 1803, with the French having officially surrendered Saint-Domingue the month prior, the French government sent

Ferdinand to the orphanage. A month later, in January 1804, following the declaration of Haitian independence, the French government committed Tante Marie to the infamous French mental asylum, La Salpêtrière. She died there a year and a half afterward.

Tante Marie never did get to tell her own story about what happened to her and her nephew. An eyewitness account furnished to the Martinican jurist and naturalist M. L. E. Moreau de Saint-Méry by Praxelles, friend of Tante Marie's and godmother of one of Christophe's daughters, fills in many gaps about what happened. According to Praxelles, Ferdinand and his aunt arrived in France in the fall of 1802 with plenty of "gold, jewels, and other merchandise," which Christophe had provided for their pension.[140] The events that led young Ferdinand to go from the rich son of a supposedly respected French general to the despised offspring of a newly hated Haitian rebel shook the child's world like an earthquake.

Much like Isaac and Placide, Ferdinand received an invitation to Tuileries to dine with the Bonapartes. Tante Marie and her young nephew graciously accepted to appear before the first consul. Although Bonaparte claimed he wanted to keep Ferdinand nearby so that he could watch over him, not long afterward Decrès arrived to shutter the Collège. Having tried with difficulty to learn of her friend Marie's whereabouts, as well as that of the child over whom she had guardianship, Praxelles learned that the French government had locked up Marie in La Salpêtrière, with unknown pretext, forbidding her any visitors. Praxelles did not know Ferdinand's whereabouts. She later learned from a Madame de Saint-Joseph, the woman in charge of the ward where Marie was confined, that the government had relegated Ferdinand to the Maison des Orphelins, appropriately nicknamed La Pitié, or Pity. When Praxelles went to see how young Christophe fared, he seemed bewildered about all that had befallen him. Insistent that his father was a friend of Bonaparte's, the child remonstrated against accusations that Christophe had been deemed a "huge brigand who was massacring whites in Saint-Domingue." Ferdinand also asserted that his father had provided for his subsistence and that he had no need to rely on the state.[141]

Ferdinand and his aunt should have had more than enough money to survive without the French government's support. A July 9, 1805, letter informing Cossé, an official at the orphanage, of Tante Marie's death explained, "Young Christophe, one of the students at your hospice, has just lost his aunt, the negress Marie, with whom he had come from Saint-Domingue. The effects that belong to him are to be found with those of his aunt and I urge you to claim them. . . . I must also warn you that according to what Marie told me several times, there is a fairly considerable sum of gold belonging to her and to her nephew deposited with Mr. Lambert." The letter writer tried to contact Lambert and retrieve the goods, but Lambert refused. "You may have more luck by announcing to him that you are the person responsible for securing the interest of the minor," the French official counseled.[142]

In July 1805, Cossé sent the letter, along with a more detailed one, to a higher-ranking official with oversight over French orphanages. Neither letter mentioned that Ferdinand had already died. In recounting the child's arrival at the orphanage two days before Christmas in 1803, Cossé revealed that it was Lambert who had Ferdinand removed from his home and placed in the orphanage:

> The child's aunt, who had accompanied him on his voyage, deposited with Mr. Lambert a sum of 100 louis to meet the expenses relating to the education of her nephew. Shortly afterward, coming upon the heels of the all too true news that the blacks were insurgent and that General Christophe was at the head of the revolt, it seems that Mr. Lambert informed the government that the young Christophe and his aunt were residents in his Paris and that subsequently the minister intervened, by virtue of which this child was sent to the orphanage and his aunt to Salpêtrière, where she has just died. This woman kept with her young Ferdinand's trunk, which contains linen, clothing, and one or two pieces of silverware, marked with the name of the child, who now claims this trunk and all that it contains, as well as the effects of his aunt.

If this story was a ruse on the part of Cossé, designed to confiscate Christophe's belongings and conceal the death of the child in his care, it was an elaborate one. The letter continued with the claim that before she died, Tante Marie told Lambert to expect a communication and funds from Christophe to facilitate his son's return to independent Haiti:

> As for that which concerns Mr. Lambert, Ferdinand's aunt declared that over a month or about six weeks ago, she received several letters proving that Christophe sent [Lambert] a fairly high sum for the education of his son, and failing that, for his return to Saint-Domingue. This declaration coincides perfectly with the opinion, recently communicated to me, that an American was ordered to kidnap the young Ferdinand and take him to the United States and thence to Saint-Domingue but that this captain, under suspicion by the government, left hastily without being able to carry out his abduction project.[143]

Lambert, who was the first to house Ferdinand and his aunt when they arrived in Paris, and who seemingly betrayed them both, never did relinquish more than a few objects to French authorities. Praxelles implied that Lambert stole the money and shamelessly bought a large house on the Champs-Élysées that Praxelles called "richly furnished."[144] When questioned by authorities about the rest of the Christophe child's effects, Lambert claimed that the abbé Collin only ever gave him a sum of 100 louis for Ferdinand and his aunt. The abbé Collin, for his part, claimed to have been duped by Christophe, who never furnished him with the promised money for the young ward and his guardian, landing Ferdinand in the orphanage, or so Lambert testified. Lambert also denied knowing anything about a scheme for Ferdinand to be repatriated.[145]

Throughout August 1805, the French government tried to find the money and objects that Christophe sent. After that, Ferdinand disappeared from French records. Although the head of the orphanage and the government seemed to express genuine concern for the objects and funds, putatively for the items to be returned to Ferdinand, it is curious that no mention is made in any of the documents of Ferdinand's actual whereabouts at the time. Was the French government trying to cover up Ferdinand's death just as it had tried to do with Louverture's?

Praxelles, for her part, strongly condemned the French government for Ferdinand's death, saying that in reality he died *before* his aunt, who took her last breath on July 8. After Ferdinand refused to work in a shoemaker's shop, protesting that he did not need government support nor an apprenticeship and continuing to insist that his father sent ample money, the shoemaker reportedly beat the then eleven-year-old boy in the streets of Paris. Praxelles testified that Ferdinand Christophe "was beaten so severely that his body formed several abscesses, from which he died."[146] Other putative eyewitnesses reported that Ferdinand died on July 7, 1805, the day before his aunt, which is the date of his death listed in official documents from the kingdom.[147]

"Oh, unfortunate father, console yourself," Vastey later counseled Christophe. "It is better for your dear and beloved son to be dead than to have him be alive but in the power of those monsters." Imagining how the French might have tried to use Ferdinand to coerce Christophe into submission, Vastey reminded the king, "You would have seen them dangle him before you, as they did with General Toussaint; they would have put you in the same cruel agony; they would have forced you to weigh his life against the salvation of your country!" Suggesting that the future king would never have chosen his children over the nation, Vastey told Christophe, "We know of your greatness and the magnanimity of your soul; you would not have hesitated for a moment to make this painful and generous sacrifice."[148]

Is it possible that Christophe had already been forced to make this trade, though? Although he appeared to follow French military orders until late September 1802, by early October generals and soldiers in the French army, as well as ordinary citizens—many of whom believed that Christophe never truly joined the side of the French—openly acknowledged that Christophe had defected to the side of the "rebels."[149]

Christophe never wavered in his stance that slavery had to remain forbidden on the island of Saint-Domingue, but he knew that Bonaparte had not shown commitment to abolition elsewhere in the Caribbean. Perhaps Christophe waited to officially defect until his son had left the island precisely because Ferdinand's life hung in the balance, or perhaps events on the ground made it impossible for him to continue on in the French army after September 1802. After all, we have only Leclerc's account of what ultimately occurred during his decisive meeting with Christophe that April. In that letter published in *Le moniteur universel,* Leclerc described a fawning and obsequious Christophe, inexplicably more in love with France than ever after having ardently expressed his disdain for that same France by burning down its most important colonial port.

Christophe and Marie-Louise, who welcomed daughters in 1798 and 1800 and a second son in 1804, remained for many years unaware of the fate of their firstborn child. Confirmation of Ferdinand's death did not reach Christophe until closer to the time he became king of Haiti in 1811. Years of fruitless inquiry, plus knowledge about the treatment of Louverture and his family, could not have given the elder Christophe much hope that he would ever see his son alive again. On March 28, 1805, the *Political and Commercial Gazette of Haiti,* the state-run newspaper under Dessalines, reprinted a January 5 news report from the *New York Herald.* The report, based on a British newspaper article from the autumn of 1804, detailed how the French government chained and jailed Madame Louverture and kept the news of her husband's death from her. When under interrogation she claimed to know nothing about the 300,000 pounds that the French accused Toussaint of having hidden somewhere in Saint-Domingue, the French subjected her to "instruments of Torture . . . *while in a state of pregnancy . . .* which resulted in a premature labor," causing the baby to be stillborn. After reprinting the story, the editor of the *Gazette* asked, "If it is true that Madame Toussaint experienced the torments related in the following report, what idea should we form of the present government of France? And what methods should we permit ourselves to use to prevent their return to dominate us, which would occasion only that every Haitian could be subjected to a similar fate as that of which this poor woman has been the victim?"[150]

French efforts to hold on to Saint-Domingue, like those the French later used to recapture it, remained violent and unyielding. "We say it, and we repeat it continuously in front of the blacks," reads the account of one genocidal supporter of the French mission, "that we must massacre every last one of them."[151]

As Louverture frequently noted in his letters to French officials and in his memoir, he tried to compromise with French authority, and even accepted some blame, but the French punished him anyway. In the letter he wrote to Bonaparte aboard the *Héros,* Toussaint implored, "Citizen First

Consul, I will not conceal from you my faults: I have committed several. Is any man exempt from them?" Louverture also noted that, having accepted Leclerc's assurance of amnesty and retired to his lands, as promised, he was tricked and summarily arrested by the French.[152] The betrayal had therefore been all on France's side. Alluding to Bonaparte's allowance of slavery in parts of the French Caribbean in May 1802, and despondent over his forced estrangement from his family, Louverture told Caffarelli while in prison, "Saint-Domingue is a huge treasure, but to bring it to its full potential, you need . . . the peace and freedom of the blacks. But oh! General, I don't care about treasures, because I have lost things far more precious than treasures."[153] Christophe, too, would find that all the treasures in the world could not make up for the loss of his son, whose death the future Haitian king considered the "darkest betrayal and the most infamous perfidy" of his life.

The many pages of documents that detail how Louverture died contain not only the tale of a tragedy that befell one man. Within Toussaint's death is also a story about the unexpected and ultimately unknowable effect of a single bad decision, ricocheting like scattershot, leaving deadly holes everywhere in its wake. Christophe's initial reunification with the French side haunted nearly every aspect of his life like an angry specter. The grandest and most tragic of the consequences of this defection, for him, was the death of his own son. Ferdinand's loss was a forever reminder of Christophe's role in the events that led to the wrongful death of his onetime friend and commander, Louverture. While the error of defection was his father's alone, Ferdinand, eerily, shared the fate of the storied ex-general Toussaint: a cold and lonely death in France.

Much later, the official court musician, Juste Chanlatte, wrote a song lamenting the death of Christophe's son to be sung by Ferdinand's brothers: Eugène, Christophe's son from a previous relationship, and Prince Victor-Henry, heir to the throne. "Ferdinand! . . . noble Ferdinand!" the royal prince sang. "This cry launched at our walls / Will be the resounding signal of tears, blood, and battles." "Ferdinand!" said his brother Eugène in refrain, "cowardly atrocity! I swear to follow you soon, / Or not to let impunity survive after your death." Ferdinand's shadow also cast its deathly pall over Chanlatte's song written in praise of the royal princesses. The song both represented a battle cry meant to remind the kingdom's subjects of all they had sacrificed in the name of freedom and independence and stood as a reminder that the royal family had not been spared the personal losses experienced by all Haitians who survived the revolution:

Tremble, Frenchman! Two armed sisters
For a brother the ramparts haunted.
Tremble . . . from his alarming loss

Dangers they do cause.
Of the most august victim
Of a kind and magnanimous Prince
They made the iron thunder,
Ferdinand! . . . O mortal pain!
Thunderstorm! O criminal fury!
Yes, your sisters have the bolt of lightning in their hands.
Appease yourself, darling Shadow!
Calm your regrets, your pains;
Your noble Parents, the Fatherland
Do not limit themselves to tears
Do you see Madame Première
From Mars face the quarry
To try to avenge you,
The young and proud Athénaïre
Of Bellona taking control,
For you, to all danger scorn?

Electrified by their example
See our bold hearts
Serving at the temple of your virtues
Aspire only to the glorious day
Where tyrants taming rage
They will be able to wash away from such a great outrage
All the shame and the pain.
Ferdinand! . . . your name, your memory,
For us, to the cogs of glory,
Will be the cry of valor.

—lines penned by Juste Chanlatte for the
deceased Ferdinand, October 10, 1817[154]

7

AMERICA AVENGED

While the lives of both Toussaint Louverture and Ferdinand Christophe hung in the balance in France, the situation back in Saint-Domingue had been deteriorating. Was the loyalty to France of most of the Black generals of the colonial army genuine or duplicitous? Some of the formerly enslaved freedom fighters never realigned themselves with the French colonial army or did so only briefly before deserting definitively. We will follow the custom of Haitian historians and call these latter men and women the independents. They were still openly fighting the French military, including the Black colonial army. When the Black generals of the colonial army officially, and definitively, separated from the French for the final time in the fall of 1802, France was once again forced to fight two separate wars on this tiny sliver of land—one against the Black soldiers and officers who had defected from the French colonial army, and who would eventually reconstitute themselves under the title of the armée indigène, *and another against the independents, who only reluctantly later joined the* armée indigène *in their shared quest to make Haiti free. The French had to contend also with an unfavorable climate where yellow fever spread faster than the fires that had once ravaged the cane fields. Of course, Leclerc and his successor, Rochambeau, had no idea that the now united Black freedom fighters of Saint-Domingue, coupled with a disease that the Haitian revolutionaries believed was heaven-sent, would ultimately doom him and his mission. Instead of retreating from this evil expedition to bring back slavery, under Rochambeau's leadership, the French army committed terrors and tortures worthy of only the most hellish fiends. Luckily for Haiti, the French were no match for Dessalines, who led the Haitians to victory in declaring, "I have avenged America."*

Passing the law to reinstate French slavery in the colonies was far easier than trying to apply it.[1] After all, the loyalty of the Black generals and officers to the French army was tenuous. Most had only agreed a few weeks before the May 1802 law's ratification to lay down their arms, and only after Leclerc publicly declared that Bonaparte did *not* have plans to reinstate slavery in Saint-Domingue. If Bonaparte wanted Leclerc to reinstate slavery on Saint-Domingue, as Richepanse did on Guadeloupe, it would have to be done *without* the assistance of the Black generals from the colonial army.

Leclerc made his first attempt to reinstitute slavery by issuing a new rural code. Like Hédouville's, it mandated that laborers, most of whom were formerly enslaved and darker-skinned Black people, had to return to the plantations upon which they had previously been enslaved, which is to say the lands of their former enslavers. Next, Leclerc set about disarming the laborers. He tried to enlist Christophe and Dessalines in this task, which was difficult because the laborers in the interior and mountains of the colony, the so-called independents, intended to keep fighting against the French military and the colonial army.[2] Growing more desperate by the day, Leclerc resorted to the most unthinkable measure: genocide.

In Leclerc's February 17, 1802, proclamation—the one in which he declared Toussaint and Christophe "outlaws"—the captain general specified that "General Augustin Clervaux, who commands the department of Cibao, having recognized the French government and the authority of the captain general, is maintained in his grade and his command."[3] However, soon after Louverture's arrest, Leclerc ordered Clervaux to take the Sixth Demi-brigade back to Cap to reinforce the city. Just before he handed down this order, Dessalines called both Clervaux and Christophe to Haut-du-Cap and tried to convince them that, considering Louverture's arrest, they could no longer trust Leclerc and should cease following the captain general's orders, at least that is how Dessalines's secretary Boisrond-Tonnerre told the story. According to Boisrond-Tonnerre, Christophe agreed completely. Clervaux was not so sure. Boisrond-Tonnerre suspected a dispute between Clervaux and Christophe had resulted in Clervaux's ambivalence. Ultimately, and much to his detriment, Clervaux followed Leclerc's order rather than Dessalines's, and that same day the French military drowned all two hundred members of the Sixth Demi-brigade, men previously under Clervaux's command.[4] Leclerc had ordered any soldiers suspected of disloyalty to be arrested, drowned, or hanged. *The Times* of London printed one British officer's report of these executions: "Leclerc had disarmed, shipped, and drowned the whole of the 6th Regiment, with a great number of the Town Negroes, together with their wives and children; no trial was wanting at this time, their color condemned them, innocent and guilty, and their corpses floating in the harbour occasioned such a pestilence, that General Leclerc was compelled to retire out of the garrison."[5]

News of these drownings inspired even more insurrections. As accounts spread, more laborers joined the independent soldiers in Moustique, Port-de-Paix, and Plaisance, rising up against the French army trying to kill them and against the colonial army trying to disarm them. In response, Leclerc dispatched General Brunet, nicknamed the "*gendarme* of Leclerc," to Plaisance, where he reportedly perpetrated a massacre so heinous that not a single soul remained alive. Brunet repeated the same operation in Gros-Morne and Gonaïves. From this moment forward, the French military's tactic involved total extermination. Leclerc claimed that Bonaparte's reinstatement of slavery in Guadeloupe left him without other options. One month before his death, he wrote to Bonaparte to complain that news of French reinstatement of slavery in Guadeloupe had reached the colony to the most worrying effect. Though he remained concerned, he had a novel tactic in mind: depopulating the colony of all current people of color. "If my position has turned from good to critical," Leclerc wrote, "it is not just because of the yellow fever but also from the premature reestablishment of slavery in Guadeloupe, as well as the newspapers and letters from France that speak of nothing but slavery. Here is my opinion on this country: We must destroy all the blacks in the mountains—men and women—and spare only the children under twelve years of age. We must destroy half of those in the plains and must not leave a single colored person in the colony who has worn an epaulet."[6]

The effects of this policy struck immediately, and fatally. Tales of the French military's mass drownings of "the blacks" and "men of color" were reported by Haitian eyewitnesses like Vastey and Boisrond-Tonnerre, who evoked these episodes as proof that violence could only meet violence and excess only excess in revolutionary Saint-Domingue. Multiple white eyewitnesses, including French military officers, noted that the French had decided to "kill anyone who could kill us."[7] Marcus Rainsford, another British military officer stationed in Saint-Domingue during the English occupation of the island, reported, "The [French] government at this period . . . assumed a complexion more sanguinary and terrible than can be conceived among civilized people. . . . In attempting to disarm the black troops . . . the most barbarous methods were practiced, shiploads were collected and suffocated in the holds. In one instance, six hundred being surrounded, and attempting a resistance, were massacred on the spot; and such slaughters daily took place in the vicinity of Cap-Français, that the air became tainted by the putrefaction of the bodies."[8] The Scottish author Leitch Ritchie, who claimed to have received a similar firsthand account from a British traveler, characterized the Leclerc expedition as "a scene of blood and torture . . . such as history had never before disclosed, and compared with which, though planned and executed by whites, all the barbarities, said to have been perpetrated by the insurgent blacks of the north, amount comparatively to nothing." He continued, "Unsparing massacre and the refusal of all quarter became the order of the renewed hostility on both sides;—but for the African and his descendants were reserved deaths the most horrible. Thousands were nightly carried out in their harbours and drowned, or they were thrown alive, men, women, and children, to bloodhounds, to be torn limb from limb and devoured.

No torment was considered too excessive; no mode of destroying life too dreadful to be inflicted."[9]

Some French military officers, like the Martinican-born white French soldier Joseph Élysée Peyre-Ferry, seemed at first to justify the executions by claiming that Dessalines had long been assassinating whites, nearly indiscriminately. Even so, Peyre-Ferry's own testimony about France's attempted genocide corroborates British reports. Peyre-Ferry noted that he had orders "to exterminate and annihilate on the spot . . . the rebels wandering in the plantations." He was also forced to attend such executions and often found himself surrounded by the bodies of dead "negroes." In an account he wrote after the fact using notes from a journal he kept while stationed in Saint-Domingue, Peyre-Ferry outright condemned that "the black troops who found themselves in Cap were disarmed, embarked, then swallowed up by the sea." "Oh, barbarity!" he lamented. "Was it necessary to add this crime to those already committed! . . . Twelve to fifteen hundred unfortunates died on this occasion of this sort of cruel death. These executions, as unjust as they were impolitic, were repeated in multiple places, and everywhere caused to surge up against us swarms of enemies."[10]

Alongside the drowning of the Sixth Demi-brigade, one of the most infamous tales of execution came from the French general Jean-Pierre Ramel, who served under General Morpas for the colonial army. He reported that in August 1802, after Morpas's submission and defection to the French, Leclerc summoned him to Cap, as the latter had done with Clervaux. Unlike in the case of Clervaux, who survived the execution of his brigade, Leclerc proceeded to have Morpas and his entire family drowned. Forty-eight hours after Morpas, previously commander over the city of Port-de-Paix, arrived in Cap, Ramel learned that Morpas, "his wife, and his very young children were thrown into the sea." "Never had any news made me so sad," he lamented. "I recalled that when I accompanied Morpas to the port and at the moment we were about to separate, he embraced me and said he believed they wanted to kill him."[11] Chanlatte's account of this horrifying execution adds other painful details. Having been conducted on board a ship harbored in Cap, Morpas "was moored to the huge mast." Afterward, "the French fastened two epaulets to his shoulders and an old general's hat to his head, with nails of the kind that are utilized in the construction of large ships."[12] This is how Morpas was treated before his death, even though, as a *French* general, he previously declared he would never again "separate himself from France and asked [General Ramel] to write to Leclerc seeking permission for him to go to France."[13] Yet, just as with the other Black generals, Morpas's stated devotion to France had not been constant, nor were his loyalties to the republic professed without ambiguity.

Christophe is undoubtedly the most famous of the Black generals to have resisted the initial arrival of the Leclerc expedition. But Morpas, too, had refused to surrender his post to the French, before he rejoined the republican army. Writing directly to the French general Jean-Joseph-Amable Humbert on February 9, 1802, Morpas responded to Leclerc with a menacing tone that rivaled Christophe's. "Citizen General," he wrote, "I have just received your letter this instant. I cannot acquiesce to your request to place troops here without an immediate order from my superior. Consequently, I warn you that I will receive none of them." "I therefore warn you to withdraw or else I will salute you with a cannonball," he finished. Humbert was not deterred. The next day, the city fell to the French, and eventually Morpas surrendered and began working on their behalf to disarm the cultivators.[14]

Despite his professed loyalty to the French republic, in November 1802 Morpas found himself arrested and imprisoned on the ship that was to be the scene of his gruesome death. Before the French army killed him, Morpas wrote directly to Rochambeau to protest his treatment and plead his innocence. Attributing the suspicion that led to his arrest to the "color that differentiates us, which you seek to punish me for," Morpas insisted that he did not want to be sent to France, even on the strength of the promised "commendation" to be sent to the first consul. "If I were here alone, without a family, I wouldn't mind being transported to a faraway land," he pleaded. "Allow me instead, General," he continued, "to retire and live as a simple private individual, either in Cap or on La Tortue, or in any other place occupied by the French." "I feel strong enough to forage in the bosom of the earth for the sustenance necessary for my family," he concluded. Morpas's pleas had no effect. Not long after he wrote this letter, the French murdered Morpas's wife and children in front of him, before nailing the pair of epaulets onto his naked shoulders.[15]

After French troops murdered Morpas, they confiscated his papers, as they did with Louverture. Included in his official dossier held at the French Overseas Archives are his certificate of service for the French military and the documents listing the plantations he leased under the French affermage system, to be sequestered after his death. Within these papers we also find precious details about his life and family as well as an incredibly precise list of his personal effects.

From his marriage certificate, dated January 6, 1801, we learn that Jacques Scipion Morpas, born in Mornet in the dependency of Acul, a commune of Cap, was the *fils naturel* of the late citoyen Scipion and citoyenne Rose. His wife, Marie-Louise, a native of Marmelade, was also a *fille naturelle*. Her parents were Jean Baptiste Julien and Citoyenne Denne Julie. At the time of their marriage, Morpas and his wife adopted each other's children from prior relationships.[16]

Morpas, who leased several plantations, must have been quite wealthy at the time of his death. When the French government raided his home in Port-de-Paix, they claimed to find more than thirty large trunks, bags, and money boxes, which contained fancy embroidered clothing, including dresses and skirts made of imported silk and lace, collared shirts, hats, scarves, shoes, baskets, and military garb of all kinds, as well as "a gold slavery necklace," acquired by Marie-Louise. Above all, they found a considerable amount of jewelry, including one necklace described as having "twenty large gold grains and eight grains of blue crystals"; there were other bejeweled gold necklaces, pearls, earrings, rings, and bracelets, along with numerous medallions, and one had a portrait of Morpas on one side and his wife on the other.[17]

Christophe spoke highly of Morpas, whose savage death, he later said, could "excite indignation in the heart least accessible to pity." Christophe described the deceased brigadier general as having "a soft and easy disposition," saying he was "honest and highly regarded by his fellow citizens."[18] It was all the more curious that the French killed him, because Morpas was still serving their interests, even helping the French to put his commander on board the ship. About a week before the French put Morpas to death, General Brunet wrote to Leclerc, on October 24, 1802, to explain how he tricked Morpas, reassuring him that the operation in Port-de-Paix, with Morpas and his brigade now captured, was complete. "All the colonial troops" had been "embarked on the frigate the *Créole* and the *Guerrière*," Brunet reported. "All this was done without noise and without problem." "General Morpas assisted me perfectly," Brunet continued. "He had his wife and family embarked with everything belonging to him." Suspecting nothing, Brunet boasted, "he even said to me that the captain general knows that I am faithful to the government and attached to his person." Brunet finished by telling the captain general, "Every suspect person in Port-de-Paix has been put on board, and they have all been taken to Cap." "I observe, however, that Morpas will undertake the campaign with me. I answer you to take him to Cap, unless he is killed during the affair," Brunet added.[19] Although the French military later labored to paint officers like Morpas as rebels in need of punishment, according to Brunet's own account, Morpas seemed to follow French orders. Perhaps he learned while on the ship of the French army's genocidal intentions and objected. Or perhaps he never protested until it was too late.

General Ramel reported that during this time the French military systematically massacred Black officers and civilians not in rebellion: "Who were the men whom we drowned in Saint-Domingue? Blacks who had been captured as prisoners on the fields of battle? No; Conspirators? Even less so! Nobody was convicted of anything: because of a simple suspicion, a report, an equivocal word, 200, 400, 800, up to 1,500 blacks had been thrown into the sea."[20] The French repeated their massacres of people of color in the colony in Léogâne, Petit-Goâve, Jérémie, and Petit-Trou.[21]

The situation grew so dire in the south of the colony, where a French general named Berger ordered every single nonwhite person in Les Cayes to be drowned, that Boisrond-Tonnerre made the following arresting observation: "If every city of Saint-Domingue had been subject to the orders of such a man, the island would have been depopulated in twenty-four hours." Boisrond-Tonnerre subsequently described "forests turned into hanging grounds," "ships turned into jails," "hundreds of blacks and mulattoes being led to their deaths daily."[22] These were not soldiers simply running amok of their superiors. General Leclerc told Rochambeau on August 6, 1802, that such terror was the point. "Have any man who comes under suspicion ruthlessly arrested: let these arrests not be made all at once if they are for important people," Leclerc warned. "If anyone objects, hang them," he continued. "Inspire great terror, it is the only way to keep the blacks in check."[23]

The French also invented new instruments of torture to carry out these executions. These included using sulfur fumes produced by ship's vapors. The French army used this method to poison with sulfur gas the hundreds of victims they imprisoned in the holds of ships at the same time. Nineteen Black prisoners Berger kept captive aboard a single French frigate lost their lives in this manner.[24] These floating prisons, also called *étouffoirs,* were perhaps the first gas chambers used in an attempt to commit genocide in modern history. Every day the cadavers of the victims washed ashore, empty vessels of those unfortunate souls.[25]

Peyre-Ferry, hardly a sympathetic observer, painted a picture of this tragedy made only more gruesome by his racism. After the suffocations were complete, the French simply emptied their victims into the sea: "All those bodies, swollen due to the water, skin dissolved due to the heat of the sun and the friction of the sand, had undergone a change in color from black to livid white, making their corpses appear even more hideous."[26] The more people they killed, the more military honors French officers and soldiers acquired. "To arrest, to drown, or to hang, all signified the same thing," Boisrond-Tonnerre reported. "To them, drowning two hundred individuals was a national glory; to hang someone meant obtaining a promotion."[27]

The Baron de Vastey also personally witnessed some of the French army's executions during the Leclerc expedition. On one particularly gruesome day, Vastey recalled that French military scheduled three men to be burned alive at the Place Royale in Cap. As the rumor of their impending deaths circulated throughout the city, a huge crowd flocked to the public square to watch what Vastey called "this horrible auto-da-fé." Some were drawn there, no doubt, by curiosity, he said, others stood shocked and fascinated at the same time by "how far the barbarity and cruelty of our tyrants could go." "On arriving at the Place Royale, I saw two poles planted in the ground," Vastey wrote, "one with two iron rings, and the other with only one ring, where the necks of the three victims were to be placed." "Piles of wood were artfully arranged around the poles, shavings were placed on them, tar was thrown on them to make the material flammable, and the fire more active and violent," he continued. "Everyone stood around the pyre, some with their heads down, afraid to raise their eyes to stare at the terrible device; others, the ex-colonists and their acolytes, burst into joy." At three o'clock in the afternoon the general in command of the city approached the stake accompanied by a large entourage. The three victims awaited in a nearby guardhouse until the general gave the order to lead them to the stake. Drums sounded "as if on a triumphal march," Vastey lamented. With a sugarcane in their hands, the victims were secured on the pyre and attached to the posts, while the crowd fell silent. Then the general ordered the pyre lit. "Immediately the flame fizzed, the captives' feet began to catch fire," Vastey wrote. "We could immediately hear their screams and see them struggling in horrible torment. . . . Soon they were enveloped in flames; their bodies split open, grease dripping onto the pyre; thick smoke rising with the smell of roasted flesh." A scene too gruesome for the spectators, they afterward "fled and scattered in horror." The executioners alone remained in the square and "withdrew only when their victims were completely reduced to ashes!" Vastey concluded.[28]

With general insurrection taking place throughout the colony, and the bodies of the young and old piling up, fire was visible from nearly every port. From Port-au-Prince, all that could be seen in the distance was ominously rising smoke.[29] At the same time, mosquito-borne yellow fever was decimating French military forces, particularly in Saint-Marc. On August 27, 1802, a French captain in the city announced the death of almost an entire battalion. Shortly thereafter, more than six hundred men from another French battalion died of yellow fever in Cap. The Seventy-First Battalion experienced the greatest losses, being completely annihilated by the disease.[30]

On November 2, 1802, General Leclerc succumbed to the hemorrhagic fever. In its final stages, yellow fever can cause bleeding from the nose, mouth, and eyes. The Haitian revolutionaries wholeheartedly welcomed the vampiric Leclerc's vampiric death. "It was important for humanity that the number of tyrants should be diminished, and his disappearance . . . was ultimately good," said Boisrond-Tonnerre, though he acknowledged that Leclerc was succeeded by one of the worst monsters on earth.[31] General Rochambeau immediately assumed the role of interim captain general and continued his predecessor's campaign of attempting to drown, gas, hang, or shoot all the people of color in the colony under the slightest pretext, or none at all.[32]

On January 10, 1803, Rochambeau issued an order "to exterminate the negro generals, black soldiers and officers, along with the former laborers." Three and a half months later, he wrote to the French minister of the marine that he needed even more troops to complete the extermination. "We must support the war of the whites against the two other colors in this colony, so as to create a new order. Without this, we will have to start over again every two or three years. . . . I am here now. . . . I understand this execrable colony. . . . I believe that my plan is the only one to adopt in order to sail this infernal hell into port."[33] Christophe had been a nightmare for the French ever since he ordered the burning of Cap, which was why it had been so important for Leclerc to win him over to their side. General Jean Hardy, commander of the divisions of the north for the French, recognized as much when he wrote to Leclerc on April 2, 1802, after his men lost several hundred troops to Christophe near Saint-Michel: "In the nine years that I have been in the war as a general officer, I can assure you that I have not yet seen an action as cruel as these. I have many brave people to regret, my division has been weakened by nearly four hundred men, both killed and wounded."[34] This was not to be the last time that the French military officers complained of Christophe's military prowess.

Another general informed Rochambeau on January 27, 1803, that earlier that morning he learned with certainty that Christophe had worked to breach French camps and take Fort-Liberté: "Christophe's projects, which were widespread before my arrival, froze the Spaniards with fear."[35] The same day, at five o'clock in the evening, Chef de brigade Louis Labelinaye announced a bounty on Christophe's head:

> The principles of the French government have never changed; it has always been just: but if monsters, such as your leaders, have had enough preponderance to overwhelm you with evils, here is the day when your vengeance must burst forth. You must capture Christophe; there is a price for his head. Whoever brings it to the general in chief will receive 1,000 *portugaises*. However, I do not pretend to put pecuniary interests first, but rather that of all your brothers, who are also ours. Destroy the tyrants and receive from me the assurance of the kindness that General Rochambeau is willing to offer you, and know that the destruction of the infamous Christophe will put an end to all the evils of which we have been suffering for a long time.[36]

By the time the French decided to offer cash for his head, Christophe had emerged as a seasoned military man, and the mishap at the Battle of Savannah seems to have taught him something about cease-fires. Christophe knew the French to be capable of many ruses, and he intended to undertake his own, regardless of the reputation for ferocity it earned him.

Shortly after he rejoined the Black colonial army, Christophe wrote to Chef de Brigade Baron, commander of Limbé, demanding that he surrender the post. "The First, Second, Tenth, and Thirteenth Demi-brigades are in front of our entrenchments. . . . If you are determined to make yourself a prisoner of war, in this case you will be sent to Cap . . . and, on the contrary, resistance on your part would expose you to an attack whose advantage will not be on your side," Christophe wrote. "You can count on my promise; I repeat you will be treated in the customary way."[37] Baron replied immediately that he had zero intention of surrendering but surprisingly asked for a cease-fire. "I have resolved to defend myself unless you grant me twenty-four hours' delay and your word of honor that no hostility will be committed during this delay, and I promise you on my side that none will be committed by the troops I am commanding during the twenty-four hours."[38] When Chef de Brigade Baron tried to explain to General Brunet why he lost the battle, he noted that Christophe told the bearer of the letter that Baron needed to accede to his conditions and sent a letter to that effect demanding an immediate reply. Baron said he intended to defend himself right away, but before he could give orders, he heard "the battery discharge and soon after the brigands appeared and the fusillade began." By rejecting a cease-fire, Christophe ensured that more blood would be shed on the other side than on his own. Baron recalled blood everywhere, while only three "brigands" were wounded. They were subsequently questioned about the number of their troops and the generals who were commanding them. They all reported that "the demi-brigades directed by Christophe were those who started the attack; that there might have been 900 men including three companies of grenadiers and that among the troops many were insurgents, partly armed and partly unarmed." "The twenty-four hours that I had asked Christophe for were to give me time to bring in 150 men that I had placed in lower Limbé," Baron confirmed.[39]

In April 1803, Rochambeau wrote to Bonaparte to request yet more troops not only to help him eliminate Black leaders like Dessalines and Christophe and finally reinstate slavery but to bring an effective end to what he termed a race war between "blacks" and "whites." Rochambeau claimed that he needed "three strong expeditions combined and arriving nearly at the same time to combat, disarm, and chain the Negroes for the future." "Slavery must be proclaimed again in these parts, and the black code made much more severe. I even think that for a time the masters must be given the right of life and death over their slaves," he continued. "This war and that of the whites against the Negroes is murderous, and more difficult than one imagines in Europe. . . . Permit me then, General, that I ask of you to send me only officers who are young, active, and hungry for glory." Obviously unaware that Louverture had recently died, Rochambeau gave some advice to the first consul about what to do with him and other deported officers of color: send them back to Rochambeau for punishment. "The return of Toussaint, Rigaud, Pinchinat, Martial Besse, Pascal, Bellegarde, and others would have a positive effect here," he wrote. "I would hang them from the highest gallows."[40]

For Rochambeau, Leclerc's already horrific tactics of deportation and genocide were not enough to bring the project of extermination to fruition. In a journal written by one of the soldiers from the Polish legion that Bonaparte dispatched to supplement the French army, the officer described Rochambeau's infamous usage of dogs imported from Cuba trained to "eat the blacks." Polish sous-lieutenant Weygell reported:

War is undertaken here differently than it is in Europe—three days ago two hundred dogs from the Spanish colonies were brought here . . . tomorrow we are hoping for four hundred more. . . . They are unleashed every day upon living blacks, whom the dogs tear apart without pity as they devour them.[41]

This "auto-da-fé" of terror, perpetrated by the man whom Chanlatte referred to as the "worthy student of Robespierre," led to the defection of most of the Polish legion and the former free people of color from wealthy plantation-owning families, like Vastey. Vastey, in fact, witnessed some of these canine executions. The first victims of this "scene of horror," in Vastey's recollection, were those living in Cap, upon whom Rochambeau's chief of staff unleashed dogs in front of his own home and at the religious convent. After this, the terrible execution by dog tactic moved to Haut-du-Cap. There, the French trained more of these dogs to eat human flesh, right on the Charrier plantation, previously leased by Jacques Coidavid, stepfather of Christophe's wife. On the day of the executions, several high-ranking officials "dressed up in their uniforms, and donned their municipal scarves, to go to the scene, accompanied by a crowd of bipedal mastiffs, curious to witness the horrible slaughter by quadrupedal mastiffs, a thousand times less ferocious than themselves," Vastey averred:

Several days in advance, they had taken the precaution of having the dogs fast, to stimulate their hunger; from time to time, a victim was presented to them, who was removed as soon as the dogs wanted to pounce on him to devour him; finally, the fatal moment arrived when a few men or women were to be definitively handed over to them; these unfortunate people were tied to posts, in the presence of the commissioners, to prevent them from being able to run away or defend themselves.

Once the dogs were unleashed, they attacked their "prey" immediately, and "in an instant the victims were torn apart, their palpitating flesh in tatters, their blood streaming on all sides; while all that could be heard were their cries of pain and horrible agony." Eventually, "the victims' voices died away, their moans only scarcely heard any longer, while their emaciated corpses still throbbed." The French officials finished off those victims who still breathed with a stab of the dagger. "From one end of the island to the other, the same cruelties were committed by the French," Vastey concluded.[42]

Another free man of color, who, like Vastey, held out his defection from the French army until 1803, General Ferrand Ferou (sometimes spelled "Ferrou"), also chastised the French for the mass killings. His disdain for the unheard-of tactics led him to put himself at the head of a troop of Polish defectors who fought for the Black revolutionaries during the war in Saint-Domingue.[43] The Baron de Vastey explained in explicit terms how the French policy of exterminating all people of color, even those who, like him, previously fought on the side of the French, caused him and many other *hommes de couleur* to turn their backs on the republic for good. Vastey, son of a white Frenchman from Normandy and a free woman of color from Marmelade, daughter of one of the wealthiest planters in Saint-Domingue, described how France's genocidal war of racial extermination immediately affected his life. After fighting against the Black revolutionaries for years, he suddenly joined them in early 1803, "in order to avoid the death that our executioners were preparing for me," he said. "What remorse did I not feel in their midst," when, "forgetting my ingratitude or rather my error, the [Black army] welcomed me among them. . . . From that moment forward I uttered an oath never to separate my cause from that of my fellow men, and I will perish in these sentiments."[44]

Vastey provided an even more painstaking description of another of Rochambeau's novel and sadistic terror tactics. Infamous because of his criminal sexual exploits—which, in the context of slavery and colonialism, meant sexually harassing, assaulting, and raping women—Rochambeau invited women of color to lavish parties in ballrooms decorated only in black shrouds and lit with black candles. Once there, with their husbands and other companions prevented from stepping inside, Rochambeau announced to the women that they were going to attend the funerals of their loved ones. He then killed their lovers and family members in front of them.[45] Vastey, Chanlatte, and Boisrond-Tonnerre all complained about Rochambeau's infamous balls. Officer Peyre-Ferry, who confirmed this disgusting practice with unequivocally damning language, also confessed bewilderment about Rochambeau's funeral parties: "Never was such a party more messianic, more inopportune, and at the same time more ridiculous . . . in a city whose ruins were still fuming with smoke and streets still tainted with blood."[46] Members of the army also reported that while waging this genocidal war, Rochambeau managed to live in extravagant abundance. He filled his home with luxurious draperies, curtains, and pillows and purchased elaborate wallpaper and myriad decorations for his balls, including two Turkish divans "with English-style quilting."[47] The murders he ordered were dreamed up in the cold blood of a capitalist.

The French military's brutal tactics pushed the Black generals, at least overtly, back to the side of the independent Black army. Back on October 15, 1802, just before he openly rejoined Christophe, who had already abandoned the colonial army, Dessalines wrote to General Brunet to complain about Leclerc's army's horrific massacres, which had begun to personally affect his family. First, expressing his devotion to France and to Leclerc, Dessalines observed that the island had exploded once more into fully blown revolution with the ports in the south surrounded. "I am informed that the rebels are saying loudly that they would rather perish [in war] than be assassinated . . . and that they had been cruelly deceived, and [the French] were assassinating them instead of protecting them," he wrote. "Such are the reports that have been made to me." "I was also told that almost all of the officers called to Port-Républicain to join the companies had been embarked. . . . One of my eighteen-year-old nephews was part of this . . . and I was even told he was hanged . . . !!!!" "See how much I have suffered!" he lamented. The horrific circumstances of his nephew's death, Dessalines reassured Brunet, were not enough to make him rebel. "I will remain faithful to my oaths and to the government! . . . I believe this is the best way to take revenge on my persecutors," Dessalines wrote. He did offer an avenue to prevent future bloodshed, however. "The rebels are still saying, according to the information I have obtained, that so long as they are left free and rid of those who caused the most troubles on this island through their cruelties, they are ready to give proof of their submission to the captain general," he concluded. "The government has been horribly misled about the situation in Saint-Domingue; I don't know why, but it can only be the work of the enemies of France, our mother country."[48]

It might be difficult for the modern reader to contemplate the magnitude of these atrocities, and what the cities, towns, streets, rivers, ports, and mountains must have looked like during this period. Those who lived through these bloody events had no problem remembering even decades later. Ten years after the end of the war, Chanlatte wrote that he could scarcely banish the images, sounds, and thoughts from his mind. Lamenting that many of the French colonists and soldiers watched these "spectacles" with "glee," Chanlatte implored the world to have pity for the war of independence that the revolutionaries correspondingly unleashed upon the French with matching furor. "Detractors of our cause!" he exclaimed. "If you had glimpsed those deboned chests, those scattered limbs, those pulsating shreds, flesh murdered and dragged by predatory quadrupeds, you would no longer speak of your kind treatment! You would no longer be surprised by the righteousness of retaliation!"[49] Chanlatte ended his dramatic narration of these "unheard-of executions" with a punishing declaration. Although he hated Bonaparte, Rochambeau, and Leclerc with equal fervor, Chanlatte reserved his deepest and most profound indignation for the French soldiers who carried out their orders. "It is difficult to understand," he wrote, "how the more than sixty thousand men involved in this expedition could have degraded themselves to the point of simply becoming blind executioners."[50] Never one to soften his words, Chanlatte ended with this damning conclusion: "Where is the man who would not blush to be of the same species as these accursed devastators and who would not regret having lived to see the day when these bloodthirsty excuses for men were given their turn on earth?"[51]

—

France's war of extermination against the Black revolutionaries was not the only threat to the success of Haiti's fight to end slavery and colonialism. Infighting and fractures within the ranks of those who opposed the French—the independents, many of whom had declined to join Leclerc's forces or had long since defected, and the Black and mixed-race generals of the colonial army like Dessalines, Clervaux, and Christophe, whose relationship to the French army constantly wavered—meant the loss of a coherent strategy for a time.

Before he died, Leclerc sought to further deepen those fractures and revive old ones, including sowing divisions between "blacks" and "mulattoes." Believing that Dessalines harbored ill will toward Black Saint-Dominguans with light skin, in Boisrond-Tonnerre's retelling, Leclerc told Dessalines that the "men of color" constituted the real enemies of both the whites and the Blacks. In their first meeting, which took place the day before Louverture's arrest and was also the first time Dessalines saw Leclerc in person, the captain general flattered Dessalines and exalted him with disingenuous praise. "You are really needed here," Leclerc remarked, insinuating that he did not know which Black officers were "the true enemies of the French government." After suggesting that the white colonists were essentially harmless, "their real interests" being back in metropolitan France, Leclerc boldly asked Dessalines, "Is it not really the men of color to whom we owe all our misfortunes?" Dessalines only feigned agreement with the question, which was actually a declaration, according to Boisrond-Tonnerre. Since they were assumedly of the same mind, Leclerc told Dessalines, "I think the only way forward is to exterminate all of them." He subsequently offered Dessalines 500 louis to support the expedition to bring his final solution to fruition.[52] Did Dessalines carry out any of these executions? After all, he was the last major general of the Black colonial army to join the independents.

While Dessalines's storied secretary denies that the future emperor followed Leclerc's orders, Officer Peyre-Ferry accused Dessalines of being just as prone to killing other people of color, including Black Africans, as he was to killing white people, including women and children.[53] Throughout the summer of 1802, it is clear that Dessalines continued to receive Leclerc's and Rochambeau's orders. Whether he carried them out is another story. At the end of the month of July 1802, Leclerc's second-in-command wrote to Dessalines and referred to an interrogation of five men from the French National Guard that Dessalines undertook under Rochambeau's orders. Acknowledging that he received Dessalines's report and that Dessalines had asked him for further orders, Rochambeau commanded Dessalines to have the men shot in the Place de Saint-Marc. He concluded by instructing Dessalines to immediately arrest another man named Charlot.[54]

It is not clear if Dessalines followed these orders, but according to Saint-Rémy, between August and September 1802, Dessalines, like Christophe and Clervaux, disarmed laborers on behalf of the French military. Saint-Rémy, who claimed to have received this testimony in part from Dessalines's wife, Marie-Claire Heureuse, reported that Dessalines's troops were also ravishing plantations, thereby depriving women and children of necessary subsistence. General Brunet also furnished a report to Leclerc in late August 1802 suggesting that at least from what he understood to be the case, Dessalines put all his energy into disarming the cultivators. "Things with General Dessalines are still going strong," Brunet wrote. "He has already sent me five hundred rifles, and he has rid the country of more than a hundred incorrigible scoundrels." "More than three hundred men or women have been beaten by Dessalines, who wanted intelligence from them: none have been able to give him any," Brunet grimly concluded.[55] Pétion, though no favorite of Dessalines's, evidently approached him to inquire about the behavior of the troops under his command. Pétion supposedly urged Dessalines to cease such excesses, warning him that "everything was pointing in the direction of the reestablishment of slavery." "Maybe we should rally all our forces together," Pétion reportedly said, "to save our lives and our honor."[56]

Whether or not the constellation of accusations against Dessalines was entirely accurate—Saint-Rémy accused him of "hunting down our unfortunate uncles"—we do know that French officers claimed Dessalines had been instrumental in the arrest and execution of General Charles Belair and his wife, Suzanne "Sanite" Belair (also spelled "Sanité"), both of whom are today considered heroes of the Haitian Revolution. The likeness of Sanite Belair, who rebelled against the French with her husband and was called that "brave heroine" by Christophe's administration, graces the 10-gourde banknote issued in honor of the bicentennial of Haitian independence in 2004.[57]

The wives of prominent revolutionaries like Belair tended to remain near their husbands, often hiding in the woods in perilous circumstances. In March 1802, General Dessalines wrote to General Louverture that both their wives had hidden in the forest "with nothing," trying to escape French capture.[58] The wife of the revolutionary general Charles Belair was not nearly as fortunate. "I surprised Diaqoué, Belair's brother-in-law, hiding in a ravine, after questioning him without success I immediately entered the woods with my national guard and after a little searching I found Madame Charles Belair concealed behind a tuft of tall grass," wrote Faustin Répussard, a free man of color, commander over the French National Guard in Verrettes, located in the Artibonite valley. "Immediately I escorted her out of the woods and I walked with her to find Belair, who I was told was entrenched in one of the brigands' camps, but he, upon seeing his wife a prisoner, appeared before me riding bareback on a horse." In October 1802, the French executed both General Belair and his wife.[59] The story, or rather stories, told by chroniclers about whom to blame for their deaths is anything but straightforward.

Like Christophe and Dessalines, Charles Belair, who previously surrendered to the French army, participated in disarmament while professing ardent "attachment to the French government" in his missives as late as August 20, 1802.[60] At some point that summer, however, Belair openly broke with the French. In late August, Dessalines received a report that Belair had taken up arms against the French to avenge the arrest of his uncle. A month earlier, Belair had evidently written a letter to that effect to Generals Christophe, Dessalines, and Clervaux.[61]

Belair had been one of his uncle's favorites, particularly after Moyse's death. In February 1801, Toussaint wrote to Bonaparte from Santo Domingo to request that Belair, along with Paul Louverture, be officially promoted to the rank of brigadier general. "Though he may be young," Louverture said, "he is no less courageous and has always fulfilled with enthusiasm, zeal, and exactitude the duties of this office, which for a long time he has been engaged in with me, and it will be easy for me to convince you of his merits by presenting an account of how he behaved with wisdom and prudence in the mission that I charged him with . . . taking possession of the Spanish part [of the island]."[62]

While many of the Black generals expressed devotion to the French government that promoted and paid them—even after Louverture's arrest and deportation—reports from the white French generals tell a deeper and more complicated story about these loyalties. Louverture, Dessalines, Christophe, Morpas, Besse, and so many others appeared loyal to France at various points after they agreed to stop fighting the French army, while taking steps that caused the white French officials and other onlookers to suspect their devotion to the republic. On July 29, 1802, for example, Leclerc issued an "Ordre du Jour" declaring that General Besse, whom Leclerc had sent to the island of La Tortue to put down an insurrection, had instead "dialogued with the rebels," which only "delayed the submission of that island." According to Leclerc, French troops were then "forced to kill a large number of cultivators." As for Besse, "this officer will no longer be employed in the army of Saint-Domingue" and "will be sent back to France," Leclerc decreed.[63]

A few months earlier Leclerc had even had André Rigaud, whose return to the colony he initially authorized, deported to France. "In bringing General Rigaud to Saint-Domingue, I had no intention of stirring up his party, against that of Louverture," Leclerc wrote to one of his top generals, Charles Dugua, on March 28, 1802. Yet although Leclerc had counseled Rigaud to stay far away from the southern part of the colony, reminding him of all the ills his actions had previously caused there, "this general has defied my orders," Leclerc announced. "He has sent emissaries to the south to slow down cultivation and inspire terror in peaceful citizens," he continued. "With an attitude like this, General Rigaud cannot contribute to the reestablishment of the colony of Saint-Domingue," Leclerc declared, before issuing an order for Rigaud's embarkation "on the first ship destined for France with his family." Rigaud's deportation may have solved one problem, but it created others. Not having captured or deported Rigaud's son, Louis Cyrille, in December 1802 Rochambeau received a report that the "scoundrels in Rigaud fils's party" continued to attack the French military around their home city of Aux Cayes.[64]

French military officers were not the only ones to report that just as quickly as the Black officers had seemingly reunited with the colonial army, they seemed to be either defecting again or putting obstacles in the way of the French army they supposedly joined. In January 1803, the British agent in Port-Républicain, Edward Corbett, sent home a long report of events following Christophe's capitulation to the French, which he indicated had been dictated to him by an eyewitness. The unnamed "gentleman" reported that after Louverture's arrest "things continued quiet for some time till Maurpas [sic] raised the negroes." According to the unnamed observer, Morpas and his band allegedly "destroyed the plantations in the island of Tortugas," then "burned Port-de-Paix and destroyed as much as possible the adjacent Country." The French soon dispatched Dessalines to stop them, but he "always contrived to let his Stores and Ammunition fall into the hands of the Enemy." When those rebelling against French authority grew even "bolder" and began to burn plantations near Cap, Corbett's informant claimed that "Christophe was sent against them but he let them get possession of his Camp and Stores as Dessalines had done before."[65] Whether the most prominent Black and other generals of color were truly loyal to France previous to and following Louverture's arrest cannot be known for certain. Yet one thing is clear: the French successfully sowed division and distrust in the ranks of the Black generals, officers, and soldiers, leading to great divides that persisted in independent Haiti.

The French remained far more unified in their shared and duplicitous goal of trying to reinstate slavery than the Black generals were decided in the methods needed to stop them. One element of the French plot to restore slavery involved creating deep distrust between and among the Black officers and generals. It was the ever duplicitous and perhaps most fair-weather French official of them all, Colonel Vincent, who overtly counseled Leclerc in November 1801, shortly before the latter set out for Saint-Domingue with the expedition, to play Louverture and Dessalines against each other. "The great achievement would be, if necessary, to drive a wedge between General Dessalines and the general in chief [Toussaint Louverture], and I believe there is the possibility of doing so," Vincent wrote:

> Everyone has seen in all the newspapers a letter from the general in chief to the first consul in which he asks that Moyse be recognized as division general prior to Dessalines; I am convinced that the latter would be incensed by such a proposal, and nothing would be wiser than to repeatedly print the entire article in the *Moniteur,* which is very favorable to Toussaint but where Dessalines would surely notice the insulting preference given to a man he does not like: this feeling of rivalry . . . would yield the greatest good.[66]

The plan seems to have worked, to a certain extent, at least from the perspectives of the white French generals. To understand the complicated question of Dessalines's and the other Black generals' and officers' loyalties, to one another and to the French, we must return to the arrest and execution of Charles Belair and his wife.

In August 1802, not long after he learned of Belair's resolve to defect from the French colonial army, Dessalines wrote to General Brunet, the very man who arrested Belair's uncle Louverture, asking for permission to squelch the rebellion resulting from Belair's defection back to the side of those fighting against France.[67] Although it was General Vernet who informed the French government that Belair had put himself at the head of about two hundred insurgents, "who are doing considerable damage over in Verrettes and Cahos," Dessalines wrote Leclerc directly to denounce the conduct of Louverture's nephew. "It is with as much pain as astonishment that I am learning news of the shameful defection and cowardly treason of the wretched Charles Belair," Dessalines wrote, before indicating that he believed Belair might try to escape to Santo Domingo.[68] As he continued to disarm the cultivators on the orders of the French government, Dessalines began to refer to Belair as "that brigand Charles," using one of the French's favorite words to attach to the Black freedom fighters.[69] By September 4, French military officers reported that Dessalines was marching against Belair and his allies. "If they and their supporters persist in their rebellion, General Dessalines proposes and authorizes their extermination!" reported one military officer.[70] Then, on September 8, Brunet reported that the Polish general Wladyslaw Jablonowski told him that Dessalines had successfully captured Belair. "Charles Belair and eleven men of the Eighth colonial demi-brigade are in the power of Major General Dessalines, as well as a large number of farmers who had been taken from the farms." General Jablonowski added that an ally of Belair's took flight toward Mirebalais with eight of his own men and that another ally, Larose, was "traveling alone on this left bank of the Artibonite."[71]

To decide Belair and his wife's fate, Leclerc appointed a military commission. Division General Dugua, who presided over the trial, ordered the commission's reporter to read aloud the accusations and present the evidence against Belair, after which Belair and his wife, "denounced as his accomplice," were brought into the session. The French officials questioned Charles and Sanite Belair separately. Both were allowed to present some form of defense before the French returned them to the prison. Dugua ordered the gallery dismissed before asking the commission, "Citizen Charles Belair, brigadier general, accused of being the leader of the revolt that exploded in Verrettes, is he guilty?" The commission responded by unanimously pronouncing Belair guilty. Asked the same question of "Sanitte [sic], wife of Charles Belair," the commission issued a unanimous verdict of guilty once more.

The conviction rendered, Dugua read a law previously issued by Leclerc, which stated that any leader of a revolt "who will have been captured taking part in armed gatherings will be hanged." The sentence was then handed down: "The commission, considering the military grade of Charles Belair, and the sex of Sanitte his accomplice, condemn the said Belair to be shot-gunned and the said Sanite [sic] his wife to be decapitated."[72] The French executed both Belairs that day, October 5, 1802.[73] Even though it appears that Dessalines had assisted the French in the Belair affair, only four days later Rochambeau wrote to complain to Leclerc that despite appearances "it is necessary to venture higher to discover the first and true engines of this disorder." "It is more than proven that this is the work of Charles Belair and Dessalines," Rochambeau insisted. "The first one can no longer do any harm," he wrote, referring to Belair's execution, "but the latter will always do harm as long as he has the opportunity to do so."[74] Belair's execution, nevertheless, as Officer Peyre-Ferry testified, "far from slowing the effects of the revolt, only served to propagate it."[75] Soon thereafter, both Clervaux and Christophe formally defected from the French army. But would the armed Black laborers—largely African-born—and the independents—many of whom had been previously enslaved and who never or only briefly joined with the French—accept their attempt to reintegrate?

In the last few months of 1802, Christophe, like Dessalines, remained wholly immersed in a controversial contest for power in which the lines between the aggressor and the defender appeared blurry. In August of that year, Colonel Jean-Baptiste Sans-Souci, as part of the independents, took up arms against the French military in Dondon. Thought to have been born in the region of Africa called the Kongo (Congo), Sans-Souci, whose name might have derived from the Sans-Souci coffee plantation between Vallières and Mombin-Crochu, where he might have been enslaved, had been a key military officer under Christophe's command. When the Leclerc expedition landed, Sans-Souci held the rank of chef de brigade or colonel in the colonial army and commanded over the region of Grande-Rivière.[76]

While Sans-Souci initially submitted to Leclerc's forces after Christophe, unlike Christophe, Sans-Souci re-defected just three weeks later, along with several other African-born soldiers: namely, Jasmin, Macaya, Sylla, and Petit-Noël. Together, these men, leaders of a now independent army, remained in control of vast swaths of the colony, particularly in the northern mountains. Leclerc, fearing their growing influence, ordered Pétion, Christophe, and Jean-Philippe Daut "to combat those rebels." Leclerc even threatened that the independents would experience the same fate as Belair and his wife if they did not immediately submit.[77] Initially, Pétion, following Leclerc's orders, succeeded in forcing Sans-Souci and his soldiers to retreat from Dondon on September 7, 1802. Christophe and Daut soon found themselves mired in combat with the independents after Pétion subsequently lost control over Dondon and fled the region. Afterward, Pétion met with Christophe in Grand-Pré, in his old neighborhood of Quartier-Morin. This was the first time that Pétion and Christophe met each other. Together, they sought to smother the rebellion of the independents in the northern mountains.[78]

However, during this strike, the independents learned of the reinstatement of slavery in Guadeloupe. The French had loudly proclaimed their "success" in that August 1802 article published in *Le moniteur universel*. This had deeply irritated Leclerc. He told Rochambeau, "General Richepanse has reestablished slavery in Guadeloupe in a manner quite impolitic for us; we are feeling it here and that is the cause of the present turmoil." "The division of Plaisance is in insurrection for the most part," he continued, before saying that he had given an order to Dessalines "to use the most violent means to scare off the rebels."[79] It was one thing for freedom fighters to consider the May 1802 decree that had allowed for slavery to continue in Martinique, where it had not been abolished, since it was held under British control in 1794. It was quite another for the French to have violently reimposed slavery on the Black inhabitants of Guadeloupe, where Black laborers had lived in relative freedom, at least without formal slavery, since the law of emancipation eight years earlier. According to Leclerc's former secretary, this information reached the colony by word of mouth as well as through newspapers.

After having subdued multiple rebellions on Guadeloupe, the French tried to deport between fifteen hundred and eighteen hundred men of color who they believed posed an ongoing threat to the colony. First, they tried to sell them to the English in Kingston, but to no avail. The British did eventually help the French to ship the men to an island off Môle Saint-Nicolas. Yet the plan had unforeseen consequences. The men ended up escaping to the mainland of Saint-Domingue from that tiny island off its coast. "The epoch marking their escape," the former secretary remarked, "coincided with the dates of the first insurrections" of the independents in August 1802.[80]

The fact that the French had not yet been able to restore slavery to Saint-Domingue, even though they had been there for months longer than the expedition sent to Guadeloupe, earned Leclerc the ire of Decrès. Leclerc complained about Decrès's criticism directly to the first consul when he asked for ten to twelve thousand additional troops with whose arrival, Leclerc said, he could "reestablish our affairs" in less than three months.[81]

Both Pétion's and Christophe's formal defections from the French army occurred not long after this, between mid-September and early October 1802. Leclerc complained about Christophe's desertion specifically in a letter to Bonaparte, though he seemed to relish reporting that Christophe's reintegration with the "blacks," or the independents, might fail given that he previously waged a cruel war against them, especially in the case of Sans-Souci, Petit-Noël, Macaya, and Jasmin. Sans-Souci and the others, according to Leclerc, refused to recognize Christophe's authority.[82]

As a general, Christophe sought less to join than to command the independent army. Even though Sans-Souci previously fought under Christophe, he harbored distinct animosity toward him. In one telling encounter between the two men, Sans-Souci accused Christophe of having hunted down fellow Black men in Plaisance. At this public accusation, Christophe unsheathed his sword. "Do you not understand that I am your chief," he angrily asked Sans-Souci. "What do you want from me, General?" was Sans-Souci's only reply. Christophe, in a huff, reportedly responded, "Well! . . . you recognize that I am your general, and you, you are not a general; I am thus your superior and you do not dare to deny it." Even though Sans-Souci's men outnumbered Christophe's, Sans-Souci reportedly retreated from this interview.[83] Perhaps it was Christophe's countenance, a mixture of haughtiness coupled with undeniable awareness of his stature and renown. Or perhaps it was merely a strategic retreat that allowed Sans-Souci time to plot his next move.

Despite Sans-Souci's objections, after their final defection from the

French, Christophe, along with Pétion, assumed command over part of the independent army. Christophe subsequently waged war upon regions of the colony still under French military rule, ordering the commanders to deliver northern cities to him.[84] Recall that at this late date, which is to say mid-October 1802, Dessalines still seemed to be carrying out some of Leclerc's orders with the colonial army. General Dessalines's formal defection from the French army only seems to have occurred after October 23, 1802, three days after Leclerc issued a damning proclamation to the inhabitants of Saint-Domingue, ostensibly decrying the defections of Christophe, Clervaux, Pétion, and the other Black generals, officers, and soldiers of color. "An unheard-of betrayal has occurred," the decree read. "Cowards, showered with goodwill by the government, have abandoned their posts to reunite with the rebels." Noting that these defectors had attacked Cap, Leclerc suggested that every French citizen was now also a soldier and authorized to fight them. The entire colony, it seemed, was being recruited to be on the side either of France or of the so-called rebels, or put another way, on the side of slavery or the side of freedom.[85]

Leclerc unmistakably considered Dessalines one of the rebels. Making little distinction, he had earlier complained to Rochambeau that all the Black officers and soldiers had "betrayed" him.[86] Unbeknownst to Dessalines, Leclerc had also issued an order for his arrest. Details of the French plot to get rid of Dessalines are provided by Edmond Bonnet, the son of Guy-Joseph Bonnet, a former general and aide to André Rigaud, who published his father's memoirs in 1864. Bonnet recounted how, on October 22, a free woman of color named Madame Pajeot, governess of a church in the parish of Petite-Rivière de l'Artibonite, saved Dessalines from a Louverturian fate.[87] Bonnet reported that after serving Dessalines his coffee, Pajeot pantomimed a person being arrested to signal to Dessalines and his ally that French troops had arrived through another door of the presbytery and planned to arrest the general. Because of Pajeot's heroic actions, Dessalines narrowly escaped capture. Upon exiting the presbytery, he mounted his horse and cried, "Aux armes!" The Black troops immediately rallied around him. Four days later, Dessalines formally united with the independents.[88]

Even without the attempted arrest, Dessalines's open defection had likely been only a matter of time. Dessalines hated Rochambeau and reportedly vowed to Brunet that "if Rochambeau were ever to command, in eight days the colony would be lost [to France]."[89] What had already been a fatal battle for the French only became more deadly due to the ravages of disease. While Christophe, Clervaux, Pétion, and the independents used every tactic trying to take Cap, that city, like so many others in the colony, broke out with yellow fever.[90] Many of the soldiers who fought in the siege, including Leclerc, soon fell ill. Most who acquired the disease did not survive. Before his own death on November 2, Leclerc dictated his final wishes to Hector Daure, the chief financial administrator of the French army, saying that he wanted Rochambeau to succeed him.[91]

As the situation grew more favorable for the independent army, there remained one key fracture within their ranks. Men forming a contingent called the *Taccos*, named after a forest-dwelling bird, had broken away from Dessalines and Christophe soon after they joined the independents. Led by Sans-Souci and comprising Jasmin, Sylla, Macaya, and Petit-Noël, the *Taccos* did not trust Christophe and resolved not to submit to his authority, which they believed stemmed from generalized prejudices against African-born troops like them. Pétion also started causing problems, at least for Christophe and Dessalines. Still professing disapproval of Dessalines's tardy defection from the French and the deadly tactics he accused him of using against innocent women and children during the disarmament phase, Pétion momentarily broke with the independents and agreed to serve as brigadier general in the newly formed *Taccos* contingent. There was only one wrinkle. Sans-Souci asked Pétion for Christophe's head, claiming that the latter's heart remained ever with the French. "This is not the time to exercise vengeance," Pétion told him in response. "The blacks and the men of color," he continued, "have commenced a national war . . . We must forget the past." "General," Sans-Souci replied, "you oppose my desire to have Christophe killed: well then! You, yourself will regret this one day." Sans-Souci had no intention to heed Pétion's warnings, and soon enough he recruited men from Christophe's own demi-brigade to aid in the assassination plot. Having caught wind of the danger, Christophe fled to Milot, where he later built his famous palace, also called Sans-Souci. Fearing for the lives of his family, the future king hid them in the Laferrière fort, where he later erected the awesome Citadelle upon which he bestowed his name.[92]

According to Dessalines's wife, during this period her husband and Pétion came to the rapprochement that ultimately led to Haitian independence. Dessalines, for his part, later claimed that Pétion's valorous conduct as one of the first generals of color to defect from the French army encouraged him to finally rally with the independents.[93] Though one potentially disastrous conflict had been averted, another arose, and this one ended in bloodshed. Sans-Souci and Petit-Noël had elevated themselves to the ranks of generals of the *Taccos* and definitively refused to recognize Dessalines's, Pétion's, or Christophe's orders.

"This conduct could be fatal to our project of independence," Dessalines wrote in late November 1802, as he continued to try and fail to persuade the *Taccos* to rejoin the independents. According to one account, Sans-Souci was initially persuaded by Dessalines's argument and even managed to persuade Petit-Noël to recognize Dessalines's authority and accept his offer of command over the Fifth Demi-brigade. However, as soon as Christophe returned to the north from Gonaïves, where Dessalines had ordered him to reinforce the city, Christophe and his men ambushed Sans-Souci at the Grand-Pré plantation. Sans-Souci died, along with his lieutenant, Jasmin. Petit-Noël staged his own opposition in Dondon afterward, surrounding the home of General Paul Louverture, commander over the city. Petit-Noël and his men succeeded in capturing and killing Paul. Following this, Petit-Noël and Dessalines struck an initial truce, but soon enough Dessalines forced Petit-Noël to surrender. Dessalines, in turn, ordered him killed.[94] More executions followed. A French brigadier general named Fressinet wrote to Brunet on January 17, 1803, to announce, "Dessalines has just been named general in chief," before adding, "Dessalines and Christophe are apparently quite in agreement, especially since the former had killed Macaya, Sylla . . . and some others who refused to give him back their ammunition, this killing took place about eight days ago."[95] Another French brigadier general, Claparède, also reported this to General Rochambeau. In a letter dated January 13, 1803, Claparède noted that Christophe and his company had just arrested Sans-Souci, Jasmin, Macaya, and Lafleur, saying he suspected if these men had not already been executed, it was only a matter of time. Four days later the French officer confirmed what he called "the slaughter of Sans-Souci, Lafleur, Macaya, and Jasmin by the other leaders."[96]

The deaths of Sans-Souci and most of his lieutenants did not immediately end the scission. Opposition persisted under Desrance in Léogâne and Larose, one of the late Belair's allies, in Arcahaie, along with an entire contingent of *ancien libre* men of color in the south and southwest who had fought with Rigaud and still simmered with anger because Dessalines and Christophe had helped Louverture defeat the general to whom they had pledged their loyalty. Dessalines only succeeded in ending the infighting in mid-January, when he solemnly proclaimed himself "general in chief of the *armée indigène*," or the indigenous army.[97] All the previous factions united under this new appellation. One of Rochambeau's reports from this era provides key details about Pétion's role in rallying those final factions to the side of the independent soldiers, the soon-to-be indigenous army. "The desertion of the colonial troops," Rochambeau wrote, "became general from the moment that Pétion penetrated into the south (in Léogâne) and revived the hopes of Rigaud's former party, over whom he was now the leader." Pétion succeeded in "reuniting the mulattoes with Dessalines's side, with whom he had made common cause . . . and he behaved toward him from that moment forward as a subordinate." From then on, "Dessalines was recognized . . . as the leader of the rebels, and they began from that time forward to agitate with more force and together."[98] The now unified indigenous army vowed not just to remain slavery-free but to become independent from France.

The pact detailing plans for independence was sealed at the Congress of Arcahaie on May 18, 1803. Commemorated as Haitian Flag Day, it was during this meeting that Dessalines reportedly ripped the white band from the middle of the tricolor French flag, leaving only the red and the blue. According to popular accounts, Dessalines commissioned a Black woman named Catherine Flon to restitch the red and blue fabric, thereby creating a new flag for the country.[99]

Between the yellow fever decimating French troops, the defection of the Polish legion, and the exhaustion and discouragement of many French soldiers, Rochambeau's chance to win the war imploded quickly. On October 11, 1803, the city of Port-au-Prince fell at last to the *armée indigène*. The indigenous army now controlled Haiti's future capital. On the seventeenth, another unlikely city fell, one with a deadly revolutionary history: Les Cayes, which now resembled a "vast cemetery," according to Boisrond-Tonnerre. Like Cap, that city had been overwhelmed by yellow fever, and dead bodies appeared strewn about the streets seemingly without care.[100] By November 1803, the indigenous army controlled most of the south, along with almost all the northern and western parts of the country. Yet French troops still fought them on multiple fronts, wherever they could manage, including in places highly guarded by Dessalines's troops.

The indigenous army had not yet captured the ultimate prize, Cap-Français. On November 18, 1803, following the Battle of Vertières—of signal importance like the Battle of Yorktown or the Battle of Austerlitz—the indigenous army took control of Cap and forced the surrender of French troops.

Vertières is located just south of the center Cap and was home to the lucrative Charrier plantation sitting on a plateau overlooking the fort. Capturing Vertières was key to Dessalines's plan to seize at last the famous port city. Dessalines is reported to have said on that day, "I want the indigenous flag to fly over the hills of Charrier within half an hour, even if I have to watch the whole of the army corps disappear one by one."[101] Leading the *avant-garde* was not Christophe but General François Capoix (sometimes spelled "Capois"), nicknamed Capoix La Mort. Dessalines ordered Capoix to advance upon the city and not stop until he breached its gates. After encountering stiff French resistance, Capoix reminded his soldiers, "We must, brave men, make ourselves masters of this mountaintop, the success of the army depends on us." "En avant!" Capoix cried out. The French could not waver, because, in the words of one French general, "if this post was breached, nothing would stop the enemy from marching to Cap and forcing entry upon us."[102] Capoix, surrounded by the bodies of his dead comrades, wanted nothing more than to succeed. He mounted his horse, launched himself at French troops, and refused to stop fighting even when his horse was shot out from under him by a cannonball. A volley of bullets ensued, coming from both sides, and many men died. Yet assisted by the demi-brigades, led by Generals Dessalines, Daut, Clervaux, Gabart, and Vernet, the indigenous army ultimately set fire to a building at Vertières, causing the ammunition to explode. The fire allowed Capoix's troops to storm Rochambeau's men, and the remaining French soldiers had to retreat.

Rochambeau understood that this failure effectively ended the expedition. Christophe already controlled the neighboring mountaintop of Vigie Saint-Martin, having established his battery there. The indigenous army was ready to take Cap. Christophe reported to Dessalines that while "in control of the heights of Cap, he had attacked the enemy all day and occupied the advantageous position of Destaing," site of the Comte d'Estaing's former plantation.

In the following days, Dessalines learned that a local officer wished to speak with him on behalf of General Rochambeau to determine Dessalines's disposition to listen to the French general's propositions for surrender. Rochambeau claimed he "could not fathom the motives for such a fierce war as the one I was waging against him," Dessalines reported. Dessalines replied that since the officer had no rank that would entitle him to negotiate with Dessalines, the officer had to withdraw and reappear in the camp only when vested with powers of negotiating, insisting that "hostilities would not cease on behalf of my army before that time."[103] On November 27, at the break of day, the same officer returned with a letter from the chief of staff of the French army. The letter confirmed that Rochambeau sought to begin negotiations for the evacuation of French troops from the city of Cap. Dessalines received everything he asked for in these negotiations, and the articles of capitulation were signed on the twenty-seventh. Although reluctant to let anyone or anything leave Cap without seeing the direct order from Dessalines, once he received Dessalines's missive announcing the armistice, Christophe, who still occupied Destaing, assented to the evacuation. Christophe's career in revolutionary wars had quite literally begun and symbolically ended with the Comte d'Estaing, first with the latter's army on the North American continent and finally on the former site of d'Estaing's plantation.[104]

As for General Capoix's valiant service as the hero of Vertières, Dessalines wrote, "General Capoix, after having had his horse killed under him, conserved, as long as the action lasted, his sangfroid and such a level head that he was admired by the army and won praise from his enemies, and in particular from General Rochambeau, who, a spectator of the attack on Vertière [sic], did not see him for a single moment abandon the ground he gained from the enemy."[105]

The Battle of Vertières, which ended on November 18, 1803, effectively destroyed the Leclerc-Rochambeau expedition to bring back slavery. Under the command of General Capoix and aided by General Vernet (nephew of

Toussaint Louverture by marriage), the indigenous army beat back the remaining French forces. The surviving soldiers retreated, and Rocham-beau, and therefore Bonaparte, surrendered five days later. On Decem-ber 4, most French troops sailed away from the island in exhausted and humiliating defeat.[106]

———

Just before the indigenous army rid Saint-Domingue of the majority of Bonaparte's troops, Generals Dessalines, Christophe, and Clervaux declared the island independent from France. The preamble to the Decla-ration of Independence signed by these men on November 29, 1803, stated, "In the name of the Black People and Men of Colour of St. Domingo. The independence of St. Domingo is proclaimed. . . . [T]he frightful veil of prejudice is torn to pieces. . . . We have sworn not to listen to clemency towards all those who would dare to speak to us of slavery."[107] This first declaration from 1803 circulated around the Atlantic, appearing in the newspapers of England and the United States, which reported this devel-opment with an equal mix of awe and stupefaction.[108] It was unprece-dented: formerly enslaved Black people on Saint-Domingue had declared themselves independent from one of the world's fiercest colonial powers. While the American colonists effectively wrote the U.S. Declaration of Independence as a proclamation of war against England, the Haitian Dec-laration of Independence narrated Saint-Domingue's newfound status as a fait accompli that ended a war. At least in theory.

French troops remained on the island; and many French colonists who had fled to places like Cuba, Jamaica, and the United States, still claim-ing to own property in Saint-Domingue, repeatedly declared their inten-tion to return. This much was acknowledged in the November Declaration of Independence. But was the declaration more a warning to them or a clarion call? Christophe, Clervaux, and Dessalines emphasized that "land-holders of St. Domingo wandering in foreign Countries" could return to assume their property as long as they recognized the island's independence and agreed to "renounce their old errors" and "abjure the injustice of their exorbitant pretensions." "Towards those men who do us justice we will act as brothers," they wrote. For the French troops and any Europeans who might want to attempt reconquest, in contrast, the signers proclaimed,

we shall be inexorable, perhaps even cruel. . . . *Nothing is too dear and every means are lawful to men from whom it is wished to tear off the first of all blessings.* Were they to cause rivers and torrents of blood to run; were they in order to maintain their liberty, to confla-grate the seven eighths of the globe, they are innocent before the tri-bunal of Providence, that has not created men, to see them groaning under a hard and shameful servitude.[109]

Although this declaration circulated around the Atlantic world, Dessa-lines seems to have found it inadequate. He presented an even more strongly worded Declaration of Independence on January 1. Believed to have been written by Boisrond-Tonnerre, this official declaration announced that the island would now be called Haiti rather than Saint-Domingue—a huge change from the November 29 declaration—and that the Haitian people had "sworn to posterity, in front of the entire universe, to renounce France forever, and to die rather than live under her domination, and to fight until their last breath for independence."[110]

Following a public recitation of the entire declaration, Dessalines addressed a crowd of formerly enslaved people and veterans of the war of independence in Gonaïves. Imagine, if you can, Dessalines pronounc-ing these next words with a saber in his hand. "It is not enough to have expelled from your country the barbarians who have bloodied it for two centuries," he said to his audience. "We must, by a final act of national authority, assure forever the empire of liberty in the country where we were born; we must take away forever from that inhumane government, which has for so long held our spirits in the most humiliating bondage, all hope of re-enslaving us; we must live independent or die." At the May Congress of Arcahaie, Dessalines had pronounced, "Liberty or Death"—famous utterances used during both the American and the French Revolutions—as he trampled the white fabric he reportedly tore out of the French tricolor.[111] Now, creolizing this classic revolutionary motto for his new country, whose indigenous name, *Ayiti* (Haïti) he restored, Des-salines shouted into the humid air, "Independence or Death . . . Let these sacred words rally us, and let them be the signal of our combat and of our reunion." One attendee of the ceremony, Chanlatte, evoked the memory of that day by referencing "the flag that we consecrated, the one that for so long should have been the only one on display." He went on to say that Haiti's new standard would "from now on be the slender, but inde-structible chain, around which a brotherly people will always be ready to rally."[112]

It must have been arresting for the audience to hear Dessalines pro-nounce such solemn words drawn from the trauma of his own experiences of slavery and the Haitian people's ardent struggle to end it: "Everything here calls forth the memory of the cruelties of that barbaric people; our laws, our mores, our cities, everything still carries the stamp of the French; what am I saying? There are still Frenchmen on this island, and you believe yourselves to be free from this republic that has made war against every nation." For Dessalines, the war with the French was not, in fact, yet over.

First, the French general Jean-Louis Ferrand had fled to the eastern side of the island, which remained occupied by French troops and stayed under French authority until 1809. Second, Dessalines understood the U.S. Dec-laration of Independence to have started the American colonists' war with

Great Britain, not ended it. A closer reading of the speech justifying the second declaration of Haitian independence reveals it, too, as a statement of war against the French. After reminding his audience of all they lost in the thirteen-year struggle—"your wives, your husbands, your brothers, your sisters, what I am saying . . . your children, your suckling babes"—Dessalines asked, "What are you waiting for before appeasing their souls . . . will you descend down into the tomb without having avenged them?" "Know this," he continued:

You have done nothing, if you do not give to the other nations a terrible but righteous example of the vengeance that will be exercised by a people proud of having restored their liberty and who are jealously guarding it; frighten anyone who dares to attempt to take it away once more; Let us begin with the French. . . . Let them tremble in approaching our coasts, if not from the cruelties that they have exercised here, at least from the terrible resolution that we are going to make to sacrifice to death, whoever, born French, would dare to soil with his sacrilegious foot this land of liberty. . . . Peace to our neighbors! But anathema to the very name of the French! Eternal hatred for France! That is our cry.[113]

As the document's scribe, if not its author, Boisrond-Tonnerre repeated as much in his 1804 memoir. "No Frenchman," he cried, "will soil with his sacrilegious foot the territory of my country." Then, his words dripping with disdain, he evoked the painful recollection of losing his family members. "And they dare to beg us for clemency?" he asked. "No! Me, too, I am also weeping over my relatives, and I invoke fury against everything that is French." He exhorted the Haitian people to, therefore, "eternalize the war that we are declaring against them, and let the presence of an armed white man be the signal of war."[114]

After the reading of the declaration, seventeen of the generals listed in the preamble signed an oath declaring their allegiance to Dessalines, Haiti's "governor-general." Vastey, appointed secretary to General Vernet, Dessalines's minister of finance, explained the effect of renaming the island and its inhabitants: "The name of the island was changed, 'the Saint-Domingue of the French' gave way to the former 'Hayti'; and from this name, the indigenous blacks and yellows adopted the generic denomination of 'Haytiens.' "[115]

André Vernet and his wife held a huge party at their home in Gonaïves after Dessalines's January 1 speech. Madame Vernet prepared a splendid feast, at which she reportedly uttered her deceased uncle Louverture's famous, if apocryphal, words before his deportation from the island. The French "had truly only cut the trunk of the tree of the liberty of the blacks," she said, "but this tree grew back because its roots were numerous and deep." The city itself was thunderous, booming with drums and banquets, amid dancing and singing that lasted all night long.[116]

Despite the festive mood, Dessalines and Boisrond-Tonnerre were right: the war with the French was not over. There were still French colonists around, and not just in the east. Every word of the Declaration of Independence seemed to testify to the difficulty of coexisting with the former colonists. "What do we have in common with that punishing people?" Dessalines asked. "Their cruelty compared to our patient moderation? Their color compared to ours? The lengths of the oceans that separate us and our vengeful climate tell us plainly that they are not our brothers, and that they never will become so, and that if they were to ever find asylum in our land, they will once again be the instigators of our troubles and divisions."[117]

In the southern cities of Les Cayes and Jérémie, Haitians were having an especially hard time mustering the forgiveness and fraternity that the signers of the November 29 declaration promised to any white French person who agreed to live in harmony with the Haitian people. Chanlatte affirmed that the government, and most of the population, intended to show clemency to any white French person who demonstrated a sincere desire to live with them as "brothers." As the first Declaration of Independence stated, all that was required was conformity with Haitian laws and not meddling in the affairs of the Haitian government. For the first few weeks following the formal January 1 Declaration of Independence, most of the remaining French complied, but soon thereafter they started to seek positions of power in the new government, "loudly murmuring" against Dessalines's authority.[118]

Dessalines had granted the remaining white ex-colonists free circulation in the cities, plains, and mountains. Still, in Jérémie, where the blood had hardly dried, reports emerged of Frenchmen trying to corrupt Haitian soldiers in garrison there and encouraging Haitian citizens to take up arms against one another.[119] General Ferou evidently foresaw the danger and took the initiative to squelch the rebellion of the disaffected French. Such a proactive attitude became a detriment rather than an attribute for the men Dessalines placed in positions of authority. Not only had the new government not yet created a constitution, but it had no penal code or other directives by which soldiers should abide. While Dessalines excelled at giving orders to his subordinates—he assigned Henry Christophe as commander over Cap; Clervaux presided over Marmelade; Vernet over Gonaïves; Gabart over Saint-Marc; Pétion in Port-au-Prince; and General Guillaume Nicolas Geffrard in Les Cayes—there was no legislative mechanism to officially govern the army more broadly.[120] The lack of an official chain of command led to several disturbances, one of which involved the conduct of General Ferou and his soldiers in Jérémie. After discovering the French plot to create confusion and dissension among the soldiers and the population, Ferou ordered the principal conspirators arrested, judged, and shot.

The same sorts of "murmurs" began to occur in Les Cayes and then in Port-au-Prince. In these cases, Haitian people from those cities complained about the French. The unhappiness of the Haitian people led them to abandon farming and commerce and to mutiny outright against the municipal authorities, as they demanded that Dessalines put a stop to "attempts" on their prosperity, saying otherwise they would pursue their own "justice." Unbeknownst to Dessalines, the inhabitants of Les Cayes had already put some of the French people they referred to as "butchers and traitors" to death.

The executions reported in Port-au-Prince, in contrast, occurred due to a circulating list of French colonists still on the island who had supported Rochambeau's succession after Leclerc's death. Some Haitian citizens correctly interpreted that those Frenchmen who approved of Rochambeau's promotion wished to see him reinstate slavery and effect a genocide. Seemingly without Dessalines's knowledge or direct orders, the people of the city took "justice" into their own hands and killed everyone on the list. Although early Haiti's nearest reporter of these events, Chanlatte, could not say for sure how many white French people were executed, he noted that Dessalines could do nothing to stop this "powerful engine" once it was set in motion.[121]

Bonnet offered a slightly different reading of what Chanlatte called the "expulsion of the French from this island." Living in Port-au-Prince just before the unveiling of the official Declaration of Independence, Bonnet served as chief of staff, or second-in-command to Pétion. Dessalines was hardly blameless, in Bonnet's recollection. He said that when Dessalines visited Port-au-Prince he brought with him an entirely "ferocious group" who "breathed only spoliation and carnage." Claiming that Dessalines promised to allow them to burn and pillage the city, previously a French stronghold, the men accused Dessalines of not keeping this promise. When these so-called ferocious men protested, Dessalines agreed to their demands, telling them to "prepare their torches." "There were nothing but cries of joy," Bonnet recalled. The men leaped over the peristyle, "like an angry sea, crashing, slamming into one another, running in a frenzy to fulfill their disposition to pillage and burn." But when "the whirlwind had dispersed," Bonnet took Dessalines by the arm, led him into the salon, and sat next to him on the sofa. "What are we doing," Bonnet asked him, "have we not just emerged from the woods, where we lived with the greatest deprivation, exposed, without shelter, to the sun, to the rain, sleeping only under the beautiful sky?" Bonnet reminded Dessalines that during the war the enemy had been everywhere, while "today we have triumphed; we are the masters of the land. Do you not see that you are living in a magnificent palace. . . . You are about to enjoy all the pleasures of a peaceful life, and you want to abandon all of that to burn the city and begin once more a life of deprivation, misery, and suffering in the forest, without cause, without necessity, ceding to the unbraked passions of a few madmen who live only for disorder? Tell me, where is the enemy that you claim you are fighting?" "You are right," Dessalines replied. "No, no, they will not burn anything down, they will not pillage." According to Bonnet, this is the sole reason that Dessalines withdrew his authorization for the executions.

For Bonnet, however, because Dessalines remained surrounded by men like Boisrond-Tonnerre, who he said breathed nothing but fury and hatred for the French, the "massacres" that took place several months later—the very ones that Chanlatte described—had been essentially inevitable. Yet unlike Chanlatte, Bonnet described Dessalines as having presided over the executions of white Frenchmen in the Port-au-Prince jail. Bonnet said that shortly after this "saturnalia," Joseph Balthazar Inginac, fellow veteran of the Haitian Revolution and director of the National Domains, invited Dessalines, Bonnet, and Boisrond-Tonnerre over to his home for a midday supper. Inevitably the conversation turned to the events of the previous days, and Boisrond-Tonnerre remarked that the war with France being eternal, all French people on the island must be slaughtered to prevent them from aiding France in reconquest.[122] Although Bonnet's account aligns with more contemporary understandings of the first four months of Haitian independence, we must remember that the memoirist's recollection is filtered through his son, who never failed to editorialize in a way that recalled more mid-nineteenth-century understandings of the supposed massacres.

The most detailed Haitian accounts certainly came from Dessalines and Christophe's hardened enemy, the self-proclaimed partisan of Pétion, Joseph Saint-Rémy. In his multivolume *Pétion et Haïti,* Saint-Rémy, who was not born until 1818 in Basse-Terre, Guadeloupe, claimed that the idea for the "general massacre of the whites" emerged at the government dinner on the night the Declaration of Independence was officially proclaimed and that Dessalines's speech had been merely its prelude. Only Pétion and Christophe, in Saint-Rémy's retelling, silently opposed the suggestion.[123]

Chanlatte, a direct eyewitness, but recalling the episode six years after it happened, might have been the source for Saint-Rémy's claim that Christophe opposed "the catastrophe that followed the expulsion of the French." Chanlatte claimed that Christophe even tried to save some of the French victims. "How many white men," Chanlatte asked, "owe only to his protection the fact they are still breathing today?" Yet before detailing how Christophe saved white Frenchmen from being drowned in the bay and averring that he even helped some of them escape the island, Chanlatte issued a reminder that he was writing this memoir in 1810, when the world had in essence disavowed Dessalines and, in so doing, disavowed Haitian independence.[124]

In 1806, the United States, encouraged by reports that Dessalines had overseen a "massacre of whites," instated a trade embargo against Haiti that eliminated a key source of goods and weapons.[125] It made sense, then, that Chanlatte would deny that Christophe, president of Haiti at the time he wrote, had participated in the massacre of white Frenchmen. Despite the general populace's alleged desire for revenge, according to Chanlatte, under Dessalines's rule Christophe's home became "the only refuge of these unfortunates." Christophe saved numerous former colonists from being drowned, leading Chanlatte to praise him by acknowledging the "effort . . . Christophe exerted to prevent these misfortunes and then to make them stop."[126] In Chanlatte's recollection, as soon as Christophe revealed his dissenting views to Dessalines, the latter put a stop to the "excesses."[127]

Yet while both Saint-Rémy and Chanlatte labored to put Christophe backstage during the "massacres," Saint-Rémy accused Chanlatte of having helped Boisrond-Tonnerre "stoke the flames" that led to the killings. According to him, Chanlatte put himself at the "head of a group of these slaughterers" who killed a white lawyer named Ango and a merchant called Ducoudray, with whom Chanlatte had a dispute despite the fact that the two men purportedly saved Chanlatte's life during Louverture's reign. The point of Saint-Rémy's story was to paint Chanlatte, whom he considered one of the architects of the Declaration of Independence, as having "with a slip of paper . . . set fire to the universe."[128]

Most early decrees from the government directed Haitian citizens to cease expressing ire for those French men and women who wished them no harm. As for colonists "guilty" of war crimes during the revolution? That was a different matter. On February 22, 1804, Dessalines issued a decree from Gonaïves ordering the military to "arrest any person believed to have taken part in the massacres and assassinations ordered by Leclerc and Rochambeau." The decree was clear that such arrests should not be carried out due to simple whim or unfounded suspicions. Government officials needed to "gather, before proceeding to the execution of such persons, all the information, research, and proof necessary." They were likewise instructed "not to confuse just and sincere reports with denunciations motivated by hatred and ill will." These names were to be submitted to the government and publicly posted.[129]

Saint-Rémy believed the above document a fraud, though. Although Dessalines supposedly dictated it from Gonaïves, where it was signed, Saint-Rémy said that numerous letters put the governor-general in the south of the country at the time, far from the Artibonite valley. Further suggesting that the document had to be fake because of the clemency and measured judgment it proposed, Saint-Rémy concluded that Dessalines's actual orders were far simpler: "to massacre everyone."[130] These massacres, according to him, began in Les Cayes in early February, and from there followed Dessalines to Jérémie, Port-au-Prince, Marchand, and finally to Gonaïves and Léogâne. When the massacres reached their "apotheosis" in Cap, women and children, previously spared execution, began to be "butchered" too.[131] In Saint-Rémy's estimation, around eight thousand white French people had died.[132]

In late April, after the alleged executions, Dessalines returned to Cap, where he met up with Christophe, who, in Christophe's own retelling of the early days of independence, tried to save some of Dessalines's "victims," and in so doing put himself in Dessalines's crosshairs. "My life, was it not exposed, as well as that of my wife and my children, because I gave asylum to some of those unfortunates who were trying to save themselves from the punishment of death?" Christophe recalled in a letter written three years later. "Were they not *insolently* massacred under my windows?—These men were known for their utility and the services that they had rendered to the country in those unhappy times!"[133] But while Christophe supposedly urged and practiced clemency in private, Dessalines issued a proclamation a week after his meeting with Christophe, in which he famously announced, "I have avenged America." Throughout the decree, Dessalines seemed to allude to the events of the first four months of independence. "At last, the hour of vengeance has sounded, and the implacable enemies of the rights of man were subjected to the punishments due for their crimes," he said. "I raised my arm, which for so long had been held back, above their guilty heads. At this signal, provoked by a just God, your hands, sacredly armed, struck the ax against the ancient tree of slavery and prejudices":

> Yes, we have returned to these true cannibals, war for war, crime for crime, outrage for outrage; yes, I saved my country, I have avenged America. . . . What does it matter, the judgment that contemporary and future races will pronounce upon me? I fulfilled my duty, the esteem I have for myself remains; that is sufficient; blacks and yellows, whom the refined duplicity of the Europeans has for so long attempted to divide; you who today constitute a sole being, a single family; make no mistake that your perfect reconciliation was of necessity sealed with the blood of your executioners.[134]

Was Dessalines acknowledging and justifying the "massacre of the whites"? Foreign newspaper editors and journalists certainly seemed to think so.

In early June, the Newark, New Jersey–based *Centinel of Freedom* declared that there had been nothing but "massacre and pillage [in Haiti], by Gen. Dessaline's [*sic*] troops," from mid-April to mid-May. "All the French inhabitants, including men, women, and children, to the number between 2,000 and 2,500, were put to the sword or bayonet at the Cape during the above period. . . . On 22nd of April, Fort Dauphin was pillaged and all the whites, to the number of about ninety men, women and children were massacred. . . . A few days after the French inhabitants of St. Jago and other parts of the interior were escorted to the Cape; and there destroyed in the most wanton manner."[135] Such accounts were repeated and/or reprinted across the United States. One of these newspaper reprints directly connected the putative massacres to Dessalines's April 28 proclamation. In mid-June, the *Connecticut Centinel* printed a notice about the "massacre at St. Domingo" before posting in English translation the entire proclamation: "The intelligence of the indiscriminate massacre of the white French inhabitants of St. Domingo is confirmed by the arrival at New York, of the sch[oone]r *Greyhound* from Cap-Francois. Letters and verbal accounts of the passengers who escaped, agree in representing it as one of the most horrid which has occurred in modern times. . . . On the 28th of April General Dessalines issued a proclamation explanatory of his motives and of his future conduction, of which the following is a copy."[136]

U.S. journalists were not the only ones to eagerly seize upon the proclamation's visceral descriptions of revenge, past and future, claiming they glimpsed therein evidence of white massacre and new proof of Haiti's intention to engage in barbarity. Interestingly, most of France's news about these "massacres" came from U.S. newspapers. On May 13, 1804, the *Journal de Paris,* citing news from Philadelphia dated March 27, reported that the governor of Jamaica "not only aided Dessalines in chasing the French from Saint-Domingue but gave him the weapons that allowed that execrable monster to do everything in his power to massacre the colonists remaining on the island." Placing the start date of this "butchery" on January 21, the article claimed that British ships assisted many of these colonists, providing them with asylum. "We have been assured that Dessalines's plan is to burn all that remains in the seaports, to establish himself in the interior, and to fortify himself in the mountains."[137] Previously, the same French newspaper printed news out of New York from March 3 claiming "the final massacre of the whites in Saint-Domingue was preceded by a proclamation that we find so curious we have reprinted it here in full."[138] The journal then printed part of the proclamation that Dessalines formally issued on April 28. On March 9, 1804, we read in the *American Citizen* out of New York that it was a "gentleman who lately escaped, with other unfortunate sufferers from Aux Cayes," who furnished the fragment of the proclamation before its official posting in Haiti.[139]

These reports and news of the contents of the proclamation also reached France. After printing the entirety of the proclamation, the Paris-based *Courrier des spectacles* reported on August 7, 1804, that it had received the April 28 proclamation from New York. "This proclamation had, as we know, the exact effect promised by its author. Independently of the

2,500 French massacred recently on the orders of Dessalines, 40 Anglo-Americans and 6 Irish established in Cap and in Port-au-Prince experienced the same fate with their families. Twelve Spaniards and 2 Danish similarly established there for some time . . . had at first been held for ransom . . . then were pitifully massacred."[140] These rumors circulated in France for some time and reached an apex that summer. Noting that this information came from "French Papers," on July 4, *The Morning Post* out of London reported that "the number of French citizens murdered up to the 20th of April, by Dessalines at St. Domingo, amounted to 26,000, including women and children. Forty Americans, and six Irishmen, settled at the Cape and at Port-au-Prince, have with their families, shared the same fate with the French." The article then repeated the information verbatim about the Spaniards, the Danes, and also a Swede allegedly ransomed and murdered.[141]

Yet, once again, almost as soon as such information appeared in the British press, it saw refutation. Five days after it reported the "massacres" "confirmed," the same *Caledonian Mercury* out of Edinburgh cautioned its readers about news from France reported as fact by papers like *The Morning Post.* "Some of the small French papers last received contain a very exaggerated account of the barbarities committed by Dessalines, in St. Domingo. It is the policy of Bonaparte to make the State of St. Domingo an object of horror in the eyes of France, and all the other nations—to efface the memory of the frightful scenes which he caused to be acted there, by an exaggerated account of present cruelties, and to make his rival tyrant more detestable, if possible than himself." The French government and the press it largely controlled painted Haitians as genocidal aggressors to shift the blame from their own actions during the Leclerc expedition. "The French papers only publish the bad actions of this black chieftain, whom we should advise not to imitate the Corsican in anything more," the *Caledonian Mercury* article continued, "and in an official *Moniteur* of St. Domingo make the world acquainted with some of the horrors committed there by Bonaparte's white slaves under the command of his brother-in-law General Leclerc."[142] The paper also advised Dessalines to publish the atrocities of the French in an official government outlet, which Boisrond-Tonnerre and Chanlatte did with their 1804 memoir and pamphlet, respectively.

When independent Haiti finally established its own official, national newspaper in November 1804, its very first article denounced the despotism of the Leclerc expedition. "A formidable squadron and the most powerful army that any power had ever yet sent to the Antilles came to descend upon every part of the island," read the article. Leclerc had "a reputation for equivocation and an incomprehensible character" and "presented himself sometimes with a threatening air, other times with the sweetest

of speeches and the most brilliant promises; the most insidious proclamations and letters swarmed from his hands; he lied; he seduced rather
than defeated most of the country's leaders; and soiled, at last, with his
infamous barbarity, the character of the nation he represents." Remarkably, seeming to defend Dessalines's belated reunion with the independent
army, the article's author continued by referring to the moment when
Dessalines, "already renowned because of his exploits," decided that he
"did not have any longer to be the tool of such a madman." "He reunited
everyone around him" and "raised the standard of disobedience and swore
from that moment forward to be the liberator of his country, or to bury
himself under its ruins; the generals of the island joined together with
him; and they marched from victory to victory, and soon enough they
took Cap, on November 29, 1803."[143]

While it is clear that the war with France—both discursive and
material—was not over on November 29, any more than it was on January 1, and therefore that Haitians were still in self-defense mode in the first
months of 1804, it is also reasonable to believe that some white French
civilians died in the four to five months following independence. How
many and in what context is the question? A U.S. captain who claimed
to have witnessed some of the "massacres" appeared before a tribunal in
St. Jago de Cuba in mid-April 1804 to report that "the general massacre
of the whites by the blacks" in Port-au-Prince began on March 20 and
continued until the twenty-third of that month. "The blacks broke down
doors and pillaged houses throughout the city," the captain claimed, then
took the inhabitants into the street and killed them with "a blow from the
saber." More than five hundred people died, he said, including "a woman
and her four children." While most of the other women were spared, the
captain professed certainty that only four white men—two businessmen,
a surgeon, and a blacksmith—survived the "massacre." The ship captain
claimed that many "mulattoes" from the city participated in these killings
as well.[144]

Some supposed eyewitnesses claimed that these killings took place on
Dessalines's direct orders, if not in his sights. At around noon on April 25,
1804, a man and a woman arrived in St. Jago de Cuba from Haiti and testified before French agents that they witnessed "massacres" in the southern
Haitian region of Les Cayes. The pair claimed that the first "massacres"
occurred during the night of January 20–21, resulting in the deaths of
about sixty people from the parish of Cavaillon. On February 9 or 10, "six
days after Dessalines entered Les Cayes," they continued, "the negroes,
on the orders of this chief, made arrests all night after which more than a
hundred whites were murdered outside the city," including the abbé Gras-
set, the curé of Les Cayes. The killings continued throughout February,
according to the two "witnesses." On the fifteenth or sixteenth, perhaps

fifteen additional white men were "massacred" in Dessalines's presence just before he left Les Cayes. The massacres continued in his absence. Dessalines allegedly left orders to a *"griffe"* named Cocoherque to arrest fifty-four white men who were "assassinated" the next day. As a result, there remained only about fifty white men left in Les Cayes, said to have escaped to Jamaica. The "witnesses" reported that despite these "moments of terror" the "white women were not insulted" and that only one, a Madame Frédéric, was killed "for wanting to save her condemned son from being massacred."[145]

French authorities similarly questioned two other alleged eyewitnesses, Fauche and Le Bell, who arrived in St. Jago de Cuba from Cap on April 18, 1804, about the status of white French people in Haiti. Among Fauche and Le Bell's allegations were that Dessalines's government was "despotic [and] arbitrary." They also confirmed that the Haitian flag, referred to as the "rebel flag," was "half red and half blue." Fauche and Le Bell claimed that when they were in Cap, back on the northern side of the island, they heard about a "general massacre" of the white population in Port-au-Prince. When pressed about British reactions and interactions with the "inhabitants or the negroes," the two men provided an ambiguous response. "Please allow us to remain silent. The captain of the frigate who rescued us did us every service and we do not want to say anything more." After this testimony, they also "refused to sign their responses."[146]

The curé of Saint-Marc, Father Dufour, claimed to have fled independent Haiti on February 15, about three weeks after he was marked for assassination. He hid for a month in the city, he said, before, disguised as a sailor, he embarked on a ship destined for Newport in the United States. Father Dufour was given up en route, however, to a French corsair that took him to Cuba. Not long after a British ship took him to Jamaica, where he claimed at the time of writing this testimony that he had been living since March 9. Unlike the other putative escapees of the massacre, Dufour did not blame Dessalines. Instead, he blamed the *hommes de couleur:* "Since the evacuation of the French, all white individuals, men, women, and children, have been massacred in Saint-Domingue. It was the factious among the men of color who plotted this general massacre and had it carried out by the blacks." "These same men, in the fourteen years since the troubles in Saint-Domingue began, have massacred several priests," he continued. "If it hadn't been for this faction, I would have had enough influence over the rest of the people of color and the entire black class to prevent this horrible massacre and to make them respect religion and its ministers." There was enough blame to go around, so long as those responsible were being painted as not white. Dufour described as "equally ferocious and bloodthirsty the blacks, former slaves, and the men of color, free by birth or *affranchis,* issued from the blacks and whites."[147]

It was perhaps only a matter of time before rumors of the "massacres" were used as fodder to fuel conjecture about ongoing political rivalries. On July 1, 1804, a British administrator furnished a report to the War Office in which he claimed to have received personal testimony of the alleged massacres from the captain of an "American vessel," lately at Les Cayes. The American captain reported that "a difference had arisen between Dessalines & Christophe. The former wanting the extermination of all the White people without distinction; the latter insisting that an intercourse with the Whites was necessary for the welfare of the country." "Upon this ground, these two chiefs had come to an open quarrel, each having a separate army," he continued. The captain went on to say that French troops still in Môle Saint-Nicolas, around five hundred of them, had joined with Christophe to fight Dessalines. Just two weeks later, on July 16, the *Caledonian Mercury* reported not simply that the massacres were "confirmed" (before correcting the story five days later) but that "DESSALINES and CHRISTOPHE are completely at variance, and have probably by this time commenced hostilities against each other, for the sovereignty of that ill-fated colony." The information, too specific to have come from another source, underscores how conjecture and unsupported rumor could masquerade as fact when it came to outlandish stories about Haitian independence.[148]

While the *Caledonian Mercury* somewhat painted Christophe as a benevolent protector, Antoine Frinquier, a French army doctor stationed in Cap under Rochambeau, said of the "massacres" on May 20, 1804, that he had personally escaped being among the "number of its victims," describing Christophe as one of the main architects. The doctor alleged that after the official evacuation in December of the year prior, when Dessalines elevated Christophe initially to division general of the north, the latter "continually exercised new acts of cruelty, either by arresting whites who displeased him and who had wealth or by slitting the throats of a few he designated." In Frinquier's account, Christophe did attempt to put some white people under his protection after Dessalines reportedly proclaimed that all white people should be massacred, including Justamont, a doctor well known to Christophe, and Pierre Roux, the most famous printer in Saint-Domingue, who worked in independent Haiti under both Dessalines and Christophe. Although Frinquier doubted that Christophe had benevolent aims toward the white people who stayed at his home, if these men had been marked for execution, Christophe's efforts to protect them must have succeeded. Both Justamont and Roux, along with Faraud, the chief architect, whose life was also spared, lived and worked in the Kingdom of Haiti.[149]

Despite the testimony of certain individuals, mediated through various transcribers, and often repeated as unquestionable truths by the era's newspapers, it is still unclear how such widescale massacres or executions might have come about, who was involved, who ordered them, and most important, who was ultimately responsible for the deaths of civilians, including women and children, if they did, in fact, occur. Frinquier cited several proclamations ordering the massacres of white people that he claimed Dessalines issued, including one undersigned by Chanlatte, Dessalines's secretary at the time, but originals of these documents have not been located, and we cannot therefore verify their authenticity or how Frinquier would have gained access to them.[150]

International newspapers, for their part, were filled with contradictory accounts of the first four months of Haitian independence. Some papers denied that any "massacres" took place at all. In mid-March 1804, the *United States' Gazette* from Philadelphia reported having learned from "the schr. *Eagle,* from Aux-Cayes that Dessalines had arrived there from the Cape and that tranquility was restored. No massacres had taken place since the sailing of the *Ann:* and there was a reasonable prospect, from the interference of Gen. Dessalines, of a restoration of 'order and good government.' Proclamations were distributed that the whites should be protected in their lives and property."[151] Another article, this one from *Poulson's American Daily Advertiser* (reprinted from a Boston paper) in late March, cast even more doubt upon the alleged eyewitness accounts. "A gentleman of information, recently from the West-Indies," reported "that no credit ought to be given to the accounts circulated in the United States, of the massacres in cold blood of the whites in the devoted colony of St. Domingo." While he admitted that "in the moment of assault and engagement some excesses have been committed," since the departure of the French forces "the blacks have treated the whites who have not been in arms against them with hospitality and good faith." "Many of the enormities reported, were committed by the mortified and chagrined French," who then blamed Black people for them. Moreover, "the fragment of the Proclamation said to have been issued by Dessalines, our informant declares to be a forgery," the article concluded. "The blacks shew no resentment against any whites, excepting the French soldiery; and them they will destroy with the rage of infuriated men"; in contrast, "foreigners, particularly Americans, trading with them, are sure to meet with hospitality and fair dealing."[152]

Another account in the U.S. press supports the idea that most people in Haiti did not participate in the executions of innocent people (as opposed to former French soldiers or colonists hostile to the new Haitian government). Captain Fowler, commander of the *Eagle,* referenced in the newspaper above, reported that Dessalines arrived in Les Cayes from Port-au-Prince the day before his schooner was to leave, and "on his arrival, he ordered the late commandant to be arrested, and thrown into prison; and thus terminated the work of destruction which for some time back had been progressing in that unfortunate island."[153] In this account, the commander of Les Cayes, rather than Dessalines, ordered the executions, while the governor-general put an end to them. The account seems more believable when we consider that even Saint-Rémy was willing to admit that Dessalines "recoiled in horror" when some of his men proposed that "the white race must be finished off."[154] While this newspaper article and others call into question the claim that Dessalines ordered any "massacres" in Les Cayes, additional eyewitness accounts contradict the claims that the governor-general ordered innocent women and children killed and that whatever took place in the four or five months following independence constituted "Caribbean genocide."[155] A census from October 1804 for the city of Gros-Morne, one of the only known censuses from early Haiti, reported that at least six hundred "blancs," or white people, lived there. Breaking down the categories of the census shows that white women and children, as well as white men, were well represented in the city. The census, taken by government order, was quite detailed, listing the profession and age of each citizen.[156]

There is evident hyperbole in claims that Dessalines exterminated the entire white population of the island; the October census from one Haitian city alone contests the idea of white extermination. Yet this myth persists in popular culture.[157] This is partly due to a famous 1812 fictionalized account written in French, *The History of the Saint-Janvier Sisters, the Only Two White Women Saved from the Massacres in Saint-Domingue,* which circulated around the world, eventually being translated into German and adapted for the stage many times over.[158] Foreigner commentators and journalists like Sir James Barskett of England, author of *History of the Island of St. Domingo* (1818), undoubtedly also helped this narrative to circulate and stay alive.[159] Yet as we have seen, accounts of Dessalines's putative "massacres" proliferated in mid-nineteenth-century histories of the early days of Haitian independence published in Haiti as well. But Haiti's most well known historians of that time, including Beaubrun Ardouin, Thomas Madiou, and Saint-Rémy, used newspaper accounts from the era to narrate how the supposed executions unfolded. Of the mid-nineteenth-century Haitian reports, only one, that of Adjutant General Bonnet, as reported by his son, could be linked to first-person testimony.[160]

Those who lived in Haiti at the time proceeded with more deliberate circumspection. On April 8, 1804, a woman living in Cap who signed her name Veuve Bellony Pardieu wrote to Marie Bunel (née Mouton), a woman of color born in Saint-Domingue and wife of a white Frenchman named Joseph Bunel de Blancamp (called simply Bunel), former treasurer under Louverture and a close friend of Christophe's. Marie Bunel had fled to Philadelphia after Rochambeau released her from prison from charges connected to the revolution in November 1803. Addressing Marie as "my dear and cherished friend, my daughter," Pardieu lamented, without revealing the reason, "I am writing to you with a heart full of pain, sorrow, and misery." A relative of Joseph's wrote to Marie from Cap around the same time, on April 12, 1804, to express joy at Marie's successful arrival "on the continent," before cautioning, "I will not tell you anything about what is happening in this country." On April 17, 1804, a white merchant named Maurin, who had done business with Marie, also wrote to her that he had safely arrived in Cuba from Cap, but only after "having been obliged to leave practically every possession behind." Maurin revealed only of his sudden departure that the city of Cap had since been "evacuated" and continued to "experience one event after another." Joseph Bunel did not seem to be too concerned, however, either about the letters his wife had received, or U.S. newspaper reports of the putative executions, which he undoubtedly read. Joseph returned to the island from Philadelphia on September 2, 1804, with Dessalines's approval, just in time to witness "the governor proclaimed emperor." A hundred cannon shots accompanied the announcement, Bunel reported to his wife, followed by twenty-one shots from the ship transporting him, and twenty-one more from another already in the harbor at Gonaïves.[161]

Dessalines himself, it turns out, provides us with the most suggestive context for understanding whatever occurred in the first few months after independence. In the April 28 proclamation that countless observers cite as proof of the massacres, Dessalines reminded his audience that the project of general "extermination" was not merely dreamed of by the French but put into practice by them. In the proclamation, undersigned by Chanlatte, whose voice and style of writing echo throughout, Dessalines reminded the Haitian populace that "the massacre of the entire population of this island was conceived of in silence and cold blood by the [French] cabinet." Referring to Leclerc's attempt to convince Dessalines to eliminate the "men of color," which is to say the people of *mixed race,* Dessalines underscored that "the execution of that atrocious project" was "proposed to me without any embarrassment, and had already been begun by the French." Further contextualizing, perhaps even justifying whatever happened since January, Dessalines reminded his people that while Leclerc and Bonaparte repeatedly promised not to bring back slavery, assuring that all people in Saint-Domingue, regardless of skin color, would remain free, the French turned around and reinstated slavery in neighboring Guadeloupe. He evoked the freedom fighter Louis Delgrès's failed opposition to the French military, which resulted in mass suicide in Guadeloupe: "the brave and immortal Delgresse [*sic*], who preferred to dissipate into the air along with the debris of his fort, rather than to accept chains once again." Dessalines also reminded the audience of French "plots recently hatched" to sow division in Jérémie, land of death during the revolution, land of discord after it, which resulted in a "terrible explosion . . . despite the generous forgiveness granted to those incorrigible beings when the French

army was expelled; their emissaries in the other cities responded correspondingly to excite a new internecine war." After evoking the awful fate
experienced by "our brothers deported to Europe," among them Toussaint Louverture, Dessalines pronounced that the French, after the Treaty
of Amiens, sought to extend slavery instead of abolishing it in the newly
reacquired Martinique.

Dessalines concluded by renewing his eternal declaration of war against
France while reaffirming that he had no intention to harm innocent French
colonists who chose to remain in the country and become Haitians. His
policy offered "clemency" to all white French people who had the means
to support themselves and the desire to live peacefully in Haiti:

> Because it is repugnant to my character and my dignity to punish any
> innocent people for the faults of their fellow men, a handful of white
> people commendable because of the religion they have always pro-
> fessed, who moreover have taken an oath to live with us in the woods,
> experienced my mercy. I am ordering that they be spared the sword
> and that no harm come to their properties nor their lives.

Dessalines, playing both chronicler and statesman, effectively confirmed that no policy of his in the past or the present provided for innocent
French people to be killed because of either their nationality or their skin
color and that no such policy would exist in the future. Later, Dessalines
made Christophe responsible for ensuring that city dwellers could provide
their own subsistence, and if not, to ensure that they could find positions
as farm laborers in the countryside.[162] Finally, at the end of the April 28
proclamation, Dessalines ordered all department-level and local military authorities to assist, encourage, and protect "all neutral nations and
friends that want to establish commercial relations with this island."[163]

Despite the messiness of firsthand accounts casting doubt upon the
who, what, when, where, why, and how of the supposed "massacres,"
many contemporary commentators have often been all too willing to
believe and promote those narratives that support the allegation that Dessalines ordered "genocide" of the white French population in the months
following independence.[164] This claim is in direct contradiction with history. Even if Dessalines ordered some executions, there is wild discrep-
ancy in the purported death count, between three hundred and twenty-six
thousand. Moreover, as we will see in the following chapter, Haiti existed
not in merely a metaphorical state of war with France but in armed conflict, calling into question the language we should adopt with respect to
deaths in this period. The only people who ever committed genocide on
the island of Saint-Domingue were the Spanish. The only ones who ever
attempted it again, as Dessalines pointed out, were the French.

Even as Chanlatte evinced disdain for what he called a "catastrophe"—

albeit one he said largely occurred without Dessalines's knowledge or direct orders—he also defended Haitian conduct during the earliest days of independence by reminding his readers of France's atrocities against the Haitian people.[165] Chanlatte knew that his memoir, written in French and dedicated to the French abolitionist abbé Henri Grégoire, would be read by white French people on the island and back in France. It was more of a *j'accuse* than an apology. "It is you, with the crimes that you have aroused in this country, who have given birth to our reprisals," he said, before asking, "Upon whom should we place the blame [and] the responsibility for these scourges, if not upon the very people who provoked them?" He reminded the French of the genocidal plot their countrymen recently conceived, and "in great measure executed," to produce the "total destruction" of the Haitian people, even after Dessalines "pardoned" them. Since the French who remained in Haiti after independence also "sought to divide us and to arm us against one another," Chanlatte concluded, "should we not have been permitted to get revenge?"

It is over, white men! who have for so long wronged and immolated us! the veil of credulity has fallen, the reign of foreign tyranny has for us ended. The last Haitian will have taken his last breath before we see, once again, planted in this land the flag of slavery. It is only by treating us as free men, by making us forget, on the strength of virtue, your past errors, that you can ever hope to share with us the treasures of this island, in reciprocal exchange. [166]

8

EMPIRES RISE . . .

Heavy may be the head that wears the crown, but heavier still is the one that, bearing nearly all the crown's duties, enjoys hardly any of its glories. Haitian independence began auspiciously with a war against France. Yet not all Haiti's problems involved Napoléon Bonaparte, who, in 1804, declared himself emperor of France for life. That same year, the Haitian military elevated Dessalines to Emperor Jacques I. Although the eastern part of the island remained under French occupation, its Spanish inhabitants soon found themselves under siege from their neighbors in the west. Louverture had ruled over the whole island, and like him Dessalines wanted the sea to be the only limit of his realm. Dessalines chose Christophe to wage this war of destruction, fire, captivity, and even death against the Spanish occupants in the east. Oscillating between compassion and brutality, fortitude and exasperation, Christophe remained at bottom a military man, and he had orders to lead an army. Would the final vestiges of compassion in his heart become the ultimate victim of Dessalines's military empire? The prize for adopting Dessalinian strength? Yet more responsibilities as general in chief of the Haitian army, in a state pitted against a nation.

Amid the ongoing fighting across the island, Haiti's new leadership still needed to tackle the question on so many minds: What shape would the new Haitian government take? The United States famously created a republic led by a president and a congress after its revolution. France had also previously transformed itself into a republic, with various head governing bodies, but not a president. Under Louverture, the colony, albeit as part of the French republic, had been ruled by a governor-general. And so, even though republics were on the rise and monarchies remained the world's most common form of governance, Dessalines initially chose the title governor-general of Haiti. Some of his contemporaries right away considered this a problem. First, Louverture held that title when the island sat under French rule, and it denoted that Louverture stood under the command of a superior authority, in his case, the three consuls of France. Second, as Vastey observed, the title "general" suggested that Haiti was to have neither a monarchy nor a republic but a "purely military" government. Would the world respect a new country whose "legislators" seemed to announce they were "better at wielding the sword than the pen"?[1]

Though it declared its independence as if by bullhorn, Haiti's government had not yet convinced the world that Haiti was a reality, and "Saint-Domingue" was no more. Perhaps this is why, in late January 1804, André Vernet, seconded by more than a dozen generals and officers from the army, wrote an open letter to Dessalines imploring him to adopt a different title. "Persuaded that supreme authority cannot be shared, and that the interest of the country demands that the reins of the administration be placed into the hands of he who inspires us with confidence, and that the title of governor-general does not fulfill, in a satisfying manner, the wishes of the public, because it supposes a subordinate authority, dependent upon a foreign power," they wrote, "Let us now confer upon citizen Jean-Jacques Dessalines the title of emperor of Haiti with the right to choose and name his successor."[2] Dessalines accepted this nomination three weeks later, saying he believed he deserved "the august title that your confidence bestows upon me." Nevertheless, he rejected the laws of hereditary descent that characterized most monarchies. Instead, in the event of his demise, he said he preferred "to transmit my authority to those who have shed their blood for the nation." As he declared, "I renounce, yes, I officially renounce the unjust practice of passing the power down to my family." "I will never have regard for this kind of outdatedness," he concluded. Both letters are dated several months before Bonaparte announced his intentions to create the Empire of France in May 1804. However, the official Haitian newspaper did not print the letters until November 1804. Notably, Dessalines signed the nomination acceptance using the title of governor-general. Vastey, like many later historians, used that title and the date of the letters to argue that Dessalines only took the title emperor after Napoléon assumed it in late 1804, the latter being crowned that December.[3]

Although many foreign newspapers painted Dessalines as a power-hungry Napoléon-like authoritarian, with the advent of its own national newspaper the Haitian government could now convey that the public approved Dessalines's new role.[4] Alongside the nomination documents, the official newspaper under Dessalines, called the *Political and Commercial Gazette,* published a poem titled "Couplets Chanted and Presented to His Majesty Jacques Ier, Emperor of Haiti," written by Télémaque, the controller of the department of the north and previously the mayor of Cap-Français. Télémaque called Dessalines "he who punished the arrogance / of the French, our true enemies; / And whose sweet clemency, out of his subjects makes friends."[5] Having a national newspaper also allowed the Haitian government to directly communicate foreign news and ongoing developments within the state, along with new laws and important cabinet appointments. The very first issue of the *Gazette* announced

Christophe's role as commander over the northern division. His station was to be at the fort called Laferrière, site of his future Citadelle Henry. The article praised this storied general of the revolution, whose name carried such "renown" that it, along with that of Dessalines, "was destined to be transmitted down to our last descendants."[6]

Dessalines also put Christophe in charge of overseeing his ordinance of October 1804, which required a census taken in each city. On October 23, Christophe instructed all the inhabitants of Cap to immediately report to the Champ de Mars on the Place d'Armes. He subsequently determined that around fifteen hundred of the people who showed up did not have the required means to live in the city, which is to say that they did not have proper employment and ability to provide for their own subsistence. This conflicted with the third article of Dessalines's new ordinance, which required all those lacking means of subsistence be sent to the countryside to farm. The fourth article also designated how many "domestics" individual city dwellers could keep at their service. "Those who have need of domestics," the ordinance stated, "can keep only the number necessary for their needs; any surplus are to be sent back to the farms in order to work, without exception, under the responsibility of the inspectors and heads of the ateliers."[7]

Preventing idleness was not the only goal. According to a separate article in the same issue, the people Christophe identified as without work had been stealing from others precisely because they were unable to provide for themselves in town. After interrogating them, Christophe sent the identified individuals to various plantations in need of hands. This program immediately restimulated the Haitian economy. The coffee plantations began to flourish, along with the cultivation of grains. The *Gazette* declared the successful redistribution of the population from the cities to the countryside as good for international commerce and trade.[8]

The *Gazette* also announced the new Haitian constitution, once it was finished in May 1805, along with the newly established military penal code. Before the *Gazette* printed the constitution, Dessalines sought Christophe's approbation. This was not merely a sign of Dessalines's admiration for the general he put in command over the northern division; it also foretold Christophe's promotion to general in chief of the Haitian army the following month.[9] On June 11, 1805, Christophe wrote to Dessalines to acknowledge having received several copies of the constitution and the penal code. He expressed immediate approval: "For so long, the people of Haiti have had their eyes on you, asking for the beneficent laws that you have just presented. At last, they have arrived! May they endure forever and be the cause of admiration for posterity, and I hope that they make our enemies desperate . . . when they realize the carnage that we will put in place to defend them, as a means of renouncing their unjust enterprise, which is to enslave us and to efface us from the realm of free peoples!" Christophe said that he remained "more than ever convinced that these laws must be executed and followed, be they for protection or punishment. The unwavering rule of my conduct will be to submit myself to them and to hold myself to their entire execution." Another harbinger of his eventual promotion to general in chief of the entire Haitian army can be found in Christophe's seemingly insignificant inquiry to Dessalines before closing the letter. Christophe asked if Dessalines sent the constitution and penal code to Port-de-Paix, because he did not have enough copies to send them himself.[10] Dessalines had granted command of Port-de-Paix to another illustrious fighter, the hero of Vertières, General François Capoix, who eventually became the source of considerable trouble for Dessalines and Christophe.

Capoix's style of leadership can be characterized as disorganized, and he exhibited tendencies of insubordination. On April 30, 1805, Christophe wrote to Capoix imploring him to accept the punishment that Dessalines had ordered due to his insubordination. He told Capoix that as a military man he had to remember that he was a subordinate who could be punished if he did not wait for Dessalines's orders before taking certain actions. "You have no cause for chagrin," Christophe told him.[11] Capoix expressed little willingness to accept General Christophe's reassurance and slight admonishment. On May 6, Christophe learned from Vernet, the minister of finance, of rumors that the people of Port-de-Paix were preparing to mutiny against Dessalines under Capoix's orders. Christophe expressed incredulity. He wrote immediately to Colonel Michel Pourcely, second-in-command over that city, to find out who to blame for this rebellion, asking if General Capoix had really given orders outside the chain of command. Christophe had already warned Capoix that if any trouble occurred in Port-de-Paix, he would hold Capoix personally responsible. Christophe advised Vernet likewise to authorize the arrest of any person coming from Port-de-Paix and the surrounding area of Borgne who did not have permission from Colonel Pourcely. Christophe also ordered that Vernet forbid all dragoons from that area to enter Cap.[12]

While Christophe wanted to believe that his friend Capoix had not organized the alleged rebellion, he felt unsure of Pourcely's position. Christophe remarked to Pourcely, therefore, that he had learned "with difficulty" that the people of Port-de-Paix sat on the cusp of mutiny and that General Capoix was possibly still giving orders there, and in addition that Colonel Pourcely had allowed their execution. Christophe told Pourcely that if this were true, Pourcely was doubly at fault: first, for having received the orders without informing Christophe; and second, for allowing these orders to be executed. Christophe ordered Pourcely to answer for this immediately with an update on the situation on the ground.[13] The rumors of insurrection in Port-de-Paix might have been a misunderstanding. Christophe wrote to Dessalines two days later, on May 8, to report that life now seemed tranquil in the northern division, including in Port-de-Paix, where the atmosphere remained "perfectly calm."[14] Later, when Christophe visited Port-de-Paix, he learned that the rumors likely stemmed from the soldiers' tardy return from the campaign on the eastern side of the island, Santo Domingo.[15]

Christophe had been suspicious because military abandonments did sometimes occur. In June 1805, the commander of Cap sent Christophe a list of soldiers from the First Demi-brigade, in garrison in the city, who had recently abandoned their posts without permission. Christophe sent General Paul Romain the list so that he could punish these soldiers.[16] Capoix's behavior, the rumors of possible insurrections and mutinies, and actual desertions all contributed to Dessalines's urgency in issuing a constitution and a separate penal code that also provided laws for the military.

As commander over the northern division, Christophe also had to address theft, insubordination, and general disorder from military officers under his command. As Christophe's letters show, he oscillated between compassion and severity, clemency and rigidity. Sometimes those traits converged. Though he acknowledged that the army and populace alike committed crimes at times, the general seemed distressed whenever the officers under his command took the law into their own hands. For example, Christophe continued to receive complaints that soldiers and officers illegally confiscated the animals and sometimes the property of various farm owners. Some officers doled out arbitrary punishments to the troops under their command, too, like Colonel Raymond, who evidently put a soldier in his demi-brigade to death for supposed desertion. Christophe grew increasingly troubled by both summary judgments and overly harsh punishments.[17] Both thrilled and hopeful that the constitution and the penal code would make his command easier, Christophe wrote to the empress Marie-Claire Heureuse shortly after he received copies of the documents. He expressed his profound respect for her and his elation about the constitution. In congratulating her and her husband for the creation of the constitution, he wrote, "I am fulfilling a duty so sweet and truly dear to my heart!"[18]

The new constitution was remarkable not only for its own time but for the enduring principles it set forth for the world. Haiti trampled right over the long-standing hurdle to permanent abolition when it became the first state in the world to forever ban slavery. Like the 1801 constitution issued under Louverture and the 1804 Declaration of Independence, Haiti's first constitution robustly circulated across the Atlantic world, because of the novel principles of humane sovereignty it mandated.[19] The 1805 constitution, issued by the emperor Jean-Jacques Dessalines (and undersigned by Chanlatte), declared, "Slavery is forever abolished." In concert with Dessalines's new laws that allowed non-French foreigners to gain Haitian citizenship, the *Gazette* reported that several foreigners living in the empire had renounced their former citizenships. The May 25, 1805, issue of the *Gazette* reported that a Mr. James Phipps, then living in Port-au-Prince, "*fils naturel* of Lord Molgrave," renounced his British citizenship and declared his intention to reside in the Empire of Haiti and to submit himself forevermore to its laws. On September 5, 1805, the *Gazette* reported that A. M. Mullery, a businessman in Cap, sought to renounce his Danish citizenship and become Haitian.[20]

Even though Christophe does not appear to have had a hand in constructing either the imperial constitution of 1805 or the military penal code, his enthusiasm for their principles and laws resounded. On June 11, 1805, Christophe sent memoranda and around a dozen copies of the penal code to Colonels Joachim and Raymond, as well as the commander of the city of Cap, instructing them to distribute the code among the various battalion chiefs and to the captains, lieutenants, and sous-lieutenants of the demi-brigades over which each of them had command. "You are receiving also a copy of the constitution that will bring happiness to our empire," he wrote. To ensure that the principles of the constitution would be instilled in the army and the general populace alike, Christophe ordered all the military men in the arrondissement to recite it for three Sundays in a row, beginning on the sixteenth of the month. Christophe specified that this should be done in the presence of all the citizens of the area regardless of age and sex, "who will be summoned for this purpose." Christophe ordered the military penal code read aloud and published immediately in every major city too. Finally, he ordered the colonels to provide a copy of the penal code to the captain of the artillery company of their quartiers and to instruct them to follow the constitution's directives to the letter.[21] That same day, Christophe sent a similar memo and instructions, along with a copy of the constitution and several copies of the penal code, to other colonels and commanders.[22]

With the military informed of the new laws, the government prepared to make public the constitution and the penal code. Per Dessalines's wishes, at dawn on Sunday, June 16, citizens gathered on the Champ de Mars in every quartier of the country to hear the constitution and penal code. The judicial and administrative authorities met up at General Christophe's home in Cap. From there, they traveled to the Champ de Mars. Troops lined the public square, filled with men and women who lived in the city. At six o'clock in the evening the publication of the documents was announced to the sound of the artillery discharging their weapons all at once.

Adjutant General Étienne Mentor, Dessalines's aide-de-camp, then read the constitution. The *Gazette* reported that Mentor's "sonorous timbre" and "expressive voice" encouraged the enthusiasm of the people who listened with "tender affection and appreciation to the pact that was to ensure forever their joy and future happiness." As he finished, thousands of cries rang out: "Long live the emperor!"[23] After the constitution, the penal code was read. While acknowledging the "severity" of the document, the *Gazette* reported that the crowd seemed to appreciate the "paternal solicitude of the supreme chief, who, not content to be the liberator of his country, wanted yet to add to his signal accomplishments, that of creating, for his people, a civilization."[24] The celebration was repeated for the next two Sundays.

The *Gazette* printed the full text of the constitution in the June 27 edition, prefaced with a note of approbation, signed by twenty-three generals from the Haitian army. The first name was Christophe's. The statement read, in part, that these generals had come together to declare that the "tenor of the present constitution represents the free, spontaneous, and invariable expression of our hearts and the general will of our constituents." Haitians, who had been living in virtual freedom from bondage since 1793, were not surprised to find "slavery abolished forever" in article 2 or "equality under the eyes of the law incontestably acknowledged" in article 3. In some ways, article 12, in the "General Dispositions" section, highlighted a more significant development: "All property that formerly belonged to white Frenchmen is incontestably and rightfully confiscated for the benefit of the state." Article 28 justified such a provision by reiterating the Haitian government's stance that their country remained at war with France: "At the first sound of alarm, the cities will vanish and the nation will stand up." The twenty-three generals who signed the constitution at Dessalines's imperial palace on May 20, 1805, finished by "paying homage to friends of liberty, philanthropists of every country," before thanking God, "who, by way of his immortal decrees, provided us with the opportunity to break our chains and to constitute ourselves as a free, civilized, and independent people."[25]

Translation of the constitution appeared in more than a dozen British newspapers.[26] England's national newspaper, *The Times,* had this to say: "The Constitution of Hayti, which we communicated to the public yesterday, will be read by politicians with some degree of interest." While calling it "the outline of an arbitrary . . . military government," the paper ultimately judged the constitution to offer "a much milder system of despotism than that established by the European rival of DESSALINES"— Napoléon Bonaparte. *The Times* particularly approved of article 36, or the anti-conquest clause: "The declaration that the Haytians will not attempt to make conquests, or disturb the peace of the European Colonies is both just and politic." If the British reporter in this instance found "most illiberal" article 12, which banned "white men from acquiring property," he seemed to understand and even justify the principle upon which it was based. "This we conceive to be only an effusion of resentment for the injuries they have so lately received from Buonaparte and his emissaries," the writer said, before ultimately surmising, "Perhaps, for the present [it is] a necessary measure of caution."[27]

The French press, on the other hand, seemed entirely unimpressed and acknowledged the constitution only reluctantly. On September 3, 1805, the *Courrier des spectacles* printed a pithy article, drawn from a London newspaper: "Letters arriving from North America have announced that Dessalines has provided the island of St. Domingue with a new constitution."[28] Despite the French consistently referring to independent Haiti as "Saint-Domingue," the world clearly understood the warning that Haiti had sounded to France with its new constitution.

Haiti's first constitution emerged simultaneously as a charter for a novel kind of liberal society that forbade the mainstays of the Atlantic world—slavery, color prejudice, and conquest—and a declaration of war. Yet according to one onlooker, this seeming contradiction was not the constitution's most serious problem. The minister of finance's secretary, the future Baron de Vastey, had a front row seat to developments in Haiti, and he later identified several contradictions within the constitution itself, ultimately concluding that the empire's political design contained the fatal mistakes that led to the emperor's demise.

Vastey observed that although Dessalines rectified the error that led him to inappropriately adopt the title governor-general, the title emperor remained similarly problematic: "It suggests that the one who possesses it holds power over vast territories and peoples." He argued that the constitution Dessalines's government ratified was, in effect, a "political monstrosity," because while Dessalines eschewed the right to pass down his reign to his descendants, he was appointed emperor "for life." Moreover, the constitution spoke of the formation of three different governmental bodies—legislative, executive, and judicial—but in the same breath stated that these "three powers . . . were reunited in one hand," that of Dessalines. "There was in name a council of state," Vastey added, "but it was essentially null and without duties, per the constitution itself." He concluded, "The empire was a republic, and in the constitution were principles diametrically opposed to the republic, and that could not at all be appropriate, except for a purely *despotic* government; what's more, with a strange overturning of ideas, the constitution consecrated the most democratic of principles."[29] In the end, Haiti's citizens suffered the most because of these legislative errors. "As in every country," he wrote, "it is the people who are always the victims of the mistakes their lawmakers make; it is always they who are forced to pay for them with their tears, their blood, and their livelihood."[30]

The Haitian people truly suffered during the next episodes of Haitian independence. Despite Christophe's attempt to protect and serve his fellow citizens, he could neither shield them from the ongoing war with

France—which Christophe was about to lead once more, on the eastern side of the island—nor prevent the violent misfortunes that eventually led to the emperor's assassination. Citing U.S. newspapers by way of London, the *Gazette de France* mistakenly reported in December 1805 that Dessalines had died and that Christophe had taken over.[31] It was, perhaps, an uncanny portent of the momentous events that resulted in Christophe's becoming Haiti's second head of state in just under three years of independence.

—

On July 30, 1805, Christophe wrote to Dessalines to thank him for elevating him to the position of general in chief of the Haitian army. Remarking that he understood "the grandeur" of the occupation, Christophe promised to carry out his new duties with all the "zeal and energy of which I am capable."[32]

In addition to ensuring the proper function and installation of the judicial system, Christophe had, since Dessalines made him division general during the earliest days of independence, reorganized, evaluated, and directed the Haitian army in the northern part of the country.[33] He also oversaw the construction and reinforcement of several important forts. Dessalines and Christophe were convinced that a reinvasion by the French army was not only possible but inevitable. Christophe particularly concerned himself with fortifying the fort called Laferrière, where he would one day oversee the construction of the famous Citadelle he named after himself.

Although Haitians won their independence in 1804, France refused to recognize the new nation, and the French populace, like French officials, never stopped scheming for the "restoration of Saint-Domingue." In concert with that goal, in February 1805, a former French general named François-Marie Perichou de Kerversau, stationed in Saint-Domingue during the Leclerc expedition, sent detailed reconquest plans to Napoléon. Like his predecessors, Kerversau spoke of "exterminating" the entire population, including the children. No conciliations for the "negroes" should be made at all. "They want to be free," but "the honor of the French name, the security of the West Indies, and indignantly outraged humanity cannot allow it," he declared. "The aura that once guaranteed the safety of the master and allowed one man to live in peace among two hundred slaves is gone. The black man knows today that a white man is only a man." Kerversau, drawing on the Haitian Declaration of Independence, claimed that Haitians and the French would remain natural enemies as long as Dessalines stayed in charge. "Swearing eternal hatred for France is the national oath of this new state," Kerversau warned. "The decree of death against all Frenchmen . . . who would dare to trample with a sacrilegious foot the land of Haiti is the fundamental law. Dessalines reigns there with absolute control, Dessalines, the fiercest of Africans and our deadliest enemy." Kerversau believed, however, that France's mission could be aided by pitting the Black inhabitants of Haiti against one another. He cited newspaper reports to that end describing Christophe and Dessalines as at odds over the so-called massacres. Kerversau went on to call Christophe "the richest, shrewdest, and most intelligent of black leaders," saying "because of this very fact, he is the most ardent enemy of the governor"—meaning Dessalines, who was in fact an emperor. Though Christophe appeared to serve Dessalines, for now, in Kerversau's estimation, "he would murder him if the murderer's hand could remain hidden and if he had no rivals or avengers to fear," enabling the French to possibly "take advantage of his ambition and his avarice—but not make use of it directly." Kerversau acknowledged that the French would have to proceed carefully, since it was Christophe who "burned Cap on the arrival of the French," referring to the 1802 arrival of the Leclerc expedition, "and he was one of the main instigators of the second revolt." Christophe was, in the French general's view, nevertheless, "too criminal to be irreconcilable."

Kerversau's reconquest plan adds necessary context to Dessalines and Christophe's desire both to augment the army and to gain control over the eastern side of the island, still occupied by the French. "Despite Christophe's hatred and jealousy of Dessalines," Kerversau continued, "I do not know how easy it would be to drag him into an open scission and sustain him there long enough to achieve some results. For if he is the most ambitious of the blacks, he is also the most defiant and cunning, and he fears us even more than he hates his rival. Besides, the game would be far from equal. Christophe has made himself odious to the mulattoes and suspect to his people; Dessalines has made himself terrible to all, his audacity and his impetuosity make up for his talents, and the general terror he inspires makes him far from popular." Since Christophe could not easily be won over, Kerversau believed, the French government should exploit divisions in Haiti behind the scenes.

France's best chance for reconquest lay in provoking the western and the southern parts of the country, commanded by those Kerversau referred to as the "men of color," to rebel against the north, which he said was "commanded by the negroes, their sworn enemies." Exacerbating if not creating regional—in other words, color—divisions was the principal aim: the "two parties . . . could cancel each other out with their forces and wear each other out with combats that would become each day more violent and more fierce and would end by leaving them at the mercy of the government when we are ripe to regain possession of Saint-Domingue." Dessalines's rise would allow the French to "inflame Christophe's ambition, to launch him against his enemy, and to finish destroying the blacks by the blacks themselves," Kerversau wrote, before reiterating, "But the most important thing is to raise up the mulattoes." Kerversau knew that color and region were not the only differences that could be used to divide independent Haitians. Prior disputes between those Black soldiers who had resisted the Leclerc expedition and those who joined it before defecting to the indigenous army also suggested to Kerversau how reconquest could be achieved. "In the mountains bordering the French and Spanish sides there are a troop of Negroes filled with a desire to avenge the assassination of Sans-Souci, their leader, which caused them to take up arms against Dessalines and Christophe." These "Congos" remained there out of fear and hatred of those two men (as well as "the love of wandering, and the thirst for plundering"), except when they "unexpectedly come over the plains, wreaking havoc when they have the numbers, and flee when they are attacked," ostensibly back into the remote and inaccessible mountains, "where it is impossible to encircle them." Kerversau estimated that there were two to three thousand members of this "new tribe," including "several chiefs, almost independent of each other . . . and the only one who has any ability at all is a young negro from the Prieur plantation known by the name of Petit-Noël."[34]

Kerversau further explained that these "Congos" were the only "brigands" who did not participate in the alleged general massacre of the whites. While their proposed union with the French would be circumstantial and temporary, "their irreconcilable hatred for Dessalines and Christophe, and the certainty of their inevitable loss if they ever had the misfortune to fall into their hands, would encourage their loyalty to us." Kerversau therefore proposed "heighten[ing] their zeal and the affection of their leaders with a few presents," including "ammunition and arms," which would allow them "to feed the war, to desolate the northern part, . . . to ruin farming, to tire Dessalines's Negros by making the country uninhabitable for them." This strategy would be "an infinitely useful diversion" to "facilitate the uprising of the west and the south against the north," which Kerversau counseled would be "the truest means of reducing the colony by using the colony against itself." France would be saved "a great consumption of men and money," and its soldiers would be spared "a war of extermination that is repugnant to our national character." This same Kerversau also proposed the massacre of all children and declared that "the hordes of brigands" must be regarded not merely as "lost men but as tigers whom the very cause of humanity authorizes us to exterminate."[35]

As time wore on, the reconquest plans submitted to the French government by former Saint-Dominguan officials—who claimed to have the most plausible ideas to reinstate slavery given the length of time they spent on the island—took on more, not less, genocidal verve. In 1806, the former Saint-Domingue finance administrator, Henry Perroud, sent Napoléon his own detailed plan for reconquest. "If we only listened to revenge and justly irritated spirits," Perroud admitted, "we would have to destroy every person in Saint-Domingue, beyond the age of eight." Though aware that many in France welcomed such an extermination, Perroud proposed instead that "only those who dare to fight should be destroyed. We could deport, to a colony not yet settled . . . anyone wearing an epaulet." Whether they pursued deportation or extermination, the first step was to assassinate Haiti's leader. "As long as Dessalines exists," he wrote, "we will never attain our goal." Perroud also imagined involving Christophe in a conspiracy to kill the emperor of Haiti. "If, as we have been assured, the negro Christophe has broken with his leader, we can hope to use his influence to dissolve the rebel troops and take possession of all the fortified spots in the north of the colony, without losing a single Frenchman." The proposed extermination would spare only Christophe among the military officers. "All the black and mulatto leaders in revolt cannot be allowed to remain there: they must be deported, as well as all the officers who are under their orders. Christophe alone should be spared, if he behaves as the government will require," Perroud wrote. Christophe would then "become the principal instrument which we must use to destroy the powers of the other leaders, and his influence would be used to restore all the cultivators to their respective dwellings." "Christophe has always been feared by the blacks: he only socialized with whites. All the districts where Christophe was in control were the best cultivated and the calmest," Perroud said. As an "isolated leader," the French could "force" Christophe "to crack down on lazy farmers and ill-behaved subjects," who would come to hate and fear him. Because of this, "Christophe would always be obliged to reside near the governor."

In the most telling and alarming passage of Perroud's already disturbing plan, he proposed using a deeply personal travesty to manipulate Christophe—the detention of his son in France. Unaware that Ferdinand had already died when he wrote the initial report, Perroud said, "This black chief's son is in an orphanage. If the emperor [Napoléon] wishes to grant me permission to see him, that will be the first means of leading the father to the path of duty. Christophe loves his son very much." Then, in a footnote that Perroud must have added just before sending the document to Napoléon, he wrote, "A few days ago, I was informed that Christophe's child has died. His aunt is also dead."[36] It is unclear whether Perroud considered the death of Christophe's child an obstacle to his earlier plan or a boon.

Despite the alleged divisions between the emperor and the man he appointed general in chief of the Haitian army, Christophe's promotion had less to do with his prior responsibilities than with his leadership in the siege of Santo Domingo: the campaign to bring the eastern side of the island into the empire. Christophe led this important military operation, the goal of which was to end French occupation of the island, thereby further eliminating Napoléon's continued efforts to reconquer independent Haiti, of which these reconquest plans stand as proof.

Today, Santo Domingo is the capital of the Dominican Republic, but in the early nineteenth century it was shorthand for the entire eastern side of the island. Following Haitian independence, the east fell under the command of the French general Ferrand. Spain had ceded the eastern side of the island to France with the Treaty of Basel in 1795, and Louverture had been instrumental in ensuring French domination over the entire island during his rule as governor-general. Since independence, however, the Haitian military had never managed to extend its empire into Santo Domingo.

Most of the French troops and colonists left the island after Rochambeau's capitulation in November 1803. Yet two noteworthy French generals stayed behind. One of them, Louis Marie Antoine de Noailles, at Môle Saint-Nicolas, led the remaining French troops, who retreated to the northwestern side of the island—a dangerous position for multiple reasons. First, Noailles's presence breached Dessalines's treaty with Rochambeau, which allowed French troops a ten-day grace period to evacuate starting November 19, 1803. Dessalines initially offered protection to any Frenchman who sought to remain in Haiti after that date. To "tranquilize the fears" of white French citizens, Dessalines pronounced, "The war we have continued to wage up to this day has no relation whatever to the inhabitants of this Unhappy Colony. I have uniformly held out protection and security to the inhabitants of every complexion; and on the present occasion you shall find me adhering to the same line of conduct." Those who wanted to leave, he said, were "free to do so." French ships, on the contrary, would be subject to British authority.[37]

This treaty complicated things for Noailles, who did not at first know of its existence, since he was stationed way up at Môle Saint-Nicolas on the westernmost tip of the northern peninsula. Even after learning of the treaty, Noailles refused to surrender. When Colonel Pourcely attacked the city, on behalf of the indigenous army, Noailles took to the seas, where he encountered another adversary: the British. A British ship pursued Noailles in a bloody and deadly naval campaign. Noailles ended up escaping and steered his ship safely into port in Havana, but not before having received the gunshot wound that took his life only a few days after he reached the Spanish slave colony.[38]

Instead of trying to reach Cuba, General Ferrand, for his part, stayed on the eastern side of the island.[39] At the time of the armistice, Ferrand was in Monte Cristi, east of the river that separates Haiti from Santo Domingo. Upon learning that the entire expeditionary army agreed to evacuate Cap, Ferrand quickly made his way to the city of Santo Domingo, in General Kerversau's command. Ferrand, who outranked Kerversau, took over command and Kerversau fled to France with the rest of the French convoy.[40]

Such was the situation when the indigenous army declared the whole island independent of France on January 1, 1804. Since Louverture had ruled over the eastern side of the island, Dessalines likewise considered

Santo Domingo a natural part of his newly constructed empire. Ferrand held a contrary opinion. The French general had determined to do everything in his power to preserve the eastern two-thirds of the island for France. But having received no reinforcements from Bonaparte, Ferrand was left to defend the regions of Cibao, Saint-Jago, and Santo Domingo against the British for over a year with nothing more than his own fortitude and that of the inhabitants, who, Ferrand claimed, fearing Dessalines, preferred French slavery to Haitian independence.[41]

To prevent Bonaparte from attacking, Dessalines believed that he needed to drive the French military out of the east and reunite the island under one government. The emperor explained that he remained "determined to recognize only those borders of the island traced by nature and the seas," because "persuaded that as long as even one enemy still breathes in this land, I still have a duty to fulfill with dignity the role to which you have elevated me." Dessalines therefore authorized a military campaign to "recover the entire portion of my territories." He considered the mission especially urgent in light of the damning implications of General Ferrand's decree of January 6, 1805. Ferrand had declared outright that he was at war with neighboring Haiti and "remained preoccupied with the proper measures of reducing the blacks in the colony of Saint-Domingue." This decree, Dessalines said, convinced him that the Haitian army had to "eliminate, until the last vestiges, all idols of the European."[42] With his decree, Ferrand had offered an audacious and draconian reminder that French slavery still existed in Santo Domingo. Not only did Ferrand order the soldiers under his command to "diminish the population" of Haiti through a combination of combat, deportation, and starvation, but he ordered any captured male children under the age of ten, along with "all negresses and mulatresses" over the age of twelve, to remain in the colony to work on the plantations or be sold. Captured male adolescents between the ages of ten and fourteen, along with "negresses" and "mulatresses" between the ages of twelve and fourteen, were to be exported for sale, too, to prevent them from joining the Haitian army. All "blacks" and "people of color" who "escaped these formalities" would be "considered stolen objects and confiscated or reclaimed wherever they may be found in the colony of Saint-Domingue, as well as in the neighboring colonies."[43]

Remarkably, Dessalines first attempted to negotiate with the man who had sworn to bring French war once more to Haitian shores. "Because it is contrary to the laws and to the independence of the colony that any portion of the French army remains on the island," Dessalines wrote, "General Ferrand is summoned to surrender the city of Santo Domingo in twenty-four hours: if, at the expiration of this time, the city has not been evacuated, it will be subject to pillage, and all the inhabitants will be pierced with the sword."[44] Ferrand did not dare send any of his men to transmit his refusal to Dessalines; this likely would have resulted in the death of the emissary. So it was that physical warfare with France began once more on February 16, during the second year of Haitian independence. Although the campaign ultimately failed to bring the entire island under Dessalines's authority, the Haitian government still regarded the siege—whereby many of the eastern cities bordering Haiti were captured and burned—a success. "The city of Santo Domingo, the sole to survive the disaster and devastation that I have spread far and wide in the former territory of the Spanish, will no longer be able to serve as a retreat for our enemies, nor as a tool for their plots," Dessalines declared.[45] Dessalines, Pétion, and many of Haiti's most illustrious generals fought in the campaign, and Christophe kept a detailed record serialized in the *Political and Commercial Gazette* that summer.[46] Christophe's letters to various Haitian military officers and the emperor suggest that this campaign encouraged Dessalines to promote Christophe to the second-highest position in the land.

The Empire of Haiti received essential weapons and other munitions from the United States and England, which it used in the siege. Because of Haiti's intricate and delicate relationships with both countries, it was essential that neither quasi-ally interfered. Just before the strike began, Christophe reached out to Thomas Richardson, a British merchant, to ask if he thought British ships would protect the Haitians from Ferrand's attack. Richardson replied that the Haitian government could count on nothing from England and seemed to admonish the division general for having asked. Richardson's reasoning—that the British did not want to be involved out of fear that Haitians might next bring "an insurrection to their colonies"—displeased and frustrated Christophe. Christophe reported to Dessalines on February 14, 1805, that although he found Richardson frank and a man of honor, the British merchant could be giving him misinformation, or rather, it was more than possible that British agents were doing so through him.[47]

Even without assurance of protection from the British, Christophe believed he had enough troops in the northern division to join the campaign. It would take his men some time to reach the eastern side of the island, though, since heavy rains had made the river in Limbé impassable. This initially prevented the troops from gathering in Cap.[48] Christophe came up with an alternative plan. He asked General Romain, whom he had recently accused of negligence, to provide him with eighty strong and robust men who would not become fatigued by the long route and who could carry the munitions.[49] Christophe ordered most of the colonels to join the First and Second Demi-brigades of Grande-Rivière and await further orders in Fort-Liberté.[50]

The weather still refused to cooperate with Christophe's mission to Santo Domingo. On February 20, Christophe reported to Vernet that near-constant rains tortured him and his men and that he himself had almost drowned the day before.[51] Once the weather cleared up, Christophe was finally able to leave and resume his march into the eastern side of the island. After a few lengthy detours, he reached the left bank of the river just outside the city of Santo Domingo. Christophe appeared wary. Some unidentified boats had docked near his men. Preparing for conflict, Christophe ordered the chef de brigade to bring his troops to the left bank to assist him.[52]

The next day, the situation grew violent. Christophe's troops fired on a ship that seemed too close to the border separating the eastern and western parts of the island. Already, the day before, Ferrand's men had fired a cannon at them. Christophe, trying to prevent the French troops from encroaching onto the western department of Haiti, established five batteries that night within shooting range of the city.[53] They hit some of Ferrand's troops, who then retreated, but this was not Christophe's only success. Since Ferrand lived close to the border, Christophe had a fortuitous opportunity to glimpse his French rival mounting his horse that very morning as he took a long detour to enter the city. Christophe reported to Dessalines that if he had enough ammunition, he planned to fire on Ferrand and his men as soon as he spied them again. This vantage point revealed other information as well: the night before, Christophe witnessed the French military boarding people on ships, followed by their horrible cries as they were drowned.[54] This traumatic reminder of the genocide the French attempted to perpetrate under Leclerc and Rochambeau encouraged the Haitians to refuse any possible armistice.

Around this time, Christophe received news that many inhabitants of Santo Domingo desperately sought to flee the island. Some of the people living in the commune of La Vega were embarking on ships with their families for Samaná and from there hoped to reach Puerto Rico. The commander of La Vega himself escaped on a U.S. ship, along with several other soldiers and officers.[55] To prevent more people from fleeing, Dessalines ordered Christophe to determine the intentions of the inhabitants. Christophe sent his adjutant general and chef de brigade with soldiers to the Cibao region to ascertain if the Spanish there should be considered enemies or friends of the Empire of Haiti.[56] Unfortunately, Haitian troops found few friends in the east. Dessalines, displeased, ordered the apprehension and imprisonment of all "malicious" actors. Any others who were captured were to be sent to Dessalines directly.[57]

As in any war, the ordinary inhabitants suffered most during this campaign. On March 18, seemingly on the cusp of victory, Christophe sent Dessalines several men and women his troops captured on the French-Spanish side of the island. Some of the women could not be sent immediately, however, because they were pregnant and about to give birth; others simply fled.[58] But the Haitian military, especially Christophe's division, operated relentlessly and with much luck on their side. For one thing, their position—a fort with only a river separating it from the city—was disadvantageous to their adversaries. When Ferrand's troops discovered and attacked them, no one on the Haitian side was wounded, and Christophe's men were able to fire in return. Christophe also discovered sixty Black men and women hiding in the nearby woods, whom he rounded up and sent to a nearby plantation occupied by the Haitian army to await the emperor's orders.[59] From March 18 to 26, Haitian troops saw nothing but victory and French troops little else than losses. The end of the war seemed near. Christophe even wrote to Dessalines on the twenty-first to say that he, like the emperor, hoped they would soon see a successful end to the siege of Santo Domingo.[60]

Yet Christophe had set his sights even higher than retaking the eastern side of the island. Before the war's end, he wanted Ferrand's head. On March 22, he wrote to tell Dessalines that he planned to fire upon Ferrand's house the next day. However, this plan failed, only frustrating Christophe.[61] Other problems soon arose. The northern division had captured many people from the eastern side, and Christophe issued order after order for their confinement, subsistence, and even their protection. He told his chef de brigade to ensure that none of the captives were bothered or put to work on any plantations. He told Captain Étienne Albert specifically not to allow anyone to enter the quarters where the Spanish were held. Later, Christophe ordered Albert to round up all male and female laborers and send them to "His Majesty, the Emperor."[62] Christophe, a devout Catholic, gave Chef de Brigade Tabarre a different mission: to take the two captured priests to the commune of La Vega to provide Mass to the troops. Christophe reminded Tabarre to continue to arrest any deserters and all the "devastators" causing disorder in the arrondissement.[63]

Dessalines's tactics, in contrast, seemed contrary to Christophe's orders. On the twenty-fifth, Dessalines issued a command to the commanders over the regions and cities captured by the Haitian army to gather and imprison all the inhabitants of the conquered communes, "in order to, in his words, force them, along with their cattle and animals, back onto the Haitian side of the island."[64]

Meanwhile, the war for Santo Domingo raged on. It seemed all but assured that the Haitian army would be victorious, but the missed opportunity of capturing Ferrand had unexpected consequences. On March 23, Christophe's troops had shot at a ship flying a French flag. The Haitian military had not expected to see the ship off in the distance and fired too soon while it remained out of range.[65] Christophe's men soon learned of many more French ships on the horizon. On March 27, Christophe hastily informed Dessalines that the night before three French vessels entered the harbor at Santo Domingo. That day, seven more French ships arrived and could be seen in the harbor. All ten docked outside the range of Christophe's guns and cannons. Dessalines already knew about the French flotilla, having learned of it from Generals Pétion and Geffrard. At around four o'clock in the afternoon, the French ships of war assaulted Haitian troops. The combat lasted only two and a half hours, but it was devastating. French troops were prevented from gaining land, and cadavers were strewn about with several Haitian soldiers lying wounded on the ground.[66]

Although victory had earlier seemed nigh, momentous events far beyond the shores of the island had brought a mighty French fleet to Ferrand's aid at the last minute, forcing Dessalines to accept that continuing to fight Ferrand would only lead to more French attempts to directly overthrow his empire. The reason for the fleet's sudden appearance was simple: France and England had reached another peace agreement, which meant that the Haitian army could no longer rely on the British, still patrolling the waters near Haiti, to attack any French ships they encountered on the way to the island. The day after his men repelled the French army's initial attack, the emperor ordered the Haitian army to retreat.

The campaign journal of General Laurent Bazelais, who also participated in the siege, reveals the logic behind this seemingly precipitous decision. Dessalines knew that "two other squadrons were ready to leave French ports for an unknown destination" and he had been "warned by foreign relations" of the consequences of "the sudden development of peace in Europe," Bazelais wrote. Dessalines also considered "the imminent flooding of the rivers that would make his retreat impracticable." In light of these two factors, Dessalines chose not to "sacrifice, out of a vain ambition for conquest, the safety and security of that part of the seat of his empire. . . . He ordered the principal leaders to evacuate, and two hours after dinner the cavalry spread out in all directions, destroying and burning everything in their path." In concert with Dessalines's orders, the Haitian army captured the remaining inhabitants, along with their animals, and reduced all the villages and cities to ashes, "bringing everywhere devastation, gunfire, and flames, sparing only those individuals that His Majesty decided to make prisoners."[67]

Christophe took part in the final phase of the failed siege of Santo Domingo. On March 31, he met up with his dear friend General Clervaux, whom he ordered to round up the inhabitants of "Cotuy" (Cotuí) and "Macory" (Macorís) as well as the commanders over those towns, and then "burn [both villages] to the ground." Christophe also ordered his men to pillage La Vega and "Saint-Yagues" (Saint-Jago). The division general wanted every region emptied of inhabitants, and he told Clervaux to kill anyone who refused to go with Haitian troops into Dessalines's territory and to do everything to prevent such individuals from escaping into the woods.[68]

Christophe then used the same tactic he once deployed to set ablaze his own beloved city of Cap. He told the chefs de brigade Albert and Raymond to go with two battalions to Les Cayes, taking with them along the way all the Spanish people of both colors and both sexes as well as their animals. Albert and Raymond had instructions to burn everything they encountered on their way back. Christophe issued a similar order to Chef de Brigade Jean-Jacques Barile in La Moca.[69] After evacuating much of the eastern part of the island of people and animals, Christophe said he ensured each locale had been "overturned . . . from top to bottom." "I made other troops responsible for burning the city of Saint-Yagues, and the surrounding areas," he wrote, "which they succeeded in perfectly razing to the ground. Even though this city was built in the Roman style, everything was consumed by the flames, even the five cathedrals in the city."[70]

By April 2, Christophe started to make preparations to return to Milot, where Colonel Jacques Antoine had orders to take all the Spanish he captured. While Christophe ordered the city of La Vega burned to the ground, "without leaving a single vestige of it," his letters to the men under his command urged them to show compassion, kindness, and care for the captives.[71] He told Colonel Antoine to ensure that none of the troops "vexed" or bothered the men and women he led to Milot. He also ordered Colonel Louis Achilles of Ouanaminthe to secure "victuals" for the captives and those he referred to as "unfortunate mothers and their families."[72] Christophe also designated a certain quantity of bananas, potatoes, and cassava for the nearly six hundred Spanish from the French side held captive under Commander Achilles.[73] In addition to holding massive numbers of French-Spanish captives from the east—both Black and white—the army confiscated thousands of farm animals. On April 3, Christophe ordered the three thousand cows and donkeys confiscated from sugar plantations in the east delivered to the government for redistribution. Similar orders went out to General de Brigade Toussaint Brave, Chef de Brigade Pourcely, and the commanders of Ouanaminthe and Fort-Liberté.[74]

Christophe now felt ready to return to the empire, later reporting that no obstacle prevented his march back into Haiti. The only thing left to do was to explain, nay spin, this loss as a victory for the Haitian people, rather than the failure the international press described.[75] On May 22, 1805, Christophe received fifty copies of Bazelais's campaign journal and promised to give it the most publicity possible. Christophe sent a memo to all the generals and division commanders the same day, ordering them to read and publish throughout their districts the pamphlet called *Journal of the Santo Domingo Campaign,* which ostensibly also included the report Christophe wrote, and to distribute one copy each to all their direct subordinates. Christophe asked Generals Romain and Brave to choose someone who knew how to read and write from among the young people in their arrondissements and to send him to Dessalines, who would "have the report printed at the press belonging to the empire to inform the state of what happened."[76]

In his report, Bazelais concluded by alluding to Dessalines's statement that the unexpected peace treaty between France and England caused the emperor to issue the cease-fire, not an impending loss to the French. "Thus ended a campaign during which the advantage was on our side throughout, in which the enemy at every turn was completely defeated. Thus was lifted the siege of a site whose only salvation was owing to an event that was as fortuitous as it was unexpected, and a concurrence of circumstances more worthy than such a conquest."[77] Christophe, for his part, bragged in the account he published in the *Gazette* that he had marched back into Haiti not as one of the conquered but as a conqueror: "I had with me, as I passed through all the different sides, 349 men and 1,350 women, 430 male children from the age of one to fifteen, and 318 girls of the same age." Christophe had also captured a surgeon identified as Monsieur Roulet, along with five Catholic priests. He returned to Cap-Haïtien with this hapless entourage of captives on April 9, 1805.[78]

Back in the east, Santo Domingo sat in shambles, with many other villages and locales completely burned. Much of the population had fled or remained captives of the Haitian government. And the campaign to bring Santo Domingo into the Empire of Haiti did not win Dessalines any friends in the international community. Roundly criticized in both the U.S. and British presses, Dessalines became newly aware of Haiti's lonely position in the world.

U.S. merchants had allowed Dessalines to purchase the weapons he used in the strike against Ferrand. Now these newspapers criticized the campaign and worried about what it might augur for the future of Haiti: "They proved their want of discipline and courage before the walls of the city of St. Domingo; where their numbers were ten times greater than that of the force by which they were attacked," said a Baltimore newspaper. News of Dessalines's captives also appeared in the much circulated story. "Above 200 Spaniards taken by the blacks from time to time in the neighborhood of St. Domingo city have been sent prisoners to the interior, and have been employed on the plains of the *Artibonite* and on the fort of *Camp Marchand*, whither the emperor contemplates to retire in the last resort of an attack by a French army or domestic insurgents," reported the *Aurora General Advertiser.*[79]

Turning away from the goal of reincorporating the east into Haiti, Dessalines's primary occupations from this moment forward were fortification and cultivation, which he saw as crucial to Haitian sovereignty. Christophe's promotion to general in chief, on the heels of the failed siege of the east, meant that he would oversee the reinforcement of existing forts and the development of new ones, along with the revival of Haiti's labor system designed to promote plantation agriculture. The task of managing the army took Christophe away from the cities, where old factions were becoming new enemies of the Haitian state.

CRACKS IN IMPERIAL
AUTHORITY

A little under three years after the formation of the Empire of Haiti, the country's citizens found themselves mired in war once again, but this time an internal one, with Christophe less at its head than right in its center. Shortly after declaring the island independent, Dessalines moved the capital of Haiti to Marchand, which he renamed Dessalines after himself. Located in the middle of the country, the city of Dessalines seemed almost to enable its namesake to view all sides of the peninsular island at once—the better to stay abreast of near-constant threats to his power. As the failed siege of Santo Domingo lingered in the air, General Christophe had the opportunity to test the strength of the new empire's laws and demonstrate his ability to enforce them. Did repeated challenges to his authority convince him that the only choice was to discipline and punish? Most of Christophe's letters from 1805 until Dessalines's assassination in 1806 suggest that it was now the general in chief's fortitude, compassion, and humanity that came under siege, from the citizens of Haiti, the captives of Santo Domingo, and Dessalines's very own soldiers. Shockingly, it was the famous Capoix La Mort who most tested the new Haitian government. Did Capoix betray the emperor into forcing his nickname, the Death, bestowed on him after the famous Battle of Vertières, to become both their realities, or did Christophe learn something about Capoix that caused the emperor to inflict a final punishment, unaware that it would precede by only a few days his own?

On July 15, 1805, the Empire of Haiti celebrated Christophe's fete, or royal birthday, in the city of Cap-Haïtien. Haiti's most important military officers attended, and the principal administrator of the north, Roumage *jeune*, led the ceremony. The emperor attended the celebration, too, which took place at a hotel in Cap owned by Christophe. According to some chroniclers, the hotel Christophe owned would have been none other than La Couronne, the very establishment where he had been employed under French rule. Dessalines's "august presence" at the hotel celebration, reported the *Gazette*, "spread happiness among all the citizens of that city." Several foreign businessmen profited from the occasion to pay their respects to the emperor. Roumage then pronounced a flattering speech to Christophe, the evening's guest of honor:

> Yes, General, we feel at every moment the inexpressible good fortune we are enjoying by having you in our midst; we also appreciate the great advantage resulting from the harmony and happiness that you are procuring for your citizens, who find in you a good father, a virtuous leader, enlightened and impartial, the comforter of the unfortunate and their supporter, as well as a magistrate for whom humanity guides every action.[1]

The emperor expressed satisfaction with Christophe as well. Dessalines had ordered the revival of cultivation, or farming, in November 1804. But the siege of Santo Domingo temporarily turned the government's attention, and especially Christophe's, away from that enterprise. Taking advantage of a distracted Christophe and Dessalines, many laborers, enjoying less stringent surveillance, moved around the country as they pleased. Some even sought work in the cities. Part of Christophe's renewed mission to revive agriculture after his return from the east involved ensuring the adequate staffing of plantations by not only encouraging laborers to return to the farms they deserted but compelling them.

Christophe had received orders from Dessalines to assemble all the male and female laborers who might have gathered in the city or otherwise absconded from farms and return them to the countryside. In June 1805, Christophe ordered all the military commanders of the northern division to arrest every male and female laborer in the city, even those employed by officers' wives, and imprison them until they could be sent back to the farms where they were originally employed. "Any laborer from a particular commune who is found in another must be sent back," the order read. "Take care to delegate this work to trusted officers who must visit each plantation . . . and obtain from the manager the names and places of refuge of any workers who, be they sick or well, are missing." This operation would be long and painful, Christophe counseled, "but when we compare it to the great good that it will do for farming and commerce, we must not neglect any method." The general in chief asked his men to inform him of the measures they took to increase farming in their arrondissements. "Accelerate the agriculture," he wrote, "and be sure to follow the method that I have just traced for you and to maintain this order of things, which I place under your personal responsibility."[2] The following month Christophe issued order after order and penned missive after missive about farm deserters and the best methods for bringing them back to work.

The arduous mission to redistribute laborers to farms across Haiti saw numerous mishaps, both minor and major. Some of these mistakes involved people who, according to the law, had been improperly rounded up and sent to the farms. Christophe rebuked Colonel Joachim, for example, for taking a Mademoiselle Sophie to a plantation where, as a city dweller, she had not previously labored.[3] Cases of mistaken identity like this were perhaps inevitable in a system that relied on common knowledge of who had been a laborer prior to independence. These kinds of blunders also resulted due to the empire's heterogeneous composition. All kinds of Haitians lived in the country—foreigners who had renounced their citizenship, white ex–French colonists, people formerly called the *gens de couleur libre,* and of course those who had been enslaved, most of them Black Africans from the continent and their descendants. Immediately or definitively determining a person's status under the previous colonial affermage system often presented problems of knowing.

Other breaches of rules at times involved the conduct of military officers. General Capoix—promoted to division general on July 28, 1805—and his men sat at the heart of some of these disputes.[4] In December, Christophe received complaints that the officers of the Twenty-Ninth Demi-brigade had engaged in illegal requisitions on plantations in the quartier of Vallières, including taking the manager, two drivers, and several others from one plantation and enlisting them in the army. Two of the men, Henry Jean Baptiste and one known only as Narcisse, had been forced to join the Twenty-Ninth Demi-brigade. Christophe was incensed. While he had ordered the troops to recruit men for the military, his orders also forbade them to force laborers to join the army. "I am pained to see that despite the strict orders that I have given in this regard, people are still being allowed to engage in requisitions on the plantations, which is frightening and horrifying the laborers." Christophe ordered Capoix to do everything in his power to end such abuses and to send the manager and the two drivers back to their plantation. "It is time," he told Capoix, "for you to put an end to these vexations and to put at ease the laborers so that they will be able to work in safety. Follow my instructions from now on, which permit only the commander and the inspector of the quartier to engage in requisitions for the completion of the troops."[5]

While the siege of Santo Domingo had failed to bring the east under Dessalines's rule, the "new hands" captured from Santo Domingo became integral, at least in Dessalines's mind, to Christophe's mission to accelerate farming. Yet just as many Haitians did not want to perform the backbreaking labor of sugar and coffee cultivation, the captured Spanish seemed ill-inclined to engage in such work either. As a result, many of them tried to return to the east. Christophe reluctantly admitted to Dessalines that despite all the measures he had taken for their care and protection, it had been impossible to prevent many of the captives from returning to the eastern (French) side. He said people from throughout the country, including Haitian citizens, concocted schemes to help the captives escape to Santo Domingo, using little roads and paths that only the French-Spaniards knew about.[6]

When protection and care did not work, Dessalines turned to brutality. "Instructed . . . that the Spanish we brought here at the close of our campaign [in Santo Domingo] keep running away," Christophe wrote to General Brave in September 1805, "you are ordered to have shot immediately any individuals whom you capture and who have already been arrested or that you catch in the act of running away." Dessalines's orders to Christophe had been clear in this regard: "This is the only way to prevent them from running away. They must be shot in the place where they were residing and in the presence of the other Spanish people."[7] Yet this system of arresting and punishing contradicted Christophe's spring 1805 orders that his army not mistreat the French-Spanish captives.

Callousness soon replaced compassion across the empire. Upon hearing that the French military killed some of the captives who returned to the eastern side of the island, Christophe told Dessalines in September 1805, "I do not really think there is anything wrong with this. On the contrary, they are getting rid of traitors for us, who could only be odious to both sides."[8] The goal, nevertheless, at least for Christophe, had been to prevent the captives from running away, not to cause or allow their deaths en masse. The emperor wanted hands, so to speak, that could contribute to planting and farming on state-run plantations.

By November, Christophe had implemented an entire system of surveillance to prevent the French-Spanish laborers from leaving their assigned plantations. He asked General Capoix to establish a patrol "from Laxavon to the interior of the area surrounding the river [called "Dajabón" in Spanish] without crossing the river under any circumstances, to bring back all the people and to set fire to all the *ajoupas* and other houses that are established there and to despoil any rations that might exist there." Christophe stressed that with these measures he hoped to increase cultivation, not kill the cultivators. Initially, he did not order any of these captives to be shot, but instead mandated their arrest upon capture. Christophe told Capoix that any arrested individuals should be sent to him directly, and he reminded Capoix to ensure that the men under his command carried out Dessalines's orders to take the French-Spaniards back to the workhouses on the Haitian side. Any soldier or officer not following the guidelines would be arrested and taken to Laferrière. Christophe also sought to ensure that the generals in charge of these operations understood how "easy" it would be to determine if any of the workhouses were missing people. All they had to do, Christophe reminded them, was examine the ledger of people whom Dessalines ordered to return and see if it matched the number of people there. Christophe particularly worried about the border region because he observed the general neglect of farming and saw many abandoned plantations there, which threatened the acceleration of agriculture.[9]

Believing it the more humane path, Christophe conceived a plan to arrest the escapees rather than execute them. On November 20, he wrote to Dessalines to inform him that the French-Spanish they sent to plantations in the eastern part of the empire frequently ran away or tried to do so almost daily. Christophe ordered them arrested, despite Dessalines's order to have the fugitives shot, as an example to the other captives. Christophe justified the change in plans by noting that the threat of death had not acted as a deterrent. Christophe told the emperor that instead he "ordered Division General François Capoix to have them all arrested, on the same day and at the same time." If they refused to farm and become dutiful Haitian citizens, Haitian soldiers should treat them as enemies and send them to remote regions of northwestern Haiti, "which will hopefully prevent them from deserting and from providing damaging information to our enemies," Christophe wrote.[10]

By the following week, the Haitian military had put into operation Christophe's new plan. Christophe reported that his soldiers delivered 142 Spanish men and women from the French side of the island directly to him. The military then escorted the captives to Port-de-Paix, on the other side of the country, and from there to remote Moustique and Jean-Rabel. None of the captives could be permitted to leave. "This measure is being taken to put an end to their escapes and to any meetings they might have with the Spanish, our enemies; at the very least, once they are confined in this region so far from whence they came, they will no longer try to flee and at least if they do keep trying to run away, we will be more certain of being able to arrest them," Christophe told General Romain.[11] The extensive operation continued into the new year. In March 1806, Christophe sent to the north nine more French-Spanish prisoners with strict orders to prevent their escape, as many had already done, even all the way from Port-de-Paix.[12]

The question of what to do with the captives was only one of Christophe's problems as he tried to balance carrying out Dessalines's commands while preventing the abuse and torture of the populace. The general in chief continued to worry about both the army's mistreatment of laborers and the harsh extralegal punishments that citizens and soldiers received from high-ranking officers. Despite his sense that the law had to be applied uniformly and fairly, Christophe continued to exhibit compassion. In June 1805, several laborers escaped from a plantation in the Artibonite and were caught hiding in woods farther north. When Dessalines learned of this, he ordered the fugitives sent to him immediately for punishment. Christophe, responsible for ensuring their arrival, wrote to the emperor to say that he could send only three of the individuals, Augustin, Isidore, and Adélaïde. Citoyen Plutus and citoyenne Minerve could not be sent, Christophe warned, since they were more than eighty years old "and sending them on the road would be to leave them to perish from the fatigues of the journey."[13] The law remained the law, however, and Christophe had to repeatedly remind his officers to follow the military penal code rather than determine their own punishments.[14] He also felt compelled to almost constantly remind the army not to "brutalize" people, in his words, especially women and children.[15]

Christophe found respite during these difficult days with his friends, most of whom fought alongside him during the revolution. One of his longest-standing friendships was with the man who later helped install him as president: Dessalines's minister of finance, General Vernet. Vernet, like Capoix, had led a valiant demi-brigade during the Battle of Vertières. Tied to an illustrious revolutionary family, Vernet had married one of Toussaint Louverture's nieces, Marie-Augustine Chancy.[16] A native of Gonaïves, Vernet was widely respected by those who knew and worked with him. Boisrond-Tonnerre called him "the greatest jurist" and practitioner of "every military and social virtue." Vastey, the future baron and Vernet's undersecretary, lauded him also as a "virtuous citizen, filled with honor." Christophe, too, had nothing but affection for Vernet, whom he frequently called "my dear comrade."[17]

Christophe remained similarly close with many other administrators and military officers who fought alongside him during the revolution. His letters reveal his affection and care for their well-being, and his sorrow when he learned of their deaths. Christophe experienced devastation when General Augustin Clervaux died in May 1805. Lamenting the passing of the man who co-signed Haiti's preliminary Declaration of Independence, Christophe called Clervaux a "brave division general and councilor of the state." His death meant the loss of "a friend of liberty and of our own, indeed!" It was also the loss of one who shared the same father's grief. Clervaux, like Christophe, never saw his son again after he sent him to France with Ferdinand Christophe in 1802. Concerned for Clervaux's property and family, Christophe told Dessalines that he intended to ensure that Clervaux's effects did not fall into a state of dilapidation and that Clervaux's wife and remaining children had all they needed.[18]

In November 1805, when Christophe learned that yet another storied military officer had taken ill, General Gabart, Christophe sent Capoix with doctors and a surgeon in the hopes of restoring Gabart's health. Christophe expressed distress upon learning that his efforts failed. "Sire," he wrote to Dessalines on November 6, 1805, "I have just learned through an indirect channel that we have had the misfortune to lose Division General Gabart. If this news should prove to be true, I am losing a mate, a friend in all things, and Your Majesty is losing an intrepid defender of our country."[19]

This news compounded other more personal losses. Dessalines's daughter Cérine had also recently died. Christophe attempted to console the emperor, testifying to his own sadness upon learning this devastating news. He told Dessalines that he could relate. "I am a father, and I have learned by experience . . . that we cannot prevent ourselves from having natural feelings," he said. "Sire, please be assured of my most respectful attachment, it is as sincere as the friendship I offer to you." Dessalines's mother-in-law also died around the same time.[20] "So much misfortune, in such a short amount of time, cannot but afflict Your Majesty's heart in the most sensible manner," Christophe wrote. "The loss of a distinguished officer, like the late General Gabart, is difficult to repair, and has become a grief for the entire army, that of a beloved child and one so worthy of being so, must overwhelm your sensitive, paternal heart. Still, [the death] of your mother-in-law, together with all this, has to have struck the most overwhelming blow that one could feel and whose example is rare in the memory of men." Christophe continued to console his friend, the emperor, in writing:

These unfortunately irreparable losses are not less painful for me than for you, I must assure you, due as much to the ardent interest I have in anything that involves you as to the most intimate friendship that linked me to these individuals. . . . We must support each other with bravery and resignation for that which we cannot prevent, and we must not allow our souls to become defeated by sadness.[21]

Yet more sadness was in store for both men. The next year, on May 31, 1806, Division General Geffrard, another hero of Vertières, passed away. The greatest defenders of the country appeared on the verge of dying one by one. "It seems that misfortune is enjoying its ruthless pursuit of us and is going after the most ardent defenders of our country! The loss of a military man so experienced can only be mourned by all the most sincere friends of Haiti," Christophe wrote to Generals Romain, Capoix, and Dartiguenave. "As soon as you receive this letter, order a twenty-cannon salute to announce this terrible development, and the next day order twenty more."[22] Christophe subsequently wrote a letter to Dessalines similarly filled with sadness and disbelief, verging on anger:

Sire, I do not even know how to express to Your Majesty what pain I experienced upon learning of the death of our unfortunate comrade Geffrard; I can only think of how many deaths there have been in such a short period of time and what fatalism has caused so many of the greatest defenders of the empire to disappear like so. . . . I carried out the order that you gave to me to have this afflicting news announced with a twenty-cannon salute that will be repeated the next day.[23]

Christophe did not reserve his compassion solely for his friends. Several times, he had to report to Dessalines the painful reality that some of the empire's soldiers killed one another. "I pity enormously the fate of such soldiers," he told Dessalines, "who should have had the opportunity to die while doing something useful for their country."[24]

Perhaps because Christophe had been wounded in battle before, he also showed compassion for and concern with the sick and dying in the empire's hospitals. "For the good of humanity," he said, "the aid that we must provide to the soldiers wounded in the army" required the utmost attention of the state. Christophe worried that soldiers wounded in battle had not received adequate care, especially those who participated in the siege of Santo Domingo. They bravely served their country but now languished in the most profound misery, Christophe said. Consequently, he ordered Roumage to frequently visit the hospital to ensure that the sick and wounded were not neglected.[25] In June 1805, Christophe visited the Hôpital de la Providence and grew dismayed to find the patients still suffering and in misery, wanting for everything, having nothing at all to drink even. He insisted that Roumage pay more attention to the deplorable situation because, in Christophe's words, "this branch of service involves me personally."[26]

Later, as king, Christophe famously prioritized the education of Haiti's youth, and this concern seems to have germinated in the early days of independence. On April 4, 1805, the *Political and Commercial Gazette* announced that Monsieur Laborie in Cap "will instruct his students such that they will have a perfect understanding of grammar and religion, and he will make alternative arrangements with anyone wanting instruction in the English language or the other sciences." Laborie established a boarding school, home to several students already and hoped to enroll even more.[27] This news encouraged Christophe to thank Dessalines for not neglecting education in establishing the empire's priorities. "The education of the youth," Christophe wrote, "is worthy of the attention and care of the government in every way." Education was useful not just for creating a knowledge base that could ultimately serve the government but would also help the citizens to "practice the social virtues that would come to shape their spirits and their hearts." "For me, faithful to the instructions that you have given to me, I will oversee the public education that will lead to this goal," Christophe told the emperor.[28]

Dessalines, for his part, instructed Christophe to find some young people to learn the trade of printing. Taking this mission to heart, Christophe identified four young men at Monsieur Laborie's school. Although the young men could read and write, Christophe observed they could not spell, a skill essential for the work of the state printer. Laborie promised that within six months he could perfect their orthography.[29] Afterward, General Romain sent Christophe two additional young men to learn the printing press, whom the future general in chief sent to Dessalines, remarking that they wanted to learn the "business of printing" and to "study orthography," which he once again called "indispensable to the state."[30]

With the establishment of a preliminary education system, the reorganization of the army under way, and the redistribution of the labor structure essentially in place—all under Christophe's watchful gaze—by the end of August 1805 the Haitian government confidently reported to the Haitian people that the empire prospered. "The administration of the country is regular and orderly," the *Gazette* reported. Commerce with foreign merchants remained lucrative, the crops were favorable, the army functioned smoothly, and public revenue was sufficient to cover the government's expenses. In only a little over a year of independence, the army had grown to sixty thousand men fully equipped with the resources needed to defend Haiti. The Haitian government publicized these feats with the aim of persuading the Haitian people to agree to pay nominal taxes as much to show off to the foreign world powers who refused to recognize Haitian independence. The editor of the *Gazette* expressed astonishment, in fact, that the Haitian state was able to thrive, given that there were no taxes levied in the country, other than the requirement that property owners and farmers submit a quarter of their proceeds to the state.

While private property existed in the empire, as indicated in the *Gazette*, the government also owned many plantations and other estates. The *Gazette* acknowledged that revenues from these state-run farms, under the system of affermage, could be considered "immense, surpassing by a lot even certain countries in Europe, without even counting what was received from customs, which is always a fruitful method for a government to enrich itself." Trade remained robust, despite no other country having officially recognized Haitian independence. The citizens of Haiti were told that this lucrative international commerce would eventually trickle down and contribute to the "prosperity" and "opulence of all citizens."[31]

The relationship between foreign trade and diplomatic recognition from the rest of the world greatly preoccupied the empire's officials. They sometimes seemed to plead for official recognition from the United States and England; at other times, they declared Haiti's independence a fact regardless of foreign opinion. On August 8, 1805, the *Gazette* published an article signed "By a Haitian," which stated that whether any foreign nation recognized Haitian sovereignty or not, "the island is in effect independent; its independence resides in its strength and does not depend on any recognition of it from Europe. In such a matter, fact is everything, the law is nothing."[32] But what if the Haitian people adopted that perspective of fact versus law vis-à-vis the empire's regulations?

———

Though he enjoyed high-ranking status as general in chief, Christophe remarkably oversaw many different parts of the new government and its laws. In addition to the empire's school system, he oversaw the establishment of the justices of the peace and the fortifications of Haiti's numerous forts. The construction and fortification of these fortresses, located throughout the country, required tremendous human and animal labor to transport massive amounts of bricks, nails, tools, wood, and charcoal. Dessalines consistently ordered Christophe to accelerate the work, saying these forts were necessary for the defense of the country in case the French should try to invade, either from the east or from the sea. The most important of these forts had been erected at Laferrière, the future site of Christophe's famous Citadelle.

The empire's backbreaking labor system did not mark the return to chattel slavery, since no one was bought or sold or shipped across the Atlantic for that purpose. However, it did constitute a "corvée," which is the word that Christophe himself used, or labor required in lieu of taxes. When requesting four hundred pounds of three-inch-long plank nails for the work going on at Fort Laferrière, Christophe asked Roumage for "a corvée of eight men who could bring him the requested materials." Many other noteworthy forts in Haiti were built using corvée labor, too, including one in the capital, Marchand, the city renamed Dessalines.[33]

If the freedom of the previously enslaved population was fragile, so was Haiti's agricultural system. As in the days of colonial affermage, a plantation labor system worked by "free hands" depended upon the willingness of the laborers to work. Simultaneously, the system also depended on the effectiveness of the military commanders and soldiers in charge of the cultivators, who were responsible for encouraging them to labor, based on the profits they could earn, and more dubiously, in the event the laborers were unwilling, to compel them, sometimes using force. While work on the plantations was often less than voluntary—recall that laborers needed to remain on their assigned plantations—so was military service.

Dessalines also put Christophe in charge of outfitting the military in proper attire, ensuring that soldiers and officers had appropriate rations, and maintaining a system of rotation that provided regular, prolonged periods of rest for the army.[34] Christophe had frequent occasion to admonish his commanders for not providing proper rations or for allowing the rations to be pillaged. His reactions to problems in the empire reveal his exasperation at what he characterized as the near-constant incompetence of some of the men he entrusted with important tasks.

In August 1805, Christophe wrote to his commanders in the cities of Borgne, Port-Margot, and Trou, astonished that they had not yet furnished Roumage with the necessary rations for the garrison in Cap. Christophe enjoined each of them to no longer neglect this part of the military's operation. Consequently, he issued a command for Colonel Pourcely to send Roumage weekly rations from the Île de la Tortue meant to provide subsistence for the troops housed in Cap. The general in chief's irritation was perhaps never more apparent than when he learned that despite his orders the troops were not regularly being rotated out of service.[35]

In May 1806, Christophe admonished General Brave because, after relieving one detachment and replacing it with another, he sent the former to work on Fort Gandon instead of allowing the soldiers to plant subsistence crops for their own use. Christophe reminded Brave to give the relieved detachments the actual resting periods owed them every twenty days.[36] About a year earlier, Christophe had issued a memo to all the generals and military commanders specifying the exact rations to be furnished gratis for the empire's troops and which were to be offered by the farmers of each plantation. The commanders of each arrondissement remained responsible for ensuring that the chief inspectors of each quartier secured sufficient rations. Christophe counseled the military officers to encourage the commanders and inspectors to plant abundant foodstuffs on the plantations. "For you very well know that if this measure is neglected, the troops will be on the verge of dying from starvation," he wrote.[37]

The empire's affermage system permitted the cultivators to plant subsistence crops as well—that is, if Christophe could get the military to follow his orders. In August 1805, Christophe reminded two of his chefs de brigade to issue clear orders for their soldiers not to pillage the subsistence crops of the laborers. To prevent the soldiers from engaging in such illegal raids, he told them to allow their soldiers to plant their own subsistence crops after their Thursday night exercises, as long as they returned to the army by Saturday night and did not disturb the crops of the laborers working on the plantations.[38] Despite the continuation of what he often referred to as "disorders," Christophe frequently ended his letters to the emperor by reporting that tranquility reigned from one end to the other in the country. In those same letters he often simultaneously disclosed serious instances of neglect, defiance, fugitivity, theft, disorder, and insubordination.

Not only did Christophe spend much time disciplining Haiti's military officers and citizens, but as general in chief he still had to worry about the world's constant discursive and material warring with independent Haiti. Under Toussaint Louverture, Saint-Domingue had a favorable trade relationship with the United States. Dessalines hoped this would continue. For this purpose, he wrote to President Thomas Jefferson, on June 23, 1803, before Haitian independence had been declared. The future Haitian emperor all but asked Jefferson to bless the impending rupture with France. "The people of Saint-Domingue, tired of paying with our blood the price of our blind allegiance to a mother country that cuts her children's throats," Dessalines wrote, "and following the example of the wisest nations, have thrown off the yoke of tyranny and sworn to expel the torturers." The countryside, he said, "is already purged of their sight. A few cities are still under their domination but have nothing further to offer to their avid rapacity." Even if Dessalines wanted nothing to do with the French, he still needed the weapons and everyday foodstuffs from U.S. ships. This letter was meant not only to announce Dessalines's plan to make Saint-Domingue independent but to put the U.S. government at ease so that this favorable trade could continue. "Commerce with the United States, Mister President, offers a market for the huge harvests we have in storage and the even more abundant ones that are now growing. Your country's shippers are calling for it. Your nation's long-standing relations with Saint-Domingue are evidence of the loyalty and good faith that await your ships in our ports," he continued. Dessalines finished by underscoring "the eagerness with which I will exert all my authority for the safety of the United States' ships and the benefits they will reap from trading with us."[39]

From the Haitian government's perspective, Saint-Domingue had been a de facto outpost for the United States during the Adams administration as the two entities had engaged in a reciprocal trade arrangement that cost the U.S. government almost nothing to maintain.[40] Jefferson seemed to share that perspective initially, proposing that an independent "St. Domingo" could become informally co-opted into U.S. territory, if it did not become a quasi-extension of it. In December 1803, Jefferson offered that the Louisiana Territory might provide a suitable location for freed and/or rebellious enslaved persons whom the government felt could no longer be safely worked on southern U.S. plantations. Noting that "St. Domingo has undergone important changes," Jefferson commented that, like the Louisiana Territory, Haiti might provide the solution to a problem.[41]

However, not long after the Louisiana Purchase between France and the United States became official, the relationship between independent Haiti and the United States cooled. An article published in Haiti's *Political and Commercial Gazette* presciently analyzed the broader significance of the changes U.S.–Haitian trade relations underwent under Jefferson. The author of the article wrote that the United States would one day "occupy a distinguished rank among the masters of the sea." Foreseeing the inevitable decline of France and England, the writer warned, "The same thing will befall the powers that are presently dominant; they will undergo an unmistakable decline, while the United States will assume the rank to which it is destined. But this era will become deadly for the Caribbean. It will simply change masters. It will come under the yoke of the United States." As for ongoing U.S. slavery, "in the states of the south, [it] is a fire that smolders under the ashes, the eventual explosion of which will one day make tremble the hardened and deaf masters who still maintain it, despite the prudent advice of their fellow citizens of the north." Like Boisrond-Tonnerre, who observed that the "key to liberty" for the still enslaved across the Americas could be found "in their own hands," the writer from the *Gazette* prophesied that one day "some audacious avengers will reclaim with interest their natural rights that have been violated." While most Haitians believed that France was their greatest enemy, this article asked the Haitian people not to ignore or dismiss the serious danger next door in North America:

> [France's] attempts will come crashing down like the waves of the sea at the foot of the rock of our independence, and from the mountains our rescue squad will descend upon them. But a more hidden danger, and one far less apparent, because it is still distant for now, threatens us anyway. It will not be from Europe that our ills must come, if we are to ever experience them; it will be from the continent of the United States: their proximity, the constant comings and goings of their citizens in our ports, the ambitions that they will bring with them, if our government does not restrict them, must open our eyes to the plots that they may one day attempt against us.

The writer did not seek "to place a cloud over the conduct of the Americans, nor do I think at all that, either the present government or the individuals who are linked to it through commercial relations with that country, have thus far had any plans to dominate us, nor to meditate on our enslavement." Yet, he said, "it is no less true that the possibility of such a combination could arise from a concurrence of circumstances, if ever the United States were to erect itself to become a maritime power."[42]

Imperial rage followed the publication of this astonishingly prescient article. Dessalines ordered Christophe to discover the identity of the author and to have him sent to Marchand/Dessalines immediately. Dessalines worried that openly and publicly criticizing the United States might propel the trade embargo being debated on the floors of Congress.[43] Christophe soon learned from the empire's printer, Pierre Roux, that the author was Joseph Rouanez, the official English translator in the empire and editor of the *Gazette*.[44] Dessalines must not have punished the newspaperman too harshly. Rouanez continued to work as editor of the *Gazette*; and despite Dessalines's evident displeasure, events on the ground made it difficult to deny the new geopolitical threat Rouanez outlined.

On February 14, 1806, Christophe sent Dessalines several extracts from U.S. newspapers, one of which contained a message from the president of the United States to the U.S. Congress, concerning the French government's complaints about Americans engaged in commerce with Haiti. U.S. senators had impassioned debates on the Senate floor, many of which were "favorable to our cause," Christophe said.[45] Less than two weeks later, however, Christophe wrote that the United States, under pressure from the French, was about to announce a complete embargo against Haiti. "I am of the same opinion as Your Majesty," he wrote to Dessalines on

February 26, 1806. "The Congress of the United States, out of deference to France, could very well forbid commerce between its subjects and our country."[46]

Christophe received this information by unsealing the letters of foreigners doing business on the island, particularly letters from the United States.[47] By unsealing one set of letters, he learned that the bill for the trade embargo had passed. Surveillance for the purposes of gathering foreign intelligence led to censorship for the purposes of preventing that intelligence from spreading. For the first time in his correspondence, Christophe ordered information hidden from the Haitian people. "I have received with your letter," he wrote to Rouanez, "a copy of the debates that took place in the United States Senate. I do not think it would really be appropriate to have this inserted in the *Gazette*. . . . Gather together all the newspapers that you have received that discuss this material, and upon my arrival in Cap remit them to me, for these are insignificant developments that we do not need to print in our newspapers."[48] Christophe did send a copy of one of the U.S. newspapers to the emperor. "I make haste to inform Your Majesty, that I just learned from [this] U.S. newspaper . . . that the bill to suspend commercial relations between the United States and our country has passed." Though he previously downplayed the seriousness of the bill, Christophe observed that several U.S. businesses had already written to their correspondents in Haiti asking for the return of their funds. Christophe once again learned about this through his surveillance tactics. He reported to Dessalines that he "unsealed several letters" and would send them to the emperor as evidence.[49]

The embargo did not end trade between Haiti and the United States completely, but it did lead to scarcity on the island. Haiti had suffered a flour shortage for some time, and the government stockpiles remained totally depleted. Luckily, a U.S. ship had just docked in Haiti from Baltimore. Christophe wrote to Vernet that the ship's fortuitous arrival would provide immediate balm for the "subsistence of the sick and wounded" of the country, who were "barely hanging on and subjected to the greatest of deprivations."[50] Yet in his letter to Dessalines, informing him of the passing of the trade restrictions by the United States, Christophe testified to a more acute problem: the French. Not only were they at least partly responsible for the increasingly cold and distant relationship between Haiti and the United States, but Napoléon had not completely given up his designs of reconquering the entire island. Since the French still occupied Santo Domingo, their military ships remained a constant and immediate concern as well.

In March 1806, French corsairs captured three Haitian ships and seized some of the men on board. The French eventually released eight of the men and two of the ships, but not before having dismantled and otherwise destroyed them. A distressed Christophe urged Dessalines to take steps to prevent such sabotage. Otherwise, "I foresee that every kind of evil might arise," he said. "The war that we are in with the French being eternal to the death, our ships, since they are weaker, should rather crash into the side of these corsairs and the indigenous should prefer to drown themselves than to allow themselves to be captured." Going forward, Dessalines, who believed that some of the men had consorted with the French and intentionally allowed the seizures, said to imprison any man returned to Haiti by the French as a punishment.[51] Eventually, Dessalines decided that it was not enough to simply imprison the returned Haitians. He ordered to be shot anyone guilty of suspected collusion with the French.[52] This drastic punishment was a reinforcement of a previous policy of the emperor's. In October 1804, Dessalines had announced that despite receiving protection from the Haitian government, foreign commercial agents sometimes "facilitated the escape of men and women of color, natives of this country." He therefore passed a series of laws stating that the captain of any foreign ship found carrying Haitians to other countries would be arrested, imprisoned, deported, and forbidden to return to Haiti, while the state would confiscate the ship and its cargo. Moreover, "any indigenous [Haitian] taken aboard the aforementioned foreign ships will be shot in the public space."[53]

Suspicion and fear coursed through the top ranks of the Haitian government like smoke from a wildfire. This was hardly the first time that the French engaged in such operations, and Christophe and Dessalines expressed exasperation.[54] The sudden policy change might have been more due to the identity of one of the victims, however, than to general frustration. On March 8, 1806, French corsairs captured Juste Hugonin, a noteworthy printer who eventually oversaw subscriptions and the publication of the yearly almanacs in the Kingdom of Haiti under Christophe. The French released him two days later, along with thirteen other captive Haitians. Christophe convinced himself that more episodes like this could leave Haiti open to inadvertently harboring traitors on its own shores.[55]

France's discursive war against the empire represented another source of stress for independent Haiti. Determined to defame Haiti and paper the world with their hopes of reconquering "Saint-Domingue," early nineteenth-century French writers and artists wrote essays, novels, and historical works and painted tableaux all destined to convince the world that France still had rightful claim to its lost colony. In 1802, the novelist and playwright René Périn published one of the first French fictions of the Haitian Revolution: *The Burning of Cap; or, The Reign of Toussaint Louverture*. In the preface, the novelist expressed unequivocal sympathy for French colonists and white planters in writing, "I am going to take us into the middle of the city of Cap, to look there for the victims of this atrocious negro, and offer a portrait upon which, reader, you may be forced to shed many tears!!!" The novel went on to portray Louverture as having ordered Christophe to burn down Cap-Français in 1802, after which "the flames scorched the earth and the iron destroyed thousands of colonists. The blacks were at the head of the government: if we could call a government that assemblage of savages, brutes, disappointed men, who, drunk on vengeance, were thrilled to dictate the law . . . the law!. . . . Little did it matter to them that they were reigning over debris, over heaps of ashes! . . . They reigned!"[56] Though it would never see the popularity or fame of Victor Hugo's highly unsympathetic novel of the Haitian Revolution *Bug-Jargal* (1826) or Alphonse de Lamartine's melodramatic verse drama *Toussaint Louverture* (1850), the frontispiece to *The Burning of Cap* remains one of the most highly circulated images of the revolution.

Périn's novel reached independent Haiti. Christophe described it to the emperor in December 1805. Noting that the book, which he called "a little brochure," had reached him via merchant ships from the United States, he sent it to Dessalines with a note saying that it might "amuse" the emperor "in his moments of rest." He concluded by gesturing not only to the philosophical and semantic war between Haiti and the French (who persisted in calling Haiti "Saint-Domingue") but also to the physical warfare that had never really ceased:

> The contents of this brochure leave no doubt about the views of our enemies, since they do not even accord us the title of men, judging that we are not worthy of the liberty that we enjoy, that we conquered using the strength of our arms, and that no power on earth can ever take from us! But let them come, and I will give them new proof.[57]

Christophe's hatred for the French only deepened with time. When Christophe learned the following month that Napoléon had essentially declared full-on war against Europe, he could hardly hide his jubilance. Sending Dessalines a packet of newspaper clippings that he received from a foreign ship, Christophe observed, "Europe is the theater of a war that seems to be extremely inveterate." Haiti "should rejoice at what has come to pass between them. Let it please God, in the name of our tranquility, for it to last for forty years."[58]

As the French ramped up their corsair operation of sabotaging Haitian ships that spring, another French military division approached Santo Domingo. However, because England and France were once again at war, the British destroyed the entire regiment. Christophe could not have been more relieved. "It is to be hoped for," he wrote to Dessalines, "that if the war lasts even one more year between these powers, it will finish with [France] having not even one vessel left and [the country] will be irredeemably reduced in the ranks of continental powers."[59] The British had already helped Haiti thwart the arrival of a large French military division, but the danger persisted.

The empire still had problems with the French-Spaniards they had captured and subsequently attempted to incorporate into the Haitian work-force too. That the Spanish did not want to live in independent Haiti led to near-endless fugitivity. In the spring of 1806, the captives' attempts to escape had become so frequent that the Haitian government adopted drastic tactics to end this situation for good. Christophe's resolve to imprison rather than execute had weakened entirely, and he ordered the execution of the entire population of French-Spanish captives.

On March 18, 1806, Christophe told General Capoix to bring all the "Spanish" who had been arrested and imprisoned in Bayaha to Cap, to be "hanged on the scales bordering the sea." Although Christophe entrusted this order to Capoix, the letter intimated that his trust in the hero of Vertières had waned too. Earlier, Capoix had sent the general in chief some proclamations recently issued by General Ferrand, commander over the eastern side of the island. "I did not read them," Christophe admonished. "I burned them immediately; it is not prudent on your part to have unsealed such suspect missives. You should have done exactly as I did." Christophe then repeated Dessalines's order that Haitians cut off all communication with the east, and he issued his own order for Capoix to arrest three more French-Spanish people who aided those mentioned above. They, too, would be hanged by the seashore. Christophe next ordered the hangings of French-Spanish people in Ouanaminthe, who, arriving from Saint-Jago, carried what the government considered damaging letters and proclamations from the east, the same kind that Capoix had sent to Christophe.[60]

These captives did not stand alone in receiving such harsh punishment. Things started to fall apart again in April 1806, as the empire succumbed to using executions and incarceration to discipline and punish the island's own population—both self-professed Haitian citizens and some white French people still living among them. While Christophe oversaw most of these punishments, the policy to arrest and execute came directly from Dessalines. In April, Christophe, who noted he was merely obeying the emperor's wishes, ordered the head of the navy to pursue at sea anyone who had tried to escape from Cap in canoes the day before, including women and children.[61] Previously, Dessalines issued an order for the arrest of a relative of Christophe's rival Colonel Jean-Baptiste Sans-Souci. Referred to as Sans Soucy *mineur,* or minor, the young man had reportedly been on the run for two months after having been sent to work on a plantation in the Artibonite.[62] Because Sans Soucy left without permission, the government considered him a fugitive. The Haitian government required *cartes de sûreté,* or identification cards, and passports for travel, to try to prevent unauthorized movement in the country.[63] Anyone caught traveling without the proper papers was to be immediately arrested.[64]

Surveillance was constant in the empire, but so was resistance. Christophe and Dessalines seemed unable to impede the populace—whether Haitian, Spanish, or French—from organizing against the government. At one point, Christophe learned from General Capoix that the military had captured a group of Spanish and French inhabitants trying to escape to Santo Domingo. Christophe ordered not only their arrests but the creation of a surveillance post just outside Maribaroux, near the border of the French-occupied part of the island, to prevent future such attempts.[65]

The truth is that cracks in the emperor's authority had, by 1806, surfaced all over Haiti. The commanders of Gros-Morne and Plaisance submitted multiple complaints about the laborers ordered to work on farms in their jurisdictions, saying they had run off instead and found refuge elsewhere. Even though the commanders of the affected arrondissements formally requested to pursue the return of the laborers under Christophe's authorization, many of the laborers were never located. An exasperated Christophe wrote to General Romain that the only recourse for such "abuses" was to punish those involved and arrest the commanders.[66]

Yet these "abuses" continued. Christophe's letter to Dessalines on May 28, 1806, illustrates the logic behind this system of arrest, surveillance, punishment, and ultimately execution. Of additional laborers who fled their assigned posts, Christophe wrote, "All of Your Majesty's points of view on this are quite legitimate; only severity can bring back to their duty those who have deviated from it, because for some time great abuses have crept into this part [of the country]." Christophe said he would send several "officers of intelligence to annul and break up any small properties that are not valuable or pieces of land that are half cultivated by farmers. All the individuals who have run away from their plantations will be arrested, along with all those male and female laborers who have not yet returned to the plantations."[67]

Christophe's other letters from the same day provide more worrisome details about the nature of these "abuses" and where they occurred. While the east had presented problems since the beginning of Haitian independence, the western and southern parts of Haiti had been for some time sites of abandonment and outright opposition to Dessalines's authority. Laborers in these regions frequently deserted their assigned plantations. If the military caught and brought them back, many simply ran away again at the first opportunity, sometimes defecting to regions under the command of more lax military officers. To prevent them from "exercising laziness," Dessalines ordered such individuals beaten with batons upon capture because "His Majesty views this as the only means of making sure they fulfill their duty," Christophe explained. All the laborers and soldiers who deserted, many of whom were hiding in the woods, were to be arrested as well. "His Majesty has directed me to utilize all the severity necessary to execute these measures," Christophe wrote to Generals Capoix and Romain. "For it is now time to once again reestablish order in that part of the country, which is so essential to the empire." This letter foretold in some ways the tragic logic that perhaps contributed to the end of Haiti's first empire and emperor. Christophe spoke multiple times of the "foreign" laborers from Port-de-Paix who ran away, again and again seeking refuge in towns like Moustique and Saint-Louis. Out of leniency, Christophe ordered Capoix and Romain to round them up, arrest them, and send them to Laferrière, along with anyone hiding in Saint-Raphaël or Sourde.[68] This xenophobic order constitutes merely a single flash point in one of the most disturbing episodes of early Haitian independence.

In April 1806, Dessalines ordered rounded up and sent to the northern hamlet of Milot all the "white" people in Cap-Haïtien. Christophe sent an order to the commander of Cap, to that effect, on April 8, with a list of the names of all white individuals living there. To be clear, these were white French people who had remained on the island and in ostensibly good standing with the government since independence. Many of them had been useful to the newly formed state, because they were doctors, printers, tailors, blacksmiths, masons, hatters, and carpenters. Prevailing suspicions against everything French had until that point largely spared such individuals. Now they would suffer.

On the tenth of the month, Dr. Justamont (whom Christophe allegedly saved from being executed in 1804), the clock maker Calame, the hatter Buisson, a tailor, two blacksmiths, a mason called David, and a carpenter called Oguin were ordered out of the city. A white male baker, who lived by the sea, and Pierre Roux, the printer, were to have guards placed outside their homes to watch over them until such time as a chariot could be brought to help carry their effects. Each of these individuals would from now on live in Milot, where Christophe established his residence and could surveil them more closely. Two priests, Fathers Corneille Brelle and Antoine Reyes, were to stay in Cap, subject to ongoing state surveillance.[69]

A serious breach in state security precipitated these draconian measures. Although Cap appeared calm compared with many other Haitian cities, several white inhabitants had fled by canoe the previous Easter Sunday night. Among those who fled were Dr. Roulet, a man named Pouydebas, a tailor called Torrel, with his wife and his mother-in-law, and a man identified as Lafarge. Christophe only learned of their escape the next Monday morning, whereupon he ordered the harbor's own canoe, along with two sloops belonging to the Haitian army, the aptly named *Empereur* and *Indépendance,* to pursue the fugitives. The Haitian canoe had just returned from its patrol in Monte Cristi, but the sailors had failed to locate the escapees or their canoes. Christophe forced the crews of U.S. ships docked in Cap to disembark around the same time and jailed their sailors while he investigated to ensure that none of these foreign ships were missing any canoes. Convinced through his investigation that U.S. merchants and other travelers to Haiti had not contributed to the escape, he determined that other Haitians must have been responsible.[70]

While Christophe could not immediately locate those who fled, their Haitian accomplices were eventually identified as a man called L'Espérance Congo and a "man of color" named Poupoutte from Carénage. Christophe ordered both men taken to Cap immediately, and he had the wives of the white men who escaped without them put in jail too. Christophe told Dessalines that he ordered the white men and women of the city to reside in different quartiers, where they could be surveilled by the managers, drivers, and soldiers in charge of various fortifications.[71]

Christophe had wanted Roux and his press to be moved to Milot, but since Roux technically remained the state printer, for this Christophe sought Dessalines's approval. Christophe additionally reported that contrary to his initial order, he planned to leave Dr. Justamont in Cap for a little longer since many sick people remained in the hospital and needed treatment. This reprieve was likely due to Christophe's disbelief that Justamont would try to escape.[72] But both Roux and Dr. Justamont were eventually forced to leave Cap. On July 6, 1806, Christophe ordered both men taken to Fort Laferrière, the former to set up the printing press and the latter to establish a pharmacy.[73]

About a month after the escape of the white inhabitants from Cap, Christophe learned the name of the sailor who helped them. Jean Pierre, who had worked for L'Espérance Congo, confessed his involvement, leaving no doubt that L'Espérance was "one of the principal authors." Christophe ordered General Brave to conduct a perquisition and arrest L'Espérance. He also ordered the arrest of L'Espérance's wife at their home in Limonade, where she lived on the La Chapelle plantation. Christophe remained angry, however. He told Capoix that if the commander of Limonade had done his job in the first place, the commander would have already arrested L'Espérance.[74] Christophe's policy of arrestation rather than execution had been no more effective than Dessalines's capital punishments. Although their methods stood previously at odds, the continuing flights convinced Christophe that Dessalines's tactic might just be superior. Perhaps it was only the result of desperation, but from the late spring of 1806 onward Christophe seems to have become a true believer in Dessalines-style executions.

On May 3, Dessalines wrote to Christophe to inquire about the escape of the whites from Marchand/Dessalines. Once again, other Haitians must have facilitated these escapes, "because they would never have been able to undertake the route into the Spanish side if they did not have guides," the emperor said. In his reply, Christophe agreed that following Dessalines's orders seemed the only way to "remove all our worries, in this regard," though Christophe did not reveal the precise nature of the ordered punishment. "I believe just as you do, Your Majesty. Experience has proven to us that we can no longer have any sort of confidence in them; when faced with great evils, one must respond with great remedies. . . . You can be assured that I will employ great remedies."[75] The remedy Dessalines chose was once again death. The day after Christophe learned about the white inhabitants who escaped from the capital city, he echoed this language to several generals: "Experience has proven to us . . . that despite all the regard that we have shown to the few white men and women that we have allowed to remain among us, they are escaping continuously: His Majesty has just informed me about the escape of those from Camp Marchand, but due to the vigilant orders that he gave, five from the original band of fugitives were captured and hanged. Without delay, the others will soon be arrested." The white individuals named their Haitian accomplices who were then "subjected to the fate of traitors. . . . His Majesty has issued an order for the rest of them to be sent to him, whether men or women. I intend to do the same: as a result, Monday morning, see to it that all the white women that I sent you from Cap are sent [to Dessalines]." Christophe said he had no doubt that these white inhabitants were dangerous and would join the enemy at the first opportunity and "give them knowledge about our means of defense."[76] Christophe reminded General Brave specifically that the windmill carpenter and the surgeon were under his command and could remain so, even though they were ostensibly white, as long as Brave was willing to take responsibility for them.[77] Only ten days after Christophe announced his willingness to comply with the executions, the general in chief wrote to Dessalines that he had finally "removed from the white men and women all means of escaping from Haiti," clarifying, "I followed exactly the remedy that Your Majesty used in the west."[78] What happened to these white men, women, and children evicted from their homes for a second time? If precedent was followed, the government likely hanged them all.

U.S. businessmen in Haiti at the time objected strongly to these executions, fearful as to what it might mean for them. "On what basis are your fears founded? Have you experienced any disturbances on our part and about which you have complaints? If so, from whom?" Christophe asked them during a meeting about the issue. He reminded them that "the government promised safety and protection to all neutral nations and friends who maintain commercial ties with our country, and who abide by the law." "If you concern yourselves solely with commerce, you will enjoy all the consideration possible from the government. Banish your fears and have instead the greatest confidence in our loyalty," he said.[79]

Foreign spying, meddling, and other forms of interference posed a significant threat to the Haitian government, but what this chapter of Haitian history shows is that there were equally dangerous internal threats. In July 1806, Christophe started to notice that Dessalines's letters to him showed evidence of interception: many exhibited marks of having been unsealed and then resealed. Christophe also complained about not having news from the emperor for long stretches. As if this were not worrying enough, the empire had an alleged spy on its hands: a soldier named Lapointe who served under the English at Arcahaie and who evidently returned to Haiti, clandestinely, through one of the northern ports.[80] After promising to capture and arrest Lapointe, Christophe revealed his belief that U.S. citizens onshore and at sea facilitated the spy's arrival. "It is hardly shocking," he told Dessalines, "that the Americans have taken it upon themselves to enable such machinations. For gold and money, there is nothing they cannot be made to do."[81]

One thing these Americans could not do, however, is something at which they would later become quite adept: deposing a Haitian head of state. Little did Dessalines or Christophe know that the opulent independence day celebrations the empress Marie-Claire was planning were to be the emperor's last.

—

"Her Majesty, the Empress, has pleased to ask me to procure sugar and several other goods," including various cheeses and other delicacies like brandied fruits, "for the feast that she is preparing to host for the anniversary of Haitian independence," General Christophe wrote to the administrator Roumage on November 19, 1805. Later, and once more at the behest of Marie-Claire, Christophe enjoined Roumage to send him more funds for the desserts the empress ordered made for the January 1, 1806, independence day celebrations.[82] Just as he had overseen the celebrations of the first anniversary of Haitian independence, the general in chief of the Haitian army, while continuing all his other duties, helped plan Haiti's second, more elaborate independence day festivities.

On the first anniversary of Haitian independence, in 1805, Christophe spent that momentous day with the inhabitants of his home city in Cap, with the celebrations seeming to have been an afterthought. Christophe only received Dessalines's orders to organize the celebration after January 1, 1805, and the party did not begin until January 3. Still, Christophe ensured that every arrondissement marked the occasion with six days of food, wine, and other victuals. At that first anniversary of Haitian independence, the Declaration of Independence was read aloud, and a Te Deum hymn was sung for those brave soldiers and civilians who did not survive the war that made Haiti free.[83]

The first anniversary celebration of Haitian independence appeared modest compared with the second, which took place in the city of Marchand/Dessalines. This time Christophe spent the day in the company of his friend and comrade the emperor, but before that he spent his time busily confirming orders for the military. There had been too much disorder, abuse, and insubordination across the empire for Christophe to travel to the interior of the country without taking measures beforehand to ensure security. Christophe had a lot of responsibilities converging all at once. Dessalines had put him in charge of making sure that Haiti's second independence day was celebrated throughout the country. Christophe wrote to Generals Capoix and Romain on December 13, 1805, therefore, to ask them to have the day feted throughout the divisions under their authority. He also reminded them that they would be responsible for any problems that occurred in Cap in his absence.

To call to mind all they sacrificed for freedom and to compel them to continue to make sacrifices to maintain their liberty, Christophe ordered all the laborers from the plantations surrounding Cap brought to the Champ de Mars on January 1 to hear the Declaration of Independence read aloud. "Have them renew their oath to live free and independent," Christophe counseled. He also ordered Capoix and Romain to ensure the day was celebrated with "the greatest pomp and circumstance."[84] He told Capoix to have the Second Demi-brigade of Cap hear the declaration, too, but due to the security threat posed by the celebration, the soldiers should return to their posts the very next day. The same was to occur with the demi-brigades in Fort-Liberté.[85] Christophe did not seem to trust his fellow Haitian citizens.

When trouble broke out on a Milot plantation during the general in chief's absence, this only justified to Christophe his paranoia. The report Christophe received indicated a laborer had been arrested for reportedly uttering "words tending to disrupt tranquility" while wishing a commander "Happy New Year." Charges of sedition in the empire often had flimsy pretext. In mid-January, on Dessalines's orders, Christophe interrogated the laborer once again. "The result of these two interrogations," Christophe reported, "boils down to vague remarks, which were made in a state of intoxication." Nevertheless, Christophe found it "prudent to arrest the man on the supposition that there is no fire without smoke."[86] Perceptive advice coming from Haiti's second-in-command, perhaps, but Dessalines could hardly see the smoke in his own house. In fact, little fires were smoking all over the country, many of them under Christophe's watchful but sometimes too narrowly suspicious eyes.

Damaging rumors plagued independent Haiti from the beginning, which is partly why Dessalines and Christophe had been so determined to quell them. In September 1805, Colonel Joachim informed Christophe about a quickly spreading rumor that the emperor had decided to gather children to sell into slavery. Indignant that anyone would believe a lie so anathema to Haitian principles of freedom, Christophe ordered Commander Poux to pursue and arrest the authors of this "calumny." Christophe believed the rumor must have come from foreign adversaries, whom he referred to as enemies of the Haitian government. Whatever their nationality, anyone found guilty of the crime of circulating this lie, Christophe announced, would be shot to death.[87] It did not take long for someone to be accused. Only two days after Christophe's orders to Commander

Poux, he ordered the interrogation of a man and a woman whom Haitian soldiers had taken in chains to the prison in Cap for spreading "evil ideas throughout the countryside, with the capacity to alter the fortunate tranquility we are enjoying." Christophe wanted to determine if the couple had started the rumors or if they merely repeated them.[88] While Christophe and Dessalines never spoke of this situation again, both insisted that such allegations derived from foreigners within the emperor's realm.

Foreigners suspected of spying seemed to be seeping out of every corner and with near constancy. Later that fall, two Italian men, Francisco Stella and Jouannie Jordani, were charged and convicted by the empire's special military council of espionage, the punishment for which was death.[89] There were exceptions to such punishments for charges of spying, but they were few. Perhaps because of ongoing Haitian-British trade, a white Englishman named Abraham Lefevre whom the Haitian government convicted of espionage received the punishment of deportation rather than execution just one day after the Italians were sentenced to death. In mid-November 1805, Lefevre disembarked from an English frigate near the mouth of the river in Maribaroux along with several "black and yellow" women and men. They were all arrested and sent to Fort-Liberté, per Christophe's earlier orders to arrest anyone trespassing near the eastern border. Lefevre, however, ran away, occasioning a weeklong search. Christophe believed Lefevre and the others had been sent to Haiti, by whom he did not say, as a part of the "plot of our enemies to foment trouble and to gather information about the situation within the empire," which is what he told Dessalines. "I cannot fathom by what fatality the English bypassed our ports to go and furtively disembark these people at the mouth of the Maribaroux," Christophe wrote. "If it were not my duty to send them to Your Majesty, I would have had them all shot the moment they were arrested." By November 29, the military arrested Lefevre and escorted him to Dessalines. While the fate of the others sent to Fort-Liberté remains unknown, on December 3, 1805, Christophe wrote to the emperor that in compliance with his orders, he would send Lefevre back to England on the first available "English" or otherwise "neutral" ship.[90]

Foreign agents and spies did not present the only causes for concern. Christophe had to constantly extinguish outright rebellion—not mere insubordination or incompetence—within the military. In mid-December 1805, rumors of various conspiracies to overthrow the government came to the general in chief's attention by way of the emperor himself. Commander Noël Débaud, who oversaw a military brigade in Dondon, was the first to be blamed. When Christophe arrived to question Débaud at daybreak on December 17, he found the commander, who had seemed perfectly fine a day earlier, in bed. Débaud claimed to be incapable of getting up due to pain. Christophe, long impatient and inflexible in the face of perceived malingering, sent Débaud to the prison in Laferrière. Promising to take "every appropriate measure to arrest the guilty and reestablish order," Christophe told Dessalines, "You can have complete faith in me. I assure you that this brigandage will not occur." Although Christophe questioned many people, he was unable to learn who definitively participated in the alleged plot to overthrow the government. Christophe did receive a list of names of possible conspirators. He ordered their arrest immediately alongside that of Débaud. Débaud, for his part, ended up escaping and fleeing, which caused Christophe to believe even more strongly in his guilt. Christophe ordered him captured and brought back "alive or dead."[91] Disorder, sedition, and outright rebellion seemed constant. But Christophe might never have predicted at the Battle of Vertières that a hero like General Capoix would take part in the disturbances causing so much consternation and woe for his country.

Christophe constantly clashed with the man he gave the monumental task of overseeing the easternmost parts of the empire. Not all these clashes were military. Christophe was a devout and practicing Catholic. He had been married in the Catholic Church, and he and his wife had devoted themselves to raising their children as Roman Catholics. Capoix, if the reports that Christophe received are to be believed, was a *Vodouisant*, or practitioner of the Vodou faith. Capoix's religious practices became the subject of one of his more noteworthy quarrels with his military superior.

Among the many existing rifts in early sovereign Haiti, religion is perhaps the least understood. On the one hand, Haiti's first leaders professed devout Catholicism and demanded that their fellow citizens adhere to it, even though this stood contrary to the imperial laws governing freedom of religion in the country, per the constitution. *Vodouisants*, on the other hand, could be equally devout, and often Catholic as well, but far more open to religious pluralism and patently more tolerant of other faiths. Forcible conversions, for example, are not a part of the history of Haitian Vodou.[92] Force, however, is not just the tool of priests, conquistadors, colonists, and enslavers. Compelling unwilling citizens to submit to a ruler's religious ambitions comes straight from the playbook of old-world despots and monarchs as much as new-world presidents and dictators.

The imperial constitution, unlike Louverture's mandate that only Catholicism could be practiced in public, established religious freedom. One article declared, "The law recognizes no dominant religion"; and "freedom of religion is tolerated." The article also avowed the separation of church and state.[93] Though an ardent defender of the empire and its laws, Christophe seemed disinclined to accept these ideas of freedom of religion. On November 13, 1805, he wrote to General Capoix,

I have been informed, General, that *Vodun* is being danced continuously in the quartier of Bois-de-l'Anse. If this is true, that quartier needs your immediate attention, to prevent a dance so prejudicious to tranquility, and which has always been forbidden by every government. You must take, therefore, every measure necessary to prevent this dance and to arrest the performers.[94]

Christophe stood hardly alone in his opposition to and prejudices against Vodou. Although Dessalines is the only figure from Haiti's revolution to be posthumously inducted into the Vodou pantheon,[95] during his life he took measures against the religion too. Indeed, it was Dessalines who insisted that Vodou was not merely a sign of revolution afoot but a portent of revolution to come.

On November 23, 1805, Christophe had a man named Jean Pierre Narcisse from Les Cayes arrested and sent to Dessalines. Christophe described Narcisse as a "chef" or leader, residing on the Pémerle sugar plantation, "more vulgarly known there under the name of *Dieu Chaud* [Hot God]." Dieu Chaud, according to Christophe, "played the charlatan" in Les Cayes with a "great number of people." He performed the "Macanda," a dance drawn from the history of the revolutionary figure Makandal,[96] which the accused said would bring the spectators happiness and riches. "What is even more shocking about this is that respectable women from that city were going in droves to see him," Christophe told Dessalines. "This so-called Dieu Chaud" held weekly Vodou balls and "revivals and assemblies that lasted all night." That Dessalines viewed Narcisse's religious practice as dangerous to the state is foretold in Christophe's final sentence. "Such men, being dangerous and harmful to the state, I am sending him to you, in the hopes that you will bless the order to send him to join the brigade of General Geffrard."[97] While Christophe perhaps harbored personal animosity as well as political animus against Vodou—in 1811, as king, Christophe issued a circular ordering all the generals in his army to "adopt even more severe measures against any persons, whomever they may be, given over to dancing or practicing sorcery, more well known under the name of *vaudoux*"—state opposition to this practice under Dessalines emanated directly from the emperor.[98]

In May 1806, Dessalines ordered Christophe to arrest Baptiste, "a magician, performer of the *caprelata*, supposedly working to cure a headache of which *commère* Hélène was complaining." In Vodou, a *caprelata* is a "magic charm" used to cure an illness. *Caprelatas,* when used to refer to people, designated those who practiced natural medicine, integral to the health and well-being of enslaved people during the colonial era; in one historian's words these spiritual healers could be considered "medical revolutionaries." The *caprelatas,* as objects, in contrast, sometimes referred to as amulets, form part of Vodou rituals, serving as "talismans" to protect the wearer from violence.[99]

After Christophe received Dessalines's orders to have Baptiste arrested, he traveled down to Cap to arrest the man himself, but he could not locate

Baptiste. To discern the man's location, Christophe told the commander of Cap to question Hélène's brother, Mr. Prince. But the commander had earlier defied Christophe's orders, and whether the commander ever tried to find Baptiste remains unclear. He merely told Christophe that he could not find the "magician." Next, Christophe interrogated Hélène, caretaker of his children along with Dessalines's. She also professed ignorance. Christophe ultimately managed to fulfill his promise to the emperor "to discover the location of this merchant of the *caprelata*."[100] "Spies" Christophe sent to question the troops at the camp revealed Baptiste's location. The military subsequently arrested the unlucky "magician" on June 2, after which five military officers escorted him before Dessalines, and then to prison.[101]

Opposition to Vodou put the state at odds with not only the laborers on the plantations but many of its citizens and key members of the military like Capoix. On December 15 of the same year, Christophe wrote to Capoix of his "great consternation" upon learning that Capoix had ordered a Mass in which "the altar was arranged contrary to the ordinary manner, in that the ornaments of the priest were turned upside down, the saints were upside down, the candles were lit from below, and the rest of the ornaments of the church were overturned." Christophe expressed anger toward Capoix, charging, "It was in this state that you wanted the curé to say the Mass at midnight, which has never been done anywhere in the world, except for at midnight Mass on Christmas Eve." Christophe would never have believed the story, he said, if it had not "been sworn to me by someone worthy of faith." He then admonished Capoix: "You are a Catholic, you believe in the Christian religion, you should know that never has such a Mass been said!" Moreover, "you are a superior officer, you command a military division," Christophe chided. How could Capoix "set the example" when he "gives himself over to such ridiculous superstitions and demands, such that a minister at the altar humors him by lending his hands to these kinds of impieties?" It was a leader's job to be "the example of what is right and of good conduct because all eyes are fixed upon him," Christophe continued. "The least of his actions are well known and pass from mouth to mouth." Christophe's previous fatherly affection for Capoix shone through at the end of the missive. Christophe told his friend and fellow revolutionary that he felt it his duty to point out the error of his conduct.[102]

The hero of Vertières responded to Christophe by denying "the accusations . . . that he caused to be pronounced a backward Mass." Christophe seemed inclined to believe his friend and comrade. In his written response, he expressed his instinct to trust Capoix in a manner that opened the door to Capoix's further denial. Christophe told Capoix of his relief to learn that the reports of the Mass were untrue, and he invited him to come to Cap on December 27 to help prepare for the independence day celebrations in that city.[103] This was not the last time that Christophe came into conflict with Capoix. Their other problems reveal a rift deeper than religious differences.

On May 4, 1806, an exasperated Christophe told Capoix, "It is useless . . . for me to transmit my orders to you, because you are not executing any of them. I ordered you to have furnished for each quartier sixty male or female laborers, and you have not conformed at all." Christophe hardly knew what to think of Capoix's insubordination. "If, General, your heart is no longer with the service, just let me know. I will put someone else in charge of overseeing this labor," Christophe told him.[104] Capoix's military assignments were crucial to what we might call Operation Accelerate Agriculture. Not only had Christophe tasked him with rounding up Spanish laborers—sometimes overseeing their arrests and executions— but Christophe had also put Capoix in charge of ensuring that Haitian laborers were distributed throughout the northeastern and northwestern parts of the country. Although Capoix does not seem to have opposed these operations, it is true that he did not carry out some of Christophe's orders. Capoix's opposition ultimately cost him his life.

General Capoix now enters our story for the last time. Before his disappearance, he had been one of the general in chief's most frequent correspondents. He was also the military commander to whom Christophe most often turned for critical and important missions. Christophe relied heavily on Capoix for the arrests and executions of the Spanish and for reinforcing and establishing new fortifications.[105] Somewhere along the way, their goals and desires diverged.

Previously, Capoix oversaw whipping all the male and female laborers on the western side of the island determined to have been absent from their assigned plantations. The original order came from Dessalines, and Christophe transmitted it to Capoix. Christophe gave no indication that Capoix complained about this dreadful task. Yet on June 26, 1806, Capoix reported to Christophe the escape of the French-Spanish captives in Ouanaminthe. Christophe was livid. He had entrusted the surveillance of these individuals and the region to Capoix because he believed him to be one of the only military officers capable of carrying out such a duty. Although Capoix eventually located the escapees and returned them to their plantations, Dessalines's policy by then was to execute all Spanish fugitives, rather than merely arrest them. "You are playing a child's game," Christophe warned Capoix. "They should have been hanged in Ouanaminthe. As such, you should give orders right away to General Brave that he should ensure the hanging of all the Spanish in Ouanaminthe who have been caught running away." Christophe added, bewildered, "My orders have been given on this subject. But it seems that no one is following them?"[106]

Christophe had recently promoted Capoix to division general of the north, but was Capoix's heart any longer with the military, as Christophe asked him? Capoix continued to carry out his general in chief's orders and provide him with essential information throughout the first half of July. Then, on July 20, the two came into conflict once again. A division general ordinarily needed to live in the capital of the region under his command. Yet Capoix remained on the Perez plantation, which, though Christophe did not say exactly where it was located, was likely somewhere in the east, near the border, and was certainly not in Cap. Christophe therefore ordered Capoix to return to the city and establish residence there. "You are now forcing me to tell you some difficult truths," Christophe counseled. The general in chief had grown accustomed to Capoix's whims, but now he began to suspect that something more sinister lay at the root of Capoix's quixotic incompetence. "If you are sick," he told him, "you can reestablish your health there, but give up the service to keep it from suffering."[107] While Christophe gave Capoix several avenues to leave the military respectfully, the division general did not evidently take any of them.

Capoix continued carrying out orders from Christophe through mid-August, including organizing a celebration for the empress Marie-Claire's annual fete. Christophe might ordinarily have done this himself, as he had in previous years, but he told the administrator Roumage that he could not this time, having taken ill.[108] Capoix disappeared a couple months after receiving the order to plan the fete, perhaps his most pleasant assignment. The last anyone heard from him was on October 10, 1806, just seven days before the emperor's assassination.

The unruly eastern part of the island was central to the events that led to the disappearance and likely death of Capoix. On October 6, while traveling to Cap, having recently recovered from his illness, Christophe learned from his "spies" that fugitives from the French side were rebelling against Dessalines's authority again, causing destruction in Ouanaminthe. Christophe sped to the east and reached the area the next morning. Once there, he learned that fugitive French-Spanish people were being assisted by one of Haiti's own, Commander Achilles, whom Christophe had put in charge of the patrols. When the Spanish entered Ouanaminthe the previous Saturday night to Sunday morning, the army fired not a single shot at them, because the military officers had been preoccupied with hosting a dance. Their distraction allowed the invading Spanish to pillage the town and kill several inhabitants. Three days earlier, Commander Achilles learned that a fugitive Spanish man named Juan Broun, who previously escaped from being forced into service in the Twenty-Ninth Demi-brigade, had been roaming around the town with some other French-Spanish. Dessalines had already ordered any of the fugitives from the east hanged upon capture. Yet Achilles did not follow up on the information, failing even to establish a sentinel. "No resistance was put forward," Christophe reported to Dessalines. "The Spaniards had the time to plunder the town, at their leisure, since they stayed until Sunday morning." General Brave denied culpability by pleading that he had been in Fort-Liberté for several days prior, telling Christophe that as soon as he learned the news, he instructed the dragoons to pursue the Spanish. The dragoons then freed three-fourths of the Haitian people the Spanish captured. "Nevertheless, he is as guilty as Achilles," Christophe said to Dessalines. The general in chief consequently ordered Achilles arrested and sent in chains to Laferrière to await sentencing from the emperor. "If measures had been taken, not a single one of those Spaniards would have escaped," Christophe explained. "They would have been cut into pieces." To rectify this situation, Christophe convened four battalions and four companies of dragoons to pursue the remaining fugitives. He showed zero mercy to anyone even slightly involved in this affair. He ordered the arrest of all the captains and battalion leaders of the Twenty-Ninth Demi-brigade, whom, like Achilles, he sent to Laferrière for incarceration. Achilles was afterward sentenced to death, and Christophe put the brigadier chief Étienne Albert in command of the commune. Christophe said this entire affair had put him on the verge of "losing my Latin," or losing his mind, "due to the abuses that have gone on in that brigade."[109]

Capoix had been leading one of the cavalry companies that Christophe ordered to pursue the French-Spaniards "committing hostilities" in Ouanaminthe. Christophe ordered Capoix to capture and kill all the involved French-Spaniards he could find. But then, suddenly, Christophe mysteriously called Capoix off the search. Christophe explained to him rather cavalierly, "It is no longer necessary for you to travel into the Spanish part of the island. All you need to do is engage in frequent patrols with the cavalry in the surrounding area of the city and complete the order to establish security in that part of the military." What caused Christophe to change his order is not clear from any of his letters. He did, however, give an order on the same day for General Bazile to assume command of the eastern-most communes of Haiti, including Ouanaminthe, Maribaroux, and Acul Samedi.[110]

On October 9, eight days before the emperor's assassination, Christophe returned from Ouanaminthe and reported that the pursuit of the captives from the east had partially succeeded. Several had been captured, and Christophe ordered them all hanged. He told Dessalines that order had been reestablished in the eastern military brigade as well. However, "I did not have arrested the leader of the Twenty-Ninth Demi-brigade," Christophe said, "because he was garrisoned at Fort Salnave when these events took place."[111] Something momentous, disastrous even, must have happened between Christophe's penultimate order to Capoix on October 7 and his final one on the tenth. Although Christophe's letters tell an incomplete story, it is a highly suggestive one.

Christophe ordered Generals Romain and Brave and Colonel Albert to appear before him on October 10. He informed Capoix of this order and

301

told him to remain in place and patrol the border until he received new orders. Later, but that same day, Christophe declared the order he had just issued "null and void." He told Capoix, "I need to see you to transmit my orders. As such, General, please be there. I await you. General Brave will stay in Ouanaminthe."[112] Christophe never corresponded with Capoix again after this, but he did refer to him in passing as the "late General Capoix" in a letter to Toussaint Brave on October 23, six days after Dessalines's assassination. Already, on the nineteenth, Christophe had addressed a circular to Brave as commander of the second division of the north, Capoix's previous post. Perhaps more tellingly, in terms of the timeline for Capoix's death, in his letter of the twenty-third, Christophe agreed to honor Dessalines's *prior* nomination of Brave to the late general's former position.[113] Unlike with Geffrard, Clervaux, and many other military officers whose demise Christophe lamented in the most sorrowful and plaintive notes of regret, Christophe mentioned Capoix's death with nary a passing mark of anguish. The two men had fought together and had fought each other, but Christophe's previous letters to Capoix had been filled with devotion and care for the hero of Vertières. One thing consistently inspired the general in chief's murderous rage: treason or betrayal against the country. Did someone implicate Capoix in the Spanish invasion of the east? Was that someone General Brave?

We may never know. Yet Christophe's letters hint that whatever happened to Capoix had been on Dessalines's orders. Christophe wrote to the emperor on October 11, 1806, "His Excellency Division General Paul Romain and His Excellency Brigadier General Dartiguenave executed your orders yesterday at six in the evening," adding, "Capoix's three aides-de-camp are here, in the city, awaiting Your Majesty's orders."[114] The aides-de-camp were there, but not their commander, Division General François Capoix, whom Christophe had previously ordered to appear. What exactly was the order that Romain and Dartiguenave carried out for Dessalines? Capoix's execution? No one evidently saw or heard from Capoix after October 10. Just seven days before Dessalines's assassination, Christophe ended his letter to the emperor with not a single hint of any future worries in connection with this or any other affair: "Everything is perfectly tranquil. . . . You can remain at peace, sire, I will do everything that depends upon me to establish order."[115]

There was so much smoke among the military ranks because there were so many fires. As soon as Christophe extinguished one, another appeared in its place. There was also smoke that Christophe could not see, smoke gathering much closer to Dessalines's home, right in the heart of the state's own administration.

10

EMPIRES FALL . . .

While Dessalines and Christophe concerned themselves with divisions and conflicts in the east and west, a larger and deadlier conspiracy brewed in the south, just outside Dessalines's gaze, deep in the heart of Port-au-Prince. After he was lured to his death in October 1806 by once-trusted citizens and soldiers of his own army, Dessalines's lifeless body was left tattered in the bloodstained streets, not unlike the white fabric he once ripped out of the French tricolor. Dessalines so often evoked the spirits and bones of the dead, imploring them to help Haitians obtain revenge against France. Some of those ancestors, like Suzanne and Charles Belair, met their end because of Dessalines; other ghosts like that of Colonel Sans-Souci had Christophe to blame. Indeed, every hero of the revolution seemed to bring with him into independence more than his fair share of angry phantoms who never lived to tell the tale of the machinations that sent them to their graves. Christophe, though genuinely bewildered and incredulous when he learned of Dessalines's death, later found himself accused of having participated in the plot. If Christophe could turn on the First of the Blacks, the adopted nickname of Toussaint Louverture, his detractors said he was certainly capable of betraying the Avenger of America.

On July 24, 1805, Vernet, newly appointed minister of finance and the interior, issued a decree explaining to the public—and to the world—how Haiti's labor system worked, including who was to be employed on the plantations, who would oversee agricultural labor, and who was entitled to profits from farming. The decree's stated aim was to ensure that rightful property owners enjoyed the peaceful possession of their lands and to prevent illegal possessions of both state- and privately owned plantations.[1]

As early as February 1804 Haiti's officials created a system allowing military officers to make claims for and take possession of various confiscated plantations. The state knew which properties it owned, but the recognition of private property depended upon accurate record keeping. By September 1806, Dessalines acknowledged that notaries at the financial tribunals sometimes approved land claims indiscriminately. Because this could and did result in multiple people claiming ownership over a particular farm, Dessalines passed a law that the notaries could not approve land registrations without first informing the principal administrator of the relevant division. These laws pertained to farms assigned by the state and to exchanges of them between and among Haitians.[2]

Dessalines evidently issued these laws to correct problems that stemmed from prior mismanagement. The nineteenth-century Haitian historian Beaubrun Ardouin claimed that the emperor knew that either "corruption" or "negligence" had compromised the rights of public domain and that some of the properties of the ex-colonists had been assigned to individuals who were not supposed to receive them. Vernet, in Ardouin's account, was to blame for this mismanagement because he did not fully understand the title laws. Ardouin implicated Vernet's undersecretary as well, Vastey (the future baron), since Vastey oversaw much of the assignation of property. In Ardouin's account, the twenty-four-year-old Vastey took bribes from aspiring proprietors and demanded them from those entitled to register properties already in their possession.[3] Supposedly, Dessalines knew that Vernet, his comrade in arms, was hardly up to the demanding position of minister of finance. "My poor comrade," Dessalines allegedly said, "only spends his time giving lunches and making love; he relies entirely on Vastey, whose purse is growing every day."[4]

Fraud, incompetence, and outright theft connected to property claims abounded in the Empire of Haiti. For Christophe, chaos was never preferable to order, even at the price of human life. The state alone now held the power to sanction or deny ownership. Laws giving arbitrary and disproportionate power to state officials had already led to consternation in northern Haiti, as well as in the Artibonite. The east was still a mess, too, but it was the southern part of the country that caused Dessalines's demise. A new revolution was bubbling in the land of his old rival Rigaud and his new rival Pétion, and much of it was over land.

On October 15, two days before his assassination, Dessalines sent an urgent letter to Christophe about the "insurrection that has just taken place in the south." Christophe received the letter the next day and responded immediately to express his "great pain in contemplating the capital punishments that Your Majesty will be obligated to deploy . . . against the authors of this catastrophe." Dessalines had decided to travel to the south to help quell the insurrection in person. "You can have the utmost confidence in me," Christophe consoled the emperor. "I weep, Your Majesty, over the great exertions that you are going to have to experience." Concerned more about the fortifications than the so-called insurrection, Christophe said, "It can only be enemies of the state who are looking for trouble and discord to distract you from your important preoccupation of accelerating work on the forts." He ended his letter, "I have the honor of wishing you the most perfect health and to express to you, sire, with the utmost assurance, my profound respect."[5]

As if testament to their deep and enduring friendship, Christophe had sent another letter the same day, just before receiving Dessalines's note, announcing a gift of 114 mango saplings for the garden of the imperial palace. "They are enclosed in nine boxes or baskets. I hope that Your Majesty will be satisfied with them," Christophe wrote. Together, these letters comprise the last words that Christophe penned to his friend and fellow revolutionary, his son's godfather, while the emperor still drew breath.[6]

One day later, on that fateful October 17, the unsuspecting Christophe sent four letters. One was to Division General Romain repeating that an insurrection had just "exploded in the south." Asking Romain to keep this information confidential, Christophe counseled, "Redouble your zeal and surveillance to thwart the plans of the malicious and to prevent this communiqué from spreading in your division. As always, accelerate the work on the forts."[7] The second letter Christophe addressed to General Dartiguenave, to whom the general in chief reported nothing at all about the insurrection.[8] To Dr. Justamont, he sent a list of gunners with maladies who needed to be treated right away.[9] The final letter Christophe sent on the day of Dessalines's death was to General Brave with an order to replace a soldier who had recently died.[10]

Judging from his letters, Christophe did not learn of Dessalines's death until two days later, on October 19, 1806. The news came to him from Minister Vernet. Though his detractors eventually accused him of feigning ignorance and directly participating in the plot, Christophe seemed genuinely shocked. "My dear comrade," he wrote to Vernet,

> I have received with the greatest pain the afflicting news that you have just announced to me. I cannot even fathom this fatal accident, so disastrous for our country, without shuddering. You must obtain more ample information about the circumstances of this crime, to enlighten me, for in truth, I cannot begin to comprehend anything about this development, nor do I place any faith in it.[11]

As general in chief of a country whose leader had just been killed, Christophe had little time to process his anger or grief. He mostly professed bewilderment mingled with a pressing sense of urgency to confirm the news. Christophe sent seventeen letters on the nineteenth alone, each of which supports the case that he had no idea what befell the first emperor of Haiti and feverishly sought to find out. Following Christophe's journey to obtain accurate news on that day reveals not only when and how he first became aware of the emperor's assassination but the immediate difficulties that lay ahead for him as the general in chief of a nation in sudden absence of its head of state.

Details of Vernet's sparse but revelatory letter appear in Christophe's missives to Generals Romain and Dartiguenave, also written on the nineteenth, informing them of the assassination. A fuller description of the events later reached Christophe by way of Colonel Pierre Toussaint from Saint-Marc:

> It is with bloody tears . . . that I must inform you that I just learned from His Excellence the Minister of Finance, and from Colonel Pierre Toussaint, commander of Saint-Marc, that His Majesty, the Emperor, was just assassinated. He was engaged in battle from the Sibert plantation all the way until he reached Port-au-Prince; believing that the troops and inhabitants of that city were on his side, he hoped to be welcomed there but, alas, found only death.[12]

Christophe demanded more information from all his first correspondents. Still in disbelief, he stated in several letters dated from the nineteenth that he remained unsure of the veracity of the news he had received. At once seeking to learn more and fearing any further information, Christophe told Vernet that he asked General Daut to investigate and determine the authors of the "horrible crime that has been committed against the person of our emperor." Rumors of the identity of the conspirators trickled in throughout the day, and Christophe reacted to each subsequent missive with alarming rapidity.

While giving orders for the investigation, Christophe realized that the imperial family might be in danger. He sent a trusted officer to Vernet in Marchand/Dessalines to ensure that all the troops from the western division already in the capital had instructions to safeguard the ammunition, the palace, and Dessalines's family. "I believe that their lives are in danger," he told Vernet. "Give me your opinion right away," he continued, "so that I know if I should have them sent for."[13] Afterward, Christophe wrote to several of his colonels, "I am charging you with the responsibility of maintaining proper order in the capital, as well as with guarding the imperial family." He ended by announcing once again that he planned to discover the culprit or culprits responsible for killing Dessalines. "All the guilty will receive the punishments they deserve," he said.[14] But it is clear that Christophe did not know whom to charge with the murder. He wrote to Daut and Division General Cangé the same day to say that he remained "ignorant of the principal circumstances and authors" of the assassination. Considering the implications of this coup d'état for Haiti's already precarious standing, Christophe added, "I foresee in advance all the evils to which our country is to become prey." "It is of the utmost importance that the insurrection is stopped and that we learn the motives that brought it about and determine what measures can be taken to save our country," he concluded.[15]

At first, Christophe primarily concerned himself with gathering information, ensuring the safety of the imperial family, and confirming the continuation of fortifications. As the day of the nineteenth wore on and the news grew more certain, Christophe further shifted into general-in-chief mode. The insurrectionists in the south had already arrested all the generals and commanders of various cities loyal to Dessalines, Christophe learned.[16] Fearing the rebellion might spread, Christophe ordered each commander and battalion chief to have their troops at the ready and to increase patrols and surveillance.[17]

Christophe gave order after order, while still mostly unaware of what made insurrectionists in the south kill their own head of state. One of the most important southern generals who fought alongside Christophe during Haiti's war of independence was Alexandre Pétion. If Capoix had been one of Christophe's most frequent correspondents since independence, Pétion had been one of his least frequent. Pétion had congratulated Christophe for his promotion to general in chief of the Haitian army in mid-August 1805. Three weeks later, Christophe thanked "his Excellence General Pétion" infinitely for his felicitations and kindness.[18] Christophe did not send official correspondence to Pétion again until October 19, 1806, the same day he learned of the assassination, and seemingly only after he received a co-signed letter implicating Pétion.

Dated on the nineteenth, the letter was addressed to Christophe from "dissident officers," who signed their names, Vernet, Juste Chanlatte, A. Dupuy, and Diaquoi. This letter not only appears to reveal the precise moment when Christophe became aware of Pétion's involvement but also seems to have been the first time that Vernet transmitted information about the conspirators to Christophe, even though Vernet had corresponded with him throughout the day since the time he first informed him of Dessalines's death. The co-signed letter stated,

To General Henry Christophe,
General in Chief of the Army of Hayti.

Excellence,

We are writing to express both our sorrow and our revolt against this barbaric act, which brings dishonor on the glorious epic we have accomplished. In these sad and horrible moments, how can we fail to remember what we owe to the man whose energy and temerity led us to the decisive victory of November 18, 1803, over the most valiant army in the world?
How can we bear it any longer that he was so cowardly murdered by his own comrades in arms? No, a thousand times no, we would never be accomplices to Gérin and Pétion.

Confident in the feelings of honor and fairness that have always characterized you, we dare to believe that you will not accept under any pretext to take the reins of abject power.

We salute you, Honorable General, with deep respect.
Vernet, Juste Chanlatte, A. Dupuy, Diaquoi[19]

Judging from a subsequent missive he sent on the nineteenth, ostensibly after receiving the letter, Christophe took immediate action. Christophe replied to Vernet to ask him to dispatch an enclosed letter to Port-au-Prince for Pétion as quickly as possible. "And you will send me the answer to my letters by another express that you will dispatch to me," Christophe insisted, before admitting, "I am here gathering my wits. If you have any news, please let me know." He finished with a warning: "You can be sure that we'll find a remedy for this; for every serious problem there is a serious solution."[20]

In the letter enclosed for Pétion, Christophe played it cool. Addressing Pétion with a mixture of affection and concern, he wrote, "News of the troubles that have arisen in the south, my dear comrade, have indirectly reached me." "I have absolutely no idea what could have happened to lead to these difficulties, and what might be the motives. I am experiencing the greatest of worries, not having heard anything about your fate. In the difficult circumstance in which the empire finds itself, I need to have information and details about this terrible affair. It is from you that I demand it," Christophe finished. He then disclosed that Captain Hyacinthe and General Dartiguenave would not be long in reaching out to Pétion for that additional information.[21]

While Christophe grappled with what must have been complex emotions, he turned over in his mind one of Dessalines's frequent phrases and the one he had repeated to Vernet: "For every serious problem there is a serious solution." But further information would not be forthcoming that day, which is to say the nineteenth, or the day after. As he waited, Christophe could do little more than send orders to the army and ensure that the troops were properly clothed, paid, rationed, and prepared for war.

On the twenty-first, Christophe wrote perhaps the most painstaking letter of his life to Dessalines's wife, Marie-Claire Heureuse, the empress of Haiti. "It would be difficult for my heart, my dear *commère,* to express to you the sensation that I experienced upon receiving news of the troubles that have taken place, and above all, of the unheard-of attack that was committed upon the person of His Majesty, the Emperor, your husband," he wrote. "My anxiety is without equal about his fate." Christophe explained that he still lacked "any confirmed information about these terrible events" and had no idea who ordered the attack or why. "I still cannot believe that they have dared to soak their hands in his blood," he wrote. He then described his efforts to guard against the insurgency he feared might spread farther north to Marchand/Dessalines, saying in that case, "you will see me fly to your side" as soon as possible. "My dear *commère,* please do not allow yourself to be overcome with sorrow. You know me, place your complete faith in me. I will do everything mankind demands of me while trying to prevent bloodshed. The great plot of our enemies has been fulfilled; they have at last succeeded in creating divisions in the empire and at what a moment did they!" "I will do everything that duty demands of me," he told her. "With God as my witness, I will take care of your children. I have already written to the minister [Vernet]. If he believes that you and your cherished family are in any danger, he will let me know right away, and I will send for you and the children to come be near me and my wife, who is beside herself and stunned like me over this cruel event. I embrace you with all my heart and remain endlessly devoted."[22]

Unbeknownst to Christophe, someone else wrote to the empress as well: General Pétion. He struck a very different tone. "Madame," he began, "All the most sacred laws of nature, violated by him who carried the name of your spouse, the general destruction of the rightful defenders of the state, whose arrests were ordered from his guilty mouth, the excesses and crimes, at last, made oppressed citizens run to arms to deliver themselves from the most insupportable tyranny." "The sacrifice has been consummated, and the moment of vengeance was fixed by Providence for the memorable day of the seventeenth," Pétion continued. "Voilà, madame, a shortened account of the recent events, and the termination of he who profaned the title that united him with you." Pétion afterward implored the empress, "Console yourself, madame, you are in the midst of a people who would consecrate their lives for your happiness: forget that you were the wife of Dessalines in order to become the adopted wife of the most generous nation that only harbors hatred for its oppressors." He promised that her properties in the south and other possessions would be maintained for her "with the utmost care; they are protected by the love of your fellow citizens." Speaking on behalf of the army, Pétion finished by assuring Marie-Claire "of the sentiments that live within us regarding your virtues, whose traces are engraved in all our hearts and can never be erased." Not long after, the letter was printed for all the public to see.[23] Pétion had no shame.

———

General Alexandre Pétion, son of a white Frenchman and a free woman of color from Saint-Domingue,[24] was intimately involved in the plot since its inception; and he feigned neither innocence nor ignorance of the events that led to Dessalines's death. Christophe's letters, in contrast, tell the story of a man hardly on the inside, at least not yet.

The first officers Christophe sent to determine what happened to Dessalines did not procure any valuable information. Officers in the south, even Christophe's initial informants, still claimed not to know exactly how Dessalines's death came about.[25] Christophe felt desperate to learn the particulars so that he could stop any troubles from reaching the north, but with Capoix gone, there were few people he could trust to obtain intelligence. In a letter Vernet wrote to Christophe on the twentieth, the minister of finance provided him with some details, but judging from Christophe's response, he wanted information not based on conjecture. "The uncertainty in which I find myself is truly worrying," Christophe replied. "I have absolutely no idea whether His Majesty has been a victim, who the leaders of the insurrection are, what their plans and projects might be. No one so far has been able to give me any definite clarification."[26] Further complicating matters, U.S. merchants in Haiti, growing worried about their safety, planned to leave the country. The last thing Haiti needed was to be cut off from its supply chains again and to lose its most lucrative international trading partners. To allay their fears, Christophe wrote to two U.S. businessmen to reassure them that they would continue to enjoy protection and safety in the Empire of Haiti.[27]

For the first few days after Dessalines's death, Christophe seemed to oversee nearly everything, and he appeared not to have any rivals. General Louis Étienne Élie Gérin and Pétion soon exploited Christophe's take-charge attitude. Not long after the assassination, Gérin approached one of Christophe's initial sources of information, Colonel Pierre Toussaint. In a letter dated October 22, while praising Colonel Toussaint for having given him a copy of the letter Gérin originally addressed to the colonel, Christophe expressed consternation that Gérin had not written directly to him as the general in chief. "It was not you he was supposed to write to, and I am convinced you did not give him a reply," Christophe wrote. The rumor of Pétion and Gérin's involvement hinted at in the letter co-written by Vernet, Chanlatte, and company seemed suddenly to strike Christophe as quite plausible. But Christophe had a rumor circulating about him to address now too. He continued in his letter to Colonel Toussaint, "Do not be fooled by the contents of [Gérin's] letter. I have never expressed to General Gérin the ambition of becoming commander in chief. I only desire the happiness of my country and know how to submit to the laws that are established . . . because whatever the laws may be, an honest man must never fear them when he behaves honestly."[28] Referencing Gérin's letter to Toussaint in a separate missive he penned to Brigadier General Étienne Magny, Christophe reiterated that he never told Gérin that he wanted to become head of state, adding, "The leader of the faction is now known at last!"[29] This appears to be the first time that Christophe acknowledged in written correspondence the existence of a conspiracy led by Gérin.

If Christophe wanted direct contact with Gérin and Pétion, the latter to whom he had already directly written, he soon got his wish. Later, on the twenty-second, Christophe wrote to Vernet to acknowledge having received the letters from Gérin and Pétion that Vernet had dispatched to him. Pétion's letter, dated October 18, is so revealing that it must be examined in its entirety.

The first of several surprising elements revealed by the handwritten letter bearing Pétion's original signature—including Pétion's admission of guilt and motive for participating in the assassination—is that at the top, instead of "Empire d'Hayti," the letter reads, "République d'Hayti," even though Haiti had not yet officially been consecrated a republic. At the end of the letter Pétion implored Christophe to accept the reins of the government that southern soldiers had just toppled by killing Dessalines.

> Liberty or Death
> Republic of Haiti
> General-Quarter of Port-au-Prince, October 18, 1806
> Division General Pétion, Commander in Chief
>   of the Second Division of the West
> To His Excellency the General in Chief of the Haitian Army
>
> General,
>   Having escaped the destructive blows of tyranny, which the
> agents of an ungrateful and barbaric government were inflicting
> on the inhabitants of this country, we thought we should entrust
> the means of our salvation to the hands of a man who, through his
> personal travails and his own experience, could have, with wisdom,
> secured happiness for us, when, abusing our patience, he abused
> our goodwill by covering his head with the glitter of the diadem; we
> might have thought that amid greatness and power he would have
> recognized that his power was in our hands and had been won at
> the price of our courage; he even seemed to have realized this, and
> we hoped that, sheltered by the law, we would be able to enjoy in
> a peaceful state the fruits of all the sacrifices we have never ceased
> to offer up for such a long time. What was the result, General? As
> soon as he felt his authority had been consolidated, he forgot all his
> duties and, disregarding the sacred rights of a free people, seemed to
> believe that there was no true enjoyment but that exercised with the
> most despotic power and the most pronounced tyranny; our hearts
> groaned, and we sought to use only submission and docility to bring
> him back to the principles of justice and moderation with which he
> had promised to govern us. His last trip to the south finally revealed
> his plans, even to the less clear-sighted, and proved to us that we
> had no other means of self-preservation, and of opposing the
> attacks of the external enemy, than to rise en masse, if we wished
> to avoid imminent and resolute destruction. This spontaneous

movement, the impulse of our oppressed hearts, produced its effect as swift as lightning. In a few days the two southern divisions were on their feet; nothing could stop this irruption, since it was a movement as sudden as it was spontaneous and sacred, that of the right of citizens violated with impunity. We joined arms with our like-minded brothers from the south, and the army marched into Port-au-Prince in the most admirable state and with the most exact discipline, respecting property without a moment's disruption of agricultural labor or any shedding of blood.

Providence, which is infinite in its decrees, was pleased to show itself on our side in such a righteous cause by leading our oppressor to the fate that awaited him, and forced him to undergo the punishment for his crimes at the foot of the ramparts of a city he had come to with forces to empty of the blood of his fellow men, since, to use his last expressions, he wanted to reign in blood.

Our work would not have been finished, General, if we hadn't been convinced that there was a leader who could command the army with all the latitude of the power that, until now, has been in name only. It is in the name of this army, always faithful, obedient, and disciplined, that we ask you, General, to take the reins of power and government, and to allow us to enjoy the fullness of our rights, the freedom for which we have fought so long, and to be the guardian of our laws, which we swear to obey, since they will be just.

I have the honor of greeting you with respectful attachment.
Pétion[30]

The rumors Gérin spread that Christophe told him he wanted to reign, coupled with the rapid agreement to appoint him head of state, caused some in Haiti to suspect Christophe had been involved in the assassination all along. He had to tread lightly and carefully, therefore, in his response to this overture. In his October 22 letter to Vernet, who seemed distinctly opposed to any new government that involved Pétion and Gérin, Christophe described a printed document addressed to him from Gérin and Pétion. The general in chief told Vernet that after reading it, he needed to undertake "great reflections" before proceeding. "I can't make a decision yet, until I'm on the spot, to find out for myself." Christophe remained wary of traveling to the capital: first, because he feared his absence from the north could open the door to more insurrection; and second, because he suspected a trap. Vernet had counseled him to only enter Marchand, which the people were no longer calling Dessalines, accompanied by "imposing troops."[31] Vernet also worried about his own safety. Christophe therefore dispatched another officer to Marchand not only to guard the city, stores, and imperial palace but to ensure the security of Haiti's aging minister of finance, telling Colonel Barthélemy, "He is a respectable and precious man and one of our friends who has never wavered from our cause."[32] Although Christophe insisted that he could not leave Cap for fear that insurrection might take hold in his absence, by the twenty-third he had not only accepted leadership of his country but appeared also to accept Pétion and Gérin's justifications for the assassination.

The printed documents ostensibly enclosed with Pétion's missive revealed further motives for the insurrection while asking Christophe to formally lead Haiti as provisional head of state. Christophe, as a stickler for process, knew that the imperial constitution contained detailed provisions concerning succession in the event of the emperor's untimely demise. While Dessalines had the right to name his successor, his sudden death meant that he had not designated anyone. The constitution addressed the possibility of this situation by referring to the formation of a council of state.[33] Because the next head of state in the absence of a designee from the emperor needed to be determined by a formal body that did not yet exist, Christophe could not simply name himself emperor of Haiti, nor could anyone else. Only the council of state could draw up a new constitution by which a new administration could be organized, legislated, and governed. Haiti did have to be governed in the interim, though, and Generals Pétion and Gérin, having already implicated themselves in the insurrection, chose Christophe.

Christophe took only one day to reflect upon Pétion's and Gérin's letters and documents before responding. His earth-shattering response to Pétion changed everything. "The griefs that you are exposing to me concerning the conduct and arbitrary actions to which we have been witness and also victims and that placed us in a state of nullity under the reign that has just ended is worthy of the greatest attention in order to ensure the rule of law in our country." Christophe praised Pétion's "measures . . . to maintain order" and said to him, "Make it known to our brothers in the south and west that I approve their good conduct in this circumstance since order was not disrupted, which must always be the basis of our constitution." Being chosen for "the painful and honorable role of head of the government imposes the greatest of obligations upon me," Christophe continued. "No one more than you, my comrade, knows my principles and my indifference to this type of appointment; a quite powerful motive was necessary for me to determine whether to accept this enormous burden, along with the persuasion that you, in particular, have agreed to help me and lend me your knowledge when the public demands it."[34]

What crimes committed by Dessalines did Pétion and Gérin reference in that printed document to make Christophe suddenly, from one day to the next, agree that Dessalines's "arbitrary acts" not only made "victims" of those living in the southern and southwestern parts of Haiti but justified breaching article 21 of the imperial constitution: "The person of His Majesty is sacred and inviolable"?[35] Signed on October 13 in Les Cayes four days before the assassination, the printed document from the leaders of the southern army accused Dessalines of harboring animosity toward the "unfortunate class of *ancien libre* of all colors." They accused the late emperor of confiscating their lands and adding them to the empire's domains, raising troops against them, and seizing their money. "Everyone's heart was sickened; indignation was at its height. The people rose up en masse," they wrote to Christophe. "We have drawn our sword, and we will not put it back in its sheath until you demand it of us." Perhaps they chose Christophe as their successor to neutralize the threat he posed. "We do not wish to hide from you, worthy general in chief, that we believe your indignation equal to our own, and we proclaim you with joy and unanimity to be the *supreme leader* of this island, *under any denomination it should please you to choose;* every heart is with you; we swear before God to remain faithful to you and to die for liberty and for you," the statement continued. Given the seriousness of what they proposed, the authors of the document directly requested Christophe's approval: "We are not aware of what your fate and your position might be, but we hope that you will fight from this moment forward against Dessalines; we heard that you took over the treasury of Cap and that you have paid all your troops; we have just done the same; our treasurer in Cayes was overburdened with extortion demands and the ordered confiscations." The nine signers of the document—led by Colonel Jean-Jacques Wagnac, commander of the first division of the south—informed Christophe that they had invited military leaders throughout southern and southwestern Haiti, including General Gérin, to join them.[36]

Gérin's letters to Christophe, dated October 12 and 18, only arrived with Pétion's, and the printed statement, on October 22, five days after the assassination.[37] Still on the twenty-third, Christophe responded to Gérin using largely the same aloof language and tone he adopted with Pétion. However, to Gérin he wrote explicitly of the urgent need for "a regenerative constitution." For this undertaking, Christophe reminded Gérin, "it is necessary that an assembly composed of the most notable men, the most enlightened, and the most friendly to our cause be gathered together to work on this great oeuvre." Christophe wanted Gérin to know that while he had accepted the commission they offered, "I will designate the time and place where this meeting is to be held and the number of members who are to attend."[38]

Christophe knew that he next needed to inform and explain to the Haitian people the momentous events that had occurred in a little under the space of a week. He started with Vernet. The letter he wrote to the finance minister on the twenty-third suggests that Christophe had been moved by Pétion and Gérin's accounts of Dessalines's alleged abuses. The letters also suggest that Vernet was by then convinced as well. "I have received the dispatches from Generals Gérin and Pétion, which you addressed to me," Christophe wrote to Vernet. "After having read their contents, I am sending my reply. It will be carried by my aide-de-camp Georges and Monsieur Bertrand Lemoine, a wise man whom I have chosen for this mission." Christophe then noted, "I have ordered the printing and publication of these letters, of the document titled 'Resistance to Oppression,' which they have also addressed to me, and of my reply to their letter, along with other documents intended to provide information on these matters. I will send you a few copies as soon as they are printed."[39] Christophe understood the power of the press. By ordering the printing and publication of the letters he received from Gérin and Pétion, along with his response to them—and ordering that the printed document titled "Resistance to Oppression," signed by dozens of officers, be made public, too—Christophe showed distinct awareness that he needed to do more than inform the Haitian populace of the circumstances of the emperor's death. He needed to find ways of encouraging the public to accept the outcome of their emperor's assassination as righteous and inevitable, along with Christophe's ascent to head of state.

Presumably, the document printed under the title "Resistance to Oppression" would have included a second document originally addressed from the rebelling army to Christophe and dated October 21 from Port-au-Prince by which southern soldiers officially voted Christophe into the role of Haiti's new provisional head of state. Similar to the first printed letter, composed before the assassination, thirty-three men from the southern army signed the second one, dated the twenty-first, including Gérin and Pétion. This letter was far more damning and explicit, even though it did not reveal the exact sequence of events that led to the emperor's death, including who dealt the fateful blow. "General," it began, "Tyranny has been struck down along with the tyrant's head. Since the seventeenth, we are at last free." The Haitian people, amid "endless agitations constantly being rebirthed," had not "yet attained the goal that was promised to them, and at the end of which it would only then be possible to close the door to the temple of war!" To them, the principles that Christophe "always had the courage to communicate to the generals in this time of barbarity . . . were the electric sparks . . . responsible for bringing us to the moment when Jean-Jacques Dessalines, our mutual oppressor, ceased to live." Now "vengeance has been achieved, and the army is only waiting for your presence" to create a constitution "where each citizen will find a guarantee for the safety of their person and the sacred right of property, emanating from the general will, not like those laws that we have just trampled underfoot," "uniquely crafted to flatter the caprices of a single

315

man, contrary in its own wording even to the principles of liberty." "Having been abused for so long," the declaration continued, "we have sworn to never leave one another's side" until the approval of the new constitution and "we have publicly recognized you as the head of the government." They enjoined Christophe, therefore, to "satisfy the impatience of your brave soldiers" and the Haitian people, "for whom your presence alone is only missing from this moment of joy."[40]

Concerning the new constitution, Christophe, while playing coy to a certain extent by not mentioning documents already surfacing from the south referencing the "Republic of Haiti," intimated to Pétion that he wanted the crafting of Haiti's new constitution to be undertaken with more deliberation, collaboration, and reflection. Writing to Pétion on October 26, he told the division general, "It is essential that before work begins on the constitutional laws, which must unite together all that will ensure the happiness of the people of Haiti, that heads remain calm and that the silence of meditation permits us the ability to discern our rights and protect them against the passions that sometimes put themselves in their place." Remaining a bit elliptical in his opening remarks, at the end of the letter Christophe used a more direct tactic. He told Pétion that given the danger Haiti had experienced internally and the threat posed by external and international actors, composing a new constitution right away might not actually be in the best short-term interests of the country. "As soon as everything is back to normal, I will invite all the wisest, most notable men, those who possess the trust of the people, to meet in a place that I will designate for them to express their will concerning the needs of the pact that must eternally bind us and produce our collective happiness."[41] If Christophe had doubts about Pétion's motives, they seem to have been mitigated by his confidence that he could direct the Haitian state to his desire and advantage. He just needed the Haitian people to have confidence in him too.

As the state-run newspaper, the *Political and Commercial Gazette* represented the most appropriate outlet for information about the emperor's death and Christophe's promotion to head of state. Yet the October 23 issue of the paper neither mentioned nor alluded to the assassination, perhaps because Christophe did not order the paper to print this news until that very day. The next issue of the paper, ordinarily printed weekly, did not appear until November 6. It contained the first public account of Dessalines's death, which revealed the precise location and motives of the coup d'état that brought down Haiti's first emperor. "Reasons, which need not be explained, prevented us from earlier mentioning these events," the author of the article first stated. "For some time, discontent was erupting in several parts of the empire. Poor administration, various injustices, and acts contrary to the safety of the highest public officials, as well as of private individuals, aroused general disgust for the government, which has just been overthrown." According to the account, "most of the principal officers of the empire," unhappy with how they had been treated and "indignant" that soldiers went unclothed, unfed, and unpaid, while "the state's coffers had sufficient means to pay the army," decided to overthrow the government and replace it with one led by "a man distinguished by his character and his merit who would have the power to bring happiness to his fellow citizens and spread over them the advantages of a paternal administration."

The plan had been under way for several weeks, the *Gazette* reported, "until the day of the event, on October 17, when the emperor Dessalines was killed, at around nine in the morning, between Arcahaie and the city of Port-au-Prince, at the spot called Pont-Rouge, in an attempt to retreat, after having realized that he had fallen into an ambush in mistaking the people he encountered there as members of his own party." The article stressed that "the death of the ruler of the empire was *not* premeditated"; rather, the original aim of the coup had been to arrest Dessalines and charge him with crimes against the state. In accordance with article 29 of the constitution, the conspirators claimed they had wanted Dessalines to be "tried by the councilors of state, in order to depose him and to substitute another in his place." Article 29 stipulated, "Any successor who deviates from the dispositions of the previous article," which is to say article 28, would be "considered and declared to be in a state of war against society," after which he would be judged and replaced by the councilors of state. Dessalines's opponents essentially accused him of having violated article 28, which declared, "Neither the emperor, nor any of his successors, will have the right . . . to surround himself with any particular, privileged body, under the title of nobles, or under any other denomination." The southern soldiers accused Dessalines of creating a privileged class in violation of his own constitution.

The *Gazette*'s account not only set forth the legal principles behind the "revolution" but also blamed Dessalines for its fatal outcome. "The threats made by the supreme leader, his decision to retreat in order to come back with more forces, the fear that his violent character always inspired, decided his fate." According to this newspaper account, Christophe knew about the attempted coup and the plot to arrest Dessalines. Although the more than twenty letters that Christophe penned as events unfolded in the immediate wake of the assassination do not support this implication, the official record, as far as the *Gazette* is concerned, went down as such. "General in Chief Christophe was designated from the start of the army's march to occupy the head of state; he was afterward genuinely elected according to the will of the army and of the people. We will refrain from praising him here for fear of straying too far from the subject and offending his modesty," the account continued, though its author observed that Christophe's "great reputation . . . both inside and outside our country" would benefit international relations. Acknowledging it to be "no doubt surprising that this event could have been conducted with such deep secrecy," the authors of the account boasted that "Dessalines was quite ignorant of everything, as was his entire court; they saw in this uprising only the discontent of a few leaders who could have been easily defeated; the terror inspired by his name was, according to him, the most formidable weapon he could employ, and whose success was infallible." Dessalines's own words were now being used against him by the very people in whose name he had proclaimed them.

The *Gazette*'s account finished by reassuring the Haitian public that the whole affair had been undertaken with the utmost prudence. Farming and commercial operations continued, the author reported; the army was paid, outfitted, and provided with rations. The constitution that Christophe ordered was also in the works, its laws promising to be "sage and appropriate," and this new constitution, implemented by a "paternal leader and friendly administrators of the country," would help the Haitian populace to forget the ills of the past and allow them to enjoy "the happiness for which we have been thirsting for so long." The newspaper announced the promised letters and other acts associated with the event as available for sale to the Haitian public along with the "Account of the Events That Occurred in the Two Divisions of the South and the Second of the West from October 12 to 17."[42]

There were few pens in early independent Haiti capable of doing Dessalines this dirty. Rouanez, previously censured by Dessalines for his inflammatory article about the United States, is one possible candidate. Another is Juste Chanlatte, Dessalines's undersecretary, born in the south, who rather conspicuously seemed to have receded from public life by fall 1806, with Boisrond-Tonnerre undersigning the government's decrees. Chanlatte previously addressed the Haitian people in 1804, shortly after Haitian independence, with his powerful pro-Dessalines pamphlet, *To My Fellow Citizens*. An ardent partisan of Christophe's, he was later instrumental in exposing the "criminality" of the constitution that Pétion and his faction were about to create.[43] Another possible candidate was someone far less prominent.

An account written by Brigadier General Laurent Férou, commander of the arrondissement of Grand'Anse and a member of Dessalines's erstwhile army, repeated and supported the claim that the goal of the coup d'état, of which Férou approved, had not been to kill Dessalines. On October 20—three days after the assassination, but intitially penned slightly *before* Férou learned of it—he sent a letter to the governor of Jamaica, "You must be well aware of the horrors committed on this island by Dessalines. As soon as he was sure of having the power, he hastened to make himself the hero of the revolution of Saint-Domingue; giving into his ferocious and proud nature, he no longer saw the state except in himself."[44]

As a principal member of the Haitian army, Férou last saw Dessalines in July when the emperor visited the southern part of the country, notably in the cities of Jérémie and Les Cayes. On the eighth, Dessalines entered Jérémie, greeted by artillery salutes and multiple celebrations. Afterward, Dessalines stayed at his palace in that city for several weeks and even celebrated his fete (or feast day) on the twenty-fifth of that month "amid the utmost splendor and every formality possible. There was a splendid meal, ending with a quite brilliant ball."⁴⁵ Little did the emperor know that was to be his last fete and that his trusted commander Férou, who told the governor of Jamaica, "in the end there was nothing at all humane" about Dessalines, was to be one of the conspirators bent on overthrowing him.

Férou reported that the rebellion against Dessalines had been led by "the men who had already saved the people of this country from general destruction" and who "had yet again given it proofs of their devotion." In mid-October, "the entire southern department found itself delivered from the yoke of Dessalines, without the slightest disorder having been committed. Culture and commerce were not affected," though a few generals "who were found to be in favor of our tyrant" were arrested "by their own soldiers." Férou claimed that the people of the south wanted assurance that no blood would be shed in their revolution against imperial authority, although they were "certain that all those whom Dessalines has in his power and who he even suspects will be ruthlessly exterminated." The next step in removing Dessalines was to "deliver" Port-au-Prince using the great number of southern troops whom the conspirators sent there for that purpose. The final step was removing the emperor from power and installing Christophe in his place. "We will continue our march, looking for Dessalines in his farthest lairs," Férou wrote. And when the southern troops finally reunited with "the army of the north, we will recognize the leader of the island to be General Christophe, a man full of decency and dignity, whose orderly character and ability to bring about the public good is known to us all; he will be chief by our choice, the public voice calls him to duty while it has always repelled Dessalines." Although Férou's letter might seem to implicate Christophe in the plot, it does not reveal whether Christophe participated in the planning, only that he had been chosen in advance by the southern generals conspiring against Dessalines.

Férou wanted to be clear that *this* revolution's goal was not for the men of the south to seize power for themselves. It was, instead, to restore order, good mores, and "civilization." Hoping that the war between "us and Dessalines will not be long because all the troops are on our side," Férou made a specific request to the governor of Jamaica, to "authoriz[e] us to obtain from your island the objects that we may need." By permitting this trade, Férou said the Jamaican governor could "render a service to humanity" in helping the Haitian people "to get rid of a monster who has lived for too long and whose character, inclined to brigandage and disorder, could only be dangerous to his neighbors whose friendship he never sought." Férou also requested "several warships to cruise in front of spots that may still be in his power, in order to prevent [Dessalines] from receiving any assistance so that this struggle between the friends of order and those of brigandage lasts for the shortest time possible." Yet before he could send his letter, Férou learned the fateful news about the emperor and quickly scribbled a postscript on the bottom of his letter: "At this very moment a courier brought me a letter from Port-au-Prince dated the eighteenth. When our army entered that city, Dessalines, who had come to its rescue, perished. We are marching immediately to liberate Camp Marchand, where some of his supporters are still encamped."[46] Christophe was not among the Dessalines partisans at Camp Marchand that day.

Much later, Charles Mackenzie, British consul to Haiti from 1826 to 1827, directly implicated Christophe in Pétion and Gérin's rebellion. In September 1826, Mackenzie furnished his home government with a detailed handwritten recitation of Haiti's various governments since the proclamation of the country's independence. Although he admitted that he had not personally interviewed the inhabitants of the country, he claimed to have "collected information from every part of it and have diligently sifted all the evidence on which it is founded." Referring only to a vague chain of recitation, Mackenzie accused Dessalines of "disposing of every man" of "talent and reputation . . . especially those of European origin." He went on to say, "Those who could not be publickly [sic] executed, were cut off by poison, and it is recorded, on good authority, that the monster summoned the physician who had refused to administer poison secretly to the late General Pétion, to his country residence, and there inhumanly bayoneted him in the dead of night." In Mackenzie's account, after Pétion escaped this plot he "began to communicate with Christophe," who then "joined in the plot without reluctance."[47] While Dessalines's alleged attempt to poison Pétion might have just been hearsay, one thing is clear from examining Christophe's own actions in the weeks following the emperor's death: before Christophe turned against the men of the south who overthrew the emperor and caused his death, he joined with them.

According to an eyewitness report from Guy-Joseph Bonnet, the newly formed council of state believed it inadequate for the post-Dessalines government to simply explain and legally justify the coup they called a "revolution." They also wanted Christophe, their designated interim head of state, to address the Haitian people, to "expose the views of the revolutionaries" and to legitimate their choice of him as Dessalines's successor.[48] Christophe followed this advice in the address he gave in Cap on November 2, later printed in the *Political Gazette*. He first pleaded for unity: "The event that has just rendered us more worthy of your sacrifices and your labor, which in destroying the arbitrary power of which you had cause to complain, prepares a happy future for you, and must be the indissoluble knot of our union and the bulwark of our supreme happiness." Echoing the Haitian Declaration of Independence, Christophe continued, "It is to have done nothing, to destroy a bad administration without the substitution for it of a better one." Christophe's goal over the next months was to prevent disorder, anarchy, and disobedience. He told the public that Haiti's new government, led by him, would assure their rights but that it also required their obedience and help in maintaining order and unity. He promised military discipline and the execution of laws. To prevent another military rebellion, Christophe reminded the citizens of Haiti that the world still had its eyes on them, wishing for them to fail. "Do you want to lose in one day your reputation and the reward that is your destiny? Would it please you to take it upon yourself to overthrow the edifice of our independence and our freedom, and in so doing expose our downfall to the irony of nations?" Christophe said he recognized the deprivation the Haitian people had suffered of late. To farmers, he issued the following call: "You, laborers and country dwellers, whose hardworking hands provide the base for this government, your happiness is in your labor, your wealth is in the products of your farming. . . . Your happiness and that of your families is a preoccupation of the government." He asked the military, along with every inhabitant, to help rid the state of conspirators and ill-wishers, "agitators among you, actors paid by our enemies, traitors, who would seek to destroy us with the pernicious effects of their perfidious insinuations." He told his fellow Haitians to "confide right away in your leaders, with the frankness of a true Haitian. . . . Engrave in your hearts love for your country and love of order. Print there, in indelible characters, that the government wants to maintain the most perfect union and the sacrifice of every hatred, all ambition, all partisan spirit, and has only one goal, that of the salvation of the state." Christophe signed off not as emperor or even president but as "head of the government of Haiti." His signature was undersigned by that of Rouanez *jeune*, whom he announced to be the secretary of the new government, further supporting the theory that the latter contributed to the *Political Gazette*'s account of the "revolution" that ultimately deposed and killed Dessalines.[49]

———

Although the *Political Gazette*'s narration of the overthrow of Dessalines labored to portray Christophe as a member of the conspiracy's inner circle from the beginning, Christophe's private letters tell a different story, one of seeming shock, disgust, dismay, disbelief, fear, anger, and even sadness about the loss of his friend, commander, and confidant. Why, then, did he go along with the official account promulgated by the self-proclaimed councilors of state? One eyewitness account is revelatory in this regard. Vastey, who eventually became Christophe's most important secretary, later painted him as not at all the insider the southern generals tried to make him out to be. In Vastey's account, Dessalines had closed himself off from Christophe in the final months of his life, resulting in Christophe's wholesale ignorance of the problems in the south until just before the emperor's death.

Hints of Christophe's alienation from Dessalines appear in a letter Christophe wrote to the emperor on September 4, 1806. The letter also perhaps unwittingly contains a harbinger of the plot that undid Dessalines. On that day, Christophe complained about being surveilled. He reminded Dessalines that a letter Dessalines previously wrote to him from Jacmel in July had been unsealed and resealed before it reached him. Christophe now reported that Dessalines's letter from August had undergone the same fate. Someone had poorly applied a blot of wax to attempt to conceal the intrusion, also smearing wax on other parts of the envelope, which is what convinced Christophe of the subterfuge. "I do not know what strange curiosity and what motives could encourage someone to have violated the seal of Your Majesty's letters, which must be considered sacred," he said. "Mainly, they are the letters that Your Majesty has addressed to me." "It has been said that a violated letter merits the guilty one to have his hand cut off," he continued, "but the ones who have done this deserve to have their heads follow their hands."[50]

Unlike the rebellion's first chronicler in the *Political Gazette*, Vastey, who set down the history of the assassination with the most insight and proximity, but thirteen years after the fact, called people out by name. According to him, not only did Pétion constitute the soul of the conspiracy, but his faction helped alienate Christophe from the emperor beforehand. Vastey claimed that Pétion and his accomplices fabricated a letter under Christophe's name that called for the people and the troops to rebel against the emperor, which damaged Christophe's relationship with Dessalines and eventually removed him altogether from the emperor's inner circle. Christophe's ignorance of the conspiracy allowed the plot to proceed. In Vastey's recollection, the conspiracy exploded into reality on October 10, 1806, in the plain of Les Cayes when the minister of war, Gérin, led an insurrection in the south and marched with his troops to Port-au-Prince. Pétion, to maintain the illusion of loyalty, informed Dessalines. Trusting Pétion, the emperor ordered him to stop the insurrection, but to leave unaware Christophe, whom Dessalines suspected of being in on the plot because of the forged letter. Christophe's correspondence with Dessalines supports this account: the emperor did not inform the general in chief of his own army of an insurrection until October 16.

Instead of quashing the insurrection, Pétion left with his troops to join the anti-Dessalines opposition in the southern part of the country. The two sets of troops met up in Grand-Goâve and marched toward Port-au-Prince, entering the city on October 16, 1806. They were joined by Generals Yayou, Ambroise Magloire, Gérin, and several other key members of the military. On the morning of October 17, the emperor took the path to Port-au-Prince, escorted by only around twenty people. Upon reaching Pont-Rouge, outside Port-au-Prince, the emperor saw troops posted on both sides of the road, but believed they were his men, not his opponents. The emperor continued to advance, until fully surrounded. It was only then he heard cries commanding the troops to take up arms, yelling at him, "Halt, halt!" The emperor appeared to recognize his mistake. He had been betrayed. The inimitable founder of Haitian independence launched himself before the bayonets of the men standing before him and cried out, "Soldiers, do you not recognize me?" He grabbed his cane and hit and pushed the bayonets away. Just then, Gérin, Yayou, and the other conspiring generals, still in hiding, ordered the troops to fire. The emperor's horse was shot out from under him, and Dessalines fell to the ground, and died, "pierced with blows."[51]

Vastey published this account of Dessalines's assassination in 1819, by which time he filled the office of official historian of the kingdom. As part of the ongoing war of words between northern and southern Haiti, Christophe's kingdom had with near constancy portrayed Pétion, who died in 1818, as the author of this conspiracy. Yet a name that stands out in Vastey's relation is that of General Yayou.

Yayou was young. Like Dessalines, he was born in the colony of Saint-Domingue near Grande-Rivière du Nord. Unlike Dessalines, Yayou had been a partisan of Colonel Sans-Souci, the man whose death Christophe ordered during the revolution. Not only did Yayou previously fight Christophe during the internecine wars in Saint-Domingue that saw the French colonial army pitted against the independent army, but he fought Pétion, too. Nevertheless, according to Saint-Rémy, it was Yayou who persuaded Pétion to join the "insurrection." After hearing his arguments against the emperor, Pétion reportedly said, "My thoughts are not any longer in doubt: I will enter also into the insurrection; do as I do. The emperor, does he not govern us as a colonist of the worst kind would have done?"[52]

Although Christophe and Yayou corresponded infrequently, the general in chief had relied on him to crush conspiracies from time to time in the postindependence period. In October 1805, Christophe told Yayou, who then presided over the city of Léogâne, that the enemies of Haiti wanted nothing more "than to see us dragged into a civil war," and he counseled him to therefore "utilize the greatest surveillance to maintain calm and tranquility." Christophe afterward saluted General Yayou with "friendship" and a desire for him to remain in "perfect health." He even praised Yayou, calling him responsible for the arrest of the conspirators and imploring him to provide his superior officer and the emperor with a complete list of their names.[53]

Yayou now stood also among the councilors of state, post-assassination, whose name was leaked to Christophe before their official selection. Christophe wanted one of his confidants, Juste Hugonin, to discover who would be the electors for the council of state, since these men had the job of developing the constitution and officially electing Haiti's next ruler. In a November 24, 1806, letter to Christophe—which at first seems unassuming, but will later become extremely significant—Hugonin cautioned that he had just become aware of an "infinity of things that I cannot write down." He therefore dispatched to Christophe a lieutenant named Doria to transmit the information. Before closing the letter, Hugonin did say that he expected the assembly to take place on December 1. Most of the representatives were not yet known, however, Hugonin reported, except for Generals Yayou and Magloire.[54] Yayou had participated in the plot to overthrow Dessalines, and he was there on Pont-Rouge when the emperor was killed. Indeed, multiple sources report that Yayou stabbed Dessalines three times *after* he fell to the ground.[55] This same assassin would be one of the causes of Christophe's decision to rebel against the new government that the conspirators hoped to install.

By the time of the official formation of the new Republic of Haiti with its new constitution on December 27, 1806, the late emperor's reputation was as tattered as the clothing he wore on that fateful October morning. There exist several versions of what happened to Dessalines's remains. Most are tinged with the air of legend. Some sources report that Dessalines's dead body was simply left lying out in the open air. In this version, no one dared to inter the emperor's mutilated remains—his head was reportedly almost detached from his body, and the multiple stab wounds had left him unrecognizable—except for, allegedly, an impoverished older woman named Dédée Bazile, also known as Défilée La Folle, or the Crazy One.

Born to enslaved parents in colonial Cap-Français, Dédée was said to have gone crazy after she was raped at the age of eighteen. Nevertheless, she contributed to the Haitian Revolution by serving as a sutler who carried provisions for the army, afterward settling in Port-au-Prince in the postindependence period. After his death, the emperor's corpse remained at Pont-Rouge through midday, discarded like a bag of rags, his body baking in the hot Haitian sun. Taking pity on the remains, and the soul, of Dessalines, Dédée reportedly carried the cadaver alone all the way to the cemetery in Port-au-Prince. In other accounts, she assembled the remaining fragments of the corpse, placed them in a sack, and carried them to the burial grounds. To Haitians today, the name Dédée Bazile, even when she is called La Folle, calls forth the humanity and compassion this poor woman, broken by life, displayed for the material remains of the man who had the misfortune to be Haiti's first emperor.[56]

Other chroniclers of nineteenth-century Haitian history have told divergent tales of what happened to the emperor's body after his death.

Vastey did not mention Bazile or the involvement of any woman. Instead, Vastey wrote that after Gérin, Yayou, and the other "hidden conjurers" executed the emperor, "a white Frenchman named Verret, a favorite of Pétion's whom the emperor promoted to the rank of adjutant general, was seen coming forward to mutilate the inanimate body of that unfortunate man, stripping him of his watch and his jewelry." In addition to Verret, who became a commander in the south under Pétion, Vastey spoke of a man named Georges, "of execrable memory," whom witnesses said they saw "cutting off a thumb from [Dessalines's] hand and then selling it for 10 *portugaises* to a foreigner!" Dessalines had been "insulted" in life, and "he was insulted yet more after his death," Vastey lamented.[57]

The Haitian historian Saint-Rémy, in his nineteenth-century biography of Pétion, noted that two of Dessalines's closest advisers, Boisrond-Tonnerre and Étienne Mentor, were conspicuously absent from the scene of the crime, having sought refuge in Port-au-Prince. Saint-Rémy charged therefore that the two men abdicated their roles as custodians for the emperor's remains. In this account, upon learning of the "sacrilege" perpetrated against Dessalines's corpse, Pétion ordered the Eleventh Demibrigade to gather the dead emperor's remains and to bury his body in the city cemetery. General Joseph Balthazar Inginac's wife then raised a tomb for him, upon which were inscribed the words "Here lies Dessalines, dead at 48 years old."[58]

With Dessalines interred in a manner, however dissatisfying, the presumed councilors of state then went about the work of ratifying the constitution. They completed and signed the constitution of the newly minted Republic of Haiti on December 27, 1806, but without Christophe as a signatory.

11

THE DAWN OF CIVIL WAR

The new constitution for the Republic of Haiti did not mention Christophe, nor did it name the country's new head of state. Dessalines's constitution of 1805 had named Jean-Jacques Dessalines as emperor, and even Toussaint's 1801 constitution for Saint-Domingue officially named him governor-general. The omission of Christophe's name in the 1806 republican constitution, in hindsight, was perhaps a screaming harbinger foretelling that just three days after the constitution's unveiling, President Christophe—officially elected to the highest office in the land—would march on Port-au-Prince, the new capital of Haiti, and try to overthrow the very government he had just agreed to lead. This move sparked a thirteen-year civil war between one of the architects of Dessalines's demise, Alexandre Pétion, and the man chosen to succeed him, Christophe. The power struggle culminated in two presidents for Haiti. Christophe ruled in the north and Pétion in the south. Like Louverture and Rigaud, these two sons of the Haitian Revolution then fought each other mightily with words while chasing each other with bullets. The civil war they lit ablaze occasioned several high-profile casualties of former revolutionary generals, too, spreading mourning over the once-proud shores of the first country in the modern world to permanently abolish slavery. The conflict would only end once both Christophe and Pétion were dead.

Marie-Claire Heureuse Félicité Bonheur Dessalines, the Haitian empress with a joyfully long name, was born in Léogâne, some say in 1758, the same year as her husband. She received the news of the emperor's death while in the imperial palace located in the city of Marchand.[1] No doubt, sitting with profound shock and grief, Marie-Claire would have had to relate this sorrowful news to their three children. Notarial records suggest that she adopted her husband's children from a prior relationship: Célimène, Jacques Bien-Aimé, and Célestine. All three of the children were born in the 1790s before their parents' marriage.[2] Dessalines and Marie-Claire had one other child, who never lived to see the terrible day her father was brutally assassinated. Recall that Christophe had consoled

Dessalines and his wife over the loss of their daughter, Cérine, who passed away in October 1805.[3]

Having already suffered the loss of their sister, the Dessalines children were likely just as confused as their mother about whom to blame for their father's death. Marie-Claire could only have shed more tears when she received General Alexandre Pétion's fateful letter, the one accusing her husband of having ruled with "the most insupportable tyranny," at the same time as its author implored her to forget that she had been the wife of Dessalines. While Pétion's letter spoke of the emperor's death as "the moment of vengeance" finally brought to bear on the emperor who "violated" all the "most sacred laws of nature," Christophe's missive, sent two days later, had been filled with condolences and sympathy for the grieving family. The Dessalines family sat deprived of its patriarch by what Christophe referred to as the "unheard-of attack committed upon the person of His Majesty."[4]

A few days after the assassination, Madame Dessalines left the imperial city named after her husband, possibly for the last time. She traveled with her three remaining children to the city of Gonaïves, to seek the protection of her husband's dear friend and comrade in arms, General André Vernet, the minister of finance. Under his care, the empress witnessed the immediate chaos, violence, and confusion leading up to Haiti's civil war, and the most unseemly pall it cast over the independent and slavery-free land that her husband painstakingly shed his blood to secure.

Though Christophe promised Marie-Claire that he would make his way to her just as soon as circumstances permitted or send for her and the children to come to Cap, those circumstances did not arise for some time. Marie-Claire did not make her way to Cap until Christophe firmly broke with the men responsible for her husband's death. Even though Pétion had urged Christophe to immediately take the reins of power, from Christophe's perspective Pétion simultaneously directed events in a manner that suggested he wanted to make himself, and not Christophe, the highest authority in the land. According to Vastey, Pétion dismissed and replaced civil and military authorities and made use of state finances and government stores, following solely his own volition, rather than that of Christophe, the interim head of state. More seriously, Pétion condemned to death several of Dessalines's most prominent generals. Moreau and Guillaume Lafleur had their heads cut off in the cities of Les Cayes and Aquin, respectively; while General Germain and Adjutant Generals Étienne Mentor and Boisrond-Tonnerre were bayoneted in Port-au-Prince under the direct orders of, and allegedly in front of, Pétion.[5]

Boisrond-Tonnerre, who served as one of the emperor's most trusted secretaries, and who, aside from Chanlatte, showed the most literary inclinations of Dessalines's men, did not go out of the world without pleading his innocence in the plaintive tones of poetry. Prior to his death, the southern faction imprisoned Boisrond-Tonnerre along with Mentor. These arrests occurred even though the pro-Pétion historian Saint-Rémy claimed that Boisrond-Tonnerre immediately turned against Dessalines after he learned of the assassination, shouting in chorus with Mentor in the streets of Port-au-Prince, "*Vive la liberté!* The tyrant is no more!" Suspecting Boisrond-Tonnerre's and Mentor's glee to be merely a ruse, Pétion ordered their arrests. However, the night of the arrests a crowd of angry protesters reportedly invaded the prison and demanded their heads. Before his execution, Boisrond-Tonnerre scribbled a quatrain with a nail on a wall of the prison:

Damp and cold dwelling, made by and for a crime,
Where the crime, while laughing, immolates its victim,
What can your shackles and bars inspire,
When a pure heart suffers here an innocent repose.[6]

In Saint-Rémy's retelling, these lines were preserved by accident when a general named Lerebours, at the time a cavalry captain, took it upon himself to copy the poem and transcribe it on the walls of his own home.[7]

At the same time, Christophe busied himself with reassuring the Haitian people of his ability and willingness to lead them. Only two weeks after the assassination, on November 2, 1806, Christophe stood before a crowd in Cap, which included ordinary citizens and the military under his command, and spoke of the death of Dessalines as an event that made the Haitian people "more worthy of their own sacrifices" and that "prepared a happy future for them." Even if Dessalines had been as unpopular with his people as Christophe and Pétion seemed to take turns intimating, it must have been unsettling to hear of his brutal assassination at the hands of his own army. After all, Dessalines had previously been propped up in the empire as the man who bravely proclaimed Haitian independence before the world.[8]

Considering the questionable executions undertaken by Pétion and his allies, Christophe seemed determined to prove that although he was from the north, he was not a regional partisan and that he intended to govern with neutrality. Having been proclaimed the interim leader of the government the day after the assassination by the very men from the south who wanted his predecessor gone, Christophe vowed to follow the letter and law of the 1805 imperial constitution by convoking a council of state to name the deputies who would come together to create the new government and its constitution. Even knowing them to be the authors of Dessalines's demise, Christophe tasked Pétion and Gérin with convoking the assemblies of the southern province, with its two divisions, as well as that of the second division of the west. Christophe oversaw the election of councilors from the first division of the west and the entire northern department.

Christophe wanted the new seat of the government, however, to be with him in Cap, and he preferred that the forthcoming assembly take place there. This move might have allowed him to remain surrounded by a mostly loyal community. Yet to give the generals and magistrates proof of his good faith and loyalty, and to remove any suspicion that he sought to influence this assembly, Christophe reluctantly consented for it to take place in Port-au-Prince, clear on the other side of the island and far from his presence.

Christophe soon had reason to suspect Gérin and Pétion's motives. Pétion continued to delay the deliberations even though the deputies from the three divisions of the north and the first division of the west, regions loyal to Christophe, had arrived in Port-au-Prince ready to begin. Christophe quickly came to believe that Pétion had delayed the session to take control of the proceedings and ensure a clear majority for his faction. On the opening day of deliberations, when the deputies from the south and part of the west finally arrived, there were seventy-four representatives total instead of the fifty-six of which the assembly should have been composed. Pétion and Gérin somehow ensured that most of the deputies (eighteen extra) were from their side. The deputies from the divisions of the north and the first division of the west naturally protested and pointed out the illegal constitution of the assembly. Delegates from the two southern divisions and the second division of the west, now holding an absolute majority, patently rejected their opposition. Pétion's bloc went even further. Because the northern deputies, along with those of the first division of the west, protested these proceedings, both in written and in published decrees, the opposing deputies revoked seven-eighths of their number, leaving the divisions of the north and the first division of the west essentially without representation.[9]

On December 29, twenty-four deputies from the three divisions of the north and the first of the west issued a proclamation addressed to Christophe as "the General in Chief of the Army of Haiti." They included with this missive the text of their official "protestation," signed two days before, on December 27, the day the new constitution for the Republic of Haiti was completed. The undersigned deputies first described how they had appeared before the Constituent Assembly in Port-au-Prince to form the constitution. Since the second of last month, "we were supposed to have started this work," they wrote, "but General Pétion, division commander, objected that the deputies of the south had not yet arrived, and that we could not create the constitution without the participation of those from every part of the island." The deputies insisted that they remained patient until the eighteenth of the month, the day they were supposed to begin deliberating the new constitution. When that day came and went, the deputies said they expressed their impatience to Pétion, "who kept post-poning the opening of the assembly from one Monday to the next, even refusing to indicate the place where the sessions were to be held." When Pétion finally, and belatedly, opened the session, these deputies experi-enced yet more frustration, leading to consternation. "The day at last hav-ing arrived, imagine our surprise," the deputies wrote,

> after the verification of the powers, to find seventy-four representa-tives instead of the fifty-six we should have been. From that time for-ward, considering this assembly illegal, we tried to object, but our objection was rejected by the absolute majority that the deputies from the south and the second division of the west had. We knew that our protests were useless and we reserved the right to protest against anything done in the assembly, and not to make our protest known until we were in a safe place.
>
> We are therefore protesting against our signatures having been affixed to the so-called constitutional act of this day, the fruit of intrigue and malice, and against all that shall follow, until the disso-lution of the assembly, which was unlawful, and against all principles of justice and equity.[10]

By the time these councilors issued the above proclamation, Chris-tophe had already grown more than suspicious of the constitutional pro-ceedings and had expressed his outright, and public, disapproval. Under typeface that read "State of Hayti," on November 24, 1806, Christophe issued a formal "Proclamation to the People and the Army" to explain the irregular procedures in Port-au-Prince delaying the creation of the new constitution. "It is therefore only too true that these projects, which for a long time were hatched in silence, projects of which I have always been informed, and which I was reluctant to believe, have finally just now burst forth," the proclamation read. "They are no longer concealing their desire to seize supreme authority, to upset the state, and to become master of its finances." Accusing Pétion, Bonnet, and several other "vile accomplices," the proclamation, signed by Christophe and undersigned by Rouanez, charged these men with trying to "light a civil war." "They betrayed the confidence that I placed in their midst with the assembly of Haiti and want to control its deliberations," Christophe accused. He went on to explain at length how he believed Pétion's faction sought to delay the installation of the assembly to give themselves time to circumvent it, "in order to lay down before [Christophe] an odious constitution." He then issued a grave charge of election tampering against Pétion and company, who Christophe said threatened, intimidated, and manipulated the Hai-tian people living in regions over which they held command:

To better stifle the wishes of the deputies of the parishes of the north and of the first division of the west, they surrounded them with a military force, to try to extract their votes. The Third Demi-brigade, the Eleventh, the Twelfth, and the Thirteenth, coming from Jacmel, are filling the streets of Port-au-Prince and seem to be forming, in the eyes of the intimidated legislators, the apparatus and the tumult of a camp. They are daily threatened with being taken to Léogâne, if they do not agree to sign . . . and to be kept there as hostages, in the event that their municipalities refuse to sanction the infamous constitution that is being prepared for them. In the end, the situation in which these deputies find themselves is nothing other than that of being real prisoners, kept in custody.

Pétion and his faction had also threatened to march, "with arms in their hands, against the peaceful inhabitants of the countryside who cherish their liberty and do not want to submit to the new slavery that is being prepared for them," Christophe wrote, before insisting, "They have, using tactics of terror, or by other instigations, urged the inhabitants of Saint-Marc and Arcahaie to desert their homes and to join their seditious bands."

Amid this conspiracy, rumors arose that Pétion ordered the killing of Black officers who opposed him. Christophe therefore openly asked the Haitian people to rally around him. "Peaceful inhabitants and cultivators, soldiers, who have shed your blood for the freedom that has made you its idolaters, and who have weapons in hand for its defense, rally to my voice!" Christophe ordered. "The sacrilegious want to . . . throw you back into the chains, from which so many of our efforts have freed us. It is time to put an end to their attacks and destroy their plots!" After foreshadowing his own eventual defection from the Republic of Haiti and ascension to president of a separate state in the north, Christophe once more turned to reassuring the Haitian people. "Your salvation, that of the state, my own duty," he wrote, "command me to take the necessary measures for the maintenance of good order. I waited as long as I could." Christophe knew he needed to push back against the idea that he was preparing to undertake a "war of color." He also had to make it clear that he had no problem engaging in physical warfare, if circumstances necessitated it. "I declare, in the face of the whole universe," Christophe said, "that it is not the color [of the man] that I pursue but the factious, the intriguers, those who seek to disturb the good order; these are the enemies we must eradicate!" The mix of heightened severity mingled with the utmost paternal clemency was by this point in his life entirely characteristic of Christophe's oratorical and discursive style. "Peaceful men of all colors, fathers of families who love your happiness, unite against the disturbers of our peace!"

Christophe counseled. Of his enemies, however, Christophe warned, "Let them tremble to think of the means I have at hand to confound them! Let them reflect on the terrible consequences of the civil war, which they have put me in the cruel necessity of undertaking." Even though the deputies who protested the constitution did not send their letter, as such, to Christophe until December 29, it is clear from the above address that by November 24, perhaps on the strength of information relayed to him in person by Lieutenant Doria, on the same day, Christophe had already decided not to accept the outcome of the constitutional proceedings.[11]

On December 27, the councilors of state assembled by Pétion finally completed and signed a new constitution that transformed the Empire of Haiti into the Republic of Haiti. The 1806 constitution was eventually ratified and unveiled to the public on December 28, 1806, but it did *not* name Christophe as president of the newly founded republic. In the *Report Made to the Constituent Assembly by Its Constitutional Committee, in Its Session of December 27, 1806,* signed with the names of Pétion, Cézar Télémaque, Théodat Trichet, Magloire Ambroise, Bruno Blanchet, (Gabriel) David-Troy, Manigat, Bonnet, and (Charles) Lys, the deputies explained, "Entrusted by you, Citizens, to gather together the principles and institutions best suited to establish and ensure the freedom and happiness of our fellow citizens, we come to present to you the result of our work." Before presenting the constitution for the new republic, the deputies stated that the principle that most guided them remained "the separation of powers, since their concentration in one hand is what constitutes and defines despotism." As a result, they proposed to the citizens of the republic the establishment of three separate powers: executive, legislative, and judicial. They also spoke of creating a senate whose members this first time would be elected by the Constituent Assembly and in the future would be selected from among the public functionaries elected by the people. "Understand what advantages must result from this institution," the report stated. "Our laws will no longer be the expression of the whim and the will of an individual always inclined, by his own passions, to separate his particular interest from the general interest." The authors claimed that Haiti's laws would thereafter be "the work of honest and enlightened men . . . subjected to severe scrutiny, and to public discussion." The writers had no use for ambiguity. The creators of this new constitution fired a clear shot against the one created under Dessalines's reign. Stating that "the right to name the public functionaries will belong to the legislative powers," the report's authors declared, "you have not forgotten what produced, under Dessalines, that prerogative to make every appointment, which was one of his usurpations." "All leaders, it is true, do not resemble Dessalines," they admitted before warning, "but in legislation we must rely on principles, and never on men."[12]

Having essentially explained the division of the government into executive, legislative, and judicial branches, inspiration for which they claimed came from the example of the United States, Pétion and company condemned the most popular form of governance at the time, monarchies. Such a singular political formation, they argued, encouraged financial corruption and the co-optation of state money by royal families. If Haiti continued as an empire, "as in monarchies, the public treasury would become the treasury of an individual, [and] corruption would creep into the senate." Not only should the state's main advisers not be members of a royal family, they insisted, but the "executive power" should go by the "modest title of *president*." The person fulfilling that august office should initially be elected for four years and, after that, could be reelected indefinitely if the people so chose.[13]

Pétion and the other signatories then presented the constitution to the public. Not only is Christophe's noticeably absent from among the sixty-four names, but the constitution gave the newly formed Constituent Assembly the power to elect the president of the newly constituted republic. Though this self-designated assembly officially elected Christophe as the republic's first president the same day, according to an account given by the republic's secretary of state Bruno Blanchet, by the twenty-eighth Christophe was already marching toward Port-au-Prince to disrupt the proceedings and ostensibly establish himself as the state's highest authority.[14]

According to another of the signatories, Télémaque, president of the senate, Christophe's professed opposition to the constitution before it became public, stood as proof that he opposed it only because he feared it would not give him singular and "despotic" power. "He is accusing men known for their selflessness and love of freedom of being ambitious and scheming," Télémaque wrote. Christophe used as a "vain pretext" for rebellion, Télémaque charged, "a battalion that quit its garrison because of the mistreatment it received from him, and several musicians who abandoned Fort Marchand, fearing for their lives, following threats made to them after the death of Dessalines." All of this, Christophe framed as "sufficient motive to raise the standard of civil war," the president of the senate concluded. Attacking Christophe's "foreign" birth, already a well-worn tactic, Télémaque told his readers, "Only a foreigner could contemplate in cold blood the horrors [civil war] brings with it; the depths of a Haitian's soul would have been moved, and a Haitian would have at the very least wavered between his ambition and his homeland." Casting further suspicion on Christophe's devotion to Haiti, Télémaque continued, "But General Christophe has just proved to us that there are few foreigners who truly love the country they have adopted, even when this country has showered them with blessings and honors." Télémaque then claimed the "example of Dessalines, who during his reign of three years had done nothing for the people, proved that the constitution could not allow political power to reside with a single man."[15]

Christophe insisted, quite to the contrary, that Pétion's main goal in creating this constitution—which, unlike the 1805 constitution and Louverture's 1801 constitution, declined to name its head of state—remained to seize the reins of the government for himself; and Pétion's goal in encouraging Christophe to travel to Port-au-Prince for the official swearing-in, Christophe feared, constituted a trap designed either to set the conditions for his eventual arrest or to have him outright assassinated. To avoid this fate, Christophe turned against the government the assembly appointed him to lead and directed an army to undertake a siege of Port-au-Prince.[16]

Before resorting to this drastic solution, Christophe issued a proclamation, dated December 18, 1806, from "the head of government to the army of Hayti." In it, Christophe accused "secret agents" of trying to sow division in certain military brigades at the very moment when Christophe had convoked the assembly to work on the much-needed constitution. "It is easy to discern the goals of the enemies of our country," Christophe explained. "While they delay on one side the arrival of the deputies from the south, to have time to plot and prepare the terrain, their emissaries mingle with the troops of the brigades of the first division of the west, to persuade them to desert." Referencing the events Télémaque later accused him of using as a "vain pretext," Christophe continued, "This is how they persuaded the musicians of the Fourth Demi-brigade to quit their colors [drapeaux], and how it could have come to pass that the Third Battalion of the Twenty-Fifth Demi-brigade abandoned its garrison in Mirebalais, despite formal orders from its officers." The level of disorder in the military certainly seemed high, and the southern divisions under the direct command of Division General Pétion appeared threatened by Christophe's ability to lead.

Christophe knew if he wanted to retain the loyalty of the remaining officers and soldiers under his command, he needed to explain in plain terms the actions of the southern military in the wake of the emperor's death, all of which appeared contrary to supporting the election of Christophe as the new head of state. Insubordination was an accusation feared by every military man, and Christophe used that fear to his advantage. "The officers from the Fifteenth Demi-brigade had the audacity to go to those of the Sixteenth and propose to them an uprising against the authority of their leaders and the squandering of the public treasury, according to the report furnished by General Gérin, minister of war," Christophe said. In great contrast, directly appealing to the soldierly hearts and minds of the men he addressed, he spoke of his loyalty to the Haitian army and the many brave battles in which he led them in victory during Haiti's fight for freedom and independence. "Generals and soldiers," Christophe wrote, "you have known me by my conduct since I began my military career. Have I not always exuded the example of subordination and obedience whether I commanded or obeyed? Have I not always resisted the suggestions of the French and their deceptive caresses? Have their offers, their brilliant promises, ever been able to shake my fidelity and make me forget what I owed to my country, to my fellow citizens, to myself?" Recalling the proud moment when he ordered the city of Cap-Français burned to deny Leclerc's entry, Christophe continued, "When I was asked to use my influence to put you back in chains, did you not see me fight, on the contrary, for the preservation of our freedom?" Insisting that Haiti formed the only land of liberty in all the Americas, Christophe told his army forthrightly, "You can only hope for happiness and security in this land, which you knew how to conquer at the cost of your blood: here, true freedom reigns; this is its favorite sojourn. Far from your country, you will find only humiliation and slavery."

Christophe seemed quite aware that the Haitian army, as it had been for Dessalines, could be his salvation just as easily as it could be his downfall. He therefore used that same combination of severity and clemency, topped with more than a little bit of paternalism, to enjoin the officers and soldiers to remain by his side and to fight on his behalf against the southern faction that he said wanted to destroy Haiti by dividing it:

Soldiers of all ranks, whom I have the honor to command, your father, your best friend, wants to reveal to you the perfidious maneuvers that are being plotted against your happiness. Your enemies are those who preach disunity and insubordination to you; they seek to arouse distrust against the government; they desire only trouble and confusion, to indulge in robbery and exercise their profligacy while avoiding the surrender of their money, which a return to peace would force them to produce. Divide and rule, such is the secret of their disastrous policy.

Christophe then gave direct orders to the military to carry out the strike against Port-au-Prince, which took place just two weeks later, beginning on January 1, the third anniversary of Haitian independence. In the meantime, Christophe ordered all the soldiers to "remain under their flags, and not to leave their garrisons, under any pretext, lest they be considered deserters and punished as such." His second and third mandates squared with his tendency to make his military responsible for everything that happened in the locales to which they had been assigned or over which they had command: "I am rendering all the generals, chiefs and corps officers, the commanders of the garrisons, those of the municipalities and the districts, responsible for the execution of the present provision, and command them to employ the most exact supervision to maintain order and discipline among the troops." "Anyone caught inciting the troops to disobedience or desertion . . . whether among the military, among the farmers, or in the towns," he warned, "will be arrested by the generals or commanders of corps or municipalities, who will put them in prison." Christophe ordered this proclamation to be read, published, and posted in public places and then sent to all the division generals and corps and municipal commanders charged with its execution.

While Christophe issued his previous proclamations and addresses from Cap, this one he signed and issued from Fort Henry, which Julien Prévost, the future Comte de Limonade, later explained was at Laferrière, the same site as the future Citadelle Henry.[17]

Just as the pro-Christophe writers Vastey and Chanlatte, like Christophe himself, provided their accounts of the events that eventually led General Christophe to be elevated to "President and Generalissimo of the Forces of the Earth and Seas of the State of Hayti" in a divided country, so too did the most storied writers from the south. Dumesle, for his part, claimed that far from remaining neutral in terms of trying to influence the constitution created by the Constituent Assembly, Christophe repeatedly abused his powers and tried to influence the elections, particularly in the Artibonite. In Dumesle's retelling, despite Christophe's meddling, some of the cities in the Artibonite, namely Saint-Marc, made free choices in selecting their delegates anyway, but the majority of representatives from the northern division, he said, remained absolute partisans of Christophe, "for whom all liberty was contrary to the tranquility of the public." "Driven into the legislature by the secret machinations of Christophe," Dumesle continued, "they proposed to maintain, or rather to legitimize, the power he had usurped by placing the diadem on his head and perpetuating this power by bequeathing it to his descendants." Having been instructed on the "true intentions of the *Pretender*"—a subtle dig that Christophe already wanted to become king—the delegates from the two divisions of the south and second division of the west wanted to have the deliberations moved to the city of Port-au-Prince, where Pétion was the elected representative.

Pétion reportedly proposed the creation of a republic, inspired by the Rousseauian principles he claimed could reunite democratic forms and bring stability to Haiti's governance. Those in the west and the south evidently greeted the plan to form a republic with enthusiasm, Dumesle averred, and so did those from at least some parts of the Artibonite and elsewhere in the northern division. Dumesle recalled that when Pétion appeared before the tribunal to explain the constitutional theory of the new republic, he gave a speech filled with "noble impulses of republicanism, which will endure as long as the Haitian name. He advocated the reign of liberal ideas." Christophe took issue with the deliberations and the constitution, Dumesle said, because he was distressed by Pétion's intention to turn Haiti into a republic, information allegedly relayed to him by "spies." Those Dumesle also referred to as Christophe's "secret agents," and who were admitted into the national representation, installed a faction there, in Dumesle's estimation, led only by the maxim "divide to reign." Dumesle claimed that during the deliberations Christophe's faction, "walking always in the shadows," "consumed precious time with idle discussions, in order to facilitate the usurper's invasion of Port-au-Prince, where he had, in the midst of the carnage, exercised his will over the representatives of the people."[18]

Another writer from the republic more intimately involved in these proceedings, Blanchet, later acting as secretary of state under Pétion, wrote an account of these events that adds further details to the story of what happened from the southern perspective in between the October 17 assassination of Dessalines and Christophe's January 1 military strike, albeit without necessarily bringing clarity. Blanchet unequivocally began by charging that Christophe plainly lit the fires of a civil war. He accused Christophe of not having just been entirely aware of the plot to overthrow Dessalines beforehand, as General Férou had already charged,[19] but also of having directly collaborated with Dessalines's eventual assassins. Blanchet wrote, "After Dessalines's death, in which Christophe cooperated not by arming himself against him, he feared him too much, but by propositions that were skillfully communicated to Generals Pétion and Gérin to rid them of the tyrant, Christophe was provisionally proclaimed chief of the government." In Blanchet's retelling, Pétion and Gérin were not the ones, who, in subsequently defaming Christophe, caused him to become unpopular in the southern and western departments. Instead, inhabitants of those departments viewed as problematic Christophe's ascent to the position of interim head of state because Christophe had been named to that role "against the inclination of the soldiers of the west and south who had not forgotten the atrocities that man committed there in Toussaint's war against Rigaud." It was in fact Pétion, Blanchet claimed, who "thought it politically wise to place a black man at the head of the government, and it must be admitted that Christophe dissimulated so well throughout Dessalines's reign that he no longer seemed to be the same man."

In Blanchet's account, Christophe avoided appearing in Port-au-Prince not because he glimpsed with fear the vision of his own assassination but because he sought to skirt accountability for Dessalines's. "This mistrust came from the fact that he had avoided, under various pretenses, going to Port-au-Prince, where the army, which had done justice to Dessalines, demanded his presence because in different conversations [Christophe] stated he disapproved of the tyrant's death, which he blamed solely on the men of color, even though he had been the first to, in the end, provoke it, insofar as he distinctly let it be known that he desired to have his predecessor's power," Blanchet explained. During this time, Christophe's emissaries in Port-au-Prince informed him that the representatives were working on a constitution to enshrine separation among the different powers and give a "large range" of those powers to the senate. "Christophe, who only wanted Dessalines dead because he feared him and wanted to succeed him in his authority and omnipotence, Christophe unsatisfied with being recognized as head of a free government, unsatisfied with the considerable fortune that he possessed, and with the 24,000 gourdes that he was to receive each year, dissatisfied with a constitution that limited his powers, dissatisfied with the title of president, which he did not find grand enough, marched against us and surprised us on January 1, before the constitution was published," Blanchet concluded.[20]

Although they differed on the specific events leading up to and the reasons for Christophe's opposition to the constitution, it is clear from the turn of events that he did oppose it. On December 24, Christophe began his march on "Port-aux-Crimes," the name Christophean writers like Prévost and Chanlatte consistently used to refer to the capital of the republic. It was on January 1, still en route to Port-au-Prince and having reached its outskirts, that Christophe encountered Pétion's troops in the fields of Sibert (sometimes spelled "Cibert"). Christophe's and Pétion's troops met each other's sights with weapons in hand.[21] Christophe viewed the opposition mounted by Pétion's troops preventing his entrance into the city as usurpation of his powers as the elected president. Rouanez, in his position as secretary of state under Christophe in the north, later complained, "The authors of the late emperor's death, not content with having put him in the grave, wanted, after having vested him with supreme power, to seize power for themselves and engaged in a state of rebellion against legitimately recognized authority." "These men, at the head of whom are Pétion, Gérin, and a few others," Rouanez continued, "do not have the strength of mind to carry their plots very far."[22] Vastey, for his part, marveled at the remarkable transformation that had occurred from October 21, when Pétion and his faction had publicly proclaimed Christophe interim head of state, to January 1, when those same men called him a traitor and defied his authority. "By an inconceivable fatality," Vastey wrote, Christophe, in the eyes of the people of the south, "ceased in this short interval to be what he had been [before] in their own eyes." "A tyrant who had suddenly lost his rights, his virtues, his skill," charged "the very men who three months before had declared and deemed him only one worthy and capable of governing them!" "What a prodigious change!" Vastey exclaimed. "How could anyone . . . so voluntarily take up arms against his authority?"[23] Haitians turning their weapons against one another instead of against a foreign, invading army marked the start of the civil war's transformation from a largely rhetorical "paper war," involving debates over the best form of state governance—a republic or a monarchy[24]—into a physical battle for the soul of Haiti.

—

Sibert is a small village located in the commune of Croix-des-Bouquets in the western department of Haiti, about seven miles from Port-au-Prince. Christophe's army initially bested Pétion's at the bloody battle there, at least according to official accounts published by northern writers. In northern accounts, after being soundly defeated by Christophe's troops, Pétion's fled. On their way back to Port-au-Prince, however, they found themselves trapped in a swamp up to their necks. Christophe knew that he could have besieged that "rebellious city" at this moment. Yet "reflecting on how many conspirators he had left behind, on those who still swarmed in the army, whose incendiary words were not even concealed, and on the horrors that would result from a city taken by storm, he postponed its conquest and ordered his troops to return to their camps," Prévost explained.[25] Although Christophe's troops had not successfully carried out their mission to overthrow the government established in Port-au-Prince, Christophean historians insisted that because they forced Pétion's troops to retreat in humiliation, having obliged them to "leave their tasseled hats on the battlefield, to hasten their escape," this small victory sufficed. Christophe's clemency should therefore remain "a memory that will not soon be erased from the minds of those who were present on the glorious day of January 1, 1807."[26] Using the very best principles of spin, Christophean writers tried to turn what would have looked to any observer like an obvious loss—Christophe retreating from the battlefield—into a touted victory.

Ministers from Pétion's side recalled the Battle of Sibert in a highly divergent way while also proclaiming their defense a success. Blanchet provided the most detailed account of the January 1 battle and those of the latter part of the week. "It was on the Sibert plantation, three leagues from the town, that the first campaign took place," Blanchet explained. "Christophe had already reached Arcahaie when General Pétion was informed of his march." Claiming that Pétion sought not to be the aggressor, "at the news that Christophe was approaching, [Pétion] hoped to fight him outside the city and took his position on the Sibert plantation." Blanchet recalled that Pétion had with him at that time only about twenty-four hundred men, because the troops commanded by General Gérin had already returned to the south after Dessalines's death.

The battle began at eight in the morning and was extremely "vigorous," lasting for two hours. "Our twenty-four hundred men repelled Christophe's eight thousand three times," in Blanchet's recollection, "but because he had fresh troops to constantly oppose us, ours were forced to fall back to Port-au-Prince." In the afternoon, Christophe attacked the city, according to Blanchet, "but he had lost four very precious hours." During those lost hours, Pétion's troops had time to take up more advantageous positions and to establish several barricades. Although "the city was in no way fortified, they repelled Christophe," Blanchet concluded. "In the following days he made a few more attempts, but all were unsuccessful." The Battle of Sibert ended on January 6, when General Gérin belatedly arrived, but just in time, with a portion of the southern troops, while Christophe engaged in a general attack elsewhere, only to lose more ground. So beaten back were Christophe's troops by the seventh that on the morning of the eighth the advance of southern troops forced them to retreat altogether.[27]

In the week following the Battle of Sibert Christophe showed just how well he had studied the art of discursive self-defense. On his way back to Cap, he stopped in the city of Marchand to issue a proclamation to the people and the army. He pleaded once more his own reluctance to go to war with Pétion's faction and reminded the crowd that before engaging in combat, he "revealed the perfidious plots that a handful of wicked people dared to foment against your freedom. These men, strangers to all human feeling, forced me, despite myself, to make war on them," Christophe lamented. The level of betrayal exhibited by Pétion was not an outlier, Christophe warned. He accused Pétion of previously betraying General Louverture, who had given him a superior rank, when he rallied behind General Rigaud during Saint-Domingue's civil war. Pétion then abandoned Rigaud when he rallied to the French who came to fight them, until his own life was in danger, after which he switched to Dessalines's side and joined the *armée indigène*. Christophe went on to accuse Pétion and his current faction of not only having "massacred" Dessalines but having killed more than thirty superior officers simply because they were "black and intelligent."

The next passage of the proclamation is crucial. It addressed the supposed "white massacres" that were by that time a common charge against Dessalines. "They blamed the emperor, as well as the blacks, for the massacre of the whites; however, to whom do we owe the relentlessness of that cruel butchery, if not to those barbarians?" Christophe asked. This was an allusion to the fact that some of the first alleged executions happened in the southern city of Jérémie at the hands of the men formerly known as the *hommes de couleur,* or free people of color, who allegedly exercised their own unsparing revenge against those white inhabitants they blamed for the numerous drownings of officers and citizens of color during the Leclerc-Rochambeau expedition. "May all the women and even the children disappear," Christophe accused the men of the south of having declared. He went on to say that these southerners openly decided, "It's time we replaced the whites, and enjoyed the fruits of the labor of the blacks!" The future king then affirmed that he tried to save some of those white French inhabitants whom he considered either innocent of the crimes with which the *hommes de couleur* charged them or potentially useful, in his eyes, to the budding state. "Did not I spend my days risk-ing my own life, as well as those of my wife and my children, by giving refuge, in my house, to some of these unfortunates, who arrived there to escape proscription and death?" Christophe asked. In case of any linger-ing doubt over whom to blame for the "massacres," Christophe averred, "Everyone knows that in the two divisions of the south and the second of the west, the men of color threatened the emperor that they would withdraw themselves from his authority, if he did not exterminate even white women and children." Christophe essentially absolved Dessalines of having ordered the so-called massacres while perhaps unwittingly con-demning the emperor for not doing enough to stop them or at the very least for not resisting the call to extend them to other parts of the empire. Christophe then reiterated that he intentionally stayed away from the deliberations of the assembly, precisely so that he would not be accused of trying to influence it. Yet the deputies from the south and the second division of the west, "using a bad faith argument of which they alone are capable, tripled the number of deputies of the two divisions of the south and of the second of the west and thereby obtained a numerical majority, independently of the terror they inspired by armed force."

The people of Haiti communicated primarily by letters brought either on horseback or on ships traveling around the coastal ports from penin-sula to peninsula, but most had probably never traveled beyond the limits of the towns or parishes of their births. Christophe took this occasion therefore to provide some explanations to the people about the current governmental structure of Haiti: with western, southern, and northern provinces. This explanation, he said, would help the people better under-stand the inappropriateness (and questionable legality) of the overwhelm-ing majority the south gave itself in terms of deputies.

First, the number of representatives did not match the number of par-ishes in the south and the second division of the west combined. "The first division of the south contains the parishes of Aquin, Saint-Louis, Cavaillon, Les Cayes, Torbec, Port-Salut, Côteaux, and Tiburon," Chris-tophe said. "The second division contains L'Anse-à-Veau, Petit-Trou des Baradaires, Corail, Jérémie, Abricots, Dame-Marie, Anse d'Ainault, and Saint-Michel de Miragoâne." On the other side, "The second division of the west is made up of Croix-des-Bouquets, Port-au-Prince, Léogâne, Grand-Goâve, Petit-Goâve, Jacmel, Baynet, and Marigot." "What forms in sum twenty-four parishes for these three divisions, which should have been the total number of appointed deputies, one from each, since this was the mode of election followed in the divisions of the north and the first of the west," Christophe continued. "Far from having followed this fair rule, they tripled the number of these deputies and employed, more-over, all that is repugnant to even the vilest intrigue, to circumvent the deputies of the north and to buy their votes." That was the sequence of events that led to the Battle of Sibert, which, unbeknownst to all involved at the time, marked the start of independent Haiti's first civil war, one that lasted for thirteen long years.

To answer the question why he did not take Port-au-Prince and claim his rightful position as president with weapons in hand, Christophe offered his audience a simple explanation. In these remarks the future king exhibited his characteristic severity coupled with distinct care. He needed to remain careful with his words as he proclaimed what must have felt like a strange and fatal victory over other Haitians:

> These unworthy men forced me to draw the sword from the sheath to bring them to their senses. I marched against Pétion; I cut his army to pieces; a feeling of pity stopped me at the gates of Port-au-Prince, which I was about to enter, when I thought of the misfortunes to which this rebellious city was about to be delivered, that city where the blood of so many true friends of liberty has been shed. . . . I recoiled in horror at the sight of the Haitian blood that was about to be spilled. Despite the infinite crimes with which the rebels have inundated our country, I wanted to leave them a moment to reflect on their actions; let them take advantage of this while there is still time!

Christophe finished by evoking the language of the avenger of the Americas that also marked Dessalines's famous April 1804 proclamation. "I have the sword in my hand," Christophe stated, "I will preserve the freedom of our country, in spite of Pétion and his adherents; I will restore the tranquility and power of the law; and I will not allow myself any rest until I have seen happiness multiply among our fellow citizens."[28]

The differing accounts of how Haiti's civil war began, and who was at fault, fast became characteristic of this period in Haitian history, one where writers from the north and south consistently sought to shape international opinion as much as local and regional judgments about who was the aggressor and therefore ultimately to blame for the internecine conflict unhappily causing Haitians from the north, west, and south to view one another as enemies. As both Christophe and Pétion became simultaneous presidents over different regions of Haiti, it became even more important for them to try to shape the history of how the great schism was to be written, then and in the future. Each represented the other and his faction as having divided Haiti to the point of destroying it. The year 1807 would see several arduous military campaigns in the bloody contest for power over post-Dessalines Haiti. By that time, both Christophe and Pétion had been officially sworn in as presidents over the northern and southern parts of the country, separately.

—

Christophe returned to the north immediately after the storied Battle of Sibert and began the work of organizing the state he intended to form, with its capital in the city of Cap. Addressing the "inhabitants" and "cultivators" from his home under the title of "Leader of the Government of Haiti," on January 22, 1807, he adopted the stature and tone of a head of state when he declared that he wanted to open commerce between Haiti and different nations as soon as possible. He observed that flags from many different nations already frequented Haitian ports, and he therefore encouraged the inhabitants and cultivators to continue producing the products needed for export. "Devote yourself therefore without reserve to the work of farming," Christophe wrote. "All your hopes can be found in labor, without which there is neither enjoyment nor security for you." "May all the cultivators assemble on the plantations to which they have been assigned," he continued, "let them no longer fear being disturbed there; let the inspectors and the commanders redouble their surveillance, to prevent vexations, idleness, and vagrancy, and to encourage the work of harvesting."[29] One month after issuing this stately address, Christophe officially took office as "President and Generalissimo of the Forces of the Earth and Seas of the State of Hayti."

The constitution that officially appointed Christophe to the presidency was issued on February 17, 1807. Even though it made Haiti a state rather than a republic or a kingdom, Vastey admitted it "contained principles more monarchical than republican"; and he proclaimed the constitution's "royal glow" wholly "suitable to the tempestuous time and circumstances in which it was created." Vastey explained that a council of state composed of generals and notable citizens from the northern province and the first division of the western province assembled in Cap to create this constitution. Importantly, Christophe and his ministers used the February 17 constitution's ratification by twenty-nine of Haiti's most important officials to argue that the document made him president over the entire country, not just the north. "This council stipulated for the three provinces of the north, west, and south," Vastey explained. In other words, the council acted on behalf of the delegates from the missing provinces or departments—that is, the south and the second division of the west. "The government took the title of State of Hayti, and its first magistrate that of President and Generalissimo of the Forces of the Earth and Seas," he continued. "This office was for life and the president had the right to choose a successor among the generals only. Legislative power was vested in a council of state." According to Vastey, "generals and magistrates" from the south and southwest, including the section in Grand'Anse where Jean-Baptiste Duperrier, called Goman, commanded, came together also and equally stipulated for the three provinces of the north, the west, and the south. Yet back on the other side of the island, without even pretending to have sought the participation of any members from the northern province or first division of the west, Pétion was named the president of the Republic of Haiti in March 1807.[30]

Pétion became president of the republic under the pretext that Christophe refused to appear in the north to assume the office. Article 107 of the December 1806 constitution stated that the president, "before entering into the exercise of his functions, shall take the following oath: 'I swear to faithfully fulfill the office of president of Haiti, and to maintain with all my power the constitution.'" "If the president has not taken the above oath within a period of fifteen days from the day of his election, he is deemed to have refused," the next article stated. "The legislature will proceed to a new election, and the senate in such a case will proceed in the same way."[31] It is true that Christophe refused to appear in Port-au-Prince. The reason for his refusal was up for dispute.

According to Peltier, the editor of L'ambigu, explaining to Britain's minister of foreign affairs how the civil war came about (based on information he received from both Pétion's and Christophe's camps), "in November 1806, as soon as they realized that General Christophe did not care to be their instrument," Pétion's faction "formed the plan to assassinate him like Dessalines." "They called him to Port-au-Prince, under the pretense of accepting the constitution which they wanted to make for themselves under his name," Peltier reported, "and to be more sure of succeeding in their projects, they summoned to Port-au-Prince twice as many deputies from their quartiers as they were authorized to summon there."[32] Christophe, determined to become president, took the role he felt he rightly earned quite seriously. He began immediately reorganizing every branch of public service while insisting the section of the country under Pétion's de facto control remained under his own.[33]

Christophe announced to the Haitian people his ascent to the highest authority of the land in an address he issued the same day he made public the "Constitution of the State of Haiti," on February 17. Using his new title, "President and Generalissimo of the Forces of the Earth and Seas of the State of Hayti," Christophe explained the new laws, on the one hand, and how they came to be, on the other. "Light has begun to shine upon us, and a beneficent constitution is defeating the schemes and plots of which you were going to be the victims," he declared. "At last, a wise code suitable to our mores, our climate, our customs, has, so to speak, come out of the chaos, to fix once again the destiny of Haiti."[34]

Among its differences with the December 1806 constitution issued by the Constituent Assembly, which set up a republic, Christophe's version allowed only Catholicism to be publicly professed and mandated the creation of schools. With this constitution, Christophe, while reiterating that slavery remained forever abolished, sought at the same time to reassure Haiti's colonial neighbors in the West Indies and the imperial powers back in western Europe that the new Haitian government did not intend to disrupt slavery in their realms.[35]

Christophe knew from his time working under Dessalines, when the United States under Jefferson issued its infamous trade embargo, that the international import and export business remained tenuous where Haiti was concerned. At the unveiling of the constitution, Christophe therefore stressed the necessity of foreign trade. "Essentially commercial, because of its position, and its type of manufactures," he said, "it is necessary that [Haiti's] equity, as much as its commodities, attract the tradesmen of all the peoples of the earth." Christophe went on to note that "commerce" could be for Haitians the source of "every type of riches." He further observed that after religion, morals, agriculture, and commerce the new State of Haiti under his leadership would also need to organize and maintain a strong and threatening army. "The enemy is watching our movements and observes our processes," Christophe told his people. "The affection of our friends is still without any guarantee!" Evoking the Haitian war of independence and the civil war that recently disrupted the country, in the same breath, he averred,

Left to ourselves, all our resources are in our own midst; they are among you, soldiers, who are ready to shed your blood generously, rather than yield to a prideful enemy, the price of your courage, your freedom! They are among you, inhabitants and industrious farmers, from whom the state awaits its wealth; it is your union, your submission to the laws that must form the cement and the bond of our independence.

Let those who will want to maintain political relations or enjoy the advantages of our commerce find an equitable reciprocity; we only offer death and battles to the others. At the same time as these ideas occupy us, let us never forget that weapons alone are the guarantee of free peoples.[36]

Two days later, Christophe issued another formal proclamation, this one with an exuberant opening: "The constitution at last has just been published!" But the next sentences implied the far more damning consequences of the new laws. "The traitors and rebels of the west and the south will no longer have any pretext to support their claims," Christophe declared. "They have misled a large number of inhabitants, whom they have drawn into their party; they have forbidden these men, who are more worthy of our pity than our blame, all communications with us, and have deprived them of all means of enlightening themselves on the events taking place around them." To stop the revolt and punish those who brought it about, Christophe declared in the first article, "Pétion and Gérin are outside the law [*hors la loi*], as heads of the conspiracy and rebels against the government." Article 2 declared their accomplices and propagators "outside the law" as well; article 3 offered full and complete amnesty for all those who did not immerse themselves in the revolt but were only brought to it "by force"; and finally, with article 4, the government promised protection to all those who ceased "to rebel."[37] Christophe's overtures to the south did not produce the desired effect. Few from the south defected to the north at that time. Still, Christophe let it be known that as the new president of the State of Haiti he wanted to reunite all Haitians under one leader, and therefore to end the civil war before it could really begin.

—

Christophe had observed under Dessalines the importance of a state-run newspaper to control flows of information. May 7, 1807, marked the debut of the new state-run newspaper now seated in Cap and titled *Official Gazette of the State of Hayti*. In the very first article, Chanlatte, the editor of the weekly newspaper, provided the logic for the paper's change of name and a description of its future contents:

The insatiable ambition of certain characters who, under the mask of modesty and disinterestedness, tend only toward the devouring of the coffers of the nation and to the invasion of the powers of the state, having interrupted the circulation of the *Political and Commercial Gazette of Haiti*, the desire to be useful to my fellow citizens, to inform them of the acts of government, of the entry and exit of ships, to advise them of the various changes that our commercial relations are undergoing, and of political events, both external and internal, encouraged me to begin this paper, which will henceforth be known as the *Official Gazette of the State of Hayti*.[38]

This new *Gazette* became of invaluable use to Christophe, his administrators, and his military officials when they returned from the cities of Gonaïves and Saint-Marc, the next battlefields of the civil war.

According to Christophean chroniclers, civil warfare commenced again throughout the spring and fall of 1807 when, under Pétion's mandate to burn, pillage, and kill, General Dartiguenave arrived in the city of Grande-Rivière to excite revolt among its citizens, in the process setting everything on fire. Christophe's army flew to the scene and arrested Dartiguenave, whose death Christophe subsequently ordered. Afterward, Pétion engaged General Cangé to bring the western province to insurrection, but General Besse had become wise to these designs and stopped Cangé's rebellion, after which Christophe's men put him to death as well. Pétion's attacks on land not yet having been successful, Pétion then tried to attack by sea. In the month of September, setting his eyes on the northern peninsula, he tried to raise to insurrection the Ninth Regiment of Port-de-Paix. Pétion brought to his aid one of his best generals, André Juste Borno Lamarre, who had a considerable army under his command. Pétion gave clear orders: "Destroy everything and do all possible harm, to seize the town of Môle [Saint-Nicolas] and to fortify it." During this time, Christophe fell ill. As a result of his brief incapacitation, Lamarre made some key advances.[39]

Christophe continually received news of southern attempts to encroach on the State of Haiti's territories, as well as various setbacks, while he recovered from his illness. Determined not to see the city of Port-de-Paix or any of its environs fall into the hands of the enemy, Christophe got out of bed on the morning of September 5, when he reportedly should have remained in a state of convalescence, and left the city of Cap for the city of Borgne. Borgne lies on the coast of the same peninsula as Port-de-Paix, but slightly to the southeast. After spending the night in Borgne, the next day Christophe took the route to Port-de-Paix, where he arrived in the afternoon. The troops reacted with elation to see their commander in chief seemingly in good health standing before them. As was his custom, Christophe quickly "put the army under review" and gave his orders for the attack. That same day, General Magny, to whom Christophe issued orders to leave for Gros-Morne, reunited his troops with Christophe's état-major (general military staff) and began the ascent up the mountains of Port-de-Paix. Magny's troops successfully "toppled" and forced to disperse all the rebels they found on their way.

Because General Paul Romain was ill, Christophe gave command over the rest of the military strike to General Brave. Once the different regiments and battalions had their orders, on the morning of the eighth General Brave, with General Besse, began the mission to neutralize the southern rebels and take over the position of Démaho. Situated in the mountains of Moustique, Démaho was historically home to many maroons in the colonial and revolutionary eras. Northern soldiers considered this camp, sitting on the summit of the plantation bearing its name, "fortified by nature," because it was surrounded by woods, deep pits, and numerous ravines. Despite the many "outposts" and "ambushes" that the rebels placed along the route to make the ascent of Christophe's men more difficult, by the tenth his soldiers not only reached the camp but took it over entirely, using their leader's favorite wartime tactic: they burned it to the ground.

Lamarre, quite adept at navigating the mountains, managed to escape, and so the fighting continued in that region until September 20, when Christophe's troops soundly claimed their victory. A military secretary for the north wrote that September 20, 1807, emerged as a "memorable day . . . when eight battalions defeated twenty-one of those of the rebels, still entrenched, and who occupied the most advantageous positions."

Lamarre, for his part, also claimed victory in the battle despite the obvious defeat. Newspapers in the south repeated Lamarre's falsified claims of victory. Lamenting once more the aggression that brought Pétion's troops into northern territory, a Christophean secretary said he could only hope that these "victims," whom Pétion and his faction "are driving so relentlessly into battle and death," might one day "recognize in them the true enemies of their freedom and existence."[40]

As warfare raged on northern territory due to the arrival of troops from the south by sea, the southern republic's attacks on land continued. Pétion's soldiers simultaneously attempted to lay siege to the city of Mirebalais, very close to the southern border, about thirty-four miles from Port-au-Prince. Christophe's men once more vigorously repelled these southern soldiers, but in Vastey's retelling, Pétion did have some small if fleeting successes. Initially, Pétion "seized the city of Gonaïves through treachery," but eventually Christophe's army had him "chased out after he looted and burned the unfortunate inhabitants." Pétion's aggressions continued, bringing bloodshed to nearly every major city of the north. In October of the same year, southern troops attempted to lay siege with a huge number of soldiers to the city of Saint-Marc. Yet victory continued to elude Pétion's strivings. He ended up having to retreat from Saint-Marc, just as he had from so many other northern cities.

In the northern government's official report of the Battle at Saint-Marc, Christophe's secretary J. H. Raphaël described this battle in painstaking detail, including the many injuries suffered by northern soldiers. Christophe's men had informed him that rebels from Port-au-Prince threatened the city of Saint-Marc, the largest parish on the northwestern boundary between the State and the Republic of Haiti. To repel their efforts, Christophe sent the Twenty-Seventh Battalion, two artillery companies, and a squadron of cavalry from the Second Regiment, with "mounted guard," to the city. On October 23, at seven in the morning, he left the city of Cap to take the route to Saint-Marc, stopping over in Gonaïves to rest for the night. A consummate soldier and general, Christophe did not intend to direct events from afar or sit back and let his troops see all the action. At break of day on the twenty-fourth, Christophe continued to the impending battlefields of Saint-Marc. He arrived that afternoon, and without taking any rest or even descending from his horse, he visited every post in the city and gave orders to prepare for the attack from Pétion's men.

On the twenty-fifth, having become aware that troops from the south stood in position on the Pivert plantation, "within good shotgun range of the city," Christophe's men gathered on Saint-Marc's Place d'Armes to prepare for battle. They began their mission to defeat the rebels and secure Saint-Marc at eleven in the morning. The battle took place over several days and extended into the surrounding hamlet of Montrouis. October 25 saw the fiercest fighting. Over a period of six hours Christophe's men captured many prisoners, "several colonels, lieutenant colonels, and other officers, as well as a large number of soldiers." "The rebels left a battlefield strewn with the corpses of their people," Raphaël reported. The fighting might have ended much earlier, and definitively that day, but "nightfall favored the flight of the rebels," Raphaël wrote. "Without this darkness, their discomfiture would have been greater." By the twenty-seventh, Christophe's troops declared victory once more, "Saint-Marc being happily delivered."[41] Raphaël offered a reason for Christophe's continued victories. He said that southern leaders did not fight alongside their troops. "In the end, we understood that their troops fought alone, since their leaders never appeared," he explained.

Raphaël did not limit his criticism to painting Pétion and the other generals of his army as cowards who made war from afar. Writers from the State of Haiti repeatedly pointed out Pétion's responsibility for the physical warfare. It was his army that encroached on northern territory with armed troops, after all. "The friend of humanity, the man who loves his country and who is subject to its laws, wonders what is the goal of the rebel Pétion, in exposing to massacre the pitiful pawns of his ambition?" Raphaël asked. "What would have been the destiny of these unfortunates whom the fate of war has caused to fall into the hands of the president, if his clemency had not spared them, even though they had just pointed their arms at his own person?" Clemency and severity, war and peace, this was the high-sounding chord that Christophe's secretaries wanted the pitch of his voice to reach.

Christophe returned home to Cap on November 7 and declared undisputed victory. The people of the capital feted him with such exuberance and brilliance that it is hard not to see these extravagant celebrations as presages of the even more magnificent ones that Christophe later organized as the king of Haiti. Christophe did not arrive home in the capital until four in the morning on that day. Weary from the road and with a mind still troubled by bloody battle scenes, he learned that the civil and military corps, as well as the inhabitants of Cap, awaited him at the gates of the city with laurels to compliment him on his victory, hoping to glimpse his safe return. Christophe, a bit stunned at the ardent display of overt affection, but not in the mood to celebrate, "hastened to escape the acclamations of the people" and "left the major road and entered the city by side roads." Yet "he could not avoid the praises and blessings of the people, who no sooner noticed that his grace had already arrived than they traveled with him to his palace, in the midst of a crowd while the air resounded with cries of *Vive Monseigneur, le Président!* repeated thousands of times," Raphaël reported. That night the city glowed with a general illumination whose brightness reportedly equaled the ardor and admiration of the people for their president.

These battles were not to be Christophe's or the State of Haiti's last.

Pétion remained obstinate and determined, and the warfare between the two sides of Haiti lasted throughout 1807. Northern writers and administrators continued to express bewilderment as they faced Pétion's various attempts to capture northern cities and especially his repeated attempts on Môle Saint-Nicolas. "He is leading a strong army from the south, in the heart of the north; his troops are entirely defeated," Vastey declared in disbelief, before ending his narration of that combat with a statement conceived more as a reproach than a lament: "How many unfortunate Haitians have been decimated in these disastrous campaigns, victims of the ambition of Pétion!"[42]

Some of the foreign witnesses of the civil war, namely British and U.S. merchants and soldiers, agreed that Pétion was the aggressor. Writing on September 5, 1807, a British captain named Thomas Goodall on the ship *Young Roscius,* arrived in Portsmouth and gave a letter with an account of the civil war to Peltier. Peltier summarized this letter as part of a report he transmitted to British officials in his attempt to convince them that Christophe stood on the cusp of victory. "Pétion's attempt against S[aint]-Marc and Gonaïves in May and June, having completely failed," Peltier wrote, "the rebels of the southern part attempted a new expedition in July. Pétion's flotilla of barges and schooners left Port-au-Prince on July 6 under the orders of Admiral Panayoti, and arrived before Port-de-Paix, located 24 leagues from Cap, on July 9 of the same month; they had 1,000 men landed commanded by General Lamarre." Describing Christophe's eventual victory, Peltier, using information derived from Goodall and other eyewitnesses, seconded Raphaël's report: "At the same time as the Port-de-Paix expedition was going on, there was another expedition being directed from Port-au-Prince against Saint-Marc, under the orders of Pétion himself."[43] While foreigners also reported Pétion's repeated losses, during this time Christophe learned some surprising information about Pétion's faction, which only encouraged him to further consider his opponent in the south an artful traitor, the bane of Haiti's existence, and the architect of its disastrous civil war.

—

Writers from the State of Haiti insisted that some of Pétion's men, growing wise to his dangerous ambition, had in reality turned on him. Vastey noted specifically that some of the generals who helped Pétion plot against Dessalines had realized their error and began to speak out against him. Magloire, senator and general, was the first to do so, and became Pétion's first victim. For his agitations against the president, Pétion ordered Magloire assassinated in Jacmel, along with a group of his followers. Other executors of Pétion's orders, such as Bonnet and David-Troy, then enriched themselves on all that Magloire left behind. Soon after, Yayou, also a senator and a general, and a dear friend of Pétion's, "his henchman, the blind instrument of his passions, whom he had nicknamed the Brutus of Hayti, suffered the same fate as Magloire," Vastey said. "He was assassinated at Fort Campan in the mountains of Léogâne, by satellites sent by Pétion." After this, the assassinations accumulated. The commissioner of war in Port-au-Prince and many others were "sacrificed to the ambition of that new Robespierre, who selected and then struck down men with the haughtiest heads only to assert his authority over their bloody corpses," averred Vastey.[44]

Goodall, of the *Young Roscius,* reported similar information to Peltier concerning defections from Pétion's side, but with more precise details. Christophe seemed to have some involvement in the attempted defections of some of these men to his side. "The black General Yaou [*sic*], Pétion's 3rd highest ranking general, but who had grown favorable to President Christophe, sought to stir up Pétion's troops, and commit them to joining the plan he had made to reunite with 3,000 of Christophe's troops, who were on a strip of land about five leagues from Port-au-Prince, and thus to deliver the town and Pétion's troops over to Christophe," Goodall reported. "This plot having failed, General Yaou only had time to save himself fleeing at full gallop with his officers and aides-de-camp." At first, Yayou went to Jacmel, where General Ambroise Magloire commanded, but was allegedly secretly favorable to President Christophe. Initially, on further reflection, Yayou and Magloire might have been interested in reaching an amnesty with Pétion, but "the negotiations dragged on in Léogâne, and then there was the news of the lack of success of the Port-de-Paix expedition, which convinced Ambroise Magloire and Yaou to completely lift their masks." Eventually, the two men outright opposed Pétion's leadership: "By August they were encamped with their corps in Jacmel and Léogâne, where they held in check all the troops from Port-au-Prince."[45] Peltier believed that based on the factions growing in Pétion's republic, coupled with Christophe's recent victories in the north, the reunification of Haiti was imminent. Perhaps it is for this reason that Peltier, bolstered with Goodall's account, found the moment opportune to ask the British government to furnish Christophe's troops with weapons.

Though both Christophe and Pétion tried to win the exiled French journalist to their side, in April 1807 Christophe and Peltier reached an agreement whereby the latter officially accepted appointment as agent for the State of Haiti under the title of its chargé d'affaires. Peltier's main duty was to facilitate Haiti's relationship with the British government for the purposes of commerce but above all to secure recognition of Haiti's independence.[46] Previously, Peltier had tried to secure recognition for Haiti under Dessalines. His main correspondent under the emperor had been Alexis Dupuy, secretary of state at the time. Rouanez, the new secretary of state under Christophe, confirmed in a missive he sent to Peltier on April 1, 1807, that he received the correspondence between Dupuy and

Peltier and that Christophe charged him with responding and renewing the relationship. Rouanez, writing on Christophe's behalf, reiterated that the main purpose of Peltier's employment constituted securing recognition of Haiti's independence from the king of England. "The recognition of the independence of this state by the English government would perhaps induce other nations to imitate its example," urged Rouanez, "but the advantage of such an act would be all in favor of England," he did not fail to add.[47]

The Haitian government knew that although England had something it wanted—official recognition and continued trade—Haitians also had something that England wanted: coffee. In March 1808, Peltier wrote to Robert Stewart, the Viscount Castlereagh and Britain's secretary for war and the colonies, to explain that recognizing Haitian independence on the terms of a treaty of friendship proposed by Christophe would further encourage the already lucrative commerce between the two countries. The chart Peltier sent to Castlereagh presented an extensive list of all items imported to Haiti from Great Britain. Peltier observed that more than eighty ships had left for Haiti from ports as diverse as London, Liverpool, Bristol, Whitehaven, and Guernsey. These ships carried various kinds of items for export: "fine and common linen, all kinds of cloth, cashmere . . . silk, every genre of cotton stuffs, stockings, muslins, *batistes* [a very fine fabric], arms, saddlery, Birmingham ironwork, gallons, hats, cannon powder, jewelry, handkerchiefs, stationery, books, carriages, harnesses, furniture, glassware, salt fish, cod, herring, sardines, prize wine, port, merchandise from India, etc." Haitians paid for such goods in the most valuable currency they had, not sugar, but coffee. Though Saint-Domingue had been the most profitable sugar colony in the world, post-independence Haiti's main export crop emerged as coffee.

Part of the reason for the dominance of coffee plantations in independent Haiti had to do with how the revolution had unfolded. The majority of plantations that went up in flames were sugar plantations. Although coffee production did not rise as high as in 1789, which is to say seventy-six thousand pounds, or thirty-eight thousand gold tons per year, at the time Peltier submitted the chart, coffee exports were estimated at seventy thousand pounds, of which sixty thousand were destined for England alone. The other ten thousand went to the United States (through contraband due to the embargo) and various other islands in the Caribbean.[48]

Although Christophe remained disappointed about the U.S. embargo, he knew the value the State of Haiti brought to its relationship with Great Britain, and he touted the protection the Haitian military could afford to British sailors coasting in Caribbean waters. If Great Britain officially recognized Haitian independence and formally entered into a trade agreement, "its commerce and its navy would always find in our ports a government willing to offer them every kind of hospitality and preference over the subjects of other nations," Rouanez told Peltier. "The Haitian people have not the least intention to disturb or bring trouble to the other nations that have possessions in their vicinity, such that they have made it one of the principal articles of their new constitution, and it would be desirable that the English frequent our ports to be able to judge for themselves the consideration they will find here, if these links begin to form, and they would only become more firmly established and increasingly consolidated."[49]

To further "consolidate" their mutually beneficial relationship, Christophe formally proposed a treaty to Castlereagh, which he hoped would be submitted for the British king's approval. There was one huge caveat: without the explicit recognition of Haiti's independence and Christophe as the country's singular head of state, all propositions for the treaty with Great Britain were null. The fact that France still claimed "Saint-Domingue" as its colony did not present an obstacle, in Peltier's estimation, or at least so he argued. Extolling Christophe's leadership, Peltier wrote, "Today [Christophe] is a very different leader from his two predecessors, a chief such as England might desire to herself place at the head of the affairs of Haiti." He added that "General Christophe" was "English by nation," before arguing that trade with Haiti on the terms proposed by Christophe would be wholly advantageous to Britain:

> You have on no part of the globe either the hope or the prospect of a trade so advantageous or so extensive.
> This trade can bring you as much money as that of all your colonies together, and it will cost you neither government nor administration nor an army to assure you of these advantages. A treaty, a resident minister, and three consuls will suffice.[50]

Christophe knew that part of Great Britain's hesitation to recognize Haitian independence was related to the ongoing civil war. Peltier, therefore, had to attack the question of nonrecognition from both the commercial angle, as above, and from a far more political angle. With Captain Goodall's report front of mind, Peltier tried to convince the British government that the battle over Saint-Marc had been the civil war's last. "As to the objections which may have been made hitherto on account of the civil war, . . . the revolt of Pétion and his adherents was on the point of being terminated at the departure of Capt. Goodall who left Haiti 30 days ago."[51] Despite claiming that the war with Pétion had all but formally ended, and offering Goodall's report as proof, Peltier did acknowledge that Christophe needed assistance in a different war, the one with France. French troops, recall, still occupied Santo Domingo, in the east under General Ferrand.

Peltier submitted a formal request to the British government to supply

President Christophe with guns, ammunition, and other arms so that he could drive out Great Britain's biggest enemy: the French. "As these sorts of Petitions are ordinarily referred from the Privy Council to His Majesty's Secretary of State, I dare to beg your Lordship to be good enough to approve this petition and to grant its object, under the consideration that I am having sent out this month, for General-President Christophe, three ships, . . . which are exporting to Haiti more than 80,000 pounds of British manufactures, of which there is not a single gun," Peltier concluded.[52] While Great Britain certainly appeared disposed to help Haiti rid the island of French presence, since they were embroiled in the Napoleonic Wars, it was far more loath to intervene in the civil war between Christophe and Pétion.

Before Peltier's submission of this petition, he had defended Christophe against the charge that he was not the island's true sovereign. Writing in response to a different British minister's rejection of Christophe's overtures for friendly relations with Great Britain, Peltier's indignance shone through:

> Mr. Cooke tells me that I must know that the Government can take no action while it does not know who is the leader of Saint-Domingue. I am surprised that the British Government still affects today this ignorance about the man who is the head of Saint-Domingue, public acknowledgment, the dispatches of admirals, the relations established, the papers both printed and handwritten that we have handed over. . . . Even the Colonial Office, have informed the Government that the leader of Saint-Domingue is the General and President Henry Christophe, that there is no other; that there can be no other.

Asking who would be the leader of "Saint-Domingue," if not Christophe, Peltier destroyed the notion that Bonaparte, emperor of France, could be considered the island's veritable ruler, while also dismissing the idea that General Ferrand, still occupying the eastern side of the island from Santo Domingo, could alternatively be considered a legitimate commander. Burying the lede a bit, Peltier addressed the real sentiment behind the British minister's reservation, the notion that Pétion constituted Haiti's rightful, or at least a rival, head of state. Condemning the president of the Haitian republic, Peltier informed the British minister, "Pétion did not raise the standard of revolt until two months after appointing General Christophe as leader; and after having then unsuccessfully attempted to assassinate him." Peltier then echoed another Christophean talking point by observing that the area over which Christophe ruled remained far more extensive than the southern and western sections over which Pétion claimed to rule. "General Christophe controls all the strongholds and the best military positions of the island. His authority is unrivaled in the north and west, from Fort-Dauphin to the gates of Port-au-Prince, that is to say in ¾ of the island," Peltier insisted. "He has three times the number of troops as Pétion, who has no means except to stir up insurrections through the Mulatto cabal, who are repressed on the spot." "Pétion was forced to retreat to Port-au-Prince last September, fearful for his own life," Peltier remarked, before concluding, "To say that we do not know who is the leader of Saint-Domingue, because there are some revolts, is almost to say that we do not know who is the leader of England when there are seditious gatherings in Ireland or thieves in Hounslow Heath." Once more appealing to the *Englishness* of the president of the State of Haiti, juxtaposed with the implied *Frenchness* of the president of the republic, Peltier charged Pétion with having created "a French-style republic." Peltier concluded his letter with an appeal to emotion. "As for me, you will have rendered my position with General Christophe very embarrassing," he said of potentially having to relay British rejection to northern Haiti's president. "I have always transmitted to him verbatim the hopes and encouragements you have given me from time to time about his case," he wrote. "If today I have to destroy all these hopes with the stroke of a pen, I will be deeply affected." He finished by urging the British government to respect "the nobility and dignity" of Christophe's character and to accept "these brilliant and magnificent offers he makes to you as a great man and as an Englishman."[53]

Christophe had already proven himself a warrior, a general, and a head of state on the island of Haiti, in many different circumstances. Now he found himself on the world stage and had the opportunity to try his hand at diplomacy. Arguing on his own behalf, in February 1808, Christophe instructed Rouanez to write and send a *"mémoire,"* or long-form treatise, to Castlereagh, by way of Peltier. Skirting the question posed by Pétion's existence as the president of the republic, Rouanez concentrated on the war that Christophe waged silently against Ferrand, by way of supporting the Santo Dominguan general Don Juan Ramírez.

Rouanez opened his entreaty to Castlereagh, first, by professing his president's loyalty to Great Britain and his desire to maintain an intimate commercial and political relationship with England. "The intention and the goal of all the steps taken by President Henry Christophe, has always been to put, by way of a treaty, the island of Haiti, formerly Saint-Domingue, under the protection of the English Government." Turning to the robust and ongoing trade between the two nations, Rouanez continued, "The large consumption of the inhabitants of Haiti and the quantity of [British] foodstuffs which is exploited in this island, especially in the North, can offer advantages to trade which are not to be disdained: the position of this island, placed in the center of the greater Antilles, the ease of approaching it and reaching its ports, are advantages that the others cannot offer in terms of navigation." Echoing Peltier's earlier explanation of the larger territory occupied by the State of Haiti, compared with the republic, Rouanez explained, "The current state of things is that President Christophe has under his dominion, not only the north but a large part of the West, he holds independently all the territory from Montechrist [*sic*], Gonaïves, Saint-Marc, to the Artibonite; his reign extends, including the garrisons, as far south as Mirebalais, and he has in his possession the great woods and the mountains of these regions; and in the plain he holds Mont-Rouis [*sic*] and Arcahaye, all the way down to the plain of Cul-de-Sac, which is almost at the gates of Port-au-Prince." Finally attending to the issue of Ferrand, Rouanez spoke of the number of troops that the French general had on the eastern side of the island—only sixteen to eighteen hundred men—before revealing what he hoped would be the key point, a rumor that Ferrand was in negotiations with Pétion.

Noting that Ferrand procured all his resources from the United States, principally from Philadelphia, Rouanez outlined a plan for how Ferrand could be attacked and conquered with British and Haitian troops. He made a list of things needed, including guns and saddles, and argued that once "the last supporter of Bonaparte," which is to say Ferrand's camp, could be "chased from the island, the most lucrative commerce would be open" to Great Britain. Christophe, Rouanez insisted, "wants nothing more than to have robust trade with you, with every port open to Great Britain and the total expulsion of the agent of Napoléon Bonaparte."[54] Independent Haiti's unequivocal hatred of Napoléon was perhaps matched only by the British king's on-again, off-again war with France and consequent disdain for its self-proclaimed emperor.

Writing to British ministers again on June 18, 1808, Peltier complained that the British Parliament had provided no answer to Christophe's proposed treaty. Peltier found this to be a contradiction, or at the very least out of character, since Parliament had declared that any nation considered "enemies with the oppressor of the world, Napoléon Bonaparte," was a friend to and an ally of Great Britain. Moreover, Peltier complained that British marines seized with impunity cargo and ships from the State of Haiti, therefore exposing British subjects to alarming reprisals. Peltier did not seek any favors for the merchants, he said. Instead, "I am requesting from the government of His Majesty a declaration, an assurance that Haiti is not regarded as an enemy country, nor as being at war with England. I reiterate this appeal to you again today, in the name of humanity, in the name of British interests."[55]

Peltier continued to reiterate northern Haiti's talking points over the next two years as the civil war raged on, despite his earlier prediction of its imminent end and Christophe's certain victory. President Henry Christophe has not "ceased to have successes over his rival, Pétion, since the month of November last," Peltier wrote to Castlereagh from London on

May 5, 1809.[56] Then, on June 27, 1810, Peltier wrote to another British official, Sir Robert Peel, to ask him to transmit to Robert Jenkins on, the Earl
of Liverpool, a copy of "a book just published in Haïty [sic] by a Black and
printed there, which cannot but give a good idea of the improvement of
civilization in those quarters." The book was most likely Juste Chanlatte's
The Cry of Nature, published in 1810 and dedicated to the French abolitionist the abbé Grégoire. "At the same time I subjoin the report of the
Bulletin official of a naval affair which took place in February last between
the two squadrons of Christophe and Pétion," Peltier explained. "Another
action took place at the end of March in which Christophe's ships put to
flight those of Pétion."[57] Peltier alluded to the south's repeated and failed
sieges of the northern port city of Môle Saint-Nicolas, under the leadership of General Lamarre, who eventually lost his life in the famous battle.

Baron de Vastey remains undoubtedly the best northern chronicler of
the siege of Môle. He wrote that the fighting had taken place "with vigor
and in vain" when Lamarre addressed Pétion to solicit him to have the city
evacuated. Pétion ordered Lamarre, on the contrary, not to abandon the
terrain. Once more in vain, Lamarre asked for "relief and gave [Pétion] a
frightening picture of the situation to which his army was reduced." Yet
Pétion ordered Lamarre to continue. Lamarre then wrote a beseeching and
imploring letter to Pétion, which eventually fell into the hands of northern troops. Lamarre sued for help and reinforcements while painting a
bleak future in stark vocabulary. He said without aid the southern soldiers
would all die.

Pétion promised a battleship and several frigates, but nothing ever
arrived. At the same time, he ordered Lamarre not to abandon Môle under
any circumstances, and in a letter he wrote to Lamarre dated June 5, 1810,
the president of the Republic of Haiti told his best general to prepare to
"make a communal sacrifice" and not allow his heart to "waver." Northern troops later killed Lamarre in the battle over the port. Lamenting the
death of a man he once fought beside in the Haitian Revolution, Vastey
opined, "Lamarre, while visiting his line troops, was carried away by a
cannonball; this warrior deserved to shed his blood for a more beautiful
and just cause." Far from celebrating the death of this intrepid soldier
turned traitor, Christophe reacted with sadness: "An admirer of merit
wherever it is found, Henry praised his talents, bravery, and fearlessness."

Eveillard, another revolutionary officer who fought alongside both
Christophe and Vastey, and eventually with Dessalines's armée indigène,
subsequently took over the command of the republican strike, but several
days later he also lost his life on the battlefield and was replaced by Toussaint Boufflet. Christophe, sad to learn his former comrades in arms were
dying precipitously, proposed the republic's capitulation, but Pétion's officers rejected his offers with disdain. The result of such obstinance brought

nothing more than a torrent of bloodshed, in Vastey's retelling. It was only after a most stubborn resistance on the part of the south that the north "took over by vigorous force" the city and forts of Môle:

> The besieged, forced to abandon them, retreated and defended themselves vigorously. Surrounded on all sides by the victorious army, they were reduced to laying down their arms and surrendering. Under the laws of war these troops could be put to the sword; they had obstinately refused to capitulate; they had flown the flag without quarter until the moment they were reduced to the last extremity, without being able to defend themselves; these chiefs made themselves guilty and responsible for all the blood that their useless resistance caused to be shed on both sides; Toussaint Boufflet and Jean Gournaut, the two senior leaders, deserved to be punished by death according to the laws of war, and they were.

Writers from the republic loudly decried the terrible deaths of these men. "They were not assassinated after having surrendered," as writers from the republic "falsely affirmed," Vastey countered. Vastey concluded that in sending these southern troops into the heart of the north to take over one of its most important ports, Pétion exposed his men to certain, inevitable, and cruel destruction.

Christophe ordered no clemency bestowed upon any of the republic's officers who willingly led troops into the heart of disaster. As for the soldiers, he offered forgiveness and to wipe away any political memory of what he characterized as their former betrayal. Christophe made good on his promise. "After their surrender, the southern troops, both officers and soldiers, were organized into one corps, under the name of Legion of the South, this body today forms the Thirtieth Regiment of Sans-Souci. These troops have been consistently treated, outfitted, and paid just like the other regiments of the kingdom," Vastey reported.[58]

Pro-Pétion writers had a different story to tell. They narrated the failed siege of Môle Saint-Nicolas in far different and far more damning terms. Dumesle put Christophe right into the heart of the battle for Môle, specifically at Morne-à-Cabri, a little hill that dominates the city. Circular in form, a valley spreads out beneath it called the Gorge. Dumesle wrote that "the view of its arid and rocky terrain would be repulsive if the flower of the caper tree that lines it did not offer to the eye a more vivid color than that of topaz."[59] This beautiful setting was soon desolated by the dead bodies that Dumesle reported surrounded Christophe as he meditated his retreat, plagued by visions of "the defeat of the elite of his troops at the foot of our ramparts."[60] Lamarre, the leader of the battle, swore to die a thousand times rather than to bow his head before "that ferocious destroyer of the north."[61] And yet in July 1810, bow his head and body to the ground Lamarre did after "the fatal bullet cut short the thread of his days." "He was struck . . . and with his last murmurs he still uttered hope for the triumph of the republic," Dumesle lamented. The pro-Pétion journalist and politician's plaintive tone is reflected in the elegiac poem he penned for his fallen comrade:

On a chariot adorned with valor,
He seems radiant with glory,
Even as Victory
Had just his big heart betrayed.
Mars sees it; stops, and wonders. . . .
This god, formidable to mortals,
Fears they will not raise altars
To the hero who girds his crown;
He flies to the Palace of Destiny,
And wants, with a tragic death,
To end his heroic career.
Fate listens to him, and suddenly
He strikes . . . and Lamarre succumbs!!!
But the god seems to be frightened;
He fears that with this proud warrior
His brilliant prestige will not fall.[62]

In Dumesle's account, far from feeling anything like sadness or regret over Lamarre's death, Christophe celebrated it. Feeling satisfied, Christophe allegedly left the rest of the battle to his generals and returned to Cap. Once in his capital city, he had the southern general's death celebrated with public fetes for six days. "Certainly, he could not praise the hero more highly: for the hatred of a tyrant is the panegyric of republican virtues," Dumesle wrote with more than a smidgen of irony.

Dumesle also offered a patently different version of what happened to captured soldiers and officers from the republic after Christophe's troops defeated Pétion's. Two days after the death of Eveillard, a colonel from Christophe's army penetrated into the city of Môle with his cavalry, torches in hand, and set fire to all the houses he happened upon during his passage. Dumesle blamed Boufflet and charged him with having conceived the plan to retreat instead of continuing the resistance. Dumesle confirmed mass defection when he spoke of what happened after Boufflet's defeat. Believing that all was lost, Boufflet evidently quit his troops and took the route back to Môle, where "he surrendered at full speed and handed over his weapons to Christophe as a pledge of his capitulation!" "The army, left to itself, surrendered at its discretion," Dumesle continued. Those surrendered soldiers did not experience President Christophe's clemency. He gave the defeated instead the choice of "servitude or death." Dividing the troops into two sides, Christophe ordered "instantly the torture of the greatest number of them, and by a refinement of unheard-of cruelty he condemned the others to live, only to spend the rest of their existence in chains." As for Boufflet, Christophe ordered him sent to the Citadelle's prison. En route to the famous fortress, Boufflet begged for death instead of imprisonment, but Christophe's troops at first refused him the chance to share Lamarre's and Eveillard's fates.

"Listen to my prediction," Boufflet told them in a loud voice, stopping for a moment their march to the prison. "Hear the accents of truth, hear it beforehand," he said:

> The prestige of Christophe's authority will vanish; those who praise him will trample to the ground his scepter; his downfall will lead to that of his henchmen. . . . Yes, I predict it, the future has been unveiled before my eyes . . . ; the day of Liberty and Justice will shine . . . the blood of the victims will fall on the heads of the executioners!! . . . The avenged north will see all the attributes of despotism overthrown; they will scatter their debris on its soil, and will recall the terrible example of the expulsion of the colonists, whom Christophe tried to equal in tortures. . . . Then I will be no more, but my scattered bones, deprived of burial, will reunite, and will quiver with joy!!!

This speech was Boufflet's last. The leader of the escort, annoyed by the effect the purported prophecy had on the soldiers, cut off the southern general's head, forever silencing him.[63]

With northern troops having definitively expelled southern forces from the vulnerable city of Môle, Christophe issued a formal proclamation to the "Army of the Earth and Seas of the State of Hayti," dated October 8, 1810. "Môle Saint-Nicolas has just succumbed under the effort of your arms, the rebellion is extinguished in this region, and you have planted, on all sides, the flags of legitimate authority, so famous already for the numerous triumphs we have accomplished over the enemies of freedom," Christophe pronounced. "Twenty days of regular siege sufficed to destroy, from top to bottom, the fortresses that parricidal hands raised," he continued. Although Christophe maintained he did not seek to be guilty of the same parricide as his fellow Haitian brothers in the south, he said he felt no choice but to once and for all expel the southern soldiers from the north. "Weary of temporizing for the purpose of sparing blood, having realized that nothing could be compared to my patience and kindness, except the callousness and inflexibility of the rebels, I was forced to determine the fate of that criminal place," he explained:

Immediately the two chiefs who successively commanded there bit the dust; two of their shattered warships in the harbor resemble nothing more than their impotent carcasses; a considerable heap of guns, mortars, ammunition, and provisions of all kinds is the result of your labors, the price of your bravery; and these men who came from the depths of the south, with the intention of depriving you of the most precious possessions, obliged to surrender at their discretion, knew that your clemency was equal to your valor.

Christophe wholly denied that the southern soldiers who surrendered experienced anything other than his compassion and forgiveness. He remarked that the soldiers clearly believed that they would be greeted with outrage in the final hours before their deaths. Yet the opposite was true. Christophe said that northern soldiers, who included his brother-in-law, Noël Coidavid, shared their tents, their food, and their uniforms with those southern soldiers whom they once fought alongside during the Haitian Revolution. "They only recognized in you brothers, and your arms carefully carried their sick and wounded to the hospital, to be treated and cared for like your companions," Christophe proudly reported. "What did I say?" he asked. "The Ninth Regiment, the very one that was the first to raise the standard of revolt, as well as the remnants of the Sixteenth, Eighteenth, Twenty-First, Twenty-Second, Twenty-Third, and Twenty-Fourth, taken prisoner, are today surprised to take their rank in the army of Haiti; but let their surprise cease, let them know that even when he is punishing, a father is still a father." Then, reiterating the offer he had made to the south since the earliest days of the great scission, Christophe announced once more "GENERAL AMNESTY, which I have already offered to achieve the salvation of the state, the sole object of my ambition."[64]

The people of the north reportedly cheered Christophe on as he made his way back to the capital. Everywhere he went, from Port-de-Paix to Cap-Henry, he saw victory laurels thrown at his feet with the people spontaneously erecting *arcs de triomphe*, making his voyage home a "veritable victory parade," in Prévost's words. Once home, the president took care of the wives of deceased soldiers and educated their children at his expense. Then he got to work reorganizing the army, working on the redistribution of farms previously owned by the former colonists, and setting up the labor laws of the state.[65]

Peltier's requests for Great Britain to formally enter a treaty of "friendship" and recognize Haiti continued into the second decade of the nineteenth century, but took on a different character from trying to convince the British government that Haiti's civil war had reached its conclusion after the defeat of southern forces at Môle. In June 1811, Peltier proudly announced to British officials that at last "a revolution has just occurred on the island of Haiti." "President Henry Christophe has just been named

Hereditary King of the isle," Peltier wrote, as if this development were as usual as the sun rising. Nothing if not persistent in his capacity as chargé d'affaires for Christophe, Peltier followed up this revelation by saying that this change in northern Haiti's governance "appears likely to ensure the peace of the island, the stability of its government, and the security of commercial relations of other countries with this island."[66]

12

A KING IS CROWNED

On June 2, 1811, Henry Christophe and his wife of seventeen years, Marie-Louise, along with their seven-year-old son, Victor-Henry, rode into their magnificent coronation in a carriage pulled by eight horses. King Henry and Queen Marie-Louise's teenage daughters, Première-Améthyste and Anne Athénaïs, the soon-to-be royal princesses, traveled in a separate carriage pulled by six horses. The coronation took place during an opulent and extended Sunday Mass presided over by Father Corneille Brelle, of Brittany, who had acted as apostolic prefect of the State of Haiti under President Christophe. King Henry's creation of a corresponding nobility of dukes, counts, and barons numbered into the hundreds and left the world awestruck. But what could have brought about such a prodigious and profound change in governance? And what might the change of title augur for Christophe's ongoing negotiations to secure British recognition of Haitian independence? With Christophe now a king in a world of kings, was it possible that Britain's own monarch might smile kindly toward him and stretch his hand figuratively across the Atlantic as one sovereign to another? And what about France? Would the emperor Napoléon finally relinquish his claim over the island and stop trying to restore slavery? As it turns out, Napoléon did have something to do with the creation of Haiti's monarchy. In April 1810 an even more stunning event than Lamarre's attempted siege of Môle took place, in the southern republic, far from Christophe's purview: a civil war within a civil war. Quite auspiciously, on the seventh anniversary of Louverture's death, André Rigaud returned to Haiti, allegedly on the orders of France's infamous emperor. Rigaud's appearance exercised an outsized influence on the northern council of state's decision to create a monarchy with Christophe as king.

The work of preparing the renamed capital city, Cap-Henry, for President Christophe to become King Henry happened within the astonishing space of just two months. On March 26, 1811, Christophe issued a proclamation announcing that his council of state had just promoted him from the position of president of the State of Haiti to king of the Kingdom of Haiti. Just one week later, another edict announced the creation of the nobility, with Christophe's most cherished friends and administrators among the hundreds of dukes, counts, barons, and chevaliers named to the royal order of Saint Henry.

For the coronation, which took place on the Champ de Mars of Cap-Henry, the country's builders erected a temporary church. Two hundred fifty feet long and just as wide, the interior of the edifice was divided into nine arcades. In the center stood an eighty-foot-high cupola, in the middle of which sat the king's throne. A design feat fit to rival that of any of old Europe's creations, the seventy-foot-tall throne was positioned under a "superb baldachin" of crimson silk. Embroidered in gold and adorned with gold fringes, the opulent and oversized chair had been studded with golden stars and phoenixes, which gave it the appearance of "rising majestically," in the words of the ceremony's official recorder, Julien Prévost, now the Comte de Limonade. The interior of the church shone as well with two rows of galleries on both sides of the nave, draped entirely in silk cloth the color of celestial blue, adorned with gold fringes, and "pleasingly studded with gold stars." Tapestries bearing the king's coat of arms—two crowned lions holding a black flag strewn with stars and imprinted with a gold phoenix rising from flames hovering over a gold ribbon that read "I am reborn from my ashes"—covered nearly everything in the church. A large gold crown, not dissimilar to the one the king would don, hovered over a ribbon on his coat of arms bearing the words "God is my cause, and my sword."

The twelve-foot-long altar had on its left side a large grandstand elegantly shrouded in crimson silk, fringed with gold, intended for Her Majesty, the queen, and the people of her *maison*, or household.[1] The Maison de la Reine initially included Princess Jeanne, wife of the king's nephew, the Duc de Port-Margot, and Marie-Louise's *dame d'honneur*, or first lady-in-waiting. Marie-Louise's maison also included her second lady-in-waiting, Princess Noële, wife of her brother, Noël Coidavid, himself the Duc de Port-de-Paix.[2]

The Comte de Limonade described the front of the newly built church in extravagant prose as he tried to capture the lavish eloquence of the occasion. "In front of the main facade of the church, the arms of the king were painted six feet high, surmounted by the Haitian flag, which floated in the air," Limonade wrote. "We read these words on the sides of the galleries, 'freedom,' 'independence,' 'honor,' 'Henry'!" To the right of the Champ de Mars stood the royal tent, surmounted by two flags, also bearing the arms of the king. The interior of the tent contained three chambers, separated by curtains of green taffeta, themselves gold fringed and ornamented with stars and a gold phoenix. Surrounding the interior of the tent reigned a gallery draped once more in green taffeta, in which could be seen the *chiffres*, or initials, of the king, the queen, the prince, and the royal princesses.[3]

For weeks the entire city had prepared for this momentous occasion. The streets where the royal cortege was to pass on the way to the church had been leveled, repaved, and sanded. At the center of the Place d'Armes had been erected an eighty-foot column, topped with a transparent globe, itself eight feet high, surmounted by a crown, in the middle of which again appeared the *chiffres* of the king, queen, prince, and royal princesses. Laurels and flowers decorated the column on all sides, one part of which read, "The King, to the Army and Navy!" The four facades of the royal palace were decorated as well, garnished with lanterns arranged to look like the royal *chiffres* amid yet more stars and phoenixes.[4]

The coronation's proceedings began several days before the king and the queen were to be crowned by Brelle in the magnificent church constructed for the occasion. On May 30, the newly designated aristocracy gathered at six in the morning in front of the church on the Champ de Mars for their official swearing-in. After the king and queen arrived, the members of the nobility—namely, the princes, dukes, ministers, counts, barons, and chevaliers—successively took the following oath: "I swear obedience to the Constitutions of the Kingdom and fidelity to the King." After this oath, Christophe addressed the civil and military officers in a loud voice and commanded them to swear an oath:

> Officers, Sous-Officers, and Soldiers, you are swearing on your honor, on what is most sacred to you, to devote yourself to the service of the Kingdom, to the preservation and integrity of its Territory, to the defense of the King and the Royal Family, of the Laws and Constitutions of the Kingdom; to maintain with all your power Liberty, Independence, and to die, if necessary, to support the Throne.

The military officers raised their right hands and swore in a unanimous voice, "I swear it."[5] Afterward, on the same day, the king hosted a huge reception, replete with toasts and speeches, and attended by all the new members of the aristocracy and military officers.

This ceremony particularly moved the Comte de Limonade. He could not help but marvel at the transformation of colonial Saint-Domingue into the Kingdom of Haiti. Standing in appreciative wonder, the count watched as "those illustrious and intrepid defenders of the state, those founders of the liberty and independence of their country, covered in honorable scars and wounds received in combat for the preservation of their rights, came to modestly receive from the hands of Henry, this worthy military recompense, the prize of valor awarded by the hand of the hero who himself was decorated with it, as well as his worthy and beloved son." After the reception, and when all the chevaliers had been seated, Limonade addressed his own speech to the soldiers and chevaliers, counseling them to "peruse the annals of chivalry and find there the path that they must walk."[6]

On June 1, the celebration continued with the nobles attending Mass at the parish church in Cap-Henry to hear a sermon pronounced by Brelle, now the archbishop of the Kingdom of Haiti and the Duc de l'Anse. Afterward the attendees traveled to the king's palace in Cap-Henry, where Christophe gave a lively toast to "his faithful nobles." "To the valiant Models of his armies!" the king finished. Classical music characteristic of Christophean celebrations played in the background. One song ironically featured a French royalist hymn, "Où peut-on être mieux, qu'au sein de sa famille?" (Where is it better to be than with your own family). The court continued to play this song over the years at many fetes and independence day ceremonies across the kingdom. The minister of finance, Vernet, now the Prince des Gonaïves, gave a toast to King Henry, while another famous French song, "Vive Henry!," hummed in the background. Next the Prince du Limbé, General Paul Romain, toasted the queen, followed by a Haitian song titled "Hymne haytienne" (Haitian hymn), first performed during the inaugural celebrations of the Declaration of Independence in January 1804. Sung to the air of "Allons enfants de la patrie" (Let us go children of the country), or *La Marseillaise,* its first lines wonder, "What? you remain silent, Indigenous people! When a Hero, through his exploits, Avenging your name, breaking your chains, Forever assures your rights? Honor to his warlike valor! Glory to his triumphant efforts! Let us offer him our hearts, our torch; Let us sing with a stern and proud voice, United under this good Father, Forever reunited, Let us live, let us die, his true Children, Free and independent." Reveling in the music and sounds of Haitian freedom, the nobles drank in succession, chanting their hopes for the health of the prince and princesses.[7]

Not long after the coronation, Christophe ordered to be published the "Proceedings of the Coronation of Their Majesties King HENRY I and Queen MARIE-LOUISE," so that those Haitians not in attendance would be able to read the details of all that took place on June 2, 1811, when the first and last king and queen of Haiti were crowned. The preparations for that unprecedented day began at two in the morning when the infantry and cavalry units took up their posts, lining the avenues of the palace and the Champ de Mars, on the orders of the former Haitian revolutionary Noël Joachim, now the Duc de Fort Royal, serving also as the grand marshal of the palace. From three to four in the morning the preparations continued, with the Catholic clergy finally assembling near five o'clock. At six o'clock the royal family left the palace to the sound of church bells ringing, while the army musicians played songs of war, accompanied by a salvo of artillery that followed the royal family until they arrived at the Champ de Mars. The entire nobility and all the city's civil and military officers attended the ceremony. The royal family's cortege included the king's nephew, Jean, and the queen's brother, Prince Noël. Marie-Claire

Heureuse, Dessalines's widow, also attended and took her place among the *dames d'honneur* of the queen.[8]

The royal family passed into the nave of the church with the queen carrying the king's royal manteau. The princesses, Première and Athénaïs, held the queen's manteau. The queen's brother, Prince Noël, carried the corbeil intended to receive the king's cape. The king already had the crown on his head and carried in his hands the scepter and hand of justice. To his left side walked the beaming royal prince. The royal family entered the church to the sounds of music and artillery, which continued as they sank into the nave to take their places. Drums continued to beat as Father Brelle offered holy water to the king and queen. Behind the queen sat Première and Athénaïs, while behind them sat the stoic Madame Dessalines.[9]

The way that Christophe's court honored Madame Dessalines by seating her among the nobles shows the continued reverence and respect that existed for her in the northern part of Haiti. After the death of her husband, Madame Dessalines chose to remain in northern Haiti, in the city of Gonaïves, where she enjoyed a pension and protection, often corresponding directly with the king about personal matters.[10] With Madame Dessalines's presence painting a picture of her symbolic approval of the ascension of Christophe to the position of Haiti's monarch, a role once played by her husband, albeit under the title of emperor, Brelle opened the coronation by offering a prayer in Latin. He went on to bless all the royal paraphernalia: the scepter, cloaks, necklaces, and crowns. The aristocracy then presented the swords of the king and queen, along with other royal items, before the French priest for a blessing. Brelle pronounced the entire coronation Mass in Latin, before placing the royal robes on Queen Marie-Louise and King Henry. Prior to inviting them to take their oath, he placed the diamond-crusted scepter in Henry's hand. Finally, the moment the crowd had been waiting for arrived. Brelle topped both the king's and the queen's heads with the royal crowns, described by onlookers as "rare and precious works," whose diamonds had been set in an unusual diagonal pattern.

Christophe, ready to take his oath on the Bible, pronounced these solemn words: "I swear to maintain the integrity of the territory and the independence of the Kingdom; never to suffer, under any pretext whatsoever, the return of Slavery, nor of any feudal regime contrary to the freedom of the state, and to the exercise of the civil and political rights of the people of Haiti; to maintain the irrevocability of the privileges and sales of the goods of the Kingdom; to govern in sole view of the interest, happiness, and glory of the great Haitian family, of which I am the Head." The oath having been sworn, the grand master of ceremonies announced in a loud and proud voice, "The very great, very august king HENRY, the king of Haiti, has been crowned and enthroned. Long live the king!" "Thus took place the most solemn, the most majestic, and the most magnificent ceremony that has ever been seen in Haiti!" proclaimed Limonade.[11]

The king's cortege afterward left in the same order in which it arrived. Outside, the people of Haiti lined the streets. Citizens from every walk of life watched as the carriages of the king and queen, along with those of the prince and princesses, made their way back to the royal palace to cries of love and robust applause fitting for such an audacious ceremony. "I saw citizens of all professions weep with sensitivity and tenderness, and precious tears also flowed from the eyes of soldiers who were present at the Mass and coronation of their Majesties," Limonade recalled.[12]

After this, the king and queen hosted a party at the palace with more than six hundred people in attendance. Hundreds of nobles crowded into the castle while the people of Haiti, encouraged to look on from outside, spontaneously shouted, "Long live Henry! Long live the royal family!" Inside the courtyard the guests sat at three large tables, with two hundred settings each. The palace's staff had prepared the festivities to take place in the courtyard of the barracks' garden, under arbors of foliage set up for this purpose. The aristocracy occupied the first table, along with Spanish dignitaries, captains of British ships docked in the port, and foreign merchants. At the second table could be found members of the tribunal of justice, administrators, and the officers of the police units and other deputies present at the coronation. The third table was reserved for the officers of the army who had also been deputized to assist at the coronation.[13]

The royal family entered the garden just before the main course was served to cries of *Vive Henry!* King Henry opened the course by giving a toast in which he referred to the king of England as "my dear brother, King George III!" The Haitian king then asked God to permit his fellow British king to "always be an invincible obstacle to the unbridled ambition of Napoléon." The king and queen, along with the prince, princesses, and members of their respective *maisons,* mingled among the various tables, soaking up the air of grandeur that surrounded the entire occasion. The words to the song "Where is it better to be than with your own family?" played once more after their arrival. After the famous song "God Save the King!" started to play, the Spanish dignitaries stood up to offer toasts to unity, friendship, and fraternity, with the people of Haiti watching the grand spectacle through the gates of the royal palace.[14]

That night a different sort of spectacle took place as the king and queen made their way to the theater, where they listened to a song composed in their honor by Juste Chanlatte, now the Comte de Rosiers. The singer might have been Chanlatte's own wife, Françoise Marie Élisabeth Castaing, the Comtesse de Rosiers, a member of the Royal Theater.[15] Titled "Chant inaugural" (Inaugural song), the Comte de Rosiers's ballad showered gratitude upon the new king:

HENRY, our king, our father,
Swore the sacred oath,
On which our hope is based!
Completing its triumph, a revered couple
Is that of the new world,
And the borders of Haiti with them it have sworn.[16]

After Chanlatte's song, the kingdom's theater troupe performed a French opera in honor of the royal couple, *La partie de chasse d'Henry IV* (The hunting party of Henry IV). According to Limonade, the play was wholly fitting for Christophe, who felt he had a lot in common with the late French monarch.[17] While the Chevalier de Cincinnatus Leconte (called Cincinnatus), an ancestor of one of Haiti's future presidents, served as the superintendent of the King's Theater, Christophe's old comrade Pétigny appeared as one of the main actors, along with the Baron de Vastey and the Chevalier de Prézeau. Perhaps the songs in the play were performed to the ballet by Salinette Dessalines (full name Marie-Françoise), one of the emperor's daughters, born out of wedlock with a woman named Célestine Arène; Salinette danced as an official ballerina in the kingdom.[18]

A dazzling light show stunned the invitees and inhabitants of Cap that night when a beautiful illumination followed the evening of theater. The royal family returned to the palace just in time to witness their capital city radiating with light from the glimmering fireworks that sparkled over the Place d'Armes, representing a sun intertwined with the *chiffres* of the king and queen. A concert then ensued. The people of the capital danced all night in the humid air until the morning sun broke the spellbinding celebrations for a few hours.[19]

Continuing for the whole week, on their fourth day the celebrations featured yet more singing from prominent aristocratic women. Limonade's reportage provides precious details about those who did not usually enter the frame of the kingdom's more politically, and male, dominated scripts. "In the interval of rest between the feasts and celebrations, and to prepare for that which was to take place the following day, a single concert was commissioned at the palace," Limonade wrote. At five o'clock that evening the artists reunited at the palace with their majesties in the *Salle d'Apollon* (Apollo Salon) with all the guests invited to join them. The Comtesse de Rosiers and Mademoiselle Mills sang a cantata written by Chanlatte. The cantata had a section praising "the City of Cap-Henry" and calling Christophe "the Genius of Haiti," while also exalting the Citadelle Henry. After this, the women performed the coronation's choral music. The Comtesse de Rosiers accompanied her husband on the pianoforte. Limonade described the scene as one where "the suppleness, the lightness, the beauty of the voices of these two ladies, their roulades, the variety of tones, from grave to sweet, gave infinite pleasure to all." Vigorous applause greeted the enchanting singers after the duo sang in succession pieces from *Oedipus at Colonus.* The Spanish deputies took part as well, supplying the harmony, after which they sang some of their own "national airs," which only further delighted the guests as much as the king and queen.[20]

Christophe was not insensitive to those dignitaries unable to attend the coronation and its nearly weeklong celebrations, which lasted until June 7. After the official celebrations ended, the king invited officials from elsewhere in the kingdom to the capital to enjoy smaller dinners and gatherings. One such gathering involved a trip to the king's famous Citadelle. The dignitaries who came from afar asked to see the imposing structure whose ongoing expansion was already becoming legendary.

During Christophe's presidency, the Citadelle had undergone a huge transformation from the days when it was known as Fort Laferrière and then Fort Henry. The dignitaries stood awestruck and somewhat speechless upon glimpsing the rapid progress. "To say that they came back amazed would not be a faithful representation of the sentiments they experienced, since even foreigners cannot prevent themselves from the feelings of astonishment that the sight of this monument occasions within them, and from the great means required to complete this important work," Limonade explained, as he unwittingly confessed to the massive labor system Christophe had put into place to complete the construction of the Citadelle, the largest fortress in all the Western Hemisphere.[21]

—

In the official history the Baron de Vastey wrote for the kingdom in 1819, he remarked that the Citadelle's completion occurred in 1813, the same year as the royal family's new palace in Sans-Souci. However, references to the Citadelle Laferrière, renamed Citadelle Henry under Christophe, exist before 1813. Limonade, for example, put Christophe at the "Citadelle Henry" on the eve of his defection to the north against the republic, on December 18, 1806, when Christophe issued a proclamation to "reveal the secret agents of the conspirators agitating in every way to corrupt the troops." Much later, in 1809, the *Official Gazette* indirectly described the ongoing expansion of the Citadelle by referring to its appearance from the vantage point of "the Haitian Tivoli." In a passage that suggests the Citadelle was already built, in large part, by September 1809, we read that to the south of Christophe's castle in "Tivoli," stretching out from under the fog could be seen "the impregnable fortress that a tutelary genius has built." The Citadelle sat so high up on the mountain that, "partly masked by dark clouds," it often gave one "the impression of seeing the arsenal of the god Mars suspended in the air." The king's 1812 book of laws called the *Code Henry* also mentioned the Citadelle Henry and revealed that the king had already appointed a governor to oversee it.[22]

The *Code Henry* offers the key to understanding how Christophe expanded the military to attain the huge numbers of soldiers he needed to occupy, guard, and ultimately enlarge the famous fortress. Article 461 of the *Code* stated, "Every Haitian, from the age of twelve to sixty, who is not a soldier and in active service, forms part of the militias of the kingdom." Subsequent articles explained that every man in Haiti of fighting age was technically in the army reserves and could be called forth for military duty. Ordinary citizens of Haiti could also be called to duty, whether to aid with the construction of the Citadelle or the other impressive fortresses that dot the coasts and forests of Haiti.[23] "For eleven years," the *Gazette* reported, "we have been constantly occupied in building impregnable citadels, on the peaks of our most inaccessible mountains, which bristle with formidable artillery." "The Citadelle Henry, eternal monument of the glory, genius, and love of His Majesty for his people, is fully provided and supplied with armaments and equipment, ammunitions of war, to last for a considerable time," the *Gazette* explained. The kingdom's officials boasted of the grandeur of what the Haitian people had built with their own hands and its symbolic as much as its material power. "This famous Citadelle, erected on the peak of Ferrières [*sic*], unique in the new world, by the careful crafting of its immense edifice, has no equal in Europe," the *Gazette* boasted. "Due to its unassailable location, this formidable rock, this boulevard of independence, is worthy alone of an army of a hundred thousand men."[24]

Construction of the Citadelle Henry, which writers from the kingdom consistently referred to as "that Palladium of Liberty," began in April 1804 under Dessalines.[25] In his role as general in chief of Dessalines's army, Christophe oversaw the major work of its fortification. In 1805, the fort mainly functioned as a prison for soldiers and cultivators accused of desertion, or those in the empire who had otherwise committed grave crimes against the state, such as engaging in espionage.[26] It was a storehouse for weapons and ammunition too.[27] However, Dessalines wanted the fort to be bigger and more imposing. Because of the vast amount of labor needed to complete its transformation, under Dessalines's orders, Christophe ordered many cultivators from the farms sent up to Laferrière.[28] Christophe also oversaw the arrival of the materials needed to construct the fort, such as lumber, nails, and bricks, some of which he ordered to be taken from the nearest plantations surrounding the city of Milot. Christophe also confiscated the *cabrouets,* or two-wheeled carts or chariots, ordinarily used on sugar plantations. These *cabrouets* became essential for carrying materials up the dangerously angled mountain leading to the Citadelle. Christophe had also supervised the work of the architects and other builders, such as a Monsieur Hirel, whom he referred to as the "chief roofer."[29] So involved was Christophe with the construction that under Dessalines he visited the site almost daily to personally oversee its fortification.[30]

Christophe's former comrade from the days of affermage, Faraud, designed the architectural augmentations to the Citadelle for Dessalines. Faraud, also the chosen architect for Christophe's first grand home with Marie-Louise proposed at number 312 rue d'Égalité in Cap-Français, held the title of engineer under Dessalines. As such, Christophe wrote to him often to supply the tools and other materials Faraud needed to realize the emperor's vision for the augmentation of the enormous fort.[31]

For his role in completing the austere and magnificent edifice, King Henry made Faraud a baron in 1811. Faraud's coat of arms, boasting the term "Citadelle Henry," depicted two silver rabbits holding a green flag with a golden compass in the middle, topped with the black helmet of a chevalier of yore. Under Christophe, Faraud had several important roles. Not only did the Baron de Faraud sign the penal code of the *Code Henry* in 1812, but he served as a member of the Privy Council of the King, fulfilling at the same time the office of the intendant of the buildings of the Crown. The Baron de Béliard worked alongside him as director and intendant of the gardens, fountains, and forests of the kingdom.[32]

It is hard to fully capture the magnificence of the awe-inspiring Citadelle, with its four angled towers, which one observer described as "connected to each other, by levels of walls resembling curtains, to form an irregular quadrilateral edifice that encloses a vast *place d'armes*." Covering about one hectare, or about two and a half acres, Faraud's unrivaled design for "that majestic boulevard of independence," in Limonade's words, "was built on the ridged summit of one of the highest mountains on the island, from which one discovers, on its left side, the island of La Tortue, and the mirror of its superb channel; opposite, the hills and the town of Cap-Henry, its port, and the vast expanse of the seas; on the right, La Grange, Monte Cristi, the city of Fort Royal [Fort-Liberté], the bay of Mancenille, and the surrounding mountains."[33] It seems as if all of Haiti can be seen stretching out before the Citadelle from the top of its towers.

Not everyone at the time revered the imposing structure. Some foreign onlookers accused the Haitian king of using a form of labor that resembled slavery to build the auspicious towers. According to a British ship captain, as reported by one of the kingdom's most ardent detractors, Charles Hérard-Dumesle in his southern newspaper *The Observer,* "There reigns in this capital a sinister calm, the people are oppressed, trade is languishing, foreigners approach that city only with fear, like a city affected by the plague, and there are no establishments." Christophean writers contested this claim immediately. "Oh! how could it be that oppression, tyranny, and slavery reign in the midst of a people who have won their freedom and their rights at the cost of their blood?" Vastey asked. He went on to say it would be a bit insane, if not "the height of extravagance and human folly," to think that a slaving state could endure in independent Haiti. "Could this people proud and jealously guarding their freedom, who expelled their tyrants, admit other [tyrants] of their own color?" he wryly asked.[34]

Mentions of the laborers who built the Citadelle and other fortresses and palaces in kingdom-era writings are scarce. Limonade did allude to "the astonishing common activity surrounding this work," and he also spoke of the "vast capital" this construction required. "Fruits from the treasury's savings," large sums of money "filled the spacious coffers of the Citadelle," he wrote. In addition to his palace in Sans-Souci, Christophe eventually had a castle to serve as a home built on the grounds of the Citadelle. "I know that one of the intentions of our monarch is to tile and panel the rotunda of his palace at the Citadelle in quads," or gold coins from Spain,[35] Limonade wrote. "He's rich enough to do it." Going on to describe "this apartment of a new kind," Limonade said it "would be covered in precious drapery and would have no equal in the world." On the frontispiece of the structure, which Limonade referred to as a "monument," would be the "motto of Louis XIV: *Nec pluribus impar*" (Not unequal to many).[36]

With batteries named for Marie-Louise, the princesses, and the royal prince, and fortified with "exceptionally thick walls," the Citadelle was far more than a prison, a storehouse for weapons, or a military guard post. "The most regal structure ever raised in the New World," to quote one twentieth-century visitor, it reportedly housed more than fifty thousand guns, in addition to sabers, machetes, firearms of all kinds, darts meant to be thrown from the parapets at enemies, millions of bullets, along with thousands of tons of powder and saltpeter, all stored in its humongous depots. There were also cellars stocked with enough food to provide provisions for months. The food stores complemented the shelters that could house ten thousand individuals in case of war. Vast as a veritable city, the Citadelle housed its own military, pharmacy, printing press, and hospital too. Following the expansion of the palace at the Citadelle, it would be equipped for Henry to govern safely from its heights, with his family in tow, if necessary.[37]

While the transformation of the State of Haiti into the Kingdom of Haiti marked a significant development in the history of the Americas, the transformation of Haiti from a colony where slavery reigned into a free land where the people chose their own sovereign had no precedent. "Let us consider what we were twenty years ago, bent under the yoke of a barbarous slavery," Limonade wrote. "Let us never fear, no, never fear recalling what we were, but it is what we have now become that we should be most proud of." Limonade did not fail to sign off his account of the events that brought King Henry and Queen Marie-Louise to the throne by alluding to the civil war that led to the initial rupture with the south and that the king sought to repair with an offer of amnesty to the inhabitants of the southern republic. The germ of the logic for the creation of the monarchy, it turns out, was in that civil war.[38]

A few months after the coronation, King Henry issued an amnesty proclamation "to the inhabitants of the south and western part of the kingdom." A clear demonstration that the Haitian king still considered these regions part of his realm, he once more adopted his characteristic mix of severity and clemency. King Henry told the southerners and westerners whom he considered to be in rebellion, "Far from deploying against you the forces that I have in my power and the means entrusted to me, it is one of the necessities of my heart to have recourse only to conciliation and clemency." To prove the sincerity of his words, King Henry offered a considerable number of the names of republican defectors who "were greeted paternally" in the kingdom. He also insisted that not only had he welcomed them heartily into his realm but that they could now act as corroborating witnesses who could confirm that other defectors from the republic had not been executed, as reported in republican newspapers. "They were seen peaceful and happy, living within society, the persons hereafter designated, whom the most egregious calumnies made pass for dead, such as Messieurs Eugène, captain in the Third Regiment; Armand, Dugoir, Ferrier, Saint-Surin, Richeu, Bourdet, and Gauchier, quartermaster of the Ninth; Saint-Martin, Madame T. Boufflet, Hilaire, Tanta, Polidor Laville; finally, the officers and soldiers of the Ninth; the troops from the south who surrendered at Môle, and an infinity of other persons who have been sent back to their properties, as well as those who come daily to surrender." King Henry claimed to suffer from a helpful form of political amnesia in his dealings with these republicans now turned royalists, saying he wiped away any memory of "the outrages" they might have "addressed to the president of the State of Haiti." "Full and complete amnesty, complete forgetting of faults, and above all of the past; this is what Henry promises you on his royal word!" the king insisted. "Peace and brotherhood among Haitians; this is the glorious goal that his heart has in mind."[39]

—

After the announcement of the monarchy, Christophean lawmakers and writers worked quickly to explain and justify Henry's ascension to the throne, as much to Haitians as to foreign observers. After all, the constitution that the council of state issued in February 1807 seemed to afford Christophe every authority, when it made him "President and Generalissimo of the Forces of the Earth and Seas of the State of Hayti." But on March 26, 1811, after deliberations that began in February to revise the constitution, Christophe claimed to have been surprised when he arrived in the city of Fort-Liberté, previously known as Fort-Dauphin, and learned that the council of state had voted to confer upon him the new title of king of Haiti.[40] Two days later, the council, which consisted of Paul Romain, André Vernet, Toussaint Brave, Jean-Philippe Daut, Martial Besse, Jean-Pierre Richard, Jean Fleury, Jean-Baptiste Juge, and Étienne Magny, issued a new law explaining not just that they had changed the president's title to king but how they reached this decision. This document, signed by dozens of northern Haiti's highest-ranking officials, including Father Brelle, Hugonin, and Dupuy, provided the basis for the royal constitution of March 28, 1811.

Explaining their process of deliberation, the council recalled that at the time they created the February 17 constitution, "the state found itself, strictly speaking, without a social pact, and the storms of civil war brewed with such force that representatives of the people were prevented from fixing in an irrevocable manner the only mode of government that really suited us." The ensuing reasons, justifications, and philosophical as well as political theories behind the creation of the monarchy, along with the new laws it mandated, were repeated verbatim in the constitution of 1811's preamble, signed the same date, but not publicly revealed until April 4. The members of the council insisted that their body had determined a monarchy "now more than ever necessary to establish a stable order of things and become the mode of government that must forever govern the country in which we were born."[41]

When the state councilors later presented the constitution to the public, in Cap-Henry, they explained that the ongoing civil war with the republic guided their main justification for creating the monarchy, because the civil war had illuminated the faults in the previous system of governance. Insisting that the council did not deliberate in secret, the councilors revealed that they called to participate alongside them "the most educated Haitians." The council encouraged the people of Haiti therefore to appreciate that this assembly "never lost sight of your happiness, to which theirs is necessarily linked." Alluding more directly to the dissension with the south, the councilors reasoned, "When the state was threatened by the conspiracies that were forming within it, which were further fanned by our cruel and bitter enemies, and the picture of chaos and general upheaval was presented before us, the great Man who governs us felt we were in need of a social pact around which all Haitians could unite." The ongoing warfare with the south initially interrupted work on this "social pact," the councilors continued, but once Christophe reestablished order and lessened the threat, the council took up their work on the code of laws Christophe requested. Feeling even more acutely the necessity of establishing stability, the councilors believed that naming Christophe king would "preserve us from those frequent upheavals, those horrible convulsions that have so smoldered and convulsed the body politic."[42]

Christophean writers like Limonade and Vastey later filled in the details, adding consistency and color to the process by which the people of Haiti were said by the council to have themselves crowned Christophe as their first king. Limonade, for his part, wrote, "For a long time the well-expressed opinion of the most respectable and enlightened citizens was to put Henry on the throne." The principal reason the people desired to have a king—a desire that formed the council's theory and justification for the crown—was that Haitians considered the title of president to lack a military quality and "the sovereign power" needed to protect Haiti. Once the council completed the revisions to the constitution, and every class of society agreed, it was only then that the council felt it appropriate to announce, on March 26, that they had bestowed the title of king upon Henry and that of queen and royal prince upon his wife and son, respectively. At the official unveiling of the constitution in Cap-Henry, which occurred at the royal palace on April 4, Romain told the Haitian people, on behalf of the council, to "lift up their stately heads [and] be no longer alarmed at your future prosperity, and give thanksgiving to heaven." Christophe responded to Romain's address by accepting the will of his people, averring, "The nation has deemed it necessary for its prosperity and its safety to raise me to the throne and to fix its inheritance in my family. I yield to its wish, since this will contribute to public happiness." Romain then turned to address Marie-Louise and said to the queen-elect, "Madame, if anything can add to the sweet sensations that thrill our souls, it is to see the eminent qualities that heaven has bestowed upon you sitting next to the throne that the love and gratitude of the Haitian people have raised you upon." To this honor, Marie-Louise graciously replied, "The name of queen that the nation has just bestowed on me binds me even more particularly to the fate of the Haitian people, for whom I have always gloried in being a tender mother." "I will not forget, on the throne, the duties imposed by the Royal Majesty, and because my family is destined to take its place there, this will be enough to impress upon me the extreme care that I must bring to their education: yes, my children will be my dearest adornment since on them must one day depend the destiny of my country."[43]

After the official ceremony to unveil the new constitutional laws, the governor of the capital, Jean-Pierre Richard, the Comte de la Bande du Nord (later the Duc de la Marmelade), the officers of the état-major, or chief of staff, and those of the regiments in garrison in the capital, along with the officers of the administration, the members of all the tribunals, and the justice department, the principal merchants of Haiti, and all the foreigners present, mingled together. Animated by the most vibrant acclamations for the new king, they took it upon themselves, accompanied by the sounds of "warlike tunes," to travel around the country and in every square and every crossroads to give readings of the constitution. Everywhere they went, the people of Haiti reportedly cried out, "Long live the king, Long live the queen, Long live the prince and the royal family!"[44]

The council also offered a political logic for the creation of this constitutional monarchy. First, they began with what was missing from past iterations of Haitian governance. Remarking that, on the one hand, one of Dessalines's principal errors had been to initially proclaim himself "governor-general," which suggested a higher authority existed, the council also pointed out flaws with his subsequent title of emperor. "On the other hand," they said, "the magnificent title of emperor given to General in Chief Dessalines, though worthy indeed of being offered to him, for the eminent services he rendered to the state, to his fellow citizens, lacked precision in its application." "An emperor is supposed to command other sovereigns," they continued, "or at least such a high designation supposes in him who possesses it not only the same capacity and the same power but also real and effective power over an entire territory, an entire population." "Finally," the council concluded, "the temporary title of president given to his successor the great HENRY, our august leader, did not capture the idea of sovereign power, and can only be applicable to an aggregation of men assembled for such functions, or to a judicial body." Leaning on French Enlightenment philosophy to further make their case, the council insisted, "We have recognized, with the great Montesquieu, how monarchical, paternal governments excel over other governments." Haitian happiness, they said, would at last begin with Christophe's ascension to the throne.[45]

The council of state did not decide to create a monarchy on a whim, Vastey added: "It was with an understanding of [state formation] in all centuries that our legislators were guided when they founded the Haitian monarchy." "They sought to make not a constitution that was beautiful in theory, the execution of which would be impossible," he continued, "but a constitution with easy application, simple and suitable for our current needs." On the collaborative nature of this decision, Vastey observed,

Sensible men, fathers of families, those who love the duration and stability of governments, because there they find happiness, their security, and their guarantee, believed that a constitutional and hereditary monarchy was the one and only means of preventing misfortunes, revolutions, and civil wars, since with this form of government, the reign succeeds peacefully, without upheaval, which closes the doors to any ambitions, and the heir to the throne, being known, becomes the focal point of convergence; that he will receive an education and have instilled principles suitable to a prince destined to reign, and will be molded in the manners and habits of government, will make him more fit to take the reins of it.[46]

This political theory had as much to do with the political instability of revolutionary and then republican France as it had to do with the tumultuous shifts in the forms of governance that Haiti had already experienced in only seven years of independence. "The history of ancient and modern republics shows us multitudes of tyrants," Vastey wrote, before asking, "Has there ever existed a more frightful tyranny than that of Robespierre, under the Committee of Public Safety and General Security, which oppressed the French republic?" As for the future Haitian people, when they "emerged out of the republican state" the French had created in the post-emancipation colonial era, "we were saddled with the vices of that wavering government," Vastey owned. "We were looking for a secure port that could shelter us from revolutionary storms. It is experience and misfortunes that have led us from a republic to a monarchy." Leaning on Montesquieu, like the council before him, Vastey insisted that just as there are not two peoples in the world who are exactly alike, no two constitutions could be precisely the same either. The form of the government did not matter, if it was "sage, just, and had good laws" made for its own people, he insisted. The Baron de Vastey's recitation of the events that brought King Henry to the throne ended with a far more material rather than philosophical reason for the creation of the monarchy, however. "Henry is mortal, and we feared that upon his death the state might be turned upside down and civil war kindled," Vastey wrote.[47] Despite these beautiful enunciations meant to justify the creation of the monarchy, it turns out that it was not just the ongoing civil war with Pétion but the civil war within the civil war mounted by Rigaud that gave Christophe and his councilors of state the primary evidence that monarchies offered more stability than republics.

Understanding this most intricate episode that influenced the creation of the kingdom will require us to travel slightly back in time, to the year and then months before and after the coronation. In an oft-skipped-over but crucially important episode, spanning April 1810 to September 1811, Louverture's ardent rival André Rigaud returned to Haiti, allegedly on the orders of Napoléon. To hear northern writers tell it, Rigaud's return, orchestrated by Napoléon to pave the way for the restoration of French rule, indelibly influenced the council of state's decision to make Christophe northern Haiti's king. In this light, the most significant consequence that Rigaud's actions had for Haiti came not during his conflict with Louverture. Nor did it come when the French arrested, deported, and imprisoned both men in the Fort de Joux in the Jura Mountains of France, where Louverture died in April 1803, just a few weeks before Rigaud's incarceration there and eight months before Haitian independence. Instead, Rigaud staged his most dramatic act in 1810, after seven years of exile, when he mysteriously returned to the island of his birth and tried to overthrow the republic in the south. Rigaud's dubious mission might not have succeeded—he died in September 1811—but in this brief episode his return changed forever his country's political destiny.

—

André Rigaud was born with free status in the city of Les Cayes on the southern peninsula of Saint-Domingue on January 17, 1761. His mother, Rose Bossy Depaa, was a formerly enslaved African woman, some say from Allada, like Louverture's parents. However, unlike Louverture, Rigaud was also the son of a white man from Provence, in France. A goldsmith by trade, according to his military service record, Rigaud first entered the stage of world history when he fought and was lightly wounded in the head in the American Revolutionary War at the Battle of Savannah in October 1779.[48] Exiled and eventually arrested and jailed in the Fort de Joux following his defeat by Louverture, who died just before his arrival at the same prison, Rigaud returned to the island of Haiti from France on April 7, 1810. Landing beforehand in the United States, he met with several French agents, who reportedly gave him a secret mission: to dismember the Haitian government in the south so Napoléon could claim the island's remains, the better to position reconquest and the reinstatement of slavery.[49]

A letter from Christophe's secretary of state, Rouanez, to the agent Peltier provides the most detailed account of Rigaud's mission and the means he allegedly used while attempting to carry it out:

Rigaud regularly receives all the money he needs . . . from the United States. There, he continually visited Sieur Beaujour, Consul-General of France in Philadelphia, who had always been in open contact with the mulattoes of Port-au-Prince and their emissaries. . . . This individual has at his disposal a considerable sum deposited in the Bank of Philadelphia, with which he provides relief to the rebels of Port-au-Prince. It is obvious that Rigaud was sent by Bonaparte to come to replace Pétion in the government of the South of Haiti, and we will not be long in experiencing the consequences which will result from these arrangements.[50]

Rigaud painstakingly detailed in several pamphlets and memoirs his involvement in the Haitian Revolution until the time of his exile. But for this part of his story—the part involving his motives for returning following his short imprisonment and long exile, after not having seen the island for ten years—we have mostly to rely on the lips of his enemies.

Rigaud found himself in the special position of being seen as suspect by both enslavers in North America and the formerly enslaved revolutionaries of Haiti. An article published in the *Federal Republican & Commercial Gazette* out of Baltimore in March 1810 described Rigaud's tortured reception in the United States: "Attention is anxiously drawn toward him, by a report that he was lately in this state. . . . It is not for the sake of persecuting an individual that we introduce this article, but the safety of this and the Southern states imperiously requires that he should be expelled, if he has really entered them, and that at any rate his motions should be closely watched."[51]

Rigaud returned to Haiti on the seventh anniversary of Louverture's death. His contemporaries were right away suspicious of his arrival—and the timing. Northerners believed that Rigaud had been permitted to leave France on condition that he facilitate Napoléon's plot. "One would have to be very blind," wrote the Comte de Limonade, "to think that an unfortunate islander (especially given his skin color) could have escaped from the dungeons where he had languished. . . . Moreover, his arrival and the means by which it was achieved remove any doubt in this regard." Although he remained under strict surveillance during his entire exile in France, in reality, the French only imprisoned Rigaud in the Fort de Joux for slightly less than a year starting on April 30, 1803. Northern Haitian writers do not appear to have known this. The French monitored all Rigaud's movements and correspondence to prevent him from having contact with anyone in Haiti. The Haitian government may have known, however, that Rigaud had sent a detailed plan for the "reconquest" of Haiti to the French minister of the marine, shortly before his release from prison.[52]

The people of the city of Les Cayes, where he was beloved and where he once held command, greeted Rigaud with tears of joy. Eventually reunited with his son Cyrille, not long after his arrival Rigaud attended the wedding of one of his longest-standing and most beloved comrades, his former aide-de-camp Guy-Joseph Bonnet. Pétion, in contrast, learned of Rigaud's arrival in the south "like a thunderbolt," Vastey reported. Hiding his discontent, Pétion invited Rigaud to Port-au-Prince, where the two former comrades in arms set their eyes on each other for the first time in almost a decade. Rigaud had once been Pétion's superior. Now he found himself subordinate to Pétion, president of the republic and therefore his commander in chief.[53]

Pétion had fought under Rigaud and could not have forgotten his new rival's bravery, capability, and above all military prowess. Moreover, Pétion understood more than anyone else, perhaps, Rigaud's popularity in the southern peninsula, particularly in the region of his home city, Les Cayes. Pétion chose the path likely to produce less resistance therefore in deciding to celebrate Rigaud's return rather than make it known that he regarded the republic's latest newcomer as a dangerous and unpredictable enemy. Bestowing upon him the title of division general of the southern division of the army, Pétion gave Rigaud as a distraction an important commission to rid the mountains above Grand'Anse of government rebels led by the Christophe loyalist Jean-Baptiste Duperrier, called Goman, who happened to be Rigaud's godson.[54] Rigaud was hardly fooled, or interested in the assignment, and he resolved on November 1, 1810, to attempt a separation with the southern republic, taking along with him part of the second division of the western province. "Sovereignty resides in the people," he reportedly told his troops, "and the people reclaim their rights whenever they please."[55]

For a time, neither Pétion nor Rigaud dared to attack the other. Eventually Pétion sent troops from the west to march against those of the south. At the same time, Rigaud gathered his troops in Aquin, and soon after he marched with them to the Pont de Miragoâne, the border between the southern and the western departments. He hoped to stop western troops from entering the south. For the first time since his election as president, Pétion sensed that it might be Rigaud rather than Christophe destined to occasion his downfall. His worst nightmare was imagining his two rivals working together against him. Pétion needed a plan, and fast. While he gleaned that Rigaud was hardly afraid of him, he correctly suspected that Louverture's former rival was, like him, afraid of Christophe, who had played a major role in his defeat during the conflict with Louverture. Pétion feigned that he had just learned that the northern army was en route to attack the south and profit from their dissension, and that divided as they were, it would be impossible to resist them. Rigaud, evidently giving much credence to "this artifice," agreed to a "federative pact," by which Pétion would command the second division of the west and Rigaud the province of the south. The two men also agreed that if the north attacked Pétion, Rigaud would come to his aid in Port-au-Prince.[56]

Rigaud's return might have been a propitious moment for Christophe to try to invade Port-au-Prince. But Christophe's ministers consistently pointed out that this was not their president's object. He had never gone on the offensive, because he did not want to spill blood, they said. Far from wanting to make war, when Christophe learned about the political scission and ensuing warfare in the south and southwest, he sent a delegation to Port-au-Prince, accompanied by "twelve soldiers from different corps in the south, who had been taken prisoner at the Battle of Môle, to inform their fellow citizens about the good treatment they had experienced in the north." Christophe charged this deputation with proposing to Pétion the reestablishment of peace by conciliatory means, which meant the republic's surrender to the kingdom. At the arrival of the deputation in Port-au-Prince, Pétion was absent, however. He had gone to the Pont de Miragoâne to meet with Rigaud. This was the coincidence that Pétion seized upon to try to make Rigaud believe that the troops arriving from the north had come to invade, leading to the federative pact. Pétion sent the deputation away without hearing them speak, saying he wanted nothing to do with peace and reunion. He also kept the twelve soldiers who should have been sent back to the kingdom.[57]

In his history of this affair, Vastey dropped a political and historical bombshell when he explained that Rigaud's attempt to overthrow Pétion's republic led the councilors of state in northern Haiti to propose in March

1811 that Christophe be crowned king of a newly minted Kingdom of Haiti. The example northerners took from the dissensions in the south and west, Vastey explained, was that "republics are fit only for fomenting trouble and bringing about civil war."[58]

The civil war between Rigaud and Pétion dramatically changed the trajectory of the country by seeming to demonstrate that monarchical rule was less susceptible to power struggles than republican political formations. Rigaud's attempt to do away with Pétion only ended when, after suffering from what Vastey called "a sickness of languor," Rigaud retired to the plain of Les Cayes. Sensing that his life had arrived at its close, Rigaud summoned his council and the most high-ranking generals to the plantation where he resided, the most noteworthy being General Bernard Borgella. At this bedside meeting, Rigaud chose Borgella as his successor, calling him the most dignified and capable of commanding.

After wasting away for some time, and despite "the most artful assistance," on September 18, 1811, Rigaud, in Vastey's words, "ended his career in death, not without the suspicion that he had been poisoned." "What further strengthened this suspicion," Vastey continued, "was that it had been rumored that at the news of Rigaud's death Pétion feigned to be painfully afflicted, but everyone saw shining through, despite his attempt, the inner joy he felt at seeing himself rid of a rival as feared as he was dangerous." Not long after his former commander's death Borgella surrendered to Pétion. Thus ended the civil war within a civil war on the island of Haiti.[59]

Although Rigaud's death and Borgella's surrender seemingly strengthened and consolidated Pétion's rule, the president of the republic, like Christophe, clearly knew that he remained in a precarious position. There was still France to contend with. And much like Christophe, Pétion strongly suspected that not only had Napoléon sent Rigaud his way, costing the republic money, territory, and lives, but Napoléon sought to create dissension in the Kingdom of Haiti, where Christophe reigned. Napoléon's plans were hardly secret at that point. Peltier reported to the Earl of Liverpool, while explaining Rigaud's momentous return to Haiti, that "two British frigates, the *Indefatigable* and the *Minerva,* have taken the American ship *George,* which had been sent for Baltimore and had 52 priests and a bishop on board, upon its leaving Bordeaux. Whatever these passengers may allege as to the purpose of their journey, I dare almost assure you, My Lord, that they could only be destined for St. Domingue. The number of 52 corresponds precisely to that of the parishes that this island once had, and the addition of a bishop to this numerous ecclesiastical mission might corroborate the suspicions I have that this episcopal envoy was meant to place the island under the powers of the Pope, true or false; but in all cases it would make null and void the current Apostolic Prefect of Haiti, the Reverend Father Corneille, whose attachment to President Henry Christophe is well known to Napoléon, as well as the veneration that he enjoys among the natives of Haiti." "It seems obvious to me that Buonaparte's purpose in sending this convoy is to pit altar against altar on that island, and to make religion serve his plans of conquest in the islands, as well as the military and his navy of corsairs," Peltier concluded. Acknowledging these ongoing existential threats to Haiti allowed Peltier to exalt the construction of the Citadelle and its ongoing expansion as marks of Christophe's enduring ability to protect Haiti from outside invaders and preserve its independence. "The impregnable citadel which he had erected at Morne Ferrière [sic], and which, like another Gibraltar, can defy all the efforts of France and its other enemies, assures President Christophe of a decided superiority over any faction which may arise in the isle, while the existence of these factions will always be precarious."[60]

After the Battle of Môle, and the temporary end of the physical part of Haiti's civil war, King Henry spent the majority of his time up at that "impregnable" Citadelle, preparing it for a different war. Not with Pétion, but with France. There, Christophe received some shocking news in October 1814. The king had been at the fortress with the royal family for several days, when he learned that his soldiers captured and jailed a French spy. The man, Christophe soon learned, had been sent to the island not by Napoléon, who had been forced to abdicate his throne earlier that year, but by Louis XVIII, the restored Bourbon king. Haiti's king had a new rival in the Atlantic.[61]

13

THREE FRENCH SPIES

The discordant clang of half-broken church bells sounded as the people of Cap-Henry slowly filed into a solemn ceremony in the royal church. Covered in shrouds of black, the nave and choir appeared prepared for a funeral. The small throng quickly grew into a crowd. But with no evidence of mourning in sight—every countenance stricken instead with something closer to menacing glee—the absence of a corpse and coffin occasioned whispers. No elegiac hymn filled the air. All that could be heard amid the uncharacteristic silence was the low hum of a Te Deum hymn of gratitude: "Oh, to you who are the Lord and Father, we give you thanks." The king and queen sat patiently watching from their thrones as the guest of honor was pushed into the hall: Agoustine Franco de Médina. The archbishop's pronunciation of this name unleashed a chorus of hisses and boos, audible swearing, the baring of teeth, and the brandishing of swords and knives. The very much alive celebrant was a captured spy from France. He had been imprisoned for weeks in one of the kingdom's towers. This was his funeral.

One hundred days. That is how long Napoléon Bonaparte lasted after overthrowing Louis XVIII in March 1815 following the first Bourbon Restoration. One hundred days. That is how the French king lost France's penultimate attempt to recover its erstwhile colony. One hundred days alone stood between the uncertainty of Haiti's eleven-year standoff with France and the Haitian king's emergence as the triumphant victor against the greatest army the world thought it ever saw. Again.

Yet the story of the king of Haiti's first defeat of the Bourbon monarch and his attempt to reduce the Haitian people once more to slavery does not begin with the emperor Napoléon's infamous one hundred days. The story starts much earlier in April 1814, when the emperor of France was forced to abdicate his throne and then saw himself exiled, for the first time, to the island of Elba, and when the newly restored king of France, Louis XVIII, evidently having learned nothing from Napoléon's ill-fated Leclerc expedition, began to prepare his own military fleet for a Saint-Domingue reconquest. To understand France's failure, we must begin with three French spies: Dravermann, Médina, and Dauxion-Lavaysse. Memorize these names, because they are the ones who would take the fall for the French king's unconscionably arrogant dream of restoring his authority and slavery once more to "Saint-Domingue."

On June 28, 1814, not three months after the long since beheaded Louis XVI's brothers benefited from England's defeat of Napoléon, which sent him into exile on the island of Elba, the Kingdom of France, led by Louis XVIII, formally opened its mission to "restore Saint-Domingue." A former French colonist and planter from Saint-Domingue, Pierre-Victor, the Baron de Malouet, oversaw the mission. Previously dismissed by Napoléon for not supporting his incursion into Russia, Malouet was immediately reinstated by Louis XVIII and appointed minister of the marine and colonies.

Under the imprimatur of Louis XVIII, in June 1814 Malouet sent a letter to Agoustine Franco de Médina (of Santo Domingo), Jean-François Dauxion-Lavaysse (of Gascogne), and Herman Dravermann (of Bordeaux).[1] The missive directed the three men to travel to the Caribbean island of Jamaica, under British rule, and from there to form a plan to approach the two different rulers of Haiti. Their mission was twofold: gain entry to either part of the island—the kingdom or the republic—to gather information that might be helpful for the planned military expedition. In the process the three needed to gauge the feelings of Haiti's two different rulers vis-à-vis the return of French authority.

Malouet instructed Dravermann to travel to the southern republic to meet with Borgella, Pétion's second-in-command, while Dauxion-Lavaysse was meant to go with him to Port-au-Prince to appeal to Pétion. The rulers of the southern republic were to be approached first because Malouet believed that both Pétion and Borgella remained open to the prospect of French return. Médina had the most dangerous mission of them all, one that he would end up paying for with his life. Malouet instructed him to go to the northern part of the island, to the Kingdom of Haiti, and try to meet with Christophe.[2]

This might have been a reasonable plan, if Christophe's state-run newspapers were not printing constant diatribes against France, warning both the ex-colonists and the French government, under the pain of death, to never return to the island whose people they once forced into bondage. Only three months before Médina's arrival in Cap-Henry, the *Royal Gazette of Hayti* gleefully announced that the emperor of France had at last been dethroned. "Our implacable enemy is no more," the article announced. "The execrable Bonaparte, who vainly tried to exterminate us, has just succumbed to the united efforts of the allied powers. . . . Europe has just broken his tyrannical yoke forever." Although the Haitian king expressed doubt about the politics of the French king with respect to Haiti, the same number of the *Gazette* issued a stern warning to all of France:

If by a false and reckless policy, owing to absurd calculations, dictated by a sordid and rapacious interest, unjust aggressors once again come to defile our territory, by placing a hostile foot here; . . . [i]f our implacable enemies, the Colonists, particularly, persist in their absurd and chimerical projects; if they do manage to entice the current government of France to wage an unjust, ruinous, and disastrous war against us; . . . [i]f they put themselves at the head of the troops to lead them here, they will be the first to be sacrificed to our revenge, and the land of freedom will rejoice by drinking the blood of its oppressors!

"It is then that we will wage a war of extermination, and we will give no quarter, spare no prisoner," the article finished.[3] Even if Médina, who previously fought under Toussaint Louverture and the French on the eastern side of the island, was not personally acquainted with Christophe, did he really imagine that after ten years of independence Haitians in his kingdom would once again consent to French domination?

Médina's counterpart, Dauxion-Lavaysse, with whom Médina traveled first to Saint Vincent and to Saint Lucia, before landing in Kingston, did not operate under any such illusion. Dauxion-Lavaysse had an interview with Napoléon sometime before his first abdication in which he called Christophe, whom he had never met, "a funny-looking king," a "very burlesque" man, "who has generals, his doctors, and his favorites beheaded at the slightest whim of his bloodthirsty desires." During their long journey from Europe to the Caribbean, which saw their ship leave from Boulogne, passing through Dover, London, and Falmouth, before landing in the West Indies, one has to wonder, then, if the men ever discussed what such a severe king, by Dauxion-Lavaysse's own estimation, might do if he were to capture them. Dauxion-Lavaysse seemed to have been able to imagine the outcome. He told Bonaparte in the same 1813 meeting, "His Christophean Majesty . . . is never more satisfied than when, as a result of his enormous temper, he has picked off some of his own subjects."[4]

It is precisely because of what he characterized as Christophe's temperamental frame of mind that Dauxion-Lavaysse first wanted to test the waters with the Haitian king by writing directly to him. On October 21, Christophe received a letter from Kingston, dated October 1 and signed by Dauxion-Lavaysse, but the epistolary interview got off to a terrible start. Dauxion-Lavaysse addressed the letter to "General Christophe," not King Henry. This kind of slight formed one of Christophe's greatest and most well-known irritations.

From a purely diplomatic standpoint, Dauxion-Lavaysse certainly showed an inappropriate lack of respect when dealing with a head of state. His blatant dismissal of King Henry's title reflected the fact that since 1804 France had remained utterly persistent in its attempt to discursively disavow—to deadname even—Haitian independence, but with drastically different consequences. Continuing to refer to Haiti as "Saint-Domingue," and to its rulers as generals, constituted simply some of the more obvious ways France sought to undermine Haitian sovereignty as it prepared to restore its own authority over "Saint-Domingue." Yet delusional dreams of French colonial reinstatement were not the sole reason that Dauxion-Lavaysse showed King Henry disrespect. Dauxion-Lavaysse was dealing with a man he did not consider his equal, racially or intellectually. In his meeting with Napoléon, he called Christophe an "ignoramus" and likened him to "other little savage leaders of the Old and New Worlds." In contrast, Dauxion-Lavaysse praised Pétion, whom he called "an educated, enlightened man of gentle mores."[5]

When the French spy's letter reached the Haitian king, Christophe noticed how it dripped with its author's barely disguised disdain. "General," Dauxion-Lavaysse's letter began, "You have been informed of the important mission with which I have the honor to be charged to your excellency; and it had been my intention on arriving here to address your excellency and General Pétion at the same moment: for I am not come, as you well know, to be the messenger of discord, but as the precursor of peace and reconciliation." Despite claiming that he came to Haiti in peace, Dauxion-Lavaysse directly threatened war not only from France but from an alliance of "the sovereigns of Europe," who he claimed, despite their differences with one another, all shared the desire to "unite their forces if necessary and contribute to the assistance requisite to overthrow all the governments that have arisen out of the French revolution, whether in Europe or the new world." Dauxion-Lavaysse implied that such an alliance of the great powers would materialize if Christophe did not consent to bring Haiti back under the dominion of the French king Louis XVIII as "Saint-Domingue." "The sovereigns of Europe . . . unacquainted with the wisdom and principles of your excellency," Dauxion-Lavaysse wrote,

> imagine you might hesitate as to the conduct you should pursue; and it was agreed that, to replace the population of Hayti, which in this case, would be totally annihilated by the forces sent against it, it would be necessary for France to continue the slave trade for yet many years, with the double view of replacing the hands wanting for agriculture, and forming soldiers in imitation of the English.[6]

This letter confirmed what King Henry long suspected: restoring slavery to the island remained the persistent goal of the French government.

Throughout his reign, Christophe had made it his mission to ensure the Haitian people would never forget the basic fact of France's obsession with enslaving them. With Dauxion-Lavaysse's letter now in hand, Christophe had unassailable proof. King Henry immediately directed the

Chevalier de Prézeau and the Baron de Vastey to draft public responses. While Vastey directed his exposé specifically at Malouet, since Malouet had sent the spies, the Chevalier de Prézeau targeted his pamphlet at Dauxion-Lavaysse.[7]

De Prézeau's response seared with multiple takedowns of the French spy's illogical overtures. "You must believe that we are completely lacking in intelligence, if you think we do not understand the goal of your maneuvers," the chevalier wrote. "Please, Sir, cease to abuse yourself; the time of our missteps and credulity has disappeared; do not believe that you will find any dupes in a nation whose memories of your past wrongs have never been forgotten."[8] This was hardly the kind of easy-to-conquer crowd that Malouet told Dauxion-Lavaysse and the other spies to expect in a land of formerly enslaved people.

Prior to writing to Christophe, Dauxion-Lavaysse had approached Pétion. He went to Pétion initially because the letter accompanying the detailed instructions that Malouet gave to the spies stated that Pétion, and his second-in-command, Borgella, because they were "mulattoes," were likely more amenable to a French takeover:

Being educated and enlightened men, . . . they will see that if the great mass of blacks are not returned to and maintained in a state of slavery, or at the very least, to a similar condition in which they found themselves before the troubles began, there will never be tranquility nor prosperity in the colony, nor safety for themselves. . . . Given these considerations, it is reasonable to suspect that Pétion and Borgella, after we satisfy them by granting them personal favors for themselves and for a small number of their kind . . . , will consent without difficulty to the fact that their caste, in acquiring almost the entirety of political rights, will remain still, in some respects, a little bit below the white caste; . . . in so doing, their caste will be more assured of dominating the free black caste, and . . . of keeping the non-free blacks at the distance required to maintain them in order. . . . As far as we can presently judge from here, it seems that the most important thing will be to come to an agreement with Pétion's side; and, once this has been done, it will be much easier to reduce Christophe's side to obedience without a great effusion of blood.[9]

Dauxion-Lavaysse, true to his racist form, dutifully approached Pétion by sending him a missive from Kingston. The letter arrived in Port-au-Prince on a British ship and bore the date September 6, 1814. Addressing Pétion as "General" and evoking the authority of Louis XVIII, Dauxion-Lavaysse said the king of France, not to be confused with that traitor Napoléon or the unfortunate Louis XVI, would give Pétion's men, if they surrendered to France, "the rights of French subjects and citizens, which is undoubtedly better than to be treated as barbarous savages, or hunted as maroon negroes."[10] Despite Dauxion-Lavaysse's evident admiration for Pétion—in his 1813 exchange with Napoléon, Dauxion-Lavaysse referred to Pétion as "one of the smartest and most wholesome men who have ever existed"[11]—the letter he sent to Haiti's president contained hardly less threatening language than the one he later sent to Christophe. Pétion's reaction, however, was altogether different from the Haitian king's. Pétion responded to Dauxion-Lavaysse with a letter dated September 24, in which he invited the Frenchman to come to Port-au-Prince. "I regretted, after reading your Excellency's dispatches," Pétion's letter stated, "that you have not undertaken a voyage in person to Port-au-Prince, where I should be better able to communicate with you on the nature and extent of your mission. Such a step I take the liberty of recommending."[12]

The French spy, believing his mission well on the way to success, arrived in the Republic of Haiti later that fall. Upon his arrival, the republic's officials transported him to a luxurious apartment and reportedly treated him with the "politeness, attention, and respect" Pétion had promised.[13] Once in Port-au-Prince, Dauxion-Lavaysse also had occasion to meet Jean-Pierre Boyer, a former journeyman tailor, then the commander of Port-au-Prince, who later succeeded Pétion as president.[14] The favorable treatment he received in the republican stronghold of Port-au-Prince increased the spy's belief that his mission to encourage Pétion to agree to French rule and the reinstatement of slavery could not but succeed.

Almost certainly adding to Dauxion-Lavaysse's unqualified confidence was his unfailing belief that men of African descent with lighter skin held unquenchable racial prejudices against "negroes." The portion of Malouet's eventually exposed instructions to Dauxion-Lavaysse and the other spies not only gave the impression that "mulattoes" like Pétion wanted the return of slavery but assumed that it would be easy to re-enslave the "black" population. Listing in bullet fashion what he desired the three spies to accomplish, Malouet stated in instruction number five, "Not only reduce to slavery, and return to their former owners, all the blacks who are currently laboring on the plantations, but bring back once again, as much as possible, those who freed themselves from this condition." Instruction number six mandated, "Rid the island of all the blacks whom it would be inappropriate to admit among the free and whom it would be dangerous to leave among those who are attached to the plantations."[15] What a stark reminder that the struggle for Haitian freedom did not end with the Haitian Declaration of Independence. These instructions were hardly the outlying musings of a madman. Malouet's entire mission sadly reflected popular sentiment in France.

Talk of "restoring Saint-Domingue" surged under both Napoléon and Louis XVIII, and remained particularly rampant in the months leading up to Malouet's mission. The former French colonist Drouin de Bercy, for instance, devoted 10 pages of his 178-page diatribe about the loss of the colony, titled *Of Saint-Domingue* (1814), to explain how "ambush," starvation, and "terror" should be "the order of the day" to "reestablish" the colony in France's name. Averring that popular opinion in France held that "the colony will never be tranquil if we do not destroy every last one of them," Drouin de Bercy proposed that "all the leaders above the rank of corporal must disappear," and "all of the black women . . . who were mistresses and prostitutes . . . should be subjected to the disposition of the government, which will send them wherever seems fit." He concluded by unequivocally counseling that after this "purge" the colony could be easily repopulated:

> When the island has been completely conquered and purged of all of those who could cause trouble . . . the government, one year afterward . . . could send on its behalf ten old ships, provisionally armed, to traffic in Africa for as long as it sees fit to reintroduce blacks into Saint-Domingue.[16]

Putting aside for the moment these terrible, and delusional, genocidal imaginings, let us now return to the first of our French travelers to reach Haiti. He was dining not with a king but with a president, whom he called general.

Boyer brought Dauxion-Lavaysse to the national palace of Haiti to meet Pétion a few days after the intrepid voyager's arrival. Perhaps it was the effects of the fever Dauxion-Lavaysse came down with in Kingston and took with him to Haiti as his unwitting companion, along with Dravermann, that made the French spy deliriously ask Pétion to enter a treaty. Or perhaps it was simply folly. For Malouet's instructions, even with all their colonial hubris, explicitly stated that none of the three men should be compelled into "signing any formal treaty." This was because, according to Malouet, to ask for a treaty would be to have de facto acknowledged the "treaty-worthiness" of Haiti's leaders, thus also de facto diplomatically acknowledging Haiti's sovereignty from France. Malouet made quite clear that this would be "a thing derogatory to the royal dignity" of the king of France. Instead, the mission of the three spies remained essentially to "poll" Haiti's leaders so that the Bourbon king could effectively determine if he required a military expedition to reconquer Saint-Domingue.[17]

By November 9, Dauxion-Lavaysse's treaty-seeking bravado had reached new heights. Presenting himself as having precisely the authority he did not have, Dauxion-Lavaysse addressed a note to Pétion and his ministers. In the note, he offered the chance for President Pétion to sign a treaty agreeing for Haiti to become a French colony once again, under the authority of "His Majesty, Louis XVIII."[18] Pétion took immediate if surprising action by issuing a public notice officially informing the Haitian people of his formal negotiations with the king of France. But nothing could have been further from the truth. Pétion was not in negotiation with the king of France. Dauxion-Lavaysse was now acting entirely off script and seemed to view himself as being on a one-man mission to recover the colony for France.

On November 12, Pétion wrote directly to Dauxion-Lavaysse, taking a few liberties of his own. First, he outright acknowledged the goal of the mission: "Alexandre Pétion, President of Haiti, has the honor to acknowledge the receipt of the note addressed to him on the 9th of the present month by his Excellency General Dauxion Lavaysse, in his capacity as principal agent of . . . his Most Christian Majesty, for the restoration of the French colony in St. Domingue." Before offering his reply, Pétion reminded the Frenchman of all the atrocities the French colonists committed in Saint-Domingue during the ancien régime, under the Bourbons, and then under Bonaparte. "It is with pain that the President of Haiti reminds His Excellency General Lavaysse that all the calamities of this country originated in revolutionary France, and that she has never ceased to provoke them by a conduct so uniformly cruel as to drive the inhabitants of Hayti to despair." The president continued by charging that Leclerc's mission had been nothing more than "an expedition of cannibals! In which the planters and the French vied with each other in their insatiable thirst for Haytian blood. The arms which they used to assist the French army in taking possession of the country were torn from their hands, while they themselves were dragged on board floating prisons called *étouffoires* [*sic*], smothered, drowned, hung, bayoneted, burned, torn in pieces by bloodhounds"—a reference to Leclerc's and Rochambeau's genocidal tactics during the final days of the Haitian Revolution, whereby they instructed French soldiers to drown or otherwise kill the entire population of color in Saint-Domingue. Pétion finished with a question: "At what conclusion do we arrive?" He said that war would be undesirable for both France and Haiti and promised to bring the "principal proposition" to the ministers of his republic for their consideration.[19]

Perhaps Pétion merely sought to play coy, but this kind of equivocal reply, rather than unequivocal rejection, only confirmed in the king of Haiti's mind that Pétion remained open not only to the restoration of French rule but to slavery too. In a decree the Comte de Limonade issued on behalf of King Henry, he reminded the Haitian people that after Dauxion-Lavaysse had issued an unequivocal threat—that if they did not submit to France they would be "*treated as barbarous savages, or hunted as maroon negroes*"—Pétion, "to whom [the threat] was addressed, welcome[d] with the kindest cordiality the man who presumed to make it." Instead of dismissing at once Dauxion-Lavaysse's menacing overture, as Christophe had done, Pétion told Dauxion-Lavaysse that he planned to convoke an assembly on November 21 to debate the matter.[20]

Dauxion-Lavaysse, in any event, not at all satisfied with Pétion's reply, replete as it was with reminders of all the Haitian people suffered under French rule, bristled even more at Pétion's enumeration of the French colonial government's crimes. In his wholly defensive response, dated November 19, Dauxion-Lavaysse expressed utter "shock" that "Your Excellency" continued to "besmirch the country of France" for crimes "committed under a tyrant," referring to Napoléon. He asked if Pétion would similarly condemn the people of Bordeaux, Nantes, Lyon, Toulouse, and Marseille for evil acts committed by self-proclaimed anarchists in their streets. The French spy went on to accuse England of attempting to sow discord between Haiti and France, and he finished by appealing to Pétion's genealogical ties to France. "We are all French, Mr. President," Dauxion-Lavaysse wrote. "Let the august name of the Bourbons be the signal of our reunification."[21]

In his reply the next day, Pétion agreed that neither Louis XVIII nor the people of France should be held responsible for the crimes of Louis XVI, the revolutionaries, Napoléon, or the ex–French colonists. "It would be unjust to ascribe to his most Christian Majesty transactions in which he had no share," Pétion agreed, "since at the time of their occurrence he was himself in exile from his dominions, as the victim of the very men who persecuted us so cruelly."[22] At the subsequent meeting of the assembly on the twenty-first, which took place one day after Pétion's strangely conciliatory response to Dauxion-Lavaysse, the president told his two closest advisers, Joseph Inginac and Jean-Pierre Boyer, that he would never consent to French reconquest. He did, however, open another fatal door when he revealed to these men that he was not opposed to paying an indemnity to compensate the former French colonists for the loss of their properties.[23]

Did Pétion really want to compensate the very men he called the "planters who excited" Rochambeau and Leclerc to spare "neither *women*, nor *infants*, nor *the aged*"?[24] Pétion's white father, Pascal Sabès, had rejected Pétion as his son and heir and denied to him the usage of the family name, simply because the child's skin color was too "tawny" for his tastes. While the naturalists of the period proclaimed that children with one-quarter "white" ancestry like Pétion were ordinarily very light-skinned, so to be indistinguishable from "pure" whites, the future Haitian president's skin evidently appeared dark enough for him to be recognized as (or at least suspected of) being of African descent.[25] For the crime of his color, Pétion's father denied him recognition.[26] This is hardly the kind of childhood experience of color prejudice likely to create a future apologist for the white colonists.

Instead, it seems that Pétion dreamed up the indemnity to avoid the war with France that Dauxion-Lavaysse threatened in his letter. Pétion gave Dauxion-Lavaysse a letter addressed to Malouet on November 27, stating that in exchange for formal recognition of Haitian independence the southern republic would agree to pay an indemnity, the amount of which would be determined by France:

> It is worthy of the greatness and enlightened philosophy of his most Christian Majesty to recognize the emancipation of a people whose misfortunes commenced with his own. . . . It will also be a source of lasting glory to his Majesty in granting to the Haytians a recognition of the independence of their rights, to reconcile it with what he owes to a part of his subjects in making others share in the benefits of a commerce whose abundant channels would promote the welfare of both countries. It is with such sentiments that I, as organ of the people over whom I have the honor to preside, will propose to your Excellency, acting in the name of his Majesty Louis XVIII and to give him a proof of the disposition which animates us, to establish the basis of an indemnity which we most solemnly engage to pay with every just security which can be required of us.[27]

Getting the Haitian government, which comprised many people France formerly enslaved, to agree to pay that same France for their freedom would have seemed like a victory to most negotiators, but not for the overly ambitious Dauxion-Lavaysse. The former French colonists were a class apart, and Dauxion-Lavaysse viewed his mission—to restore Saint-Domingue to French rule—as a complete and utter failure if he could not return to France with a signed declaration, a treaty, bearing Pétion's consent to make Haiti French again. He therefore wrote once more to Pétion on November 29 to say that he considered his business in Port-au-Prince for the moment complete and that he and Dravermann planned to return to Kingston. Dauxion-Lavaysse added that he would be certain to communicate to Malouet the disposition of the Haitians of the republic.[28]

Before Dauxion-Lavaysse left Port-au-Prince—still stricken with fever—Pétion sent his personal physician to attend to him, as a sign of continuing goodwill. Dr. Mirambeau was a Frenchman who had lived in independent Haiti since the days of Dessalines. In addition to soothing his fevers, Mirambeau gave Dauxion-Lavaysse a personal message from the president: "The republican flag protects the rights of all people," Pétion said. "I wish to, likewise, as always, show to the whites the magnanimity of my race."[29]

The king of Haiti proceeded with a far less servile attitude in the face of French threats to Haiti's freedom. Although they were not entirely unaware of the turn of events in Port-au-Prince with Dauxion-Lavaysse, kingdom officials had been preoccupied with entertaining their own French visitor in Cap-Henry, one whom they treated like the captured spy he was rather than the respectable diplomat he was not.

—

After Dauxion-Lavaysse entered Port-au-Prince, he directed Médina to go to the Spanish side of the island, still called Santo Domingo. From there, Médina entered Cap-Henry calling himself a merchant. Recall, however, that just before Médina's arrival, Dauxion-Lavaysse had attempted to sound out Christophe's intentions. Dauxion-Lavaysse knew that he could not simply send a letter and hope that it would reach Christophe through one of the king's own ministers, as he had correctly assumed with Pétion. Pondering the best approach to infiltrate the king's inner circle, while all three men were still in Kingston, Dauxion-Lavaysse acquainted himself with a French merchant named Montorsier. Much to Dauxion-Lavaysse's surprise, Montorsier revealed that he knew King Henry, having been previously arrested and released by him, and paradoxically, he confessed that he was currently employed by the Haitian king.

In 1810, Montorsier had been traveling with six other Frenchmen upon a ship leaving Cuba that stopped for a time in Cap-Henry. According to the French traveler Gaspard Théodore Mollien, living in Haiti at the time, Christophe demanded an interview with those on board, including Montorsier. Because the men were French, Christophe supposedly wanted to execute them all. Learning that Montorsier had allied with Lafayette during the American Revolutionary War, however, Christophe decided to spare his life. In exchange for this clemency, he required that Montorsier declare his "fidelity" to Christophe and fulfill certain offices for him. Errands that he gave to Montorsier included "purchasing precious objects" necessary for Christophe's impending coronation. Montorsier was in Kingston fulfilling other such business for the king when he encountered Dauxion-Lavaysse.[30]

Since he had authorization to enter Cap-Henry and could gain access to the king, Dauxion-Lavaysse asked Montorsier to take his October 1 missive to the kingdom. The spy instructed the French merchant to directly place the letter into "General" Christophe's hands and no one else's. Perhaps the French spy believed that one of Christophe's men might alter the letter, or perhaps he thought that once they read its contents, they might not transmit it to their sovereign. When Montorsier arrived that October, he sought out the Comte de Limonade and asked him if it would be possible to arrange an audience with Christophe. Probably sensing Limonade's suspicion, the French merchant insisted he carried important dispatches from the king of France and would only give them to Christophe. Limonade found off-putting Montorsier's suddenly haughty air and presumed self-importance. The count consulted Christophe's most important minister, the man with whom the king worked most closely, the Baron de Vastey.

It had been ten years since Haiti had any direct communication with the French government. Haiti's last official communication with France took place in 1804, when Dessalines announced the declaration of their independence. Does France want to "acknowledge our independence or re-enslave us"? Vastey wondered. "Does she want to repair all her wrongs?"

"But has she not already done enough to us," the baron thought, seeming to answer his own question. Despite Dauxion-Lavaysse's directive, the two men finally persuaded Montorsier to leave the letter with the kingdom's translator, the Baron de Dupuy. The officials then sent a messenger to alert King Henry, away at the Citadelle, of Montorsier's arrival. After which, the king gathered an assembly of his most important ministers to read the letter.[31]

Limonade took on the rather lugubrious task of reading the letter out loud to Christophe. It contained what the *Gazette* later reported as a "range of insults, conceits, and lies" and finished with the French government's horrifying proposition whereby it demanded the king of Haiti choose between slavery and death.[32] It must have been strange for Limonade to hear himself pronounce the threats in the letter, which also included a reference to "annihilating" the Haitian people and replacing them with "other unfortunate beings torn from the heart of Africa." Limonade would also have had to repeat the lines referring to Malouet's favorite scheme of intimidation, "co-operation of the maritime powers of Europe," and the threat that all this would happen, "should we refuse to return beneath the yoke of France and slavery."[33]

The letter, addressed "To his Excellency General Christophe, supreme Chief of the government of the North of Hayti," did not start out this monstrous. After several pretentious flatteries of the king of France, including an attempt to absolve Louis XVIII once again of anything that happened during Haiti's war of independence, Dauxion-Lavaysse wrote, "I come then, general, by the orders of my august sovereign, to bear to you words of satisfaction and peace. And while from the height of a throne the most splendid in Europe, he commands an army of five hundred thousand men, he sends me alone to negotiate with you about your true interests." After asking the king of Haiti, whom he continued to address as a "general," to "proclaim Louis XVIII" as his king, Dauxion-Lavaysse provided an expansive portrait of how, failing that, France would carry out war against Haiti with its stated army of 500,000:

Compel us not, general, to make soldiers of the negroes we are now importing from Africa; compel us not to have recourse to all possible means of destruction. Do not expose yourself to behold the desertion of your battalions who will soon learn that French discipline, the most perfect in the world, employs not that excessive severity with which you so often exercise. . . .

I believe you to be too cool headed, too enlightened and too noble, not to be satisfied with becoming a nobleman and a general officer under the ancient dynasty of the Bourbons, which Providence has seen fit, contrary to all human calculation, to continue upon the throne of our dear France. . . .

The last consideration which I shall offer to your excellency is the integrity which distinguishes the present minister of the marine. All the world knows that in the time of the constituent assembly, in which he was always one of the most strenuous defenders of the cause of the king, he insisted on the justice of ameliorating the lot of the blacks and the men of color. To pronounce the name of Malouet is to awaken the recollection of the highest virtues, and the most inflexible integrity. Every promise made by such a man will be as sacred and as certain as if it were (pardon the expression) the Divinity himself who uttered it.

Accept, general, the sentiments of high respect wherewith I have the honor to be your excellency's most obedient humble servant.

DAUXION LAVAYSSE

P.S. Colonel Médina, an associate of my mission, will repair to your excellency, whose entire confidence he merits. In proof of the candor with which I act, I subjoin a copy of my letter to Pétion. Hardly had I written it before I felt ill, which deprived me of the honor of addressing your excellency at the same time.[34]

This is how, as Christophe later acknowledged, using as proof the copy of Dauxion-Lavaysse's letter to Pétion, the king of Haiti learned of the king of France's opinion that the inhabitants of the island were merely "maroon negroes." Dauxion-Lavaysse's letter to Pétion had ended with the following threat disguised as counsel:

Let us repose our confidence in this enlightened, generous, and loyal King. HE WILL EXTEND TO US THE RIGHTS OF FRENCH SUBJECTS AND CITIZENS WHICH IS UNDOUBTEDLY BETTER THAN TO BE TREATED AS BARBAROUS SAVAGES, OR HUNTED AS MAROON NEGROES.

"Make these reflections, this soliloquy, General," Dauxion-Lavaysse had told Pétion, "instill them into the minds of reasonable men who merit your confidence, and you will deserve the most honorable testimony of your Sovereign's satisfaction, and the gratitude of your country and the inhabitants of Hayti, whom we must ever regard as French."[35]

Complete silence reigned after the reading. By turns shocked and indignant at the audacity, Christophe and his men found that Dauxion-Lavaysse's enclosed letter to Pétion confirmed what they already knew deep in their hearts: bringing Haiti under French authority meant only one thing, the return of slavery. The French emissaries presented their choices as to submit to France or to continue to be treated as "maroon negroes."

And what to make of the bizarre threat to recruit Africans from the continent to fight with the French army against Haitians? "Compel us not, general, to make soldiers of the negroes we are now importing from Africa," the letter said. The Chevalier de Prézeau, who authored the October 1814 response, laughed at such a ridiculous proposition. "Asking Africans, our brothers, sir, to fight us would truly be to make a mistake right before our eyes; for that would only lead our ranks to swell," de Prézeau replied. The suggestion *was* patently absurd given that most Haitians at the time of the revolution had been born in Africa.[36]

Christophe, for his part, sat in a glimmering rage. Many of the men standing before him in the room carried scars from the chains the French had forced them to wear as slaves. Others were painfully reminded of the mass drownings and hangings they witnessed, along with having to watch their family members eaten by the dogs purchased from Cuba to hunt down the "insurgents."[37] Dauxion-Lavaysse had clearly and unmistakably threatened war, but he also made the threats personal when he implied that harm could come to the king's family. Dauxion-Lavaysse wrote that he was "certain that the welfare of your country, of yourself, and of your family and friends will serve as the rule of your conduct." Moreover, while trying to prove the French would not behave with racial prejudice toward those Haitians awarded free status, Dauxion-Lavaysse unwittingly confirmed they would. He claimed that under French laws some of the people of African descent like Christophe could be designated as *white men*. As such, they would escape the prejudices to which the French summarily subjected Black people in the colonies and in France:

> But I am aware, that there are among your generals some who fear that the chiefs sent by the king, . . . yielding to the influence of creoles and emigrants, may gradually re-establish the reign of prejudice. But believe me, general, the reign of prejudice is at an end for ever. . . . The king . . . will act, you need not doubt, like the monarchs of Spain and Portugal, who using *lettres de blanc,* can raise an individual of any complexion to the condition of a white man. His royal power . . . is equally capable of rendering a black or colored man not only in the sight of the throne and the law, but also in social discourse, equal to the whitest men of Picardy.[38]

De Prézeau's reply to this was unequivocal. "We do not desire to become white," he scoffed. "We pride ourselves on being the color that it has pleased God to paint our faces." "We demand only," he insisted, "the natural rights of man and the political rights that every other independent and free nation enjoys."[39]

Haitian consternation was no match for French arrogance. Almost unbelievably, Montorsier stayed in the Haitian capital after relinquishing the letter, and he persisted in his attempt to meet face-to-face with Christophe. Montorsier hoped to explain the contents of the letter to the king himself and justify France's mission. Even more incredibly than Montorsier's misplaced faith in the righteousness of the requests turned threats contained in the letter, Christophe agreed to meet alone with Montorsier.

"Do not worry," King Henry told his principal officers. "I will make him vomit up everything in his stomach."[40]

Knowing that Montorsier was quite mercenary, did the Haitian king try to account for the fact, or at least convince himself, that Montorsier must have had economic motives to explain how the man whose life the king once saved could stand before him as a messenger on such a dubious errand? Perhaps Christophe reminded Montorsier of how he earlier spared his life, or perhaps he threatened to surely end it this time. Whatever transpired in the minds of the two men standing in the room, the meeting ended with Montorsier's exposing all the French government's plans. "You will have as your property total sovereignty over the island of La Tortue," Montorsier said. "You will be able to stay there, or you will be permitted to retire, be it in France, be it in the United States, or wherever in the world you would like to go; the benefits of Louis XVIII will follow you." "You must destroy all of those in your party, though," Montorsier warned him. "It is the only way to save yourself!"

To say that King Henry lost his Latin once more upon hearing these words come out of the mouth of the audaciously unarmed Frenchman standing right before him, as if he were confronting a flower rather than a warrior, would be too tepid a way to describe the circumstances as they were. King Henry rose and angrily cried, "They want to take away the freedom of Haitians; they dare to propose that I destroy all of you; to annihilate you!" The king's officers, waiting in a room next door, ran toward the direction of the angry shouts. By the time Vastey entered the chamber, he witnessed Montorsier trembling. The Frenchman's constitution was "pale and bleak," Vastey recalled, and the officers clearly wanted to execute him. They tried to throw him off the balustrade and into the street.

"No," King Henry ordered. "Let him go. His atrocious plans have been discovered."[41]

———

Montorsier's failure to recruit the king of Haiti to the side of the king of France did not mark the end of the affair. True to Dauxion-Lavaysse's letter, Médina arrived in Santo Domingo, in the city of Saint-Jago, sometime in late October or early November 1814. Médina subsequently traveled to Cap-Henry, seemingly unaware of what happened to Montorsier. Would he have aborted the mission had he known of the fit Christophe threw after learning the contents of Dauxion-Lavaysse's letter? No matter, Médina had instructions, and unlike Dauxion-Lavaysse he intended to follow them. Médina presented himself in the kingdom as a merchant, not as an official negotiator or diplomat sent on behalf of the king of France. All the king's men already knew exactly who he was, though, owing to Dauxion-Lavaysse's treacherous letter.

Vastey was the first official from the kingdom to encounter the Spanish stranger traveling under the French standard. Vastey knew him by reputation: Médina had previously been adjutant general under General Ferrand. Vastey had also performed reconnaissance on Médina before his arrival, and learned that Médina had been accused of killing women and children in the Haitian city of Ouanaminthe during an attack ordered by General Ferrand.[42]

Although it is true that he was only one man, the sight of Médina showing up in the kingdom produced an effect not unlike the sight the Leclerc expedition produced on Louverture, when in 1802 he glimpsed the French army's numerous fleet hovering off the coast of Saint-Domingue, with its tens of thousands of soldiers on board. Observing the stark, bright sails of the enormous armada, dotting the deep blue of the Atlantic with crisp white, Louverture reportedly stated, "The whole of France has come to Saint-Domingue. . . . She comes to avenge herself and force the blacks back into slavery."[43] Dauxion-Lavaysse's letter, too, had newly called forth the sordid, traumatic, and not at all forgotten history of Louverture. Blaming Napoléon for the arrest and deportation of Louverture, Dauxion-Lavaysse evoked the memory of the most betrayed man of the revolution when he wrote, "Louis XVIII, has lamented more than anyone, the atrocious measures adopted against General Toussaint."[44] Dauxion-Lavaysse's evocation of France's duplicity vis-à-vis one of Haiti's most regretted revolutionary heroes likely struck a nerve with Christophe, if it did not entirely unleash a torrent of complicated emotions.

Even if remembering Louverture's fate did not cause feelings of guilt to stir within Christophe's breast, the evocation of the title of his onetime friend would almost certainly have brought up unhappy recollections. The end of Louverture's life, tricked as he was at the hands of the French, could only have seemed like a disturbing portent of the future awaiting King Henry should he similarly allow himself to be seduced into any meeting or formal treaty with France.

The mood of the kingdom concerning the infamous prison neglect and death of Louverture is well captured in the Chevalier de Prézeau's response to Dauxion-Lavaysse's reference to Louverture:

You may want to make us believe that you sincerely deplore his loss. As if! . . . I have never seen in any French writing the murder of this worthy Chief mentioned when the crimes of Napoléon are spoken of; on the contrary, he receives congratulations for this. So, sir, allow me to tell you that I find it hard to believe that what you are saying is true; if correcting this misdeed was so much on his mind and given such consideration by your monarch, why has he not performed a funeral service for him?[45]

The biggest misstep Dauxion-Lavaysse made in mentioning Louverture was the fact that writers from the kingdom had already accused Médina of having betrayed Louverture in 1802. As governor-general, Louverture had named Médina mayor of the city called La Vega on the eastern side of the island. Once Leclerc arrived, however, Médina, unlike Christophe, immediately joined the French plot to unseat Louverture.[46]

Not only would this have been hard to forget for Christophe's men, most of whom fought in the revolutionary wars—and some of whom probably felt guilty for later betraying Louverture themselves—but no one in Haiti who heard the story of the horrific abuse that the French heaped on Louverture's wife, Suzanne, reported in the *Political and Commercial Gazette* in 1805, had likely forgotten that either. It was one thing to have turned their backs on Louverture in 1802 under uncertain skies, not having any idea of the consequences of their actions. It was quite another thing to continue to be allied with the very French forces responsible for the horrific and highly publicized treatment of Louverture and his family.[47]

The same kind of French trickery and torture that ended in Louverture's death found strange reflection in the eventual punishment meted out to Médina. Vastey decided to perform his own ruse to force the guileless Médina into revealing his true intentions. The baron, whose skin color was described as pale white, used his ambiguous appearance to create a feeling of fraternity between himself and Médina. Disguising his unfailing admiration for Christophe, Vastey described King Henry as a mercurial tyrant, warning the Frenchman to stay out of his way. Maybe Médina really did think that Vastey considered himself a white man, like him. Whatever caused the spy to speak so freely, he felt charmed enough to reveal that during his commercial negotiations he hoped to be able to report back to the French government about life in the kingdom.[48] Médina was subsequently given a passport to roam the island freely, and he even attended several dinners at the homes of important noble men and women of the kingdom. This seemingly friendly treatment completely disarmed the spy. In the words of one observer, "Far from seeing the trap that lay ahead, he imagined that he was being honored due to his prior reputation as a soldier and that they wanted to pay homage to the representative of the king of France: in a word, he was enchanted."[49] Unbeknownst to the beguiled Médina, he was also under constant surveillance.

Fearing that the ruse had gone on long enough, on November 11, Christophe issued orders for the arrest of the Frenchman, who came to be known as one of Louis XVIII's spies. Haiti's *Gazette* outed Médina as a spy on November 19, 1814: "A spy sent by the Baron de Malouet, minister of the marine and the colonies, of His Majesty Louis XVIII, to spread discord among us and to inquire about our internal means, was arrested while carrying out his execrable enterprise; first, he presented himself under the assumed name of Médina, but he was known to be the infamous *Agoustine Franco.*"[50] In reporting Médina's arrest, the article indicated that on November 16 officials in Cap-Henry called the king, who had been at the Citadelle with his wife and children, back to Cap-Henry. Once there, Christophe assisted in the interrogation of Médina, which lasted for multiple days and yielded other painstaking revelations, whereby Médina not only left no doubt about France's perfidious intentions to bring back slavery but was found in possession of the remarkably precise step-by-step written instructions describing how France planned to accomplish the "restoration."

The kingdom's officials discovered the instructions in Médina's effects despite Malouet's order that he memorize and then destroy them; they immediately read the directives in the presence of the king and the other nobles. The instructions spelled out how France hoped to re-create the racial caste system operative in the colony before 1789:

Instructions for MM. Dauxion Lavaysse, de Médina, and Dravermann, from the Baron de Malouet, Minister of the Marine:

Negotiate with Pétion not only the return of Haiti to French rule, but a return of the caste system that was in effect before 1789.

It is extremely important to conserve for the whites every preeminence over the men of color, as a first order.

If Pétion agrees to rank the men of color, exclusively up to the mulatto, just a little bit below white people, it will be so much easier to restrict the privileges of the caste just below it (composed of those mixtures between the mulattoes and the negroes) and the free blacks. . . .

With respect to the most numerous class, that of the blacks responsible for the cultivation and planting of sugar, indigo, and so on, it is necessary that things return to the state in which they were before 1789. . . . Means should be devised with the aid of Pétion to make the greatest possible number of blacks return to the plantations and to our subordination, in the hopes of lessening the number of free blacks. Those whom it will be inadvisable to admit into this last class, and who might continue to carry with them a dangerous spirit of insurrection, should be transported to the Isle of Ratau,[51] or elsewhere.

Malouet ended by providing a bulleted résumé of how France would organize the restored colony and what would happen to Haiti's current leaders. Given the generalized way that Haiti and its leaders are defamed in popular discourse, it is important to provide in English translation a full rendition of the instructions that detail France's constant aggressions against Haiti:

We have sketched the desired political organization of St. Domingue with these instructions to give the agents an idea of what the king of France will consent to in negotiations:
1. For Pétion, Borgella, and a few others (provided that their skin color is close to that of the whites) complete assimilation with white men and all the honorific advantages thereof, as well as those of fortune.
2. To the rest of their caste, as it exists at present, the enjoyment of the same political rights as the whites, with a few exceptions that will rank them just below white men.
3. For all those who are not quite as white as the true mulatto, the above political rights, to a lesser extent.
4. For those who are free, but entirely black, still a little less of these advantages.
5. Attach to the land, and give them back to their former owners, all the blacks who are still working on the plantations, and, to the extent that it is possible, bring back all those who freed themselves from this condition.
6. Rid the island of all the blacks whom it would be inappropriate to admit among the free and whom it would be dangerous to leave among those attached to the plantation.
7. Restrict the creation of any new free people of color.
. . .

Signed, Malouet[52]

Two subsequent directives appeared below these bullet points. In them, Malouet clarified that after implementation of the above the former French colonists could reassume the properties they owned before the revolution. Thanks to these instructions, Malouet, despite Dauxion-Lavaysse's letter claiming he possessed the "highest virtues" and "inflexible integrity," became known in Haiti as "the most abominable being in France and the whole universe."[53]

After the reading, King Henry grew even more angry. Instead of submitting to unmitigated rage, he formed an ingenious plot. First, he ordered the instructions to be published. He wanted no Haitian to ever have any doubt about the continued need for a strong army, numbering more than thirty-five thousand men. Christophe next moved to ensure the publication of the French scheme around the world, especially in France. The kingdom's ability to circulate information across international lines about France's desire to bring slavery back eventually won Christophe key supporters.

Perhaps surprisingly for a world of slavery, global public opinion overwhelmingly moved over to Christophe's side. One French newspaper, the *Journal des débats,* deriving its details from a British newspaper, acknowledged, "Christophe had published a manifesto on October 20 in which he assured his black companions that he would die rather than to see a foreign power be established in Saint-Domingue." "Christophe does not fear at all France's attempts to dethrone him," the writer concluded, before wondering if France was about to "commit for a second time its error of 1803."[54] *The Times* of London issued even more harsh and direct criticism. Noting first that Dauxion-Lavaysse approached Christophe with "ferocious and sanguinary threats," the writer concluded, "Had we not been accustomed to the extravagant falsehoods of the revolutionary orators . . . , we could hardly have believed that any human being could have so flagrantly insulted truth and common sense, as is done in the preceding extracts from M. Lavaysse's letter: but the Negro Sovereign and his Council were not so stupidly credulous as this weak man thought them."[55] U.S. newspapers not only reported the story and printed the instructions but published articles by writers who ardently defended and praised the Haitian king's conduct in the face of France's absurd threats. "The Island of St. Domingo is at this hour the Kingdom of Hayti, who live free and happy under a government duly organized with Constitutional laws, and a national representation to maintain them," one such article read. "These slaves converted into men by their liberty, and into men of energy, and friendly to peace, exhibit at the present moment, the view of a flourishing people, that could defend their liberty against Napoleon himself," the article's writer concluded, before going on to condemn the failed "mission of Gen. Dauxion Lavaysse."[56]

King Henry's ability to circulate information favorable to Haiti's cause of freedom and independence was rather impressive. Christophe directly sent all the documents and letters to his antislavery friends and allies across the Atlantic, and he told the Comte de Limonade to send Malouet's instructions to Peltier, who printed them in the appendix of the February 20, 1815, edition of his periodical, *L'ambigu. L'ambigu* had already published a copy of the Chevalier de Prézeau's refutation of Dauxion-Lavaysse's letter, and in the February 28, 1815, issue the Baron de Vastey's response to Malouet appeared. King Henry eventually ordered the publication in Haiti of the transcripts of Médina's interrogation, too, which occurred on November 17, the same day that the Kingdom of Haiti held the Te Deum Mass in ironic honor of the still alive captured spy. The fact that Christophe effectively controlled the narrative about the French spies allowed him to damn Malouet's mission with dramatic confidence: "The whole world is acquainted with the termination of this mission of *espionnage* and perfidy, to the disgrace of the government and minister who sent it."[57]

The day after Médina's interrogation—in which he admitted that "the minister said that the negroes must be made to return to the plantations, and that the planters should be put in possession of their properties, as in Martinique and Guadeloupe," adding that he believed and that Malouet told him anyone who did not submit to France would "*be exterminated,*" even the children—the king transported his entire family to church in Cap-Henry to witness the unusual living wake unfold.[58] All Christophe's most important ministers were present, accompanied by their wives, dressed in their Sunday best.

The church in Cap-Henry had been erected in seventeenth-century colonial Saint-Domingue. Rebuilt at the end of the eighteenth century after its partial destruction by an earthquake, the building was crushed again during the 1842 temblor that brought down much of the city, only to be rebuilt once more in 1876. The church has its own fascinating, if auspicious, revolutionary history too. This was the very spot where the French government condemned Ogé and his accomplice Chavannes to die after their failed October 1790 demand for rights equal to the French colonists.[59]

On the day of Médina's living wake, the inside of the church had been decorated in shrouds of black, meant to reflect the mournful ceremony to take place within its walls. Médina stood on a dock, facing an audience that included the Royal Haitian Guard. Médina leaned his back against a column as the people sang hymns of gratitude to God for having brought this traitor so openly and plainly into their midst, facilitating his capture and thwarting his mission. Médina, for his part, pleaded for his life.

Several hundred Haitian guards stood before Médina, surrounding him and the church. Some of the guards, depending on the regiment they served, would have been cloaked in long white habits; others would have been wearing habits in the king's color of celestial blue; still more numerous would have been those of the general guard whose uniforms were red. A sea of red, white, and blue surging up before him, shrouded in veils of black, might have offered a fittingly kaleidoscopic panorama of each of the country's past and present national colors bleeding together.

Unlike Montorsier or Lavaysse, Médina apologized. The scene before him might have had something to do with his sudden remorse. Instead of a sermon—or even a eulogy—Médina had to listen as the archbishop, the Duc de l'Anse, read Malouet's deadly instructions before everyone in the room, along with the contents of Dauxion-Lavaysse's letters, both the one addressed to the king and the one addressed to Pétion. The responses by Pétion and Christophe to each of these letters were also read, portions of which had also appeared in the Chevalier de Prézeau's pamphlet.

Aside from members of the military, a huge crowd of people who traveled from all parts of the kingdom to attend the service filled the church. There was standing room only. The seats were reserved for the noble men and women of the kingdom. Many foreign businessmen in the country also attended. Lines of troops and members of the general populace covered the historic plaza outside the church as well. Once the opening hymn and readings of the letters ceased, printed copies were distributed to all in attendance. Vastey reported the event with insightful precision in the *Royal Gazette.* "Imagine the position of this spy," he wrote, "in the midst of an immense crowd, surrounded by a throng of warriors who considered him a peculiar and ferocious beast, coming to propose to them slavery or death, as he did, and chains or annihilation to any child over six years old." Médina seemed understandably terrified as he stared down visions of his death at the hands of the former revolutionaries he once fought alongside. Staggering at the sight of the armed warriors and an irate crowd out for blood, he could barely stand. He continued to pray and begged for mercy for his soul. Evoking every saint, he turned his face up to the painted ceiling and prostrated himself to God. But only Haiti's king could provide him with absolution.[60]

Deliverance from this living wake was not yet on the horizon. The kingdom was known for throwing lavish events that lasted hours, dancing often into the wee morning light. Before Médina was to know whether his fate that day included the death the ceremony augured, he had to listen to the ire of all the king's men. After the Duc de l'Anse, the Chevalier de Prézeau stood up and exhorted the Haitian people to chant with him, *Vivre libre et indépendant, ou mourir!* "Live free and independent, or die!"—an often repeated and printed refrain in the kingdom. Next, the Baron de Vastey read to the crowd from de Prézeau's refutation of Dauxion-Lavaysse's letter, which was twenty-eight pages long. Then he read out loud his own twenty-four-page response to Malouet. Haitians had abhorred the name Malouet long before seizing the French minister's dubious instructions from Médina. In 1802, Malouet published a book in which he claimed that the French needed to urgently reestablish their authority over Saint-Domingue to ward off the otherwise inevitable destruction of "the whites." Malouet justified this in writing: "At last it is known, this secret full of horror: the liberty of the blacks means their domination! It means the massacre or enslavement of whites, the burning of our fields, of our cities." Vastey had countered, "At last it is known, this secret full of horror: the colonial system means domination by whites, it means the massacre and enslavement of blacks." It was Vastey's speech rather than his reading of the pamphlets that brought Médina to his knees. "Friends! With these names of Slave and Master, nothing can stop the wrath that inflames you; the bell of freedom has sounded!" Vastey said. "Run to your weapons, to fire, to carnage, and to vengeance!" Vastey later recalled that upon hearing these words Médina, "imagining that thousands of bayonets were pointed at his chest, became overcome with fear" and subsequently fainted. "We were obliged to bring him some vinegar and a cordial in order to revive him after this necessary terror," Vastey wrote.[61]

The king, not known for being a visually expressive man, sat and watched the entire spectacle unfold with stoic but stern approval. Posterity, in contrast, did not approve this treatment. For the mid-nineteenth-century Haitian historian Joseph Saint-Rémy, this episode merely served to prove that Christophe was a "second Caligula." Albeit recognizing that Louis XVIII had sent Médina to Haiti as one of the "commissioners" meant to "prepare the island to return to French control," Saint-Rémy claimed that Christophe's men were wrong to tie Médina to a stake and subject him to insults from the crowd, before publicly whipping him. "Even though Médina was more of a spy than a diplomat," Saint-Rémy concluded, "we must rail against the barbaric way in which justice was sought."[62]

Indicting the people of Haiti for the waking funeral of Médina meant also to indict the French, who had invented such ceremonies. As the *Gazette* noted—and as Vastey pointed out—the Haitian government drew the plans for Médina's treatment straight from the pages of Rochambeau's terror tactics during the final days of the Haitian Revolution. Remember those grand balls in Port-au-Prince, where Rochambeau invited and gawked at women of color while forcing them to attend the funerals of their husbands and lovers?[63] It had been only ten years since the French committed such atrocities. Only ten years since the infamous episodes of drowning—the very ones Pétion alluded to in his response to Dauxion-Lavaysse. Only ten years stood between the Haitian people and the Carrier-style floating gas chambers reported by numerous eyewitnesses, and it had been a mere ten years since General Rochambeau sent dogs to devour the Haitian people.[64]

Only twenty years had passed since slavery formally ended on the island. Many, if not the majority, of the people in the church that day had previously been enslaved by the French. The memory of slavery was fresh and extremely vivid for those subjected to its many tortures. And enslavers around the world, but particularly in France, continued to publicly justify their horrific treatment of the people they had enslaved while publicly advocating for the return of French domination and slavery to Saint-Domingue.[65]

The threat of being tortured if "Saint-Domingue" were ever "restored," therefore, was not an abstraction in the Kingdom of Haiti but an all too possible reality in a world of ongoing slavery. "Oh, you young Haitians who have had the good fortune to have been born under the reign of laws and of liberty!" Vastey reminded his fellow citizens. "You, who do not remember these times of horror and barbarity, read this writing; never forget the misfortunes of your fathers, and teach yourselves to always defy and hate your enemies."[66]

The Haitian people appear to have been convinced. We read in the November 19 issue of the *Gazette,* after its meticulous reportage of Médina's ironic funeral Mass,

> The least clairvoyant know without a doubt that the French want to plunge us back into slavery or to destroy us; convinced of this great truth, we hear everywhere in all parts only cries to arms! the elderly, women, children are asking for weapons; already the brave soldiers of the mountains . . . have outfitted themselves with huge and long swords and pikes in order to fight the French; we hope that this example will be followed throughout the kingdom; we hear only one shout: *Because the French must come, let them come only once! the more who come, the more we will kill!*[67]

It is in some respects easy to see why the kingdom's citizens submitted to Christophe's hardened authority, given the content of their memories. They had no reason to doubt their king when he said he was the only one who could protect them from once again being forced into slavery, and they had every reason to believe the French king's intentions were to make it so. Other people around the world were also believers. *The Analectic Magazine* wrote in 1817, "It was stipulated in the late continental treaty, that France should not be interfered with, in any attempts to recover her lost possessions; and she may flatter herself with an idea, therefore, that St. Domingo can be gathered again unto her dominion; but she will learn, we apprehend,—if, indeed, she has not already been taught,—that the Haytians are resolved upon the alternative of liberty or death, and that it is going to cost as much as the island is worth, to regain possession of it."[68]

Although later Haitian historians claimed that Christophe ultimately had Médina executed, Vastey refuted this accusation. In 1817, he insisted, "Médina is still alive. For almost four years we have been keeping this spy as living proof of Pétion's loyalty to the French cabinet." A former colonist, with his own infamous reputation, named Laffont de Labédat affirmed in 1815 that Médina, at least at that point, had not been executed by Christophe's government. Nevertheless, while Dauxion-Lavaysse returned to Kingston, reportedly dejected and dispirited because of his failure, Médina's family never saw him again. Because he never returned either to France or to Santo Domingo, where his relatives lived, Médina's family received a pension from Louis XVIII.[69]

The king and his men's ire might strike today's readers as misdirected rage. After all, Christophean chroniclers knew that the real men to blame were Louis XVIII, Malouet, and the ex–French colonists papering the earth with their desperate schemes to reinstate slavery. But Médina was hardly an innocent emissary. In the letter he wrote to Malouet on June 10, 1814, he proposed that he could help to "foment a party" against Christophe. Yet while King Henry forced Médina to suffer for this, Malouet escaped having to take responsibility. Unbeknownst to King Henry, Dauxion-Lavaysse, or any of the men on the French king's ill-begotten errand, Malouet died on September 7, 1814. His death may explain how and why Louis XVIII could so easily disavow his own mission.[70]

On January 19, 1815, the French king issued a plea of innocence and self-defense and ordered it published in *Le moniteur universel:*

Official Censure upon the Mission of Lavaysse, Dravermann, and Médina, by the Minister of the Marine and Colonies.

The minister secretary of state for the marine and the colonies has placed before the king the letters inserted in the public papers, and which were addressed from Jamaica on the 6th of July, and first of October last, to the present chiefs of St. Domingo, by Colonel Dauxion Lavaysse. M. Dauxion, whose mission was altogether pacific and had for its sole object to collect and transmit government information respecting the present state of the colony, had no authority for making communications contrary to its object. The king has expressed his high displeasure and orders his disapprobation be made public.[71]

Yet the Bourbon monarch was about to contend with an even bigger problem than Haiti's accusations of French treachery reverberating around the world. The Kingdom of Haiti reacted with astonishment after learning that Napoléon Bonaparte escaped from the island of Elba, where he had lived in exile since the spring of 1814 after he was forced to abdicate his throne, per the Treaty of Fontainebleau. The *Gazette* called Bonaparte's reentry into the city of Paris on March 20, 1815, practically without obstacle, and accompanied by only around a thousand men to guard him, "an event that has no equal in history." The report continued by revealing that Bonaparte subsequently, and "tranquilly," reestablished possession of his empire, while Louis XVIII, the royal family, and the king's supporters, including numerous ex-colonists, fled. It turns out that Bonaparte's return halted Louis XVIII's planned expedition to "restore Saint-Domingue."[72] That the Bourbons, even with their army of half a million, could not defeat an army of a thousand surely bolstered the Haitian king's confidence in his ability to defend Haitian freedom.

14

THE AGE OF CHRISTOPHEAN DIPLOMACY

After his previous failed attempt to overtake Haiti, and with Napoléon in exile, this time permanently on the island of Saint Helena, Louis XVIII issued a royal decree naming yet more French commissioners to the "colony of St. Domingue." Their mission? To confer with the existing authorities in the "colony" and determine which of its agents seemed most open to negotiating surrender to the "mother country." More French commissioners? Colony? Mother country? Hardly the language of liberated understanding. The French king must have believed that the third time was the charm. King Henry would soon show him. Haiti and France for a time stood at a seemingly never-ending crossroads, as if locked in a perpetual duel that had every possibility of ending in the destruction of one or both parties. But Christophe's maneuvering seemed to temporarily break the standoff. The king of Haiti's obstinance, strength, and foresight changed the character of Haiti's encounter with the French monarch indelibly. And so we enter the age of Christophean diplomacy, a time when King Henry demonstrated to King Louis more forcefully than ever before, and for all the world to see, that Haiti and Haitians were not the playthings of the slaving powers.

In August 1816, a U.S. brig called the *Sidney Crispin* carrying exported logwood left Port-au-Prince. The ship arrived in New York City after a voyage of twenty-four days. Once back in the United States, the ship's captain, Elesha Kenn, reported some remarkable news concerning French plots to retake "Saint-Domingue." Kenn said that while he docked off the coast of the republic's capital, a French warship cruising in the region had approached the *Sidney Crispin*. The French officer on the boat informed Kenn that before he sailed from France, a French frigate carrying commissioners destined for a meeting with Pétion had preceded it.[1] Two months later, the *Sidney Crispin* returned to Haitian shores, but this time Kenn's ship landed near Cap-Henry, in the north, around the same time as the two French ships.

On the morning of October 17, the lookout for the port of Cap-Henry spied two vessels known to be warships tacking in the open sea. The look-

409

out suspected the frigate and the accompanying brig to be enemy ships since they appeared to be cruising cautiously about the port without approaching too closely. The next morning, the ships came closer, appearing about four leagues from the port. The Duc de la Marmelade, governor of the capital, mounted his horse and hurried to Fort Picolet, the better to watch the maneuvering of the two foreign ships with his own eyes. He could not mistake what he saw. The two ships hovering off the coast were French. "For the first time in twenty-seven years, the white flag has just shown itself on our shores," the *Gazette* reported about ten days later. "The sight of this despicable flag, symbol of the slavery under which we groaned for centuries, has excited in all hearts the deepest indignation." Not knowing the ship's intentions, the duke saw little choice but to wait and see what the French sailors did next.

The duke might have been initially puzzled, but he would not remain in confusion for long. That afternoon, the frigate and the brig hoisted the Haitian flag at the mizzen and the white French flag at the mainmast and made full sail for Fort Picolet. The governor of Cap-Henry, scrambling for an explanation, presumed that the ships brought French parliamentarians for the purposes of official negotiations between the French and the Haitian king. The duke therefore sent a Haitian pilot ship into the waters to await the customary missive requesting permission to come on land. When the French brig stood about two leagues from Fort Picolet, however, it slid to a halt, veered, and then fired a cannon. What was the meaning of this? No parliamentarian flag waved at the commander of the fort, who still had no idea what the two French ships wanted. Neither French boat sent any indication to the pilot that it sought to enter the port. Instead, the brig continued to maneuver in open water, firing several more cannon shots. The duke now suspected that the French ships, deviating from ordinary procedures, wanted the Haitian pilot to come aboard instead of sending their emissary to Christophe's men.

The French sailors, perhaps owing to what happened to Médina, did not intend to dock at the Haitian port. However, the governor of the capital could not in good faith send any Haitian men aboard the French ships either. How could the duke be sure that the Haitian emissaries would not be detained, as had been some of the first Black soldiers who boarded French ships at the time the Leclerc expedition arrived on the coasts of Saint-Domingue in 1802? Explaining this necessary vigilance, the *Gazette* insisted to its readers, "We must not forget that during the last war, the French used this ruse, of presenting themselves in front of our ports . . . to ask for a pilot while they tried to eliminate us from the world." The article continued, "We must never forget that Toussaint Louverture and all our unfortunate compatriots fell into the powers of the French, and only became their victims through the most monstrous of all betrayals; no, we will never forget the perfidies of the French, and they have given us too many cruel lessons for us not to be wise and prudent in our communications with them; we must always have the greatest distrust for these Greeks of modern times, who only make treaties in order to be able to violate them, who lack faith, and perjure their oaths according to their interests and circumstances."[2]

The same day, the frigate and the brig, seeming to understand that no Haitian would board their ships, began to sail away from the fort in the direction of the channel that leads toward the island of La Tortue, north of Port-de-Paix. In what was likely a chance meeting, the Haitian lookout observed that the French ships suddenly changed direction and headed toward another brig heading west. The French brig bore on that ship and sent several men aboard it who stayed for a not inconsiderable amount of time, before descending again and sailing away. The lookout, who watched the minute movements of every man on board and who continued to study the third foreign ship to try to determine its colors, soon recognized that the brigantine in question was a U.S. ship. Instead of heading west and then south, for its Port-au-Prince destination, that ship changed its direction and began prowling around the port of Cap-Henry, where it coasted for several days. From the perspective of the lookout, the ship seemed to want to dock. At times it approached so close to the port that its landing appeared imminent, but inevitably, just in time, it pushed back and steered in the opposite direction. This quixotic behavior continued for six days, until the ship's captain finally signaled that he wanted to enter the port.

The king's official translator, the Baron de Dupuy, authorized by the Duc de la Marmelade to approach the ship, boarded it to gather the necessary formalities. In the process Dupuy recognized both the ship and its captain. It was Captain Kenn, along with his supercargo, Jacob M. King. Upon seeing Dupuy, both men declared almost immediately that they carried letters for Christophe that had been given to them by the captain of the French brig. Armed with this new information, Dupuy hurriedly reported this to the governor. This surprised the Duc de la Marmelade, still observing from afar the strange actions of the ships. The duke nevertheless approached King Henry with this unexpected information.

The king naturally wanted to know the contents of the French missives and told the Duc de la Marmelade to admit the U.S. captain and his supercargo. What happened next astonished all Christophe's men, even accustomed as they were to French manipulation and duplicity. Kenn gave Marmelade two letters, neither of which was countersigned and both of which were addressed to King Henry as "General" and made reference to "Saint-Domingue," rather than Haiti. Marmelade could hardly contain his indignation. The duke found it "astonishing that Americans who had been trading with Haiti for so many years, and who enjoy the protection of the government, and who, like us, had been brought to liberty and independence, could have burdened themselves with a commission that was as dishonorable as it was disturbing for men who belong to a nation that is friends with Haiti." Because the letter did not recognize the sovereignty of Haiti, nor its sovereign ruler, the duke refused to take it to the king.[3]

The people of Haiti had by this time crowded around the port and the ship. Curious about the commotion taking place on board, they asked around to find out what was happening. As news began to spread among them that the letters from the French government were addressed to "Monsieur, the General Christophe, at Cap-Français," the crowd began to boo and hiss. Lucky for them, Kenn and King were Americans. "If these emissaries had been French, it would have been very difficult for our leaders to protect them from the fury of the people and the soldiers," the *Gazette* reported. "There is no doubt that they would have been stoned." "This is what one exposes oneself to, however, by freely taking on the task of being the bearers of insults to a free and independent people!" the paper concluded. "We are saddened that they were able to find two citizens of the United States of America who wanted to undertake such a mission free of charge, which could only be very unpleasant to them in all respects."[4]

The mission of those on board the French ships had everything to do with King Louis XVIII's second attempt to "restore Saint-Domingue." Following the forced abdication of Napoléon for a second time, and the Bourbon king's second restoration, Louis XVIII named additional commissioners to "Saint-Domingue"—the name the French, in Vastey's words, "obstinately continued to call Haiti."[5] The French colonists' pleas to the king had been as persistent as they were stubborn. We read in the French *Journal des débats* on January 16, 1815, "The determination of Christophe should not have any influence upon the only plan that can restore Saint-Domingue to France. It is the path that Pétion will take which will decide the fate of the colony." To accomplish this disgraceful mission, Louis XVIII authorized his new minister of the marine, the Vicomte de Dubouchage, to appoint several French commissioners to negotiate with Pétion on the topic of the surrender of "Saint-Domingue."[6] If it seems like a sad attempt to repeat the affair of Dravermann, Médina, and Lavaysse, it was, but with a definitive ending. This time, Christophe not only brazenly defeated what Vastey called "the colonial Hydra that troubles us once again," but he cauterized the wound to prevent its many heads from growing back.[7] In further exposing France's treacherous and ultimately impotent machinations to the public, Christophe embarrassed the French monarch and in the process won the war of public opinion.

—

Despite the turbulence of a France oscillating between Bourbon and Napoleonic rule, the French ex-colonists continued their machinations. They hardly cared who was in power. Their only concern was with the "restoration" of Saint-Domingue. It hardly mattered to Haitians who ruled in France either. Their only object was self-preservation in the name of sovereignty. "Having experienced this for twelve years, we had prepared every means of defense," the *Gazette* announced in June 1815. "We were ready for the return of Louis XVIII to France, but nevertheless when we learned of his plans, we came to believe we needed to further increase our defense preparations, to resist with equal relentlessness the relentlessness shown to us." "Meanwhile, an event unparalleled in history took place," the *Gazette* continued. "Bonaparte escaped from his exile on the island of Elba with one thousand to eleven hundred men of his guard and landed in France." Napoléon's escape and return to France caused the French royal family to flee north to Ghent (located in Belgium today). They took with them many of the ex-colonists, some of the richest property owners in Saint-Domingue. War was declared and the European allied nations were shaken, but this had been in the end a positive development for Haiti. "Farewell for the moment to the expedition with which we were threatened," the *Gazette* concluded. The Kingdom of Haiti deemed France's propitious and perpetual turmoil inconsequential to Haiti's war preparations, "since it matters little to us whether we fight the troops of Louis XVIII or those of Bonaparte, since both the one and the other are coming for our lives, and as a nation and as individuals we are on our guard, we are ready to push back any attempt against our country." The strength of the kingdom's defense lay entirely with its army, composed of the Haitian people. "Our security is in ourselves, in our energy, and above all in the courage and character of our invincible sovereign, who will never accede to any proposal that would not have as its goal the recognition of our independence," Vastey announced in the *Gazette*.[8]

Yet, without doubt, France still posed an enormous threat to Haiti. What most frightened the Haitian king and his men was uncertainty about whether Pétion's defenses remained strong enough to repel the French, on the one hand, and whether Pétion remained devoted enough to the antislavery principles of Haitian sovereignty to avoid leading the republic into a treaty that would eventually bring back slavery, on the other. A Haitian citizen newly arrived from France brought some distressing news, on this score, which proved that the intrigues of the ex-colonists in exile continued with dispatch and effect. Former colonists still had their eyes on Pétion as the surest route of restoring their lost properties and their domination over the people they persisted in claiming they owned. Referred to as Mr. Gentil, this Haitian citizen arrived in the kingdom with missives that contained details of a treaty the French hoped to convince Pétion to sign. In the first letter, dated February 16, 1815 (one month before Napoléon's return), an ex-colonist named Catineau Laroche told Pétion that under a plan recently adopted by the French king, following the restoration of "Saint-Domingue," "without question you will be named governor of the whole colony." For this to happen, Christophe had to be defeated. Not only this, but Laroche admitted that under Pétion's governorship "the system of slavery would be restored in a few years, unless contrary laws were made or the law of February 2, 1794, was confirmed."[9] Laroche meant this letter to act as a precursor, a threat, designed to encourage Pétion to accept the more moderate plan that Laroche wanted to send to the Haitian president the next day.

The day after his first missive, Laroche penned a second letter proposing a different plan from the one that he claimed France stood on the verge of sanctioning. To accompany the letter, he enclosed a draft treaty, also penned by Laroche, in which he proposed that Pétion present it to Louis XVIII to thwart the plan described in Laroche's letter from the day before. The draft treaty spoke of cutting out the minister of the marine from the negotiations, whose desire to bring back slavery was well known in both France and Haiti. Laroche acknowledged the French minister was not the only one who wanted to see the restoration of slavery. He blamed pro-slavery and pro-reconquest sentiment in France on his fellow ex-colonists. Laroche had his own opinions on the matter, however. He wrote, "It matters little whether the fields of the Antilles are cultivated by free hands or by slave hands, by blacks or by whites." "The main thing is that these lands be cultivated," he continued, "and that the products be delivered for French commerce." Under Laroche's plan, Haiti would once more become "the colony of Saint-Domingue" and France's "commercial relations with the colony would be established on the same foot as they were before 1789." Europeans would see their "respective properties" restored, and all French people would have "free access" to the island. In return for allowing France to regain control and station an army and consuls on "Saint-Domingue," the French king would "renounce, for himself and for his successors, the right to interfere in the internal administration of the colony." As for Christophe, Laroche envisioned no role for him in this new arrangement, as his first missive to Pétion made clear. The Haitian king needed to disappear.[10]

As soon as Gentil transmitted these documents to Christophe, the *Gazette* reported the plan's stark terms, laying before the Haitian people the threat the French continued to pose to them via Pétion: "New agents were supposed to go to [Pétion] and together act in concert, with the infamous intention of putting the Haitians back under the yoke of slavery." "For the price of so many perversities," the French offered him "the position of governor-general of Saint-Domingue; the command of the French troops was offered to him as well as a price for his attachment to France and to the ex-colonists, and to reward him for his atrocious services, this infamous betrayal." Christophe immediately ordered the publication of all the documents "in order that all Haitians will know about them, because, as His Majesty said with much affect, '*I have no secrets to keep from my children.*' "[11] Gentil's arrival back in the kingdom happened at a symbolic, and in some ways fortuitous, moment. The kingdom was abuzz preparing Sans-Souci palace, the home of the king, queen, and royal children, for a magnificent celebration to commemorate the fourth anniversary of their rise to the throne. In times of stress, the palace at Sans-Souci served as a balm, a relaxing respite, and a refuge, for the king and his family. In times of celebration, Sans-Souci formed the perfect locale for the king to show off Haiti's ongoing prosperity, for the sake of both the aristocracy and the foreign guests who, with any luck, might be invited by the king to sojourn at the palace or to dance the night away at one of the many parties held there.

The customary magnificence of Sans-Souci's fetes shone with uncommon splendor at the fourth anniversary of the king and queen's coronation, which took place in June 1815, the day after Christophe ordered publication of the first set of Laroche's letters. Starting the day before the celebrations, the grand dignitaries and principal civil and military authorities of the kingdom arrived in Sans-Souci. At sunset, a burst of artillery fired, and several illuminations suddenly lit the city sky as the citizens attended balls and other festivities designed to celebrate the memorable day when Christophe became king.[12]

Unlike the Citadelle, which the king clearly used for diverse purposes and in various forms before its final completion, Sans-Souci did not house the royal family regularly before 1813. In fact, at the time of the coronation, there existed only a much smaller castle-like structure at the site of the future palace. Called the Château de Sans-Souci, this building was primarily used by the kingdom to store the archives of the order of Saint Henry. The royal family continued to live at their palace in Cap-Henry throughout 1811 and 1812. The composition and unveiling of the *Code Henry* in February 1812 took place at the royal palace in Cap-Henry, too, and as late as August 1812, Christophe still signed nearly all his letters and orders from his home in the capital. By March 1813, Christophe started sending most of his orders directly from his new palace, whose name he often spelled "Sans Soucy." It was around this time that the royal family likely moved in.[13]

Located in Milot, Haiti, about ten miles from Cap, by the time of the king and queen's crowning, the awe-inspiring structure—which Vastey called proof that Haitians had not lost "the architectural taste and genius of our ancestors who covered Ethiopia, Egypt, Carthage, and Old Spain, with their superb monuments"—might not have been ready to occupy, but its expansion was clearly well on its way. The *Gazette* reported on October 12, 1809, that Christophe and Marie-Louise had returned to Cap-Henry a few days prior, after having spent several days in Sans-Souci, where their new palace was under construction. "The new palace being built there offers a magnificent sight, and every day new embellishments are being added to it," the paper reported.[14]

Limonade recalled that at the time of the coronation Christophe was preparing the city of Milot, also called Sans-Souci by him, to serve as the new capital of the kingdom. As the construction of the palace grew ever nearer to completion, "ravines were filled in, mountains were leveled, public roads were set up. This superb royal palace, the glory of Haiti, extolled the beauty and boldness of its construction," Limonade wrote. Offering yet more details, Limonade spoke of the new palace's "sumptuous apartments, with parquet floors, paneled with the finest and rarest mahogany," "amassed at great expense and with scrupulous care." Once completed, the palace was admired by Haiti's many foreign visitors, even those who had disdain for the king. The British traveler James Franklin judged that Sans-Souci palace was "little, if at all inferior to some of the most admired edifices of Europe." The New England travel writer and physician Jonathan Brown visited Sans-Souci in the 1830s, long after the king's suicide in 1820, when the palace had been completely pillaged and had fallen into utter desuetude. Even though Sans-Souci resembled only the shadow of its formerly opulent state, Brown could not help but be wonderstruck by the castle he called "a sort of Louvre."[15]

Christophe's predilection for the city of Sans-Souci can be traced to the earliest days of independence, when he still primarily referred to the city where the castle would one day be built as Milot.[16] References to the tiny hamlet dot Christophe's letters from 1805 to 1806. In April 1806, General Christophe had Pierre Roux, who ran the printing press, move his operation to Milot, and Christophe referred to a plantation of his located in Milot in another letter he wrote while serving as general in chief of the Haitian army under Dessalines.[17]

The name Christophe gave to Sans-Souci palace caused considerable speculation in the king's era, and continues to do so today. There existed several areas on the island called Sans-Souci in the colonial period, but records indicate none were at the site of the future castle. René Cossait, Jacques-Philippe Larose, and Pierre Thomas Marsan are just a few of the French planters/enslavers who owned properties in a little town called Sans-Souci located in the rural section of Mombin-Crochu, just south of Ouanaminthe. There was also a Quartier Sans-Souci in the jurisdiction of Fort-Dauphin.[18] There were and remain many locales called Sans-Souci across the Caribbean archipelago, too, including in Christophe's native Grenada. The Grenadian Sans-Souci sits in Saint George parish, not far from the *carénage* where the man who enslaved Christophe reportedly sent him on the errand that eventually led the future king away from the island of his birth.[19]

Some have looked farther afield to locate the origins and logic behind the name Christophe gave to the palace. At the time of the palace's unveiling, foreign onlookers sometimes stated that Christophe had been inspired by Frederick the Great's summer château in Potsdam, Germany, which bears the same name.[20] Christophe was a known connoisseur of literature, art, music, and especially the opera. He also enjoyed reading historical narratives and had a special affinity for the history of Henry IV. Yet it was Frederick the Great of Prussia who constituted a figure of special intrigue. The Prussian monarch's "talents, enlightenment, and dominion" were often toasted to, postmortem, at celebrations in the royal palace at Sans-Souci.[21] Christophe's admiration for the late Frederick the Great, and his successor and son, Frederick William, did not pass unnoticed by observers. At least one nineteenth-century chronicler, Jonathan Brown, argued that Christophe must have "borrowed from Potsdam" the name Sans-Souci— Frederick the Great being a "personage with whom above all others [King Henry] was captivated."[22] Some Christophe detractors found in Haiti's Sans-Souci, "named so modestly after the palace of Frederick the Great," yet more reason to heap ridicule and opprobrium on King Henry, calling the castle simply another one of the Haitian king's "burlesque ecstasies."[23] Even if King Henry did take inspiration from his Prussian counterpart, the style, manner, and design of the German Sans-Souci and the Haitian Sans-Souci bear little resemblance to each other.[24] This fact has led to other, similarly circumstantial conjectures about the logic behind the palace's distinct nomenclature.

The late twentieth-century historian Michel-Rolph Trouillot popularized the theory that the name of the palace marked Christophe's lugubrious, if unintentional, recognition of the memory of Colonel Sans-Souci, whose death Christophe had directly ordered. "Henry I killed Sans Souci twice: first, literally, during their last meeting; second, symbolically, by naming his most famous palace Sans Souci," Trouillot contended. Trouillot argued more forcefully that Christophe deliberately named the palace after his former rival as a form of revenge. Because "Christophe built Sans Souci, the palace, a few yards away from—if not exactly—where he killed Sans Souci, the man"—the Grand Pré plantation sits adjacent to Milot plantation—"coincidence and inadvertence seem quite improbable," Trouillot concluded. "More likely, the king was engaged in a transformative ritual to absorb his old enemy."[25] Yet, just as there were and are many locales called Sans-Souci in the Caribbean, Colonel Sans-Souci was hardly the only Sans-Souci in Christophe's life.

Sans-Souci (spelled with a *y* at times and with or without a hyphen) reflected a common name, both pre- and postindependence. Not only was there a city, including several *mornes,* or small mountain hillocks, called Sans-Souci, home to some of the colony's most lucrative plantations, but some white people also held the surname Sans-Souci, including one referred to as M. Sans-Souci, a hotelier.[26] At least six other white colonists bore this name, according to the parish registers. Several dozen enslaved individuals had been given the name too. Sifting through the voluminous pages of the *Affiches américaines,* with its proliferating fugitive slave notices, produces records of more than seventy enslaved individuals called Sans-Souci, or some variation thereof. Although the majority were categorized as "Congo," we also find enslaved individuals with this name described as "Mondogue," "Bambara," "Nago," "Tacoua," "Barbe," "Arada," along with other ethnic or regional specifications meant to signify birth in Africa.[27]

A "Sanssoucy" described as a "garçon forgeron," or a young blacksmith, also lived at house number 743 on the corner of rue Espagnole and rue Taranne, according to a government survey taken in 1803; and several men named Sans-Souci later held roles in Christophe's government. At one point, Christophe appointed a surgeon named Sans Souci to serve the city of Dessalines, while the king promoted a Candiau Sans-Souci, along with the Baron de Vastey and the Baron de Joseph Dessalines, to the Royal and Military Order of Saint Henry on October 28, 1815. A Colonel de Sans-Souci, later identified as having the first name Pierre, was posted during the same year to a regiment in Limbé.[28]

As auspicious as Christophe's execution of Colonel Sans-Souci seemed to Trouillot, it may not have been as memorable for Christophe. The war involved so many factions, turns of fate, and outright reversals that it is hardly surprising that many of its events, both momentous and minor, faded from memory with time. Christophe did mention the Colonel Sans-Souci he ordered killed (which he spelled "Sans Soucy") briefly in two letters he penned in 1805. In one of them, addressed to Dessalines on September 6, Christophe expressed regret that he could not furnish the information about the colonel that the emperor requested. "I hasten to respond in honor of your letter of today, in which you ask me the precise time when Sans Soucy made the first strike toward insurrection at Grande-Rivière," Christophe wrote. "I am very sorry not to be able to tell you more about it, that era not being foregrounded in my memory and having lost my papers relating to this affair at the Choiseul plantation, where I had my effects looted." In a prior letter, written in January of the same year, Christophe wrote to another individual to ask if the late Colonel Sans-Souci had taken flour belonging to a woman named Catherine Paquin during that time when "disorder and pillage were the order of the day."[29]

Rather than evoking strong emotions, Christophe's recollections of Sans-Souci, the man, seem to have evoked none at all. The king's indifference to this particular death is perhaps explainable by recalling the many military battles in which Christophe took deadly part. Christophe was a warrior, and he and Sans-Souci had never been friends, much less true comrades. Moreover, Christophe made many enemies during the revolution, and he would make many more before his own death in 1820. While it seems unlikely that Christophe named his palace after his rival, this minor quibble does not detract from the main point of Trouillot's argument—that the significant opposition Sans-Souci led against both the French and the elite Black generals has been silenced in Haitian, as much as in world, history. Neither the king nor his many supporters appear to have been affected by Colonel Sans-Souci's memory enough to inscribe it into the official record of the voluminous documents they created to establish an official Haitian-created history of the revolution. Colonel Sans-Souci is hardly the only Haitian revolutionary figure whose memory the Christophean era effaced.

In August 1816, the king ordered the construction of a national monument erected at the center of the Place d'Armes of the Citadelle Henry. A "Column to Liberty and Independence!" according to the decree describing it, the statuesque structure was to be engraved in bronze with the entire Declaration of Independence inscribed on its edifice. The names of each of the famous document's signatories were to be listed, "with the exception of all those persons deemed traitors to the kingdom." Their names were to be "erased."[30]

The palace was believed by some to have been designed by German and French architects, but the *Royal Almanac* for 1814 listed its architects as André, Décourtil, François Poisson, and brothers Théophile Badaillac and Jean-Baptiste Badaillac.[31] Once completed, the grounds of Sans-Souci palace included a unique domed church, several *arcs de triomphe,* and elegant gardens, amid lush greenery and an elaborate system of fountains. A dramatic double staircase flanked the castle leading to the entryway, with its two arches detailed with etchings and inscriptions. One acknowledged Henry as the kingdom's "founder." There were also several large columns with etchings praising the royal family, and two painted crowns on the principal palace facade, one for the king and one for the queen, each of which stood at sixteen feet tall. While the one on the right read, "To the First Monarch Crowned in the New World," the one on the left said, "The Beloved Queen Reigns Forever over Our Hearts." The distinctive hall of mirrors formed the centerpiece of the palace, located at the farthest reach of the enormous edifice, which all told stretched over thirteen hectares.[32]

The king's palace, which the nineteenth-century Haitian writer Demesvar Delorme described as "extending on each of its four sides like three-quarters of the facade of the Tuileries," included an adjacent connected palace for the royal prince, the seat of the council of state, the Palace of the Ministers, the Casernes, a large esplanade, an interior court, stables, and the queen's garden, preceded by large barracks. The only known likeness of the palace to render it in all its splendor in the Christophean era, long before the magnitude 8.1 earthquake partially destroyed it in 1842, remains the painting done by a young Haitian artist named Numa Desroches. According to one chronicler, Christophe informally adopted

Desroches, born in 1804, the same year as Christophe's youngest child, and raised him in the palace, providing for his education at the kingdom's Royal Academy.[33]

The kingdom celebrated the anniversary of Christophe's coronation at Sans-Souci palace every year on June 2. Despite having learned of the recent attempt on Haitian sovereignty only the day before, the king wanted the year 1815 to be no different. At daybreak on the second, a royal salute opened the formal gathering. By seven in the morning, the grand dignitaries and the civil and military authorities, in full regalia, were introduced into the throne room of the council of state's palace, the outer facade of which contained an etching that read "To reign is his duty, To govern his virtue."[34] After they had been seated according to their respective ranks by the Baron de Sicard, at eight o'clock the king and the queen appeared before the nobles with the royal children, preceded by the grand officers of their respective *maisons* to the usual chorus of "Long live the king! Long live the queen! Long live the royal family!"

After having been seated for only a moment, King Henry suddenly stood up from his throne, turned to the dignitaries, and announced, "The anniversary of the coronation presents the occasion for you to gather around the throne, where the desires of the people and the army have placed us. It is very satisfying for us to witness and participate in the renewal of this oath which you took five years ago." The king then referenced the packet of letters brought to Haiti by Gentil, which he said were proof of "the plans of our implacable enemies who want to attack our livelihood, by every means of villainy that they alone are capable of putting to use." Turning to the dignitaries surrounding his throne, Christophe explained, "Through the exhibits and documents given to us by Mr. Gentil, animated by patriotism and his love for his fellow citizens, we have acquired new confirmatory evidence of Pétion's criminal conduct, of the treaty he concluded with the French and the plots to return the region under his command to them, and the expectation he has of receiving new French spies, to act concurrently with him in the criminal intention of putting the Haitian people back under the yoke of slavery." With all eyes and ears on him, the king continued, "We have ordered the most important of these letters to be delivered to the press to be made public; you will be able to convince yourselves in reading them of the great designs that our enemies have conceived of undertaking with that great criminal." Christophe then reminded the nobles that Napoléon's astonishing return to power and Louis XVIII's corresponding flight had only momentarily halted the plans laid out in the correspondence between Laroche and Pétion. King Henry cautioned that Haiti's standoff with France had hardly come to an end. He told his guests, "Regardless, however favorable these events might be from our point of view, we must not delude ourselves into believing that we are in complete security; and let ourselves become lulled into complacency. Let us always maintain the martial and warlike attitude that we have adopted; let us be attentive and on our guard, such that any enemy who would try to subjugate and enslave us will always find us ready to defeat him and to punish his reckless audacity."[35]

For years the kingdom played this tune, whereby Christophe and his ministers painted Pétion not simply as a treacherous leader but as a man who committed treason against Haiti and the Haitian people. After printing fifteen bullet points meant to support the charge of "high treason" against Pétion, the editor of the June 29, 1815, issue of the *Royal Gazette*, after reporting on this ceremony, finished by making an appeal for a new hero to appear and free the people of the southern republic. In language that resonates with the famous "Black Spartacus" passage in the abbé Raynal's *History of the Two Indies,* the editor of the *Gazette* asked, "Does there no longer exist a man, a warrior among you, who would be generous enough to save his brothers and his country?" "Where is he, this liberator, this avenger of liberty and independence? Let him only show himself, and the country will be saved!!!" the *Gazette* declared.[36]

It turns out that King Henry and his men did not have to wait long to find another occasion to rail against Pétion's attempt to strike a deal with the French government. Following the second restoration of the Bourbon king, with Bonaparte banished for good, this time to a small island in the South Atlantic called Saint Helena, Pétion prepared to receive a visit from Laroche. In a letter to Pétion dated January 25, 1816, Laroche wrote, "There are still strong biases against Saint-Domingue in France." "The former colonists are still asking for war, and always talk of exterminating the male population of all colors," he acknowledged. Laroche explained that the ex-colonists, who had recently returned to France from London, constituted the biggest threats. Many of them had "English funds that [they] offered to the government for the first expenses of the expedition." According to Laroche, one ex-colonist, in particular, Pierre François Venault de Charmilly had asked to be named "chief administrator of Saint-Domingue." "His gold had an effect," Laroche continued, "and as soon as he proved he had it, the people around the [French] king voted for war." The French plan to exterminate the Haitian populace would come about in one way or another, if Venault de Charmilly had his way, Laroche warned: "If there was disagreement between you and King Henry, a French expedition would join one of you to exterminate the other and the victorious party would be exterminated in turn. Men of all colors and parties must expect to be sacrificed, if the colonists ever have the power."[37]

Writers from the kingdom expressed outrage upon learning that Pétion had invited to the republic someone expressing such clearly genocidal thoughts. Pétion's public silence regarding the matter did not help. That he refused to issue a comment only provided further matter for Christophean writers to cast opprobrium on his character. "It is quite astonishing that for more than six months Pétion has known that these documents were intercepted and published and that he has been proven guilty, by multiplying evidence, of a monstrous and execrable perfidy toward the Haitian people," complained the editor of the *Gazette* in February 1816: "It is very astonishing, I say, that he did not write a single word to try to justify himself regarding so infamous a form of treason; he hasn't even given a sign of life. Why then does Pétion persist in preserving the most profound silence regarding the facts of which he is accused? Shouldn't he at least do his best to justify himself?"[38]

Writers from the kingdom stared down Pétion's silence by making public Laroche's letters, along with his proposed treaty to Pétion. Writing from Sans-Souci palace, where Christophe employed him as secretary of state and minister of foreign affairs, the Comte de Limonade wrote to Vastey to formally instruct him to make public Laroche's correspondence.[39] Using his characteristic sarcasm and sardonic wit to expose this second French plot of reconquest, re-enslavement, and extermination, on February 29, 1816, Vastey formally published the letters. At the orders of the king, he also produced a separate, stand-alone pamphlet called *Official Communication of Three Letters from Catineau Laroche: Ex-colonist, Agent of Pétion, Printed and Published by Government Order*.[40] The former British soldier turned historian Marcus Rainsford, to whom a toast is given in absentia in the November 19, 1814, issue of the *Gazette*, subsequently published an English translation. With a potent combination of English translation and foreign printers all too willing to reprint the account, the story traveled and gained the king and the Kingdom of Haiti sympathy from many across the Anglophone world.[41]

The French king, perhaps because of the negative publicity brought to this case by the Kingdom of Haiti, decided in the end to try a tactic other than outright war. Not long after Vastey made the case public, President Pétion, still addressed as "General," received an official missive from the French crown dated October 2, 1816. Denouncing Bonaparte, referred to as "the Usurper," and his previous expedition to the island, the letter, signed by the Vicomte de Fontanges and Esmangart, while they were en route to Haiti, announced Louis XVIII's new French mission, one the missive characterized as "entirely peaceful."[42] With the new French expedition looming and the commissioners' imminent arrival on the horizon, Pétion could no longer afford to stay silent. Every moment he said nothing provided yet more kindling that Christophean writers could use to further inflame recrimination against him at home and abroad.

In his response to Fontanges and Esmangart's letter, dated four days later, Pétion used the tactic he had first tried with Dauxion-Lavaysse and more recently with Laroche. He started by denouncing both the Leclerc expedition and the duplicitous mission of Dauxion-Lavaysse and company, intimating that he did not believe the French king's denials; the instructions the three spies carried had been signed by Malouet, after all, "a very influential minister who was close to the king."[43] The commissioners replied from on board their boat the same day, addressing none of the accusations about Louis XVIII and the three French spies. Instead, the agents sent Pétion an official copy of the "Order of the King, Louis, by the grace of God," which formally named Fontanges, Esmangart, and two others as the new French commissioners to the island.[44]

What astonished Christophe and his ministers perhaps even more than the situation with Dauxion-Lavaysse and Laroche was that Pétion allowed the commissioners to enter Port-au-Prince. During their conference, Fontanges and Esmangart once more disavowed Dauxion-Lavaysse's mission and claimed that the latter had not been endowed with "any power from the king," going so far as to state that Louis XVIII had not even known of the mission until he learned of its failure "through public channels." Fontanges and Esmangart further insisted that Louis XVIII publicly reproved the so-called French spies and "condemned the mission and even more the conduct that had been on display." The commissioners told Pétion that neither the French king nor any of his agents would have any more to say on the matter of Dauxion-Lavaysse and company.[45]

The unsuccessful (from the French perspective) back-and-forth between the French commissioners and the president of the republic that fall led Fontanges and Esmangart, true to French form, to threaten war, exposing France's and their own complete and continuous disavowal of Haitian independence. After proposing what they called a compromise, but one that would still divest Haiti of its sovereignty and "restore Saint-Domingue," the commissioners issued a threat. "Your current independence is therefore nothing more than a veritable chimera," they wrote to Pétion, calling it "a claim which cannot be sustained, which will become fatal to you and even more fatal to the people on behalf of whose interests you stipulate." Then, admitting their actual inability to persuade Pétion to relinquish control of the republic to France, they wrote, "As for us, General, our sojourn in this country now being useless and even indecent, we are withdrawing." "We are leaving with the sincere regret of not having been able to succeed in doing what could bring happiness to this colony, and peace to the people," they wrote. "If their future is not as happy as it could be, if some new misfortune still comes to afflict them, we can blame your refusal, your resistance, but never the heart or the justice of the king [of France]."[46] Thus it was that the second mission sent by Louis XVIII, with the mandate of restoring French rule on the island, failed with less of a loud bang of war than a barely audible poof of French disappointment.

Pétion's belated opposition to the French notwithstanding, Christophe stood to win not just the war of diplomacy but the war for public opinion. Writers from his kingdom patiently and clearly documented and reported each attempt on Haitian freedom. With the eyes of the world upon the

Kingdom of Haiti, English translations of book-length writings and pamphlets from Christophean writers allowed the Haitian king to explain and justify, with Vastey as his most capable and fiery amanuensis, Christophe's actions vis-à-vis the French as he courted international opinion and formal recognition of Haiti's sovereignty. It was not uncommon to find positively flattering and fawning reviews of Vastey's writings in the U.S. and British press, for example, some of which argued outright that the leaders of these countries should recognize Haiti.[47] One U.S. writer, Caleb Cushing, repeated the kingdom's talking points about a multitude of topics: that the French were responsible for all civil strife in Haiti, that the French were trying to no avail to restore slavery and colonialism, and that the French did not deserve any compensation or indemnity for their so-called lost properties since "no man of course but a colonist can seriously think the king of Hayti was under the least obligations to restore the lands of the planters, or even give them an equivalent."[48]

The fact that the king of Haiti seemed to prevail in the war for public opinion had already led Christophe to be so bold as to send some of the writings produced out of the royal press, including his *Manifeste du roi*, to Pétion, along with another proposed treaty of amnesty. The draft document outlined how Pétion could surrender and become a member of the kingdom. Four nobles whom Christophe sent to travel to Port-au-Prince on the mission took the treaty, titled "L'olivier de la paix" (Olive branch of peace), directly to the southern republic. In the proposed treaty, Christophe offered six concessions to dissolve the civil war and reunite Haiti: the total forgetting of the past; frank and sincere reunion with all members of the Haitian population; that Pétion could keep his "grade and authority"; the conservation of the grades of the southern generals, officers, magistrates, and commanders currently in the republic; that these men would be admitted into the hereditary order of the kingdom's aristocracy; and finally, Christophe promised to guarantee all the properties of Haitian citizens in the south and the west. In an accompanying missive, the Comte de Limonade cautioned, "Reflect carefully, General, on all the considerations in my letter; it all depends on you, since this is only between you and the king." "Reflect well, and you will see if there is any other path for you to take, any other decision other than to promptly recognize royal authority and join the king to collaborate upon everything that will tend toward the happiness and safety of the Haitian people," he concluded.[49] As might very well be assumed, Pétion and writers from his republic soundly rejected Christophe's overtures, and reject them again they would under Jean-Pierre Boyer in 1818, after he became president in the wake of Pétion's sudden demise.[50]

Contemporary view of the Citadelle Laferrière (Henry) from the sky, showing its grandiose stature.

View from the top of the Citadelle taken in 2021 from one of its towers, showing the multitude of cannons and cannonballs still in place at the site.

Photograph taken at the Citadelle from another one of its towers, showing an expansive view of the island.

Christophe, somewhat ironically, admired the French king Louis XIV's motto, "Nec pluribus impar" (Not unequal to many), inscribed on this cannon at the Citadelle.

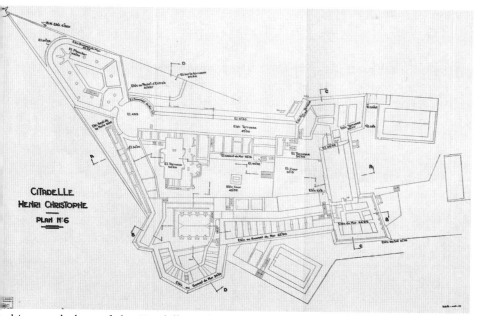

Architectural plans of the Citadelle, written in Spanish, collected by the Haitian historian Alfred Nemours. Unknown date, ca. 20th century.

Numa Desroches, *Vue du palais d'Henry Christophe à Sans-Souci* (View of the palace of Henry Christophe in Sans-Souci), ca. 1816–18.

Bust of an unknown woman, sometimes said to be a Goddess or Muse of the Theater, outside Sans-Souci palace in Milot, Haiti, 2021.

An Italian broadside, first published in Milan, probably around 1813, with an engraving of King Henry, signed by Torchiana and Dridier. The image went on to be reprinted in the book *Serie di vite e ritratti de' famosi personaggi degli ultimi tempi* (Series of lives and portraits of famous people of recent times), published by Batelli and Fanfani in Milan from 1815 to 1818.

Anonymous, early nineteenth-century portrait of the royal children of Haiti, ca. 1815. *From left to right,* Prince Victor-Henry (heir to the throne) and his sisters, Princesses Améthyste-Henry (called Première) and Anne Athénaïs.

he British artist Richard Evans briefly ved and taught painting in the Kingdom f Haiti. This is Evans's famous portrait f Christophe's son Prince Victor-Henry, eir to the Haitian throne, ca. 1816.

The British painter Richard Evans also painted the Haitian king in what is the most well known of the nineteenth-century depictions of Christophe, ca. 1816.

Nineteenth-century oil-on-canvas portrait by an unidentified artist depicting the death of Christophe, showing the palace's guards rushing into the room after the king has shot himself in the heart, ca. mid-19th century.

An image apparently drawn after the nineteenth-century painting of Christophe's death, published in Gabriel Hanotaux and Alfred Martineau's 1929 *Histoire des colonies françaises et de l'expansion de la France dans le monde* (History of the French colonies and of the expansion of France in the world). Below the engraving are the words "Christophe's Death (According to an Engraving Popular at the Time)."

Photograph taken in April 2022 of the headstone on the tomb of the Christophe women, located inside a sacristy at the San Donnino Chapel in Pisa, Italy, where the women are buried.

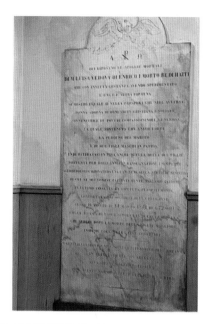

After the king's suicide in October 1820, authors and artists around the world sought to capitalize on his death. This image depicts characters drawn from J. H. Amherst's play *Christophe, King of Hayti* (1821), by William West in 1824.

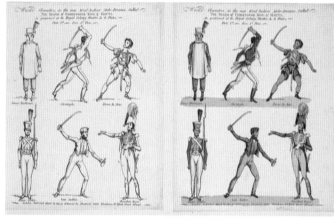

The palace at Sans-Souci, located in Milot, Haiti, was in large part destroyed by a catastrophic magnitude 8.1 earthquake that hit the city of Cap-Français in May 1842. This photograph, taken in October 2021, shows the current state of the palace, today a UNESCO World Heritage site.

Engraving from 1825 depicting a French diplomat, the Baron de Mackau, presenting the French king Charles X's indemnity ordinance (which required Haitians to pay 150 million francs to France as the price of recognition of their independence) to the Haitian president, Jean-Pierre Boyer, in 1825. Such depictions formed a part of French propaganda designed to paint the French king as the true liberator of the Haitian people.

Engraving from 1825, following the indemnity ordinance, depicting Charles X bestowing freedom on a Black man kneeling before him in chains.

Nineteenth-century engraving depicting the city of Cap-Français as it was in the colonial era, drawn by Eugène-Ferdinand Buttura, exact date unknown, ca. 1830s.

Famous lithograph depicting General Toussaint Louverture, published by François-Séraphin Delpech, after an earlier image drawn by Nicolas Eustache Maurin, 1833.

General Jean-Jacques Dessalines (later the emperor Jacques I), as depicted in an engraving published in Dantès Fortunat's *Nouvelle géographie de l'île d'Haïti: contenant des notions historiques et topographiques sur les autres Antilles* (New geography of the island of Haiti, containing historical and topographical observations on the rest of the Antilles) (Port-au-Prince: Chez l'Auteur, 1888).

Christophe crowned king of Hayti.

Engraving from an 1848 pictorial history of the Americas, written by S. G. Goodrich, depicting the June 1811 coronation of Christophe as King Henry I of Haiti. Below the engraving read the words "Christophe crowned king of Hayti."

General Alexandre Pétion (later president of the Republic of Haiti), as depicted in an engraving published in Dantès Fortunat's *Nouvelle géographie de l'île d'Haïti: Contenant des notions historiques et topographiques sur les autres Antilles* (New geography of the island of Haiti, containing historical and topographical observations on the rest of the Antilles) (Port-au-Prince: Chez l'Auteur, 1888).

Frontispiece to René Périn's *L'incendie du Cap; ou, Le règne de Toussaint-Louverture* (The burning of Cap; or, The reign of Toussaint Louverture) (1802), portraying Governor-General Toussaint Louverture presiding over the city of Cap-Français as it was burning following the February 1802 fire ordered by General Henry Christophe.

Frontispiece to the anonymously published 1816 book *Débarquement de la flotte française à Saint-Domingue, faisant suite aux révolutions de cette île* (The landing of the French fleet in Saint-Domingue, subsequent to the revolutions on that island). The image depicts the French landing by boat in the foreground and multiple figures running in the background.

15

THE AGE OF CHRISTOPHEAN PROSPERITY

The king of Haiti was riding high. With his highly publicized school system much touted and lauded around the world, he enlisted the star power of some of England's most famous abolitionists, Thomas Clarkson and William Wilberforce, along with the famous Black American antislavery activist Prince Saunders, to help trumpet his many victories over the French. The latter even immigrated to Haiti in the hopes of personally contributing to Christophean prosperity. The international press continuously reported Christophe's unlikely and extraordinary rise, too, with as much urgency as they hound the royal family of England today. Great Britain's abolitionists, for their part, became virtually obsessed with using the king of Haiti as a symbol of Black possibility after slavery. But while he was undoubtedly still considered by many a heroic man, deservingly celebrated for his contributions to Haitian independence and Black sovereignty in the Americas, Christophe has represented for many, past and present, a complicated antihero, ruling a difficult country in a difficult time, and the legacy of much of what he built during the age of Christophean prosperity begs the age-old question of whether the ends justify the means.

The age of high Christophean diplomacy coincided with an age of undeniable Christophean prosperity. On November 20, 1816, King Henry issued a proclamation that demonstrated his growing fame as he exposed numerous French plots to "restore Saint-Domingue" and publicly decried the machinations of French commissioner after French commissioner. Feeling bolder than ever in his dealings with the French, the Haitian king declared all trade between France and Haiti forbidden. He subsequently issued four articles to explain the meaning of this embargo. The first, and most important, stated, "The French flag would not be allowed in any of the ports of the kingdom, nor would any individual of that nation, until the independence of Haiti is definitively recognized by the French government." The second article of the decree mandated that Haitians entertain no "overtures or communications" from the French government, unless "they bear official form according to the rules established in the kingdom for diplomatic communications." In other words, any documents coming from France's head of state or other government officials not only had to carry official seals from the French king but had to be addressed to the king of Haiti, not to a "general of Saint-Domingue." Third, Christophe declared that he would never consent to any treaty that did not at the outset recognize the liberty and independence of Haiti, including in the south and southwest, "the territory and cause of the Haitian people being one and indivisible." Finally, the Haitian king mandated that as a sovereign he would only negotiate with the French government "on equal footing, from one power to another power . . . in matters of both government and commerce."[1] This effectively meant that in French negotiations with Haiti the relationship could not be framed as that of an imperial power to its colony.

King Henry knew that striking at the heart of French commerce would feel like a huge blow, both to the government and to the people of France, but especially to the ex-colonists. The French wanted to trade with Haiti, through back channels, without recognizing Haitian independence. King Henry's official ban prevented the French government, and the French people, from benefiting from nonrecognition. "Since the French intended to destroy us by way of commerce," Vastey wrote in 1817, "when we outlawed French trade, we destroyed all their hopes, and their chimerical edifice crumbled." King Henry was willing to take his prohibitions against French commerce further, if necessary. "Therefore, if France continues its system of insults and aggression against Haiti, if it stubbornly refuses to recognize our full and entire independence, which is the one and only guarantee we can have against it," Vastey insisted, "we would do well, after banning ships under its flag and individuals from that nation from our territory, to proscribe its goods also."[2]

The arrival of the French commissioners Fontanges and Esmangart in Port-au-Prince, and their attempt to open negotiations with the kingdom using the colonial terms of "General Christophe" and "Saint-Domingue," had been the direct catalysts for this ban. When the Haitian king made these documents public, they were accompanied by a declaration explaining to readers that France intended to introduce into the kingdom false intelligence and duplicitous maneuvers designed to trick them. The only remedy Haiti had was therefore to "no longer admit into the country any Frenchman at all, or vessel of that power, veiled or not by foreign expeditions, until our absolute independence . . . is recognized by the French government."[3]

The other colonial governments viewed Christophe's messaging around Haiti's right to sovereignty as potentially dangerous to their own, with respect to their continuation of slavery in the Caribbean. This was as true of France as it was of the seemingly friendly to Haiti nation of Great Britain. The rules governing slavery that applied in the British Isles differed from those in operation in their Caribbean colonies. In 1772 the *Somerset* decision outlawed slavery on metropolitan English territory while preserving it in England's overseas colonies.[4] This meant that while England did not consider either the Republic or the Kingdom of Haiti its enemy technically, Haiti's relationship to the rest of the British-claimed Caribbean islands stood on precarious ground. We can especially glimpse the precarity of Haiti's sovereign status as a land of freedom in a world of slavery in the Thomas Strafford affair in Kingston, Jamaica.

Strafford, a white British man, had lived in Haiti for some time when he decided to return to Kingston on December 13, 1816. After a voyage of twenty-four days, he arrived home and quickly found that the colonial Jamaican government charged him with having "publish[ed] and cause[d] to be published a most wicked, scandalous, seditious, and inflammatory libel." The indictment held by the Jamaica Archives and Records Department details the charges against Strafford, noting that on December 13, 1816, he "unlawfully quit" Haiti, "with the purpose of clandestinely landing in the said Island of Jamaica" in order to "disquiet, molest, and destroy tranquility and the good order of the said Island of Jamaica in furtherance and aid of the said Person called Christophe." The "seditious" work in question was Vastey's 1816 *Reflections on a letter from Mazères,* which had not yet been published in its formal English translation by the white British botanist William Hamilton, who lived in Haiti at the same time as Strafford.

The government accused Strafford of bringing the book to Kingston at the direct behest of King Henry for the purposes of sparking slave revolt and rebellion. Strafford's bail stood at 500 pounds, according to the lengthy indictment, and he was ordered to remain in jail "until such security be given."[5]

The trial unfolded in February 1817, and according to the *Royal Gazette of Jamaica,* the government indicted Strafford on one main charge: "uttering and publishing certain seditious publications in this island, brought by him from St. Domingo." However, in a surprising twist of events, "after a long examination of witnesses," the Jamaican court acquitted Strafford of any ill intent. The paper claimed that "a few copies of some ridiculous and contemptible publications, which had been issued from the St. Domingo press, under the direction of the Tyrant Christophe, were forced into the possession of Mr. Strafford on his leaving St. Domingo," and that Strafford only accidentally brought them to the island. The paper went on to report that even though "no evil design could be proved against him," the jury, after deliberating for only a few minutes, returned with a verdict whereby Strafford was judged "guilty of publishing the Libel, but not with an evil intent." In a passage that editorializes to a high degree, the *Royal Gazette of Jamaica* concluded its reportage of Strafford, referred to as "a very discreet and respectable character," with the kind of false information about events in the kingdom that had grown legion among Christophe detractors: "One of the witnesses noticed that the monster Christophe had, unceremoniously, shot one of his secretaries, named Lemonade [*sic*], while dining at his own table, and this is one of Wilberforce's favourites, with whom he holds a confidential correspondence!!!"[6]

This was a ridiculous and easily disproved lie. Limonade was not dead. He was alive enough at the time of the Jamaican article's publication to authorize the new royal printer, Buon, to publish the *Royal Almanac* for the upcoming year, 1818. That same year Limonade wrote to the British and Foreign Bible Society to acknowledge receipt of five boxes of Bibles. Wilberforce acknowledged the rumor himself when he mentioned having received a letter from Limonade dated March 1817, in the letter he wrote to Lord Teignmouth, president of the Society. Wilberforce noted that Limonade had made payment on behalf of Christophe for the Bibles, before observing, "Your Lordship will probably recollect that this very Count de Limonade . . . was stated in the newspaper to have been shot by King Henry at a public dinner some months ago." Denouncing this falsehood, Wilberforce declared, "King Henry has been so often represented to the British in a very unfavourable light," before concluding, "Many, I doubt not, have been the inventions of his enemies."[7]

Limonade kept up a robust correspondence with Thomas Clarkson, too. On November 20, 1819, Limonade sent an important missive to the renowned British abolitionist, in which he insisted that any request for the people of Haiti to indemnify the French ex-colonists would quite simply be "inadmissible." Limonade went on to note that Christophe did not intend to deviate even "one iota from the principles" set forth in his November 1816 proclamation banning French people and their ships from the island.[8]

Although the Jamaican newspaper had disparaged Clarkson and Wilberforce, it was Strafford who had actually lived in the kingdom and who directly accepted the king's religious, economic, and education commissions on numerous occasions. In February 1816, Strafford, along with a free man of color, the Connecticut-born abolitionist Prince Saunders, met with Christophe to inform the Haitian king of his high reputation among some of England's most famous citizens. In London, Saunders had frequented the home of Sir Joseph Banks, president of the Royal Society.[9] King Henry was gratified to learn from Saunders that the renowned British naturalist, by that time famous for his voyage around the world with Captain Cook, had asked Strafford and Saunders to transmit to him several words of "flattering praise." Christophe subsequently asked Limonade to write to Banks to express his appreciation and gratitude. "My very august and very gracious Sovereign has instructed me to thank you infinitely on his behalf and to let you know how much he appreciates the feelings of generosity and humanity that animate you," Limonade wrote with elation. "He is happy to be able to count among the number of his true friends a man as famous as you!" Limonade finished the letter by noting that he had enclosed his account of the king's coronation.[10]

By that time, the kind of celebrations that had taken place during the coronation had become legendary. In 1816, the *Gazette* had published a highly detailed description of Queen Marie-Louise's fete, which lasted for a noteworthy twelve days, beginning on August 14. These celebrations provided material and affective testimony of the kingdom's prosperity, and were at least partially designed to impress foreigners like Banks, who the king hoped might visit one day, as well as foreigners already in the kingdom, who the king hoped would return home with tales of the remarkable transformation of the colony from a torturous slave society, whose wealth was built on subjugation, into the vibrant and free Kingdom of Haiti, whose wealth they could report was achieved through sound labor laws. A master of publicity, King Henry had directed Vastey to publish the proceedings of Marie-Louise's 1816 fete in the royal newspaper, but also in book form, where the tale soon reached the United States, by design. Excerpts of the story appeared in English translation that October on the front page of the *New-England Palladium,* where the details of the party gained such traction that the *National Intelligencer* and other newspapers around the country soon reprinted the story.[11]

The formal ceremony for the queen's fete, which Strafford attended, took place on the fifteenth, followed by a Mass.[12] On the sixteenth, the festivities continued at the home of the Duc de la Marmelade, governor of Cap. At the dinner could be spied all the foreign merchants in town, who also participated in the opening festivities the day before. Strafford sat among the British merchants who attended the feast, along with several U.S. businessmen and at least one merchant from Bremen.[13] During the meal the most exquisite and expensive wines were served with toasts raised to the king of England, to "the Human Race," and to the president of the United States. Afterward, a British merchant by the name of Mr. White gave a speech praising King Henry. Met with vibrant applause, Mr. White began with an uncanny comparison, "Gentlemen, I am English and accustomed to expressing my sentiments freely":

I have seen all the sovereigns of Europe, troops from every nation; I have observed the customs and laws of the peoples of every country I have visited, and well! gentlemen, I tell you in truth, I observed the king of Haiti at the head of his troops, I examined the richness of the uniforms, the dress and the discipline of the Haitian army; I have observed the manners and studied the laws of this country; I have not seen in Europe a sovereign who appears to be better, or has better maintained or better disciplined troops, nor more order, regularity, and justice than in this kingdom.

Mr. White concluded by painting Christophe as a veritable superhero who had saved the Haitian people: "In the situation you are in, you have no enemies to fear; you are invincible!"[14]

On the seventeenth, the royal family took a brief reprieve from the celebrations, passing the day at their palace in Tivoli. Commencing the celebrations once more on the eighteenth, the entire royal family returned to Cap-Henry. Queen Marie-Louise and the children attended another Mass at the cathedral in Cap-Henry, followed by a parade on the Place d'Armes. After giving audience to the minister of finance and the interior, the king joined the parade, mounting a "splendid horse," wearing the uniform of the Haitian guards, which consisted of a long coat, red lapels, black velvet cuffs and collar, with white lining and piping, red epaulets, white short breeches, white stockings, boots, and a sako[15] bordered by a red silk braid with a plaque of the king's coat of arms. The uniform also had red silk cordons with red pompoms on the end.

King Henry had been preparing to undertake a review of the military on this occasion, but his sons captured the spotlight. Bystanders watched as the royal prince, at the head of his light cavalry, put his remarkable zeal and energy on display by carrying out with aplomb his father's commands. The *Gazette* wrote that Prince Victor "rode through the ranks on a fiery steed," with the editor concluding, "His martial and warrior-like air predicts what he will one day become and gives us the greatest hope." Of Prince Eugène, the *Gazette* observed, "We also saw him at the head of the *chasseurs de la garde*, walking with a firm step and commanding with an assured voice. This young prince, endowed with a happy disposition, educated by skillful masters, coupled with his devotion to his studies, will succeed, over time, in becoming a consummate soldier in the great art of war." The evening concluded with a magnificent ball.

On the nineteenth, the king held a dinner specifically for the foreign merchants in the capital. Christophe told the men in attendance, including Strafford, that he felt honored to have the chance to express his appreciation for all the foreigners who continued to do business in and with Haiti. A British merchant by the name of John Shoolbred praised King Henry's speech on behalf of "the foreign merchants established in the capital of the Kingdom of Haiti," offering words of admiration for Queen Marie-Louise as well: "We have often heard of the rare qualities that characterize this great princess; and it is with great sincerity that we desire that she continue for a long time to adorn the high place in which Your Majesty has succeeded in placing her by your bravery and by your wisdom; and we also hope that your eldest son, the royal prince, as well as the royal princesses can imitate the virtues of their august father and mother."[16]

On the evening of August 24, with the festivities for the day drawing to a close, the Duc de la Marmelade hosted a dinner at the Café des Étrangers (Foreigners' Café) in continued honor of the queen's fete. After finishing copious amounts of wine, the attendees once again offered toasts to foreign heads of state, culminating in the customary cries of *huzzah!* The final toast of the evening given by Mr. White in the name of King Henry's deceased son, Ferdinand, brought the room to tears. Mr. White solemnly offered these words as he raised his glass: "In Memory of His Royal Highness Ferdinand Henry, Royal Prince of Haiti, who died a victim of the villainy of the French cabinet." A deep and profound silence spread over the room. All chatter ceased as sadness stamped every face with a frown. The guests stood up in silence as they drank to the memory of the dearly regretted prince.

Vastey managed to restore the lively and energetic tenor to the dinner when after a few moments he toasted, "To the recognition that we owe to the virtuous philanthropists who have defended our cause with as much ardor as disinterestedness; if their vows and efforts are powerless, then let us use our swords to cut through the bodies of the enemies of humanity, and to uphold the rights given to us by God, nature, and justice!" The queen hosted a similarly lavish dinner in the capital the next day with fifteen hundred guests in attendance.[17]

Travelers who came from outside Cap-Henry for the celebrations and who made their way to the Citadelle and the palace might have been thrilled to see several new *arcs de triomphe* in northern Haiti. One had been erected across from the bridge and another at the end of the road from Limbé to Cap-Henry. Haiti's *Gazette* described the arches as seeming "to invite their Majesties to take the route to the capital." At the entrance to the city could be glimpsed yet another magnificent arch, replete with inscriptions to the king and queen and decorated with ornate garlands.[18]

Queen Marie-Louise's 1816 fete was outdone perhaps only by the one that occurred the next year, in August 1817, when she once more celebrated her royal anniversary with a party that lasted for twelve days. The lighting for this celebration took on even more magnificence than the dazzling light shows the inhabitants of Cap and Sans-Souci, and the kingdom's many foreign visitors, had by that time grown accustomed to witnessing on Haitian Independence Day. "The palace and the city of Sans-Souci were superbly illuminated," the *Gazette* reported. "Several pyramids had been constructed and were lit up by thousands of lanterns reflecting a thousand different colors."[19]

Not all foreign media reacted positively to these lavish parties. One racist detractor, writing for the Baltimore-based *Niles' Weekly Register*, accused Christophe of having "*aped* royalty." The writer then mocked the entire Haitian aristocracy, by referring to Vastey as the "baroness Big Bottom," to Christophe as "king Stophel himself," and to Limonade as "Lime Punch." The writer described the "vast pomposity" of Christophe's court for, he said, the "benefit of all who desire to '*laugh and to be fat,*' at the fools and knaves who applaud it—black or white." Seeming to take direct aim at the *New-England Palladium*'s coverage and interest in the queen's fete, the writer for *Niles' Weekly* went on to marvel at the U.S. newspapers that reprinted the "long account of a set of black fellows at Hayti, the quondam grooms and scullions of the 'legitimate' days, disguised as gentlemen and ladies, riding in somber processions." This article had its own life, going on to be reprinted in the southern state of Virginia.[20]

It was not just U.S. newspapers from southern states where slavery still reigned, as in Virginia and Maryland, that poked fun at the Haitian king. In 1811 a broadside engraving mocking King Henry by Dridier and Torchiana began circulating, first in Italy and then throughout the Atlantic world. The image continued to be reproduced throughout the 1810s, appearing again in 1818 in volume 2 of the Italian-language *Series of Lives and Portraits of Famous Characters of Recent Times*, accompanied by a short biography.[21] In this portrait, says one scholar, King Henry is depicted "not as a person, but as a type: a racially indeterminate mimic man, outfitted in British-styled royal finery decidedly inappropriate for the climate, self-absorbed, distant from his people, and indifferent to how he was perceived."[22]

Another flavor of attempts to paint King Henry as a ridiculous figure guilty of squandering Haiti's riches can be tasted in the *Concord Gazette* out of New Hampshire. In 1817 this New England paper printed an advertisement for a wax figure of the king of Haiti, "as large as life." The ad erroneously described Christophe as having married one of Louverture's daughters and of possessing a crown that cost $30,000.[23] The exaggerated lore surrounding the cost of King Henry's crown continued after his death. In reporting the 1843 overthrow of President Boyer, the *Barre Gazette* reported that the former Haitian president fled to Jamaica and "brought with him the crown formerly worn by the emperor [*sic*] Christophe, and that the jewels with which it was studded were worth two millions of dollars."[24]

The international press covered the queen and the royal princesses with a bit more kindness, at least while Christophe reigned. Describing their fancy accoutrements, *The Lady's Monthly Museum* applauded that the "very superb dresses" of the princesses and the queen had "just been finished by one of our fashionable dress-makers." The queen's dress evidently appeared as opulent as any wedding gown of haute couture today, containing a white satin petticoat "richly embroidered in sun-flowers, terminating at the bottom with a broad gold fringe." The train was also made of white satin and had been embroidered with the same sunflowers as the petticoat, "looped up on each side (to form a drapery) with gold tassels and bullion." A plume of white feathers topped off the already fine elegance of the dress. The British magazine described the princesses' dresses in similarly fawning terms. One dress had a petticoat of lilac satin, trimmed with rows of gold and silver fringe to form the drapery, finished at the bosom with a "gold and silver cestus, with a finely executed rose, from which is suspended an elegant sash of gold." The train offered equal room for marvel. Formed out of silver tissue embroidered at the bottom with veins of leaves in gold, it displayed large red roses with sleeves also in silver tissue. Her sister's dress had been designed in the same style, but this one had a pink corded satin petticoat with a train covered in "blonde lace, richly worked in silver." This second dress displayed embroidered French roses and lilies of the valley, with sleeves done in the same silver tissue that covered the body of the dress, finished at the bottom with a silver cestus.[25]

Marie-Louise owed her good press at least in part to widespread reports of her kindness. In its account of her 1816 fete, the *Royal Gazette* did not fail to mention that Christophe, "desiring to stamp the celebration of his beloved wife, with acts of clemency," "had several prisoners released." Such benevolence was widely acknowledged to be due to Marie-Louise's influence and was touted by foreigners and the Haitian populace alike.[26]

Although the queen saw her image far less scorned abroad, the king had too many supporters at home and across England to be overly concerned with racist mocking of his likeness or exaggerated reports of the money he allegedly spent. By 1816, the Kingdom of Haiti proliferated with foreign artists perfectly capable of rendering the king's likeness in the noble and dignified form he hoped would spread around the world. In October 1816, the British painter Richard Evans got onto the kingdom's payroll for three months at the price of 1,200 gourdes. Evans held the official title of "professor of the academy of painting." Back in England, Evans had studied under Sir Thomas Lawrence, considered at the time one of the greatest portraitists in Great Britain. Before leaving for Haiti, Evans met with Saunders at Wilberforce's home to discuss their upcoming voyage. Once in Haiti, Evans quickly helped staff and direct the Academy of Painting and Design in Sans-Souci.[27] Christophe was elated to inform his friend Clarkson back in England that the school was now open and that under Evans it was quite "active." Even though in 1817 the *Royal Almanac* listed the official "painter of the king" as a Mr. Revinchal, it is Evans's portrait of Christophe that remains the most famous and widely known image of him.[28]

Evans did not stay in Haiti for long. By 1818, the *Royal Almanac* no longer listed him as a member of the academy, and he had returned to England. That very year Evans appeared before the Royal Academy in London to display his famous portrait of the Haitian king standing august in his iconic military uniform. Evans painted at least two versions of the portrait, and possibly three. In late 1816, Christophe sent one of them, along with Prince Victor's, to William Wilberforce as a gift.[29]

At the same time Christophe appointed Evans, the king made Saunders "schoolmaster" for three months at the price of 300 gourdes. Saunders had been in Haiti earlier that year with Strafford. The *Gazette* reported his previous arrival in January and described the hearty welcome Saunders received. It was not long before Saunders made his mission in the kingdom known. Around two weeks after his arrival, the *Gazette* documented how Saunders brought smallpox vaccine to Haiti and had "begun to vaccinate many children at Sans-Souci." "His majesty has ordered several Haitian doctors to assist Mr. Prince Sanders so as to learn to administer the vaccine," the paper reported. The *Gazette* triumphantly announced, "The scourge of smallpox, which wreaks so much havoc in our country, especially in hot weather, will no longer have to be feared by us."[30]

His mission being complete for a time, Saunders had gone back to England, where he went on to direct the publication of the laudatory *Haytian Papers* (1816), which included parts of the *Code Henry*. Saunders had particularly called attention to those laws dealing with agricultural laborers and their compensation. While in England he met not only with Wilberforce and Evans but with a young British artist by the name of John C. F. Rossi. Saunders hoped to similarly persuade him to travel to Haiti, "for the purposes of carrying on works of Sculpture and ornamental parts of Buildings." Rossi, though initially enthusiastic about the possibility, later changed his mind after hearing a rumor that Christophe was about to be overthrown. He told a friend that "the government of France for the purpose of employing troops who wish to be so, proposes to send a considerable force to St. Domingo [Haiti] to support *Petion* [*sic*] against *Christophe*, & in case of success to appoint Petion, who now favour[s] the French, to be Governor of that island." Rossi declined also, he said, because he incorrectly suspected that Saunders "was not adequately commissioned by Christophe the King of Hayti to engage them." Saunders returned to the kingdom on September 21, 1816, with four other men, including Evans, but without Rossi. Like Saunders they had all been formally invited by the king to occupy important positions in public instruction.[31]

Christophe desired to set up the Haitian school system using the Lancastrian method, thereby introducing British education and "the English language to Haiti." He appointed one of the other men who traveled to Cap with Saunders, T. B. Gulliver, to public schoolmaster for 300 gourdes for three months. While Evans lived at Sans-Souci palace, both Gulliver and Saunders initially stayed in Cap at the expense of the king. The king later appointed Saunders headmaster of the school system in the northwestern coastal town of Port-de-Paix, with other headmasters appointed in Gonaïves, Sans-Souci, and Saint-Marc.[32]

Christophe regularly corresponded with Clarkson throughout this time. He wrote to Clarkson on February 5, 1816, to explain his elaborate education plans: "For a long while, my intention, my dearest ambition, has been to secure for the nation which has confided to me its destiny the benefit of public instruction." Christophe continued, "I am completely devoted to this project. The edifices necessary for the institutions of public instruction in the cities and in the country are under construction."[33] To facilitate national education, Christophe created a program to sponsor foreign artists, scientists, musicians, and mathematicians, as well as English teachers, to come to the kingdom to instruct Haitian students, both boys and girls. Christophe also mandated creation of the Royal Chamber of Instruction, appointed a minister of education, and issued an edict mandating the development of schools throughout northern Haiti.[34]

Although Christophe never succeeded in finding female instructors to educate the kingdom's female students, Christophe's education plan experienced many successes. By 1820, numerous academies and national schools thrived in diverse locales. Many Haitians found employment not only as monitors and inspectors but as directors of schools in towns as various as Gonaïves, Saint-Marc, Fort Royal, Limbé, Borgne, Saint-Louis, Jean-Rabel, and Plaisance.[35]

From a combination of the writings produced by Vastey, Limonade, and Chanlatte, along with those circulated by antislavery supporters of Haiti, like Saunders, Banks, Clarkson, Wilberforce, Strafford, and Hamilton, the international reading public learned about the royal decrees issued by the king of Haiti that described this plan for free general education. Through such reportage foreigners were able to share in the king of Haiti's remarkable vision for every city to have a national public school, not unlike what Christophe had already instituted with great success in the city of Cap-Henry. During this time, a military hospital was also erected in the capital. By 1818, the hospital instituted a chair of medicine and anatomy, and the newly created Academy of Belles-Lettres had begun to instruct students in science. In 1820, the Collège Royal counted among its instructors Dr. Duncan Stewart, whom Christophe appointed as professor of anatomy and surgery and who later saved his life following the stroke that almost ended it.[36]

Foreign influence in Haiti spanned from medicine to education to religion. Christophe had particular interest in Anglicanism, believing its preachers could help further his education plans. Sometime between 1815 and 1816, the royal press at Sans-Souci published a bilingual English-French edition of the Anglican church's *Book of Common Prayer,* its first translation into French. The book's cover read: "for the use of the Royal College and the National Schools of Haiti." And in May 1816, Christophe had a conversation with Prince Saunders in which he expressed interest in bringing "Anglican orders" to Haiti.[37]

Also in 1816, Christophe invited to the kingdom a well-known Protestant abolitionist from New York, Stephen Grellet, who had been on an extended sojourn in Port-au-Prince for the purposes of setting up a religious school in the republic. Grellet had taken several dozen Bibles with him from New York to distribute throughout the south, where he held numerous religious meetings, much to the consternation of the country's "Romish" priests. Grellet told the British abolitionist William Allen that he desired to have sent to Port-au-Prince "some qualified school masters with all the necessary apparatus for such schools." "I understand that some of my English correspondents from the Bible Society & that for education [sic] are preparing to send to the part of the Island under the dominion of King Henry the 1st Bibles and four school masters," Grellet wrote to Allen. "Now my dear friend, my request is, on behalf of this part of the Island I now visit, that you should extend a portion of your attention & bounty unto them. The president will accept it with all gratitude, for his study appears to be the welfare of this people." Grellet then thanked Allen, as well as Clarkson and Wilberforce, for providing him with the necessary paperwork to enter the Kingdom of Haiti and allowing him to extend his "religious mission."[38]

Grellet never did make it to the kingdom. He told his abolitionist friends back in London that after having experienced a hurricane in Haiti, he became ill and had to return to the United States. Before ending his letter, Grellet remarked that Pétion intended to imitate the king of Haiti by instituting the Lancastrian method and that the president was "preparing a large building where he wishes to have higher branches taught." Although he did express slight preference for the president, whom he met on numerous occasions and who had heartily welcomed him to the republic, Grellet insisted, "I may sincerely say I have no prejudice for or against the other side; pure gospel love inflames my heart towards all this people for whom I feel more than can be expressed."[39]

The Haitian king already had Clarkson and Wilberforce continually advocating on his behalf, but Christophe corresponded with the Bible Society all on his own too. In a letter from 1819, Christophe demonstrated that he was in many respects the most capable of stumping for Haiti on the world stage. King Henry wrote to the president of the Bible Society, Lord Teignmouth, to update him on the successful expansion of Haiti's school system and the introduction of the King James Bible. "Our schools are still doing very well and our young Haitians are making great progress," Christophe reported. "The Holy Bible is now in the hands of all schoolchildren in our national schools and specialized schools. Six other schools in the interior of the country are going to be established on the English system, by tutors who have been found capable of directing them."[40] Christophe's elaborate education system, as well as his intimate relationship with England's most famous abolitionists, was by 1819 well known across Great Britain, and positions in his schools were highly coveted. In November 1819 a man named Arthur Young wrote to Wilberforce to recommend his neighbor's son for a teaching position.[41] In his correspondence with the French government, urging it to consider a treaty of recognition with Christophe, Clarkson also touted what he called the king of Haiti's "task to civilize a barbarous people," which he described as "bring[ing] them by degrees from ignorance to knowledge, or from slavery to national freedom." "Such, however, is the burthen which Henry the 1st has imposed upon himself, and his success has been already so great as to leave no doubt that in a few years he will accomplish this glorious end," Clarkson proclaimed. "Professors of the arts and science, Instructors of language and teachers of the youth both in letters and religion," Clarkson continued, "are so judiciously distributed that every Haytian, who is now born will have the opportunity of being able to read and write, and many of becoming accomplished scholars."[42]

Although it received far less fanfare and media attention in the era than his school system, King Henry also created a policy whereby Haitians could apply to become the owners of the former homes, plantations, buildings, and other properties of the ex-colonists. While exports of coffee and indigo, the kingdom's staples, were strong, King Henry urged Haitians to cultivate wheat and other grains on their former colonizers' lands too. The king explained that he wanted "all Haitians without distinction, the poor as well as the rich, to have the ability to become owners of the property of our former oppressors."[43] Under the king's rule trade thrived as well. In August 1817, the *Gazette* reported that from the port of Cap-Henry alone, in just six months, there were seventy-one ships exporting "17,084,000 pounds of sugar and coffee." Another goal of redistributing the land among the people had been to make Haiti less dependent upon imports. "Growing our own means of subsistence will be the surest and most powerful way to increase and maintain the population, which is becoming more numerous day by day," the *Gazette* announced.

A different prominent Englishman celebrated Christophe for these economic successes and labor reforms. Sir Joseph Banks of England, the first director of Kew Gardens, painted Christophe, because of his labor laws, as the greatest legislator the world ever saw. Banks said that the laws Christophe instituted in the *Code Henry* constituted, "without doubt in its theory, the most moral association of men in existence; nothing that white men have been able to arrange is equal to it." Banks especially admired the portion of the *Code* dealing with the equitable treatment of laborers and their compensation. The first article listed under "Law Respecting the Culture" maintained, "The proprietors and farmers of land are bound to treat their respective laborers with true paternal solicitude." The second article stated, "The law exacts from the laborers in return a reciprocal attention to the welfare and interest of the landlord and farmer." The third article required, "In lieu of wages, the laborers in plantations shall be allowed a full fourth of the gross product, free from all duties."[44] The *Code Henry* described what was at the time, arguably, the most radically free labor system in the Americas. It seems that Christophe's contemporaries were well positioned to understand that the feudal world the *Code* created was not at all the same as the form of chattel slavery that still existed in the Euro-American world of slavery. Portuguese, Spanish, and Dutch slavers continued to kidnap Africans from the continent and force them to submit to a lifetime of violent subjugation in the American hemisphere. King Henry designed his *Code,* on the contrary, to allow workers to share in the wealth produced on state-run farms.

———

Christophe remained an attentive father to his children at the same time as he guardedly watched over Haitian institutions. The king personally concerned himself with the education of the royal prince and princesses and assigned them governesses and tutors, respectively. Christophe seemed particularly interested in the schooling of his youngest son, however. The king's letters to his heir consistently urge the royal prince, from a young age, to always take his education seriously. Yet while some of King Henry's letters to Prince Victor praised the youth, others admonished him for his lack of seriousness and attention to writing. Christophe often criticized the essays Prince Victor sent him as writing samples, for example. But the royal prince's conduct toward his instructors provided the king with greater occasion to "reproach" his son. In October 1813, King Henry wrote, "Your governor and preceptor are not pleased with you," before asking, "can you think that I could be too?" "I am informed that you have mistreated your servants," the king continued. "That is not good of you." He finished by admonishing, "If you wish to deserve my esteem & my friendship, it is not in this way that you must go about it, but rather by a wiser conduct, by a docility to your counselors, and to the lessons of people who have the capacity to instill in you patience, affability, and a friendliness that will make you cherished by everyone."[45]

Some of the prince's teachers and minders lasted longer than others. The king held special regard for Augustin Calixte, his son's steward, but felt compelled to temporarily relieve him of his assignment so that Calixte could take up a role in *Richard, the Lion Heart,* played at court in January 1814.[46] While Calixte and Victor-Henry's uncle, Prince Noël Coidavid (until his untimely death), remained the steward and governor of his education, respectively, by 1815 the prince's lead teacher had changed from a man named Dominique Bazin to the erudite, prolific, and much stricter Baron de Vastey.[47] Although Christophe continued to complain from time to time about the young prince's lack of seriousness, Vastey remained his teacher until the end of 1819.[48] In 1820, the royal prince's *maison* was shaken up entirely by Vastey's new responsibilities to the king, Prince Noël's death, and the appointment of Prince Victor's new steward, Lieutenant Colonel de Médard Mathieu. The prince still had friendly faces around him, namely, his cousins, André Coidavid and Captain Joseph

Coidavid, who fulfilled the office of his "Gentlemen," that is, his aide-de-camp and *officier de la garde-robe* (masters of robes), respectively.[49]

The prince also had a new teacher, the British instructor William Wilson. Wilson, being young himself, reported to Thomas Clarkson, that not unlike the royal prince he sometimes incited the king's ire because of his "mishaps." "Due to youthful indiscretion," Wilson told Clarkson in a letter that he later included in his memoir,

> I was summoned with a companion and asked to present myself to be reprimanded. There was nothing likable about this reprimand because the offense was great. [The king,] speaking with such passion that he was approaching closer and closer to a hole, without realizing it—the paving stones having been removed from a large square to ventilate the arcade from below—might have fallen into it if I hadn't made a gesture to attract his attention; after which, although he was still threatening toward us, and more especially toward me, vilifying me, calling me a whippersnapper, and a rascal, he turned his back to us and then smiled.

Implying that this accidentally heroic gesture saved not only the king's life but his own, Wilson concluded, "I think that after this episode I grew in his esteem, for although I continued to act very indiscreetly, from time to time, he never sent me back to prison, and on several occasions declared that I was of good breeding."[50]

While Christophe's other son, Eugène, might not have commanded the same attention from his father, the Duc de Môle (Eugène's title of nobility) certainly seems to have sought it. Eugène wrote to his father in September 1816 to send him some samples of his own writing, "in order to receive more and more the marks of your kindness." "I would count myself lucky if I could obtain your approval," Prince Eugène said to his father. This fascinating missive, written by the son of the king who could never be king, is of particular interest because of what it suggests about their father-son relationship. The enclosed one-paragraph essay, titled "Portrait of the Sultan Saladin" (Portrait du Saladin sultan), offered a short but sympathetic account of the Muslim ruler of Egypt and Syria, who famously defeated a massive army of crusaders in the Battle of Hattin, capturing the city of Jerusalem in 1187: "At the height of his power, he ruled a unified Muslim region stretching from Egypt to Arabia."[51] Prince Eugène's essay, which concluded that Saladin, "had nothing barbaric about him except his birth," was recovered in 1826, at the same time as the letter, according to a note scribbled on the manuscript in a different hand. The anonymous scribbler believed that Prince Eugène's description of Saladin had been merely a stand-in, "so to speak, for the portrait of Christophe himself." The scribbler went on to suggest that this essay landed the "poor little prince two years in prison at the famous ferrière [sic] dungeons," where "he was released by a miracle of providence." Originally collected as part of a series of rare documents and manuscripts for "an anticipated (but never written) book," by the nineteenth-century Italian jurist and academic Giacomo Costantino Beltrami, whose papers are housed at the Biblioteca Civica Angelo Mai in Bergamo, Italy, it is not clear who scribbled the note on the letter; and no other evidence of Christophe's alleged imprisonment of his son Eugène has yet to come to light.[52]

Correspondence between Christophe and one of his most trusted doctors, a man named Massicot, can also be found in the same Italian archive. While the "doctor, first class," of the king was initially a man called Turlin, Christophe later appointed Dr. Massicot as one of his primary doctors in Cap-Henry and made him a chevalier.[53] Christophe frequently ordered Massicot (who lived in Haiti until at least 1820), through Ministers de Prézeau and Limonade, to care for various people in the capital, Sans-Souci, and at the Citadelle. He also frequently dispatched Dr. Massicot to other neighboring towns and parishes. It was important to Christophe that the nobles especially received proper medical care. In April 1819, King Henry, having grown worried about one of his oldest friends in life and in combat, sent the doctor to the town of Petite-Rivière to attend to Paul Romain, the Prince du Limbé.[54]

The doctor had been employed in the kingdom since at least March 1813, and from that time forward Christophe sent him to care for many of his most trusted and valued friends and relatives, including the Comte de Borgne, the painter Manuel, the king's nephew Prince Jean, and his goddaughter Lorance.[55] The king also dispatched Massicot to care for foreigners, officers in the army, and "new Haitians," that is to say, formerly enslaved people whom the kingdom's military succeeded in liberating from slave-trafficking vessels that entered Haitian waters.[56]

King Henry's order for Dr. Massicot to treat Étienne and Lucienne, two "new Haitians," gives some clue as to how individuals rescued from slave traffickers spent their days in Haiti. The king called Étienne and Lucienne "scrubbers of my palace" (frotteurs de mon palais), who he said arrived in Haiti very sick, like many other victims of slave trafficking. King Henry expressed anger, however, that the two men, who had previously been treated at the hospital in Carénage, were sent to work without being "cured." The king therefore ordered Massicot to treat them at the "main hospital" and not to send them back to work until they had been "scrupulously examined" and cured of their illnesses, which the king figured included more than just the previously diagnosed "gall."[57] Because the Citadelle was a prison in addition to a defense fortress, Christophe sometimes needed to send Dr. Massicot there to care for prisoners. Two of those prisoners included "the ex-sous-governor Martial and the Baron de Jean Charles," both of whom, Christophe noted, "are very sick in that place." Christophe's compassion mixed with severity was once more on display in this instance, as we learn that his guards had only recently arrested the two men. Still, Christophe said "they should be treated in the dungeons where they are being held for life."[58]

King Henry also entrusted the care of his wife and children to Dr. Massicot. He sent the doctor to attend to Queen Marie-Louise in July 1815, while in March of the same year Dr. Massicot and Dr. Turlin both treated Princess Améthyste. Christophe's daughters seem to have imbibed more than a little of their mother's kindness coupled with their father's sense of duty and care. Améthyste's governess, the Comtesse d'Ouanaminthe, wrote to thank Princess Athénaïs for her concern after the countess recovered from an illness she acquired in June 1814. From this letter we learn that the Comtesse d'Ouanaminthe and Queen Marie-Louise were cousins. The countess wrote in her letter, "Comtesse de Valière, my cousin, has asked me to assure you of my attachments and asked you to inform the queen of them." Comtesse de Valière is afterward revealed to be none other than the queen's sister, Louise-Geneviève Coidavid, at the time married to Louis Pierrot, previously the Baron de Pierrot, and who by 1814 acquired the title of Comte de Valière, before finishing his career under Christophe as a duke in 1820.[59]

In August 1819, the Comtes de Valière, d'Ouanaminthe, and du Terrier-Rouge, husband of Princess Athénaïs's governess, surge into the story of the king's life in a way that potentially surfaces a crack across the otherwise smooth appearance of Haitian sovereignty and Christophean prosperity, patiently sculpted by the king for a decade and a half. On August 26, the *Royal Gazette* reported that Prince Victor left Sans-Souci at two in the morning, accompanied by one of his father's oldest friends, Jean-Philippe Daut, the Duc de l'Artibonite, along with the above-named counts, and the Baron de Monpoint and the Chevalier de Prézeau. With them, the royal prince spent the next fifteen days touring the kingdom. Prince Victor paid special attention to the cities of Gonaïves, Petite-Rivière de l'Artibonite, Montrouis, Crête-à-Pierrot, Verrettes, and Saint-Marc, where the citizens of Haiti evidently greeted him like a virtual celebrity with acclamations of "Vive le prince royal!" The young prince took time to hold audiences with people across the region, as well as with the military, before visiting the cities' forts and hospitals.

The *Gazette* reported that Prince Victor was beloved throughout the realm, explicitly setting the tone for the young heir to one day inherit his father's throne. His speeches, above all, seemed to endear him to the aristocracy. "It is pleasant and flattering for me that the king, my august and very honored father, has entrusted me with such an honorable mission as that of receiving in his name the military and civil officials of the western province, who, by their merit and the services they have rendered to the country, have been judged worthy of national awards," Prince Victor told the nobles. "You will not forget, Gentlemen, that the education of the nobility is only established in the midst of a free people to honor merit," he continued. "That all virtuous Haitians who have well served their country, whether in military or civilian life, have an equal right to it; that the nobility carries more particularly the obligation of being a good Haitian, a good father, a good son, a good husband; that your conduct should serve as an example and a model for your fellow citizens; by this, you will justify the confidence of H.M., you will honor the choice he has made of you, and you will acquire new titles to his esteem and consideration." The *Gazette* concluded of the prince's stately reception and kingly demeanor, "Satisfaction was the same everywhere the prince traveled. Haitians all being of one heart and mind, in their desire to give the prince testaments of their love." The article ended by openly declaring the prince a "worthy inheritor of the name and the throne of Henry."[60]

King Henry's absence from the tour of the kingdom seems a bit conspicuous in hindsight. Christophe had taken pride in traveling on these tours in previous years. Was his health already suffering before his stroke on August 15, 1820, leading him to position his son in such a way as to immediately assume the throne upon his feared, and perhaps anticipated, demise? Even more suggestive than the king's absence on this tour, in 1820, Chanlatte, who like Limonade survived the coup that led to the king's suicide, published an opera titled *The Hunting Party of the King,* originally performed at court as part of the independence day celebrations on January 1 of that year. Performed in front of the royal family and many members of the aristocracy, the play featured Creole-language songs danced to a calinda. But just ten months before Christophe's suicide, the plotline whereby the king goes missing during a royal hunting trip, and "the morbid imaginings" it produces in members of the court, seems strangely prophetic. Yet unlike the tragic denouement of Christophe's real life, this opera ends happily. The king is prevented from being killed by a wild boar, ensuring his safe return to the throne, and like any good romance, the performance finishes with a wedding between the maiden, Céliflore, and Zulimbo, the very man who in the play saves Christophe's life.[61]

16

CRACKS IN KINGLY
AUTHORITY

King Henry, at heart paternal and inclined toward clemency, could be exacting and unforgiving toward anyone who dared to openly betray him. Christophe's rift with two of his most trusted Frenchmen, Joseph Bunel and Father Corneille Brelle, illustrates the perils of this not always complimentary character contrast. These cases also point to the inherent vulnerability of northern Haiti in a world of slavery and colonialism. In hindsight, Brelle's and Bunel's betrayals—although they took place years apart—surfaced deeper cracks forming across Christophe's realm, fissures that, each in its own way, stood as portents for the end of the king and kingdom. But there was something else, something far more auspicious and of a seemingly providential nature, that took the king by surprise in 1818 and ended up in the most unlikely manner paving the way for the kingdom's eventual demise. On March 29, the Republic of Haiti announced the sudden death of President Alexandre Pétion, after an illness of eight days. Over in the republic's capital, Port-au-Prince, never had a funeral been undertaken with more solemnity; but over at Sans-Souci never had a death given King Henry more hope for the future. Alas, Haiti's reunification was not to be. At least not until the Haitian king found his own grave.

Marie-Louise Christophe kept up a lively correspondence showing mutual reciprocation and affection with the French merchant Joseph Bunel's wife, Marie. The Bunels had a long history on the island. In the colonial era, Marie Bunel had been a landowning free woman of color who owned slaves, while her husband, a white colonist from France, had been treasurer-general under Toussaint Louverture whom he helped broker a key trade agreement with the United States.[1] Joseph Bunel had helped to negotiate "Toussaint's Clause," which opened trade between the French colony under Louverture and the United States. According to General Maitland, also involved in the affair, Joseph, whom he called "a man of bad character," owed the "weight" he had with Louverture almost entirely to his wife, a "near relation" of Louverture's.[2]

As a landowning free woman of color, Marie Bunel, whose birth name was Marie-Françoise Mouton, was quite wealthy at the time that Joseph married her, allegedly, "to make his fortune."[3] In addition to owning several plantations, on the eve of the revolution Marie Bunel also ran the Hotel du Bon Chasseur (previously run by Mongeon and Gaye), which brought even more earnings. She also possessed a considerable amount of social capital. Marie and her extended family, the Grandjeans or Grand Jeans (one member of whom, Stephen Grandjean, married Joseph Bunel's sister Mary Frances), consorted with many of Cap's most prominent families of color, including the Boyers, the Viltons, and the Coidavids. Christophe quite likely made the acquaintance of the Bunels through Marie-Louise's stepfather, Jacques Coidavid, whom Antoine Grandjean selected as god-father for his daughter Antoinette in 1787. Respected and admired for her jovial personality, Marie owned and lived in a home in Cap on the same street where Dessalines's wife Marie-Claire Heureuse, a *marchande,* lived with Rosillesse and Marie-Jeanne Dessalines in 1803. Beloved equally for her sugary jams and business acumen, both Dessalines and Marie-Claire knew the Bunel family well and implored Marie to return to the island following the much touted exuberance with which they greeted Joseph when he returned in September 1804.[4]

Despite having so many beloved friends and many family members who still resided in Cap—including her niece, Orphise Bunel, her sister, Hélène Mouton, and her nephews, Ambroise Grandjean and Diaquoy—Marie Bunel undoubtedly felt some level of ambivalence about returning to the island of her birth.[5] After all, if she and her husband had escaped consequences for Bunel's role in helping to broker Louverture's storied trade agreement with the United States, the same could not be said of Joseph's role in assisting Christophe at the outset of the Leclerc expedition. Not unlike Louverture, both Bunels found themselves incarcerated, separately, after the fire that Christophe ordered in Cap.

On the day he ordered the fire, Christophe wrote to treasurer-general Bunel to order him to hand over "all the money that you have in the treasury." Bunel complied, relinquishing to Christophe 41,000 gourdes in cash.[6] When Leclerc landed and demanded that Bunel turn over the funds to him, Bunel informed him that he had already given the money to Christophe. For this, Leclerc had him arrested and then deported to France, where officials sent him to Besançon, "with the city for a prison." Though their fates diverged, this was the same region where Louverture saw his own incarceration and experienced his demise in the Fort de Joux.[7] As for Marie Bunel, she had also been arrested, but after appealing to Rochambeau she saw release shortly before the revolutionaries declared independence in November 1803. Yet not long after her release, a mysterious visitor appeared at her home, warning that her life stood in danger, and counseled her to depart immediately for the United States, which she did, eventually reuniting in Philadelphia with her husband.[8]

After independence, Joseph Bunel lived off and on between northern Haiti and Philadelphia from 1804 to around 1812, while Marie Bunel remained in Philadelphia until 1810. The Christophes and the Bunels, nevertheless, remained intimate associates. Christophe addressed his letters to Bunel with the kind of affection and familiarity he reserved for his most respected and cherished friends—in one instance he called him "mon cher diplomatique," or "my dear fellow." Lauded by the Comte de Limonade, his "old friend," for his ever "constant love of liberty," Bunel seems to have lived a comfortable life in Haiti under Christophe's rule, where he also counted the Vasteys as friends and business associates. When Marie returned in 1810, the Bunel and the Christophe families continued to spend time together, enjoying a mutually beneficial personal and commercial relationship.[9]

Marie-Louise Christophe had continued to write to Marie Bunel while she remained in Philadelphia. In September 1810, Marie-Louise wrote to send her friend some ingredients for making "compotes" of mango, guava, lemon, and "other fruits." Marie-Louise also promised to send her jams "of every type." In return, she hoped to receive from Marie Bunel, "if it is possible, 49 pairs of cotton stockings, very fine, and very wide."[10] Joseph Bunel, for his part, remained in Cap while his wife lived in Philadelphia, traveling back and forth to visit her. On June 12, 1810, Christophe wrote to Marie Bunel to reassure her not only that her husband had arrived safely in the capital but that his health was improving.[11] At some point after Marie Bunel moved back to Haiti, the relationship between the two husbands changed considerably.

At the height of Christophe's civil war with Pétion's republic, and at a time when northern administrators were busy devoting their energy to the creation of the *Code Henry,* the kingdom got wind of a conspiracy afoot involving Bunel and other foreigners living in the north. To hear Vastey tell the story, several partisans of the French entered the north during this period and eventually established themselves in various merchant houses. Among these foreigners, Vastey listed Bunel, the infamous Montorsier, and Étienne Viart (sometimes spelled "Viard"), also a good friend of the Bunels. The first two were Frenchmen, and the third Vastey described as an "homme de couleur, by skin, but French by his principles."[12]

Following Dessalines's assassination, Bunel came and went from the island, seemingly as he pleased, but at one point he returned to Haiti with several other Frenchmen, "for the purpose of plotting against the government," Vastey charged. The conspiracy was vaster and had greater implications than Christophe and his allies first realized. Bunel and his accomplices reportedly sought to introduce dissension into the north and encourage rebellion, while Viart and the other accomplices encouraged revolution in the western province of the kingdom. But who was responsible for this conspiracy, and on whose behalf was it undertaken? "In the end, it was French partisans, armed with the dagger of treason and covered with the mask of hypocrisy, who were stirring things up again in our midst, and who made incredible efforts on both sides, to further excite the fire of discord and civil war," Vastey lamented. Christophe ordered some of the men, like Montorsier, arrested and taken to the jailhouse. Yet writers from the kingdom, as we have seen, claimed that Christophe later allowed Montorsier to go free, provided that he agreed to work on Christophe's behalf.[13]

However, the southern newspaper *The Observer*, edited by Dumesle, who referred to Christophe as "his very ferocious Majesty" and the "angel exterminator of the north," asserted that the king did not liberate Montorsier at all. Citing a report published in pamphlet form in Paris in September 1819, written by a man who claimed to have lived in the kingdom when these events occurred, and who signed his name as P.-P.-P. Duluc, Dumesle asserted that Christophe had Montorsier executed. Providing a long list of Frenchmen and other white foreigners allegedly killed under Christophe's orders, Duluc had claimed that although Montorsier had been a long-standing business associate of the king's, "that barbarian" "disappeared him over night."[14] As for Mr. Bunel, his fate after being discovered as a conspirator is not known for certain.

What we do know is that in early January 1811, Christophe ordered the confiscation of 11,252 gourdes' worth of merchandise and money belonging to Bunel. Bunel's property had gotten entangled in an 1810 general sequestration that Christophe had ordered of all U.S. belongings and goods to compensate for the fraud committed by several U.S. merchants who Christophe claimed robbed him of more than $100,000 in gourdes in money and coffee combined.[15] We also know that at some point Marie Bunel returned to Cap-Henry, where she lived as late as the spring of 1812, according to at least one letter she received there that April. That the last known record of the Bunels occurred in 1812, the same year as the conspiracy, suggests an unhappy fate for both.[16]

One of the men whom Christophe accused of concerting with Bunel, a man called Papalier, had previously been implicated in the republic's attack and capture of one of Christophe's most prized ships, the *Princesse Royale Améthyste,* named after the king's firstborn daughter. This event sparked renewed hostilities between the north and the south. In early January 1812, Christophe dispatched the *Princesse Royale* and two other ships to waters surrounding the southern department, in one nineteenth-century Haitian historian's words, "to explore the coastline," but "the harsh treatment meted out to the squadron's crews gave rise to great discontent and a plot to hand it over to the republicans in the west or south." When the fleet passed La Gonâve, the inhabitants of Port-au-Prince spread a rumor that Christophe intended to lead an expedition against the republic. On January 12, Pétion called the troops and national guards to arms. At the same time, an English frigate anchored in the bay of Port-au-Prince set sail for Gonaïves to inquire about the ship and any proceedings emanating from the king. King Henry then received the distressing information that having passed by Miragoâne, the crew aboard the *Princesse Royale* surrendered to the republic, followed by the other two ships in the squadron. Yet in a surprising turn of events, Christophe learned that the commander of the English frigate called the *Southampton,* after consulting with President Pétion, had traveled on to Miragoâne and attacked the *Princesse Royale.* The English ship afterward seized Christophe's boat entirely and escorted it to Port-au-Prince. Christophe blamed this event on a French conspiracy similar to the one involving Bunel, averring Papalier plotted and led the attempt on the ship named after Christophe's daughter. For this, the king ordered Papalier executed. That March, Christophe declared he would lead a strike on Port-au-Prince, at the same time as he announced the republic's capture of the *Princesse Royale.*[17]

Despite the economic prosperity the kingdom enjoyed, the year 1812 had simultaneously brought more fruitless war with the southern republic, amid seemingly endless conspiracies against the king. In June 1812, in the middle of the ongoing campaign in Port-au-Prince, three of the king's military divisions from the Artibonite, amounting to about two thousand men, abandoned the kingdom and defected to the republic.[18] With Christophe ultimately forced to retreat from Port-au-Prince and its environs, other desertions and defections to the republic reportedly followed, including that of five hundred soldiers near Ouanaminthe and other townships along the eastern border in 1813.[19]

The constant tumult is perhaps responsible for the fact that not a single issue of the kingdom's *Gazette* has yet been recovered for the year 1812. Northern Haiti's official newspaper seems to have been off the grid, or at least very irregular, after January 1811, just prior to King Henry's announcement that he would take the title of king. The paper's disruption appears to have lasted well into the first months of 1813, when the fighting between the kingdom and the republic reached a temporary end, but with neither side able to declare a definitive victory against the other.[20]

The collapse of his relationship with Bunel around this time had to have more than irritated the king, since he had allowed, against his greater instincts, this white Frenchman to occupy a role in his inner circle. Christophe would not experience less disappointment or personal distress to learn that he had made another miscalculation with a different white Frenchman, Father Brelle. Not only had he made Brelle archbishop of the kingdom, but he bestowed upon him the title of the Duc de l'Anse.

Since the beginning of Christophe's reign over northern Haiti, Brelle, first as apostolic prefect and then as archbishop, represented one of his most ardent defenders. On March 8, 1807, Brelle issued a pastoral letter to the clergy and "all his faithful," under his new official title of "Apostolic

Prefect of the State." Brelle appealed to the people of northern Haiti by stating that the priests were on their side. Brelle further vowed that Christophe had been called to duty by God and that Haiti's clergy took up the call to make it happen. "The Catholic religion supported Christophe," the French priest said: "We have only to adhere to the intentions of the government and to imitate the example of His Excellency, the President and Generalissimo of the Forces of the Earth and Seas of the State of Hayti; sentiments recorded in his every address, in all his proclamations; feelings too precious, too consoling, not to make an impression on our hearts." Echoing an article in the 1807 constitution, Brelle finished, "The government knows no religion other than the Catholic, apostolic, and Roman religion in the State of Haiti."[21]

Brelle also participated in the northern state's ongoing war of words with the southern republic. Tackling criticism from Pétion's side that Christophe had pompously taken the title "President of the Earth and Seas," Brelle responded directly in the pages of the *Official Gazette* with this stinging barb: "At what kind of school, good God! did you study? Our president has never said that he commands over the earth and the sea; he knows that God alone has that power; but he says that he is the generalissimo of the earth and sea forces of his state. That is quite different, is it not, my brother?"[22] In the earliest years of his rule, Christophe fully mobilized the Catholic faith on his behalf, and Brelle was his main warrior.

Christophe also advocated for Brelle to the pope. Throughout its run, the *Official Gazette* updated readers about the unfolding drama between Napoléon and Barnaba Chiaramonti, Pope Pius VII. The November 23, 1809, issue of the *Gazette* opened with an article from London announcing that the pope had excommunicated Napoléon. Because French forces had captured the pope earlier that July, the London paper observed that the papal decree was toothless. The pope's imprisonment lasted until Napoléon was forced to abdicate his throne, for the first time in 1814.[23] The pope returned to Rome on May 27 of that year. The news traveled lightning quick. On June 10, 1814, King Henry, with the Comte de Limonade as his signing secretary, addressed a letter directly to the newly liberated pope. "Most Holy Father, The extraordinary events which have just taken place in Europe, the fall of the impious Napoléon, have resounded even in our climes," the letter began. "We rejoice with all Christianity to see our most mortal enemy, and the most implacable to Hayti, that frightening colossus, toppled from the height of his power." "We adore with humility the decrees of divine Providence, which raises and breaks thrones at the whim of its immutable and eternal wisdom, and which, for having made the holy religion suffer through tribulations, has emerged more pure and more glorious than ever from the abyss where profane hands had wanted to plunge it forever," the letter continued. King Henry took that occasion to reiterate his faith and fidelity to the Catholic Church and its human amanuensis, the pope. "Receive, therefore, most holy Father, our warm and sincere congratulations on the happy return of your holiness to the capital of the Christian world, where we presume that this dispatch will find your holiness in full possession of his states, honored, cherished by his peoples, whose satisfaction we form an idea of by that which we ourselves experience." Before closing the letter, King Henry sought to remind the pope of some unfinished business of his own, namely, an official apostolic decree naming Father Brelle the archbishop of Haiti.[24]

On April 12, 1811, King Henry, by way of Limonade, had addressed a missive to the captive pope through Christophe's agent Peltier. Peltier, we presume, sent it on to the archbishop of Palermo, reportedly living in Sicily at the time. In the April letter, King Henry informed the pope that the people of Haiti and the Haitian army had elevated him to the position of king. "Faithful to the holy religion we pride ourselves on professing and jealous to propagate its sacred decree," the king told the pope how, as king, he had made it a priority to create an archbishop's seat and three episcopal seats, endowed with 60,000 livres for the former and 40,000 livres each for the latter. While the king had not yet designated other priests to occupy the three lesser episcopal seats, Henry alluded to Father Brelle as his choice for the archbishop role. "The minister on whom we have set our eyes to occupy the seat of dignified archiepiscopal is a zealous missionary who, for twenty years, has been working with untiring ardor to consolidate here the standard of the cross and is the only one of the Lord's sacred anointed who, at the risk of his life, has defended his precepts and his law," King Henry wrote. He then directly asked the pope "to send us good and valid seals of election so that we may consecrate this glorious goal." The letter concluded by asking the pope to please name the archbishop of Santo Domingo, Jean de Dieu Gonzalés, later the queen's chaplain, to one of the other three positions.[25]

King Henry's June 1814 letter reveals that despite rumors that the pope entirely ignored his entreaties, in September 1811 the archbishop of Palermo had responded positively to Christophe's April 1811 missive.[26] The archbishop promised to do everything possible to make official within the Catholic Church the archbishop's seat and that of the three episcopal seats requested by the Haitian king. Perhaps attributing the lack of communication since that time to the pope's incarceration, in the June letter Christophe followed up by, among other things, noting he had named Father Brelle archbishop of Haiti. Christophe was steadfast enough in his faith, however, to insist that for this archbishop seat to be official in the eyes of the church (and ostensibly God), the pope needed to send sealed documents to that effect. Only the pope had the right to erect episcopal seats. Christophe reminded the Holy See, therefore, that in April 1811 "we solicited the bounties of His Holiness in favor of our faithful and beloved Corneille Brelle, Duc de l'Ance [sic], archbishop of Hayti, our grand chaplain, an estimable priest who has been working for twenty years for the propagation of the faith, who enjoys general consideration and ours in particular, and who deserves it in every respect." In the interim, "we have appointed him archbishop of Hayti and our grand chaplain," Christophe informed the pope. "We reiterate once more to you most Holy Father, in his favor, our pressing solicitations for the confirmation of his nomination, and his seals of election, and that it may please His Holiness to designate and send such archbishops as His Holiness may deem suitable to consecrate him with this dignity."[27] These entreaties, though they did not lead to Brelle's official ordination, or that of any other bishops serving in Haiti, were not ignored either.

The archbishop of Anagni sent Christophe's letters to the pope, along with two reports on Haiti by way of Cardinal Ercole Consalvi, the pope's most trusted and important official.[28] The official report given to Consalvi called "Coup d'oeil sur Hayti" (Brief description of Haiti) described Henry's laws in terms not unlike those used by Joseph Banks. "A code of simple, clear, precise laws, adapted to the morals, customs, and character of the people to whom the sovereign has given his name, constitutes the legislation of the nation," the report stated. As for the agricultural laws specifically, the writer noted, "A code of agriculture, of which there is no similar example among any people, a project that has occupied the entire solicitude of the sovereign, regulates the reciprocal duties of owners, farmers, and cultivators, the policing of residential workplaces, the cultivation, manufacture, and exploitation of commodities, according to their type, and encompasses everything that constitutes the rural economy." The report concluded, "The principles of this code rest on justice and equity, inseparable companions of humanity," and praised the fact that the Kingdom of Haiti thrived economically: "It is perhaps today the only government that, through the organization of its finances, owes nothing to anyone but to which, on the contrary, immense capital is owed."[29] Haiti was not yet the debtor nation it would become due to the indemnity just a decade later.

In his two letters to the pope, Christophe stopped just short of asking for official recognition of Haiti's sovereignty. Yet had the pope officially anointed Brelle or any of the priests in Haiti, this would have amounted to de facto recognition of Haitian independence and sovereignty from France. Yet the Holy See—despite what a blow it would have been to Napoléon—was not willing to take such a drastic measure, out of step with the rest of the world. No other nation yet recognized Haitian independence. The Holy See did not plan for Rome to be the first. In fact, the Vatican was one of the last. It did not recognize Haitian independence until 1860.[30]

Christophe's friend and ally Brelle, on whose behalf the king sued to the pope multiple times, had not only physically crowned Christophe king but assisted in important state functions, celebrations, and funerals, until his conspicuous absence at the August 12, 1817, funeral of the king's nephew Prince Jean, the Duc du Port-Margot. Father Gonzalés, the queen's chaplain, gave the service that day instead. Gonzalés, with Brelle absent once again, performed the Mass that year for the queen's fete too, which began three days later on August 15. Yet Brelle still technically occupied the role of the Duc de l'Anse, archbishop of Haiti, at least on paper, at the time the *Royal Almanac* for the year 1817 was printed. However, the almanacs for a particular year were usually printed at the end of the year prior. Revealingly, in the 1818 almanac, although Brelle remained listed as a duke and one of the "princes of the kingdom," the title of archbishop had been granted to Gonzalés; and Gonzalés, rather than Brelle, remained in this position in 1820, the year of the king's stroke at the church in Limonade, where, as archbishop, Gonzalés was saying Mass.[31]

Duluc counted Brelle among the numerous white foreigners Christophe allegedly "killed during a period of more than seven years!!" Duluc claimed that Christophe sentenced his chaplain, "the reverend Father Brelle," to death as the "price of his excessive condescension." Duluc also defended Agoustine Franco de Médina in the affair with Dauxion-Lavaysse, saying, "Whatever propositions that envoy might have been charged with making, [he] was only guilty of a crime against Christophe."[32] Duluc's highly ideological defense of the indefensible Médina—who carried genocidal instructions for reconquest and the return of slavery into the kingdom in 1814—casts suspicion on his understanding and interpretation of what might have happened to Brelle.

Despite claiming to have been present for many of the events he described, in his pamphlet Duluc offered little more than an unverified list of people whom Christophe had supposedly wronged with hardly any detail and no evidence. For example, Duluc also condemned Christophe for the conflict with Nicolas Moline that had occurred during Louverture's war with Rigaud and that the agent Roume had complained to Louverture about. Yet unlike Christophe, who furnished Louverture with written evidence that Moline had engaged in rebellion against the *French* republic, for which Christophe was at the time a *French* general, Duluc resorted to ad hominem accusations against the Haitian king. "During the dissensions between Rigaud and Toussaint-Louverture, Christophe was the executioner of all the *hommes de couleur* who fell into his power in the city of Cap," the Parisian pamphleteer charged. "The last one he put to death was Molines [*sic*], his old friend and fellow gambler." Perhaps most egregiously, while offering no other explanation, Duluc claimed that the death of Christophe's firstborn and much regretted son, Ferdinand, had not been due to the French government's malfeasance. "It is quite true that Christophe sent one of his sons to France," wrote Duluc. "It is false that this son, who died in France, was deprived of all means of existence there. . . . The French government, on the contrary, granted him all possible subsistence, as His Majesty continues to do daily for the children of Toussaint-Louverture."[33] Duluc sought to refute the contents of a letter printed in the French newspaper *Le constitutionnel* in August 1819, which had defended Christophe's conduct during the revolution. The paper said of Christophe, "He was not a barbarian, he who was the first to surrender to French authorities [in 1802], and he gave them as a token of his faith his son Ferdinand, whom he loved as does an excellent father and who died in France bereft of all assistance."[34] Yet unlike in the days of the Moline rebellion, Christophe controlled his own press that he could use to not just refute accusations against him but take control of spurious narratives about him, his family, and his kingdom.

In 1817, the Baron de Vastey published his widely read *Political Reflections,* whose first chapter began with a public condemnation of the French government's treatment of young Ferdinand and the other Black students from Saint-Domingue who attended the Collège de la Marche. "We could hardly believe," Vastey wrote, "that a respectable government could have defiled itself and committed such a horrible act as killing children by subjecting them to poverty and poison." Referring to testimony from unnamed "eyewitnesses" who confirmed that none of the children in question survived, Vastey continued, "Unfortunately nothing is more notorious nor more true; not one of those unfortunate children has reappeared in this country."[35] *Le constitutionnel* likely derived its information about what happened to the unfortunate Ferdinand directly from the kingdom's sources.

One document from the kingdom that more immediately, and more faithfully, speaks to the rift that had formed between the king and the archbishop Brelle can be found in an October 1816 letter that Christophe wrote to Father Brelle. In the letter, written after the death of Toussaint Dupont, the Comte de Trou, Christophe accused Brelle of trying to profit from state funerals. "If the price of funerals does not decrease, particularly the funerals of dignitaries, it would be better for the family of said dignitaries for the deceased to be interred without the benefits of a church service, since those services, which they can well do without, will reduce them to becoming beggars." "There is enough in this matter, I aver, to become a Huguenot, even an atheist," Christophe concluded. The letter ended abruptly with Christophe's signature and contained none of the usual and customary niceties that stamp his other personally signed missives.[36]

The date of this missive corresponds to a time when Christophe had initiated a full-throated effort to push the northern kingdom not only into a more Anglophone sphere of influence but amid his concerted efforts to change the religion of Haiti from Catholic to Anglican. Christophe wrote to Wilberforce on November 18, 1816, "I have always spoken about this to my fellow citizens, I have always made them feel the necessity of having absolutely nothing in common with the French nation, of embracing the Anglican religion as the most sublime, as that where we find generally the most virtuous, most honest, and most enlightened clergy." Anglican priests behaved "very different in this respect from the Roman Catholic clergy, whose dissolution of morals is known," Christophe said before calling Catholic priests "the apostle[s] and defender[s] of slavery." King Henry then insisted that he would use all his influence to persuade the Haitian people to accept the Anglican religion, writing, "I have been assured in advance that they will happily embrace this great reform, when the time has arrived, that is to say, when knowledge of the English language is widespread."[37]

Although this more practical reason adds much to our understanding of the chasm that eventually separated Christophe and Brelle, it is also true that King Henry felt betrayed by him, and he clearly wanted to punish the archbishop, rather than merely sideline his religious influence. On July 19, 1819, the *Gazette* officially announced Brelle's death and referred to him as "the ex-archbishop of Haiti." Before revealing his cause of death, the article informed readers that Brelle had previously been "in detention at his hotel in the capital," where he died of "the chronic illness he had suffered from for a long time (scorbutic diarrhea)." It turns out that it was not the exorbitant prices he charged for funerals that led the king to order Brelle defrocked. The *Gazette* informed readers that the king had "suspended [Brelle] from his spiritual and temporal duties for preaching doctrines subversive to the state." The kingdom accused Brelle of having "sought to sow unrest and civil war among the citizens of towns and the countryside."[38]

Continued conspiracies led and encouraged by foreigners, along with bona fide foreign spying, internal insubordination and betrayal of the kingdom's laws by members of the nobility, were only a few of the cracks that by the later 1810s had begun to spread across the kingdom. By the time Carl Ritter landed in Haiti in April 1820, he recollected that to his "great disappointment . . . the sovereign of the northern portion of the island, never permitted strangers to explore his dominions; because in his jealousy, he regarded every white as a spy."[39] The monarch and all he built soon crumbled under the weight of so many fissures, along too many different lines.

One of the more unexpected events that can be linked to the king's eventual downfall was the death of President Pétion.

—

"The president of Haiti is dead!!!" someone screamed in the city of Les Cayes on March 29, 1818. "What did you say! Good God!" screamed another, reacting to the same surprising news as it spread around the city. "Those shouts of lamentation made all my being tremble!" said a general of the army a few days later in Les Cayes as he recalled the sounds of the voices in distress that had traveled, as if by telephone, to announce the death of the president.[40] President Pétion, ill for eight days with a fever, laid down his head for a final time and took his last breath at half past four in the morning on March 29 in the national palace in the city of Port-au-Prince. "O death! what a terrible blow you have dealt us!" read an obituary published in *The Telegraph* the week after the president's death. "Children who have lost a cherished father cannot shed more tears, more cries, more sobs than the people of Haiti!" Going on to describe the entire city as resounding with groans produced by the most profound sadness, the newspaper reported that those living in the countryside mourned with equal ardor. "The fields were abandoned, and the cultivators, bringing their wives and children, crowded into the roads and transported themselves to the city of sadness in order to, for the last time, glimpse the inanimate body of he who did not think of them as would a great king with respect to the peasants of his kingdom: a thought all at once trivial, sublime, and sentimental."[41] The reportage of Pétion's death in Haiti's first periodical, the twice-monthly *L'abeille haytienne* (The Haytian Bee), edited by two of King Henry's most ardent enemies, Jules Solime Milscent and Noël Colombel, was not less tinged with distress. "Alexandre Pétion, president of Haiti, has ended his career!" said the magazine. "March 29 was the last day of his life." "Pitiless death reaped our father, our friend, our consoler, one of the strongest supporters of our country," the editors lamented. Immediately following his death, the clang of the church bells that had sounded every morning since the president fell ill on the twenty-second of the month, rang out with a lugubrious chord at daybreak. Afterward, several cannons were fired at various intervals to confirm to the people of the capital that their president was no more.[42] Pétion's corpse soon after lay on display in the national palace, which had been transformed into a chapel. The late president's funeral opened at eleven in the morning on March 31 with the apostolic prefect of the republic, R. P. Gaspard, presiding. "March 29!" Gaspard pronounced. "A day forever consecrated among us to mourning and the deepest sadness! a day of our most unfortunate memories! you will not be erased from our recollections." "Alexandre Pétion, once president of Haiti, is nothing more than a cold and lifeless body," Gaspard concluded. According to Pétion's wishes, the republic interred his body in a vault at the foot of the famous Tree of Liberty, where Polverel announced general emancipation in September 1793.[43]

These funeral arrangements had certainly preoccupied the minds of the administrators of the republic in the hours and days immediately following the president's death. However, at the same time, these administrators had to turn their attention to the pressing matter of Pétion's successor. The day before the funeral, at ten o'clock in the evening, the republic's senior officials made their decision, and twenty-one cannon shots soon announced a decree had been issued by the senate. It named Division General Jean-Pierre Boyer the president of Haiti.[44] The senate immediately announced their rationale for replacing Pétion so quickly. "We had to consider that it would expose public affairs to an obvious danger, if we deferred the election of the citizen who will now have to lead as the executive power, in order to replace the virtuous Alexandre Pétion, who is now deceased," the senate explained.[45]

The senate formally swore in Boyer to the office of the president on April 1, the day after Pétion's funeral and three days after his death. "My soul is also torn with the memory of the forever deplorable loss we have just suffered," Boyer said in his first speech as president. "In this circumstance of mourning, I nevertheless feel the need to self-abnegate, to think only of my homeland," he told a crowd filled with public functionaries, commercial agents, ordinary citizens, and foreigners alike. "The elevation with which your choice honors me imposes upon me obligations that might frighten me in light of my feeble means," he continued, "if I did not have the hope of being enlightened by your knowledge, assisted by the generals, my comrades in arms, and strengthened by the confidence of my fellow citizens." Boyer finished by trying to reassure the worried public, concerned about what Pétion's unexpected death might augur for the future of their state: "The republic can count on my zeal. All acts emanating from our august benefactor will be religiously respected. I will follow in his footsteps."[46]

Back in the north, King Henry did not receive word of Pétion's death and Boyer's appointment as president until later in the first week of April, after journals and newspapers from the republic reached the kingdom. Even though the republic's reports clearly described the president as having died after eight days of fever, this did not stop the Baron de Vastey from claiming that Pétion died after having been "eaten away by remorse and grief [and] disgusted with an odious life." "He let himself die of starvation, without having wanted to receive any food or any medicine, until his last moments," Vastey claimed. Vastey gathered evidence for this supposition surprisingly from a detail contained in the *Haytian Bee*. Editors Milscent and Colombel reported that after the president grew ill on March 22, "we devoted ourselves to the most attentive care of him; but he refused the remedies presented to him; he did not even want to take any food, despite the strongest entreaties from his family and friends." Vastey concluded from this report that the president no longer saw any value in his leadership of the republic or in his own life.[47]

Yet an even stronger feeling among the king's men was that despite all the "base and flat adulations" pronounced at his funeral and reported in the republic's newspapers, there was opportunity in the late president's passing. The people of northern Haiti would never forget Pétion's "crimes of high treason," but the kingdom's officials remained more interested than ever in reunification. Disregarding the reported process that brought Boyer to the presidency, Vastey claimed that Boyer had been anointed, rather than chosen by senate vote, to the position, "much as the Praetorian Guards appointed Roman emperors." Pétion had reportedly designated his successor with a sealed letter concealed in a secret box, which was quickly discovered by the senators. Because the person Pétion named was not Boyer, the senators dispensed with the letter and proceeded to elect Boyer, their favored division general anyway. At least that is how writers from the northern kingdom told the story.[48]

King Henry was in Port-de-Paix, on his customary annual tour of the kingdom, when he learned of Pétion's death. Believing that this might have been the opening he longed for, Christophe quickly dispatched three of his most trusted administrators to travel on a mission to the republic. The king designated Dessalines's son, the Baron de Dessalines, along with the Baron de Bottex, and a commissioner named Armand, all of whom Christophe tasked with carrying a proclamation into the republic with which the king hoped to bring about at last the reunion of the north and the south under the Kingdom of Haiti.[49]

Written from Saint-Marc on June 28, 1818, the king's proclamation was accompanied by a letter addressed to "Messieurs the Generals and Magistrates." The king first sought to remind these officials from the republic that the kingdom had never "provoked civil war" with them. "It has always been repugnant to our hearts, because it is not only contrary to the true interests of the Haitian people but also nourishes the enemies of Haiti in the criminal and barbaric hope of destroying us by using us against each other and reducing those who will have survived to a complete state of slavery." The king urged his interlocutors therefore to "pay attention to the means of operating the reunion of all Haitians, of extinguishing our dissensions, in order to bring back tranquility, unity, and happiness among us."[50] The accompanying June 9 proclamation addressed "to the Haitians of the West and the South" explicitly invited the people of the republic to join the kingdom and put their civic fates into the hands of King Henry. In exchange for their loyalty, the king offered to guarantee their persons and property and to maintain the civil, military, and other government functionaries in their current ranks and positions. The proclamation also addressed the false rumor that in the days after Pétion's death, Christophe's emissaries had traveled to the republic while the king waited at the border in Saint-Marc to prepare for his impending invasion of the republic. "We have been informed that malevolent people who wish to see the horrors of civil war renewed are spreading the word that under the pretext of touring the kingdom, we are taking advantage of the new circumstances that have just arisen to march an army against Port-au-Prince," the proclamation stated. "While the real object of the tour that we are now undertaking in the kingdom, accompanied by our family, is to assure ourselves, with our own eyes, of the situation of the people and of agriculture, to ensure the reign of law, order, and justice."[51]

On March 31, before news of Pétion's death reached the kingdom, the *Gazette* had reported that the king, queen, and royal family, as well as the entire court, were preparing to undertake "a general tour to visit in person the people of the towns and countryside and ascertain the improvements that have taken place in all branches of the administration of the kingdom," concluding, "All preparations for the journey are being made with the greatest activity."[52] Nevertheless, the generals and magistrates of the republic did not allow much time to pass before they responded to the king with a stiff rebuke.

Directing their reply to "General Christophe," they opened their missive by saying the king's letter filled them with the "feelings of the most profound indignation." Boyer evidently read the proclamation aloud in the presence of his deputies, who responded with immediate incredulity. They could not believe that Christophe "dared to propose to them to betray their oath, to declare themselves in a state of revolt against the leader they have chosen, whom they have recognized, whom they have sworn to obey according to the law, which is the expression of the general will." Going on to remark that Christophe must be "delusional" to think that this tactic would work, the generals said that by the end of Boyer's reading they could hardly contain their emotions. "Oh! what does General Christophe want from us?" they asked. "What can he offer us? We are free, independent, and republican." They demanded to know, therefore, "What is he asking us for? That we recognize him as leader, we reject him." Accusing the king of causing "innocent blood" to spill, they finished with an unequivocal rejection of Christophe's peace offering: "We declare, in a word, that nothing can ever disunite us; that it is in vain that General Christophe will use all the means at his disposal to achieve this, and that we will all die rather than submit to him."[53] The north and the south, even with Pétion gone, seemed destined to continue to straddle a political and civil impasse, much to Christophe's consternation.

Christophe's frustration with Boyer's newly declared rule over the republic only increased as time went on. Not only did the king have to combat misinformation about the kingdom put out by the Republic of Haiti, and especially by Dumesle in his newspaper, but there was also the matter of the international press. *Niles' Register* printed an erroneous article in October 1818 reporting it had "received accounts here from *Hayti*, stating that *Boyer* had totally defeated the army under *Christophe*, between St. Marks [*sic*] and Port-au-Prince," and that four thousand of the king's soldiers had been killed in the battle.[54] Then, after his brother-in-law Noël's death, due to the terrible lightning storm that struck the Citadelle that fall, the king felt obligated to issue a statement refuting the claims of certain Jamaican newspapers describing the Citadelle's total destruction as a result of the fire. An easily disproven claim, the *Gazette* reminded its readers that the sheer elevation of the Citadelle, which could be seen "from more than twenty leagues on all sides," meant that if the structure had disappeared, the many foreign ships coasting off the harbor of Cap would have immediately noticed its absence. "The ships that are passing along our coasts and the travelers on them have been able to convince themselves with their own eyes that the structure of the Citadelle suffered no damage," the *Gazette* insisted. There was some destruction to the city below, the paper admitted, but "the houses that were destroyed are already rebuilt, and in a more solid state than they were before."[55] As for the king's eyes, they seemed impossibly turned in several directions at once.

While Christophe had occupied himself with land reforms since the earliest days of his presidency—namely, redistributing the plantations and other properties of the ex-colonists among the nobility and eventually the army—during the latter years of his rule, as king, he sought to advance more extensive reforms that would benefit even more people. The royal newspapers for 1817, 1818, and 1819 are filled with charts and tables describing to whom the government had newly assigned individual coffee, indigo, sugar, and cacao plantations. Christophe also personally oversaw the construction of new school buildings in Jean-Rabel, Saint-Louis, Borgne, Limbé, and Plaisance, and he directed the reorganization of the kingdom's finances.[56]

Perhaps responding to criticism of his rule and ignorance about the nature and extent of his reforms, the king sought to remind the kingdom's farmers, whose laborers were almost entirely responsible for his wealth, how much he, as their sovereign, valued and appreciated them. In August 1819, Christophe authorized a sum of 200,000 gourdes to be distributed to the manufacturers and farmers of "the castles and dwellings of the Crown," in several districts. "We glimpse with satisfaction the well-being of our fellow citizens of the countryside who are enjoying the abundance and the fruits of their vigorous labor" the *Gazette* announced.[57] The king personally involved himself with military and aristocratic promotions, too, announcing the promotion of the Chevalier de Prézeau to the rank of baron and, more auspiciously, that of Dr. Stewart to field marshal of the army and chief surgeon of military hospitals.[58]

The best of times in the Kingdom of Haiti seemed nearly always to coincide with the worst of times. Despite all this kingly prosperity, and Christophe's uncanny ability to thwart France's colonial games of manipulation, the biggest threat to the kingdom's sovereignty remained, in many respects, on Haiti's own shores. In September 1819, the *Royal Gazette* reported that, according to some Parisian journals, Boyer had opened negotiations with Louis XVIII. The papers implied that the conversation was trending in a "favorable" direction for the ex-colonists: "We have been assured that Boyer's envoy has arrived in Paris with certain proposals, whereby the value of the amount of all the properties belonging to the French, in that part of Saint-Domingue where he commands, will be reimbursed to the dispossessed colonists, per term, in twenty years." "King Henry does not appear to be disposed to such an arrangement like President Boyer," one of the French papers is quoted as having wryly concluded. The kingdom responded to this news more with disdain than surprise: "As we can see, Pétion's successor is following in his footsteps; he wants to make the people of the southwest beholden to the ex-colonists!"[59]

Despite such reports, the king felt perfectly capable of standing his ground on the world stage, even when friends like Thomas Clarkson urged him to consider a treaty of indemnity with France. Christophe and his writers in the kingdom had very publicly insisted that the Haitian people could not and would not indemnify the French colonists—who had once put them in chains and tortured them in body and mind—since the time that Pétion first proposed it. The *Royal Gazette* printed this stern rebuke: If Pétion "tallied up the pain and torture" the ex-colonists exacted upon the people they enslaved on the island, "he would see on what side there should be compensation, if there were to be any." And besides, "What link could still exist between the master and the slave who has broken his chains?" the paper asked. In his writings, Baron de Vastey repeatedly insisted: "It is the recognition of our independence that will forever protect us from the tyranny of our oppressors! Without this precondition, no treaty, no agreement," he said. "We want to be free and independent; and we will be despite the dishonorableness of the colonists. Our independence will be guaranteed by the tip of our bayonets!"[60] Yet Clarkson clearly saw the matter differently.

Clarkson acknowledged receiving an earlier missive from the Comte de Limonade, written on behalf of King Henry, in which the Haitian aristocrat and statesman rejected Clarkson's suggestions for a treaty between Haiti and France precisely because it included an indemnity. Still, Clarkson reached out in March 1820 to Baron Turckheim, his friend and a politician in France, to insist that the king of Haiti might in fact be open to negotiating on this point. This was more than a little bit of duplicity on the British abolitionist's part. Clarkson suggested that the biggest threat to the king's ability to offer stability, security, and prosperity to his people remained "the apprehension that France may wish some time or other to recover Hayti by force of arms." "On this account he is under the necessity of keeping up a large standing army both of horse and foot," Clarkson continued. "The greater part of which he would disband and employ in agriculture, if this apprehension were removed from his mind." Clarkson immediately clarified, "I do not mean to imply by this that he is afraid of the French armies. He is well assured that France can never conquer Hayti, but while he continues in this suspense, he seems to be prevented from making the same improvements in agriculture as in literature and the sciences." Clarkson believed that he had the answer to this most enormous crack in the Kingdom of Haiti's sovereignty: France's refusal to recognize it. Clarkson told Turckheim that he understood that France had sustained financial "loss" because of the Haitian Revolution and had tasked itself "with the maintenance of some hundreds of the ex-colonists," most of whom were awarded "annual pensions from the French government." Clarkson reminded his interlocutor that while the pensions of these colonists undoubtedly cost France a lot of money, they were not anywhere near as costly as the loss of trade with Haiti, which could resume if the two nations could find a way to exist on "friendly terms."

The British abolitionist knew he needed to walk into this conversation carefully but sternly. "The French name is odious in Hayti," he reminded Turckheim. "Think for a moment of the misery which France inflicted upon this unhappy island under the reign of Buonaparte!" Clarkson then rehearsed the atrocities that had become familiar talking points in abolitionist circles owing to the publication of papers, letters, and books from the Kingdom of Haiti. "How many hundreds were hunted down and given alive to blood-hounds, who were taught to enjoy their flesh! How many hundreds were confered [sic] in the holds of ships, and purposely suffocated there by the fumes of brimstone! How many hundreds were taken out to sea and thrown overboard, or purposely sunk with the vessel itself!"

Lest Turckheim attempt to blame Napoléon for these atrocities, Clarkson brought up the matter of Dauxion-Lavaysse and the situation with the three French spies, which had taken place under the current king of France, Louis XVIII. Clarkson then offered to act as a neutral agent to broker the treaty King Henry had already rejected. He ended his letter with all but a wink and a nod in concluding, "Permit me to observe, that I have no interest in offering my mediation, nor any motive but humanity and goodwill, as it relates both to France and Hayti, and that King Henry is entirely ignorant of my writing this letter."[61] It was Clarkson's turn next to be ignorant of affairs taking place in Haiti. In December of the same year, Clarkson learned that the man on whose behalf he had so ardently pleaded for some five years suffered a stroke in August, followed by his suicide two months later.

A KING IS GONE, BUT
NOT FORGOTTEN

Drastic conflict followed the sudden death of President Pétion in March 1818, at the age of only forty-seven. Pétion's successor, Jean-Pierre Boyer, also a former general from Haiti's war of independence, had far less patience with the great schism and began plotting an attack on the war-weary kingdom. But Boyer believed he first needed to crush an opposition that had existed in his region since 1807. Although it was commonplace in the nineteenth century to describe Haiti as a country split in two, the political divisions were far more complicated and had everything to do with the king's, and kingdom's, eventual demise. On the northern half of Haiti's southwestern peninsula lies a mountainous region called Grand'Anse. Since the beginning of the great divide, a formerly enslaved man named Jean-Baptiste Duperrier, called Goman, known as the "god of the forests," controlled Grand'Anse. Partial to his godfather, General André Rigaud, during the Haitian Revolution, Goman pronounced Grand'Anse independent from the other Haitian states at the beginning of the dissension between the north and the south. Even when Rigaud declared himself the leader of a third political entity on the southern side of the peninsula in 1810, Goman refused to surrender either his authority or the approximately seven hundred square miles over which he claimed sovereign power. In February 1820, President Boyer's expedition sent to crush those "rebels" succeeded when Goman leaped to his death from a mountaintop to escape capture. Encouraged by his first attempt at unifying fractured Haiti, Boyer waited for an opportune moment to send his army to overtake the northern kingdom. To hear the king's enemies tell it, Providence soon provided one. On August 15, 1820, the same day that a fire raged across the republic's capital in Port-au-Prince, King Henry collapsed after suffering a major stroke in Limonade. The king's doctor, the Scotsman Duncan Stewart, revived Christophe, but he remained partially paralyzed on one side. Two months later the king was dead.

The queen prayed over the inert body of her husband, Henry Christophe, the now lifeless king of Haiti. Her teenage children—Prince Victor-Henry and Princesses Première-Améthyste and Anne Athénaïs—knelt by her side, softly weeping. Only moments earlier, the king's men told Queen Marie-Louise what she long feared. Christophe, betrayed by his own military and nearly all his closest confidants, had shot himself. Night had fallen, and the palace exuded alarming quiet. The site of the king's death was cloaked in the kind of incongruous, placid calm that rarely accompanies the sudden discovery of a suicide. Christophe's blood had stained his white shirt; his eyes were fixed open in a wide, sad stare. The serenity of the scene was interrupted only when the king's doctor and several of his oldest advisers entered the bedroom. The palace's gates would at any moment be breached. The royal family needed to hide Christophe's body if they hoped to save it from the terrible fate that had befallen the king's predecessor, the emperor Jean-Jacques Dessalines, whose corpse was reportedly torn to pieces when it was dragged through the streets of Port-au-Prince after his assassination nearly fourteen years earlier. The king's personal guards, the Royal Dahomets, were summoned to assist the queen and her children as they attempted to carry the body up to Christophe's famous fortress.

The long gravel road to the Citadelle, less than five miles from Sans-Souci palace, winds up the mountain at a barely passable, dangerous thirty-five-degree angle. Once the cortege reached the top of the Citadelle, Christophe's guards helped Marie-Louise and her children dig a shallow grave in an interior courtyard. There, they buried the king's remains before pouring lime over him.[1] Barely a dozen people attended the makeshift interment that marked the unceremonious end of the man proclaimed the "first monarch crowned in the New World."[2]

As often happens, the victor—in this case the Republic of Haiti—provided some of the most detailed accounts of the minute series of events that led King Henry to take his own life. Purporting to draw on eyewitness testimony from former members of the aristocracy, one southern magazine, *The Haitian Propagator* (Le propagateur haïtien), reported that Christophe had not attempted to offer an "olive branch" to Boyer after Pétion's death. Instead, Christophe sought to overthrow him, with the letter inviting southern generals and magistrates to yoke their fates to the king standing as evidence. Disappointed when southern officials rebuffed his entreaties, Christophe remained hopeful that time might change their minds. "I shall withdraw for a few days, and soon I will be called to put peace among them," the king reportedly assured himself.[3] Reunification clearly did not happen at that time, and in fact Boyer had his eyes on a different prize.

Despite refusing official incorporation into any of Haiti's separate states—recall that Rigaud died in 1811 and the section he ruled was shortly thereafter absorbed into the Republic of Haiti—Goman did accept gifts from King Henry, including an opulent throne and a gold cross of the order of Saint Henry. He also signed his letters as the Comte de Jérémie, the title that Christophe bestowed upon him.[4] Goman's seeming deference to the king of Haiti—Dumesle pointed out that Goman referred to his "camp" as the "Province of the South," which is how the region under his governance was listed in the *Royal Almanac*—led to more conflict with the neighboring republic.[5]

During his reign, Pétion had tried and failed to overthrow Goman, and after Pétion unexpectedly died in March 1818, President Jean-Pierre Boyer decided to make another attempt. At the start of 1819, Boyer launched an official campaign to find and capture Goman, then known to be hiding in the treacherous Mamelles mountains. By June 1819, under the title of the "Expeditionary Army"—almost too ironically, the same name used by Leclerc and his invading army—soldiers from the republic had Goman entirely surrounded, such that many from his camp reportedly began to surrender, with *The Observer* reporting, "We have them so well covered that it is impossible for the rebels to cross the line of demarcation, which prevents them from entering the arrondissements neighboring Jérémie." As for the Comte de Jérémie, the paper stated that he could be considered practically defeated since "Goman is hiding even from the very people who were once in his confidence."[6] By August 1, *The Observer* all but assured its readers that with more prisoners captured every day, Goman's defeat was imminent. "The famous Goman is a fugitive," the paper reported. "He enjoys no security, even in the deepest caverns. He is being harassed by our troops, who are searching for him with great eagerness."[7]

By the start of November, the Expeditionary Army triumphantly announced that two leaders from Goman's camp had surrendered.[8] By December 1, 1819, the Expeditionary Army had conquered or eliminated nearly all Goman's followers. While acknowledging that the Comte de Jérémie remained at large, *The Observer* announced that soldiers from the republic had cut off the heads of five prominent leaders who had fought them in Grand'Anse.[9] The campaign had lasted at that point for nearly a year, and Goman's faction grew ever wearier. "Accustomed to living in the woods for fourteen years, many of these victims of error and ambition had gone savage there," *The Propagator* later explained. "In the plan declared against them, force and persuasion worked together. Starting on February 1, 1819, they were attacked with vigor and at the same time they were offered concessions in conformity with their interests." "Those simple men were overtaken, and the whole of their operation was destroyed," concluded the southern magazine. The siege only ended when Goman, surrounded by Boyer's troops, leaped to his death from a mountaintop into the gulf below.[10]

In rebellion since the post-Dessalines era, Grand'Anse was now "entirely pacified," or so the republic announced. Boyer had much praise for the republican soldiers who took part in the "pacification." When he greeted the victorious soldiers in coastal Jérémie in March 1820, he said to them, "You will return to your respective quarters to unwind after the painful campaign you have just finished. In the midst of the relaxation you are about to enjoy, remember always that if you overcame difficulties in Grande'Anse that seemed insurmountable, there is still much more to do!" Reading from the proclamation he issued on February 18, 1820, upon learning of the Expeditionary Army's success, Boyer intimated that this was but the first victory in his plan to reunite all of Haiti. "There remains more yet for you to do!" he said. "Forever listen for my voice and be ready, at the first signal, to march with me to consolidate stability and national glory."[11] To hear the king's contemporaries tell it, the republic had Providence on its side.

It was not long before Christophe learned from his informants of the death of Goman, the man he had appointed commander over the southern division.[12] The news struck a plaintive chord in his heart. The king considered Goman both an ally and a friend who "raised the standard of fidelity and honor in the mountains of Grande'Anse of Jérémie, who rallied his brothers, enlightened them, undeceiving them of calumnies," and who recognized Christophe as "the only leader whom he wants to and must obey."[13] Christophe also received a report of the republic's "pacification" of Grand'Anse from the British admiral Sir Home Popham, who gave him Boyer's February 1820 proclamation. Christophe read and reread the proclamation, as if in disbelief, before he sighed with exasperation and said, "What a blow I am being dealt!"[14] According to *The Propagator*, it was not just the loss of his ally Goman that further assaulted the king's spirit. The king's constant parties, frequenting of "courtesans," and total abandonment of any sliver of religiosity made him putatively more severe, irritable, and filled with paranoid disquietude than usual. Around that time, Popham, after having gone from Jamaica to Cap, traveled from Cap to Port-au-Prince. In his meetings with Boyer, Popham tried to convince the president that the republic had great advantage over the northern kingdom. But Popham recommended to Boyer that the two sides of Haiti simply recognize each other and try to live independently and in peaceful coexistence. Popham held similar meetings with Christophe, who seemed to be abandoning, albeit reluctantly, the idea that the two states would ever be reunited.[15]

Christophe was in his fifties at this point. More a battle-wearied and quickly aging man than a hardened soldier, he was still a father and a husband. Growing increasingly somber by the day, the king had become prone to daydreaming, which sometimes led his thoughts to trend toward paranoia and suspicion. As his inner circle grew ever smaller, his faith and confidence in his son grew larger. Because Christophe had become susceptible to fits of uncontrollable rage, his other family members tried to rally the archbishop Don Gonzalés to his side in the hopes of calming the king's soul and lessening the phantoms plaguing his waking reveries.

Father Gonzalés frequently prayed with the king, offering him pious consolation and speaking to him of religion as the ultimate refuge against fear and remorse.

The border separating the kingdom from the republic continued to haunt Christophe's dreams, however, and he spoke often of the possibility that the southern army might breach northern Haiti's boundaries. The king therefore wanted Saint-Marc, Verrettes, and Petite-Rivière fortified to guard against the republic. These thoughts made him even more single-minded. From April to August 1820, Christophe ceased to be approachable as he personally oversaw the work of fortification with his army. A pause in this effort seemed afoot only due to Queen Marie-Louise's impending fete, always celebrated with unsparing magnificence. The queen's fete coincided that year with the Feast of the Assumption, on August 15. On that day, the king and his family traveled to Limonade to begin the celebrations. The royal family stayed at château Bellevue-le-Roi amid the preparations. Although he seemed in a terrible mood that morning, scolding his wife and children for not moving quickly enough, Christophe's health reportedly showed no signs of alteration. For this occasion, the king donned a green uniform, richly embroidered in gold. On his chest shone a large diamond plaque of his order of Saint Henry. Later, sitting on his throne, in the middle of the church, Christophe complacently listened to Father Gonzalés's sermon.[16]

"We see before us, the great, the good, the incomparable Henry, our king, our father, whom God created explicitly to save us from all the evils with which we were threatened," Gonzalés announced. As those final words left Gonzalés's lips, the king appeared suddenly struck with a "thunderous apoplectic attack." An officer lunged forward to support him and prevent him from falling. This officer, while succeeding in cushioning the king's fall, could not fully prevent it. "Christophe hit his head violently against the wall as he fell to the ground, leaving the imprint of his blood there," recalled an eyewitness. "Dread seized all those in attendance; the priest himself fainted, and only recovered in time to fall prey to a devouring fever, which, in the space of three days, led him to the tomb." As a fire raged on the other side of the island in the capital of the republic, King Henry suffered what was later determined to have been a major stroke. After his collapse, the king's doctor, the Scotsman Duncan Stewart, succeeded in restoring Christophe's respiration. Yet alarm spread as onlookers realized the king seemed partially paralyzed.[17]

Christophe continued to receive prompt medical care from Dr. Stewart, who saved his life and restored his health, reportedly "by bleeding him from arm to foot." Afterward, the king was taken to the château at Bellevue-le-Roi. His head still weak and wobbly for many days following the attack, the severe and stern king now seemed afraid. The stroke only further increased his paranoia. He did not want anyone to walk behind him and required all those in his presence to always appear in front of him. The king lamented having no friends and accused his servants of unfaithfulness to him. "It is in vain that I bestow favors and titles of dignity upon those around me, my good deeds are forgotten," Christophe said to the Baron de Vastey one day. "If God restores my health, I will remember how to deal with these ingrates." "Sire, I am going to the palace to find a spot which might present some cool air," Vastey said in reply. "You are trying to play me," Christophe answered with a mixture of haste, anger, and unintelligibility. "You will give me the coolness of soul of which I am deprived or you will pay dearly for it," the king scolded. Vastey, one of the king's oldest and most trusted advisers and friends, bristled at this reply but could find nothing to say that might soothe the irritating imaginings in the king's mind. The next day, he proposed that the king return to Sans-Souci, where he might avoid some of the boredom and ennui the baron believed had augmented Christophe's anxiety.[18] Yet when the king returned to Sans-Souci in early September, Dr. Stewart observed that Christophe had reached an even higher state of paranoia.[19]

Perhaps the inaction of not being able to govern was to blame. The month before his stroke, King Henry personally occupied himself with distributing land sequesters and ensuring fairness in the process.[20] But as Prince Victor's tutor, William Wilson, reported to his father back in England, in a letter dated October 1, 1820, the stroke that had caused an earthquake, shattering the king's brain, occurred coterminously with the yellow fever epidemic that struck the island. Wilson reported that he had also recently recovered from the illness. "Full half of the whites" died from the malady "some time ago," and the "number is now greater," he told his father. Wilson remained grateful if not incredulous that he survived the "Black vomit" that "denotes mortification in the stomach," which usually leads to death within the hour. Dr. Stewart, who treated Wilson, explained his improbable recovery by observing that Wilson's "inflammation" had actually been in his throat, due to "excessive retching," not the progression of disease. After six days of incapacitation, "I was out of immediate danger," Wilson reassured his father. "The king I regret to say," Wilson continued, "has for more than two months been indisposed." "But he is now convalescent," the young prince's teacher reported, "and attends as before to the affairs of his government in which he is assisted by the Prince, my pupil." Written seven days before the king's suicide, Wilson's letter contained little harbinger that anything like a rebellion was afoot. Wilson told his father that although he had not yet seen the young prince since his own recovery, he believed their lessons would resume shortly. He also felt that he had finally earned the good opinion of the king since Prince Victor spoke well of him to his father and had made "great progress." Wilson boasted at the end of the letter that the prince "now speaks English so well as to procure me a great deal of praise."[21]

The next letter that Wilson wrote to his father carried a far more despondent and worrying tone. "I have seen in the space of ten days a powerful and most absolute monarch shaken from the throne on which he had had the peculiar merit of placing himself," Wilson wrote. "I have seen his son dragged to prison and there assassinated; and I have seen his family, who but a few days—nay, hours—before knew not the extent of their own riches and power of enjoyment, condemned to comparative poverty. Murder and robbery have not only been tolerated, but applauded; no kind of injustice was too flagrant to be committed." "My unfortunate pupil," he repeated with lamentation, "was murdered in prison, ten days after the death of his father."[22] Wilson had already written to Thomas Clarkson to transmit news of the "revolution" that he said removed the king from power and resulted in the end of his life. Though Wilson wrote in haste, and in a hurried, uncertain state with respect to his own future, because he was "known to be attached to the prince," he did not miss the chance to inform Clarkson of the man behind this upheaval. Wilson named Jean-Pierre Richard, the Duc de la Marmelade, who, after having pillaged Christophe's palace, now refused the title the king gave to him, demanding to simply be called "General Richard."[23]

Once he found himself in a more secure and reassuring position in the renamed city of Cap-Haïtien, Wilson provided Clarkson with a much longer and more highly detailed account of Christophe's stroke, along with a narration of his understanding of the insurrection in Saint-Marc that he said began with a Colonel Paulin. The story, Wilson owned, might seem a bit chaotic, because what he had to relate from those terrifying days would be "difficult to be believed." Wilson's account largely matches the one written by Dr. Stewart, as well as the one published by *The Propagator.*[24]

After his return to Sans-Souci the king claimed to have learned through informants that Boyer continued to plot an attack on the city of Saint-Marc, the largest stronghold in between the kingdom and the republic, on the southwestern border.[25] On September 14, the still-recovering king received two high-ranking officers from the Eighth Demi-brigade of Saint-Marc, General Jean-Claude and Colonel Paulin, each of whom accused the other of colluding with the republic to bring down the king. Fond of the saying "Where there's smoke, there's fire," Christophe was known for punishing people on mere suspicion. Without hearing Paulin's full testimony, Christophe sided with Jean-Claude and sent Paulin to prison. The regiment in Saint-Marc remained partial to Paulin, however, and retaliated by murdering Jean-Claude. The border troops then delivered Jean-Claude's head to President Boyer when they voluntarily surrendered and offered to join the republic's army.[26]

When Christophe learned of the defection of the entire Eighth Demi-brigade, he dispatched troops from the neighboring town of Montrouis to oppose them. Instead of defending the kingdom, they joined the southern army, reportedly cheering in the streets, "Vive la République! Vive le Président!" By October 6, the insurrection had spread north all the way to Cap-Henry, where Wilson said he heard villagers shouting, "Down with the Tyrant!"[27]

On the morning of October 8, Christophe sent one last military brigade to crush the rebellion, but when he learned that those troops had also defected and joined the republican army, he told Dr. Stewart with resignation, "I well know what I have to do." The fatal shot rang out from his bedroom, depending on the account, sometime between 7:30 and 10:30 that night.[28] By the time the dead king's cortege reached the top of the Citadelle, his wife's and children's shoes had long since been torn from their feet due to the sharp stones covering the gravel path; their hearts were no doubt in tatters as well. Christophe's guards helped Marie-Louise and the prince and princesses dig a shallow grave to bury the body. In most accounts, they placed the king's remains in the limestone walls of the battery bearing the name of the royal prince.[29]

When the royal family returned to the palace after having buried the king, they found their home had been invaded. Inhabitants from Cap and Milot had plundered the royal residence, stealing its expensive furniture and imported jewels and looking for hidden treasures. Soldiers shot at the ceiling of the Salle des Chefs, ruining the mural painted by the British artist Richard Evans. Far from trying to prevent this pillage, the king's soldiers took part in it.[30]

The next day, the soldiers arrested Marie-Louise and her daughters along with Prince Victor and Prince Eugène. The nobles who remained loyal to the king, including the Baron de Vastey, the Baron de Dessalines, the Comte de Laxavon, and Ducs Joachim and Daut, were also jailed.[31] Although Boyer ordered the republican army to avoid bloodshed while securing the city of Cap, the directive came too late.[32]

General Richard, the Duc de la Marmelade under King Henry and the head of the conspiracy against him, ordered the male prisoners' deaths at around ten o'clock on the night of October 18. An eyewitness watched Prince Victor plead for his life. The teenager reminded his father's former friends that his "only crime was to be the son of their enemy." Richard responded by explaining that although the prince was just sixteen years old, as the heir to his father's throne "the tranquility of the state demanded his life." "Well then I am at peace," the prince replied. The twenty-two-year-old prince Eugène went next and did not deign to speak; "a spiteful gaze was all he gave his executioners."[33]

Wilson blamed Christophe's stroke for much of the conspiracy that formed in its wake with Richard at its head. While the king had remained under the care of Dr. Stewart in Limonade, about fifteen kilometers from Cap, Richard and another of the king's men named Prophète hatched the plan to overthrow the man they helped make "the most absolute monarch in the world." Then Christophe's health had suddenly improved, much to their consternation, and the king had returned to his capital, unaware of the plot formed in his absence. "It was Friday evening, the 6th of October, that, as I was returning home from the house of a friend, my attention was roused by the appearance of many soldiers hastening from every quarter, with arms in their hands, to the Place d'Armes before the palace, shouting *Vive la Liberté! Down with the Tyrant! Down with Christophe! To your houses! To your houses!*" Wilson recalled. "And suddenly every door was closed; while the assembled military passed the night, some in consultation, others in dancing and riot, and many in mad efforts to excite their comrades to plunder. That night no one slept in the Cape," Wilson continued. The king did not learn about the revolt planned by the Duc de la Marmelade until ten o'clock in the morning on Saturday, the seventh. Although somewhat in disbelief, by four o'clock that afternoon Christophe's loyalists finally managed to convince him of the report's veracity.

At the same time, rumors started to spread throughout the capital and Sans-Souci that the king wanted to massacre all the whites, which Wilson did not believe. The insurgents nevertheless marched to Haut-du-Cap, several miles off the road to Sans-Souci, "and there encamped themselves with a river in front and lofty mountains behind, throwing up such fortifications as the haste of the moment would permit." "No more than seven chiefs at first appeared in the conspiracy. Of these Marmelade was, as I before observed, the head, with his old name of Richard. The cry was '*Down with the King! No nobility! No Tyranny!*' and every chief tore from his breast the cross of St. Henry, which he trampled under his feet. Every mouth was opened against the king," Wilson wrote.

Despite his previous report to his father about the king's ability to rule with the help of his son during his convalescence, Wilson described King Henry in his letter to Clarkson as having been almost too weak to stand. Since he could not very well mount a horse and fly to the scene, as he would have done in the past, the king dispatched Prince Joachim, the chief officer of his guard, to march with twelve hundred infantry and four pieces of cannon against the troops at the bridge of Haut-du-Cap. Christophe promised his men $4 each for this service and more if they could successfully beat back the rebels.

The rebels stood at about four thousand in number, in contrast, and some from among them were from the light cavalry of the king's own household troops, commanded by none other than Prophète. The rebels answered the letter Joachim brought from the king by demanding "their liberty." They said they had "broken the chains of slavery, and that they would no longer have a king." The rebels then fired on Joachim, who ordered his men to attack. The king's troops, "instead of obeying the order, threw away their arms, and joining the opposing force, cried out *Vive la Liberté! Break the chains of slavery!*" Wilson recalled. "This affair took place on Sunday, the 8th of October, and it was at half past eight that evening that the King received the news of the defection of his household troops."

The king had arrived at an impossible crossroads, the choice that would constitute his final act. Which was the path to take? Stay and fight, come what may, or end his time in this world and leave his fate in the next one up to God? "Since the confidence which the Haytians once reposed in me is no more, I well know what I have to do," Christophe only then told Dr. Stewart. The flailing monarch, aching in body and soul, called his children into his chamber, said a few words to each of them, and then asked them to leave him to his own thoughts. Moments after this last family gathering the sound of the gunshot rang out. The king had used a pistol to pierce his own heart.

It was the fate of his young pupil Prince Victor that seemed to affect Wilson the most. The prince's tutor went on to describe the tragic scene of the queen and princesses hurrying their father's corpse up to the Citadelle to inter his body. A terrible scene of pillaging at the palace followed the royal family's flight, with jewels and riches amounting to more than $6 million confiscated. When the royal family returned, the army arrested them all. The queen, princesses, and princes were taken to Cap, where they were insulted and shown scorn by a populace that once seemed to admire them. "I saw the Prince led into the town, his most interesting figure covered with dust and sweat, suffering under regret for the death of his father, his mother's misfortune," Wilson said. After this, the prince was "conducted from his own house to a loathsome prison, where on the 18th at midnight he was assassinated by Richard, Prophète, and other chiefs, to their eternal disgrace and the degradation of the whole people, who received the news with savage shouts of exultation." Wilson shook as he wrote this part of the letter. "His body, with those of the others who died with him, was afterwards thrown upon a dunghill, and there exposed till it began to be decomposed."[34]

Wilson's sadness over the death of his sixteen-year-old pupil does not appear to have been performative. A year later, he wrote to Mrs. Clarkson to lament the sorrows of Queen Marie-Louise, whose "peace of mind" had been disrupted by the "utterly careless" men who seemed to have no qualms about "murder[ing] her son." Wilson remained particularly struck by the presence at the execution of Prophète and Nord Alexis, the latter of whom had reportedly married one of Christophe's illegitimate daughters, though Wilson does not mention this.[35] Prophète and Alexis, former revolutionaries who fought under Dessalines, had a few days earlier vowed to protect Madame Christophe, who they insisted remained entirely innocent. "Madame Christophe, in common with all Haytian females, is distinguished by a douceur, an humanity, which shudders at violence," Wilson wrote.[36]

Dr. Stewart offered Clarkson his own version of the story. Writing from Cap on December 8, Stewart told Clarkson what he no doubt already knew: "King Henry died by his own hands; finding himself reduced to a helpless state by paralytics and deserted by all his troops, he shot himself through the heart." Stewart reported that he had been nearly always by the king's side since the stroke and "attended him by night and by day." "He suffered much in body but very much in mind, and his impatience became quite insupportable to all about him," Stewart reported. Stewart claimed that following his recovery, Christophe had seemed suddenly in good spirits. The king seemed "quite collected to the last, and sometimes quite cheerful." "I used often to converse with him for hours," Stewart revealed. "He seemed sensible that he had used his people harshly and that he ought to have been more liberal to his soldiers." According to Stewart, the king had acknowledged the large crack forming in his authority, but the revelation came too late. Offering more specific details about the last years of Christophe's life, Stewart said the king had been "barbarously cruel" and "very avaricious." He described Christophe's behavior as "very licentious" and said he "prostituted the wives of most of his nobility." Stewart then reported that in his estimation fifteen of the king's most trusted administrators saw execution by the republic on the eighteenth. The republic accused them of having executed "his oppressive orders," and made them suffer "together with both his sons." "The Queen and her daughters are taken care of by the Present [government] and have gone to Port-au-Prince," Stewart wrote, before revealing the real object of his letter. "At his death, King Henry was due me three months salary besides about $20,000 for attendance on his family and nobility, this he promised to pay me and three days before his death he told the Baron de Dupuy that he intended to give me $40,000," Stewart stated. The doctor concluded, "I understand from the Baron that you have some of the late King Henry's money in your hand." Stewart signed off by asking Clarkson not to pay out any other claims until Stewart could ensure "that my claims are just."[37]

Wilson also repaired to the Clarksons to try to obtain the salary he claimed Christophe owed him. Unlike Stewart, Wilson professed genuine concern for the eventual fate of Queen Marie-Louise and her daughters. Wilson pleaded on behalf of the Christophe women, citing their "acts of humanity" and the good opinion of them across Cap. Wilson believed that the Christophe children, including King Henry's now deceased sons, reflected the kindness and generosity of their mother while holding on to the "natural greatness of mind" characteristic of their father. Like Stewart, Wilson complained about some of the king's behaviors. He was clear, however, in stating that the king, despite his many faults, had been a good father. "He loved his children and was particularly careful of their education . . . even in their earliest infancy," Wilson said.[38]

As for the queen, Wilson continued to be in her confidence. Queen

Marie-Louise, as he told Mrs. Clarkson, was convinced that the Baron de Dupuy, who survived the "revolution," had played a role in the death of her husband. Wilson expressed sympathy toward Marie-Louise, but he could not believe her charges against Dupuy, who, he said, "we must remember with admiration, . . . did not desert the queen & her family, that he attended them in that distressing march to the Citadelle, & that he suffered himself to be confined a prisoner to the Cape where 1,000 were insisting upon his destruction."[39]

Marie-Louise rightly suspected those of the king's men who managed to survive the executions that took the lives of her sons. When King Henry had tried to corral his personal guards and closest officers to facilitate his voyage to Saint-Marc, he found many of his previous confidants had deserted the kingdom. Julien Prévost, the former Comte de Limonade, had once been one of Christophe's most ardent defenders, and yet he sat in this camp. Prévost joined the conspiracy against Christophe and went on to edit an anti-Christophe newspaper, *The Concord* (La Concorde), while enjoying an illustrious military career. Under President Boyer, Prévost participated in the mission that had by turns been both Dessalines's and Christophe's goal: reunification of Santo Domingo and Haiti.[40]

News of Juste Chanlatte's defection must have hit the queen particularly hard. Chanlatte had been one of Christophe's most important secretaries, helping him to found the state-run newspaper, the *Official Gazette of Hayti*. This same Chanlatte performed an immediate about-face, penning diatribe after diatribe, and even some poems, to defame his former king. That the king must have been turning in his grave does not constitute too strong an expression. Given the rank and title of general under Boyer, Chanlatte died of natural causes in 1828, but not before appearing at the ceremony in which the president unveiled the 1825 indemnity treaty, whereby the French king, Charles X, exacted 150 million francs as the price of recognition of Haiti's sovereignty and independence.[41]

Although alone when he shot himself, in some ways Christophe did not die alone. His most trusted friends, Vastey and Daut, remained at his side in the hours before he took his life. For this loyalty, the republic executed them. And as is naturally the case, only those nobles who turned their backs on the king lived to talk about it. Without offering a chain of recitation, Marceau Louis, biographer of Queen Marie-Louise, identified the guards who rushed in at the sound of the gunshot as de Prézeau, Dupuy, Vastey, and the Chevalier de Sévère-François.[42]

A remarkable nineteenth-century painting by an unknown artist depicts in oil on canvas the moments after the discovery of the king's suicide, providing additional clues about the potential identities of those present. In the tableau, King Henry holds a pistol in his right hand and appears slumped over while sitting in an ornate brown and gold wooden chair. His left hand hangs lifelessly by his side; his blue velvet desk is topped with several books, papers, and ink for writing. A painting of the king that seems to have been drawn after the famous portrait by Evans hovers in the background. In the foreground, one of the guards has ripped the gold helmet with a white plume from Christophe's head and holds it high in the air as if wanting to preserve it, or plunder it. The other three men appear dressed in blue and red military uniforms characteristic of the formal Haitian Guard; still others wield sabers in their hands, as if they rushed into the room to protect the king. Other guards or nobles stand like shadows in the doorway ready to pounce upon the potential intruder who might have fired at their king. The king, they all learned, by the blood staining his white shirt and the pistol in his hand, had been his own executioner.

The painting's portrayal of the death of King Henry might have been drawn after the portrait outlined in the Republic of Haiti's state-run paper, *The Telegraph*, the first publication to offer a precise description of the hours and moments before and after the king's death, including what the king was wearing. When Christophe retired to his bedroom, after having "caressed his daughters a little," he reportedly "asked his wife for white linen and looked attentively at his son, without saying anything to him. He begged them all to withdraw, saying he needed to rest." "Then he was given water with which he washed his hands and arms, as if he wanted to purify himself," *The Telegraph* editorialized. In the painting Christophe is wearing pants and a white chemise, just as described in the newspaper, although what he was wearing on his head differs in *The Telegraph*'s account. "He put on a shirt, with white trousers, and put a white handkerchief on his head." It was only then that Christophe "dismissed the servants caring for him, asking them to close the bedroom door after them. Immediately afterward the pistol shot was heard, which ended his life; they ran in and found him dead, bathed in his own blood."[43]

—

Queen Marie-Louise enjoyed the friendship and kindness of Dr. Stewart while he remained in Haiti, but her life in the republic quickly grew insupportable. She had painful memories of the events that changed her life in a more personally momentous way than the bloody revolution she had already survived. She found herself grieving strongly while trying to understand all that had befallen her country in less than two decades since independence. Now a different sort of trial was to begin as she witnessed open celebrations of her husband's death.

The October 22, 1820, issue of *The Telegraph* debuted a headline that must have felt to her like a stab in the eye: "Death of the Tyrant and the End of Tyranny." Referencing the coincidental fact that Dessalines had also died in the month of October, the paper gleefully printed, "October will be a memorable month for us. It has seen twice, in the space of four-teen years, liberty triumph over tyranny, and two tyrants succumb under the efforts of the republicans." Some of the information *The Telegraph* initially reported was later determined to be erroneous. "On the eighth of this month, between 10:00 and 11:00 a.m., CHRISTOPHE the cruel, BLEW OUT HIS BRAINS," the newspaper reported. But Christophe, according to eyewitnesses, shot himself in the heart that night, not in the morning. Perhaps Marie-Louise took solace when she learned that Gen-eral Romain, the Duc de Limbé and one of her husband's oldest and dear-est friends, had not surrendered to the republic, as previously reported. "This leader has declared himself to be in a state of rebellion, and he is trying to form a party. However, he will not be able to succeed, since the few people he had with him are coming over to our side daily," *The Tele-graph* reported. The republic did eventually capture Romain and after-ward held him prisoner in Léogâne until republican guards killed him in 1822 after his attempted escape.[44] As for anyone imprisoned by the late king before his death, estimated at around four thousand men, the repub-lic set them all free.[45]

The day before the executions of Prince Victor and Prince Eugène, along with the other Christophe loyalists, *The Telegraph* printed a memo issued by President Boyer, who took his turn at publicly celebrating King Henry's death. "The tyrant is no more: he has performed justice upon himself," Boyer announced at his national palace in Saint-Marc on Octo-ber 17, 1820, the day before the Christophe children were executed and on the anniversary of Dessalines's assassination. "Christophe's reign covered in sorrow the north and west until he took his own life Sunday last on the eighth of the month, by a pistol shot, at the news of the defection of what he called his military household, which, instead of fighting General Richard and his troops from the garrison in Cap, who declared themselves on the sixth to be against his despotism, embraced them and swore, on reuniting with the republic, to live henceforth united, and as a people of brothers and friends," Boyer said. He went on to use one of Christophe's tactics when he announced that any not yet surrendered northern mili-tary officers and soldiers could now capitulate without fear. "The repub-lic is merciful because it is strong: it has only children to reunite and no enemies to fight," the president said. Boyer claimed that going forward he forbade anyone to harm former members of Christophe's administra-tion or to "make their blood flow": "The president of Haiti must travel throughout the entire northern part of the country with imposing forces; not to conquer, but to reconcile and pacify. The people want to be free: they will be; the constitution alone can guarantee them of this precious advantage, because the constitution of the republic is the work of their representatives."[46] That Boyer intended to offer clemency to her husband's former friends and comrades in arms must have been hard for the queen to accept in light of the callous way her children were killed, the very day after Boyer's speech, by men with whom she had shared her home and to whom she previously entrusted her life.

Harder still to absorb for the queen and her daughters, alongside the seemingly endless articles damning their patriarch that continued to be printed in *The Telegraph,* or the betrayals of Chanlatte, Prévost, de Prézeau, and the others, might have been Boyer's desire to paint himself as the benevolent protector and benefactor of the Christophe women. In July 1821, Boyer answered a letter written to him by Clarkson inquiring about the fate of the former queen. "Madame and Mesdemoiselles Christophe have obtained after the fall of the northern government all the protection to which great misfortune entitles them," Boyer told Clarkson. "They expressed to me the desire to go and spend some time in England to take care of their health; I gave them permission to that effect." Boyer continued by revealing that he furnished the Christophe women with a passport and agreed that Clarkson was the one who could "be most useful to them" in their sojourn across the Atlantic.[47]

Marie-Louise did not take long to leave after she received Boyer's permission. The former queen left Port-au-Prince, where she had been living with her girls, on August 1, 1821. The day before her departure she wrote directly to Boyer to thank him for his attention and care. The letter, which Boyer reprinted in the September 23, 1821, issue of *The Telegraph,* seems genuine enough, but the fact that Boyer wanted to make it public suggests that the president sought to do damage control. While King Henry had undoubtedly been unpopular in the south, it might have been hard for many citizens to understand the teenage prince's execution. About a week after Richard and his entourage killed the prince and other members of the aristocracy, Boyer issued a proclamation asking the Haitian people to not seek glory in carrying out revenge. He specifically referenced the executions of Vastey and the royal prince. "I regret that blood, of which I never want to spare, flowed on the eighteenth of this month: with every bit of my solicitude I did not intend for this to happen. My Order of the Day for the seventeenth, sent expressly to Cap by my aides-de-camp, did not get there soon enough to save the lives of Christophe's sons and a few officers who made themselves too conspicuous by executing his barbaric orders," Boyer explained, before concluding, "Haitians! The past has been forgotten."[48] But Marie-Louise did not forget.

Frédéric Martin, a Parisian who immigrated to Haiti under Pétion and who, after that, worked at a trading house run by Guy-Joseph Bonnet, said he visited the queen and the princesses in Port-au-Prince before their departure. While he described the queen as "calm and resigned," her daughters, and especially Athénaïs, he said, "seemed to harbor beneath a proud and almost savage posture a thousand projects of revenge."[49] Unable to hide their anger and grief, the Christophe women still had to live among the citizens of the republic. The people of Port-au-Prince, in their turn, had to witness and stare at the sorrow of the former queen and princesses. Perhaps their neighbors listened with sympathy to the lamentations of the widow and fatherless children. Perhaps they were indifferent altogether.

In her letter to Boyer, the former queen seemed determined to mask her sadness with a veil of appreciation and gratitude. "To His Excellence the President of Haiti," her letter began,

On the verge of leaving for some time this beautiful country, this homeland which saw our births and which we will never cease to cherish, my daughters and I, we felt the need to express to you, other than in person, all the gratitude and our appreciation for the generous procedures Your Excellency has put in place for us for the past nine months.

Please accept, President, these new and solemn assurances of the deep memory that we will preserve.

In our misfortunes, we have found in you a protector, a friend, a brother. . . . Our hearts are filled with admiration.

Marie-Louise left her properties and other effects in the care of Étienne Magny, the former Duc de Plaisance, who fought beside her husband in the war of independence and had been one of his most trusted officers. An interesting choice. Even Magny had turned on the king and joined with Boyer. Still, the queen bequeathed her affairs to his trust. Before closing her letter, she implored Boyer to show kindness to her family members still in Haiti, including her sister, cousin, nephews and nieces, and at least one grandson. "I am leaving part of my family and that of my late husband in Cap; I recommend them to all your benevolence," she wrote, before signing, "Widow Henry CHRISTOPHE."[50]

The former queen consort, as the British referred to her, might have stayed in Haiti instead of fleeing, seeking solace in her daughters and other relatives and dear friends, like Dessalines's widow, Marie-Claire. Marie-Claire remained in Haiti on a government pension under the reign of Christophe, which continued under the reign of Boyer and all subsequent administrations until her death in 1858.[51] Marie-Claire and Marie-Louise were, in fact, old friends, who together witnessed the birth of their new country under their husbands, before watching as that new country became their spouses' tombs.

Before Marie-Claire was the queen's honored guest at court, the empress had invited Marie-Louise to dine at her table. Marie-Louise and Henry, then a general, attended a dinner at the theater in Cap hosted by the merchants of the city on February 15, 1804. The women wore flowers and beads in their hair and adorned their bodies with gold bracelets and other expensive trinkets and jewels. After a spectacular display of balloons, fireworks, and "rockets," the two women, future partners in the widow's sorrow, shared a comedic moment. While guests danced, an eyewitness reported that "the bench upon which Madame Dessalines and Madame Christophe, with other great ladies, were sitting, gave way, and laid their ladyships sprawling on the floor." An unseemly and potentially embarrassing sight, the music stopped as all the guests looked around in slight confusion. "Is she hurt?" everyone seemed to exclaim at once. Mesdames Dessalines and Christophe only laughed off the whole accident, and the party went on as before.[52]

Marie-Louise might also have shared the journey that is a new widow's grief with the wives of the other nobles who lost their husbands in the same "revolution." There was Aglaë Vastey and her two daughters, Aricie and Malvina, with the late Baron de Vastey; there was also Marie Barbe, wife of Jean-Philippe Daut, whose son Pierre had married Dessalines's daughter Célestine.[53] Yet although they had all just lost their husbands, and at the hands of the same men, there was one key difference. A chasm too enormous for anyone who has not experienced it to breach separated their fates by several bounds. The children of those other widows had not been killed. Even Suzanne Louverture, though consigned to a life of exile in Agen, France, where she died on May 19, 1816, at the age of seventy-four, was spared the ultimate misery of having her sons executed by her husband's enemies.[54] How could Marie-Louise, in contrast, be expected to continue in Haiti, to live out every day under such staggering despair while having to stare into the faces of the men who committed such an unforgivably eternal act?

If her personal grief was not enough to lead her to look to other shores for solace, the continued anti-Christophe screeds coming from *The Telegraph* and the Cap-Haïtien-based *The Concord* might have been enough to send her over the edge. *The Concord* repeatedly ran stories cataloging the arrest, conviction, and execution of former members of the king's army whom the republic deemed guilty of "sedition."[55] More disturbingly, encountering this paper might have forced the queen to confront what was perhaps the most uncomfortable truth of her life.

Marie-Louise's husband had caused other women, children, and parents to experience the same pain that swiftly changed her identity from happy mother and wife to grieving and despondent widow. In the June 10, 1821, issue of *The Concord,* an anonymous author described the terrors of what he called the eighteen years of "servitude" that Christophe forced upon the people of the north, such that they felt their lives "differed little from that in which we were immersed under the colonial regime." There was reason for more than scorn in the loss of the lives of hundreds of laborers who built the enormous Citadelle, after having conquered independence, he said, only to find "themselves in oppression." The author recalled

those long lines of women farmers coming from the various com-munes, from Bombarde to Fort-Liberté and Ouanaminthe, most of them clothed with the rags of misery, exhausted by hunger, having consumed along the journey to La Ferrière almost all the food they loaded for the chores they had to perform, forced to carry rocks, sand, and other materials, from dawn until sunset, without the one who was employing them, and who lived in opulence and abundance of all kinds, thinking of coming to their aid!

In rain or sunshine, whether the path was muddy or filled with barely passable rocks, the march to the top of the Citadelle continued for those consigned to the corvée. "How many of those unfortunate women died on the road, returning to their homes?" the author asked. "How many were deprived of the sweet pleasure of seeing the objects of their affections again, a mother embracing her daughter, a wife her husband, a sister her brother and her parents?" Even after the completion of the Citadelle, the work continued, particularly after the lightning storm that set the edifice on fire, killing Marie-Louise's brother Noël. The queen's sorrow was so great on that occasion, but so was that of the people forced over the next two years to rebuild the Citadelle. "There is not a stone of that fortress that has not been stained with the blood and bathed with the tears of these unfortunate people," the writer charged. "There is not a single work of fortification that does not conceal the curses of the wretched labor-ers who built them, forced to perform such hard labor under the baton, having only a few puny roots for food, and asking heaven for lightning to strike again and topple those walls, and annihilate them to end their deplorable existence!"[56]

Accounts like this did not exist only in *The Concord* or other pro-Boyer newspapers. There were some foreigners who claimed to have witnessed the harsh labor regime used in the kingdom, not just to build or rebuild the Citadelle, but for everyday farming and other ongoing state projects. A British lieutenant in Haiti with Sir Home Popham reported that on one of Christophe's "plantations" the "overseers," "he is quite positive . . . were provided with whips." He said they used them quite liberally. On this par-ticular plantation, which sat about five miles from Cap-Henry and had 150 cultivators working the land, the lieutenant claimed to have witnessed several "mulatto women employed carrying stones to build a church, driven by a black woman who had a whip with which she impelled their speed when she thought necessary."[57] Yet what distinguishes the account in *The Concord* from many others, including that of this lieutenant, is the chronicler's ability to name the names of those who suffered under what he characterized as pure Christophean oppression.

Because the Citadelle was also a prison, those who entered its walls ordinarily never left them. Haunted by those ghosts, the writer for *The Concord* called out to the "plaintive and errant shadows of Toussaint Boufflet, Jean Gourneau, Pierre Lelong, Vindiau Hatrel, and other unfortunate leaders," who lost their lives within the Citadelle's walls. The writer, using the well-worn tactic of the Baron de Vastey vis-à-vis the French colonists, said he deliberately wanted to name these prisoners, victims of "Christophe's crimes." "And you, Pierre Toussaint, forced by hunger to devour one of your own limbs in the dungeon where you were confined; Raphael, Jean-Charles, Martial, Achilles, Bernardin, Magloire, Genty, and all of those unfortunate people immolated under the slightest pretext," the article continued. "Be comforted," the writer called out to them in the grave. "Your tyrant sleeps among you. He is no longer defiling the day; the earth is rid of this scourge; humanity is avenged at last!" Before closing the account of what he said constituted the true history of the Citadelle, and with a heart "afflicted with pain," the writer called attention to the name and story of one more victim, whose memory, he lamented, brought cause for "fresh tears." "What heartbreaking memory will come to color my tears yet?" he asked. "It is of you, young Souverain-Brun, whose knowledge was ahead of your years." "You died in the flower of your life, taken from a beloved wife! You died precipitated in the abyss; your broken bones scattered, and you would also be deprived of a burial!" the author cried out.

Perhaps Marie-Louise's pain, and that of her daughters, was not the most important, after all. The author ended his testimony with a curse more than a wish, "I say as a farewell to La Ferrière these verses that the chemist Lavoisier engraved the day before his death on the walls of his prison":

Under the scythe of Time, everything perishes at random,
It absorbs the strong, ravishes the courageous,
And the man, yesterday a child, tomorrow will be an elder.
Reflect, Tyrants, and see how all fades away on its path,
Ah! only virtues perish not.[58]

KINGDOM OF THE
NEXT WORLD

The year after the king's suicide saw a proliferation of anti-Christophe diatribes published across a range of different media, emanating from and circulating in diverse locales. In Haiti, Port-au-Prince's The Telegraph *and* The Haytian Bee *almost immediately printed articles not just defaming the former king but purporting to reveal the minute details that led up to his suicide. From 1822 to 1823, informed by the sordid accounts of British ship captains like Sir Home Popham, in port at the time of the suicide,* The Haitian Propagator *began a series called "On the Fall of Christophe," followed by another series in 1823 and 1824 called "Christophe and His Admirers." If any of these articles reached Marie-Louise, then residing in England, at first with the Clarksons at Playford Hall in Suffolk, and later with her daughters on Weymouth Street in London's Marylebone district, would she have refused to read them or shrugged them off, either in irritation or in indifference, or simply set them aside with a weary sigh? It had been a few years, after all, and the former queen—still unable to shake those terrible moments when her sons were ripped from her—had vowed to live out the remainder of her life in sorrow and exile.*

Although the queen had stood by Christophe's side since the earliest days of the Haitian Revolution, and eventually outlived most of her immediate family, dying in 1851, hardly any of the kingdom's many chroniclers bothered to consult her tale. Much later, while living in exile in Italy—as one of the only "black faces," in her words—she at last told her story to a British acquaintance, a frequent visitor at the former palace. She lamented that she had suffered through the deaths of her husband and her sons, including that of her eldest, François Ferdinand, who died in Paris in 1805. Seeking neither recognition, nor glory, nor pity, nor wealth, she said with a sigh, "I have lost a husband, an empire, and [nearly] all my children . . . sorrow has quite weaned me from the vanities of this life; at my age and in my situation, I can only look forward to the next world, as a place of rest and peace."[1]

Although Marie-Louise told other visitors, too, that she sought only to lead a life of solitude, soon after she arrived in Europe, an unflattering spotlight seemed suddenly to turn in her direction. Almost immediately after news of King Henry's suicide reached Europe, the Nîmes-based *Journal du Gard,* which drew its information from Popham's account, published a notice about the "fall of Christophe." Afterward, the editor inserted a short, desultory paragraph about the former queen and her daughters and their famous, or perhaps infamous, corps of *Amazones.* "Among all the oddities which the black king introduced into that part of Saint-Domingue, which groaned under his yoke, one of the strangest, no doubt, was his regiment of *Amazones,*" the paper stated:

> Madame Christophe (the queen) was its colonel, and her daughters held the ranks of captains and lieutenants. Every rich lady was obliged to enter this corps at the age of sixteen, to mount and equip herself at her own expense. Because the sword was too heavy for these new *Herminies* [female Hermans or army women], it was decided to arm them with small blades made of a very light wood. One of the greatest pleasures of Her Majesty was to make this female regiment maneuver at full gallop.[2]

The Haitian royal family's image did not necessarily fare better in England. The Christophe women arrived in London in the fall of 1821 to a British public primed with curiosity about the sordid story of the king's death.

On December 11, 1820, Britain's *Morning Chronicle,* clearly informed by Haitian newspapers, reported that one of the "first advantages that will be derived by humanity from the late revolution in the north side of Hayti, and the Death of Christophe, is the liberation of several victims, who, in the character of political enemies of his late sable Majesty, have long dragged a miserable existence in the dungeons of his citadel of Sans Souci [*sic*], who possibly had lost all hopes of ever again seeing the light of the sun."[3] *The Times,* out of London, drawing its material from New York City newspapers, and without mentioning the execution of Prince Victor, reported that the Christophe family initially fled to the Citadelle. The only resistance that President Boyer experienced came from General Romain, "who had taken post in the mountains of Gros-Morne, near Gonaïves, with the assumed title of General-in-Chief." In the end, the paper finished, "the fortress of Ferriere [*sic*] appears, however, to have been at last, quietly given up to republican troops, together with the members of Christophe's family, and the whole of the ex-King's treasures."[4]

While news of Christophe's death had not yet reached England, by November 4, U.S. newspapers reported the king's demise based on reports given to them by American ship captains. The reports might not have been immediately considered trustworthy. U.S. newspapers had previously reported the erroneous death of Christophe, namely, in 1818, after

Pétion's death.⁵ Much of the early reporting about the king's actual death contained flawed if not false information as well. For example, several newspapers reported that King Henry's death occurred on July 5 and "was kept secret," while attempts were made to "Crown his son."⁶ By November 6, *The New-York Columbian* corrected this misinformation when it flatly announced "the recent death of Christophe," with little hint of the drama the king's life and death soon inspired around the world.⁷

The Christophe women initially intended to stay with the Clarksons for only a few weeks, but they ended up extending their sojourn for half a year. During that time all three women suffered from bowel complaints and frostbite, unaccustomed as they were to such a cold and rainy environment. The Clarksons had played patient and sympathetic hosts. They sought medical care for their guests and brought in tutors in French and Italian for the princesses. Clarkson also helped Marie-Louise attend to her finances. With his assistance, she obtained a credit account, and for a time life in England seemed to suit the grieving family. The Christophes even had dinner at the home of their former patriarch's friend William Wilberforce in 1822, before they moved to a more secluded cottage in the seaside town of Hastings. Away from London's hustle and bustle, they hoped to avoid the stares of strangers, undoubtedly curious about the presence of these stately and finely dressed Black women.⁸

The friendship between the Clarksons and the Wordsworths eventually grew strained in connection with the presence of the Christophe women. The Wordsworths were more than a little scandalized by the presence of this Black queen in England. Hardly hiding their opinion of what they considered the inappropriateness of her presence, William's sister, Dorothy, wrote a letter to Mrs. Clarkson in October 1822 in which she enclosed a racist poem mocking Queen Marie-Louise, written by William Wordsworth (author of the famous sonnet "To Toussaint L'Ouverture") and his sister-in-law Sara Hutchinson. "My dear Friend," the letter began,

At the end of my letter I must copy a parody (which I hope will make you laugh), that William and Sarah [*sic*] threw off last Sunday afternoon. They had been talking of Mr. Clarkson's kindness to every human being, especially of his perseverance in the African cause, and of his last act of kindness to the distressed negro widow and her family. Tender thoughts of merriment came with the image of the sable princess by your fireside. The first stanza of Ben Jonson's poem slipped from William's lips, a parody, and together they finished it with much loving fun. Oh! how they laughed! I heard them in my room upstairs, and wondered what they were about; and, when it was finished, I claimed the privilege of sending it to you. . . . Ben Jonson's poem begins "Queen and huntress chaste and fair." You must know it.

Queen and negress chaste and fair!
Christophe now is laid asleep
Seated in a British chair.
State in humbler manner keep
Shine for Clarkson's pure delight
Negro princess, ebon bright!

Let not "Willy's"[9] holy shade
Interpose at envy's call,
Hayti's shining queen was made
To illumine Playford hall,
Bless it then with constant light,
Negress excellently bright!

Lay thy diadem apart,
Pomp has been a sad deceiver.
Through thy champion's faithful heart
Joy be poured, and thou the giver,
Thou that mak's't a day of night
Sable princess, ebon bright.[10]

Surprised at the brazen and overt racism, the Clarksons stopped speaking to the Wordsworths. This estrangement continued for several months until Dorothy apologized, with a hint of sarcasm, for "our joke on poor fallen royalty."[11]

Unable to reconcile with the climate, both racial and social, Marie-Louise opted to take her daughters to Italy. According to Catherine Clarkson, who later lost touch with the Christophe women, Marie-Louise remained in contact with her grandson, Prince Eugène's child, and she hoped to spend the final years of her life back home in Haiti.[12]

Though the climate of Italy suited her well, Marie-Louise still suffered much in body and mind. Her daughters were unwell, and all three women continued to be subjected to ridicule and derision. In an article quoted in the Black American newspaper *Freedom's Journal* on May 11, 1827, the author refuted an inflammatory account of Marie-Louise, first published in the *New-York Enquirer.* In that newspaper, the ardent racist Mordecai Manuel Noah[13] denounced as improbable a rumor that Madame Christophe was engaged to a German prince,[14] since readers must "remember she is a fat, greasy wench, as black as the ace of spades, and one who would find it difficult to get a place as a Cook in this city." "So much for royal taste," he concluded. The author of the refutation in *Freedom's Journal,* the first Black-owned newspaper in the United States, defended Madame Christophe against "this calumny" by writing, "We are induced, from a personal acquaintance with Madame Christophe for many years previous to and after she was elevated to the rank of Queen of Hayti, to bear testimony against the above illiberal and unjust representation." "We do not hesitate to say, that no just person acquainted with the Ex-Queen could have thus characterized her, and that there are many Americans who will unite with us in this declaration," the author wrote, before professing:

Although not so graceful and dignified in her person as the Ex-Empress of Hayti, Madame Dessalines, her person and manners were very agreeable, and she always sustained the reputation of a good and virtuous wife, an affectionate mother, and an amiable friend, and a hospitable and charitable lady, who sought for and improved every opportunity of exercising these good qualities to all the foreigners, residing and visiting at the Cape, and particularly to the Americans. She was always extremely neat in her person, and when not compelled by etiquette to appear in regal attire, was very modest in her dress and deportment. We particularly regret that such misrepresentations should originate in the United States, as it must have a tendency to injure Americans in the estimation of the black population of Hayti; who have been, and continue to be the friends of all friendly foreigners, especially the Americans.

Going on to speak of her reputation in Europe and of the rumor of her engagement, the author concluded,

We also know that since Madame Christophe has resided in Europe, her hospitality and courtesy, have induced gentlemen of the highest respectability to pay their respects to her. She has estates in Hayti, of which Gen. Magny, the Commandant of the North, regularly remits the revenues; and wherever she resides she supports an elegant and respectable establishment. We should conjecture that some mistake has been made in the foreign paragraph; and that it is her eldest daughter, also a very accomplished and well educated woman, of about the age of 26, who is the intended bride of the German Prince. As an act of justice to the lady who has been traduced; and to the feelings of the great majority of the Haytien people, who are in amity with us, we trust that this statement of facts will not be denied a place in the papers which have circulated this calumny.[15]

Freedom's Journal also reprinted another series of articles about Marie-Louise on June 27, July 4, and July 11, 1828. In these accounts, a former acquaintance of the queen's claimed to have spied her on the streets of Florence, where the Christophe women were then residing, later saying he saw Marie-Louise eating at a "trattoria" with her daughter. The "acquaintance" described the queen as having the appearance of "a poor deserted black woman, eating her macaroni in a miserable 'Trattoria' an object of derision to the vulgar, and of curiosity to all."[16]

The renewed attention to the story of the king of Haiti, and the fate of his widow, seems almost entirely owing to the above article, originally published in *The New Monthly Magazine and Literary Journal,* based in London. The unnamed author wrote that he was walking down the via dei Calzaiuoli in Florence when the sight of Marie-Louise's "black face" in a white crowd suddenly caught his eye and stunned him. Overhearing the woman speaking French, he at once remembered where he had seen her before. Getting her name and title wrong, he guessed the woman was the "Ex-Empress of Hayti, Marie Therese! The wife of or rather widow of the late Henri Christophe, 'the Great,' Emperor and King of Hayti." Claiming to have known her in "happier times," the author followed the former queen until she reached a "second-rate" trattoria, where Marie-Louise met her daughter and another "café-au-lait coloured" woman. The man watched as the three women sat at a small table eating macaroni. This putative former acquaintance of King Henry's, still without speaking to them, followed the women back to their apartment and afterward asked their landlord how this spot came to be their residence. "They had been brought to his house by a valet de place in his interest, and had regularly dined there at the same hour every day, paying most magnificently for whatever they had," the man reported. "They are great people, I believe, in their own country, although not of the same colour with us," he said. "This is the last time they dine here, and I am really sorry to lose them, as they have taken the Marchese Guigni's first-floor near the Santa Felicita Church."

The British tourist owned that he had only positive recollections of the former king and his family, perhaps tinged by youth and his tendency to view life from the "couleur de rose." "Christophe himself was a most wonderful man," the visitor wrote. "He was plain and gentleman-like in his person, somewhat inclined to corpulency, and might be said to have a sort of benevolence of manner which was quite extraordinary in an uneducated negro." Going on to compare him to King George III, whom he knew Christophe admired, the man continued, "I have heard it remarked that he bore a very strong resemblance to our late King, with the exception of colour and features of course, which he endeavoured to increase as much as possible by dress. He usually wore a blue coat with red cuffs and collar, exactly like the old Windsor uniform, with a star on the left breast, and riband of the order of St. Henri. He had short crisp curled hair like all black people, but his was whitened by age, which added considerably to the respectability of his appearance; and he had the most intelligent eyes I almost ever encountered—they appeared to look through one."

Not content to have glimpsed the former queen from a distance, the traveler later sought an audience with her at the Palazzo Guigni.

"Madame Christophe would be happy to receive you," her lady-in-waiting told the curious man. When the traveler walked into the well-appointed drawing room, he saw one of Marie-Louise's daughters seated and doing embroidery. He still had trouble absorbing these Black faces in what he considered a white space. "She was very lively, and pleasant, but by some extraordinary misapplication of judgment, she had selected a white dress, which came up to the throat, and made the colour of her face more singularly conspicuous," he thought. "We entered into some common-place conversation about the weather and the heat, until we were joined by her mother, who came in leaning on the arm of her Dame de Compagnie, and seated herself by me on the sofa," he continued. "She was much altered in her appearance since I last saw her; time and grief had left their usual mark upon her countenance, yet there was an air of suppressed dignity about her, which seemed to say, that she had made up her mind to forget her former situation, and bear with her present, if not with cheerfulness, at least with resignation." When the traveler referred to Marie-Louise as a "queen," she rebuked him, saying "that if I were not an Englishman, she should have supposed that I was ridiculing her." "I am now only la veuve Christophe," she said placing her hand gently upon the visitor's arm, "and all I have to do is to court obscurity as much as possible." The former queen did not hold back in recalling the worst moments of her life. She purportedly spoke to the visitor of her agonizing memories and the terror she experienced when her children were ripped from her. "One son, a gallant youth, made a more desperate resistance than the rest," she told him. Afterward, "she heard her eldest son begging for his life," but his pleas were ineffective since they were addressed to men "unacquainted with mercy." "One volley and all was over," she concluded. "The hopes of the mother were cut off in their dawn," the visitor editorialized, "and this very promising young man fell a victim to the capricious ambition of his father. The poor lady had not even the consolation of burying her murdered children, their mangled remains were dragged away by the enraged populace, and treated with every possible indignity."[17]

Marie-Louise and her children made every effort to live with dignity during their long exile. Having spied them in 1830 in the vacation spa town of Carlsbad (Karlovy Vary), part of the Austrian empire at the time, the French writer François-René de Chateaubriand could not help but to take his turn gawking at and then writing about the Christophe women. Of Athénaïs, Chateaubriand wrote that "she was very educated and very pretty." "Her ebony beauty rests free under the porticos among the myrtles and cypresses of Campo Santo, far from the field of cane and mangrove trees, in the shade of where," he added, "she was born a slave."[18] Of course, lucky for them, Chateaubriand was mistaken: the Christophe girls had never been enslaved. Still, they did not escape sorrow.

The Christophe womens' exile across the Atlantic took them from

England, to Austria, to the Italian cities of Rome, Florence, Turin, and Pisa. Amid their many wanderings, Marie-Louise and Athénaïs experienced a new tragedy when in October 1831, shortly after the three women took up residence in Pisa, Améthyste passed away from complications of an enlarged heart. Athénaïs passed away even more tragically eight years later, in the city of Stresa where she had been vacationing with her mother and where they had become friends with the Italian philosopher Antonio Rosmini. On September 10, 1839, Athénaïs reportedly hit her head so violently during a fall that she died. After Marie-Louise returned to Pisa, lonely and childless, with her late daughter's corpse in tow, a friend of Rosmini's lamented, "I very often see the unfortunate ex-queen of Haiti here."[19]

Occasional visitors, like the Englishman Robert Inglis, sometimes graced Marie-Louise's doorstep, but for the most part the former queen passed her remaining days alone. Inglis tried to persuade Marie-Louise to return to England with him, but by that time she was perhaps too infirm due to her own health issues, or too deeply resigned to think of starting over again. She did appear to humor Inglis's entreaty. He said, "We pressed her to think of coming back: she said that she had never liked any country so well as England; that she would never have left but for the health-sake of her daughters; but that now she had only to lie down & die, that she was daily endeavouring to prepare for it." During their last meeting, Inglis recalled with an air of wispiness, "I again took her hand & kissed it . . . she embraced me; & said that I was like her son, that her son would just have been of my age."[20]

If she did not want to return to England, Marie-Louise did seek to return to Haiti. Addressing a letter to President Boyer from Turin on November 7, 1839, Marie-Louise confessed, "A final and frightful misfortune has just put a climax to the calamities by which it has pleased divine Providence to cause me to experience." "The last of my daughters, Madame Athénaïse [sic] has just succumbed," she continued, before imploring, "In the state of isolation and abandonment in which I find myself, my thoughts and my wishes naturally turn toward my dear homeland, love for which has never faded from my heart." Adding that she hoped to spend her final days among those with whom she shared "blood ties and who do not regard me as a foreigner," she also asked for a passport for her sister Geneviève Pierrot. Boyer ended up denying Marie-Louise's request to return to Haiti, but he did authorize Geneviève to travel to Italy, where both remained for the rest of their days.[21]

Marie-Louise, unfortunately, had more suffering to do. Even with the consolation of a sister by her side, her health continued to decline. Likely a complication from diabetes induced gangrene, Marie-Louise had her left foot amputated in 1842. Afterward, like so many Black women in the nineteenth century who found themselves in Europe, forcibly or of their own volition, she became the unwitting victim of scientific observation.[22] Ferdinando Bellini, the surgeon who operated on Marie-Louise, donated her amputated limb to the museum at the University of Pisa. According to a notation in the museum's archives, the Black female "chambermaid" that Marie-Louise had with her in her final days, Zefferina, and to whom she bequeathed 400 Spanish pillar dollars in her will, also ended up in the museum after her death in 1855.[23]

A deeply pious woman, Marie-Louise had donated money for a small church to be built in Pisa called San Donnino, where she buried both her daughters under marble headstones in a dedicated sacristy, and where she herself was buried after her death on March 14, 1851.

Thanks to the efforts of scholar Miriam Franchina, there are now two historical markers commemorating the Christophe women in Pisa; the first, outside the chapel where the women were interred and the second in front of Marie-Louise's last known residence at Piazza Carrara, belated homage to Haiti's first and last queen.[24]

—

Perhaps Marie-Louise closed herself off in her final years not just from her desire to escape persistently racist gazes but to avoid traumatic representations of her life and family, by turns caricatured, romanticized, or otherwise marketed for public consumption and personal aggrandizement. After *The New Monthly Magazine* published the British traveler's long article detailing his alleged encounter with the former queen, new interest surged in the life of the royal family and late king of Haiti. The article was reprinted around the world the same year it was published, and it was also immediately translated into French and Italian.[25] Apparently seizing on the opportunity created by the furor over the story, a Mr. Stanley in London held a public auction for what he claimed was "the royal mantle of the Queen Consort of Christophe, King of Hayti."[26] This was not the first time the queen's effects had been put up for auction. In January 1822, notices appeared in *The Times* "Sales by Auction" section announcing the sale of "a Brilliant Tiara. A suit of Rubies and Brilliants, a large single stone brilliant pin, a necklace, earrings, stars, and other valuable Jewels, the property of the Ex-Queen of Hayti."[27] After she returned to London and took up residence on Weymouth Street, another for-sale-by-auction notice appeared in *The Times*.[28] This one, which announced that the Christophe women were "leaving England," unwittingly revealed the luxurious surroundings that Marie-Louise and her daughters enjoyed, no doubt the result of the sale of their jewels, coupled with the remittances Marie-Louise received from the Bank of England:

The furniture, which is of the most modern and very best description and manufacture comprises lofty 4-post and other bedsteads with rich hangings, capital seasoned down and goose feather beds, best horsehair and white wool mattresses, clean bedding, elegant drawing room chairs, sofas, and tables, brilliant chimney glasses, Spanish mahogany dining tables, ditto chairs French stuffed in morocco, sideboard, excellent chamber furniture, elegant china and glass, large India china jars, French lamps, &c. with the usual description of kitchen requisites.[29]

Perhaps encouraged by the public display of her wealth, one man, seeking the money that Christophe had entrusted to Clarkson for his education plan (and which Clarkson deposited for Marie-Louise), claimed to be the deceased Haitian king's brother. On February 21, 1837, a man calling himself Louis Alexandre Henri Christophe arrived in Swansea on a ship called *Psyche*.[30] His certificate of arrival stated that he was a "native of St. Domingo" and that the country from which he had directly sailed was "Cuba." This Christophe appealed to Lord Glenelg, secretary of state of His Majesty's Colonies, with the sad tale of his dejection since the time of the death of his alleged brother, the king of Haiti.

Louis Alexandre said not only that he was King Henry's brother but that he commanded the king's army for several years prior to the king's death, after which he had "passed the chief part of his time as a State Prisoner in Hayti." Upon his release, he went to Cuba, he said, "for the purpose of endeavoring to obtain information as to the property of his late Brother King Christophe." However, much to his surprise, "he was arrested and detained for the space of twenty-three months—an inspection of his papers having caused suspicion that he proposed exciting discontent among the black populations." After serving his sentence, Louis Alexandre claimed he was put on board the *Psyche* and taken to Swansea. He asserted that he was entitled, "by the Laws of Hayti," along with the queen consort and the "Princesses and the Daughters of his said late Majesty," to the "considerable sums of Money" that Christophe had sent to England.[31]

Louis Alexandre told Lord Glenelg a family history that he hoped would convince the British official of the veracity of his claims. "My Lord," he began, "I am brother of the late King Christophe of St. Domingue and have to state that having resided in the island of Trinidad during ten years, my Brother sent for me." The governor of Trinidad ordered both Louis Alexandre and the bearer of Christophe's letter arrested, and he was "thrown into Prison to satisfy the Inhabitants of the island which wished me to be destroyed." Upon his release three months later, the governor "advis[ed] me to quit without delay and join my brother saying I was lost if I remained at Trinidad." He then traveled to "St. Domingo," where "my sister the queen, wife of the king, asked me where I had been all the time since they had sent for me." Louis Alexandre replied that he had been in southern Haiti waging war on Pétion. Louis Alexandre said he afterward left "St. Domingo" for Piedmont, Italy, "where my sister-in-law then and does now reside," until she told him to "*return to Trinidad & do what your Brother did in St. Domingo*, afterwards, return to England and receive the large fortune which he made and which is in the Bank of England. I replied I was now too old and too tired with war and refused her advice." After a fruitless audience with the king of Piedmont, Louis Alexandre claimed he left Italy for Trinidad "in order to receive money, but I was forbidden to enter the Port." From there, he went to Cuba, where he was again imprisoned for a year before leaving. "I am now arrived in England and I request your Lordship will aid me in causing an opposition to be put on the money in the Bank to enable me to pay debts I have contracted in England. I am an Immigrant. I can neither return to St. Domingo or Trinidad. I have the honor to be your Lordship's servant."[32]

Lord Glenelg was not disposed to offer any assistance or assign any credibility to Louis Alexandre's tale. But even after learning that Lord Glenelg "has no means at his disposal by which he could render you assistance in investigating your rights to the property to which you lay claim," Louis Alexandre remained determined to acquire the money.[33] Adding several interesting (but unlikely to be true) details to his tale, Louis Alexandre claimed that he and King Henry were born on the island of Saint Vincent, where their father was "chief." Writing from London on September 3, 1838, Louis Alexandre said he needed government assistance until he could prove his story with the corroborating documents, which were "seized at Trinidad" upon his arrest. These supposedly included "a Letter written by the late King Christophe to myself—and of Family Documents proving the Marriage of Henri my Father (Chief of the Island of St. Vincent previously to its occupation by the English) and the births of King Christophe and myself—by which Documents alone I shall be enabled to substantiate my claims to the Funded Property of my late Brother King Christophe." He implored the British lord, "Until the above Documents which have been so detained arrive in England I trust your Lordship will order due provisions to be made for me for which I will give your Lordship Security upon the property of the Royal Family of Christophe in England." The answer to this additional entreaty was the same as the first: "It is not in Lord Glenelg's power to make any provision of the maintenance of the writer."[34]

Louis Alexandre was as persistent as he was cunning and inventive. The first clue that something was off were his repeated references to "St. Domingo," a term sometimes used to refer to Haiti in Great Britain, France, and the United States but never by the inhabitants of Haiti and certainly not by those from the kingdom. King Henry and his ministers were known to deny entry to and/or negotiations with any foreign government or its emissaries, as well as any foreign merchant, who referred to

"Cap-Français" instead of Cap-Henry or the "island of Saint-Domingue" instead of the Kingdom of Haiti. In the words of the Haitian minister of foreign affairs, this outdated colonial terminology constituted "expressions improper and offensive to His Majesty's Government."[35] Yet perhaps the signal error the impostor Christophe made was to claim that he had command over the royal army, which was easy to disprove since the royal almanacs listed every member of the Haitian nobility and military. These almanacs circulated widely, especially in England.

Louis Alexandre's charade as male heir to Christophe's fortune continued for more than a decade. In 1848 the *National Anti-slavery Standard*, drawing on a London *Times* article, reported his ongoing shenanigans, including charges of fraud for which he was imprisoned. Those who testified against him, including British merchants and abolitionists who knew the king, publicly refuted Louis Alexandre's story. One such individual, referred to only as "a gentleman who held for many years a situation in Hayti," testified to the chief clerk of the court that the king of Haiti "never had a brother, and that the prisoner himself had never been at Hayti." Before being condemned and remanded to custody, the impostor brother was told, "There is no doubt you are a very designing man, and this system of swindling must be put a stop to."[36]

Incredibly, another man claiming to be Christophe's "beau-frère," or brother-in-law (married to Christophe's sister), surfaced in 1843. Instead of suing to the British government, this man, Michel Scipion, went directly to ex-president Boyer, then living in exile in France after the coup d'état that unseated him that March. Acknowledging and dismissing the claims of the impostor Louis Alexandre, who falsely "said he was the brother of the king," Scipion insisted that he constituted Christophe's sole and rightful male heir. Scipion gave himself away much like Louis Alexandre not simply by referring to Haiti as "St. Domingue," but by claiming that Christophe was "a negro from Africa." Scipion also reported that he had approached Marie-Louise during her residence in London. "She also refused to recognize me," he wrote, before confessing that she gave him money to go away.[37]

Authors, publishing houses, and theater companies also pounced on the opportunity to make a quick coin, or name, for themselves by preying upon the death of the first and last king of Haiti.

The French playwright and poet Pierre-Jean de Béranger ill-estimated the opportunity presented by the king's death, and found himself in trouble with French authorities, after he published an air titled "The Death of King Christophe, Notice Presented by the Nobility of Haiti to the Three Great Allies." The song's critique of monarchies was perhaps too overt:

Princes, avenge that good Christophe.
A king worthy of all your regrets.

Dons Quixotes of the arbitrary,
Zounds! come on, valor!
This monarch was your brother;
Kings are all of the same color.

The French government quickly forbade distribution of Béranger's song after it was printed in a book in 1820. But while Louis XVIII's censors confiscated the original handwritten manuscript, too, five thousand copies of the book had already been sold.[38] Béranger must have remained in the French government's crosshairs; he later found himself jailed because of his lyrics.[39]

Béranger was not the only Frenchman to find his writing about Haiti censored in the year and wake of Christophe's death. French officials around the country censored shortly after it appeared Civique de Gastine's brochure titled *Letter to the King on the Independence of the Republic of Haiti, and on the Abolition of Slavery in the French Colonies.*[40] The interior minister of France and the general police of Paris confiscated the brochure on April 4, 1821, saying, "Here is the work of one of those maniacal revolutionaries, one of those furious Jacobins from the past. He wants the king [of France] to proclaim the independence of the Republic of Haiti . . . but he has chosen this subject only to have occasion to insult either the king's government, or religion and its ministers . . . or kings in general, and finally to incite all peoples to arm themselves against all thrones."[41] Civique de Gastine died in Haiti on June 12, 1822. "Persecuted by his government, for his passionate writings, which dealt at bottom with the happiness of the human race, in general," he was eulogized by Haiti's *The Telegraph* as follows: "He was not afraid to speak the truth to kings. Grateful Haiti will never obscure the memory of what he did for us. He believed that he could not better prove his friendship to the Haitian people than by coming to live among them."[42]

The tone of and tolerance for writing about Haiti, and especially its late king, was less fraught over in London. In England the dead ruler's reign had a kind of mysterious cachet about it, which seemed to invite readers to want to know more about the world Christophe created and lost. By turns parodied and romanticized, Christophe's story was marketed for both the stage and the page in 1820s London. On January 29, 1821, a comedic play (at least it was designed to be) titled *Death of Christophe*, written by a London dramaturge by the name of J. H. Amherst, appeared on the stage at London's famous Coburg Theatre. The play offered nothing more to spectators than a sad minstrel show, unworthy of one so talented as Ira Aldridge, who played the king in the second premiere. Featuring a combination of drunken Black soldiers, portrayed as hapless and incompetent, the play parodied all the king's men. The short length of time between Christophe's reported death and the staging of the play may explain its hasty ending. Christophe's demise is abruptly announced on the final page of the handwritten manuscript with a clumsily scribbled sketch of a tombstone "surmounted by a flag of truce." The caption to the image reads, "We submit the King has destroyed himself." The title of Amherst's play waffled over time. Some magazines advertised the play only as *Christophe, King of Hayti;* while others used an alternative title, listing the play as *Death of Christophe, King of Hayti.* What is clear from the change of title is that either the play's author or the Coburg Theatre, where it continued to be staged into the 1830s, sought to capitalize on and profit from the death of King Henry.[43]

Amherst's play was not the first time a forthcoming fiction had its title altered to respond to changing circumstances in Haiti. The three-volume *Zelica, the Creole* (an adaptation of Leonora Sansay's 1808 *Secret History; or, The Horrors of Santo Domingo*) saw publication in London the same year as Christophe's death. By 1821, the novel, which makes no reference to Christophe's death, even though he is a central character in its narration, was advertised in several British periodicals under the erroneous title *Zelica, the Creole, or the Death of Christophe.*[44] *The Times* of London took the false advertising further by claiming that in the novel "the death of Christophe and the catastrophe are described with the greatest degree of interest."[45] This title might have hit Marie-Louise particularly hard. Though Marie-Louise's mother was named Marie-Jeanne, she was known as Zulica, a name exoticized and popularized by several novelists in eighteenth-century France.[46]

Writers in southern Haiti also capitalized on the literary possibilities of Christophe's demise. In September 1823, a sixteen-year-old writer, Jean-Baptiste Roman, presented to President Boyer a draft of his play, *The Death of Christophe, Tragedy.* The president hoped to have it one day staged at the capital's theater. In act 1, scene 1, later printed in *The Propagator,* Jean-Philippe Daut, the former Duc de l'Artibonite, arrives at the palace to tell Christophe that Jean-Claude's head was delivered with glee to the western and southern army after Christophe arrested Colonel Paulin and ordered him executed over their dispute. King Henry tells him in reply,

Friend, I do not fear all these vile scoundrels:
They will receive a prize for their dark attacks.
I live; and that is enough for their perfidy
To stop believing it will remain unpunished for a long time to come,
But, since when, tell me, by honor animated,
In Brutus, in Cato, my subjects transformed
Wanting to avenge the withered majesty of the laws,
Speak of liberty, of glory, and of country?
Who then revealed to them all these mighty words
Whose true meaning their feeble reason fails to understand?[47]

Christophe's line "I live," when the title of the play evokes the contrary truth, aptly reflects the Shakespearean-like irony of the betrayal suffered by the former king, whose motto was "I am reborn from my ashes."

Queen Marie-Louise might have been more surprised to find herself as a literary character in an 1842 short story in the decade before her own death. In September 1842, "The Prince of the Fan" appeared in the Parisian newspaper *Le courrier français*. Drawing on *The New Monthly Magazine*'s ever popular "Madame Christophe" article, this short tale signed by Louis Lurine, revolves around the former queen's fictional encounter in Italy with King Henry's former personal secretary and translator, Jean "Dupuis" (supposed to be the Baron de Dupuy). Dupuis, the eponymous Prince of the Fan (Prince d'Éventail), who marries Queen Marie-Louise's fictional and still living daughter "Antoinette," like other fictions about the king, criticizes him. "Christophe started very low, madame, and arrived very high, in the twinkling of an eye, by the enchantment of freedom," the prince says to "Marie-Thérèse." "He had grown up, he had suffered, he had wept in a slave's hut . . . and the brightness of the crown came to conceal suddenly, on the face of a black man, the shameful trace, the still bloody blight of slavery." The narrator then intervened: "One reproached [His Majesty] for having a policy that was always severe, often inexorable, but he simply wanted to be the founder of a government and a dynasty."[48] Though filled with the usual biographical errors, stereotypes, and racist assumptions in accounts penned about Christophe by his detractors—such as claiming King Henry could not read or write—Lurine's characterization ultimately revels in what is perhaps one of life's most simplistic truths. Hardly anyone is unequivocally *good* or *bad*, the majority falling somewhere on the long continuum in between.

Contemplating the legacy of Christophe's life and reign, as much as his death, requires sympathetic yet critical identification. A heart can be filled simultaneously with understanding and admiration, condemnation, and indignation. Even the famous French abolitionist Victor Schoelcher, hardly inclined to show sympathy for King Henry, could not help but lament the utter state of desuetude that the institutions Christophe built for the benefit of the Haitian people had fallen into in his absence. "While the king of the north used violent and barbaric means to curb indiscipline [and] suppress theft," he "restored culture, raised up from the ruins, founded factories, and covered his kingdom with free schools, for which he appointed foreign professors."[49] Pétion's and Boyer's inability to do the same remained the French abolitionist's primary reproach. "What have you done for the young nation you were charged with leading?" Schoelcher asked. "No more schools: the ones Toussaint and Christophe had opened, you voluntarily closed them; no more roads, no more trade, no more industry, no more agriculture, no more relations with Europe, no more order, no more society, no more anything, there is nothing left." Schoelcher found much to admire, in contrast, in Christophe's dreams. "It is impossible to deny," he wrote, "that Christophe was of a higher order of mind. The country under his terrible reign was marching rapidly toward civilization." "People worked," he continued. "The ports of Cap were filled with ships that came to exchange fine merchandise for sugar and coffee; schools were established in all the towns and received large numbers of pupils; a chair of medicine and anatomy, where hygiene and surgery were taught, was established in the capital of the kingdom; entire books were published in three still active printing presses," Schoelcher wrote.[50] Yet Christophe's dream to rule over a free and prosperous land was at war with his means in a world of slavery and colonialism.

Diplomatic nonrecognition, the return of slavery to the French colonies, and the threat of foreign occupation made governing Haiti complicated. And the existence of a free and sovereign Black nation in the Americas so frightened the slaving powers that its realization brought repeated threats and punishments to Haiti. At the same time, the entangled nature of Atlantic capital from slavery and the slave trade meant that even though he never did reinstate chattel slavery, the king of Haiti profited from the institution. Because of trade with some of the colonial and slaving powers, he did not succeed in fully breaking with the capitalist order the freedom fighters of Saint-Domingue attempted to destroy.

The king's rule was full of all kinds of contradictions, to be sure. Unfortunately, the end of Christophe's reign resulted in a far less sovereign Haiti than the one King Henry left behind. We will never know how things might have unfolded if Christophe had not chosen to end his life, but we have seen what happened without him. Christophe had adamantly refused to pay any reparations to the French.[51] After his death, in what could be considered the greatest heist in history, France succeeded in extorting Haiti for the liberty the Haitian revolutionaries had fought so hard to secure.

EPILOGUE: THE GREATEST
HEIST IN HISTORY

On July 3, 1825, at ten o'clock in the morning, three years after President Boyer succeeded in reuniting the entire island into the Republic of Haiti—incorporating not just the north and the south but the eastern part of the island (today the Dominican Republic)—a French frigate, followed by two other boats, entered the waters of Port-au-Prince. While the other two boats sailed under the French flag, the frigate had at its mizzenmast a Haitian flag. The colonel in charge of the port soon learned that the French ships were on a diplomatic mission bearing the seal of Louis XVIII's successor and brother, Charles X.

Having agreed to meet with the French king's emissaries, including the Baron de Mackau, the diplomat responsible for the mission, Boyer hardly knew what to expect. From a distance the potential encounter seemed to augur war more than diplomacy. Only nine months earlier, Boyer had issued a circular in which he denounced as a "pretension" the French government's "incredible" claim that it had the right to "suzerainty" over Haiti. Boyer told the Haitian people to remember what he told them earlier that year: they needed to prepare the country for war. "Hurry to finish all the necessary work," the president wrote. "Ensure the weapons are in order, maintain good condition of the artillery, and prepare ammunition of all kinds." "Put in requisition the workmen of the corps, and even, if necessary, private individuals, for the prompt execution of the cannon mounts," he continued. "Make sure, finally, in case of invasion by the enemy, that you are not behind on any of these things."[1]

Boyer's fears seem to have materialized. Mackau appeared on the Haitian horizon, eventually supported by a daunting naval fleet of fourteen armed ships under the command of Admiral Pierre Roch Jurien de la Gravière carrying more than five hundred cannons.[2] On April 17, 1825, the French king had signed an ordinance, which Mackau's mission was to present to Boyer. The ordinance was short and contained only a brief preamble and three articles, the second of which stated the terms of the mission unequivocally: "The present inhabitants of the French part of St. Domingue shall pay to the Caisse Générale des Dépôts et Consignations de France, in five equal installments, from year to year, the first due on

December 31, 1825, the sum of 150 million francs, destined to compensate the former colonists who will claim an indemnity." In exchange for this compensation, article 3 declared that France would recognize "for the current inhabitants of the French part of the island of Saint-Domingue, the full and complete independence of their government."[3]

Boyer's previous obstinance—in his circular he had written, "War to the death to the implacable enemies who would place a sacrilegious foot on our territory"—dissipated with surprising rapidity on sighting the French diplomat.[4] On July 11, 1825, Boyer formally signed the fatal treaty that changed the course of his country forever and put another "first" in its column. This time in the negative category. In the accompanying proclamation that Boyer issued to announce the end of Haiti's de facto war with France, the president tried to frame this startling development in positive terms. "A long oppression was weighing Haiti down," Boyer told the Haitian people. "Our courage and heroic efforts ripped us, twenty-two years ago, from degradation and raised us to the level of an independent state." "But what your glory lacked was another triumph. The French flag, by coming to greet this land of freedom, consecrates on this day the legitimacy of your emancipation."[5] Christophe and his ministers had insisted that Haitian independence was a "fatal truth" that could only be denied by the delusion of the other world powers.[6] Yet here was Boyer proclaiming that French recognition legitimized Haitian freedom.

Following this "agreement," the French immediately began to frame Charles X as the true founder of Haitian independence. Several poems and engravings glorified the French king as an antiracist liberator, even though slavery continued in France's American colonies throughout Charles X's rule and that of all his successors until the French Revolution of 1848. A stanza in Nicolas-Vigor Renaudière's "The Haitian Canto: Homage to His Majesty, Charles X, on the Occasion of the Emancipation of Haiti" (1825) stands as a prime example of the genre:

Oh, Charles X, my King, whom I love and admire,
Over the hearts of the French, reign in all empire;
No, hear you no offense in the word liberty,
As you alone today, reclaimed its purity. . . .
No more slavery, then, . . . all people become free;
Laws and the gracious prince ensure equity! . . .
And history will say a great and generous King,
Made none but happy men, the blacks emancipating.[7]

A famous engraving by Signet followed suit. It depicts an enslaved Black man in chains, kneeling before King Charles, bestowing freedom upon him. Another nineteenth-century engraving by Jean-Charles Develly unwittingly undercut the narrative of French benevolence by depicting the enormous French fleet in the background of the meeting between Boyer and Mackau.

Some journalists from the era questioned the circumstances by which the indemnity had come about, condemning France for using "force." Boyer and the Haitian press did not like this narrative, however, and consequently dismissed the idea that their country, which they said "had done everything on our own," would suddenly give in to French demands out of fear. "It is known to the world that the Haitian government, of its own free will and for several years, has proposed to that of France an indemnity and to favor trade with the first nation that would recognize our full and complete independence," an article in *The Telegraph* stated. Addressing the idea that Boyer felt threatened by the massive French fleet accompanying Mackau, the article continued, "As for the appearance of this squadron in our port, one must agree that it is one of the last *pretensions of dignity*, or that rather there was a little bit of ostentation in saying that *it was necessary that the noble and generous determinations of the king of France, be accompanied by an apparatus of force*." The writer for *The Telegraph* knew that the fleet had seemed imposing to the Haitian people and attempted to discredit the idea that the fleet had come with the determination "either to fight us, if we did not accept the ordinance, or to recognize our independence, if we did accept it." "But this squadron was so little proportioned to the urgent means that would have been necessary to put into execution for a plan of attack that it is unnecessary to even speak of it," *The Telegraph* concluded. Before closing the article, the author did not let pass an opportunity to extol Haiti's world historical significance: "Without a regenerated Haiti, the slave trade, that traffic in human flesh, would still exist."[8]

The fact that the Haitians had proclaimed their independence and freedom to the "universe" under Dessalines did not stop French writers from continuing to suggest that the Haitian people owed everything to France. A stanza in Joseph Joachim Victor Chauvet's "Haiti, Lyrical Song" (1825) reads, "From Africa, Haitians, you received your existence / But your laws, your arts, you owe them all to France."[9] Some Haitian writers also contributed to this narrative. Parroting Boyer's talking points, Juste Chanlatte provided the most unexpected example. Though he was from a family of enslavers on both his mother's and his father's sides, Chanlatte had established himself as one of the most highly visible trumpeters of Haitian independence from the start.[10] His 1804 pamphlet, published immediately after the Declaration of Independence, finished with unequivocal support for Haiti's new leader, Dessalines: "Long live Haitian independence! Long live the governor-general!"[11] After Dessalines's assassination, Chanlatte joined ranks with Christophe and praised him throughout his reign as the "august leader" of the Haitian people, dedicating many poems and plays to court life.[12] Yet immediately after the king's suicide, Chanlatte began publishing nasty diatribes, in verse and prose, about the late Haitian king, whom he called an "absolute tyrant" who "sullied and massacred" "my dear country."[13] Worse still, Chanlatte discursively betrayed everything he wrote in his 1810 history of Haiti and abolitionist pamphlet *The Cry of Nature* to defend Haitian sovereignty when at a formal dinner in January 1826 that Boyer gave to welcome the newly appointed French consul general to Haiti, Chanlatte ventriloquized Boyer's propaganda about the indemnity. In a song he composed for the occasion, Chanlatte praised Charles X, of the still slaving France, as a "philosopher," a lover of "liberty," who with the 1825 treaty put his "immutable seal" on Haitian rights. Chanlatte finished by singing the lines "It is only by plowing these fields, / That we can remain free."[14]

The belief that the French king emancipated the "slaves" of "Saint-Domingue" with the indemnity ordinance was as delusional as the French belief that the Haitian government and its people owed the French colonists compensation for the loss of their income. In a later lawsuit, the colonists claimed that the indemnity covered only one-twelfth of the value of their lost "properties," including the people they forced to work as their slaves. Yet the instructions given to Mackau reveal that the determined sum of 150 million francs was meant to provide merely one year's revenue for any colonist with a documented claim, not to cover the entire sum of their alleged losses.[15] The ex-colonists had dreamed of economic restitution since the earliest days of Haitian independence. In fact, they are the ones who first proposed an indemnity in 1805, in the astounding amount of 700 million francs, which they, with a false gesture of generosity, proposed the Haitian state could deliver to them gradually.[16]

On the question of whether Boyer truly believed he had no choice but to sign the ordinance or go to war, in his own recollection of the mission Mackau admitted that the French government had not sent him to negotiate with Boyer. The French diplomat had orders to deliver the ordinance to Boyer as a fait accompli. "My mission to the people of our former colony is not a negotiation," Mackau explained. "I am limited to explaining . . . on what conditions His Majesty [of France] consents to grant their independence, fully and entirely." "I lack the powers to make the slightest modification to the proposals of which I am the bearer." The accompanying ships of war, he revealed, had been sent to "excite distress in the government of Haiti." The instructions given to Mackau by the French minister of the marine, marked "very secret," stated that if the Haitian government "did not demonstrate gratitude for what His Majesty deigns to do for them," Mackau was to "announce to the leaders of that government that henceforth they will be treated as enemies of France; that already a squadron is ready to establish the most rigorous blockade in front of the ports of the island; that this squadron will soon be reinforced by other vessels sent from our ports; and that the interruption of all maritime commerce will cease for Saint-Domingue only after this island will have submitted, without conditions, to the domination of France."[17]

Boyer had known for some time, long before the failed 1824 negotiations, of this looming multivalent threat from France and the possibility that things might come down to paying for freedom or going to war. Admiral Popham, stationed in Jamaica at the time, wrote to President Boyer just prior to King Henry's death to tell him that Haitian liberty and independence were under direct threat from the French due to the "influence that the colonial party has obtained over the councilors of His Very Christian Majesty who may try to take over this country sooner or later because of the unfortunate division that exists between the northern part and the western and southern part of the island [of Haiti]."[18] When the French colonists learned that Popham proposed to Boyer that he enter into an agreement of amnesty with Christophe, hoping this might remove obstacles to international recognition of Haitian independence, the French began immediately scheming to ensure that Louis XVIII remained in favor of "restoring Saint-Domingue," rather than recognizing Haiti's independence.

Louis XVIII's brother Charles X became king of France in September 1824, following his brother's death. Prior to his coronation, the colonists had spent much of their time pleading for the "rights" and putative restitution they believed they were owed because of what they had lost in Saint-Domingue. In March 1821, the colonists had even prepared a presentation for the French government, which included letters between Popham and Boyer that had fallen into their hands, the goal of which was to indicate "several effective and specific means" to put into effect "in the interest of France reconquering this colony."[19]

In the ensuing years, with the obstacle of Christophe gone, President Boyer repeatedly tried to negotiate France's recognition of Haitian independence. Yet these missions failed because Louis XVIII had been determined to gain at least suzerainty over the island, which would have made Haiti a protectorate of France. Just one month before Louis XVIII died, his ministers rebuked the two commissioners Boyer sent to Paris to try to negotiate in exchange for recognition a "pecuniary indemnity."[20] Once Boyer's delegates returned to Haiti, the government printed a pamphlet summarizing the different demands over the years made by the French government vis-à-vis its lost colony. "In 1814, they wished to impose upon us the absolute sovereignty of France," the pamphlet began. "In 1816, they were satisfied with constitutional sovereignty; in 1821, they demanded only a simple suzerainty." Then, "in 1823, during their negotiations with General Boyer, they confined themselves to asking for, as a sine qua non, the indemnity, which we had previously offered." The pamphlet's author questioned therefore why suddenly the French were asking for suzerainty again in the summer of 1824. "Through what kind of return to a spirit of domination, do they want, in 1824, to subject us to an external sovereignty? What then is this external sovereignty?" he asked. "It is composed, in our view, of two kinds of rights: one that is restricted to a protectorate, which is the one presented to us; the other that extends to external relations, either political or commercial, and that subsequently they would not fail to enforce." The author concluded by clarifying, in an unequivocal tone, that Haitians did not intend to give up their sovereignty: "But from whatever side we consider this suzerainty, it seems to us injurious or contrary to our security; that is why we reject it."[21]

Not long after Louis XVIII's death his brother Charles X, the new French king, caving to the pleas of the ex-colonists, decided to accept the offer of indemnity, but he set the amount. The nonnegotiable conditions required Haiti to also agree to not only pay the exorbitant sum of 150 million francs but to extend most favored nation status to France, which ended up hurting Haiti's trade with Great Britain.[22] There was also the question of whether the agreement would be kept and under what terms, and what France's recourse would be if the Haitians did not pay. Newspapers from nineteenth-century France reveal that the French king knew the Haitian government could not make these payments.[23] Onlookers did not fail to deem the amount absurd. One British journalist noted that the "enormous price" constituted a "sum which few states in Europe could bear to sacrifice." "One effect of this foolish treaty—foolish only on the part of Boyer—is, that by purchasing the acknowledgment of what was before an undisputed fact, he has brought the fact itself into question, for he has afforded room to doubt that Haiti had the means of keeping that which she had begged herself to buy," the writer concluded.[24] Boyer's own framing of his acceptance of the indemnity ordinance reinforced this reading. In announcing the indemnity, he told the Haitian people,

A special Order of His Majesty Charles X, dated April 17 of this year, recognizes the full and complete independence of your government. This authentic act, by adding the formality of law to the political existence you had already acquired, legalizes, in the eyes of the world, the rank in which you have placed yourselves, and to which Providence has called you.[25]

Haiti did not have the money to pay, however. Consequently, the French government required Haiti to borrow 30 million francs from French banks to make the first two payments. Haiti defaulted soon thereafter. Yet France remained undeterred in its mission to make Haitians pay for having dared to be free. In 1838, the new French king, Charles X's cousin Louis Philippe, sent another expedition with twelve warships to address the Haitian government's default. The 1838 revision, labeled "Traité d'amitié"—or "Treaty of Friendship"—reduced the outstanding amount owed to 60 million francs, for a total indemnity of 90 million instead of 150 million, but the Haitian government was once again ordered to take out high interest loans to pay the balance.[26] After news of this superseding treaty, foreign newspapers reported that war had been narrowly avoided between the two countries.[27]

The Haitian people suffered the most from France's extortion. After the 1825 treaty *The American Monitor* out of London worried that "a second consequence" of the indemnity agreement—the first being that the agreement called into question Haiti's a priori political existence—would be that "by so large a drain of resources from the public," Haiti would deprive itself "of the means of enforcing the very right for which she stipulates."[28] Indeed, Boyer levied draconian taxes in order to pay back the loans, and using special labor laws he created in 1826, called the *Rural Code,* he required the Haitian people to redouble their efforts at farming.[29] While Christophe had been busy during his reign developing a national school system, along with hospitals and roads, under Boyer and all subsequent presidents such projects ceased. Perhaps more dire for the Haitian people was the fact that the Haitian government found itself unable to invest in new technologies to make the work of farming and agriculture less arduous.

Because Boyer's *Rural Code* was based on a similar style of feudalism as the previous administrations under Louverture, Dessalines, and Christophe (adapted from the one imposed by Sonthonax, Polverel, and Raimond), the government heavily taxed Haiti's agricultural workers. According to the Haitian intellectual Anténor Firmin, "To pay the French debt, the masses, composed mostly of the black population who worked the land, were alone overloaded with an indirect tax on the exportation of coffee (a staple product of Haitian foreign trade), made worse by an issue of paper money which prevented the farmer from knowing exactly what the exchange value offered to him would be for the product of his labors."[30] As Schoelcher had observed, compounding the problem in the face of existing deficits, the Boyer administration had decided to print paper banknotes, which, because they were not backed by gold, led to the rapid devaluation of the Haitian gourde in the international market.[31]

The independence debt and the resulting drain on the Haitian treasury not only resulted in the underfunding of education in Haiti but also contributed to the country's inability to develop public infrastructure.[32] Contemporary assessments reveal that with the interest from all the loans, Haiti did not finish paying the indemnity debt until 1947. Recognizing the gravity of this scandal, the French economist Thomas Piketty has argued that France should pay at least $28 billion to Haiti in restitution.[33] A more recent investigation by *The New York Times* under the title of "Ransom" shows that though the amount had been reduced to 90 million francs, after interest and other fees, Haiti ultimately paid France 112 million francs, or more than 500 million U.S. dollars, which, adjusted for inflation, the *Times* has calculated to be approximately 22 billion U.S. dollars.[34]

The Haitian historian, novelist, and politician Demesvar Delorme wrote that Boyer's apparent assent to the indemnity agreement at first provided Haitians with hope. "This administration, which held the entire island in peace for twenty-five years," Delorme wrote, "as a result of the treaty concluded with Charles X, saw itself freed from apprehensions of a new war with the former metropole, which had hitherto preoccupied the public mind."[35] Even so, some Haitians disagreed immediately, especially in northern Haiti, where the memory of Christophe's resistance to the French remained strong and where public opinion about him was not nearly as negative as in the south. Delorme remarked that the former city of Cap-Henry remained "filled with former soldiers, officers, and influential generals from the war of independence," who "only accepted with great difficulty the treaty between Boyer and Charles X." "In the generous thoughtlessness owing to their national pride, they argued in 1825 that it should be at least stipulated in a separate act that the republic itself was offering the indemnity in its benevolence to dispossessed colonists." In other words, these generals believed that Boyer could make this agreement for the republic, perhaps, but should not have been able to obligate the Haitian people to pay.[36] Most Haitians only came to publicly disagree with the indemnity more gradually. As time wore on, some of the functionaries in Port-au-Prince, watching the country's gold and silver stores constantly sent aboard foreign ships, marched through the streets crying out, "You see! How can we alleviate your misery when we are forced to give everything to France?" Aversion to the indemnity remained most pronounced among the working and middle classes who were made to pay the largest share of Haiti's taxes.[37]

Boyer, for his part, seemed to genuinely believe that recognition of Haiti's independence from France would lead to recognition from the rest of the world. However, this did not happen for some time; and Boyer ultimately had to pay for his role in making Haiti indebted to France for freedom. He was overthrown in 1843. Yet it is the Haitian people of yesterday and today who have paid the dearest price.

French presidents, from Jacques Chirac to Nicolas Sarkozy, to François Hollande, to Emmanuel Macron, have a history of punishing, skirting, or downplaying Haitian demands for recompense.[38] Chirac, president of France in 2003, when the Haitian president, Jean-Bertrand Aristide, demanded formal restitution from the French government in the amount of $21 billion, threatened the Haitian government by suggesting it might want to "take care over the nature of the actions of their regime."[39] Worse, Chirac sent one of his ministers, Régis Debray, to Haiti to undermine support and momentum for Aristide's claims. Debray reported back to Chirac that Aristide's demands had "no legal basis."[40] Many Haitians believe that the French government under Chirac subsequently helped orchestrate Aristide's removal because of the international cadre of lawyers he engaged to study the nineteenth-century independence indemnity. Aristide's group calculated back in 2003 that France owed Haiti 21 billion U.S. dollars in reparations. Speaking to the *New York Times,* Thierry Burkard, France's ambassador to Haiti in 2004, acknowledged that Aristide's removal from office that year—following Haitian protests against his rule—was effectively "a coup," orchestrated in part by France. It was, he said, "probably a bit about" the Haitian president's request for reparations.[41]

After the 2010 earthquake that devastated the city of Port-au-Prince and killed more than 200,000 Haitians, the French president, Nicolas Sarkozy, visited the country, becoming the first French president ever to do so. While pledging to aid the ailing nation, Sarkozy did not address growing Haitian demands for reparations. Aristide, then living in exile, responded in an interview by saying, "When President Sarkozy went to Haiti after the earthquake, Haitians were not begging for cents, they were asking for the US$21 billion because it is a question of dignity. Either we have dignity or we don't, and Haitians have dignity. That means we respect your dignity, so you should also respect our dignity. We will not beg for cents. Cents will never solve the problems of Haiti." "After 200 years of independence, we are still living in abject poverty. We still have what we had 200 years ago in terms of misery. It is not fair. So if we want to move from misery to poverty with dignity, France must address this issue with Haitians and see what kind of agreement will come out from this important issue," he insisted.[42]

The conversation with the French government seemed to have a breakthrough in May 2015, when Sarkozy's successor, François Hollande, became only France's second head of state to visit independent Haiti. While in the country he publicly stated that France needed to "settle the debt."[43] Later, realizing he had unwittingly provided fuel for the legal claims already prepared by the attorney Ira Kurzban on behalf of the Haitian people, Hollande clarified that he meant France's debt was merely "moral."[44] For Hollande to deny that the consequences of slavery were also material was to deny French history itself.

France belatedly abolished slavery in 1848 in its remaining colonies of Martinique, Guadeloupe, Réunion, and French Guyana, which are still territories of France today, called *départements.* After abolishing slavery, the French government demonstrated once again its perverted understanding of slavery's relationship to economics when it financially compensated former "owners" of enslaved people instead of the people the French enslaved. The resulting racial wealth gap is no metaphor. In metropolitan France, 14.1 percent of the population lives below the poverty line.[45] In the former slave colonies of Martinique and Guadeloupe, in contrast, where more than 80 percent of the population is of African descent, the poverty rates are 38 percent and 46 percent, respectively.[46] The poverty rate in Haiti is even more dire at 59 percent.[47] Whereas the median annual income of a French family is $31,112, it's only $450 for a Haitian family.[48] These discrepancies are the concrete consequence of stolen labor from generations of Africans and their descendants.

Yet in the face of growing calls for reparations, particularly after the 2020 murder of George Floyd, the tactic of France's current president, Emmanuel Macron, has been simply to continue to "silence the past." When Élysée, shorthand for the official residence of the French president, was asked by a reporter from ABC News about the indemnity, the response was, "There'll be no reaction from Elysee [sic] on that matter."[49] Reporters for the United States' self-declared paper of record, *The New York Times*, were unable to get Macron's administration to even issue a "no comment."

—

On May 7, 1842, the city of Cap-Haïtien suffered a magnitude 8.1 earthquake whose tremors were felt as far away as Arkansas.[50] The quake crumbled the former Kingdom of Haiti's capital and unleashed a deadly tsunami. Nearly ten thousand people died, and virtually every structure suffered catastrophic damage. Delorme, only eleven years old at the time, recalled that around 5:30 p.m. "a deafening thud, a distant, mournful rumbling, as if emerging from a deep abyss, was heard." "The bell tower of the cathedral began to sway in the air, the bell's chimes were ringing in full blast, sinisterly, without rhythm; a horrible death knell," he continued. "Then the bell tower crumbled, the upper part first. Then the church came down altogether, and all the surrounding houses, and all the houses for as far as I could see; and all the streets came down afterward, and finally the whole city."

King Henry's former palace, located about ten miles from the epicenter, was not spared. Amid the untold human suffering, Delorme could not help but grieve the loss of the enormous edifice. Delorme associated the upheaval caused by the quake with the overthrow of President Boyer the following year. "This event had produced in our spirits a commotion difficult to name. In Cap, we were almost as stunned as we were by the earthquake."[51] Yet Delorme clearly believed that, unlike the earthquake, the coup d'état might bring positive developments. "President Boyer had been in power for twenty-five years; he governed the entire island," Delorme wrote. "He was the most perfect personification of authority that had ever been known in this country, and that we could know in this country. This president of the republic was a king." Delorme continued by saying that all that was missing from Boyer's reign was the concept of "heredity," and that while his "power had the appearance of being determined by a constitution, it was in reality without limit." "Louis Philippe resembled more a president than Jean-Pierre Boyer," Delorme concluded.[52]

Historically, guides in Haiti who lead visitors up to the Citadelle and through the ruins of Sans-Souci have had no trouble explaining the triumphs and failures, the paradox and the promise, of Haiti's all too real king. "King Christophe, our great black leader was too ambitious for the people of Haiti," said guide Louis Mercier to a group of tourists, as reported in a famous *New York Times* profile in March 1941. "He built schools, castles, palaces, roads, churches, hospitals, but in the end the people were driven to work too hard and they turned on him." The "awed" tourists then listened as Mercier concluded, "He refused to outlive his glory and despised Napoleon for being so weak that he was willing to fall alive into the hands of his enemies. Our king took his own life, in one of the rooms of this palace, with a silver bullet. It was a proud ending." Contemporary voyagers who travel to see Sans-Souci from around the world remain in awe of the remnants of its combined baroque and neoclassical style too. After visiting the ruins, the Harvard professor Henry Louis Gates Jr. remarked, "Though a devastating earthquake destroyed much of it, it remains a grand, imposing, gorgeous structure, something right out of a fairy tale."[53] Although Christophe's equally imposing Citadelle has rightfully been called the "eighth wonder of the world," it is Sans-Souci that holds the intrigue and mystery of a time, and a man, now largely forgotten.

ACKNOWLEDGMENTS

The COVID-19 pandemic threw my world—personal, mental, and physical—into disarray. I could not have written this book without the support of my husband, Samy, editor extraordinaire who was with me on the marvelous day when we found an image of Christophe's home in Cap at the French Overseas Archives in Aix, and the patience and bright-eyed interest of my children, Samy Mozart and Sébastien Franck. The friendship and spirit of sharing and camaraderie of Julia Gaffield is truly unmatched. I could never properly thank her for all the documents she sent my way as we both embarked on the journey of writing biographies of famous Haitian revolutionary men without initially being able to travel to archives. I would have been lost in so many ways without the careful eye of Grégory Pierrot, a collaborator and dear friend; he has a remarkable ability to make words out of even the sloppiest eighteenth- and nineteenth-century French handwriting. To Chelsea Stieber, thank you from the bottom of my heart for sharing your Library of Congress documents with me and for your spirit of kindness and generosity, and above all your humor and grace. LeGrace Benson is the definition of a gracious scholar, ever at the ready to discuss all things Queen Marie-Louise and to share her findings, especially the remarkable portrait of Christophe's death. Nicole Willson has been doing remarkable, essential work on the queen as well, and her encouragement has been so heartening. Laura Wagner saved this book at the eleventh hour from being tens of thousands of words longer, and her keen editorial eye pulled me from the dregs of "historian brain." Laurent Quevilly was incredibly generous in sharing his Vastey family letters with me; Cameron Monroe shared the Christophe letter book; Miriam Franchina was so kind as to share the Bergamo, Italy, letters and other documents from the Christophe era with me, a relative stranger at the time. Lewis Clorméus has been an invaluable colleague and friend, never failing to put me in touch with archivists and librarians in Haiti or sending me key historical documents. Anne Eller and Edward Rugemer were kind enough to invite me to workshop a chapter from this book at the Race and Slavery Seminar they run at Yale University. I am so grateful to all in attendance that day including David Blight and Westenley Alcenat and all the graduate students, colleagues, and others I could not see on the Zoom webinar. I benefited from the invaluable assistance of Taylor Berkoski at the Historical Society of Pennsylvania, archivists at the Connecticut Museum of Culture and History, Lela Sewell-Williams and Benjamin Talton at the Moorland-Spingarn Research Center of Howard University and Marie-Catherine Vencatasin and the entire team of archivists and librarians at the Archives Nationales d'Outre-Mer in Aix-en-Provence. At an early phase of this project, Aura Díaz López at the Nemours Archive at the University of Puerto Rico at Río Piedras was essential. She allowed me to consult the archive after I showed up completely green and virtually out of the blue one day in autumn nine years ago. I remain ever grateful to her. I owe so much gratitude to so many other archivists and librarians at the Archives Nationales in Paris, too, most of whom I never met because they were working behind the scenes, but I am especially grateful to the Chargés d'études documentaires Dr. Fadi El Hage and Matthias Millon. Eternal admiration and gratitude are owed also to Katie Orenstein, Lauren Sandler, Angela Wright-Shannon, and everyone at the OpEd Project for believing in me and Haiti and trusting that I could do public writing. Thanks also to fellow writers Lauren Z. Collins, Jaime Fuller, Kaitlyn Greenidge, Joshua Rothman, and Malaika Jabali; and fellow travelers on the journey to bring more of Haiti's culture and history to light, Michel DeGraff, Nathalie Pierre, Matthew Smith, Malick Ghachem, Chantalle Verna, and Alessandra Benedicty-Kokken. Erroll McDonald, Brian Etling, Simon Lipskar, and Geri Thoma made the book publishing happen.

Laurent Dubois has been hearing about this book probably for too many years; his expertise and advice on all things Haitian Revolution were indispensable, and I especially enjoyed being able to discuss with him even the most obscure revolutionary figures. Kaiama Glover and Alex Gil were cheerleaders and sounding boards; they are both, all around, simply wonderful people for any scholar to know. Alyssa Sepinwall, Carolyn Fick, and Amy Wilentz championed this project from afar in so many ways, and I am ever grateful. Jean Casimir, Misty Schieberle, Gina Rho, Anne Garland Mahler, Charlotte Rogers, Carmen Lamas, Njelle Hamilton, Régine-Michelle Jean-Charles, Robert Fatton Jr., Claudine Michel, Claire Payton, and Jonathan Katz were wonderful colleagues and friends. Thanks also to Paul Clammer and Tabitha McIntosh for sharing a few issues of Haitian newspapers early on with me, and to Henry Stoll who did so more recently. Flora Cassen was right there with me to discuss this project, provide advice, and generally listen from the very beginning. She is a person I can always count on, and I so wished we lived closer to each other. My best friend, Maxine, may not know it, but she helped sustain me in some of the most painful, lonely days of the pandemic. She is one of my biggest encouragers, and I will always cherish our friendship. I have the best siblings in the world. Special thanks to my older brother Rodney for helping me to conceive of the initial idea for this book, including refining the book proposal. I couldn't have done it without you, bro. Tatiana, where are the words, you were a second mother to my children when we lived in California. You will always be my best friend. Austin, baby brother, oh, how I hold you dear. What a wonderful father and friend you are; I have loved watching you mature and grow to be the kind and wonderful man you are today. Veronica, my dear, what can I say, you keep me laughing and you are an inspiration. My mother and stepfather, Leydy and Don, have always taken care of me and my children. I know what people mean when they say there are no words to express their gratitude, but let me try. I love you both dearly, and there are so many things I could not have done without you.

This book was inspired by my love for my father, Rod, and my desire to write something he would want to read. I hope you enjoy this, Pops.

I only wish my uncle Mo and my grandma Elvira St. Rose were here to read this book too. I hope I made our ancestors proud.

The First and Last King of Haiti was supported by a Ford Senior Fellowship from the Ford Foundation, a grant from the Robert B. Silvers Foundation, and the memory of the blood, sweat, and tears of the Haitian revolutionaries who sacrificed their lives, and sometimes their souls, so we could all be free.

NOTES

LIST OF ABBREVIATIONS

AGH: Association de Généalogie d'Haïti, Montréal, Canada
ANF: Archives Nationales de France, Paris, France
ANOM: Archives Nationales d'Outre-Mer, Aix-en-Provence, France
BCAM: Biblioteca Civica Angelo Mai e Archivi Storici, Bergamo, Italy
Beinecke: Beinecke Rare Book and Manuscript Library, Yale University
BFBS: British and Foreign Bible Society Archives, Cambridge University Library
BL: British Library, London
BPL: Boston Public Library
CHS: Connecticut Museum of Culture and History (previously Connecticut Historical Society), Hartford, Connecticut
Gironde: Archives Départmentales de la Gironde, Bordeaux, France
HL: Haverford College Quaker and Special Collections, Haverford, Pennsylvania
HSP: Historical Society of Pennsylvania, Philadelphia
TNA: The National Archives of the United Kingdom, London
Nemours Collection: Colección Alfred Nemours, University of Puerto Rico, Río Piedras
SHD: Service Historique de la Défense, Ministère des Armées, Vincennes, France

PROLOGUE: KING HENRY'S DRAMA

1. "Crowds Jam Streets as 'Macbeth' Opens: Police Open Way Through the Throng to Let Audience into the WPA Drama in Harlem," *New York Times*, April 15, 1936, 25; "The Play That Electrified Harlem," Library of Congress, Washington, D.C., accessed Sept. 6, 2023, www.loc.gov.
2. *Macbeth*, in *Orson Welles on Shakespeare: The W.P.A. and Mercury Theatre Playscripts*, ed. Richard France (New York: Routledge, 2001), 97n1; see also Richard France, "The 'Voodoo' Macbeth of Orson Welles," *Yale/Theatre 5*, no. 3 (Summer 1974): 67.
3. "Eighth wonder of the world" quotation from Guillermo de Zéndegui, in *Image of Haiti* (Washington, D.C.: Organization of American States, 1972), 11; also quoted in a ca. 1970s-vintage pamphlet purchased on eBay, "Haiti: Cap Haïtien . . . and the Mighty Citadelle." See also Victor-Emmanuel Roberto Wilson,

"The Forgotten Eighth Wonder of the World," trans. Jacqueline Van Baelen, *Callaloo* 15, no. 3 (Summer 1992): 849–56.

4. Henry Louis Gates Jr. and Andrew S. Curran, *Who's Black and Why? A Hidden Chapter from the Eighteenth-Century Invention of Race* (Cambridge, Mass.: Harvard University Press, 2022), 10–12.

5. Numbers taken from Slave Voyages database: www.slavevoyages.org.

6. "The Declaration of the Rights of Man and of the Citizen," Aug. 26, 1789, Élysée, www.elysee.fr.

7. David F. Marley, *Wars of the Americas: A Chronology of Armed Conflict in the Western Hemisphere,* 2nd ed. (Santa Barbara, Calif.: ABC-CLIO, 2008), 2:533.

8. Quoted in Laurent Dubois, *Avengers of the New World: The Story of the Haitian Revolution* (Cambridge, Mass.: Harvard University Press, 2004), 223.

9. Christophe to Leclerc, Feb. 2, 1802, in *Manifeste du roi* (Cap-Henry, Haiti, [ca. 1814]), 21–22; see also Charles Malo, *Histoire d'Haïti (Île de Saint-Domingue), depuis sa découverte jusqu'en 1824* (Paris: Janet and Ponthieu, 1825), 211–12.

10. Gauvin Alexander Bailey, *The Palace of Sans-Souci in Milot, Haiti (ca. 1806–1813): The Untold Story of the Potsdam of the Rainforest* (Munich: Deutscher Kunstverlag, 2017), 67–73.

11. [J. H. Amherst], *Christophe, King of Hayti, a Drama in 3 Acts* (1821), Houghton Library, Harvard University, TS 3111.225; David Worrall, *Harlequin Empire: Race, Ethnicity, and the Drama of the Popular Enlightenment* (New York: Routledge, 2016), 72.

12. William Edgar Easton, *Christophe, a Tragedy in Prose of Imperial Haiti* (Los Angeles: Press Grafton, 1911); Errol G. Hill and James V. Hatch, *A History of African American Theatre* (Cambridge, U.K.: Cambridge University Press, 2003), 138–39; for *Emperor Jones,* see Ruby Cohn, "Black Power on Stage: Emperor Jones and King Christophe," *Yale French Studies* 46 (1971): 41–47; and Mary A. Renda, *Taking Haiti: Military Occupation and the Culture of U.S. Imperialism, 1915–1940* (Chapel Hill: University of North Carolina Press, 2001), 217.

13. Vandercook's book was released to rave reviews and was chosen by the Literary Guild as its March 1928 book of the month. See "Black Majesty," *Houston Chronicle,* Feb. 26, 1928; John W. Vandercook, *Black Majesty: The Slave Who Became a King* (New York: Scholastic Book Services, 1963), n.p.; see also Renda, *Taking Haiti,* 217.

14. Charles Forsdick and Christian Høgsbjerg, "Sergei Eisenstein and the Haitian Revolution: 'The Confrontation Between Black and White Explodes into Red,'" *History Workshop Journal* 78, no. 1 (Fall 2014): 159, 171–72. For more on Eisenstein's attempt to make a film about the Haitian Revolution, see Alyssa Goldstein Sepinwall, *Slave Revolt on Screen: The Haitian Revolution in Film and Video Games* (Jackson: University of Mississippi Press, 2021), 89–90.

15. Quoted in Forsdick and Høgsbjerg, "Sergei Eisenstein," 172.

16. John Houseman, *Run-Through: A Memoir* (New York: Simon and Schuster, 1980), 185.

17. Brooks Atkinson, "'Macbeth,' or Harlem Boy Goes Wrong, Under Auspices of Federal Theatre Project," *New York Times,* April 15, 1936, 25; "Colored Macbeth: Negroes in Shakespeare Play," *Atlanta Daily World,* April 27, 1936, 2.

18. Bosley Crowther, "'Macbeth' the Moor," *New York Times,* April 5, 1936, sec. 9, 1.

19. Simon Callow, *Orson Welles: The Road to Xanadu* (London: Random House, 1995), 222; France, "'Voodoo' Macbeth," 69.

20. William Woodis Harvey, *Sketches of Hayti: From the Expulsion of the French to the Death of Christophe* (London: L. B. Seeley and Son, 1827), 185–86, 403–4.

21. May Miller, *Christophe's Daughters*, in *Negro History in Thirteen Plays*, ed. May Miller and Richard Willis (Washington, D.C.: Associated Publishers, 1935), 251–64. The future king was also depicted as one of the Haitian revolutionaries in many other plays, including in the Trinidadian writer C. L. R. James's *Toussaint Louverture*, first performed in Westminster, England, in 1936, and in 1961 in the Martinican poet Édouard Glissant's *Monsieur Toussaint*. James's *Toussaint Louverture* was written in 1934 but published for the first time in 2013 by Duke University Press. See C. L. R. James, *Toussaint Louverture: The Story of the Only Successful Slave Revolt in History, a Play in Three Acts*, ed. Christian Høgsbjerg (Durham, N.C.: Duke University Press, 2013); and Édouard Glissant, *Monsieur Toussaint* (Paris: Seuil, 1961).

22. William Du Bois, *Haiti*, in *Federal Theatre Plays* (New York: Random House, 1938), 1–80; "Brilliance Reigns at 'Haiti' Opening: Opening Night at the Lafayette Brings Out Harlem's Elite," *Amsterdam News*, March 12, 1938, 16; " 'Haiti' Passes 'Beth' Record," *Amsterdam News*, March 19, 1938, 19.

23. Selden Rodman, *The Revolutionists, a Tragedy in Three Acts* (New York: Duell, Sloan & Pierce, 1942); Dan Hammerman, "Henri Christophe," unpublished MS, New York Public Library, MSS 1984-011.

24. Richard Durham, *Black Hamlet*, Richard Durham Papers, Accession no. 1998/02, box 3, folders 2 and 3, Vivian G. Harsh Research Collection of Afro-American History and Literature, Chicago Public Library. Recordings of the episodes, numbers 30 and 31, are available at the Internet Archive: "Destination Freedom," archive.org.

25. James Forsyth, *Defiant Island: A Play Based on the Life of Henry Christophe of Haiti* (Chicago: Dramatic Publishing Company, 1975), 148.

26. Derek Walcott, *The Haitian Trilogy: "Henri Christophe," "Drums and Colours," and "The Haitian Earth"* (New York: Farrar, Straus and Giroux, 2002); Derek Walcott, *Henri Christophe: A Chronicle in Seven Scenes* (Bridgetown, Barbados: Advocate, 1950), 58; and Derek Walcott, *What the Twilight Says: Essays* (New York: Farrar, Straus and Giroux, 1998), 12.

27. Aimé Césaire, *La tragédie du roi Christophe* (Paris: Présence Africaine, 1963), 16; and Aimé Césaire, *Nègre je suis, nègre je resterai: Entretiens avec Françoise Vergès* (Paris: Albin Michel, 2005), 57.

28. Alejo Carpentier, *The Kingdom of This World*, trans. Harriet de Onís (New York: Farrar, Straus and Giroux, 2006), 114, 142. The scholar Roberto González Echevarría has observed that along with the novel's historical inaccuracies Carpentier makes Christophe the "Satan" of the text. See Echevarría, *Alejo Carpentier: The Pilgrim at Home* (Ithaca, N.Y.: Cornell University Press, 1977), 131–42, 147.

29. Tabitha McIntosh, "White Ghosts and Silver Bullets: Imaginary Objects and the Haitian Revolution," Age of Revolutions, April 8, 2019, ageofrevolutions.com.

30. Fannie B. Ward, "Cape Haytien City: Vicissitudes of 'the Paris of the West Indies,' " *Daily Inter Ocean*, Dec. 23, 1894, 14.

31. Vincent Towne, "Henri Christophe: The Black Hitler," *Pittsburgh Post-Gazette*, Aug. 26, 1942, 23. For the golden bullet in Vandercook, see *Black Majesty*, 150.

32. Guillermo de la Parra and Manelick de la Parra, with illustrations by Antonio Gutiérrez, *Fuego: Majestad negra*, nos. 191 and 192 (1983). See also Enrique García, "The Uses of Henri Christophe in the Work of Derek Walcott, Aimé

Césaire, and Alejo Carpentier, and His Visual Representation in the Melo-dramatic Mexican Comic Book *Fuego*," in *Paroles, textes et images: Formes et pouvoirs de l'imaginaire,* ed. Jean-François Chassay and Bertrand Gervais (Montreal: University of Quebec, Center for Research on Text and Imagination, 2008), 180, oic.uqam.ca.

33. Michel-Rolph Trouillot, *Silencing the Past: Power and the Production of History* (Boston: Beacon Press, 1995), 31–32; for the gravestone, see Wilson, "Forgotten Eighth Wonder of the World," 855.

34. Hénock Trouillot, "Le gouvernement du Roi Henri Christophe," *Revue de la société haïtienne d'histoire, de géographie et de géologie* 35, no. 117 (Oct.–Dec. 1972): 9; Wilberforce quoted in Robert Isaac Wilberforce and Samuel Wilberforce, eds., *The Life of William Wilberforce by His Sons . . . in Five Volumes* (London: John Murray, 1838), 5:108; Vandercook, *Black Majesty,* n.p.

35. Peter Slevin, "World's Oldest Black Nation 'Ruthlessly Self-Destructive,'" *Miami Herald,* Oct. 16, 1994, 21.

36. Nancy Heinl and Robert Heinl, *Written in Blood: The Story of the Haitian People, 1492–1995* (Lanham, Md.: University Press of America, 1996), 6; David Brooks, "The Underlying Tragedy," *New York Times,* Jan. 14, 2010.

37. "État des bâtimens étrangers entrés dans le Port du Cap-Henry depuis le 1er janvier, 1817 jusqu'au 10 août inclusivement," *Gazette royale d'Hayti,* Aug. 14, 1817, 3–4.

38. Colombian Cruises pamphlet titled "Sans Souci & the Citadel of the Black King: Henri Christophe," ca. 1930s, from author's private collection.

39. Catherine Porter et al., "Haiti 'Ransom' Project," *New York Times,* Nov. 16, 2022, www.nytimes.com.Haiti.

INTRODUCTION: ON DOING JUSTICE TO CHRISTOPHE'S STORY

1. Wendell Phillips, *Toussaint L'Ouverture,* Dec. 1861 (Stamford, Conn.: Overbrook Press, 1963).

2. See, for example, John Relly Beard, *The Life of Toussaint L'Ouverture, the Negro Patriot of Hayti* (London: Ingram, Cook, 1853).

3. "Par le General Chanlatte, aîné. A Present from Mr. St. Aude of Gonaïves: 'Henry Christophe,'" Sc Rare 972.94-B, Schomburg Center for Research in Black Culture, New York Public Library (hereafter NYPL); for an original, see [Juste Chanlatte], *Henry Christophe* (Cap-Haïtien: Imprimerie du Gouvernement, 1820), Moorland-Spingarn Research Center, Howard University, Washington, D.C. This item has been miscataloged as written by Chanlatte's brother, François Desriviers Chanalatte [*sic*].

4. "From St. Domingo," *Bermuda Gazette,* March 10, 1821; Juste Chanlatte, *La partie de chasse du roi, opéra en trois actes* (Sans-Souci: Imprimerie Royale, 1820).

5. "Les vingt premiers jours du mois d'octobre 1820 an 17: Est-ce un rêve?," *Le télégraphe,* Nov. 5, 1820, 4.

6. Charles Hérard-Dumesle, *Voyage dans le nord d'Hayti, ou révélations des lieux et des monuments historiques* (Aux Cayes: Imprimerie du Gouvernement, 1824), 264, 236, 226.

7. Dumesle, *Voyage,* 227–34.

8. Dumesle, *Voyage,* 225.

9. James Franklin, *The Present State of Hayti (Saint Domingo), with Remarks on*

Its Agriculture, Commerce, Laws, Religion, Finances, and Population, Etc. Etc. (London: John Murray, 1828), 214.

10. Charles Mackenzie, *Notes on Haiti Made During a Residence in That Republic,* Vol. 1 (New York: H. Colburn and R. Bentley, 1830), 1:49.

11. Gaspard Théodore Mollien, *Haïti ou Saint-Domingue* (ca. 1830), ed. Francis Arzalier, 2 vols. (Paris: L'Harmattan, 2006); William Woodis Harvey, *Sketches of Hayti: From the Expulsion of the French to the Death of Christophe* (London: L. B. Seely and Son, 1827); Carl Ritter, *Naturhistorische Reise nach der westindischen Insel Hayti* (Stuttgart: Hallberger, 1836); see also a three-part article in English translation published under the name Charles Ritter as "Observations on the State of Hayti at the Conclusion of Christophe's Reign," in *The Repository of Arts, Literature, Fashions, Manufactures, &c,* January 1, 1825, 23–26; February 1, 1825, 91–96; and March 1, 1825, 151–55; for de Frese, see Fredrik Thomasson, "Sweden and Haiti, 1791–1825: Revolutionary Reporting, Trade, and the Fall of Henry Christophe," *Journal of Haitian Studies* 24, no. 2 (2018): 4–35.

12. William Hamilton, *Memoir on the Cultivation of Wheat Within the Tropics* (Plymouth, U.K.: Henry H. Heydon, 1840); and "Advertisement: By the Translator," in Baron de Vastey, *An Essay on the Causes of the Revolution and Civil Wars of Hayti: Being a Sequel to the Political Remarks upon Certain French Publications and Journals Concerning Hayti,* trans. William Hamilton (Exeter: Western Luminary Office, 1823); Prince Saunders, *Haytian Papers: A Collection of the Very Interesting Proclamations, and Other Official Documents; Together with Some Account of the Rise, Progress, and Present State of the Kingdom of Hayti* (London: W. Reed, 1816); George W. C. Courtenay, "Iphigenia, Port Royal, June 6, 1819," in "Christophe, Late Emperor of Hayti," *Blackwood's Edinburgh Magazine,* Aug.–Dec. 1821, 546–52; see also an account given by Courtenay to Frances Williams Wynn and published as a summary in "Christophe, King of Hayti," *Diaries of a Lady of Quality, from 1797 to 1844,* edited with notes (London: Longman, Green, 1865), 173–83.

13. Thomas Clarkson, *A Letter to the Clergy of Various Denominations and to the Slave-Holding Planters, in the Southern Parts of the United States of America* (London: Johnston and Barrett, 1841), 13.

14. Vincent to Clarkson, Paris, October 17, 1820, Clarkson/170, St. John's College Library, Cambridge University.

15. Reprinted in "Christophe et ses admirateurs," *Le propagateur haïtien,* Oct. 15, 1823, 8.

16. "Fin du détail sur le voyage de S.A.S.," *Gazette officielle de l'État d'Hayti,* Jan. 3, 1811, 2–3.

17. See José Luciano Franco, *Comercio clandestino de esclavos* (Havana: Editorial de Ciencias Sociales, 1996), 106.

18. *Gazette royale d'Hayti,* Oct. 10, 1817, 2–3.

19. Derek Walcott, *What the Twilight Says: Essays* (New York: Farrar, Straus & Giroux, 1998), 13.

20. Baron de Vastey, *Essai sur les causes de la révolution et des guerres civiles d'Hayti, faisant suite au Réflexions politiques sur quelques ouvrages et journaux français concernant Hayti* (Sans-Souci, Haiti: Imprimerie Royale, 1819), 203–239, 250–63, 273; 302–04. See also Marlene Daut, *Baron de Vastey and the Origins of Black Atlantic Humanism* (Basingstoke: Palgrave Macmillan, 2017), 50–54.

21. Patrick Bellegarde-Smith, *Haiti: The Breached Citadel* (Boulder, Colo.: West-view Press, 1990).
22. Arlette Farge, *The Allure of the Archives*, trans. Thomas Scott-Railton (New Haven, Conn.: Yale University Press, 2015), 76.

CHAPTER 1: A FUTURE KING IS BORN

1. *Almanach royal d'Hayti pour l'année 1814, onzième de l'indépendance, et la troisième du règne de Sa Majesté* (Cap-Henry: P. Roux, 1814), 5; Ralph T. Ester-quest, "L'Imprimerie Royale d'Hayti (1817–1819): A Little Known Royal Press of the Western Hemisphere," *Papers of the Bibliographical Society of America* 34 (Jan. 1940): 171–84.
2. Vastey, *Essai*, 158.
3. Vastey to Clarkson, March 24, 1819, in *Henry Christophe and Thomas Clark-son: A Correspondence*, ed. Earl Leslie Griggs and Clifford H. Prator (Berkeley: University of California Press, 1952), 136; Prévost to Clarkson, Sept. 3, 1819, in ibid., 153. For circulation of Vastey's writing, see Marlene L. Daut, "The 'Alpha and Omega' of Haitian Literature: Baron de Vastey and the U.S. Audience of Haitian Political Writing, 1807–1825," in *The Haitian Revolution and the Early United States: Histories, Textualities, Geographies*, ed. Elizabeth Maddock Dil-lon and Michael Drexler (Philadelphia: University of Pennsylvania Press, 2016), 287–313.
4. Baron de Vastey, *Le système colonial dévoilé* (Cap-Henry: P. Roux, 1814), iii.
5. Clarkson to Christophe, July 10, 1820, Papers of Thomas Clarkson, Add Ms 41266, BL. This letter is also transcribed in Griggs and Prator, but the editors of the volume redacted it and it therefore lacks several phrases from the original. See Clarkson to King Henry, July 10, 1820, *Correspondence*, 200–207.
6. For Chanlatte, see *Henry Christophe*, 1.
7. Cathcart to Maitland, Nov. 26, 1799, CO 245/1, TNA.
8. Joseph Saint-Rémy, *Pétion et Haïti: Étude monographique et historique* (Paris: Auguste Durand, 1857), 4:150. In 1839, Saint-Rémy published in Paris a twenty-page essay on Christophe, which opened with a statement acknowledging the complicated dynamics involved in writing Christophe's biography: "History perhaps does not present a character more difficult to judge than General Chris-tophe; on the one hand, very honorable testimonies elevate him to the rank of the greatest men; on the other hand, voices commendable in all respects have only a cry of anathema to issue against him." See Saint-Rémy, *Essai sur Henri-Christophe, général haïtien, par le citoyen Joseph Saint-Rémy, des Cayes (Haïti)* (Paris: Félix Malteste, 1839), 1.
9. Saint-Rémy, *Pétion et Haïti*, 4: 151n1. One early source that contributed to this "misconception" was the 1807 *Biographie moderne; ou, Dictionnaire biographique*, wherein we find Christophe described as a "Black general born on the English island of St. Christopher." The English translation of the vol-ume published in 1811 repeated the same information. See "Christophe, H.," in *Biographie moderne; ou, Dictionnaire biographique de tous les hommes morts et vivans qui ont marqué à la fin du 18è siècle et au commencement de celui-ci, par leurs écrits, leur rang, leurs emplois, leurs talens, leurs malheurs, leurs vertus, leurs crimes, et où tous les faits qui les concernent sont rapportés de la manière la plus impartiale et la plus authentique*, 3rd ed. (Leipzig: Paul-Jacques Besson, 1807), 1:461; and "Christophe, H.," *Biographie Moderne: Lives of Remarkable Characters Who Have Distinguished Themselves from the Commencement of*

the French Revolution to the Present Time. From the French. In Three Volumes (London: Longman, Hurst, Rees, Orme, and Brown, 1811), 1:275.

10. Daniel Paterson, *A Topographical Description of the Island of Grenada; Surveyed by Monsieur Pinel in 1763, by Order of the Government, with the Addition of English Names, Alterations of Property, and Other Improvements to the Present Time* (London: W. F. Faden, 1780), 5.

11. Marriage act of Philippe Rose Roume de Saint-Laurent and Marianne Elizabeth Rochard, February 19, 1799, Port-Républicain, CO 23/38, TNA.

12. Paterson, *Topographical Description of the Island of Grenada*, 9.

13. Roume to Toussaint Louverture, Oct. 24, 1799, CC9A/26, ANF. Thanks to Julia Gaffield for sharing this document.

14. Paterson, *Topographical Description of the Island of Grenada*, 4.

15. William F. Keegan and Corinne L. Hofman, *The Caribbean Before Columbus* (Oxford: Oxford University Press, 2017), 57–58.

16. Paterson, *Topographical Description of the Island of Grenada*, 4.

17. Paterson, *Topographical Description of the Island of Grenada*, 4; Beverley A. Steele, *Grenada: A History of its People* (London: Macmillan Education, 2003), 34.

18. Keegan and Hofman, *Caribbean Before Columbus*, 212; Steele, *Grenada*, 34–35.

19. Transatlantic Slave Trade Estimates, Slave Voyages database, www.slavevoyages .org.

20. Paterson, *Topographical Description of the Island of Grenada*, 10, 13.

21. *Annual Register for 1768*, 6th ed. (1800), 210; D. Polson, "The Tolerated, the Indulged, and the Contented: Ethnic Alliances and Rivalries in Grenadian Plantation Society, 1763–1800" (PhD diss., University of Warwick, 2011), 245–46. See also "Sir Francis Laurent: Profile & Legacies Summary (????—1784)," Centre for the Study of the Legacies of British Slavery, www.ucl.ac.uk.

22. Bridget Brereton, *An Introduction to the History of Trinidad and Tobago* (London: Heinemann, 1996), 15, 17.

23. Roume to Louverture, Nov. 25, 1799, CC9A/26, ANF.

24. Christophe later observed in a letter to William Wilberforce that he could "perfectly understand English," before insisting, "it is in this language that I desire for you to continue to correspond with me." "Résultat de l'expédition de Saint-Domingue. Conduite de Général Leclerc," *L'ambigu*, no. 22 (1803): 87; Christophe to Wilberforce, Nov. 16, 1816, in Robert Isaac Wilberforce and Samuel Wilberforce, eds., *The Correspondence of William Wilberforce, edited by his sons* (London: John Murray, 1840), 358.

25. *Le peuple de la République d'Hayti, à Messieurs Vastey et Limonade* (Port-au-Prince: Imprimerie du Gouvernement, 1815), 2. The pamphlet was signed by several dozen men living in Pétion's republic, including Bazelais, Boyer, Magny, Borgella, B. Inginac, and D. Chanlatte (Juste Chanlatte's brother). Ardouin, however, identifies this pamphlet as having been authored by Sabourin under the orders of Pétion. See Beaubrun Ardouin, *Études sur l'histoire d'Haïti* (Paris: Chez L'Auteur, 1858), 8:153–54.

26. Saint-Rémy, *Pétion et Haïti*, 4:150–51.

27. For Grenada's absentee society, see Paterson, *Topographical Description of the Island of Grenada*, 6–12; Vastey, *Essai*, 160fn1.

28. Dumesle, *Voyage*, 227–29.

29. Noël Colombel, *Examen d'un pamphlet, ayant pour titre: Essai sur les causes de la révolution et des guerres civiles d'Haïti, etc.* (1819), 11; for the confusion with another family member, see Marlene L. Daut, *Baron de Vastey and the*

Origins of Black Atlantic Humanism (Basingstoke: Palgrave Macmillan, 2017), 41, 47–50.

30. "Départs," *Affiches américaines/Feuille du Cap-Français,* May 4, 1791, 220; Jean Vastey to Pierre Vastey, May 12, 1795, private collection of Laurent Quevilly (hereafter cited as LQ); Jean-Pierre Vastey to Pierre Vastey, Aug. 15, 1796, LQ. Many thanks to Laurent Quevilly for sharing these letters. See also Laurent Quevilly, *Le Baron de Vastey* (Books on Demand, 2014), 149, 167, 192, 218.

31. Noël Colombel, *Réflexions sur quelques faits relatifs à notre existence politique; suivies de la réponse des généraux, officiers supérieurs de l'armée, et principaux magistrats de la république, réunis au Port-au-Prince, à la lettre que Christophe leur a écrite* (Port-au-Prince: Imprimerie du Gouvernement, 1818), 13.

32. Courtenay, "Iphigenia," 551.

33. Mollien, *Haïti ou Saint-Domingue,* 2:63.

34. Charles Henri d'Estaing, Reports of the French Fleet in North America, 8–10, AM.6422, HSP.

35. Armand Louis de Gontaut, duc de Biron, *Mémoires du duc de Lauzun, édition complète, précédée d'une étude sur Lauzun & ses mémoires,* ed. Georges D'Heylli (Paris: Édouard Rouveyre, 1880), 211–18. De Lauzun had previously served in Corsica. See Gaston Maugras, *The Duc de Lauzun and the Court of Louis XV, from the French of Gaston Maugras, with Portrait* (London: Osgood, McIlvaine, 1895), 164–73.

36. "Tableau des vaisseaux & frégates composant l'escadre de Monsieur Le Comte d'Estaing Vice-Amiral de France lors de son départ de Toulon," in Reports of the French Fleet, AM.6422, HSP; "Nouvelles politiques. Amérique," *Affiches américaines,* Aug. 17, 1779, 1–2; D'Estaing, Reports of the French Fleet, 14; Biron, *Mémoires,* 213–15.

37. D'Estaing, Reports of the French Fleet, 1, 10.

38. Charles Henri d'Estaing, "Relation de la prise de l'isle de la Grenade," MAR/C/7/101/A, ANF.

39. D'Estaing, Reports of the French Fleet, 18–21.

40. D'Estaing, Reports of the French Fleet, 22.

41. Draft of d'Estaing's report on the siege of Savannah, MAR/C/7/101/A, ANF.

42. Ritter, who lived in Haiti at the time of the king's suicide, is likely the source for Leconte's claim that Christophe had free status at the time of his birth in Grenada. Vergniaud Leconte, *Henri Christophe dans l'histoire d'Haïti* (Paris: Berger-Levrault, 1931), 1–2; Charles [*sic*] Ritter, "Observations on the State of Hayti at the Conclusion of Christophe's Reign," *The Repository of Arts, Literature, Fashion, Manufactures,* February 1, 1825, 91.

43. "État . . . des habitations en activité du Département du Cap où sont portées les sucres et sirops qu'elles ont livrées à l'administration depuis le 10 octobre 1793 . . . jusqu'au 30 germinal de l'an 3ième de la République française, une et indivisible," May 20, 1795, 10 DPPC 188, ANOM; René Phelipeau, *Plan de la plaine du Cap François en l'Isle St. Domingue* (1786), Library of Congress, www.loc.gov.

44. "Les Administrateurs des Domaines nationaux de la Colonie de Saint-Domingue, au Citoyen Colleau, Préposé à la Petite-Anse. 24 prairial an VII (June 12, 1799)," 10 DPPC 132, ANOM.

45. Leconte, *Henri Christophe dans l'histoire d'Haïti,* 2.

46. W. E. B. Du Bois, "Did You Know?," *Crisis,* Aug.–Sept. 1951, 468; Cathcart to Maitland, Nov. 26, 1799, CO 245/1, TNA.

47. Saint-Rémy, *Pétion et Haïti*, 150–51; Dumesle, *Voyage*, 227–28; Mackenzie, *Notes*, 1:159.

48. Hubert Cole, *Christophe, King of Haiti: A Biography* (New York: Viking Press, 1967), 31.

49. J. B. F., "Notice sur Henry Christophe, Général, Roi, avec réflexions," *Feuille du commerce, petites affiches, et annonces du Port-au-Prince*, March 13, 1842, 3–4.

50. Michel-René Hilliard d'Auberteuil, *Considérations sur l'état présent de la colonie française de Saint-Domingue; Ouvrage politique et législatif; présenté au ministre de la marine*, 2 vols. (Paris: Grangé, 1776), 2:63.

51. Hilliard d'Auberteuil, *Considérations*, 1:144.

52. "Arrêt du Conseil d'état, qui supprime un ouvrage intitulé: Considérations sur l'état present de la colonie française de Saint-Domingue, du 17 décembre 1777," in Vastey, *Le système*, 88n1.

53. Vastey, *Le système*, 87–88.

54. For natal alienation, see Orlando Patterson, *Slavery and Social Death* (Cambridge, Mass.: Harvard University Press, 1982), 5–6.

55. Mary Prince, *The History of Mary Prince, a West Indian Slave. Related by Herself. With a Supplement by the Editor. To Which Is Added, The Narrative of Asa-Asa, a Captured African*, 3rd ed. (London: F. Westley and A. H. Davis, 1831), 3–4.

56. Charles Moran, *Black Triumvirate: A Study of Louverture, Dessalines, Christophe—the Men Who Made Haiti* (New York: Exposition Press, 1957), 125–26.

CHAPTER 2: A CHILD IN A WORLD OF SLAVERY AND REVOLUTION

1. "Liste des bâtiments de guerre perdus par Sa Majesté britannique depuis le commencement de la guere [*sic*] avec l'Amérique," *Affiches américaines*, Jan. 26, 1779, 4.

2. "Nouvelles politiques. Amérique," *Affiches américaines*, Feb. 2, 1779, 2.

3. "Nouvelles politiques. Amérique," *Affiches américaines*, Feb. 9, 1779, 4.

4. "Nouvelles politiques. Amérique," *Affiches américaines*, Feb. 16, 1779, 3.

5. "Nouvelles politiques. Amérique," *Affiches américaines*, April 6, 1779, 4.

6. "Nouvelles politiques. Amérique," *Affiches américaines*, July 20, 1779, 4.

7. Charles C. Jones, ed., *The Siege of Savannah in 1779, as Described in Two Contemporaneous Journals of French Officers in the Fleet of Count d'Estaing* (Albany, N.Y.: Joel Munsell, 1874), 10; "Nouvelles Politiques. Amérique," *Affiches américaines*, Aug. 10, 1779, 3–4; "Frégates, flûtes, ou corvettes arrivées avec M. le Comte D'Estaing, ou qui se sont trouvés en station aux Isles du Vent," MAR/C/7/101/A, ANF; Alfred J. Nemours, *Haïti et la guerre d'indépendance américaine* (1952; Port-au-Prince: Fardin, 2012), 46.

8. "Avis Divers," *Affiches américaines*, Jan. 29, 1766, 40; Jean-Marie Collot d'Herbois, *Les Français à la Grenade, ou, L'impromptu de la guerre et de l'amour; Comédie-divertissement en deux actes et en prose, mêlée de chants, de danses, et de vaudevilles. Composée à l'occasion des avantages remportés par les armées de Sa Majesté Très-Chrétienne en Amérique, pendant la campagne de l'année 1779. Jouée sur les théâtres de Lille & de Douay le 20 septembre de la même année, & successivement sur les autres théâtres de province* (1779), n.p.; "Spectacle," *Supplément aux Affiches américaines*, Dec. 1, 1784, 1.

9. "États-Unis," *Supplément aux Affiches américaines*, Dec. 10, 1785, 2.

10. Alexander Atkinson, "Character Sketch: Charles Henri d'Estaing," MS 2019 box folder 20: 422, Alexander Atkinson Papers, Georgia Historical Society.

11. Moran, *Black Triumvirate*, 125. John W. Vandercook writes, in contrast, dismissing Vastey's account entirely, "No one knows where King Christophe was born. . . . His name, Henry Christophe, piles up considerable evidence for the St. Kitts party. The Henry, spelled always with the English 'y,' and 'Christophe' after St. Christopher, of course . . . so they argue." John W. Vandercook, *Black Majesty: The Slave Who Became a King* (New York: Scholastic Book Services, 1963), 4–5.

12. "Extrait des registres de l'état civil de la Commune de Ravel," Ministre de la Marine et des Colonies, MAR/C/7/101/A, ANF.

13. "Caractère de M. le Comte d'Estaing, Vice-Amiral," *Affiches américaines,* Feb. 5, 1783, 1.

14. "Brevet d'Amiral, pour Charles Henri Théodat d'Estaing, vice amiral des mers d'Asie et d'Amérique," MAR/C/7/101/A, ANF.

15. Nemours, *Haïti et la guerre d'indépendance américaine,* 8.

16. "Caractère de M. le Comte d'Estaing," 1–2.

17. Vastey, *Le système,* 41–43.

18. Alex Dupuy, "French Merchant Capital and Slavery in Saint-Domingue," *Latin American Perspectives* 12, no. 3 (1985): 91.

19. For the property keeping this name throughout the eighteenth century, see folder "Becht ou Destaing [*sic*], l'habitation de ce nom sise au haut du morne du Cap," 10 DPPC 90, ANOM; Jean-Baptiste Romain, *Noms de lieux d'époque coloniale en Haïti; Essai sur la toponymie du nord à l'usage des étudiants* (Port-au-Prince: Imprimerie de l'État, 1960), 81.

20. "Biens et effets à vendre," *Supplément aux Affiches américaines,* June 6, 1778, 3.

21. In Saint-Domingue, a *carreau de terre* was a little more than three acres. See Médéric-Louis-Élie Moreau de Saint-Méry, *Description topographique, physique, civile, politique et historique de la partie Française de l'isle Saint-Domingue.* 1798. Revised and edited by Blanche Maurel and Étienne Taillemite (Paris: Société de l'Histoire des Colonies Françaises et Librairie Larose, 1958), 14n.

22. "Biens et effets à vendre," *Affiches américaines,* Oct. 24, 1780, 4.

23. "Avis divers," *Affiches américaines,* April 16, 1766, 140.

24. "Nègres marons," *Affiches américaines,* Feb. 12, 1766, 54.

25. "Avis divers," *Affiches américaines,* Aug. 27, 1766, 304.

26. "Avis divers," *Affiches américaines,* Nov. 12, 1766, 392.

27. "Biens et effets à vendre," *Affiches américaines,* July 1, 1767, 208.

28. "À bail ou à louer," *Supplément aux Affiches américaines,* Aug. 14, 1769, 280.

29. "Nègres marons," *Affiches américaines: Avis du Cap,* March 15, 1769, 82.

30. Jean Fouchard, *Les marrons du syllabaire: Quelques aspects du problème de l'instruction et de l'éducation des esclaves et affranchis de Saint-Domingue* (Port-au-Prince: H. Deschamps, 1988), 85.

31. "Esclaves en maronage," *Affiches américaines,* Dec. 13, 1769, 288.

32. "Esclaves en maronage," *Supplément aux Affiches américaines,* May 29, 1781, 2.

33. "Nègre marons," *Affiches américaines,* Jan. 16, 1782, 1.

34. "Esclaves en marronnage," *Supplément aux Affiches américaines,* Aug. 14, 1781, 4.

35. "Effets à vendre," *Supplément aux Affiches américaines,* Aug. 24, 1779, 1.

36. "Esclaves en marronage," *Supplément aux Affiches américaines,* July 31, 1781, 2.

37. Mollien, *Haïti ou Saint-Domingue,* 2:64.

38. "Ordonnance du Gouverneur Général Mr. de Bory Portant établissement d'un corps de chasseurs volontaires. Du 29 avril 1762," in Nemours, *Haïti et la guerre d'indépendance américaine*, 23–24.

39. "Ordonnance du Gouverneur Général Comte d'Estaing portant création d'un corps de troupes légères dit première légion de Saint-Domingue, 15 janvier 1765," in Nemours, *Haïti et la guerre d'indépendance américaine*, 26–27.

40. "Nouvelles politiques. Amérique," *Affiches américaines*, April 6, 1779, 4.

41. "Ordonnance du Gouverneur Général portant formation d'un corps de chasseurs volontaires de Saint-Domingue du 12 mars 1779," in Nemours, *Haïti et la guerre d'indépendance américaine*, 31–32.

42. "Ordonnance du Gouverneur Général Comte d'Estaing," 27.

43. Rigaud was a goldsmith by trade, according to his official *état de service*, which confirms that he fought at the Battle of Savannah, where he suffered a light wound to the head. See "État de service d'André Rigaud," folder Rigaud, Dec. 1, 1795, GR 8YD 638, SHD.

44. Saint-Rémy, *Pétion et Haïti*, 1:27.

45. Thomas Madiou, *Histoire d'Haiti*, 8 vols. (Port-au-Prince: Henri Deschamps, 1985–91), 4:397; Énélus Robin, *Abrégé de l'histoire d'Haïti*, 2 vols (Port-au-Prince: Imprimerie Vve J. Chenet, 1894), 1:54.

46. T. G. Steward, *How the Black St. Domingo Legion Saved the Patriot Army in the Siege of Savannah, 1779* (Washington, D.C.: published by the Academy, 1899), www.gutenberg.org.

47. George P. Clark, "The Role of the Haitian Volunteers at Savannah in 1779: An Attempt at an Objective Overview," *Phylon* 41, no. 4 (1980): 356–66; Leara Rhodes, "Haitian Contributions to American History: A Journalistic Record," *Journal of Haitian Studies* 7, no. 1 (2001): 46–60; John Garrigus, "Catalyst or Catastrophe? Saint-Domingue's Free Men of Color and the Battle of Savannah, 1779–1782," *Review/Revista interamericana* 22 (Spring–Summer 1992): 109–25.

48. Clark, "Role of the Haitian Volunteers at Savannah in 1779," 357.

49. Vastey, *Essai*, 160n1; Clark, "Role of the Haitian Volunteers at Savannah in 1779," 361.

50. "État de services d'André Rigaud."

51. André Rigaud, *Mémoire du général de brigade André Rigaud, en réfutation des écrits calomnieux contre les citoyens de couleur de Saint-Domingue* (Aux Cayes: Lemery, 1797), 8.

52. See John D. Garrigus, "Saint-Domingue's Free People of Color and the Tools of Revolution," in *The World of the Haitian Revolution*, ed. David P. Geggus and Norman Fiering (Bloomington: Indiana University Press, 2009), 58; and Stewart King, *Blue Coat or Powdered Wig: Free People of Color in Pre-revolutionary Saint-Domingue* (Athens: University of Georgia Press, 2011), 277–78.

53. Dumesle, *Voyage*, 76–77.

54. Julien Raimond, *Correspondances de Julien Raimond avec ses frères; de St.-Domingue, et les pièces qui lui ont été adressées par eux* (1793–94), 63, 63n1.

55. In an article originally published in *Le Temps* (July 1933), republished by the Association Généalogique d'Haïti, Clément Lanier, citing "a biographical notice from the *Etant de Port-au-Prince*," specified that Ogé, too, fought in Savannah alongside the "indigenous fusiliers from Georgia." Lanier revealed the chain of recitation for this claim as originating from the "papers of the notary François Lanier, whose father, Joseph Rémi Lanier, property owner in the lower Artibonite, had been in Savannah in 1779 in the ranks of the Grena-

diers Volontaires." "A brief note recalls that during the public audience granted the evening of October 8, 1816, by Pétion to the Viscount de Fontanges, sent by Louis XVIII with the intention of winning over the president to the idea of surrendering to France," Lanier wrote, "the moment became truly troubling when the Haitian coast guard commander, Paul Panayoti, who had served in the campaign, in the regiment of Guadeloupe, adroitly evoked, among so many memories, the episode of the American war, while receiving the hand of the former major of the expedition who was accompanied by Mr. Esmangart, the chevalier de Saint-Louis, Mr. de Laujon, and a retired officer from Cap, Jules Duc, a former Chasseur-Volontaire in the same battle in Georgia." See Clément Lanier, "Les nègres d'Haïti dans la guerre d'indépendance américaine," *Genèse: Journal généalogique et historique*, April 25, 1933, www.agh.qc.ca.

56. Garrigus, "Saint-Domingue's Free People of Color," 58.

57. Jacques de Cauna, "Dessalines, esclave de Toussaint?," *Outre-mers: Revue d'histoire* (2012): 319–22; Philippe R. Girard and Jean-Louis Donnadieu, "Toussaint Before Louverture: New Archival Findings on the Early Life of Toussaint Louverture," *William & Mary Quarterly* 70, no. 1 (Jan. 2013): 52, 54.

58. "État des services tant militaires civiles que militaires troupes soldées de Jeanvier Dessalines," COL E 129, ANOM.

59. "Ordonnance du Gouverneur Générale portant formation," 34.

60. Garrigus, "Catalyst or Catastrophe?," 113.

61. "Nouvelles politiques," *Affiches américaines*, March 21, 1780, 4.

62. Garrigus, "Catalyst or Catastrophe?," 115.

63. "Décorations miltaire et civile accordées aux noirs et mulâtres libres. Ordonnance du gouverneur général comte d'Estaing portant règlement pour servir à la distribution de la récompense sous le nom de médailles de la valeur et de la vertu, 15 janvier 1765," in Nemours, *Haïti et la guerre d'indépendance américaine*, 28–29.

64. Baptismal notation for Julien Raymond, État civil de Baynet (1744), digitized records, ANOM.

65. Julien Raimond, *Observations sur l'origine et les progrès du préjugé des colons blancs contre les hommes de couleur; Sur les inconvéniens de le perpétuer; La nécessité, la facilité de le détruire; Sur le projet du Comité colonial, etc.* (Paris: Chez Belin, Desenne, Bailly, 1791), 2–10.

66. See the "Règlement des administrateurs concernant les gens de couleur libres," from June 24 and July 16, 1773, in Vastey, *Le système*, 75–78.

67. Vastey, *Le système*, 77 and 77–78n1.

68. Quoted in Vastey, *Le système*, 87.

69. Vastey, *Le système*, 78–79.

70. "Esclaves en marronage," *Supplément aux Affiches américaines*, July 30, 1783, 4.

71. Cole, *Christophe, King of Haiti*, 31.

72. Reports of the French Fleet, 23–24; Anon., "Siege of Savannah," in Charles Colcock Jones, Jr., ed. *The Siege of Savannah as described in two contemporaneous journals of French officers in the fleet of d'Estaing* (Albany, N.Y.: Joel Munsell, 1874), 11–12.

73. "Nouvelles politiques. Amérique," *Affiches américaines*, Aug. 10, 1779, 4.

74. Reports of the French Fleet, 23–24.

75. "Siege of Savannah," 11; Nemours, *Haïti et la guerre d'indépendance américaine*, 20 .

76. Reports of the French Fleet, 24; "Siege of Savannah," 12–13.

77. "Siege of Savannah," 13.

78. Franklin, Arthur Lee, and John Adams to de Sartine, Nov. 12, 1778, MAR/ C/7/101/A, ANF.
79. Nemours, *Haïti et la guerre d'indépendance américaine*, 15–16.
80. Nemours, *Haïti et la guerre d'indépendance américaine*, 16.
81. Marquis de Brétigny to d'Estaing, July 17, 1779, MAR/C/7/101/A, ANF.
82. D'Estaing to de Sartine, Aug. 21, 1779, in Nemours, *Haïti et la guerre d'indépendance américaine*, 14.
83. D'Estaing to Rutledge, Aug. 31, 1779, MAR/C/7/101/A, ANF.
84. Jean Bart (1650–1702) was a famous Dutch-born ship captain who later served in the French navy as a commander.
85. De Brétigny to d'Estaing, Sept. 23, 1779, MAR/C/7/101 A, ANF.
86. Antoine François Térence O'Connor, "Relation du siège de Savannah capitale de la Nouvelle Georgie, Province du Sud de l'Amérique septentrionale," MAR/ C/7/101/A, ANF.
87. "Relation du siège de Savannah."
88. "Siege of Savannah," 13 and 13n4.
89. "Relation du siège de Savannah."
90. "Extract from the Journal of a Naval Officer in the Fleet of Count d'Estaing, 1782," in Jones, *Siege of Savannah,* 59.
91. M. E. McIntosh and B. C. Weber, ed., Introduction to *Une correspondance familiale au temps des troubles de Saint-Domingue: Lettres du Marquis et de la Marquise de Rouvray à leur fille, Saint-Domingue-Étas-Unis (1791–96)* (Paris: Société de l'Histoire des Colonies Françaises et Librairie Larose, 1959), 9. Roberta Leighton says he was born in 1735, see "Meyronnet de Saint-Marc's Journal of the Operations of the French Army Under d'Estaing at the Siege of Savannah, September 1779," *New-York Historical Society Quarterly* 36, no. 3 (July 1952): 274n
92. D'Estaing to de Sartine, Feb. 29, 1780, COL E 278, ANOM.
93. "Relation du siège de Savannah"; "L'instruction donné à M. de Rouvray," COL E 358BIS, ANOM.
94. Pechon, *Journal de la campagne de Savannah en 1779,* John Carter Brown Library, Providence, Rhode Island.
95. "Relation du siège de Savannah."
96. "Relation du siège de Savannah"; "Siege of Savannah," 22.
97. "Relation du siège de Savannah."
98. Pechon, *Journal,* 9.
99. "Siege of Savannah," 22.
100. Pechon, *Journal,* 20–21.
101. "Siege of Savannah," 24–25.
102. "Relation du siège de Savannah."
103. Lincoln and d'Estaing to Prévost, Oct. 6, 1779, MAR/C/7/191/A, ANF.
104. "Relation du siège de Savannah."
105. "Relation du siège de Savannah."
106. Pechon, *Journal,* 20.
107. "Relation du siège de Savannah."
108. "Relation du siège de Savannah."
109. "Copie des ordres donné par M. d'Estaing aux frégate La Fortunée . . . en rade devant Thibée en Georgie," Oct. 23, 1779, MAR/C /7 101/A, ANF.
110. De Rouvray to de Sartine, Dec. 12, 1779, COL E 278, ANOM.
111. "Journal du siège de Savanah avec des observations de M. d'Estaing," MAR/ C/7/101/A, ANF.

112. Garrigus, "Catalyst or Catastrophe?," 119.
113. "Nouvelles politiques. Paris," *Affiches américaines,* July 4, 1780, 3.
114. "Du Cap," *Affiches américaines,* May 2, 1780, 3.
115. "Nouvelles politiques. Amérique," *Affiches américaines,* Sept. 21, 1779, 3.
116. "Extrait d'une lettre de Williamsbourg en Virginie, du 9 octobre dernier," *Affiches américaines,* Nov. 9, 1779, 4.
117. "Nouvelles politiques. Amérique," *Affiches américaines,* Nov. 16, 1779, 4.
118. "Tableau de vaisseaux et frégattes [*sic*] arrivés au Fort Royal pendant notre séjour audit lieu & qui ont resté sous les ordes de M. le Cte. D'Estaing," in Reports of the French Fleet, AM.6422, HSP; "Nouvelles politiques. Amérique," *Affiches américaines,* Dec. 14, 1779, 4.
119. De Rouvray to de Sartine, Dec. 12, 1779.
120. "Colonies, Versailles le 4 juillet 1780," COL E 278, ANOM.
121. De Sartine to de Rouvray, July 14, 1780, COL E 278, ANOM.
122. "Avis divers," *Supplément aux Affiches américaines,* Jan. 12, 1779, 3.

CHAPTER 3: TRACING GENEALOGIES TO THE FUTURE KING

1. "Christophe, H.," in *Biographie moderne; ou, Dictionnaire biographique,* 1:461.
2. "Christophe (Henri)," in *Biographie des hommes vivants; ou, Histoire par ordre alphabétique de la vie de tous les hommes qui se sont fait remarquer par leurs actions ou leurs écrits. Ouvrage entièrement neuf, rédigé par une société de gens de lettres savants* (Paris: L. G. Michaud, 1816–17), 178; for the Dureau father and son, see Marie-Adélaïde Nielen, "Fonds La Croix et Dureau, 478 AP, Répertoire numérique détaillé" (Paris: Achives Nationales, 2009), 5, 20.
3. "Christophe (Henri)," in *Biographie universelle; ou, Dictionnaire historique des hommes qui se sont fait un nom par leur génie, leurs talens, leurs vertus, leurs erreurs, ou leurs crimes* (Paris: Gautiers Frères, 1833), 3:445.
4. "Détail des habitations," folder Bineau-Dureau, 10 DPPC 219, ANOM. See also folder Dureau, 10 DPPC 162, ANOM; folder veuve Dureau, 10 DPC 245, ANOM; and the Dureau family papers, 478AP/5, ANF. For Christophe again linked to Dureau de la Malle's plantation, see, for example, "From the British Monitor. Memoirs of Henry the First, Late King of Hayti," *American Mercury,* April 22, 1822. For location of plantation in Bois-de-Lance, see Romain, *Noms de lieux d'époque coloniale en Haïti,* 79.
5. Mollien, *Haïti ou Saint-Domingue,* 2:63.
6. Marceau Louis, *Marie-Louise d'Haïti* ([Port-au-Prince], 1951), 2–3; Cole, *Christophe, King of Haiti,* 31; Louis-Émile Élie, *La vie tragique d'Henri Christophe* ([Port-au-Prince]: C3 Editions, 2020), 26; Leconte, *Henri Christophe dans l'histoire d'Haïti,* 2.
7. Dumesle, *Voyage,* 228–29.
8. Baptismal notation for Jean-Baptiste, Quarteron, Dec. 12, 1780, État civil du Cap, ANOM.
9. "Recensement des maisons de la ville du Cap François," June 27, 1776, and "Table du cartulaire des maisons de Cap" [1787], in *Cadastres des maisons de la ville du Cap 1776 et 1787,* 5 DPPC 49, ANOM. Pétigny *père* is listed as the owner of house number 458 on the rue d'Anjou (Taranne) in the 1803 government survey of Cap; while Pétigny *fils* owned or rented house number 476 in neighboring La Fossette. *État nominatif des contribuables de la ville du Cap*

Français, tant pour la contribution de guerre que pour celle communale, pour l'an 11ième, 50 DPPC 50, ANOM.

10. Marriage notation for Claude Pétigny and Emmanuelle Gaury, Oct. 27, 1739; Baptismal notation for Étienne Joseph Pétigny, Feb. 3, 1743; Death notation for Étienne Joseph Pétigny, April 13, 1743; Baptismal notation for Pierre Jacques Pétigny, July 18, 1746; Baptismal notation for Pierre Noël Pétigny, March 13, 1749; Death notation for Claude Pétigny, Nov. 26, 1749, all in État civil for Ouanaminthe, ANOM.

11. For other Pétignys including Célestin Pétigny's son's death and mention of a Sergy Pétigny, see Death notation for Charles Joseph Bélonière Pétigny, July 29, 1851, État civil d'Haïti, AGH, www.agh.qc.ca. Delorme mentions Belonière Pétigny's promotion to colonel under Boyer as having occurred just before the 1842 earthquake in Cap. See Demesvar Delorme, *1842 au Cap, tremblement de terre* (Cap Haitien: Progrès, 1942), 1. For another of Célestin Pétigny's sons, born in Cap on June 20, 1803, see Birth record for Guilhaume Laurent de Pétigny, April 6, 1817, État civil d'Haïti, AGH.

12. Marriage notation for Jean Célestin Pétigny and Marie-Jeanne-Félicité Daut, April 7, 1817, État civil d'Haïti, AGH.

13. For Pétigny *fils* on the constitution, see "Constitution du 27 décembre 1806," mjp .univ-perp.fr; *Almanach royal d'Hayti pour l'année 1814*, 33, 109, 126. See also *Almanach royal d'Hayti pour l'année 1817, quatorzième de l'indépendance, et la sixième du règne de Sa Majesté* (Cap-Henry: P. Roux, 1817), 116. For the Chevalier de Pétigny as singer and amateur, see "Royaume d'Hayti. Du Cap-Henry, le 18 juillet," *Gazette royale d'Hayti*, July 22, 1813, 1; for the royal academy, see "Chambre royale d'instruction publique," *Gazette royale d'Hayti*, Dec. 28, 1818, 4.

14. Clive Cheesman, ed., *The Armorial of Haiti: Symbols of Nobility in the Reign of Henry Christophe* (London: College of Arms, 2007), 184.

15. "État des habitations qui ont été accordées par la Commission de Vente et d'Aliénation des Biens Domaniaux du Royaume, aux personnes qui les ont soumissionnées," *Gazette royale d'Hayti*, Aug. 20, 1817, 4.

16. Death record for Charles Joseph Bélonière Pétigny, July 29, 1851, État civil d'Haïti, AGH; *Almanach royal d'Hayti pour l'année 1820, dix-septième de l'indépendance, et la neuvième du règne de Sa Majesté, présenté par Buon* (Sans-Souci: Imprimerie Royale, 1820), 19, 130.

17. Death record for Jean-Baptiste Pétigny, Sept. 17, 1824, État civil d'Haïti, AGH.

18. Colonial livres, or pounds, were a largely theoretical, noncirculating currency used primarily for administrative purposes. See Robert Lacombe, *Histoire monétaire de Saint-Domingue et de la république d'Haïti, jusqu'en 1874* (Paris: Larose, 1958), 14, 21. For Pétigny, see Gauvin Alexander Bailey, *Architecture and Urbanism in the French Atlantic Empire: State, Church, and Society, 1604–1830* (Montreal: McGill-Queen's University Press, 2018), 110, 522n48.

19. Bailey, *Architecture*, 107.

20. Bailey, *Architecture*, 114, 524n72.

21. "Esclaves en maronage," *Supplément aux Affiches américaines*, Dec. 26, 1772, 626. An error in the newspaper's pagination has this notice on page 616.

22. "État des nègres épaves qui doivent être vendus à la Barre de Sénéchaussée de Saint-Marc, le samedi 11 avril 1789," *Affiches américaines*, March 12, 1789, 137. Repeated in the April 15, 1789, issue.

23. The main form of currency in colonial Saint-Domingue was Portuguese (*des*

portugaises) money made in Brazil of minted gold. Although the currency conversion rate from *portugaises* to colonial livres fluctuated enormously, in 1790/1791 one gold portuguese was equivalent to 66 colonial livres. See *Almanach général de Saint-Domingue pour l'année commune de 1791* (Port-au-Prince: L'Imprimerie de Mozard, 1790), 181; and Lacombe, *Histoire monétaire*, 14, 20. For the notice in the *Affiches*, see "Esclaves en marronage," *Supplément aux Affiches américaines/Feuille du Cap-Français*, April 25, 1789, 4. For recent Christophe chroniclers on the notice see Jean-Hérold Pérard, *Henry Christophe, un grand méconnu* (Imprimé au Canada, 2018), 29; and Paul Clammer, *Black Crown: Henry Christophe, the Haitian Revolution, and the Caribbean's Forgotten Kingdom* (London: Hurst, 2023), 33–34.

24. Saint-Rémy, *Pétion et Haïti*, 4:150–51.

25. "Esclaves en maronage," *Supplément aux affiches américaines*, Jan. 16, 1781, 2.

26. Leconte, *Henri Christophe dans l'histoire d'Haïti*, 2; Cole, *Christophe, King of Haiti*, 31; Élie, *La vie tragique d'Henri Christophe*, 26.

27. Leconte, *Henri Christophe dans l'histoire d'Haïti*, 2–3.

28. Cathcart to Maitland, Nov. 26, 1799, CO 245/1, TNA.

29. Alfred de Laujon, *Souvenirs de trentes années de voyages à Saint-Domingue, dans plusieurs colonies étrangères et au continent d'Amérique*, 2 vols. (Paris: Schwartz and Gagnot,1835), 1:355; for Laujon in Port-au-Prince, see title page of A. P. M. Laujon, *Précis historique de la dernière expédition de Saint-Domingue, depuis le départ de l'armée des côtes de France, jusqu'à l'évacuation de la colonie; suivi des moyens de rétablissement de cette colonie* (Paris: Le Normant, [1805]).

30. Saint-Rémy, *Pétion et Haïti*. 4:150–51.

31. Guy-Joseph Bonnet, *Souvenirs historiques de Guy-Joseph Bonnet, général de division des armées de la République d'Haïti, ancien aide de camp de Rigaud: Documents relatifs à toutes les phases de la révolution de Saint-Domingue, recueillis et mis en ordre par Edmond Bonnet* (Paris, 1864), 369; Anon., "Observations d'un français sur la traite des noirs, et sur l'état actuel de Saint-Domingue," in Frédéric Schoell, *Recueil de pièces officielles destinées à detromper les François sur les événemens qui se sont passés depuis quelques années* (Paris: Librairie Greque-Latine-Allemande, 1815), 7:287.

32. Dumesle, *Voyage*, 229–30.

33. Mollien, *Haïti ou Saint-Domingue*, 2:64.

34. "Avis divers," *Feuille du Cap-François, supplément aux Affiches américaines*, June 2, 1787, 3; "Société entre le Sr Doubrere Félix, le Sr Gay aussi écrit Gaye (Jean Pierre) et la demlle Mongeon (Luce)," Sept. 18, 1784, 7 DPPC 6164, ANOM.

35. "Avis divers," *Avis du Cap: Affiches américaines*, Nov. 14, 1768, 187; "Avis divers," *Supplément aux Affiches américaines*, Dec. 25, 1769, 507; "Avis divers," *Affiches américaines*, Feb. 27, 1781, 2.

36. *Affiches américaines*, March 19, 1766, 107–8.

37. "Avis divers," *Supplément aux Affiches américaines*, Dec. 25, 1769, 507.

38. "Avis divers," *Affiches américaines*, Feb. 27, 1781, 2.

39. "Effets à vendre," *Affiches américaines*, Jan. 22, 1783, 4.

40. "Avis divers," *Supplément aux Affiches américaines*, May 14, 1783, 1.

41. "À vendre ou à affermer," *Affiches américaines*, Sept. 10, 1783, 4.

42. "Avis divers," *Supplément aux Affiches américaines*, March 31, 1784, 2.

43. "Biens et effets à vendre," *Affiches américaines*, April 28, 1784, 4.

44. "Avis divers," *Supplément aux Affiches américaines*, June 2, 1784, 1; see also the

record of the "society" recorded by Cassanet, notary of Saint-Domingue, on September 18, 1784, under "Société entre le Sr Doubrere Félix, le Sr Gay aussi écrit Gaye (Jean Pierre) et la demlle Mongeon (Luce)," 7 DPPC 6164, ANOM.

45. "Avis divers," *Supplément aux Affiches américaines*, Sept. 15, 1784, 4.

46. *Cadastre des maisons de la ville du Cap*, 5 DPPC 49, ANOM; Charles Vincent, "Plan de l'état actuel de la ville du Cap, servant à indiquer les progrès de ses reconstructions" (1800), GE SH 18 PF 149 DIV 4 P 23/1, BNF.

47. For Alexandre Abraham Faxardo's successful inheritance, see "Au Cap, Lettre Commune, Aubaine, No. 70, Duplicata," Feb. 16, 1781, and "Mémoire pour le receveur des aubaines du Cap-Français . . . St. Domingue, rélativement à la succession de Salomon Pierre Faxardo, Espagnol," 10 DPPC 163, ANOM; for the lawsuits, a family tree, and evidence presented, including lack of circumcisions, see *Mémoire pour le Sieur Alexandre Faxardo, neveu & légataire de Salomon-Pierre Faxardo, appellant de sentence du juge du Cap du 27 mars 1779, aux fins d'arrêt & exploits des 19 & 21 juillet suivant: Contre le receveur actuel de l'aubaine, intimé, & principal demandeur en nullité du testament fait par le Sieur Faxardo*, 10 DPPC 163, ANOM. For the laws in France as they relate to this family, see also Zosa Szajkowski, *Jews and the French Revolutions of 1789, 1830, and 1848* (New York: Ktav, 1970), 228–29.

48. "Bail de maison par le Sr. Faxardo aux Sieurs Monier et Meyere [*sic*], devant M. Tach, le 17 juillet 1784," Nov. 13, 1826, 10 DPPC 250, file 49: Indemnité Faxardo, ANOM; "Bail à loyer, Sr. Faxardo aux Srs. Monier et Meyere," July 17, 1784, 7 DPPC 7428, ANOM; for Meyer's first name as Charles, see a later lease, "Bail à loyer, Sr. Faxardo au Sr. Meyere," Dec. 15, 1785, 7 DPPC 7429, ANOM.

49. "À louer ou à affermer," *Feuille du Cap/Supplément aux Affiches américaines*, June 21, 1786, 4.

50. "Avis divers," *Supplément aux Affiches américaines*, Sept. 15, 1784, 3. A sign designating "Stables of the Hôtel de la Couronne" is described in "Bail à loyer, Sr. Faxardo au Sr. Gaye," May 24, 1787, 7 DPPC 7431, ANOM.

51. While the previous lease agreement had been in both Meyer's and Monier's names, the notary Tach recorded a lease for the property in only Meyer's name on December 15, 1785. "Bail à loyer, Sr. Faxardo aux Srs. Monier et Meyere," July 17, 1784; "Bail à loyer, Sr. Faxardo au Sr. Meyere," Dec. 15, 1785.

52. "Suite des avis divers," *Supplément aux Affiches américaines*, Jan. 19, 1785, 6.

53. "Avis divers," *Supplément aux Affiches américaines*, Jan. 25, 1786, 2.

54. The lease agreement between Faxardo and Meyer documents the expansion. See "Bail à loyer, Sr. Faxardo au Sr. Meyere," Dec. 15, 1785.

55. "Avis divers," *Supplément aux Affiches américaines*, April 19, 1786, 2.

56. "Demandes," *Supplément aux Affiches américaines*, Feb. 15, 1786, 3.

57. "Suite des avis divers," *Supplément à la Feuille du Cap-Français*, Feb. 17, 1787, 2.

58. "À vendre," *Moniteur général de la partie française de Saint-Domingue*, April 22, 1792, 646.

59. For Morepas/Maurepas, see "Esclaves marrons entrés à la géole," *Supplément aux Affiches américaines/Feuille du Cap-Français*, June 20, 1789, 1.

60. "Bail de maison par le Sr. Faxardo au Sr. Gay [*sic*], devant M. Tach, le 24 mai 1787," Nov. 13, 1826, 10 DPPC 250, file 49: Indemnité Faxardo, ANOM; "Bail à loyer, le Sr. Faxardo au Sr. Gaye," May 24, 1787, 7 DPPC 7431, ANOM; "Avis divers," *Feuille du Cap-Français/Supplément aux Affiches américaines*, June 2, 1787, 3.

61. "Dissolution de société entre le Sr. Doubrere et du Sieur Gaye et la demoiselle Mongeon," Nov. 27, 1784, 7 DPPC 6164, ANOM.

62. "Esclaves en marronage," *Supplément aux Affiches américaines*, Feb. 16, 1785, 6.

63. "Esclaves marrons entrés à la géôle," *Feuille du Cap-Français/Supplément aux Affiches américaines*, July 14, 1787, 2; "À vendre," *Supplément aux Affiches américaines*, Dec. 14, 1785, 5.

64. "Avis divers," *Moniteur général de la partie française de Saint-Domingue*, Dec. 24, 1792, 152.

65. "Départs pour la Nouvelle Angleterre," *Affiches américaines*, July 11, 1793, 8.

66. Last will and testament of Alexandre (Abraham) Faxardo, "Extrait des minutes du Greffe du Tribunal civil du département du nord," July 23, 1794, 7 DPPC 7508, folder 31, ANOM; "8 fructidor an 7ème [Aug. 25, 1799], mise en possession du Citoyen Grenier des emplacements et maisons dont deux incendiées, et une intacte, reservée, rues Francaises sous les numéros 786, 787, 788, appartenant à Citoyenne Faxardo, femme Pereire," Aug. 25, 1799, 10 DPPC 109, folder Fexardo, ANOM.

67. "Au Cap-Français, le vingt quatre thermidor an 7 [Aug. 11, 1799], Faxardo maisons numéros 786, 787 et 788," Aug. 11, 1799, 10 DPPC 109, ANOM; "8 fructidor an 7ème [Aug. 25, 1799], mise en possession du Citoyen Grenier des emplacements et maisons dont deux incendiées, et une intacte, reservée, rues Francaises sous les numéros 786, 787, 788, appartenant à Citoyenne Faxardo, femme Pereire," Aug. 25, 1799, 10 DPPC 109, ANOM; "Bail à loyer, Sr. Faxardo au Srs. Monier et Meyere," July 17, 1784, 7 DPPC 7428, ANOM.

68. For Lagrange's many plantations, see "État des capés entrés dans le Magasin général du Gouvernement à la Petite-Anse, depuis le 16 du mois de fructidor, an onze, jusqu'au 22 dudit inclusivement," *Gazette officielle de Saint-Domingue*, Sept. 21, 1803, 207, and similar tables listing his full name in the *Gazette officielle de Saint-Domingue*, Sept. 3, 1803, 287, and Sept. 14, 1803, 299. For LeGrand's petition, see "No. 481 Acte de la présentation renvoyons le petitionnaire à l'éxécution des articles premier et second de l'arrêté du général en chef le 26 pluviôse dernier et pour l'éxécution du second commettons les citoyens Artaud et Dardan, au Cap 1 germinal an 10," March 22, 1802, 10 DPPC 109, ANOM.

69. "Cartulaire des maisons de la ville du Cap," 1803, Papiers Bougainville, 135AP/4, ANF; *État détaillé par la commission chargée de répartir l'indemnité attribuée aux anciens colons de Saint-Domingue, en exécution de la loi du 30 avril 1826*, esclavage-indemnites.fr.

70. "No. 481 Acte de la présentation."

71. In the same judgment, she received another, much larger one of 16,250 francs for her brother's former coffee plantation in Borgne, as his universal heir. See *État détaillé par la commission chargée de répartir l'indemnité attribuée aux anciens colons de Saint-Domingue.*

72. "Avis divers," *Feuille du Cap-Français; Supplément aux Affiches américaines*, June 16, 1787, 2.

73. "Avis divers," *Supplément aux Affiches américaines/Feuille du Cap-Français*, Jan. 27, 1790, 2.

74. See, for example, "Avis divers," *Moniteur général de la partie française de Saint-Domingue*, March 14, 1792, 490.

75. See Hanneton, shop owner, in "Avis divers," *Supplément aux Affiches américaines/Feuille du Cap-Français*, April 10, 1790, 2; the abbé Bonamici in "Départs," *Supplément à la Feuille du Cap-Français*, March 15, 1788, 2; for apothecaries, see Batilliot frères in "Avis divers," *Supplément aux Affiches américaines*, April 26, 1786, 2; for businessmen, see M. de Nard, in "À vendre,"

NOTES

Supplément aux Affiches américaines, April 19, 1788, 4; for human traffickers, see notice for "a young and beautiful quadroon," being sold by M. Hallai, leather merchant, no. 789 rue Espagnole, next to the Hotel de la Couronne, in "Biens et effets à vendre," *Supplément aux Affiches américaines/Feuille du Cap-Français,* Sept. 30, 1789, 2.

76. "Spectacle," *Affiches américaines,* Sept.11, 1781, 1; for segregation and enslaved people at the theater, see "Amérique. S. Domingue," *Affiches américaines,* April 23, 1766, 145–46; and Julia Prest, *Public Theatre and the Enslaved People of Colonial Saint-Domingue* (Cham, Switzerland: Palgrave Macmillan, 2023), 12.

77. "Avis divers," *Supplément aux Affiches américaines/Feuille du Cap-Français,* June 23, 1790, 2; "Avis divers," *Supplément aux Affiches américaines/Feuille du Cap-Français,* July 3, 1790, 2.

78. Reprinted in Thomas Southey, "Courier, July 26th; November 15, 1815, American Papers," *Chronological History of the West Indies,* 3 vols (London: Longman, Rees, Orme, Brown, and Greene, 1827), 3:590; "Christophe, Late Emperor of Hayti," *Blackwood's Edinburgh Magazine,* Aug.–Dec. 1821, 590.

79. For a convent and a dentist, see "Avis divers," *Affiches américaines,* March 19, 1766, 107. For another dentist, see notice concerning Sieur Moretti from Aix-en-Provence offering his services and residing with M. Tastet, saddler, rue Espagnole, vis-à-vis the Couronne hotel in "Avis divers," *Supplément aux Affiches américaines,* Jan. 2, 1790, 1. For the veterinary school, see "Etablissement vétérinaire," *Supplément aux Affiches américaines/Feuille du Cap-Français,* June 19, 1790, 2; for the goldsmith Barrème, see "Suite des avis divers," *Supplément aux Affiches américaines,* Feb. 8, 1786, 5; for the sale of "a very beautiful dye factory, located on Rue Espagnole, consisting of four large boilers," see "À vendre," *Supplément aux Affiches américaines,* July 19, 1786, 3; for the boarding school, see "Avis divers," *Supplément aux Affiches américaines,* Feb. 13, 1782, 1.

80. *Almanach royal d'Hayti pour l'année 1814,* 5; Louis, *Marie-Louise d'Haïti,* 2–4.

81. See the folder for Bédou, 10 DPPC 91, ANOM.

82. Mollien, *Haïti ou Saint-Domingue,* 2:64–65.

83. Document transcribed and reprinted in Georges Servant, "Ferdinand Christophe, fils du roi d'Haïti, en France," *Revue de l'histoire des colonies françaises,* Jan. 1913, 221–22.

84. Dumesle, *Voyage,* 230–31. Saint-Rémy repeats this, including the misspelled name "Codavid," in his *Essai sur Henri-Christophe,* 4.

85. Vandercook, *Black Majesty,* 13–14; Charles E. Waterman, *Carib Queens* (Boston: Chapple, 1932), 95–96; Moran, *Black Triumvirate,* 127.

86. "Will of Maria Luisa Christophe Otherwise Marie Louise Christophe Heretofore Coidavid, Spinster of Weymouth Street Portland Place, Middlesex," July 8, 1851, PROB 11/2135/332, TNA. Transcription available at the Fanm Rebèl project: www.fanmrebel.com. In 1778, the year of the future queen's birth, but on July 19, there is a baptismal record for a Marie-Louise, "négritte, eight days old, fille naturelle of Marie-Jeanne, free Negresse." As was the custom for children born outside marriage, Marie-Louise's father was not listed. Her godfather, however, was Joseph Pevrette, "free negro," and her godmother was "Marie-Louise, Free Mulatress." Baptismal notation for "Marie-Louise, négritte," July 19, 1778, État Civil du Cap, ANOM.

87. "Bail à ferme à la maison no. 326," Dec. 31, 1794, folder Picard, 10 DPPC 138, ANOM.

88. Jean Valentin Vastey to Pierre Vastey, May 14, 1798, LQ.

89. "Saint-Domingue, Département au Nord, au nom du gouvernement Français," June 30, 1803, folder Christophe, 10 DPPC 98, ANOM. For the factory near the bell tower, see Christophe to Toussaint Louverture, n.d., 10 DPPC 98, ANOM; "Titres de propriété de Christophe pour la maison qu'il a acheté de la fabrique contigue à l'église paroissale du Cap," 10 DPPC 98, ANOM; and "Requisition . . . ," Oct. 4, 1801, 10 DPPC 98, ANOM; for the price of the property, see "Dépot d'un renovation d'un estimation d'un terrain appartenant à la fabrique par le Citoyen Dardeau . . . ," Nov. 9, 1801, 10 DPPC 98, ANOM. For the renovation, see "Marché de construction entre le général Christophe et le citoyen Faraud," Feb. 1, 1802, 10 DPPC 98, ANOM.

90. For Picard's plantation in Plaisance, see Toussaint Louverture's response to the petition of Citizen Léonard Picard, July 16, 1801, 10 DPPC 138, ANOM; for Christophe as married to Marie-Louise Malgrin, see "Vente de portion de terrein . . . ," Jan. 18, 1802, 10 DPPC 98, ANOM.

91. "Acte au notariat pour constater l'authenticité d'un terrain appartenant à la paroisse du Cap," Oct. 23, 1801, 10 DPPC 98, ANOM; "Marché de construction entre le général Christophe et le citoyen Faraud"; for the streets, see "Requisition . . . ," Oct. 4, 1801, 10 DPPC 98, ANOM.

92. "Saint-Domingue, Département au Nord . . . ," June 30, 1803; "Vente d'emplacement situé au Cap par Charles Picard pour lui et la dame Boudet et sa soeur à Mme Christophe," Sept. 29, 1801, 10 DPPC 98, ANOM; see also "Marché de construction entre le général Christophe et le citoyen Faraud."

93. For Suzanne's properties, see "Extrait des régistres du Greffe du Tribunal du département du Nord," Jan. 13, 1798, folder Toussaint Louverture 10 DPPC 149, ANOM. For Christophe's confiscated properies, see folder Christophe, 10 DPPC 98; see also "Au nom du gouvernement Français," *Gazette de Saint-Domingue*, July 6, 1803, 22.

94. "République Française, Saint-Domingue, Département du Nord, au nom du gouvernement Français," June 29, 1803, 10 DPPC 98, ANOM; Marie-Louise was referred to as the "common wife" of the "rebel Christophe, ex-general," in several other documents issued concerning the confiscation of the property she had acquired on rue Dauphine (renamed rue d'Égalité) and the Place d'Armes. See "Extrait des pièces déposées aux Archives de la Direction des Domaines Nationaux, bien séquestrés et vacants du département du Nord de Saint-Domingue," June 24, 1803, 10 DPPC 98, ANOM; and "St. Domingue, Dépt. du Nord, au nom du gouvernement française," 10 DPPC 98, ANOM.

95. "St. Domingue, Dépt. du Nord"; a public announcement for the sale of the home also appeared in the *Gazette de Saint-Domingue,* see "Au nom du gouvernement français," *Gazette de Saint-Domingue,* July 6, 1803, 22.

96. "Vente d'emplacement"; "Vente de portion de terrain par les maires et officiers . . . de la ville du Cap à la Dame Christophe," Jan. 18, 1802, 10 DPPC 98, ANOM; Ministère de Finances, *État détaillé des liquidations opérées à l'époque du 1er janvier 1828, par la commission chargée de répartir, l'indemnité attribuée aux anciens colons de Saint-Domingue, en exécution de la loi du 30 avril 1826 et conformément aux dispositions de l'ordonnance du mai suivant* (Paris: Imprimerie Royale, 1828), 98.

97. Benoît Joachim, "L'indemnité coloniale de Saint-Domingue et la question des rapatriés," *Revue historique* 246, no. 2 (Oct.–Dec. 1971): 359–76.

98. "Vente d'emplacement"; for the opulent plans for the home and Faraud's involvement, see "Marché de construction."

99. *Almanach royal d'Hayti pour l'année 1814*, 5.

100. Vastey, *Essai*, 160–61.

101. "Extrait des régistres du controle de la marine du Cap. Coidavis chef de brigade et commandant militaire au Fort Bellair [*sic*] et Dépendances aux commissaires délégués par le gouvernement français aux Isles sous le vent," Oct. 2, 1796, folder Coidavis, 10 DPPC 99, ANOM; and for his children, see Nadine and Vincent Coidavis to the Commission des Domaines Nationaux de Saint-Domingue, Jan. 11, 1800, 10 DPPC 99, ANOM. For Coidavid as a Black officer, see "Rapport du Général Hédouville, agent particulier du Directoire à St. Domingue, au Directoire Exécutif," AB/XIX/5002, ANF: ("Citoyen Coidavid (noir), commandant le fort Bélair qui domine la ville").

102. "Coidavie, Jacques. Extrait des régistres du controle de la marine du Cap;" "État de service militaire présenté au Général Hédouville, agent du Directoire française," COL E 86, ANOM.

103. "Extrait des régistres . . . Coidavis chef de brigade"; "Arrêté de la commission l'an 4 qui accorde au Citoyen Coidavid la concession provisoire du terrain en question," 10 DPPC 99, ANOM.

104. Marriage notation for Jacques Coidavi [*sic*] and Marie-Jeanne, Oct. 30, 1783, État civil du Cap, ANOM; *Cadastre des maisons de la ville du Cap*, ANOM, 5 DPPC 49. For Belley, see chapter two in Christine Levecq, *Black Cosmopolitans: Race, Religion, and Republicanism in an Age of Revolution* (Charlottesville; University of Virginia Press, 2020), 75–159.

105. The family's last name is spelled erroneously on this baptismal record as "Codavy." Baptismal notation for Noël Codavy, Jan. 7, 1784, État civil du Cap, ANOM.

106. *Almanach royal d'Hayti pour l'année 1814*, 5.

107. Cheesman, *Armorial of Haiti*, 26.

108. *Almanach royal d'Hayti pour l'année 1817, quatorzième de l'indépendance, et la sixième du règne de Sa Majesté* (Cap-Henry: P. Roux, 1817), 27; Julien Prévost, *Relation des glorieux événemens qui ont porté Leurs Majestés Royales sur le trône d'Hayti; suivie de l'histoire du couronnement et du sacre du roi Henry 1er, et de la reine Marie-Louise* (Cap-Henry: P. Roux, 1811), 37.

109. "Nécrologie," *Gazette royale d'Hayti*, Sept. 27, 1818, 1–2.

110. "Will of Maria Luisa Christophe."

111. Death notation for Marie Rose Cléomène Ménard, March 1, 1850, État civil d'Haïti, AGH.

112. "Will of Maria Luisa Christophe."

113. "Nadine et Vincent Coidavis à la Commission des domaines nationaux de St. Domingue," Jan. 11, 1800, 10 DPPC 99, ANOM.

114. *Almanach de Saint-Domingue pour l'année 1765* (Cap-Français: Chez Marie, 1765), 66. See also Romain, *Noms de lieux d'époque colonial en Haïti*, 54–55.

115. Narcisse to Members of the Commission of National Domains, May 29, 1800, folder Clérisse, 10 DPPC 95, ANOM; Jacques de Cauna, "La sucrerie Clérisse à Saint-Domingue: Une histoire de famille," *Cahiers du Centre de Généalogie et d'Histoire des Isles d'Amérique* 32 (1990): 58–59.

116. "Extrait des régistres du Controle de la Marine. Bail à ferme de l'habitation Clérisse située au quartier Morin établie en sucrerie au Citoyen Coidavid," May 31, 1797, 10 DPPC 95, ANOM.

117. "Extrait . . . Coidavis chef de brigade."

118. "État général des biens nationaux et séquestrés du Département du Nord, etab-

lis en sucreries et caféyères, jardins, places à vivres, fours à chaux & guidiveries, etc. . . . dont le prix des fermes sonts payables en espèces . . ." (1797), 10 DPPC 188, ANOM; Phelipeau, *Plan de la plaine du Cap.*

119. "État général des propriétés de tout genre existantes dans la Commune des quartiers Morin . . . ," Oct. 31, 1797, 10 DPPC 189, ANOM.

120. "État général des habitations en activité du département du Cap où sont portés les sucres & sirops qu'elles ont livrés à l'administration depuis le 10 octobre 1793," April 20, 1795, 10 DPPC 189, ANOM; see also "Rapport: Le Directeur des Domaines nationaux, bien séquestrés et vacants du départments au nord de Saint-Domingue," November 24, 1802, folder Harouard, 10 DPPC 115, ANOM.

121. "État des maisons affermées par l'administration depuis le premier frimaire jusques et compris le dix neuf nivôse" (1794), 10 DPPC 188, ANOM; "État des animaux et instruments . . . provenant des habitations nationales et séquestrées, affermées . . . ," n.d., 10 DPPC 189, ANOM.

122. "État général des biens nationaux et séquestrés du Département du Nord"; "États des biens affermés dans l'Arrondissement du Cap, an 5 et an 6," 10 DPPC 188, ANOM; Phelipeau, *Plan de la plaine du Cap.*

123. "État de l'habitation Mazères que nous envoyens au Citoyen Commandant Raymond," Aug. 2, 1797, folder Mazères, 10 DPPC 167, ANOM.

124. Narcisse to Members of the Commission of National Domains, May 29, 1800.

125. Nadine et Vincent Coidavis to the Commission of National Domains, Jan. 11, 1800, 10 DPPC 99, ANOM; De Cauna, "La sucrerie Clérisse à Saint-Domingue," 58. De Cauna cites a document located in the French overseas archives (ANOM), but he mistakenly lists Marie-Louise Coidavid as Jacques Coidavid's sister.

126. Untitled note signed "Gast," Jan. 14, 1800, folder Coisdavis, 10 DPPC 99, ANOM.

127. "Rolle des habitations avoisinant la ville du Cap," 10 DPPC 188, ANOM.

128. "Will of Maria Luisa Christophe"; Supplice, *Dictionnaire,* 595–96; Aisha K. Finch, "Cécile Fatiman and Petra Carabalí, Late Eighteenth-Century Haiti and Mid-Nineteenth-Century Cuba," in *As if She Were Free: A Collective Biography of Women and Emancipation in the Americas,* ed. Erica L. Ball, Tatiana Seijas, and Terri L. Snyder (Cambridge, U.K.: Cambridge University Press, 2020), 296.

129. "Will of Maria Luisa Christophe"; for royal staff, see *Almanach royal d'Hayti, pour l'année bissextile 1820* (Sans-Souci: De L'Imprimerie Royale, 1820), 13.

130. He is listed as a witness on a marriage notation for Louis Augustin Octavien Hyppolite and Marie Rose Élisabeth Jean Joseph, Oct. 31, 1857, État civil d'Haïti, AGH.

131. Delorme, *1842 au Cap,* 2.

132. "Esclaves en maronage," *Affiches américaines,* July 29, 1767, 248.

133. "Nègres marons," *Affiches américaines,* May 7, 1766, 163.

134. "Esclaves marrons entrés à la géole," *Feuille du Cap-Français/Supplément aux Affiches américaines,* July 7, 1787, 1.

135. Baptismal notation for Joseph Malgrain, Dec. 30, 1755, État civil de Gros-Morne, ANOM.

136. Baptismal notation for Françoise Malgrin, July 26, 1758, État civil de Gros-Morne, ANOM.

137. Death notation for Suzanne Malgrain, July 19, 1760, État civil de Gros-Morne, ANOM.

138. Baptismal notation for Françoise Hortense Malgrain, Dec. 2, 1781, État civil de Gros-Morne, ANOM.

139. Table décennale de 1777 à 1788 pour la paroisse du Petit Saint-Louis-du-Sud, État civil, ANOM.

140. Alfred Nemours, *Histoire militaire de la guerre d'indépendance de Saint-Domingue*, 2 vols. (Paris: Berger-Levrault, 1925–28), 2:242.

141. *Almanach royal d'Hayti pour l'année 1814*, 5; Vastey, *Essai*, 201. For Chancy as Marie-Louise's niece, see "Suite de la Fête de S.M. la Reine," *Gazette Royale d'Hayti*, Aug. 24, 1816, 1.

142. "Oraison funèbre de feu Duc du Port-Margot," *Gazette royale d'Hayti*, Aug. 14, 1817, 3.

143. Cheesman, *Armorial of Haiti*, 28.

144. "Avis divers," *Supplément aux Affiches américaines*, April 22, 1790, 1.

145. Death notation for Jean Christophe, Feb. 20, 1774, État civil de Cavaillon, ANOM.

146. Death notation for Anne Devesus (Christophe), June 26, 1794, État civil de Cavaillon, ANOM; "État nominatif, pour l'an 11ème," 5 DPPC 50, ANOM.

147. Baptismal record for Henry Christophe, Sept. 24, 1755, État civil de Croix-des-Bouquets, ANOM.

148. "Esclaves marrons entrés à la géôle," *Affiches américaines/Feuille du Cap-Français*, July 19, 1788, 1.

149. *Almanach royal d'Hayti pour l'année 1814*, 67, 75, 95. Pierre Christophe fathered a child born on December 5, 1816, with his wife, Delphine Beausoleil. Birth notation for Jean Pierre Christophe, Nov. 11, 1817, État civil d'Hayti, AGH.

150. Baptismal notation for Jean Christophe, Feb. 21, 1785, État civil du Cap, ANOM. A twenty-seven-year-old Jean Christophe, born in 1790 and bearing the title of captain, was also listed as a witness on a birth record for Jean Marseille Casimir. Birth notation for Jean Marseille Casimir, June 22, 1817, État civil d'Haïti, AGH; for more men with the name Christophe, see *Almanach royal pour l'année 1820*, 80–81, 71, 56.

151. Courtenay, "Christophe, Late Emperor of Hayti," 549.

152. Servant, "Ferdinand Christophe, fils du roi d'Haïti, en France," 220–21.

CHAPTER 4: RISING AND FALLING WITH REVOLUTION

1. "Esclaves en maronage," *Affiches américaines*, Oct. 5, 1779, 2. For *nabot*, see Gabriel Debien, "Les esclaves des plantations Mauger à Saint-Domingue (1763–1802)," *Bulletin de la Société d'histoire de la Guadeloupe*, no. 43–44 (1980): 70n2, 89.

2. Crystal Nicole Eddins, "Runaways, Repertoires, and Repression: Marronnage and the Haitian Revolution, 1766–1791," *Journal of Haitian Studies* 25, no. 1 (2019): 4–38.

3. Jean Fouchard, *Les marrons de la liberté* (Paris: Éditions de l'École, 1972), 528; Carolyn Fick, *The Making of Haiti: The Saint-Domingue Revolution from Below* (Knoxville: University of Tennessee Press, 1990), 93; Étienne Charlier, *Aperçu sur la formation historique de la nation haïtienne* (Montreal: Dami, 2009), 102n7.

4. Boukman Dutty, quoted in Fick, *Making of Haiti*, 93.

5. See Laurent Dubois, *Avengers of the New World: The Story of the Haitian Revolution* (Cambridge, Mass.: Harvard University Press, 2004), 100–101; "The Revolutionary Philanthropist," in *Haitian Revolutionary Fictions: An Anthol-*

ogy, ed. and trans. Marlene L. Daut, Grégory Pierrot, and Marion Rohrleitner (Charlottesville: University of Virginia Press, 2022), 30–37; Antoine Dalmas, *Histoire de la révolution de Saint-Domingue, depuis le commencement des troubles, jusqu'à la prise de Jérémie et de Môle St. Nicolas par les Anglais* (Paris: Mame Frères, 1814), 1:117; Antoine Métral, *Histoire de l'insurrection des esclaves dans le nord de Saint-Domingue* (Paris, 1818), 15; Civique de Gastine, *Histoire de la Republique d'Haiti ou Saint-Domingue, l'esclavage et les colons* (Paris: Plancher, 1819), 105; and *Le philantrope révolutionnaire; ou, L'hécatombe à Haïti: Drame historique en 4 actes et en prose,* MS (Portsmouth, U.K., 1811).

6. Dumesle, *Voyage,* 85–90, 300. See also Dubois, *Avengers,* 101; and Doris Y. Kadish and Deborah Jenson, eds., *Poetry of Haitian Independence,* trans. Norman R. Shapiro (New Haven, Conn.: Yale University Press, 2015), 225.

7. Carolyn Fick, "Appendix B: Bois Caïman and the August Revolt," in *Making of Haiti,* 260–63.

8. See chapter 4 in Marlene L. Daut, *Awakening the Ashes: An Intellectual History of the Haitian Revolution* (Chapel Hill: University of North Carolina Press, 2023).

9. Reprinted in "Colonies. *Lettre de l'assemblée générale de Saint-Domingue à la municipalité des Cayes* [August 23, 1791]," *Mercure universel,* Oct. 29, 1791.

10. "Saint-Domingue: Habitation de Messieurs Harouard & héritiers Meynard de St. Michel: Compte rendu par Suzeau depuis le 23 août 1791, époque de l'insurrection des nègres jusqu'au 31 décembre 1792," folder Harouard Meynard de St. Michel, 10 DPPC 164, ANOM; DuPont de Gault to Citoyen Daure (colonial prefect of Saint-Domingue), Oct. 25, 1802, folder Harouard, 10 DPPC 115, ANOM.

11. "Une relation de l'insurrection de la plaine du nord, 8 août–8 septembre 1791," reprinted in *Un monde créole: Vivre aux Antilles au XVIIIe siècle,* ed. Annick Notter and Érick Noël (La Crèche, France: La Geste, 2017), 172–75.

12. "Une relation de l'insurrection de la plaine du nord," 175, 178.

13. "Une relation de l'insurrection de la plaine du nord," 172–75.

14. "Une relation de l'insurrection de la plaine du nord," 175–76.

15. A pseudoscientific term for a person with a "pure" Black parent and a "mulatto," or half-black, half-white parent. See Marlene L. Daut, *Tropics of Haiti: Race and the Literary History of the Haitian Revolution in the Atlantic World* (Liverpool: Liverpool University Press, 2015), 89–90.

16. "Une relation de l'insurrection de la plaine du nord," 176–78.

17. Laurent François Le Noir de Rouvray to Madame la Comtesse de Lostanges, Dec. 6–7, 1791, reprinted in *Une correspondance familiale au temps des troubles de Saint-Domingue: Lettres du Marquis et de la Marquise de Rouvray à leur fille, Saint-Domingue–États-Unis,* ed. M. E. McIntosh and B. C. Weber (Paris: Société de l'Histoire des Colonies Françaises/Librairie La Larose, 1959), 39.

18. "Une relation de l'insurrection de la plaine du nord," 172.

19. In contrast, enslaved men who fought with the colonists or saved their lives sometimes achieved liberty, as was the case with a man suggestively named Christophe who saved de Rouvray's life "in pursuit of the brigands," and whose liberty de Rouvray subsequently petitioned successfully. "Procès-Verbal du 23 septembre," *Assemblée Générale de la partie de Saint-Domingue. Procès-Verbaux des séances et Journal des débats,* no. 39 (Sept. 27, 1791), 172, CO 71/22, TNA. See also the case of the enslaved man named Bazile in the same issue and that of another whose name was not given in "Procès-Verbal du 17 septembre au matin," *Assemblée Générale,* 157.

20. "Saint-Domingue: Habitation de Messieurs Harouard & héritiers Meynard de St. Michel"; "Une relation de l'insurrection de la plaine du nord," 176, 178.
21. "Une relation de l'insurrection de la plaine du nord," 176, 178.
22. "Saint-Domingue: Habitation de Messieurs Harouard & héritiers Meynard de St. Michel."
23. "Une relation de l'insurrection de la plaine du nord," 179.
24. *Le courrier extraordinaire, ou, Le premier arrivé,* Oct. 30, 1791, 1.
25. *Histoire des desastres de Saint-Domingue, précédée d'un tableau du régime et des progrès de cette colonie, depuis sa fondation, jusqu'à l'époque de la Revolution française* (Paris: Garnery, 1795), 212.
26. Reprinted in *Une correspondance familiale au temps des troubles de Saint-Domingue,* 102–103.
27. Fick, *The Making of Haiti,* 80–85, 121–22.
28. "The National Assembly Law on the Colonies with an Explanation of the Reasons That Have Determined Its Content, 1791," in *Slave Revolution in the Caribbean, 1789–1804: A Brief History with Documents,* ed. Laurent Dubois and John D. Garrigus (New York: Bedford St. Martin's, 2017), 70–71; Fick, *The Making of Haiti,* 84; Daut, *Awakening the Ashes,* 83–87.
29. Saint-Rémy, *Pétion et Haïti,* 1:106.
30. "Extrait de la séance du 16," *Moniteur général de la partie française de Saint-Domingue,* Dec. 22, 1791, 154–55.
31. [Charles Yves] Cousin d'Avallon, *Histoire de Toussaint-Louverture chef des noirs insurgés de Saint-Domingue; Précédée d'un coup d'oeil politique sur cette colonie, et suivie d'anecdotes et faits particuliers concernant ce chef des noirs, et les agens directoriaux envoyés dans cette partie du Nouveau-Monde, pendant le cours de la révolution* (Paris: Pillot, Frères, 1802), 19–20n2; Aimé Césaire, *Toussaint Louverture: La Révolution française et le problème colonial* (Paris: Présence Africaine, 1961), 179; Fouchard, *Les marrons de la liberté,* 415; Daut, *Awakening the Ashes,* 112–13.
32. Historically, members of a sultan's guard.
33. "Discours prononcé à l'Assemblée générale de St. Domingue par M. Roume l'un des commissaires nationaux le 3 décembre 1791"; "Discours de M. de Saint-Léger," *Moniteur général de la partie française de Saint-Domingue,* Dec. 4, 1791, 78–80.
34. "Assemblée générale de la partie française de St-Domingue, extrait de la séance du 19, au matin," *Moniteur général de la partie française de Saint-Domingue,* Nov. 21, 1791, 39.
35. "Assemblée générale de la partie française de St-Domingue, suite de la séance du 19, au soir," *Moniteur général de la partie française de Saint-Domingue,* Nov. 23, 1791, 45.
36. "Assemblée générale de la partie française de St-Domingue, présidence de M. de Mun, suite de la séance du 8," *Moniteur général de la partie française de Saint-Domingue,* Dec. 16, 1791, 130.
37. "Avis divers," *Moniteur général de la partie française de Saint-Domingue,* Dec. 24, 1792, 73.
38. Jean François, Biassou, et al. to the Civil Commissioners, Dec. 12, 1791, reprinted and translated in *The Haitian Revolution: A Documentary History,* ed. David Geggus (Indianapolis: Hackett Publishing Company, 2014), 87–88.
39. "Assemblée coloniale de la partie française de St-Domingue, présidence de M. de Favaranges, extrait de la séance du 21," *Moniteur général de la partie française de Saint-Domingue.* Dec. 27, 1791, 174–75.

40. "The Negotiations Break Down," in *The Haitian Revolution: A Documentary History*, ed. David Geggus (Indianapolis: Hackett, 2014), 89.
41. Jean François, Biassou, et al. to the Civil Commissioners, Dec. 12, 1791.
42. Saint-Rémy, *Pétion et Haïti*, 1:156–57.
43. "Première mission de Sonthonax à St. Domingue," AF/III/210, ANF.
44. Légér-Félicité Sonthonax, "Émancipation des esclaves: proclamation du 29 août 1793," Digithèque MJP, https://mjp.univ-perp.fr/constit/ht1793.htm; Étienne Polverel, "Proclamation relative à l'émancipation des esclaves appartenant à l'État dans la province de l'Ouest, à l'émancipation volontaire de leurs esclaves par les propriétaires et à la promesse de la liberté Générale," reprinted in "Aux origines de l'abolition de l'esclavage," in *Revue d'histoire des colonies*, 36, no. 127–128 (troisième et quatrième Trimestres, 1949): 364; Polverel, "Proclamation [relative à l'émancipation des esclaves appartenant à l'État dans la province Sud]," reprinted in "Aux origines de l'abolition de l'esclavage," in *Revue d'histoire des colonies*, 36, no. 127–128 (troisième et quatrième Trimestres, 1949): 369.
45. *Journal des révolutions de la partie française de Saint-Domingue, dédié à la république du 20 septembre 1792*, March 28, 1793, 1, D/XXI/115, ANF, italics in original.
46. Polverel and Sonthonax, "Proclamation," July 11, 1793 (Cap-Français: P. Roux, 1793), repository.library.brown.edu; *Almanach royal d'Haïti pour l'année 1814*, 5.
47. Saint-Rémy, *Pétion et Haïti*, 1:180.
48. Saint-Rémy, *Pétion et Haïti*, 1:193–94.
49. Saint-Rémy, *Pétion et Haïti*, 1:194–95, quote from 195.
50. On a ship with two sails, the mizzenmast is the second and lower of the two. Saint-Rémy, *Pétion et Haïti*, 1:195–97, quotation from 197.
51. Saint-Rémy, *Pétion et Haïti*, 198–99; Ch. Warin, "Plan de la ville du Cap Français dans l'isle de Saint Domingue, sur lequel sont marqués en teinte noire les ravages du premier incendie; et en rouge les islets, parties de l'islets, edifices &c qui existent encore. Le 21 juin," BNF, gallica.bnf.fr.
52. Jeremy Popkin, *You Are All Free: The Haitian Revolution and the Abolition of Slavery* (Chicago: University of Chicago Press, 2010), 194.
53. Saint-Rémy, *Pétion et Haïti*, 4:151.
54. For Denard's arrest, see "Commission nationale-civile . . . Ordonnons que Denard sera arrêté et conduit en prison," June 13, 1793, D/XXV/7, ANF; for Christophe's letter, see "No. 41. Primata. St. Domingue, Commission civile, lettre du citoyen Christophe aux Commissaires civiles," June 19, 1793, COL CC9 A8, ANOM.
55. Handwritten note ordering the head of police to seize Denard's papers, June 19, 1793, D/XXV/7, ANF.
56. Handwritten orders from the Civil Commissioners, June 20, 1793, D/XXV/7, ANF.
57. Popkin, *You Are All Free*, 15.
58. Saint-Rémy, *Pétion et Haïti*, 1:198–99.
59. Biassou did evidently meet with the commissioners on June 22, 1793, per a direct order from Sonthonax and Polverel authorizing him to be escorted to Camp Bréda "with every bit of security." See "Commission nationale-civile . . . Mettons sous la sauve garde . . . le commandant Bisassou," June 22, 1793, D/XXV/7, ANF.
60. See Sonthonax and Polverel's order to Jean-Louis Villate, and Martial Besse, authorizing them to undertake any "military operations that they judge appro-

priate for the reduction of the rebels in Cap": Decree from the Commission Nationale-Civile, June 22, 1793, D/XXV/7, ANF.

61. Saint-Rémy, *Pétion et Haïti*, 1:199–200.

62. Handwritten order from Civil Commissioners to Besse and Léveillé, June 23, 1793; document signed by Sonthonax promoting Martial Besse to commander of Terrier-Rouge, June 23, 1793, D/XXV/7, ANF.

63. Handwritten orders from the Civil Commissioners, June 20, 1793, D/XXV/7, ANF. See also Popkin, *You Are All Free*, 194. It is in fact Christophe's ability not just to sign his name but to write, in general, that permits us to distinguish him in this instance from Christophe Mornet, a man of color who previously fought at the Battle of Savannah like him but who, unlike our Christophe, could not sign his name at the time that he served as a witness to Roume's marriage in February 1799. Christophe's literacy also helps distinguish him from another Black inhabitant of the colony bearing the name Citizen Christophe. He was the manager of the Héricourt sugar plantation leased by Toussaint Louverture before his arrest, but he could not sign his name either, according to the sequestration documents issued by the French government in June 1802, when they seized all Louverture's holdings. "Extrait des registres des actes de mariage de la commune et canton du Port-Républicain," Feb. 19, 1799, CO 23/38, TNA; "Extrait des procès verbaux dressés par Corneille, sur les habitations du citoyen Toussaint Louverture, dans différents quartiers du département du nord," June 12, 1802, file Toussaint Louverture, 10 DPPC 149, ANOM.

64. Civil Commissioners to Vernet, June 24, 1793, D/XXV/7, ANF.

65. "Commission nationale-civile . . . Déclarons libres les dix neuf esclaves . . . ," handwritten note from the commissioners concerning liberation of Charles, Antoine, Izac, and Janitte, enslaved on the habitation Poque, n.d., D/XXV/7, ANF.

66. General Cezar [*sic*] Galbaud to General Galbaud (his brother), Aug. 28, 1793, box 29, Rochambeau Papers, University of Florida Libraries. The French commissioners ordered César Galbaud's arrest on June 13, 1793. See "Ordonnons que César Galbaud sera arrêté," June 13, 1793, D/XXV/7, ANF.

67. Handwritten note from the Civil Commissioners at Camp Bréda promoting Pacot and authorizing arming of slaves, June 25, 1793, D/XXV/7, ANF.

68. Étienne Polverel and Léger-Félicité Sonthonax, "Proclamation," July 2, 1793, CO 23/32, TNA.

69. "Émancipation des esclaves. Proclamation du 29 août 1793."

70. Beaubrun Ardouin, *Études sur l'histoire d'Haïti* (Paris: Dezobry et E. Magdeleine, 1853), 2:224–64; Polverel, "Proclamation relative à l'émancipation des esclaves apparentant à l'état dans la province de l'ouest."

71. Reprinted in Geggus, *Haitian Revolution: A Documentary History*, 125–26.

72. Toussaint Louverture, *Extrait du rapport adressé au Directoire exécutif par le citoyen Toussaint Louverture, général en chef des forces de la république française à Saint-Domingue*, Sept. 4, 1797, 29, BNF.

73. *Affiches américaines*, July 11, 1793, 1–4.

74. Handwritten declaration signed by Sonthonax, Oct. 10, 1793, D/XXV/12, ANF. Many thanks to Julia Gaffield for sharing this document.

75. Probably Claude Domergue, white planter and member of the provincial assembly of Saint-Domingue for the south; and Jacques Boyé, a white French colonist who was commandant de la place in Port-au-Prince in 1793 and who later served as a diplomat for President Jean-Pierre Boyer. For Boyé, see Beaubrun Ardouin, *Études sur l'histoire d'Haïti* (Paris: Dezobry et E. Magdeleine, 1853), 2:453; for

Domergue, see "Assemblée générale de la partie française de Saint-Domingue, extrait de la séance du 19," Nov. 21, 1791, 26; and "Colons de Saint-Domingue: Anciens propriétaires (1789)-D," in *Domingino-Verlag*, ed. Olivier Gliech, www .domingino.de.

76. Christophe to Citizen Magistrate of Port-au-Prince, Dec. 4, 1793, Fondo Campori dalla Biblioteca Estense Universitaria, Italy. Thanks to Miriam Franchina for sharing this document.

77. "Decret de la Convention nationale, du seizième jour de pluviôse, l'an deuxième de la République française une et indivisible," Feb. 4, 1794, www.assemblee -nationale.fr/histoire/esclavage/d%C3%A9cret_1794.pdf.

78. For Louverture, see David Geggus, *Haitian Revolutionary Studies* (Bloomington: Indiana University Press, 2002), 180; Hazareesingh, *Black Spartacus*, 66; for Biassou, see Erica Johnson, "Becoming Spanish in Florida: Georges Biassou and His 'Family'" in St. Augustine," *Journal of Transnational American Studies* 8, no. 1 (2017): 1.

79. Geggus, *Haitian Revolutionary Studies*, 182–84.

80. "Bail à ferme à la maison no. 326," Dec. 31, 1794, 10 DPPC 138, ANOM.

81. Cheesman, *Armorial of Haiti*, 140.

82. For chief engineer in the colony, see Faraud's title as listed in "Fexardo: Maison numéro 787 rue du Chantier au Cap reconstruction . . . ," May 6, 1801, 10 DPPC 109, ANOM. For the coat of arms, see Cheesman, *Armorial of Haiti*, 140; for his first name as Alexandre, see "État nominatif des contribuables de la ville du Cap français," 5 DPPC 50, ANOM.

83. "Bail à ferme à la maison no. 326."

84. "Procès verbal de mise en possession de la Salle de Spectacle, du 2 frimaire an 7e," folder Salle de Spectacle, 10 DPPC 146, ANOM.

85. "Plan de l'état actuel de la ville du Cap, servant à indiquer les progrès de ses reconstuctions," ca. 1800, BNF, gallica.bnf.fr.

86. "No. 481 Acte de la présentation renvoyons le pétitionnaire à l'éxécution des articles premier et second de l'arrêté du général en chef le 26 pluviôse dernier et pour l'éxécution du second commettons les citoyens Artaud et Dardan, au Cap 1 germinal an 10," March 22, 1802, folder Faxardo, 10 DPPC 109, ANOM. See also "État des maisons reconstruites dans la ville du Cap dont le temps de la jouissance accordé aux reconstructions . . . encore sur le coup de séquestre ont été affermées pour compte de la république par l'administration . . . ," 10 DPPC 188, ANOM; and "État nominatif des contribuables de la ville du Cap français."

87. "État des maisons affermé par l'administration depuis le premier frimaire, jusque et compris le 19 nivôse an III," Jan. 8, 1795, 10 DPPC 188, ANOM; for the structure not having been built, see "Plan de l'état actuel de la ville du Cap, servant à indiquer les progrès de ses reconstuctions."

88. Cathcart to Maitland, Nov. 26, 1799, CO 245/1, TNA.

89. For the Chabanon and Butler plantations in Limonade as leased by Christophe, see "État de situation des sucreries, affermées de ce quartier avec l'administration du 20 du mois de frimaire an 5, époque des beaux jusqu'à ce jour," 10 DPPC 188, ANOM. For the St. Michel plantation, see "État général des propriétés de tous genres existantes dans la commune des Quartier Morin . . . tant celles qui ont été séquestrées, que celles qui ont été relevées du séquestre dont les propriétaires sont présents ou représentés par des fondés des pouvoirs, et leur situation actuelle," 10 DPPC 188, ANOM.

90. "Extrait des minutes de la municipalité de la ville & banlieue du Cap. 1793.

Procès verbal de séquestre de 1. Emplacement & Guildive à l'habitation St. Michel," 10 DPPC 99, ANOM.

91. See the file marked "St. Michel, Tardy, et plusieurs autres," 10 DPPC 99, ANOM.

92. For Prioleau as American merchant, see "Offre des particuliers pour les habitations sucreries," 1797, 10 DPPC 167, ANOM; for the lease, see "État des habitations du département du nord de Saint-Domingue, établies en sucreries et affermées jusqu'à ce jour, 2 ventôse an 5," Feb. 20, 1797, 10 DPPC 189, ANOM.

93. "Mise en possession. Habitation Destruilles," folder Meneust, 10 DPPC 130, ANOM.

94. "Mise en possession. Habitation Destruilles." See also "État des habitations du département du nord de Saint-Domingue."

95. "État des habitations du département du nord de Saint-Domingue."

96. "Extrait du régistre des déliberations de l'agence Directoire exécutif à Saint-Domingue," Sept. 8, 1798, folder Meneust, 10 DPPC 130, ANOM.

97. Leclerc to Decrès, Feb. 15, 1802, in Paul Roussier, ed. *Lettres du général Leclerc, commandant en chef de l'armée de Saint Domingue en 1802* (Paris: Société de l'histoire des colonies françaises, Ernest Leroux, 1937), 91–92. For Granier as commandant, see Christophe to Commander Vilton, April 10, 1802 , in Bouvet de Cressé, *Histoire de la catastrophe de Saint-Domingue par J. Chanlatte, avec la correspondence des généraux Leclerc (beau-frère de Bonaparte), Henry-Christophe (depuis roi d'Haïti), Hardy, Vilton, etc., certifiée conforme aux originaux déposés aux archives, par le lieutenant général Rouanez jeune, secrétaire d'état, publiés par A. J. B. Bouvet de Cressé* (Paris: Librairie de Peytieux, 1824), 140.

98. Bonnet, *Souvenirs historiques,* 284n2.

99. Christophe to Vilton, April 10, 1802; for Vilton as commandant of Quartier-Morin, see "Quartier Morin. Habitation Darance," Jan. 19, 1800, 10 DPPC 132, ANOM; For Vilton's background, see Dumesle, *Voyage,* 243.

100. Vilton to Christophe, April 20, 1802, in Bouvet de Créssé, *Histoire de la catastrophe de Saint-Domingue,* 148–49; Bonnet, *Souvenirs historiques,* 284n2.

101. Christophe to Vilton, April 22, 1802, in Bouvet de Cressé, *Histoire de la catastrophe de Saint-Domingue,* 152.

102. Christophe to Vilton, April 10, 1802, in Bouvet de Cressé, *Histoire de la catastrophe de Saint-Domingue,* 144.

103. "État général des habitations en activité du département du Cap, où sont portés les sucres, sirops quelles ont livrés à l'administration, depuis le 10 octobre 1793 jusqu'au 30 germinal de l'an 3 de la république, une et indivisible," 10 DPPC 189, ANOM. For the cultivators on the Saint-Michel plantation, see "Extrait des minutes de la municipalité de la ville & banlieue du Cap. Inventaire de l'habitation Saint-Michel," folder St. Michel/Harouard, 10 DPPC 146, ANOM.

104. "Bail à ferme de l'habitation St. Michel, sise en quartier Morin au citoyen Henri Christophe, chef de brigade, commandant la Petite-Anse," June 2, 1797, folder St. Michel/Harouard, 10 DPPC 146, ANOM.

105. "Bail à ferme de l'habitation Butler, sucrerie, située au Bois de Lance, quartier de Limonade, passé au Citoyen Henry Christophe, chef de brigade"; for Noël, see "Mise en possession de l'habitation Butler sucrerie au Citoyen Christophe, du 11 fructidor an 5ème. Bois de Lance," folder Buclair, 10 DPPC 92, ANOM.

106. "Bureau de recettes des domaines nationales," April 8, 1800, folder Buclair, 10 DPPC 92, ANOM; for Grenier as "gérant," see "État supplémentaire des habitations sucrerie de la partie du nord de St. Domingue, qui ont été affermée paiables [*sic*] en sucre depuis le 7 thermidor, époque de la clôture du tableau général," Sept. 14, 1797, 10 DPPC 189, ANOM.

107. For Christophe's promotion to inspector, see Military Index, CC9B 5–7, ANF. Thanks to Julia Gaffield for sharing this document. "État de l'habitation Mazère [sic] que nous envoyons au citoyen Commissaire Raymond, nous Jacques Coidavid et Jean Louis Narcisse, tous les deux fermiers de la ditte habitation et conformement à la lettre d'invitation que nous avons reçu du citoyen Henry Christophe, chef de brigade et inspecteur," folder Mazère, 10 DPPC 167, ANOM.

108. Christophe to Raimond, Aug. 12, 1797, folder Buclair, 10 DPPC 92, ANOM.

109. Christophe to Raimond, Nov. 29, 1797, folder St. Michel/Harouard, 10 DPPC 146, ANOM.

110. Saint-Rémy, *Pétion et Haïti*, 4:152.

111. "État des derniers livrées par les différents fermiers des sucreries situées dans ce quartier à valoir et au prix . . . ," May 14, 1799, 10 DPPC 189, ANOM.

112. Christophe to Louverture, Aug. 22, 1801, folder Buclair, 10 DPPC 92, ANOM.

113. "Limonade. Habitation Buclair [sic]. Sucrerie," Aug. 26, 1801, folder Buclair, 10 DPPC 92, ANOM.

114. "Offre des particuliers pour les habitations sucrerie," 10 DPPC 167; for Christophe's promotion, see Military Index, CC9B 5–7, ANF.

115. Military Index.

116. "Bail à ferme de l'habitation St. Michel, sise au Quartier Morin au Citoyen Henri Christophe, chef de brigade, commandant de la Petite Anse," 10 DPPC 146, ANOM.

117. Christophe to Raimond, Nov. 29, 1797. On July 1, 1797, Christophe was still being referred to as chef de brigade and commandant de la Petite-Anse. See "Nous, Jean Marie Colleau, officier d'administration chargé du service à la Petite Anse, stipulant pour et au nom de la république . . . ," July 1, 1797, folder St. Michel/Harouard, 10 DPPC 146, ANOM.

118. For General Léveillé as commander of Cap, see Christian Schneider, "Le colonel Vincent, officier du génie à Saint-Domingue," *Annales historiques de la Révolution française* 329, no. 3 (2002): 102; for Toussaint on Léveillé and desire to promote Christophe, see Louverture to the Minister of the Marine and Colonies, March 24, 1799, CO/245/2, TNA. For Christophe's rank, see "Je soussigne, Commissaire de Marine, Receveur Principale des Domaines nationaux . . . ," April 8, 1799, folder St. Michel/Harouard, 10 DPPC 146, ANOM.

119. "Bail à ferme d'un bâtiment dépendant de l'habitation St. Michel située à la Petite Ance [sic], affermée au Citoyen Henry Christophe"; see also Christophe to Jolinger, June 21, 1797, folder St. Michel/Harouard, 10 DPPC 146, ANOM.

120. Lease renewal for Henry Christophe with respect to St. Michel sugar plantation as represented by Citoyen Granier, Dec. 10, 1799; for the sugar, see "Recette des domaines," Nov. 4, 1799, folder St. Michel/Harouard, 10 DPPC 146, ANOM.

121. "Toussaint Louverture, général en chef de l'armée de Saint-Domingue, vu l'aviso . . . ," July 8, 1801; for Christophe as general, see Louverture to Raimond, June 30, 1801, folder St. Michel/Harouard, 10 DPPC 146, ANOM.

122. "Aujourd'hui est comparu par devant le notaires publics du Cap Français . . . ," July 28, 1801, folder Harouard, 10 DPPC 115, ANOM.

123. [Malemond], Le Directeur des Domaines Nationaux, Biens Séquestrés et vacants du Département du Nord de Saint-Domingue, Report, Nov. 15, 1802; for the previous price of the rents, see DuPont de Gault to Daure, Oct. 25, 1802, folder Harouard, 10 DPPC 115, ANOM.

124. DuPont de Gault to Daure, Oct. 25, 1802.

125. "Le Chef d'Administration de la Marine et des Colonies, Sous-Préfet du Départment du Nord," Jan. 21, 1803"; Le Ministre de la Marine et des Colonies certifie à qui il appartiendra que la citoyenne Marie-Anne . . . ," June 27, 1800; "Depot de la procuration de Veuve Butler, femme divorcée Cormier par le citoyen Dupont de Gault," Dec. 12, 1802, folder Butler, 10 DPPC 90, ANOM.

126. "L'an cinquième de la République française . . . ," May 5, 1797; Moyse to the administrators of National Domains of Saint-Domingue, May 14, 1800, folder Bréda, 10 DPPC 91, ANOM.

127. The child over whom Christophe became guardian mysteriously disappears from mentions of Christophe's life after this. For Moyse's plantations and Christophe's guardianship over the child, see "Expédition du séquestre de l'habitation de ci-devant Général Moyse, à Porto-Plata," folder Moyse, May 10, 1802. For Moyse's residence, see "Procès verbal d'apposition de séquestre sur la maison Moyse, sise Quai St. Louis," Jan. 6, 1803, folder Moyse, 10 DPPC 131, ANOM.

128. Bill of sale to Suzanne Louverture, April 12, 1799; for Marie-Thérèse Coyotte as "femme de confiance," see "Procès-verbal d'apposition . . . de l'habitation de l'ex-général Toussaint, Canton d'Ennery," folder Toussaint Louverture, 10 DPPC 149, ANOM.

CHAPTER 5: COMPLICATED VICTORIES

1. "Serment prise par le Chef de Brigade Maurepas, à sa promotion du grade de général de brigade," June 8, 1801; see also the promotion certificate for Morpas, issued June 8, 1801, folder Morpas, 10 DPPC 131, ANOM. Louverture wrote to Bonaparte on February 10, 1801, to ask the first consul to sanction the promotions to brigadier general of Morpas, Christophe, Paul Louverture, and Charles Belair. See Louverture to Bonaparte, in Joseph Élisée Peyre-Ferry, *Journal des opérations militaires de l'armée française pendant les années 1802 et 1803 sous les ordres des capitaines-généraux Leclerc et Rochambeau* (Paris: Les éditions de Paris, 2006), 241–42; see also Ardouin, *Études*, 4:331.

2. Vincent, "Series of reports gathered by Vincent," document 145, Rochambeau Papers, box 20.

3. Dumesle, *Voyage*, 150–51; Saint-Rémy, *Pétion et Haïti*, 1:239.

4. Leconte, *Henri Christophe dans l'histoire d'Haïti*, 29–30; Saint-Rémy, *Pétion et Haïti*, 1:268–69.

5. Tom Reiss, *The Black Count: Glory, Revolution, Betrayal, and the Real Count of Monte Cristo* (New York: Crown, 2012).

6. Saint-Rémy, *Pétion et Haïti*, 1:252, 282; "Exposé sommaire, présenté au Directoire éxécutif par Pierre Pinchinat, député de St. Domingue, au corps législatif," AF/III/21, ANF; "État de services d'André Rigaud," folder Rigaud, Dec. 1, 1795, GR 8Yd 638, SHD.

7. "Les officiers & soldats de l'armée sous les ordres de Toussaint L'Ouverture, général de brigade des armées de la république, à la Convention nationale," Dec. 5, 1795, microfilm, CC9A 11 (1/2), 12 (2/2), ANF. Thanks to Julia Gaffield for sharing this document.

8. Saint-Rémy, *Pétion et Haïti*, 1:267 and 282–84; for Louverture's promotion to lieutenant governor and as liberator, see "Proclamation d'Étienne Laveaux, général en chef et gouverneur de Saint-Domingue," April 1, 1796, 5B,N.127, Archivo General de Indias, ESTADO.

9. Raimond to Georges René Le Peley de Pléville, minister of the marine, Sept. 10,

1797, AF/III/210, ANF; for the printed version, see *Rapport de Julien Raimond, commissaire délégué par le gouvernement français aux Isles-sous-le-vent, au Ministre de la Marine* (Au Cap Français: P. Roux, 1797).

10. Raimond to Le Peley de Pléville, Sept. 10, 1797; for plantations leased to Generals Dessalines, Toussaint Louverture, Paul Louverture, Belair, Clervaux, and numerous other officers, see "État général de l'ouest de Saint-Domingue," 10 DPPC 190, ANOM; and folder Petit-Goâve, "État général des biens séquestrés dans l'arrondissement du Petit-Goâve, affermés par l'administration des Domaines nationaux jusques et compris le 30 floréal an 10," 10 DPPC 191, ANOM.

11. Raimond to Le Peley de Pléville, Sept. 10, 1797; for the accusation against Raimond, see Eustache Bruix, "Rapport: Le directeur des Domaines nationaux, bien séquestrés et vacants du départments au nord de Saint-Domingue," Jan. 6, 1799, AF/III/210, ANF.

12. Raimond to Le Peley de Pléville, Sept. 10, 1797; for Louverture's children, see Bernard Gainot, "Un projet avorté d'intégration républicaine. L'institution nationale des colonies (1797–1802)," *Dix-huitième siècle* 32 (2000): 372–73; "Rapport de vendémiaire an VIII," quoted in ibid., 374–75.

13. Raimond to Le Peley de Pléville, Sept. 10, 1797; Sonthonax to public, civil, and military functionaries in the commune of Cap, Aug. 20, 1797; Louverture to Sonthonax, Aug. 22, 1797, AF/III/210, ANF.

14. "Extrait du registre des délibérations de la commission déléguée par le gouvernement français aux Isles sous le vent, au Cap le 3 fructidor, l'an 5ème," Aug. 20, 1797, AF/III/210, ANF; for the letter with original signatures, see "Au Cap, le 3 fructidor l'an 5ieme . . . Le général en chef et les officiers composant l'état major de l'armée de St. Domingue," Aug. 20, 1797, GR7, B1, SHD. Thanks to Julia Gaffield for sharing the latter document.

15. Copy of Louverture's letter to citizens composing the municipal administration of Cap, Aug. 22, 1797, AF/III/210, ANF.

16. Louverture, "Rapport au Directoire exécutif. Toussaint Louverture, général en chef de l'armée de Saint-Domingue au Directoire exécutif. Au Cap-Français le 19 fructidor an cinq [Sept. 5, 1797] de la République française," AF/III/210, ANF.

17. Louverture to Vincent, Oct. 21, 1797, AF/III/210, ANF.

18. Sonthonax to the Executive Directory, Jan. 6, 1798, AF/III/210, ANF.

19. "Extrait du Bulletin officiel de Saint-Domingue, du 4 floréal l'an 6ieme de la RF. . . . Cap-Français, Discours du commissaire Raimond adressé au Général Hédouville, agent du Directoire exécutif de la RF à son arrivée au Fort-Liberté," April 17, 1798; and "Réponse du Général Hédouville au Citoyen Commissaire," n.d., AF/III/210, ANF.

20. For Christophe as interim, see Louverture to Christophe, April 3, 1798, AT-7, Nemours Collection.

21. "Numéro 64. Extrait du Bulletin officiel de Saint-Domingue. Du 19 thermidor, l'an 6, Le général de division agent particulier du Directoire exécutif à St. Domingue aux administrations municipales, aux tribunaux correctionnels et de la paix, aux Commissaires du Directoire exécutif, aux officiers généraux, aux commandants d'arrondissement, aux officiers supérieurs de la gendarmerie," AF/III/210, ANF.

22. "Arrêté concernant la police des habitations et les obligations réciproques des propriétaires et fermiers et des cultivateurs. Extrait du registre des délibérations

de l'agence du Directoire exécutif à Saint-Domingue," July 24, 1798, AF/III/210, ANF.

23. "Extraits du Bulletin officiel de Saint-Domingue. Du 24 vendémiaire l'an 7 . . . Cap Français. Instructions en forme d'arrêté concernant les mesures préliminaires à prendre pour la formation de la gendarmerie, du 22 vendémiaire an 7. Extrait du régistre des délibérations de l'agence du Directoire exécutif à Saint-Domingue," Oct. 13, 1798, AF/III/210, ANF.

24. Saint-Rémy, *Pétion et Haïti*, 2:16.

25. "Rapport du Général Hédouville, agent particulier du Directoire à St. Domingue, au Directoire exécutif," AF/III/210, ANF; Saint-Rémy, *Pétion et Haïti*, 2:17–18.

26. Vincent to Clarkson, Oct. 17, 1820, Clarkson/170, St. John's College Library. For the precise location of the Héricourt plantation, see S. Rouzier, *Dictionnaire géographique et administratif d'Haïti . . . ou guide général en Haïti* (Port-au-Prince: Aug. A. Héraux, 1927), 3:15.

27. "Arrêtés et proclamations relatifs aux événements du Fort-Liberté, dans les journées des 24 et 25 vendémiaire, an 7," AF/III/210, ANF; Saint-Rémy, *Pétion et Haïti*, 2:18.

28. For Moyse's condition upon arrival at Héricourt, see Rouzier, *Dictionnaire géographique*, 3:15.

29. "Arrêtés et proclamations relatifs aux événements du Fort-Liberté, dans les journées des 24 et 25 vendémiaire, an 7."

30. "Proclamation, le délégué de l'agence du directoire aux citoyens du Fort-Liberté," AF/III/210, ANF.

31. "Arrêtés des différentes communes de la colonie de Saint-Domingue, adressées à l'agent particulier du Directoire, au Général en chef et à l'administration Municipal du Cap," AF/III/210, ANF.

32. "Arrêtés des différentes communes."

33. "Arrêtés des différentes communes"; see also, Daut, *Awakening the Ashes*, 147–48.

34. "Arrêtés des différentes communes."

35. Hédouville sent as evidence this proclamation from Oct. 22, 1798: "Proclamation. Le Général de Division Hédouville, agent particulier du Directoire exécutif à St. Domingue, aux habitants de cette colonie," AF/III/210, ANF; see also Saint-Rémy, *Pétion et Haïti*, 2:21–22.

36. "Rapport du Général Hédouville, agent particulier du Directoire à St. Domingue, au Directoire exécutif," AF/III/210, ANF.

37. Louverture, "Exposition de l'événement du Fort-Liberté, des causes qui l'ont produit, et analyse des pièces y relatives," AF/III/210, ANF.

38. "Rapport du Général Hédouville."

39. André Rigaud, *Réponse du général de brigade André Rigaud à l'écrit calomnieux du Général Toussaint Louverture* (Aux Cayes: Lemery, 1799), i–iii.

40. André Rigaud, *Réponse à la proclamation de Toussaint Louverture, datée, au Port-au-Prince, le 20 brumaire an VIIIème* (Aux Cayes: Lemery, 1799), 1–3.

41. Rigaud, *Réponse du général de brigade*, ii.

42. Rigaud, *Réponse à la proclamation de Toussaint Louverture*, 4.

43. Daut, *Awakening the Ashes*, 157–58.

44. Louverture to Coisnon (director of the National Institute in Paris), Nov. 12, 1798; "Rapport fait par Toussaint Louverture, général en chef de l'armée de St.-Domingue, au Directoire exécutif," AF/III/210, ANF. For designated successor, see Saint-Rémy, *Pétion et Haïti*, 2:25.

45. Louverture to the French minister of the marine, March 24, 1799, CO 245/2, TNA.
46. Saint-Rémy, *Pétion et Haïti*, 2:23, 26–27, 29.
47. Quoted in Saint-Rémy, *Pétion et Haiti*, 2:35.
48. For secret treaty, see Hazareesingh, *Black Spartacus*, 136–37.
49. Roume to Louverture, Nov. 25, 1799.
50. "Rapport du Chef de Brigade Grandet, au Citoyen Ministre de la Marine et des Colonies," June 29, 1799, microfilm, CC9A 22, ANF. Thanks to Julia Gaffield for sharing this reel of documents.
51. Roume to Louverture, April 6, 1799; see also Roume to Louverture, March 29, 1799, CO 245/2, TNA.
52. Roume to Bruix, April 17, 1799, CO 245/2, TNA.
53. Roume to Christophe, Aug. 21, 1799, reel CC9A 25, microfilm, ANF.
54. Christophe to Roume, Aug. 27, 1799, reel CC9A 25, microfilm, ANF.
55. "Cap-Français, le 17 thermidor an 7 [Aug. 4, 1799], Nous chef de bataillon adjoints aux adjutants généraux de l'armée, en vertu des ordres du citoyen Henry Christophe, chef de brigade et commandant en chef l'arrondissement du Cap, en date de ce jour . . . ," reel CC9A 25, microfilm, ANF.
56. "Copie de l'ordre donné au Citoyen Charles, capitaine du 1er régiment de prendre le commandement d'un détachement pour aller aux Gonaïves chercher des prisonniers pour conduire au Cap," reel CC91 25, microfilm, ANF.
57. "Copie du procès verbal fait par le citoyen Charles, capitaine au 1er régiment, commandant le détachement chargé de conduire des prisonniers conspirateurs des Gonaïves au Cap," Aug. 17, 1799, reel CC9A 25, microfilm, ANF.
58. "Copie de l'ordre donné au Citoyen Raymond, pour aller avec son détachement au Borgne prendre des prisonniers sortant de Port de Paix, pour les conduire au Cap," reel CC9A 25, microfilm, ANF.
59. "Copie du procès verbal fait par le citoyen Raymond, commandant le détachement qui a conduit des prisonniers-conspirateurs du Borgne au Cap"; "Copie de l'ordre donné au général de brigade Moyse," reel CC9A 25, microfilm, ANF.
60. "Copie de l'ordre donné au général de Brigade Moyse," reel CC9A 26, microfilm, ANF.
61. Leconte, *Henri Christophe dans l'histoire d'Haïti*, 40–41.
62. Roume to Louverture, Oct. 24, 1799.
63. Louverture to Roume, Oct. 20, 1799, reel CC9A 26, microfilm, ANF.
64. Roume to Louverture, Oct. 24, 1799.
65. For Louverture's rebukes, see Louverture to Christophe, Feb. 16, 1798, AT-11, Nemours Collection; and Louverture to Christophe, April 3, 1798, AT-7, Nemours Collection.
66. Louverture to Roume, Nov. 19, 1799, reel CC9A 26, microfilm, ANF.
67. Roume to Louverture, Dec. 25, 1799, reel CC9A 26, microfilm, ANF.
68. Cathcart to Maitland, Nov. 26, 1799, CO 245/1, TNA.
69. Leconte, *Henri Christophe dans l'histoire d'Haïti*, 42; Saint-Rémy, *Pétion et Haïti*, 2:97.
70. "Adresse. Toussaint Louverture, général en chef de l'armée de Saint-Domingue, à tous les citoyens du département du sud," April 20, 1800, MMC-2814, Celestine Bencomo Collection, Library of Congress. Thanks to Chelsea Stieber for sharing scans of the Bencomo collection.
71. Gardner Weld Allen, *Our Naval War with France* (Boston: Houghton Mifflin, 1909), 205–6; Bonnet, *Souvenirs historiques*, 92–93.
72. Leconte, *Henri Christophe dans l'histoire d'Haïti*, 42.

73. Louverture to Christophe, May 13, 1800, AT-6, Nemours Collection.
74. *Almanach royal d'Hayti pour l'année 1814*, 5; Saint-Rémy, *Pétion et Haïti*, 2:132–33.
75. Louverture to Don Joaquín García (captain general and president of the former royal army), Feb. 1, 1801, Bencomo Collection.
76. Leconte, *Henri Christophe dans l'histoire d'Haïti*, 46.
77. Leconte, *Henri Christophe dans l'histoire d'Haïti*, 49–50.
78. Louverture to Citizen Madelmond (Master of Lands, in Cap), Sept. 5, 1801, Haiti/1872/I.1, CHS.
79. Claude Auguste, "Indépendantisme louverturien et révolution française," in *La Révolution française et Haïti*, ed. Michel Hector (Port-au-Prince: Société Haïtienne d'Histoire et de Géographie, 1995), 1:244–45, cited in Christian Schneider, "Le colonel Vincent, officier du génie à Saint-Domingue," *Annales historiques de la Révolution française* 329 (July–Sept. 2002), journals.openedition.org.
80. Copy of the marriage notation for the agent Roume and Marianne Elizabeth Rochard, Extrait des registres des actes de mariage de la commune et canton du Port-Républicain, Feb. 19, 1799, CO 23/38, TNA.
81. Saint-Rémy, *Pétion et Haïti*, 3:2–3.
82. "Extrait d'une lettre du C. Roume, agent particulier du gouvernement français à Saint-Domingue, au C. Gr****, membre de l'Institut national," *La décade philosophique, littéraire et politique*, March 31, 1802, 55.
83. Saint-Rémy, *Pétion et Haïti*, 3:3; Louverture to Bonaparte, Aug. 25, 1801, AF/IV/1213, ANF.
84. Roume to Forfait (minister of the marine), Dec. 2, 1801, Microfilm BN08270, Rochambeau Papers, University of Florida Libraries.
85. *La décade philosophique, littéraire et politique*, Sept. 7, 1802, 504.
86. Daut, *Awakening the Ashes*, 177–78.
87. Quoted in Saint-Rémy, *Pétion et Haïti*, 3:5–6.
88. Schneider, "Le colonel Vincent."
89. Louverture to Bonaparte, July 16, 1801, AF/IV/1213, ANF.
90. Bonaparte to Louverture, March 4, 1801, Unprocessed Haiti Collection, Moorland-Spingarn Research Center, Howard University, Washington, D.C.
91. Louverture to Bonaparte, Aug. 24, 1801; Louverture to minister of the marine and colonies, Aug. 24, 1801, AF/IV/1213, ANF.
92. Farming regulations reprinted in Beaubrun Ardouin, *Études sur l'histoire d'Haïti* (Paris: Dezobry et E. Magdeleine, 1853), 4:248–53; Leconte, *Henri Christophe*, 51.
93. Reprinted in Ardouin, *Études sur l'histoire d'Haïti*, 4:248–53.
94. "République française. Arrêté. Toussaint Louverture, général en chef de l'armée de St. Domingue," April 3, 1801, AF/IV/1213, ANF.
95. "Suite du coup d'oeil politique sur la situation actuelle du Royaume d'Hayti," *Gazette royale d'Hayti*, Aug. 27, 1816, 1–2.
96. Reprinted in "Moyse's Rebellion," in Geggus, *Haitian Revolution: A Documentary History*, 164–65.
97. Plantation located in Soufrière and owned in the colonial era by the white planter Étienne-François Bailly, according to an indemnity payout as listed in *État détaillé des liquidations opérées à l'époque du 1er janvier 1832, par la commission chargée de répartir l'indemnité attribuée aux anciens colons de Saint-Domingue, en exécution de la loi du 30 avril 1826 et conformement aux dispositions de l'ordonnance du 9 mai suivant* (Paris: Imprimerie Royale, 1832), 84.

98. Toussaint Louverture, *Récit des evénements qui se sont passés dans la partie du nord de Saint-Domingue, depuis le 29 vendémiaire, jusqu'au 13 brumaire, an 10 de la République française, une et indivisible (4 novembre 1801)* (Port-Républicain: Chez Gauchet, Lagrange & c., Imprimeurs-Libraires du Gouvernement, [1801]), 8–11, CO 137/106, TNA.
99. Louverture, *Récit des evénements*, 11–13.
100. Whitefield to Major General George Nugent, Dec. 9, 1801, CO 137/106, TNA.
101. Folder Moyse, 10 DPPC 131, ANOM; for gold stores, see Whitefield to Major General Nugent, Dec. 5, 1801, CO 137/106, TNA.
102. "Procès-verbal de séquestration de la maison No. 548," Feb. 16, 1803, folder Moyse, 10 DPPC 131, ANOM.
103. "Expédition du séquestre de l'habitation de ci-devant Général Moyse, à Porto-Plata," folder Moyse.
104. Leconte, *Henri Christophe dans l'histoire d'Haïti*, 51.
105. "Expédition du séquestre de l'habitation de ci-devant Général Moyse, à Porto-Plata"; Louverture to Christophe, July 24, 1801, AT-5, Nemours Collection.
106. Rouzier, *Dictionnaire géographique*, 15, 485.
107. Henry Christophe and Julien Prévost, *Manifeste du roi* (Cap-Henry, Haiti, [ca. 1814]), 4.
108. "Proclamation, 4 frimaire X," in Geggus, *Haitian Revolution: A Documentary History*, 166–67; Leconte, *Henri Christophe dans l'histoire d'Haïti*, 52–3.
109. Saint-Rémy, *Pétion et Haïti*, 1:267; Laveaux quoted Raynal's famous *Histoire des deux Indes* to exalt Louverture to the rank of the second-highest official in the colony, but did not call him Spartacus, as is sometimes reported. See "Proclamation d'Étienne Laveaux, général en chef et gouverneur de Saint-Domingue," April 1, 1796, 5B, N.127, Archivo General de Indias, ESTADO; for an analysis of this proclamation in relation to Raynal's work, see Grégory Pierrot, *The Black Avenger in Atlantic Culture* (Athens: University of Georgia Press, 2017), chap. 3.
110. Tartuffe is a famous con artist in a play by the seventeenth-century French playwright Molière called *Tartuffe*.
111. Roume to Forfait (minister of the marine and the colonies), Dec. 2, 1801, BN08270, Rochambeau Papers, University of Florida Libraries.
112. Vincent, "Series of Reports," Rochambeau Papers, box 20.
113. Louverture had written to the French minister of the marine in early 1801 to request the return of his children. See Louverture to the minister of the marine, Feb. 12, 1801, 61/J/18, Gironde.
114. Vincent to Leclerc, Nov. 20, 1801, BN08270, microfilm, Rochambeau Papers, University of Florida Libraries.
115. Dessalines to Louverture, May 5, 1802, Haiti Collection, Unprocessed collection: 23C, Moorland-Spingarn Research Center, Howard University, Washington, D.C.
116. Louverture, *Récit des evénements*, 3–4.

CHAPTER 6: LOVE, LOSS, AND BETRAYAL UNDER UNCERTAIN SKIES

1. Quoted in Dannelle Gutarra, "Toussaint Louverture's Captivity at Fort de Joux," *Journal of Caribbean History* 49, no. 2 (2015): 144.
2. "Extrait des minutes de Greffe . . . ," April 7, 1803, TL-3A4, Nemours Collection.

3. Toussaint Louverture, *Mémoires du général Toussaint Louverture*, ed. Daniel Desormeaux (Paris: Classiques Garnier, 2011), 142–43.
4. Quoted in Gutarra, "Toussaint Louverture's Captivity at Fort de Joux," 142–43.
5. Quoted in Stéphen Alexis, "Le crepuscule d'un dieu: Quelques scènes des derniers moments de Toussaint Louverture au Fort de Joux," *Cahiers d'Haïti* (April 1944): 6.
6. Madison Smartt Bell, *Toussaint Louverture: A Biography* (New York: Vintage Books, 2007), 58–60.
7. The date given by Isaac slightly contradicts a marriage certificate Louverture signed on February 19, 1799, when he acted as a witness at the agent Roume's marriage. Louverture signed the certificate listing him as fifty-four years old at the time, which would have put his birthday in either 1744 or 1745. Isaac Louverture, "Notes divers d'Isaac sur la vie de Toussaint Louverture," in *Histoire de l'expédition des Français, à Saint-Domingue, sous le consulat de Napoléon Bonaparte, par Antoine Métral; suivie des mémoires et notes d'Isaac Louverture, sur la même expédition, et sur la vie de son père; ornée du portrait de Toussaint et d'une belle carte de Saint-Domingue* (Paris: Fanjat Aîné, 1825), 325–26; "Extrait des registres des actes de mariage de la commune et canton du Port-Républicain," Feb. 19, 1799, CO 23/38, TNA.
8. Bell, *Toussaint Louverture*, 76; Jean-Louis Donnadieu, "La famille 'oubliée' de Toussaint Louverture," *Bulletin de la Société archéologique et historique du Gers* 401, no. 3 (2011): 357–65.
9. Gainot, "Un projet avorté d'intégration républicaine," 373.
10. *Mémoires historiques et secrets de l'impératrice Joséphine Marie-Rose Tascher-de-La-Pagerie, première épouse de Napoléon Bonaparte*, ed. Marie Le Normand (Paris: Chez L'Auteur, 1827), 2:102–3.
11. Louis Joseph Janvier, *Les constitutions d'Haïti, 1801–1885* (Paris: C. Marpon et E. Flammarion, 1886), 1–2.
12. Reprinted in Joseph Saint-Rémy, *Mémoires du général Toussaint-L'Ouverture écrits par lui-même* (Paris: Pagnerre, 1853), 87n1.
13. Bonaparte to Leclerc, Nov. 19, 1801, in *Correspondance de Napoléon Ier, publiée par ordre de l'empereur Napoléon III* (Paris: Imprimerie Royale, 1861), 7:412–13.
14. Leclerc to Christophe, Feb. 3, 1802, in Roussier, *Lettres*, 61.
15. In the Haitian sources, both Leclerc's and Christophe's letters were sent on February 2, but Leclerc's account suggests that whenever the response was written, he did not receive Christophe's reply the same day. See Leclerc to the French minister of the marine, Feb. 9, 1802, in Roussier, *Lettres*, 69; Christophe to Leclerc, Feb. 2, 1802, in Christophe and Prévost, *Manifeste du roi*, 21–22; see also the same letter in Juste Chanlatte, *Le cri de la nature* (Cap-Henry: P. Roux, 1810), 81–83. Both Leclerc's and Christophe's letters are quoted in Charles Malo, *Histoire d'Haïti (Isle de Saint-Domingue), depuis sa découverte jusqu'en 1824, époque des dernières négociations entre la France et le gouvernement haïtien* (Paris: Janet et Ponthieu, 1825), 211–12. Malo claims that Leclerc did not receive Christophe's reply until February 4.
16. P. A. Cabon, *Notes sur l'histoire religieuse d'Haïti de la révolution au concordat (1789–1860)* (Port-au-Prince: Petit Séminaire Collège Saint-Martial, 1933), 38–39, 68n1. For Brelle's birth name, see ibid., 69n1.
17. "Ministère de la Marine. Extrait du régistre des délibérations de l'administration municipale du Cap. Séance du 16 pluviôse an 10 de la République française (5

février 1802)," reprinted in *Le moniteur universel,* April 22, 1802, 1–2. The original account of the entire affair cited in the newspaper that led to Christophe's order was written by the mayor of Cap, Cézar Télémaque, and other municipal authorities and printed in pamphlet form as "Extrait du régistre des délibérations de l'administration municipale du Cap. Séance du 16 pluviôse an 10 de la République française (5 février 1802)," CO 137/108, TNA.

18. Louverture to Leclerc, Feb. 14, 1802, AB/XIX/5002, ANF.

19. Isaac Louverture, "Mémoires d'Isaac, fils de Toussaint Louverture, sur l'expédition français, sous le consulat de Bonaparte," in *Histoire de l'expédition des français,* 233–34.

20. Louverture, *Mémoires,* ed. Desormeaux, 97–98.

21. Alexis, "Le Crepuscule d'un dieu," 4, 3.

22. Louverture to Leclerc, Feb. 14, 1802.

23. Louis Félix Boisrond-Tonnerre, *Mémoires pour servir à l'histoire d'Haïti* (Dessalines: Imprimerie Centrale du Gouvernement, 1804), 6–7.

24. Anonymous letter given to Governor Nugent, dated Feb. 13, 1802, CO 137/107, TNA.

25. Christophe to Vilton, April 10, 1802, in Chanlatte, *Le cri de la nature,* 103.

26. Anonymous letter given to Governor Nugent, dated Feb. 13, 1802. In a letter Dessalines wrote to General Agé from Léogâne at the time of Leclerc's arrival, Dessalines spoke of having "raised" the city, saying he "burned everything" near the mountains surrounding Croix-des-Bouquets. Dessalines to Agé, Feb. 10, 1802, 61/J/18, Gironde.

27. Louverture, *Mémoires,* ed. Desormeaux, 115.

28. "Proclamation au quartier général du Cap, le 28 pluviôse, an X," Feb. 17, 1802, in Roussier, *Lettres,* 98–99.

29. Louverture, *Mémoires,* ed. Desormeaux, 115.

30. Louverture, *Mémoires,* ed. Desormeaux, 122n2 and 122.

31. Christophe to Louverture, March 19, 1802, Haiti Collection, Unprocessed collection: C14, Moorland-Spingarn Research Center, Howard University, Washington, D.C.

32. *Le moniteur universel,* May 22, 1802; *Le moniteur universel,* May 28, 1802, 1022.

33. "Ministère de la Marine," *La clef du cabinet des souverains,* March 19, 1802.

34. Leclerc to Louverture, Feb. 12, 1802; and Leclerc to the French minister of the marine, Feb. 15, 1802, in Roussier, *Lettres,* 85–86, 87; Louverture, *Mémoires,* ed. Desormeaux, 109.

35. Quoted in I. Louverture, "Mémoires," 241.

36. I. Louverture, "Mémoires," 229–30.

37. Jean-Louis Vastey, *Réflexions politiques sur quelques ouvrages et journaux français concernant Hayti* (Sans-Souci: Imprimerie Royale, 1817), 3.

38. Pamphile de Lacroix, *Mémoires pour servir à l'histoire de la révolution de Saint-Domingue* (Paris: Pillet Ainé, 1819), 2:125–26.

39. See Chanlatte, *Le cri de la nature,* and Christophe and Prévost, *Manifeste du roi.*

40. Chanlatte, *Le cri de la nature,* 77.

41. See "Extraits des registres des délibérations des consuls de la république," Nov. 8, 1801, in Leclerc, *Lettres,* 63–65.

42. General Leclerc, "Proclamation," Feb. 17, 1802, in Roussier, *Lettres,* 98–100.

43. Vincent to Leclerc, Nov. 18–20, 1802, "Unpublished Papers of Generals Leclerc

and Rochambeau During the War of Independence in Haiti, 1802–3," GEN MSS 1576, box 32, Donatien Marie Joseph de Vimeur, Vicomte de Rochambeau Papers Relating to the French West Indies, Beinecke.

44. Christophe to General Hardy, April 22, 1802; Leclerc to Christophe, April 24, 1802, in Chanlatte, *Le cri de la nature*, 94–95.
45. Christophe to Leclerc, April 22, 1802, in Chanlatte, *Le cri de la nature*, 85.
46. Christophe to Vilton, April 22, 1802, in *Le cri de la nature*, 110.
47. Reprinted in Joseph Élisée Peyre-Ferry, *Journal des opérations militaires de l'armée française pendant les années 1802 et 1803 sous les ordres des capitaines-généraux Leclerc et Rochambeau* (Paris: Les Éditions de Paris, 2006), 263; see also an image of the original handwritten document in "Unpublished Papers of Generals Leclerc and Rochambeau During the War of Independence in Haiti, 1802–3," 33; and a handwritten copy submitted to the British government in CO 137/138, TNA.
48. Saint-Rémy, *Pétion et Haiti*, 3:43; I. Louverture, "Mémoires," 276.
49. Christophe agreed to meet Leclerc on the twenty-sixth in his letter of April 25, 1802, in Chanlatte, *Le cri de la patrie*, 87–88; see also Duraciné Vaval, "Le roi d'Haïti Henri Christophe: L'homme et son oeuvre de gouvernement," *Revue de la Société d'histoire et de géographie d'Haïti* 2, no. 3 (June 1931): 6.
50. "Armée de Saint-Domingue. Arrêté," April 26, 1802, GR 7B 3, Chateau de Vincennes, SHD. Thanks to Julia Gaffield for sharing this document with me.
51. Magon to Rochambeau, April 27, 1802, "Unpublished Papers of Generals Leclerc and Rochambeau During the War of Independence in Haiti, 1802–3," 35.
52. Leclerc to Denis Decrès (minister of the marine), reprinted in *Le moniteur universel*, June 13, 1802.
53. I. Louverture, "Mémoires," 276–77.
54. Leclerc to Christophe, April 19, 1802, in Chanlatte, *Le cri de la nature*, 83.
55. Leclerc to Decrès, in *Le moniteur universel*, June 13, 1802.
56. Boisrond-Tonnerre, *Mémoires*, 33–34.
57. I. Louverture, "Mémoires," 277–79. A letter from Louverture to Christophe dated April 28 suggests that Louverture did read the letter immediately but only peremptorily. Asking Christophe to return, Louverture wrote, "Occupied, my dear General, in chatting with you, I hadn't had a chance to think about the content of General Leclerc's letter. After you left, I realized that I neglected to ask you about several sentences in his letter, which I need to know more about and discuss with you in order to be able to reply." Louverture to Christophe, April 28, 1802, 61/J/18, Gironde.
58. Saint-Rémy, *Pétion et Haiti*, 3:42.
59. I. Louverture, "Mémoires," 279.
60. Dessalines to Louverture, May 5, 1802, Haiti Collection, Unprocessed collection: 23C, Moorland-Spingarn Research Center, Howard University, Washington, D.C.
61. Christophe to Louverture, Feb. 8, 1802, Haiti Collection, Unprocessed collection: C1, Moorland-Spingarn Research Center, Howard University, Washington, D.C.; Christophe to Louverture, Feb. 22, 1802, Haiti Collection, Unprocessed collection: 12C, Moorland-Spingarn Research Center, Howard University, Washington, D.C.
62. Christophe to Louverture, March 8, 1802, Haiti Collection, Unprocessed collection: C13, Moorland-Spingarn Research Center, Howard University, Washington, D.C.

63. Christophe to Louverture, March 19, 1802, Haiti Collection, Unprocessed collection: C14, Moorland-Spingarn Research Center, Howard University, Washington, D.C.; for the Lamartinières, see Hazareesingh, *Black Spartacus*, 310–11.

64. Christophe to Louverture, April 2, 1802, Haiti Collection, Unprocessed collection: C17, Moorland-Spingarn Research Center, Howard University, Washington, D.C.

65. Christophe to Louverture, April 14, 1802, Haiti Collection, Unprocessed collection: C18, Moorland-Spingarn Research Center, Howard University, Washington, D.C.

66. Christophe to Leclerc, May 1, 1802, Haiti Collection, Unprocessed collection: 22C, Moorland-Spingarn Research Center, Howard University, Washington, D.C.

67. Quoted in Marie-Lucie Vendryes, introduction to Cheesman, *Armorial of Haiti*, 2.

68. Vastey, *Essai*, 25.

69. Leclerc, "Arrêté," May 1, 1802, reprinted in *L'observateur, ou, Gazette du Port-Républicain*, May 16, 1802, CO 137/108, TNA.

70. In the letter he wrote to Leclerc on April 29, Louverture also referenced "General Christophe's submission to the Republic with troops under orders" and mentioned having read Leclerc's orders to Christophe in addition to the letter from Leclerc that Christophe brought addressed to Louverture. Louverture to Leclerc, April 29, 1802, AB/XIX/5002, ANF. Thanks to Julia Gaffield for sharing this document.

71. Dessalines to Louverture, May 4, 1802, Haiti Collection, Unprocessed collection, Moorland-Spingarn Research Center, Howard University, Washington, D.C.

72. Laujon, *Précis historique de la dernière expedition de Saint-Domingue*, 71; Saint-Rémy, *Pétion et Haïti*, 3:44.

73. Quoted in I. Louverture, "Mémoires," 289.

74. "Dépêche télégraphique," *Le moniteur universel*, July 12, 1802.

75. Saint-Rémy, *Pétion et Haïti*, 3:45.

76. Boisrond-Tonnerre, *Mémoires*, 46, 37.

77. Vastey, *Essai*, 29–34.

78. I. Louverture, "Mémoires," 282.

79. Louverture, *Mémoires*, ed. Desormeaux, 127.

80. Leclerc to Decrès, in *Le moniteur universel*, July 13, 1802; Desormeaux, *Mémoires*, 155n2.

81. Leclerc to Bonaparte, June 6, 1802, in Roussier, *Lettres*, 161–62.

82. Leclerc to Decrès, June 11, 1802, in Roussier, *Lettres*, 168–69. See also reprint in *Le moniteur universel*, July 13, 1802.

83. Chanlatte, *Le cri de la nature*, 43.

84. Leclerc to Bonaparte, June 6, 1802, in Roussier, *Lettres*, 161–62.

85. A reference to the Greek stoic, Diogenes, known for walking around Athens with a lantern in broad daylight in search for an "honest man." Christophe to Vilton, April 10, 1802, in Chanlatte, *Le cri de la nature*, 103.

86. Boisrond-Tonnerre, *Mémoires*, 35–36.

87. Brunet to Louverture, June 3, 1802, Haiti Collection, Unprocessed collection: 24C, Moorland-Spingarn Research Center, Howard University, Washington, D.C.

88. Dessalines to Rochambeau, June 14, 1802, 61/J/18, Gironde.

89. Brunet to Rochambeau, May 23, 1802; Brunet to Rochambeau, Sept. 13, 1802,

"Unpublished Papers of Generals Leclerc and Rochambeau During the War of Independence in Haiti, 1802–03."

90. Brunet to Leclerc, June 19, 1802, and archivist's note on page 9, "Unpublished Papers of Generals Leclerc and Rochambeau During the War of Independence in Haiti, 1802–03."

91. Louverture to Brunet, June 5, 1802, 135AP/6, ANF.

92. Brunet to Louverture, June 7, 1802, TL-2A3b, Nemours Collection.

93. Louverture, *Mémoires,* ed. Desormeaux, 137.

94. Brunet to Leclerc, June 7, 1802, "Unpublished Papers of Generals Leclerc and Rochambeau During the War of Independence in Haiti, 1802–3," 9.

95. Brunet to Leclerc, June 9, 1802, Haiti Collection, Unprocessed collection: C25, Moorland-Spingarn Research Center, Howard University, Washington, D.C. A catalog of some of Toussaint's captured papers, as well as an extensive list of Paul Louverture's effects and papers, exists in the folder for Toussaint Louverture, 10 DPPC 149, ANOM.

96. Vastey, *Essai,* 28–27.

97. Louverture, *Mémoires,* ed. Desormeaux, 138–39; "Arrestation et renvoi en France de Toussaint-L'Ouverture et de toute sa famille," *Le citoyen français,* July 15, 1802; Georges Le Gorgeu, *Étude sur Jean-Baptiste Coisnon: Toussaint-Louverture et Jean-Baptiste Coisnon* (Paris: Pedone-Lauriel, 1881), 31.

98. Reprinted in Desormeaux, *Mémoires,* 153n2.

99. Placide Louverture to Suzanne Louverture, Aug. 12, 1802, AF/IV/1213, ANF.

100. For the transfer order and that he be held incommunicado, see "Décret," July 23, 1802, in *Correspondance de Napoléon Ier,* 7:676; for Bonaparte's instructions to Caffarelli, see Bonaparte to Caffarelli, Sept. 9, 1802, in *Corréspondance de Napoléon Ier, publiée par ordre de l'empereur Napoléon III* (Paris: Henri Plon, 1861), 8:30.

101. Reprinted in Alexis, "Le crépuscule d'un dieu," 4.

102. Autopsie cadavérique, April 7, 1803, C-2, Nemours Collection.

103. Boisrond-Tonnerre, *Mémoires,* 48; Vastey, *Essai,* 28.

104. "Ministère de la Marine. Rapport au gouvernement de la république. Paris, le 4 floréal an 11 de la République française," *Le moniteur universel,* April 25, 1803, 960.

105. "Paris, 7 floréal," *Journal des débats et loix du pouvoir législatifs,* April 28, 1803, 2.

106. "Paris, 8 floréal," *Le courrier des spectacles,* April 29, 1803.

107. Hélène Maspero-Clerc, *Un Journaliste contre-révolutionnaire, Jean-Gabriel Peltier (1760–1825)* (Paris: Société des Etudes Robespierristes, 1973), 155, 160; Peltier used the title "Chargé d'Affaires of General Henry Christophe, President of Haiti," in his letter to Lord Liverpool, June 24, 1810, MS38245, BL. Thanks to Julia Gaffield for sharing this document.

108. "Résultat de l'expédition de Saint-Domingue. Conduite du Général Leclerc et autres," *L'ambigu,* no. 22 (1803): 88.

109. Leclerc to Decrès, Oct. 7, 1802, "Unpublished Papers of Generals Leclerc and Rochambeau During the War of Independence in Haiti, 1802–3."

110. "Toussaint Louverture Is Dead," *Times,* May 2, 1803, 3.

111. "New York—June 16," *Telegraph and Daily Advertiser,* June 20, 1803, 2.

112. "Proclamation au peuple et à l'armée," *Gazette officielle de l'État d'Hayti,* June 4, 1807, 18.

113. "Fin du coup-d'œil politique sur la situation actuelle du Royaume d'Hayti," *Gazette royale d'Hayti,* Oct. 17, 1816, 4.

114. Leclerc to Decrès, reprinted in *Le moniteur universel,* July 13, 1802.
115. Leclerc to Decrès, reprinted in *Le moniteur universel,* Aug. 12, 1802.
116. Servant, "Ferdinand Christophe, fils du roi d'Haïti, en France," 222–23.
117. Roume to Bruix (minister of the marine and colonies), March 16, 1799, CO 23/38, TNA; Copy of the marriage notation for the agent Roume and Marianne Elizabeth Rochard. See also Gainot, "Un projet avorté d'intégration républicaine," 388.
118. Servant, "Ferdinand Christophe, fils du roi d'Haïti, en France," 219–20.
119. Leclerc to Bonaparte, Aug. 9, 1802, in Roussier, *Lettres,* 207.
120. Leclerc to Bonaparte, Sept. 26, 1802, in Roussier, *Lettres,* 246.
121. Lacroix, *Mémoires,* 2:226–27.
122. Bonaparte to Leclerc, July 1, 1802, in *Correspondance de Napoléon Ier,* 7:640–41. For Bonaparte's original instructions to Leclerc, see Rafe Blaufarb, ed., *Napoleon, Symbol for an Age: A Brief History with Documents* (New York: Bedford/St. Martin's, 2008), 163–64.
123. Bonaparte to Leclerc, March 16, 1802, in *Correspondance de Napoléon Ier,* 7:525–26.
124. Decrès to Leclerc, June 14, 1802, "Unpublished Papers of Generals Leclerc and Rochambeau During the War of Independence in Haiti, 1802–3," 16.
125. Bonaparte to Leclerc, July 22, 1802, in *Correspondance de Napoléon Ier,* 7:675.
126. Leclerc to Bonaparte, Sept. 26, 1802, in Roussier, *Lettres,* 246.
127. Bonaparte to Louverture, Nov. 18, 1801, in *Correspondance de Napoléon Ier,* 7:410–11.
128. Bonaparte to Decrès, Oct. 7, 1801, in *Correspondance de Napoléon Ier,* 7:351–52.
129. Bonaparte to Louverture, Nov. 18, 1801; Bonaparte to Talleyrand, Nov. 13, 1801, in *Correspondance de Napoléon Ier,* 7:410 and 406–7.
130. Bonaparte to Leclerc, Nov. 19, 1801, in *Correspondance de Napoléon Ier,* 7:412–13.
131. For Bonaparte's reinstatement of the slave trade, see "6055. Deuxième annexe à la pièce 6053, Note," April 27, 1802, in *Correspondance de Napoléon Ier,* 7:568.
132. Quoted in Saint-Rémy, *Pétion et Haiti,* 3:76–77.
133. Servant, "Ferdinand Christophe, fils du roi d'Haïti, en France," 222–23.
134. Reprinted in Alphonse de Lamartine, *Toussaint Louverture* (1850), ed. Léon-François Hoffmann (Exeter: University of Exeter Press, 1998), 9.
135. "Picture of St. Domingo," *Literary Magazine and American Register for 1803–4* (Philadelphia: John Conrad, 1804), 1:446–50.
136. Bernard Gainot, *Les officiers de couleur dans les armées de la république et de l'empire (1792–1825)* (Paris: Karthala, 2007), 161–62.
137. For Clervaux's son's trajectory, see Gainot, "Un projet avorté d'intégration républicaine," 398–99.
138. Quoted in Gainot, *Les officiers de couleur,* 162.
139. Reprinted in Le Gorgeu, *Étude sur Jean-Baptiste Coisnon,* 45.
140. Servant, "Ferdinand Christophe, fils du roi d'Haïti, en France," 222–23.
141. Servant, "Ferdinand Christophe, fils du roi d'Haïti, en France," 223–24.
142. Laporte Lalanne to Cossé (agent de surveillance à l'hospice des orphelins), July 9, 1805, reprinted in Servant, "Ferdinand Christophe, fils du roi d'Haïti, en France," 227.
143. Cossé to Desportes (membre de la commission chargée des Hospices), July 9, 1805, in Servant, "Ferdinand Christophe, fils du roi d'Haïti, en France," 225–26.
144. Servant, "Ferdinand Christophe, fils du roi d'Haïti, en France," 224.

145. Report furnished to the French minister of the interior, Aug. 31, 1805, in Servant, "Ferdinand Christophe, fils du roi d'Haïti, en France," 232.
146. Servant, "Ferdinand Christophe, fils du roi d'Haïti, en France," 224.
147. Vastey, *Réflexions politiques*, 5–6.
148. Vastey, *Réflexions politiques*, 6–7.
149. Jean Valentin Vastey mentioned that he believed Christophe, Dessalines, Paul Louverture, and Clervaux had never truly given up the "party of hatred." See Jean Valentin Vastey to Pierre Vastey, Dec. 9, 1802, LQ.
150. "Madame Toussaint," *Gazette politique et commerciale d'Haïti*, March 28, 1805, 61–63.
151. Quoted in "Résultat de l'expédition de Saint-Domingue. Conduite de Général Leclerc," *L'ambigu*, no. 22 (1803): 88.
152. Louverture to Bonaparte, July 20, 1802, AF/IV/1213, ANF.
153. Quoted in Alexis, "Le crépuscule d'un dieu," 4.
154. Comte de Rosiers [Juste Chanlatte], *Recueil de chants et de couplets à la gloire de leurs majestés et de la famille royale d'Hayti, etc. etc. etc. à l'usage de la cour et des Haytiens* (Sans-Souci: Imprimerie Royale, n.d.), 11, 27–28; "Lines Penned by Juste Chanlatte for the Deceased Ferdinand," *Gazette royale*, Oct. 10, 1817, 3.

CHAPTER 7: AMERICA AVENGED

1. "Loi relative à la traite des noirs et au régime des colonies," May 20, 1802, 1 LEG 1, ANOM; Arrêté consulaire du 27 messidor an X (16 juillet 1802), Papiers de la secrétairerie d'état impériale, AF/IV/379, ANF.
2. Peyre-Ferry, *Journal des opérations*, 135; Boisrond-Tonnerre, *Mémoires*, 49–50.
3. Leclerc, "Proclamation to the Inhabitants of Saint-Domingue," Feb. 17, 1802, reprinted in Peyre-Ferry, *Journal des opérations*, 262.
4. Boisrond-Tonnerre, *Mémoires*, 49; Saint-Rémy, *Pétion et Haïti*, 3:102.
5. "St. Domingo," *Times*, Feb. 1, 1803, 3.
6. Leclerc to Bonaparte, Oct. 7, 1802, in Roussier, *Lettres*, 256.
7. Lacroix, *Mémoires*, 2:238.
8. Marcus Rainsford, *An Historical Account of the Black Empire of Hayti* (London: Albion Press, 1805), 326–27.
9. Leitch Ritchie, "State of the Country through the Subsequent Revolution Ending in the Independence of the Haitian Republic," in *The Slave King, from the Bug-Jargal of Victor Hugo*, translated by Leitch Ritchie (London: Smith, Elder, and Company, 1833), 308–310.
10. Peyre-Ferry, *Journal des opérations*, 76, 148, 152, 231.
11. Quoted in Victor Schoelcher, *La vie de Toussaint Louverture* (Paris: Karthala, 1998), 368.
12. Chanlatte, *Le cri de la nature*, 48.
13. Schoelcher, *La vie de Toussaint Louverture*, 368.
14. Morpas to Humbert, Feb. 9, 1802; for the city falling the next day, see archivist's summary of accompanying letter (on page 40) from Humbert to Leclerc, dated Nov. 11, 1802, "Unpublished Papers of Generals Leclerc and Rochambeau During the War of Independence in Haiti, 1802–3"; for Morpas's initial resistance, see also Morpas to Louverture, Feb. 6, 1802, 61/J/18, Gironde.
15. Morpas to Rochambeau, Nov. 20, 1802; see also archivist's note concerning Morpas's and his family's deaths, "Unpublished Papers of Generals Leclerc and Rochambeau During the War of Independence in Haiti, 1802–3," 41.

16. Marriage notation for Scipion Morpas and Marie-Louise, Jan. 6, 1801, folder Morpas, 10 DPPC 131, ANOM.
17. "Procès-verbal d'inventaire des effets de Maurepas," Dec. 2–9, 1802; for the gold necklace of slavery, see "Madame Morpas Doit . . . ," folder Morpas, 10 DPPC 131, ANOM.
18. Christophe and Prévost, *Manifeste du roi,* 11.
19. Brunet to Leclerc, Oct. 24, 1802, Papiers Rochambeau, 135AP/6, ANF.
20. Reprinted in Lamartine, *Toussaint Louverture,* 9.
21. *Literary Magazine and American Register;* Boisrond-Tonnerre, *Mémoires,* 74.
22. Boisrond-Tonnerre, *Mémoires,* 75n3, 65.
23. Leclerc to Rochambeau, Aug. 6, 1802, "Unpublished Papers of Generals Leclerc and Rochambeau During the War of Independence in Haiti, 1802–3," 30.
24. Vastey, *Réflexions sur une lettre de Mazères* (Cap-Henry: P. Roux, 1816), 96–97; Boisrond-Tonnerre, *Mémoires,* 77n1.
25. Alexandre Pétion to Dauxion Lavaysse, Nov. 14, 1814, reprinted in Vastey, *Essai,* 32; see also Claude M. Ribbe, *Le crime de Napoléon* (Édition Privé, 2005).
26. Peyre-Ferry, *Journal des opérations,* 172.
27. Boisrond-Tonnerre, *Mémoires,* 71.
28. Baron de Vastey, reprinted in "Fin du coup-d'œil politique sur la situation actuelle du Royaume d'Hayti," *Gazette royale d'Hayti,* Oct. 17, 1816, 3–4.
29. Boisrond-Tonnerre, *Mémoires,* 73.
30. Peyre-Ferry, *Journal des opérations,* 138–39, 179.
31. Boisrond-Tonnerre, *Mémoires,* 61.
32. Peyre-Ferry, *Journal des opérations,* 188.
33. Quoted in Józef Kwaterko, " 'Ces brigands qui chantent la Marseillaise . . .': Les lettres des militaires polonais et la guerre d'indépendance haïtienne (1802–1804)," in "La Révolution haïtienne et ses influences dans le monde atlantique du XVIIe siècle au début du XIXe siècle," *Revue d'histoire haïtienne,* no. 1 (2019): 255n14.
34. Hardy to Leclerc, April 2, 1802, box 173, Rochambeau Papers, University of Florida Libraries.
35. Quantin to Rochambeau, Jan. 27, 1803, box 1568, Rochambeau Papers, University of Florida Libraries.
36. "À la Petite-Anse, 7 pluviôse an 11, 5 heures du soir [Jan. 27, 1803], Louis Labelinaye, chef de brigade, commandant la place de la Petite-Anse," box 1570, Rochambeau Papers, University of Florida Libraries.
37. Christophe to Baron, Oct. 17, 1802, 135AP/6, ANF.
38. Baron to Christophe, Oct. 17, 1802, 135AP/6, ANF.
39. Baron to Brunet, Oct. 19, 1802, 135AP/6, ANF.
40. Rochambeau to Bonaparte, April 13, 1803, folder 6: Pièces divers et mémoires, AF/IV/1213, ANF.
41. Quoted in Kwaterko, " 'Ces brigands qui chantent la Marseillaise,' " 259.
42. Vastey, reprinted in "Fin du coup-d'oeil politique sur la situation actuelle du Royaume d'Hayti," *Gazette royale d'Hayti,* Oct. 17, 1816, 4.
43. Jan Pachoński and Reuel K. Wilson, *Poland's Caribbean Tragedy: A Study of Polish Legions in the Haitian War of Independence, 1802–1803* (Boulder, Colo.: East European Monographs, 1986), 211.
44. Vastey, *À mes concitoyens,* (Cap-Henry: P. Roux, 1815), 18.
45. "Royaume d'Hayti," *Gazette royale,* Nov. 19, 1814, 2.
46. Peyre-Ferry, *Journal des opérations,* 238–39; quote from 112.
47. Prudot and Germont M. Tapissier, "Mémoire des ouvrages faites et fournis au

citoyen Rochambeau, général en chef de l'armée de St. Domingue," manuscript as summarized and quoted in "Unpublished Papers of Generals Leclerc and Rochambeau During the War of Independence in Haiti, 1802–3."

48. Dessalines to Brunet, Oct. 15, 1802, 135AP/6, ANF.
49. Chanlatte, *Le cri de la nature*, 53.
50. Chanlatte, *Le cri de la nature*, 54.
51. Chanlatte, *Le cri de la nature*, 55.
52. Boisrond-Tonnerre, *Mémoires*, 46–49.
53. Peyre-Ferry, *Journal des opérations*, 117.
54. Rochambeau to Dessalines, July 28, 1802, AR-1, Nemours Collection.
55. Brunet to Leclerc, Aug. 26, 1802, "Unpublished Papers of Generals Leclerc and Rochambeau During the War of Independence in Haiti, 1802–3." For Madame Dessalines, see Saint-Rémy, *Pétion et Haïti*, 3:60.
56. Saint-Rémy, *Pétion et Haïti*, 3:60.
57. Saint-Rémy, *Pétion et Haïti*, 3:61; Madiou, *Histoire d'Haiti*, 2:362; "Fin du Coup-d'œil Politique sur la Situation actuelle du Royaume d'Hayti," *Gazette royale d'Hayti*, Oct. 17, 1816, 4.
58. Dessalines to Louverture, March 9, 1802, box 147, Rochambeau Collection, University of Florida Libraries. Thanks to Julia Gaffield for sharing this document.
59. Répussard to Rochambeau, Sept. 10, 1802, box 110, Rochambeau Collection, University of Florida Libraries. See also Maurice de Young. "Jean-Jacques Dessalines and Charles Belair," *Journal of Inter-American Studies* 2, no. 4 (1960): 449–56.
60. Belair to Rochambeau, Aug. 20, 1802, "Unpublished Papers of Generals Leclerc and Rochambeau During the War of Independence in Haiti, 1802–3."
61. Madiou, *Histoire d'Haïti*, 2:361. Original of the letter, of which I have seen only a transcription, reported by Roselor François to be in the private collection of Constantin Mayard Paul.
62. Louverture to Bonaparte, Feb. 10, 1801, in Peyre-Ferry, *Journal des opérations*, 242.
63. Ordre du jour signed by General Leclerc, July 29, 1802, ALEC-1, Nemours Collection.
64. On April 2, 1802, General Hardy told Leclerc that he succeeded in deporting Rigaud. Leclerc to Dugua, March 28, 1802, in *Minerve, le bulletin officiel du département du sud de Saint-Domingue*, April 10, 1802, CO 137/108, TNA; Hardy to Leclerc, April 2, 1802, Rochambeau Papers, box 174; General Pageot to Leclerc, Dec. 4, 1802, Rochambeau Papers, box 1407.
65. Edward Corbett, "Submission and Afterwards Revolt of the Blacks in St. Domingo.—Communicated by a Gentleman on the Spot," Jan. 28, 1803, CO 137/110, TNA.
66. Vincent to Leclerc, Nov. 18–20, 1801, "Unpublished Papers of Generals Leclerc and Rochambeau During the War of Independence in Haiti, 1802–3."
67. Saint-Rémy, *Pétion et Haïti*, 3:62nn2 and 3.
68. Brunet to Leclerc, Aug. 24, 1802, 135AP/6, ANF; Dessalines to Leclerc, Aug. 26, 1802, "Unpublished Papers of Generals Leclerc and Rochambeau During the War of Independence in Haiti, 1802–3."
69. Dessalines to Brunet, Sept. 3, 1802, 135AP/6, ANF.
70. Quantin to unnamed official responsible (au particulier à cette division) for Saint-Marc, Sept. 4, 1802, 135AP/6, ANF.
71. Brunet, "Au quartier général de Saint-Marc, le 21 fructidor an 10, ordre particulier à cette division," Sept. 8, 1802, 135AP/6, ANF.

72. "Jugement du général de brigade Charles Belair et de Sanitte, sa femme," *Gazette officielle de Saint-Domingue*, Oct. 9, 1802, 2–3.
73. Saint-Rémy, *Pétion et Haïti*, 3:63.
74. Rochambeau to Leclerc, Oct. 9, 1802, "Unpublished Papers of Generals Leclerc and Rochambeau During the War of Independence in Haiti, 1802–3."
75. Peyre-Ferry, *Journal des opérations*, 230.
76. Ernesto Mercado-Montero, "Sans-Souci, Jean Baptiste," in *Dictionary of Caribbean and Afro-Latin American Biography*, ed. Franklin W. Knight and Henry Louis Gates Jr. (Oxford: Oxford University Press, 2016). Web version.
77. Saint-Rémy, *Pétion et Haïti*, 3:64–65, 68.
78. Saint-Rémy, *Pétion et Haïti*, 3:68; Romain, *Noms de lieux d'époque coloniale en Haïti*, 95.
79. Leclerc to Rochambeau, Aug. 6, 1802, "Unpublished Papers of Generals Leclerc and Rochambeau During the War of Independence in Haiti, 1802–3."
80. Quoted in Saint-Rémy, *Pétion et Haïti*, 3:73–74.
81. Leclerc to Bonaparte, Sept. 27, 1802, in *Lettres*, 251.
82. Saint-Rémy, *Pétion et Haïti*, 3:97; Leclerc to Bonaparte, Sept. 16, 1802, in *Lettres*, 230.
83. Vaval, "Le roi d'Haïti, Henri Christophe," 7.
84. Saint-Rémy, *Pétion et Haïti*, 3:98–99.
85. Saint-Rémy, *Pétion et Haïti*, 3:107; Leclerc's letter reprinted in ibid., 3:102–103.
86. Leclerc to Rochambeau, Oct. 14, 1802, "Unpublished Papers of Generals Leclerc and Rochambeau During the War of Independence in Haiti, 1802–3."
87. Possibly the same Madame Pajeot described in a French military bulletin as a "negress" called "La Vierge" who had at one point been arrested after allegedly confessing to having, while disguised in men's clothing, "killed with her own hands three white men in the affair of July 7, 1794, in Fort-Dauphin, and having animated the assassins by having them drink blood mixed with cannon powder to excite them to carnage." "Bulletin du Cap et du Fort-Dauphin," n.d., WO 1/65, TNA.
88. Bonnet, *Souvenirs historiques*, 114.
89. Brunet to Leclerc, Sept. 30, 1802, "Unpublished Papers of Generals Leclerc and Rochambeau During the War of Independence in Haiti, 1802–3."
90. Saint-Rémy, *Pétion et Haïti*, 3:116.
91. Daure to Rochambeau, Nov. 2, 1802, "Unpublished Papers of Generals Leclerc and Rochambeau During the War of Independence in Haiti, 1802–3."
92. Saint-Rémy, *Pétion et Haïti*, 3:93, 122–23.
93. Saint-Rémy, *Pétion et Haïti*, 3:124.
94. Saint-Rémy, *Pétion et Haïti*, 3:125.
95. Fressinet to Brunet, Jan. 17, 1803, box 1524, Rochambeau Papers, University of Florida Libraries.
96. Claparède to Rochambeau, Jan. 13, 1803; Claparède to Rochambeau, Jan. 17, 1803, "Unpublished Papers of Generals Leclerc and Rochambeau During the War of Independence in Haiti, 1802–3," 13.
97. Saint-Rémy, *Pétion et Haïti*, 3:153.
98. Quoted in Saint-Rémy, *Pétion et Haïti*, 3:153–54n2.
99. Saint-Rémy, *Pétion et Haïti*, 3:182–84; Colin Dayan, *Haiti, History, and the Gods* (Berkeley: University of California Press, 1995), 51–52; Nicole Willson, "Unmaking the tricolore: Catherine Flon, material testimony and occluded narratives of female-led resistance in Haiti and the Haitian *Dyaspora*," *Slavery & Abolition* 41.1 (2020): 131–48.

100. Boisrond-Tonnerre, *Mémoires*, 83.
101. Quoted in Romain, *Noms de lieux d'époque coloniale en Haiti*, 51.
102. *Rapport des événements qui se sont passés au Cap Français, Isle St. Domingue, depuis le 20 brumaire an XII jusqu'aux 8 frimaire (12–30 novembre 1803) suivant adressé par le général La Poype au ministre de la guerre*, in "Vertières: Suite de l'ultime bataille l'armée expéditionnaire, rapport et prétextes," special issue, *Bulletin de L'ISPAN* (Nov. 2020): 15–21.
103. Dessalines, *Journal de la campagne*, 7, CO 137/111, TNA; H. Pauléus Sannon, *Études historiques: La guerre d'indépandance* (Port-au-Prince: Chéraquit, 1925), 75.
104. Dessalines, *Journal de la campagne*, 8–9.
105. Dessalines, *Journal de la campagne*, 6.
106. Saint-Rémy, *Pétion et Haïti*, 3:240–49.
107. David Geggus, "The 29 November 1803 Declaration of Independence," haitidoi.com. An earlier handwritten version exists, dated Nov. 19, 1803, and signed with the additional signatures of Pétion, Vernet, and Capoix. See "19 November 1803 Proclamation," haitidoi.com.
108. "St. Domingo," *Times*, Feb. 6, 1804, 3; "French Oppression," *New York Morning Chronicle*, Jan. 2, 1804. There exists a later handwritten transcription of the proclamation, too, dated May 8, 1804. "Proclamation. 8 mai 1804," GR7, B11, SHD. Thanks to Julia Gaffield for sharing the latter document.
109. "Translation," *New York Evening Post*, Jan. 6, 1804.
110. Acte d'indépendance, Jan. 1, 1804, mjp.univ-perp.fr. All translations mine unless otherwise noted. For an English translation of the 1803 version, see Geggus, "29 November 1803 Declaration of Independence."
111. Saint-Rémy, *Pétion et Haïti*, 3: 183–84.
112. "Acte d'indépendance," January 1, 1804; [Juste Chanlatte], *À mes concitoyens* (1804), 5.
113. "Acte d'indépendance," January 1, 1804.
114. Boisrond-Tonnerre, *Mémoires*, 92–93.
115. Vastey, *Essai*, 43.
116. Saint-Rémy, *Pétion et Haïti*, 4:17.
117. "Acte d'indépendance," January 1, 1804.
118. Chanlatte, *Le cri de la nature*, 56.
119. Chanlatte, *Le cri de la nature*, 57.
120. Vastey, *Essai*, 44.
121. Chanlatte, *Le cri de la nature*, 57–59.
122. Bonnet, *Souvenirs historiques*, 125–31.
123. Saint-Rémy, *Pétion et Haïti*, 4:25.
124. Chanlatte, *Le cri de la nature*, 59–60.
125. "An Act to suspend the commercial intercourse between the United States, and certain parts of the island of St. Domingo," Library of Congress, https://maint.loc.gov/law/help/statutes-at-large/9th-congress/session-1/c9s1ch9.pdf; Marie-Jeanne Rossignol, translated by Lillian A. Parrott, *The Nationalist Ferment: The Origins of U.S. Foreign Policy, 1792–1812* (Columbus, OH: The Ohio State University Press, 2004), 128, 133; Julia Gaffield, *Haitian Connections in the Atlantic World: Recognition after Revolution* (Chapel Hill: University of North Carolina Press, 2015), 148.
126. Chanlatte, *Le cri de la nature*, 60.
127. Chanlatte, *Le cri de la nature*, 60–61.
128. Saint-Rémy, *Pétion et Haïti*, 4:26, 37, 29.

129. "Décret relatif aux individus qui ont provoqué ou qui ont pris part aux mas-sacres et aux assassinats ordonnés par LECLERC et ROCHAMBEAU," in Lin-stant Pradine, *Recueil général des lois et actes du gouvernement d'Haïti*, 2nd edition (Paris: A. Durand, 1886), 1:15.
130. Saint-Rémy, *Pétion et Haïti*, 4:31–32.
131. Saint-Rémy, *Pétion et Haïti*, 4:36–41.
132. Saint-Rémy, *Pétion et Haïti*, 4:52.
133. Reprinted in Saint-Rémy, *Pétion et Haïti*, 4:39.
134. Jean-Jacques Dessalines, "Proclamation: Jean-Jacques Dessalines, gouverneur général aux habitants d'Haïti," April 28, 1804, Haiti and the Atlantic World, https://haitidoi.com/2015/10/30/dessalines-reader-28-april-1804/.
135. "Intelligence: Foreign and Domestic," *Centinel of Freedom*, June 4, 1804.
136. "Massacre at St. Domingo," *Connecticut Centinel*, June 14, 1804.
137. "Nouvelles étrangères," *Journal de Paris*, May 13, 1804, 1517.
138. "Nouvelles étrangères," *Journal de Paris*, May 6, 1804, 1467.
139. "Fragment of a Proclamation by General Dessalines," *American Citizen*, March 9, 1804.
140. "Nouvelles étrangères. Amérique Septentrionale," *Courrier des spectacles*, Aug. 7, 1804, 3.
141. "From the French Papers," *Morning Post*, July 18, 1804.
142. *Caledonian Mercury*, July 16, 1804; "London—July 18," *Caledonian Mercury*, July 21, 1804.
143. "Empire d'Haïti," *Gazette politique et commerciale d'Haïti*, Nov. 15, 1804, 1–2.
144. "Extraits du registre des déclarations faites à l'agence française de Santiago de Cuba concernant le massacre des blancs," 10 DPPC 697, ANOM.
145. "Extrait du registre des déclarations faites à l'agence française de St. Jago de Cuba," 10 DPPC 697, ANOM.
146. "Réponses des Citoyens Fauches et Le Belle, tous deux arrivant du Cap, aux questions à eux faites par le citoyen Baschée Boisgely, agent française à St. Yagues de Cuba," 10 DPPC 697, ANOM.
147. Cabon, *Notes sur l'histoire religieuse*, 90–91.
148. G. Hallam to War Office, July 1, 1804, WO 1/75, TNA; *Caledonian Mercury*, July 16, 1804.
149. Antoine Frinquier, "Relation des événements du Cap-Français depuis l'évacuation de l'armée commandée par le général Rochambeau, jusqu'au 20 mai 1804, 32 jours après le massacre général des blances de cette colonie," GR 1 M 597–98, SHD. Thanks to Julia Gaffield for sharing this document.
150. Frinquier, "Relation."
151. "New York, March 10," *United States' Gazette*, March 12, 1804.
152. "Blacks of St. Domingo," *Poulson's American Daily Advertiser*, March 26, 1804.
153. *Republican Gazette and General Advertiser*, March 23, 1804.
154. Saint-Rémy, *Pétion et Haïti*, 4:39.
155. Philippe R. Girard, "Caribbean Genocide: Racial War in Haiti, 1802–4," *Patterns of Prejudice* 39, no. 2 (2005): 138–61.
156. 1804 Census, Gros-Morne, Haiti, Haiti and the Atlantic World, haitidoi.com; "Empire d'Haïti, Ordonnance, Jacques Ier," *Gazette politique et commerciale d'Haïti*, Nov. 29, 1804.
157. See Julia Gaffield, "Five Myths About the Haitian Revolution," *Washington Post*, Aug. 4, 2021, www.washingtonpost.com.
158. [Adèle de Falaiseau], *Histoire de mesdemoiselles de Saint-Janvier, les deux seules blanches sauvées du massacre de Saint-Domingue*. 1st ed. (Paris: J. J. Blaise,

1812). Adaptations include the German Johanna Franul von Weissenthurn's *Die Schwestern St. Janvier. Schauspiel in fünf Aufzügen. Nach einer wahren Begebenheit, aus den Schreckenstagen auf St. Domingo* (1821) and Alexandre de Saillet's *Lucile de Saint-Albe, épisode de la révolution de Saint-Domingue* (1848).

159. James Barskett, *History of the Island of St. Domingo* (London: A. Constable, 1818), 313.

160. Bonnet, *Souvenirs historiques,* 136.

161. Dessalines's coronation reportedly took place a month later on October 8, 1804. Veuve Bellony Pardieu to Marie Bunel, April 8, 1804; Relative of Bunel's, per contents of the letter with illegible signature, to Marie Bunel, April 12, 1804; Maurin to Marie Bunel, April 17, 1804; Joseph Bunel to Marie Bunel, Sept. 7, 1804; Grandjean to Marie Bunel, Sept. 19, 1804; HSP, Arthur C. Bining Collection (#1811), MSS.695; Marie Bunel to Rochambeau, Nov. 23, 1803, box 1363, Rochambeau Papers, University of Florida Libraries; see also Philippe R. Girard "Trading Races: Joseph and Marie Bunel, a Diplomat and a Merchant in Revolutionary Saint-Domingue and Philadelphia," *Journal of the Early Republic* 30, no. 3 (2010): 369–70.

162. "Empire d'Haïti, Ordonnance, Jacques Ier," *Gazette politique et commerciale d'Haïti,* Nov. 29, 1804.

163. Jean-Jacques Dessalines, "Proclamation. Jean-Jacques Dessalines, gouverneur-général, aux habitans d'Haïti," April 28, 1804.

164. Philippe Girard, "Caribbean Genocide: Racial War in Haiti, 1802–4," *Patterns of Prejudice* 39, no. 2 (2005): 138–61; Jon Levine, "Columbus Haters Led Effort to Rename Street for Murderous Haitian Emperor," *New York Post,* May 22, 2001, nypost.com.

165. Chanlatte, *Le cri de la nature,* 59.

166. Chanlatte, *Le cri de la nature,* 62–64.

CHAPTER 8: EMPIRES RISE . . .

1. Vastey, *Essai,* 42–43.

2. "Empire d'Haïti, Du Cap, le 21 novembre," *Gazette politique et commerciale d'Haïti,* Nov. 22, 1804, 7.

3. "À Dessalines, le 15 février, 1804," *Gazette politique et commerciale d'Haïti,* Nov. 22, 1804, 7–8; Vastey, *Essai,* 47.

4. "London," *Salisbury and Winchester Journal,* Nov. 19, 1804.

5. "Couplets chantés et présenté à Sa Majesté Jacques Ier, empereur d'Haïti," *Gazette politique et commercial d'Haïti,* Nov. 22, 1804.

6. "Empire d'Haïti," *Gazette politique et commerciale d'Haïti,* Nov. 15, 1804, 2.

7. "Empire d'Haïti," *Gazette politique et commerciale d'Haïti,* Nov. 29, 1804, 4.

8. *Gazette politique et commerciale d'Haïti,* Nov. 29, 1804, 4.

9. Christophe to Dessalines, July 30, 1805, Christophe Letter Book, Henri Christophe, King of Haiti. Copie de lettres (manuscript) 1805–6, FCO Historical Collection, FOL. F1924 HEN, King's College, London Library (hereafter Christophe Letter Book).

10. Christophe to Dessalines, June 11, 1805, Christophe Letter Book.

11. Christophe to Capoix, April 30, 1805, Christophe Letter Book.

12. Christophe to Vernet, May 6, 1805; Christophe to Pourcely, May 6, 1805, Christophe Letter Book.

13. Christophe to Pourcely, May 6, 1805, Christophe Letter Book.

14. Christophe to Dessalines, May 8, 1805, Christophe Letter Book.

15. Christophe to Dessalines, May 14, 1805, Christophe Letter Book.
16. Christophe to Romain, June 7, 1805, Christophe Letter Book.
17. Christophe to Raymond, June 4, 1805, Christophe Letter Book.
18. Christophe to Sa Majesté, L'Impératrice, June 11, 1804, Christophe Letter Book.
19. Deborah Jenson, "Dessalines's American Proclamations of the Haitian Independence," *Journal of Haitian Studies* 15, no. 1–2 (Spring/Fall 2009): 77; for Haiti's principles of humane sovereignty, see Daut, *Awakening the Ashes*, 218.
20. "Empire d'Haïti," *Gazette politique et commerciale,* May 25, 1805; "Déclaration de M. Mullery, négociant au Cap," *Gazette politique et commerciale,* Sept. 5, 1805.
21. Christophe Circulaire to Cols. Joachim, Raymond, and Commandant de la place du Cap, June 11, 1804, Christophe Letter Book.
22. Christophe Circulaire to Col. Étienne Albert, to Commandant des guerres de la Grande-Rivière, to Commandant Jasmain and Lolotte Poux and Commandant d'artillerie Tiphaine, June 11, 1804, Christophe Letter Book.
23. Christophe to Dessalines, June 16, 1805, Christophe Letter Book.
24. "Empire d'Haïti," *Gazette politique et commerciale d'Haïti,* June 20, 1805, 112.
25. "Empire d'Haïti," *Gazette politique et commerciale d'Haïti,* June 27, 1805, 113–16; Constitution du 20 mai 1805," Digithèque MJP, https://mjp.univ-perp.fr/constit/ht1805.htm.
26. "Foreign Official Papers," *Cobbett's Weekly Political Register,* Aug. 24, 1805; "Friday's Post," *Ipswich Journal,* Aug. 24, 1805.
27. "Lord Nelson Attended Yesterday Morning at the Admiralty . . . ," *Times,* Aug. 24, 1805, 2.
28. "Angleterre—Londres, 24 août," *Le courrier des spectacles,* Sept. 3, 1805, 3.
29. Vastey, *Essai,* 48.
30. Vastey, *Essai,* 49.
31. "Nouvelles etrangères. Angleterre. Londre," *Gazette de France,* Dec. 1, 1805.
32. Christophe to Dessalines, July 30, 1805, Christophe Letter Book.
33. *Gazette politique et commerciale d'Haïti,* July 18, 1805, 127–28.
34. Recall that Dessalines had Petit-Noël killed around the time of the conflict with Sans-Souci, according to Saint-Rémy. Saint-Rémy, *Pétion et Haïti,* 3:125.
35. François-Marie Perichou de Kerversau, "Observations politiques et militaires sur la colonie de St. Domingue et sur les moyens les plus analogues aux circonstances de venir à son secours," ca. January 1805, AF/IV/1213, ANF.
36. Henry Perroud, "Organisation d'une armée et plan de campagne pour reprendre Saint-Domingue, présenté à Sa Majesté l'empereur des Français, roi d'Italie par l'Ordonnateur Perroud," ca. 1805, AF/IV/1213, ANF.
37. Reprinted in "West Indies," *Scots Magazine,* Feb. 1, 1804, 145.
38. Madiou, *Histoire d'Haïti,* 3:130–31.
39. Madiou, *Histoire d'Haïti,* 3:136.
40. Ardouin, *Études sur l'histoire d'Haïti,* 3rd ed. (Paris: Dézobry et E. Magdeleine, 1854), 5:473–74.
41. Madiou, *Histoire d'Haïti,* 3:197–98.
42. "Adresse de Sa Majesté l'empereur aux habitants de l'île d'Haïti, à son retour de la campagne de Santo-Domingo," *Gazette politique et commerciale d'Haïti,* May 30, 1805, 97.
43. "Arrêté [*sic*] lancé par Ferrand," *Gazette politique et commerciale d'Haïti,* May 30, 1805, 98–99.

44. "Amérique Septentrionale. *Philadelphie,* 15 mai," *La clef du cabinet,* July 2, 1805, 1.
45. "Adresse de Sa Majesté l'empereur aux habitants de l'île d'Haïti, à son retour de la campagne de Santo-Domingo," 98.
46. "Journal de campagne tenu pendant l'expédition de Santo-Domingo," *Gazette politique et commerciale d'Haïti,* May 30, 1805, 100.
47. Christophe to Dessalines, Feb. 14, 1805 [a], Christophe Letter Book.
48. Christophe to Dessalines, Feb. 14, 1805 [b], Christophe Letter Book.
49. Christophe to Romain, Feb. 16, 1805, Christophe Letter Book.
50. Christophe to multiple colonels, including Joachin, Feb. 18, 1805, Christophe Letter Book.
51. Christophe to Vernet, Feb. 20, 1805, Christophe Letter Book.
52. Christophe to Dessalines, March 12, 1805; Christophe to Antoine, March 12, 1805, Christophe Letter Book.
53. "Journal de campagne," *Gazette politique et commerciale d'Haïti,* June 20, 1805, 109.
54. Christophe to Dessalines, March 13, 1805, Christophe Letter Book.
55. Christophe to Dessalines, March 16, 1805, Christophe Letter Book.
56. "Journal de campagne," *Gazette politique et commerciale d'Haïti,* June 20, 1805, 110.
57. Christophe to Chef de Brigade Tabarre, March 16, 1805, Christophe Letter Book.
58. Christophe to Dessalines, March 18, 1805 [a], Christophe Letter Book.
59. Christophe to Dessalines, March 18, 1805 [b], Christophe Letter Book.
60. Christophe to Dessalines, March 21, 1805, Christophe Letter Book.
61. Christophe to Dessalines, March 22, 1805; Christophe to Dessalines, March 23, 1805 [a], Christophe Letter Book.
62. Christophe to Poux, March 22, 1805; Christophe to Albert, March 23, 1805; Christophe to Albert, March 25, 1805, Christophe Letter Book.
63. Christophe to Tabarre, March 23, 1805, Christophe Letter Book.
64. "Journal de campagne," *Gazette politique et commerciale d'Haïti,* June 6, 1805, 104.
65. Christophe to Dessalines, March 23, 1805 [b], Christophe Letter Book.
66. Christophe to Dessalines, March 27, 1805, Christophe Letter Book.
67. "Journal de campagne," *Gazette politique et commerciale,* June 13, 1805, 105.
68. Christophe to Clervaux, March 31, 1805, Christophe Letter Book.
69. Christophe Order, April 2, 1805: To Chef de Brigade Étienne Albert and Chef de Brigade Raymond; Christophe Order, April 2, 1805: To Chef de Brigade Jean-Jacques Barile, Christophe Letter Book.
70. "Journal de campagne," *Gazette politique et commerciale d'Haïti,* June 20, 1805, 111.
71. Christophe Order, April 2, 1805: To Chef de Bataillon Jason with two battalions from the First and one battalion from the Twenty-Eighth, to maintain order in la place de la Vega, Christophe Letter Book.
72. Christophe Order, April 2, 1805: To Chef de Bataillon Col. Antoine and "sous-bataillon," Christophe Letter Book.
73. Christophe to Achilles, April 2, 1805, Christophe Letter Book.
74. Christophe Order, April 3, 1805: To Citoyen Hilaire Gaston; Christophe Order, April 3, 1805: To General de Brigade Toussaint Brave; Christophe to Commandant d'Ouanaminthe, April 3, 1805; Christophe to Commandant de Fort-

Liberté, April 3, 1805; Christophe Order, April 5, 1805: To Chef de Brigade Pourcely, Christophe Letter Book.

75. See "Empire français, Paris, 25 messidor," *Courrier des spectacles,* July 15, 1805, 1; *Aurora General Advertiser,* July 19, 1805.

76. Christophe to Bazelais, May 22, 1805; Christophe Circulaire to Generals and Military Commanders, May 22, 1805, Christophe Letter Book.

77. "Suite du journal de campagne tenu pendant l'expédition de Santo-Domingo," *Gazette politique et commerciale d'Haïti,* June 13, 1805, 105.

78. Christophe, "Journal de campagne," *Gazette politique et commerciale d'Haïti,* June 20, 1805, 111.

79. *Aurora General Advertiser,* July 19, 1805; *Federal Gazette,* July 23, 1805.

CHAPTER 9: CRACKS IN IMPERIAL AUTHORITY

1. *Gazette politique et commerciale d'Haïti,* July 18, 1805, 128.

2. Christophe to Generals de Brigade and to the Commandant militaires des deux division du nord, June 22, 1805, Christophe Letter Book.

3. Christophe to Joachim, Aug. 31, 1805, Christophe Letter Book.

4. "Ordres généraux," *Gazette politique et commerciale d'Haïti,* Aug. 8, 1805, 140.

5. Christophe to Capoix, Dec. 18, 1805, Christophe Letter Book.

6. Christophe to Dessalines, June 7, 1805, Christophe Letter Book.

7. Christophe to Brave, Sept. 2, 1805, Christophe Letter Book.

8. Christophe to Dessalines, Sept. 10, 1805, Christophe Letter Book.

9. Christophe to Capoix, Nov. 14, 1805, Christophe Letter Book.

10. Christophe to Dessalines, Nov. 20, 1805, Christophe Letter Book.

11. Christophe to Romain, Nov. 26, 1805, Christophe Letter Book.

12. Christophe to Romain, March 11, 1806, Christophe Letter Book.

13. Christophe to Dessalines, July 6, 1805, Christophe Letter Book.

14. Christophe to Brave, July 17, 1805; Christophe to Capoix, Sept. 4, 1805, Christophe Letter Book.

15. Christophe to Capoix, Sept. 24, 1805, Christophe Letter Book.

16. *Almanach royal d'Hayti pour l'année 1814,* 5; Vastey, *Essai,* 202.

17. Boisrond-Tonnerre, *Mémoires,* 50n1; Vastey, *Essai,* 202; Christophe to Dessalines, May 22, 1805, Christophe Letter Book.

18. Christophe to Dessalines, June 13, 1805; Christophe to Dessalines, June 15, 1805, Christophe Letter Book. For Clervaux's son, see Gainot, "Un projet avorté d'intégration républicaine," 399.

19. Christophe to Dessalines, Nov. 6, 1805, Christophe Letter Book.

20. Christophe to Dessalines, Oct. 31, 1805; Christophe to Dessalines, Nov. 6, 1805; Christophe to Dessalines, Nov. 7, 1805, Christophe Letter Book.

21. Christophe to Dessalines, Nov. 7, 1805, Christophe Letter Book.

22. Christophe to Romain, Capoix, and Dartiguenave, June 10, 1806, Christophe Letter Book.

23. Christophe to Dessalines, June 11, 1806, Christophe Letter Book.

24. Christophe to Dessalines, Dec. 13, 1805, Christophe Letter Book.

25. Christophe to Roumage, May 7, 1805, Christophe Letter Book.

26. Christophe to Roumage, June 28, 1805, Christophe Letter Book.

27. "Maison d'éducation," *Gazette politique et commerciale d'Haïti,* April 4, 1805, 68.

28. Christophe to Dessalines, June 11, 1805, Christophe Letter Book.

29. Christophe to Dessalines, June 7, 1805, Christophe Letter Book.

30. Christophe to Romain, June 7, 1805, Christophe Letter Book.
31. "Du Cap, le 21 août," *Gazette politique et commerciale d'Haïti,* Aug. 22, 1805, 147.
32. "Empire d'Haïti," *Gazette politique et commerciale d'Haïti,* Aug. 8, 1805, 139–40.
33. Christophe to Roumage, May 23, 1806, Christophe Letter Book.
34. Christophe Circulaire to Generals and Commandants Militaires, July 20, 1805; Christophe to Roumage, Aug. 2, 1805; Christophe to Joachim, Oct. 17, 1805, Christophe Letter Book.
35. Christophe to Roumage, Aug. 2, 1805; Christophe to Dessalines, May 22, 1805, Christophe Letter Book.
36. Christophe to Brave, May 4, 1806, Christophe Letter Book.
37. Circulaire to Generals and Commandants Militaires, July 20, 1805, Christophe Letter Book.
38. Christophe to Chef de Brigade Pierrot of the Fifth and Chef de Brigade Marinier of the Sixth, Aug. 8, 1805, Christophe Letter Book.
39. Dessalines to Jefferson, June 23, 1803, Founders Online, founders.archives.gov.
40. "Du Cap," *Gazette politique et commerciale d'Haïti,* Oct. 17, 1805, 175.
41. Jefferson to John Page, Dec. 23, 1803, Founders Online, founders.archives.gov.
42. "Du Cap," *Gazette politique et commerciale d'Haïti,* Oct. 17, 1805, 175–76. For the Boisrond-Tonnerre quotation, see Boisrond-Tonnerre, *Mémoires,* 93.
43. Christophe to Dessalines, June 26, 1805, Christophe Letter Book.
44. Christophe to Dessalines, Oct. 31, 1805, Christophe Letter Book.
45. Christophe to Dessalines, Feb. 14, 1806, Christophe Letter Book.
46. Christophe to Dessalines, Feb. 26, 1806, Christophe Letter Book.
47. Christophe to Dessalines, Sept. 5, 1805, Christophe Letter Book.
48. Christophe to Rouanez, March 19, 1806, Christophe Letter Book.
49. Christophe to Dessalines, March 20, 1806, Christophe Letter Book.
50. Christophe to Vernet, May 28, 1806, Christophe Letter Book.
51. Christophe to Dessalines, March 20, 1806, Christophe Letter Book.
52. Christophe to Capoix, March 27, 1806, Christophe Letter Book.
53. "Empire d'Haïti," *Gazette politique et commerciale d'Haïti,* Dec. 13, 1804, 4.
54. Christophe to Dessalines, Aug. 29, 1805, Christophe Letter Book.
55. Christophe to Dessalines, March 8, 1806; Christophe to Dessalines, March 11, 1806, Christophe Letter Book.
56. René Périn, *L'incendie du Cap; ou, Le règne de Toussaint-Louverture* (Paris: Marchand, 1802), xiv, 119–20.
57. Christophe to Dessalines, Dec. 13, 1805, Christophe Letter Book.
58. Christophe to Dessalines, Jan. 12, 1806, Christophe Letter Book.
59. Christophe to Dessalines, March 8, 1806, Christophe Letter Book.
60. Christophe to Capoix, March 18, 1806; Christophe to Brave, March 24, 1806, Christophe Letter Book.
61. Christophe to Chef de Division de Marine Masson, April 7, 1806, Christophe Letter Book.
62. Christophe to Capoix, March 11, 1806; Christophe to Dessalines, March 11, 1806, Christophe Letter Book.
63. Christophe to Generals Romain and Brave, Jan. 10, 1805; Christophe circular to Generals Brave and Romain, and to the Commandants of the military, May 7, 1805, Christophe Letter Book.
64. "Empire d'Haïti," *Gazette politique et commerciale d'Haïti,* Nov. 21, 1805, 192.
65. Christophe to Capoix, Nov. 11, 1805, Christophe Letter Book.

66. Christophe to Romain, Nov. 12, 1805, Christophe Letter Book.
67. Christophe to Dessalines, May 28, 1806, Christophe Letter Book.
68. Christophe to Romain and Capoix, May 28, 1806, Christophe Letter Book.
69. Christophe to Commandant de la place du Cap, April 8, 1806, Christophe Letter Book.
70. Christophe to Dessalines, April 9, 1806, Christophe Letter Book.
71. Christophe to Dessalines, April 9, 1806, Christophe Letter Book.
72. Christophe to Dessalines, April 9, 1806, Christophe Letter Book.
73. Christophe to Commandant de la place du Cap, July 6, 1806, Christophe Letter Book.
74. Christophe to Capoix, May 9, 1806, Christophe Letter Book.
75. Christophe to Dessalines, May 8, 1806, Christophe Letter Book.
76. Christophe to Generals Romain, Dartiguenave, and Lamérince, May 9, 1806; Christophe to Brave, May 9, 1806, Christophe Letter Book.
77. Christophe to Brave, May 9, 1806, Christophe Letter Book.
78. Christophe to Dessalines, May 18, 1806, Christophe Letter Book.
79. Christophe to U.S. businessmen in Cap, May 15, 1806, Christophe Letter Book.
80. Christophe to Romain and Brave, July 13, 1806; Christophe to Dessalines, July 13, 1806, Christophe Letter Book.
81. Christophe to Dessalines, July 13, 1806, Christophe Letter Book.
82. Christophe to Roumage, Nov. 19, 1805; Christophe to Roumage, Dec. 20, 1805, Christophe Letter Book.
83. Christophe to Dessalines, Jan. 3, 1805; Christophe to Romain and Brave, Jan. 3, 1805; Christophe to Roumage, Jan. 5, 1805; Christophe to Brave, Jan. 5, 1805; Christophe to Raymond, Jan. 5, 1805; Christophe to Dessalines, Jan. 12, 1805, Christophe Letter Book.
84. Christophe to Capoix and Romain, Dec. 13, 1805, Christophe Letter Book.
85. Christophe to Capoix, Dec. 28, 1805, Christophe Letter Book.
86. Christophe to Dessalines, Jan. 11, 1806; Christophe to Dessalines, Jan. 23, 1806, Christophe Letter Book.
87. Christophe to Poux, Sept. 3, 1805, Christophe Letter Book.
88. Christophe to Dessalines, Sept. 5, 1805, Christophe Letter Book.
89. Christophe to Romain and Capoix, Dec. 2, 1805, Christophe Letter Book.
90. Christophe to Dessalines, Nov. 18, 1805; Christophe to Dessalines, Nov. 23, 1805; Christophe to Dessalines, Dec. 3, 1805, Christophe Letter Book.
91. Christophe to Dessalines, Dec. 17, 1805; Christophe to General Dartiguenave, Dec. 18, 1805; Christophe to Adjutant General Gérard, Dec. 18, 1805; Christophe to Dessalines, Dec. 18, 1805, Christophe Letter Book.
92. Nadege Green, "The Black Religion That's Been Maligned for Centuries," *Atlantic,* June 29, 2022, www.theatlantic.com.
93. "Constitution d'Haïti," *Gazette politique et commerciale d'Haïti,* June 27, 1806, 115.
94. Christophe to Capoix, Nov. 13, 1805, Christophe Letter Book.
95. Laurent Dubois, "Dessalines Toro d'Haïti," *William and Mary Quarterly* 69, no. 3 (2012): 541–48.
96. Legendary fugitive from slavery François Makandal was convicted in 1758 of allegedly using a vast network of maroons to poison planters and their families, as well as other enslaved people, living in the northern plain. Legend has it that when colonial authorities tried to burn Makandal at the stake he suddenly leaped out of the fire, transformed himself into a mosquito, and then flew away. Contemporary scholars have argued that Makandal likely never poisoned

anyone, with the planters misinterpreting his religious rituals and looking for causes for what was in reality epidemic disease. See John Garrigus, *A Secret Among the Blacks: Slave Resistance before the Haitian Revolution* (Cambridge, Mass.: Harvard University Press, 2023).

97. Christophe to Dessalines, Nov. 23, 1805, Christophe Letter Book.
98. Christophe to the Prince du Limbé (General Paul Romain), May 5, 1811, reprinted in Supplice, *Dictionnaire*, 419–20.
99. Karol K. Weaver, *Medical Revolutionaries: The Enslaved Healers of Eighteenth-Century Saint Domingue* (Urbana: University of Illinois Press, 2006), 125.
100. Christophe to Commandant de la place, May 16, 1806; Christophe to Dessalines, May 18, 1806, Christophe Letter Book. For Hélène as caretaker, see Christophe to Dessalines, March 6, 1806, Christophe Letter Book.
101. Christophe to Dessalines, June 3, 1806, Christophe Letter Book.
102. Christophe to Capoix, Dec. 15, 1805, Christophe Letter Book.
103. Christophe to Capoix, Dec. 21, 1805, Christophe Letter Book.
104. Christophe to Capoix, May 4, 1806, Christophe Letter Book.
105. Christophe to Capoix, May 10, 1806, Christophe Letter Book.
106. Christophe to Capoix, June 26, 1806, Christophe Letter Book.
107. Christophe to Capoix, July 20, 1806, Christophe Letter Book.
108. Christophe to Roumage, Aug. 11, 1806, Christophe Letter Book.
109. Christophe to General Dartiguenave, Oct. 11, 1806; Christophe to Brave, Oct. 12, 1806, Christophe Letter Book.
110. Christophe order, Oct. 6, 1806: Division General Capoix; Christophe to Capoix, Oct. 7, 1806; Christophe order, Oct. 6, 1806, Christophe Letter Book.
111. Christophe to Dessalines, Oct. 9, 1806, Christophe Letter Book.
112. Christophe to Capoix, Oct. 10, 1806, Christophe Letter Book.
113. Christophe to Brave, Oct. 23, 1806; Christophe circular to Romain, Brave, and Dartiguenave, Oct. 19, 1806, Christophe Letter Book.
114. Christophe to Dessalines, Oct. 11, 1806, Christophe Letter Book.
115. Christophe to Dessalines, Oct. 11, 1806, Christophe Letter Book.

CHAPTER 10: EMPIRES FALL . . .

1. "Le Ministre des finances et de l'intérieur," *Gazette politique et commerciale,* Aug. 15 1805, 144.
2. "Empire d'Haïti. Décret relatif aux testaments et autres actes portant donation des biens fonds," *Gazette politique et commerciale d'Haïti*, Oct. 2, 1806, 152.
3. Beaubrun Ardouin, *Études sur l'histoire d'Haïti* (Paris: Dezobry et E. Magdeleine, 1856), 6:164.
4. Ardouin, *Études sur l'histoire d'Haïti*, 6:240.
5. Christophe to Dessalines, Oct. 16, 1806[a], Christophe Letter Book.
6. Christophe to Dessalines, Oct. 16, 1806[b], Christophe Letter Book. For Dessalines as godfather to Victor-Henry, see Christophe to Dessalines, July 2, 1805, in ibid.
7. Christophe to Romain, Oct. 17, 1806, Christophe Letter Book.
8. Christophe to Dartiguenave, Oct. 17, 1806, Christophe Letter Book.
9. Christophe to Justamont, Oct. 17, 1806, Christophe Letter Book.
10. Christophe to Brave, Oct. 17, 1806, Christophe Letter Book.
11. Christophe to Vernet[a], Oct. 19, 1806, Christophe Letter Book.
12. Christophe to Romain and Dartiguenave, Oct. 19, 1806; Christophe to Pierre Toussaint, Oct. 19, 1806, Christophe Letter Book.

13. Christophe to Vernet, Oct. 19, 1806[b], Christophe Letter Book.
14. Christophe to Colonel Jean Louis Longueval, Oct. 19, 1806, Christophe Letter Book.
15. Christophe to Daut and Cangé, Oct. 19, 1806, Christophe Letter Book.
16. Christophe to Colonel Marinier and Chef de Bataillon Brochard, Oct. 19, 1806, Christophe Letter Book.
17. Christophe to Romain, Oct. 19, 1806, Christophe Letter Book.
18. Christophe to Pétion, Sept. 3, 1805, Christophe Letter Book.
19. Dissident officers to Christophe, Oct. 19, 1806, Supplice Private Collection; see photo of document in Supplice, *Dictionnaire*, 417–18. Thanks to Lewis Clorméus for sharing an original image with me.
20. Christophe to Vernet, Oct. 19, 1806[c], Christophe Letter Book.
21. Christophe to Pétion, Oct. 19, 1806, Christophe Letter Book.
22. Christophe to S.M., L'Impératrice, Oct. 21, 1806, Christophe Letter Book.
23. Pétion to Marie-Claire Heureuse Félicité Dessalines, Oct. 19, 1806, in Saint-Rémy, *Pétion et Haïti*, 4:147.
24. Saint-Rémy, *Pétion et Haïti*, 1:23.
25. Christophe to Vernet, Oct. 21, 1806; Christophe to Besse, Oct. 21, 1806, Christophe Letter Book.
26. Christophe to Vernet, Oct. 21, 1806, Christophe Letter Book.
27. Christophe to Mr. Groguine, Oct. 21, 1806; Christophe to John Darcy, Oct. 21, 1806, Christophe Letter Book.
28. Christophe to Toussaint, Oct. 22, 1806, Christophe Letter Book.
29. Christophe to Magny, Oct. 22, 1806, Christophe Letter Book.
30. Pétion to Christophe, Oct. 18, 1806, Supplice Collection; see photograph of document as reproduced in Supplice, *Dictionnaire*, 412–16. Thanks to Lewis Clorméus for sharing a scan of the original.
31. Christophe to Vernet, Oct. 22, 1806, Christophe Letter Book.
32. Christophe to Barthélemy, Oct. 22, 1806, Christophe Letter Book.
33. "Constitution d'Haïti," *Gazette politique et commerciale d'Haïti*, June 27, 1805, 116.
34. Christophe to Pétion, Oct. 23, 1806, Christophe Letter Book.
35. "Constitution d'Haïti," *Gazette politique et commerciale d'Haïti*, June 27, 1805, 113.
36. "Les chefs de l'armée du sud au général en chef," Oct. 13, 1806, in Saint-Rémy, *Pétion et Haïti*, 4:124–25.
37. The date reads the sixteenth in the copy of the letter where Christophe mentions having received Pétion's first letter, but this was likely Christophe's secretary's error in miscopying the date, since Pétion's letter is clearly dated the eighteenth.
38. Christophe to Gérin, Oct. 23, 1806, Christophe Letter Book.
39. Christophe to Vernet, Oct. 23, 1806, Christophe Letter Book.
40. Reprinted in Saint-Rémy, *Pétion et Haïti*, 4:159–60. For the document titled "Resistance to Oppression," see also Madiou, *Histoire d'Haïti*, 3:390–94.
41. Christophe to Pétion, Oct. 26, 1806, Christophe Letter Book.
42. "Isle d'Haïti," *Gazette politique et commerciale d'Haïti*, Nov. 6, 1806, 169–70; for articles of the constitution, see "Constitution d'Haïti," *Gazette politique et commerciale d'Haïti*, June 27, 1805, 114; for Christophe's order for the account to be printed, see Christophe to Vernet, Oct. 23, 1806, Christophe Letter Book.
43. "Relatif aux testaments et aux autres actes portant donation des biens fonds," *Gazette politique et commerciale d'Haïti*, Oct. 2, 1806, 152; Juste Chanlatte,

Réflexions sur le prétendu Sénat du Port-au-Prince (Cap-Haïtien: P. Roux, 1807); See also Chanlatte, *À mes concitoyens.*

44. Férou to Sir Eyre Coote, Oct. 20, 1806, CO 137/117/4 No. 65, folios 12–23, TNA.

45. "Empire d'Haïti, de Dessalines, le 4 octobre," *Gazette politique et commerciale d'Haïti,* Oct. 16, 1806, 162–63. For Dessalines in Les Cayes, see Dessalines to M. John Downie (English merchant), Aug. 15, 1806; for Dessalines at his palace in Jérémie, see Dessalines to Downie, July 20, 1806, WO 1/75, TNA.

46. Férou to Sir Eyre Coote, Oct. 20, 1806.

47. Mackenzie to the British government, Sept. 9, 1826, CO 318/102, TNA.

48. Bonnet, *Souvenirs historiques,* 143–44.

49. "Isle d'Haïti," *Gazette politique et commerciale d'Haïti,* Nov. 20, 1806.

50. Christophe to Dessalines, Sept. 4, 1806, Christophe Letter Book.

51. Vastey, *Essai,* 53–63.

52. Saint-Rémy, *Pétion et Haïti,* 4:133–34.

53. Christophe to Yayou, Oct. 12, 1805; Christophe to Romain, Nov. 7, 1805; Christophe to Dessalines, Nov. 13, 1805, Christophe Letter Book.

54. Hugonin to Christophe, Nov. 24, 1806, ACL-4 (Letters to Henry Christophe), Nemours Collection.

55. Saint-Rémy, *Pétion et Haïti,* 4:140.

56. Jana Evans Braziel, "Re-membering Défilée: Dédée Bazile as Revolutionary *Lieu de Mémoire*," *Small Axe* 9, no. 2 (Sept. 2005): 57–85.

57. Vastey, *Essai,* 63–64.

58. Saint-Rémy, *Pétion et Haïti,* 4:140.

CHAPTER 11: THE DAWN OF CIVIL WAR

1. Clément Lanier, "Claire Heureuse, de son vrai nom Claire Félicité Guillaume Bonheur. Conférence prononcée le dimanche 23 juillet 1933," *Revue de la Société d'histoire et de géographie d'Haïti,* Jan. 1, 1934.

2. Birth notation for Célimène Dessalines, "fille de Jean-Jacques Dessalines," February 2, 1806, La Bibliothèque Haïtienne des Spiritains, Haïti. Document as cited in Julia Gaffield's forthcoming biography of Dessalines, tentatively titled *Jean-Jacques Dessalines and the Haitian Revolution,* with Yale University Press. Thanks to Julia Gaffield for sharing a scan.

3. On the illness and death of Cérine, see Christophe to Dessalines, Oct. 3, 1805; Christophe to Dessalines, Oct. 31, 1805, Christophe Letter Book.

4. Pétion to Madame Dessalines, Oct. 19, 1806, BNF, gallica.bnf.fr; Christophe to S.M., L'Impératrice, Oct. 21, 1806, Christophe Letter Book.

5. Saint-Rémy, *Pétion et Haïti,* 4:146; Vastey, *Essai,* 75–76.

6. Saint-Rémy, introduction to *Mémoires pour servir à l'histoire d'Haïti par Boisrond-Tonnerre, précédés de différents actes politiques dûs à sa plume, et d'une étude historique et critique par Saint-Rémy (des Cayes, Haïti), avocat aux cours impériales de l'ouest et du sud* (Paris: Libraire, 1851), xv–xvi. Poem on xvi, ibid.

7. Saint-Rémy, introduction to *Mémoires pour servir,* xvi n1.

8. "État d'Hayti: Adresse au peuple et à l'armée," Nov. 2, 1806, reprinted in *Gazette officielle de l'État d'Hayti,* May 14, 1807, 7–8.

9. Vastey, *Essai,* 78–80; Juste Chanlatte, "Quelques réflexions sur le prétendu Sénat du Port-au-Prince," *Gazette officielle,* July 2, 1807, 35.

10. "Port-au-Prince, le 29 décembre 1806. Les députés des divisions du nord et de la première de l'ouest, à Son Éxcellence le général en chef de l'armée d'Haïti," *Gazette officielle,* Aug. 20, 1807, 63–64.

11. "État d'Hayti. Proclamation au peuple et à l'armée," Nov. 24, 1806, reprinted in *Gazette officielle,* May 21, 1807, 11–12; for the rumors of killings, see Vastey, *Essai,* 76; for Lieutenant Doria, see Hugonin to Christophe, Nov. 24, 1806.

12. Alexandre Pétion et al., "Rapport fait à l'Assemblée constituante par son comité de constitution, dans sa séance du 27 décembre 1806," in *Constitution d'Haïti du 27 décembre 1806, et sa révision du 2 juin 1816, an 13 de l'indépendance* (Port-au-Prince: Imprimerie du Gouvernement, 1816), i–iv.

13. Pétion et al., "Rapport," iii, vi–vii.

14. Blanchet to Monsieur Peltier, July 31, 1807, WO 1/79, TNA; "Constitution du 27 décembre 1806," Digithèque MJP, mjp.univ-perp.fr. See also the confirmation that Christophe had been "confirmed to be the first magistrate of the State, in being named to preside over the Haitian Republic," in Cézar Télémaque et al.'s "Adresse du Sénat, au peuple et à l'armée," Jan. 24, 1807, 1, 4, N.13, PAIRS Spanish Archives, Archivo General de Indias, ESTADO.

15. Cézar Télémaque et al., "Adresse du Senat," Jan. 25, 1807, 2, PAIRS.

16. Vastey, *Essai,* 79–81.

17. "État d'Hayti, Proclamation, le chef du gouvernement à l'armée d'Hayti," Dec. 18, 1806, reprinted in *Gazette de l'État d'Hayti,* May 7, 1807, 2–3; on the Citadelle Henry, see Prévost, *Relation,* 3.

18. Dumesle, *Voyage,* 34–36.

19. Férou to Sir Eyre Coote, Oct. 20, 1806.

20. Blanchet to Peltier, July 31, 1807.

21. Prévost, *Relation,* 4.

22. [Rouanez], "Extrait. Haïti liberté et indépendance. Aux Gonaïves le 25 avril 1807, l'an quatre de l'indépendance. Le secrétaire d'état à Mr. Peltier," WO 1/79, TNA.

23. Vastey, *Essai,* 84–85.

24. See Chelsea Stieber, *Haiti's Paper War: Post-independence Writing, Civil War, and the Making of the Republic, 1804–1954* (New York: New York University Press, 2020).

25. Prévost, *Relation,* 4; Vastey, *Essai,* 81n1.

26. "Suite du rapport sur l'expédition des Gonaïves," *Gazette officielle,* July 16, 1807, 44.

27. Blanchet to Peltier, July 31, 1807.

28. "État d'Hayti. Proclamation. Au peuple et à l'armée," Jan. 14, 1807, reprinted in *Gazette officielle,* June 4, 1807, 19–20.

29. "Adresse. Le chef du gouvernement d'Hayti, aux habitants et cultivateurs," Jan. 22, 1807, WO 1/79, TNA.

30. Vastey, *Essai,* 88–90.

31. "Constitution du 27 décembre 1806."

32. Peltier, "Hayti, trois mémoires remis à Lord Castlereagh, octobre 1807," WO 1/79, TNA.

33. Vastey, *Essai,* 91.

34. "Adresse. Henry Christophe, Président et Généralissime des Forces de Terre et de Mer de l'État d'Haïti," Feb. 17, 1807, WO 1/79, TNA.

35. "Constitution du 17 février 1807," Digithèque MJP, https://mjp.univ-perp.fr /constit/ht1807.htm.

36. "Adresse. Henry Christophe," Feb. 17, 1807.

37. "Proclamation. Henry Christophe, Président et Généralissime des Forces de Terre et de Mer de l'État d'Haïti," Feb. 19, 1807, WO 1/79, TNA.

38. "Avis," *Gazette officielle,* May 7, 1807, 1.

39. Vastey, *Essai,* 96–97; "Rapport. Fait par le Chef de l'État Major de l'Armée, à Monseigneur le Président et Généralissime des Forces de Terre et de Mer de l'État d'Haiti, sur la campagne du mois de séptembre, faisant suite à celle de la prise du Port-de-Paix," Oct. 1, 1807, 1, WO 1/79, TNA.

40. "Rapport. Fait par le Chef de l'État Major de l'Armée," Oct. 1, 1807, 2–9.

41. "Rapport. Fait par le Chef de l'État Major de l'Armée, à Monseigneur le Président et Généralissime, rélativement à la victoire remportée le 25 octobre devant Saint-Marc, sur les révoltés du Port-aux-Crimes," Nov. 8, 1807, 1–5, WO 1/79, TNA.

42. "Rapport," Nov. 8, 1807; Vastey, *Essai,* 97.

43. [Peltier], "Situation d'Haïty, à 5 septembre 1807, suivant les lettres du Cap et le rapport du Capitain Goodall, du Young Roscius, arrivé à Portsmouth," WO 1/79, TNA.

44. Vastey, *Essai,* 99.

45. [Peltier], "Situation d'Haïty, à 5 septembre 1807, suivant les lettres du Cap et le rapport du Capitain Goodall, du Young Roscius, arrivé à Portsmouth," WO 1/79, TNA.

46. Peltier to Lord Castlereagh, June 8, 1807; "Confirmation des pouvoirs envoyés le 2 avril 1807, à M. Peltier, par le gouvernement de Hayti. Extrait d'une depêche du secrétaire d'état, M. Rouanez jeune, à M. Peltier au Cap, le 28 août 1807," WO 1/79, TNA.

47. "Extraits des dépêches reçues d'Hayti, par M. Peltier, de la part du secrétaire d'état, M. Rouanez jeune, au nom de S.E. le Général Henry Christophe. Président de l'État d'Hayti . . . ," WO 1/79, TNA.

48. "Orders in Council Their Operation with Respect to the Future Trade with Haity [*sic*]," WO 1/79, TNA. For the trade prohibition, see Julia Gaffield, *Haitian Connections in the Atlantic World,* 146–48.

49. "Extraits des dépêches reçues d'Hayti."

50. Peltier to Castlereagh, Oct. 28, 1807, WO 1/79, TNA.

51. Peltier to Castlereagh, Oct. 5, 1807, WO 1/79, TNA.

52. Peltier to Castlereagh, Jan. 21, 1808, WO 1/79, TNA.

53. Peltier to E. E. Cooke, Note verbale, Nov. 10, 1807, WO 1/79, TNA.

54. Rouanez, "Mémoire présenté par l'ordre de Monseigneur le Président et Généralissime des Forces de Terre et de Mer de l'État d'Haïti à Right Honorable Lord Castlereagh, One of His Majesty's Principal Secretaries of State &c &c."; Peltier to Castlereagh, Feb. 7, 1808; Peltier to Castlereagh, Feb. 5, 1808, WO 1/79, TNA.

55. Peltier to E. E. Cooke, June 18, 1808, WO 1/79, TNA.

56. Peltier to Lord Castlereagh, May 5, 1809; see also Rouanez, "Extrait d'une dépêche de M. Rouanez, secrétaire d'État d'Haïty, à M. Peltier à Londres, datée au Cap, le 17 mars 1809," WO 1/79, TNA.

57. Peltier to Sir Robert Peel, June 27, 1810, WO 1/79, TNA.

58. Vastey, *Essai,* 107–112.

59. Dumesle, *Voyage,* 21, 11.

60. Dumesle, *Voyage,* 13–14.

61. Dumesle, *Voyage,* 23.

62. Dumesle, *Voyage,* 23–24.

63. Dumesle, *Voyage,* 25–28.

64. "Proclamation. Henry Christophe. Président et Généralissime des Forces de Terre et de Mer de l'État d'Hayti," Oct. 8, 1810, in Prévost, *Relation,* 30–34. For Noël having fought in the Battle of Môle, see "Ode sur la prise du Môle Saint-Nicholas," in Prévost, *Relation,* 37n2.

65. Prévost, *Relation,* 34.

66. Peltier to Peele, June 1, 1811, WO 1/79, TNA.

CHAPTER 12: A KING IS CROWNED

1. Prévost, *Relation,* 113–14.

2. Prévost, *Relation,* 102; see also *Almanach royal d'Hayti pour l'année 1814,* 31.

3. Prévost, *Relation,* 114–15.

4. Prévost, *Relation,* 115–18.

5. "Procès verbal de la prestation de serment des grands dignitaires, officiers civils et militaires, des troupes de terre et de mer du Royaume d'Hayti, à Sa Majesté," in Prévost, *Relation,* 116–17.

6. Prévost, *Relation,* 121, 122–23.

7. Prévost, *Relation,* 126; "Hymne haytiène [*sic*]," CO 137/11, TNA.

8. Prévost, *Relation,* 127–28, 131–32.

9. Prévost, *Relation,* 132–33.

10. "Suite du rapport sur l'expédition des Gonaïves," *Gazette officielle,* July 16, 1807, 44. Marie-Claire, signing as Veuve Dessalines, wrote to Christophe to complain that Madame Cincinatus, out of jealousy, was preventing her husband (the Chevalier Cincinatus Leconte) from visiting the widow at her home. Marie-Claire Heureuse to Christophe, March 1813, La Bibliothèque Haïtienne des Spiritains, Haiti. Many thanks to Julia Gaffield for sharing this document with me, which she received from Patrick Tardieu.

11. Prévost, *Relation,* 153–54.

12. Prévost, *Relation,* 155.

13. Prévost, *Relation,* 155–56.

14. Prévost, *Relation,* 157.

15. *Almanach royal d'Hayti pour l'année 1814,* 139; for the Comtesse Chanlatte's full name, see Grégory Pierrot, "Juste Chanlatte: A Haitian Life," *Journal of Haitian Studies* 25, no. 1 (Spring 2019): 51.

16. Reprinted in Prévost, *Relation,* 159–62.

17. Prévost, *Relation,* 162.

18. *Almanach royal d'Hayti pour l'année 1814,* 140. For Marie-Françoise Salinette's parentage, see the marriage notation for Louis Étienne Neptune and Marie Françoise Salinette Dessalines, July 2, 1835, digitized at familysearch.org.

19. Prévost, *Relation,* 163.

20. Prévost, *Relation,* 178–83.

21. Prévost, *Relation,* 192.

22. Prévost, *Relation,* 3; "Le Tivoli haytien," *Gazette officielle,* Sept. 28, 1809, 155; "Loi Militaire," *Code Henry* (1812), 103.

23. "Loi Militaire," *Code Henry,* 105. For images and locations of many of northern Haiti's forts, see Stephanie Curci, "Mapping Haitian History," www.mappinghaitianhistory.com.

24. "Royaume d'Hayti. Du Cap-Henry, le 15 août," *Gazette royale,* Aug. 16, 1814, 3–4.

25. "La Citadelle Henry: 'Un monument qui le mît debout,' " *Bulletin de l'ISPAN,* Sept. 1, 2011, 2.

26. For the fort as a prison, see Christophe to Dessalines, Nov. 13, 1805; Christophe Order to Capitaine Jean-Baptiste Noël, Nov. 18, 1805; Christophe to Commandant Fidèle, Dec. 15, 1805; for cultivators who deserted the farms and were sent to work at the fort, see Christophe to Romain, June 16, 1806, Christophe Letter Book.

27. Christophe to Captain Boisson, Aug. 27, 1805, Christophe Letter Book.

28. Christophe to Poux, Aug. 11, 1805, Christophe Letter Book.

29. Christophe to Colonel Joachim, Dec. 21, 1805; Christophe to Capoix, Sept. 13, 1805; Christophe to Commandant Jasmain, Aug. 20, 1805; Christophe to Commandant Benjamin, Aug. 20, 1805; Christophe to Colonel Baptiste Michel, Aug. 28, 1805, Christophe Letter Book.

30. Christophe to Dessalines, Feb. 17, 1806, Christophe Letter Book.

31. Christophe to Faraud, June 28, 1805; Christophe to Faraud, April 30, 1805, Christophe Letter Book.

32. "La Citadelle Henry," 4; Cheesman, *Armorial of Haiti*, 140; Prévost, *Relation*, 102; "Loi pénale militaire," *Code Henry*, 27; *Almanach royal d'Hayti pour l'année 1814*, 14, 29.

33. Prévost, *Relation*, 17.

34. Dumesle quoted and response in "De Sans-Souci, le 25 octobre," *Gazette royale d'Hayti*, Oct. 28, 1819, 1–2.

35. *Quadruples d'espagne* (also known as *quadruples pistoles*), or quadruples from Spain, were an extremely valuable form of currency: coins layered with thick gold. Boyer evidently found a "considerable amount" of them in Christophe's coffers after his suicide and used them to finance his own siege of the eastern side of the island, which ended in the reunification of Haiti from 1822 to 1843. See Lacombe, *Histoire monétaire*, 16, 20, 58n2.

36. Prévost, *Relation*, 19–20.

37. "La Citadelle Henry," 4; Mercer Cook, "A Visit to Christophe's Citadel," *Negro History Bulletin 9*, no. 3 (1945): 53, 70; Christophe to Dr. Massicot, March 7, 1813, Documenti di Haiti, cc.3r-4v, BCAM.

38. Prévost, *Relation*, 199.

39. "Proclamation. Henry, par la grâce de Dieu et la loi constitutionnelle de l'état, roi d'Hayti, aux habitans du sud et de partie de l'ouest du royaume," Sept. 3, 1811, in Prévost, *Relation*, 194–97.

40. Prévost, *Relation*, 45.

41. "Loi constitutionnelle du Conseil d'État, qui établit la Royauté à Hayti," March 28, 1811, WO 1/79, TNA; "Constitution royale du 28 mars 1811," Digithèque MJP, http://mjp.univ-perp.fr/constit/ht1811.htm; "Le Conseil d'État, au peuple et à l'armée de terre et de mer d'Hayti," April 4, 1811, WO 1/79, TNA.

42. "Le Conseil d'État, au peuple et à l'armée de terre et de mer d'Hayti."

43. Prévost, *Relation*, 44–49.

44. Prévost, *Relation*, 56–57, 64.

45. Prévost, *Relation*, 60–61.

46. Vastey, *Essai*, 149, 143–44.

47. Vastey, *Essai*, 148, 149, 147, 143.

48. Saint-Rémy, *Pétion et Haïti*, 1:83n1. The marriage record for André Rigaud and his wife, Anne Villeneuve, lists Rigaud's parents, André Rigaud and Rose Bossy, as "both deceased, native to this department [Les Cayes] on one side." Rigaud's record of service offers more precise information, listing his father as originally from Provence and his mother as "originaire d'affrique[sic]"

(originating from Africa). Marriage notation for André Rigaud and Anne Villeneuve, June 5, 1799, État civil des Cayes, ANOM; "Etat de Services d'André Rigaud."

49. Claude B. Auguste, *André Rigaud et la saga des anciens libres* (Montréal: CIDHICA, 2008), 248; Prévost, *Relation*, 23–24.

50. Quoted in Peltier to Lord Liverpool, "Note Sur la Situation de l'isle d'Haity, (Saint Domingue) à la fin d'avril 1810," June 24, 1810, MS38245, BL. Thanks to Julia Gaffield for sharing this document.

51. The article was reprinted in *Repertory*, April 3, 1810; *Connecticut Mirror*, April 9, 1810; *Berkshire Reporter*, April 11, 1810; and *Sun*, April 21, 1810.

52. Prévost, *Relation*, 24; Auguste, *André Rigaud et la saga des anciens libres*, 248, 254, 254n504.

53. Bonnet, *Souvenirs historiques*, 244; Marriage notation for Guy-Joseph Bonnet and Victoire Adélaïde Emelie Péan, May 2, 1810, État civil d'Haiti, AGH; Vastey, *Essai*, 113.

54. Bonnet, *Souvenirs historiques*, 237; Vastey, *Essai*, 115.

55. Quoted in Vastey, *Essai*, 117.

56. Vastey, *Essai*, 129–32.

57. Vastey, *Essai*, 141–42.

58. Vastey, *Essai*, 143.

59. Vastey, *Essai*, 170–72.

60. Peltier to Earl of Liverpool, June 26, 1810, MS 37870, BL. Thanks to Julia Gaffield for sharing this document.

61. "Royaume d'Hayti. Du Cap-Henry, le 20 novembre," *Gazette royale d'Hayti*, Nov. 19, 1814, 1.

CHAPTER 13: THREE FRENCH SPIES

1. Bernard Gainot, "Jean-François Dauxion-Lavaysse (vers 1770–1830). De la reconnaissance de terrain à la reconnaissance sociale," *Annales historiques de la Révolution française* 385, no. 3 (2016): 67–86; Friedemann Pestel, *Kosmopoliten wider Willen: Die "monarchiens" als Revolutionsemigranten* (Olenburg: De Gruyter, 2015); Vastey, *Essai*, 205.

2. Jean Brière, *Haïti et la France: Le rêve brisée, 1804–1848* (Paris: Karthala, 2008), 61–62; Vastey, *Essai*, 205–207.

3. "Royaume d'Hayti," *Gazette royale d'Hayti*, Aug. 16, 1814, 2–3.

4. Quoted in Saint-Rémy, *Mémoires de Toussaint*, app., 125. For their voyage, see Vastey, *Essai*, 205.

5. Quoted in Saint-Rémy, *Mémoires de Toussaint*, app., 127, 126.

6. Dauxion-Lavaysse to Christophe, Oct. 1, 1814, in Vastey, *An Essay on the Causes*, app. F/2, xcvi.

7. Baron de Vastey, *Notes à M. le Baron V. P. de Malouet* (Cap-Henry: P. Roux, 1814); Chevalier de Prézeau, *Réfutation de la lettre du général français Dauxion Lavaysse* (Cap-Henry: P. Roux, 1814).

8. De Prézeau, *Réfutation de la lettre*, 4–5.

9. Madiou, *Histoire d'Haïti*, 5:261–65.

10. Dauxion-Lavaysse to Pétion, Sept. 6, 1814, in Vastey, *An Essay*, app. B/1, xv.

11. Quoted in Saint-Rémy, *Mémoires de Toussaint*, app., 128.

12. Pétion to Dauxion-Lavaysse, Sept. 24, 1814, in Vastey, *An Essay*, app. B/2, xvi–xvii; see also Madiou, *Histoire d'Haïti*, 5:249.

13. Pétion to Dauxion-Lavaysse, Sept. 24, 1814, in Vastey, *An Essay,* app. B/2, xvii.
14. For Boyer's occupations, see Charles Mackenzie to British government, Sept. 9, 1826, CO 318/102, TNA.
15. Reprinted in Madiou, *Histoire d'Haïti,* 5:266.
16. Drouin de Bercy, *De Saint-Domingue* (Paris: Chocquet, 1814), 53–63.
17. "Instructions for MM. Dauxion Lavaysse, de Médina and Dravermann," in Vastey, *An Essay,* app. C/1, xxxiv, xxxiii. For Dauxion-Lavaysse's fever, see Dauxion-Lavaysse to Pétion, Nov. 19, in Vastey, *An Essay,* app. B/5, xxiv. For "treaty-worthiness," see Gaffield, *Haitian Connections in the Atlantic World,* 6.
18. The "Official Censure upon the Mission of Lavaysse, Dravermann, and Médina, by the Minister of the Marine and the Colonies" was published in the *Moniteur de France,* Jan. 19, 1815, in Vastey, *An Essay,* app. F/3, ci; Dauxion-Lavaysse to Pétion, Nov. 9, 1814, in Vastey, *An Essay,* app. B/3, xix–xx; see also Madiou, *Histoire d'Haïti,* 5:250.
19. Pétion to Dauxion-Lavaysse, Nov. 12, 1814, in Vastey, *An Essay,* app. B/4, xx–xxiv.
20. "Kingdom of Hayti. Declaration of the King," in Vastey, *An Essay,* app. F/1, lxxxv–xcvi; Pétion to Dauxion-Lavaysse, Nov. 12, 1814, in Vastey, *An Essay,* app. B/4, xxiii–xxiv.
21. Reprinted in Madiou, *Histoire d'Haïti,* 5:252–53.
22. Pétion to Dauxion-Lavaysse, Nov. 20, 1814, in Vastey, *An Essay,* app. B/6, xxvi–xxvii.
23. Madiou, *Histoire d'Haïti,* 5:254.
24. Pétion to Dauxion-Lavaysse, Nov. 12, 1814, in Vastey, *An Essay,* app. B/4, xxi.
25. Saint-Rémy, *Pétion et Haïti,* 1:23–24.
26. Saint-Rémy, *Pétion et Haïti,* 1:23–24.
27. Pétion to Dauxion-Lavaysse, Nov. 27, 1814, in Vastey, *An Essay,* app. B/7, xxviii–xxix.
28. Dauxion-Lavaysse to Pétion, Nov. 29, 1814, in Vastey, *Essay,* app. B/8, xxix–xxx.
29. Quoted in Saint-Rémy, *Mémoires de Toussaint,* app., 126n2.
30. Mollien, *Haïti ou Saint-Domingue,* 2:119–22; De Prézeau, *Réfutation de la lettre,* 5.
31. Vastey, *Essai,* 207–9.
32. Vastey, *Essai,* 208.
33. "Kingdom of Hayti. Declaration of the King," lxxxvii.
34. Dauxion-Lavaysse to Christophe, Oct. 1, 1814, xcvi–ci.
35. "Kingdom of Hayti. Declaration of the King," lxxxvii; Dauxion-Lavaysse to Pétion, Sept. 6, 1814, xv–xvi.
36. De Prézeau, *Réfutation de la lettre,* 21–22; John K. Thornton, "'I Am the Subject of the King of Congo': African Political Ideology and the Haitian Revolution," *Journal of World History* 4, no. 2 (1993): 181–214.
37. Vastey, *Essai,* 215.
38. Dauxion-Lavaysse to Christophe, Oct. 1, 1814, xcix.
39. De Prézeau, *Réfutation de la lettre,* 21.
40. Mollien, *Haïti ou Saint-Domingue,* 2:121.
41. Vastey, *Essai,* 210–12.
42. Vastey, *Essai,* 205.
43. Lacroix, *Mémoires pour servir à l'histoire de Saint-Domingue,* 2:63.
44. Dauxion-Lavaysse to Christophe, Oct. 1, 1814, xcvi.
45. De Prézeau, *Réfutation de la lettre,* 8–9.

46. "Royaume d'Hayti," *Gazette royale d'Hayti,* Nov. 19, 1814, 1.

47. "Madame Toussaint," *Gazette politique et commerciale d'Haïti,* March 28, 1805, 61–63.

48. Madiou, *Histoire d'Haïti,* 5:259. For Vastey's appearance, see Courtenay as quoted in "Christophe, King of Hayti," in Frances Williams-Wynn, *Diaries of a Lady of Quality,* 177.

49. Mollien, *Haïti ou Saint-Domingue,* 2:122.

50. "Royaume d'Hayti," *Gazette royale d'Hayti,* Nov. 19, 1814, 1.

51. In his later interrogation, Médina explains that the Isle of Ratau was Malouet's euphemism for extermination. See "Process verbal of the examination of Agoustino Franco, surnamed de Médina, a French spy," in Vastey, *An Essay,* app. C/2, xlii.

52. Reprinted in Madiou, *Histoire d'Haïti,* 5:266–67; see also Jean Baptiste Guislain Wallez, *Précis historique des négociations entre la France et Saint-Domingue; suivi de pièces justificatives, et d'une notice biographique sur le général Boyer, président de la République d'Haïti* (Paris: Ponthieu, 1826), 172.

53. "Royaume d'Hayti," *Gazette royale d'Hayti,* Nov. 19, 1814, 1.

54. "Grande Bretagne," *Journal des débats politiques et littéraires,* Dec. 14, 1814, 1.

55. "M. Auxion [*sic*] Lavaysse, of Whom We Yesterday Spoke," *Times,* Jan. 5, 1815, 3.

56. "Translated for the N.Y. Evening Post," *Evening Post,* Jan. 6, 1815, 2; "Instructions for Messieurs Dauxion, Lavaysse, De Medina, and Dravermann," *Poulson's American Daily Advertiser,* Jan. 9, 1815, 3; "Translated for the N.Y. Evening Post. Instructions for Messrs. Dauxion Lavaysse, De Medina, and Dravermann," *Boston Daily Advertiser,* Jan. 14, 1815, 2; quoted material appears in "From the Salem Register," *National Advocate,* Aug. 28, 1816.

57. "Appendix. Instructions de M. Malouet saisies sur les Agens du Gouvernement Français envoyés à Hayti," *L'ambigu,* Feb. 20, 1815, 3–12; "Réfutations de la Lettre de Dauxion Lavaysse, par le Chevalier de Présaux [*sic*]," *L'ambigu,* Jan. 10, 1815, 20–28; "Appendix. Note de M. Malouet en réfutation de ses Mémoires sur les Colonies, par le Baron de Vastey, Sécretaire du Roi d'Hayti," *L'ambigu,* Feb. 28, 1815, 434–36; Quote from "Kingdom of Hayti. Declaration of the King," lxxxvi.

58. "Process Verbal of the examination of Agoustino Franco."

59. Jean-Hérold Pérard, *Le Cap-Haïtien: 350 ans d'histoire, 1670–2020* (Canada: [Publishing house not identified], 2020), 27–28; John Garrigus, " 'Thy Coming Fame, Ogé! Is Sure': New Evidence on Ogé's 1790 Revolt and the Beginnings of the Haitian Revolution," in *Assumed Identities: The Meanings of Race in the Atlantic World,* ed. John Garrigus and Christopher Morris (College Station: Texas A&M University Press, 2010), 19–45.

60. "Royaume d'Hayti," *Gazette royale d'Hayti,* Nov. 19, 1814. For the uniforms of the guards, see Prévost, *Relation,* 88–93.

61. Malouet quoted in Vastey, *Notes à M. le Baron V.P. de Malouet,* 14; original in Pierre Victor Malouet, *Collection de mémoires sur les colonies, et particulièrement sur Saint-Domingue* (Paris: Baudouin, 1802), 4:46; Vastey, *Le système,* title page; Vastey, *Essai,* 217; "Royaume d'Hayti," *Gazette royale d'Hayti,* Nov. 19, 1814, 1–3.

62. Joseph Saint-Rémy, *Essai sur Henri Christophe, général haïtien* (Paris: Imprimerie de Félix Malteste, 1839), 16–17.

63. "Royaume d'Hayti," *Gazette royale d'Hayti,* Nov. 19, 1814.

64. Sara E. Johnson, "You Should Give Them Blacks to Eat: Waging Inter-American Wars of Torture and Terror," *American Quarterly* 61, no. 1 (March 2009): 65–92.
65. See, for example, the numerous pamphlets advocating for an invasion of Haiti published immediately following the Bourbon Restoration by an ex-colonist from Saint-Domingue, Pierre-Louis Berquin-Duvallon, among which were *Le Retour des Bourbons, ode adressée à S.M. Louis XVIII . . . lors de son entrée dans la capitale au noms des colons de Saint-Domingue, réfugiés en France* (Paris: Chez Charles, 1814); *De Saint-Domingue considéré sous le point de vue de sa restauration prochaine* (Paris: Fanckoucke, 1814). For Berquin's many other writings on the topic, see, Daut, Pierrot, et al., "Pierre-Louis Berquin-Duvallon," in *Haitian Revolutionary Fictions*, 149–50.
66. Vastey, *Le système*, 90.
67. "Royaume d'Hayti," *Gazette royale d'Hayti*, Nov. 19, 1814, 4.
68. "Article V—*Reflexions sur une Lettre de* Mezeres [sic], *ex-colon français, addressee à M. J. C. L. Sismonde de Sismondi*, etc.," *Analectic Magazine*, May 1817, 403.
69. Vastey, *Réflexions politiques*, 145n1; Madiou, *Histoire d'Haiti*, 5:223, 269; Brière, *Haïti et la France*, 68. On the background of the infamous colonist Laffont de Labédat, see De Prézeau, *Réfutation de la lettre*, 6.
70. Médina quoted in Brière, *Haïti et la France*, 61–62; William S. Cormack, "Malouet, Pierre Victor (1740–1814)," in *Encyclopedia of the Age of Political Revolutions and New Ideologies, 1760–1815*, ed. Gregory Fremont-Barnes (Westport, Conn.: Greenwood, 2007), 447.
71. "Official Censure," in Vastey, *An Essay*, app. F/3, ci; original published as, "Paris, le 18 janvier," *Le moniteur universel*, Jan. 19, 1815, 2.
72. "Royaume d'Hayti," *Gazette Royale d'Hayti*, June 2, 1815, 1–2.

CHAPTER 14: THE AGE OF CHRISTOPHEAN DIPLOMACY

1. "Nouvelles extérieures. New-Yorck [sic]. 21 août," *Gazette royale*, Aug. 27, 1816, 1.
2. "Apparition du pavillon blanc," *Gazette royale*, Oct. 27, 1816, 1–2.
3. "Apparition du pavillon blanc," 2; See also Vastey, *Essai*, 351–56. This event was widely reported in the U.S. press. See *New-England Palladium & Commercial Advertiser*, Dec. 3, 1816; *Albany Advertiser*, Dec. 4, 1816; *Boston Patriot and Morning Advertiser*, Dec. 4, 1816; *Essex Register*, Dec. 4, 1816; *American Advocate and Kennebec Advertiser*, Dec. 7, 1816; *People's Advocate*, Dec. 7, 1816; *Weekly Visiter* [sic], Dec. 7, 1816; *Recorder*, Dec. 10, 1816; *Newburyport Herald*, Dec. 10, 1816; *American*, Dec. 11, 1816; *Burlington Gazette*, Dec. 12, 1816; *Merrimack Intelligencer*, Dec. 14, 1816; *Columbian Register*, Dec. 21, 1816; *American Beacon and Commercial Diary*, Dec. 23, 1816; *People's Advocate*, March 22, 1817. See also the captain's defense of his actions, which was printed in several U.S. newspapers: *Commercial Advertiser*, Dec. 3, 1816; *Baltimore Patriot*, Dec. 5, 1816; *Boston Daily Advertiser*, Dec. 6, 1816; *New-England Palladium*, Dec. 6, 1816; *Alexandria Gazette*, Dec. 9, 1816; *Lancaster Journal*, Dec. 9, 1816; *American Beacon and Commercial Diary*, Dec. 10, 1816.
4. "Apparition du pavillon blanc," 3.
5. "Des Gonaïves, 20 octobre," *Gazette royale*, Oct. 27, 1816, 3.
6. "Grande-Bretagne. Londres, 11 Janvier," January 16, 1815, 2; Louis XVIII's

ordinance naming new commissioners to St. Domingue, in Vastey, *An Essay,* app. E/4, lxi–lxii; Vastey, *Essai,* 348–50.

7. Vastey, *Essai,* iii.

8. "Royaume d'Hayti. Du Cap-Henry, le 1er juin 1815, ans 12," *Gazette Royale,* June 2, 1815, 2.

9. Laroche to Pétion, Feb. 16, 1815, in *Collection de pièces relatives a l'histoire de la république et du royaume d'Hayti,* 72–73, Osterreichische Nationalbibliothek, 8.G.33.

10. Laroche to Pétion, Feb. 17, 1815, in *Collection de pièces relatives a l'histoire de la république et du royaume d'Hayti,* 74–79.

11. "Royaume d'Hayti. Du Cap-Henry, le 1er juin," 2.

12. "De Sans-Souci, le 3 Juin [*sic*], *Gazette Royale,* June 2, 1815, 3.

13. Prévost, *Relation,* 83; see Christophe to Baron de la Tortue (Bursar of the Province du Nord), March 3, 1811, ACH-3; Christophe to Baron de la Tortue, Jan. 1, 1812, ACH-2; Christophe to Baron de la Tortue, July 21, 1811, ACH-4; Christophe to Baron de la Tortue, Aug. 7, 1812, ACH-6, Nemours Collection; Christophe to Baron de la Tortue, Aug. 6, 1812, ACH-5, Nemours Collection; Christophe to Comte de la Taste (Minister of Finances and the Interior), March 31, 1813, ACH-7, Nemours Collection. See also Order from the King to Dr. Massicot, March 7, 1813, Documenti di Haiti, BCAM.

14. Vastey, *Essai,* 201; "État d'Hayti, Du Cap, le 11 octobre," *Gazette officielle,* Oct. 12, 1809, 161.

15. Prévost, *Relation,* 19; Franklin, *Present State of Hayti,* 291; Jonathan Brown, *The History and Present Condition of St. Domingo,* 2 vols. (Philadelphia: William Marshall, 1837), 2:187.

16. See, among many letters, Christophe to Local Commander of Cap, Jan. 19, 1805; Christophe to Colonel Joaquim, Jan. 20, 1805; and Order from General Christophe, April 2, 1805, Christophe Letter Book.

17. Christophe to Dessalines, April 9, 1806. For Christophe's home in Milot, see Christophe to Roumage, Oct. 4, 1805; Christophe to Colonel Joachim, April 14, 1806; for the plantation called Milot, see Christophe to Dessalines, Jan. 11, 1806, Christophe Letter Book; and Gauvin A. Bailey, *The Palace of Sans-Souci in Milot, Haiti (ca. 1806–1813): The Untold Story of the Potsdam of the Rainforest* (Berlin: Deutscher Kunstverlag, 2017), 75.

18. For Cossait, Larose, and Marsan, see Romain, *Noms de lieux d'époque coloniale en Haïti,* 58, 113, 130. For the quartier Sans-Souci, see "À vendre," *Supplément aux Affiches américaines,* May 5, 1787, 2; and for its location in the jurisdiction of Fort-Dauphin, see "Avis divers," *Supplément aux Affiches américaines/Feuille du Cap-François,* Sept. 23, 1789, 3.

19. See, for example, on the island of Saint-Vincent, "Plan of the Sans Souci Estate," www.loc.gov. Sans Souci in Grenada is today a residential area in Saint George parish; see Paul Crask, *Grenada: Carriacou and Petite Martinique,* 3rd ed. (Guilford, Conn.: Bradt, 2017), 85. There is also a Sans Souci in the northeastern corner of Trinidad, birthplace of the Toronto-based poet and fiction writer Dionne Brand, who set one of her short stories in the town of Sans Souci on an unnamed Caribbean island in her collection called *Sans Souci.* Dionne Brand, *Sans Souci, and Other Stories* (Ithaca, N.Y.: Firebrand Books, 1989).

20. Bailey, *Palace,* 77.

21. "Suite de la fête de Sa Majesté la Reine," *Gazette royale,* Aug. 22, 1816, 4.

22. Brown, *History and Present Condition,* 216. This information went on to be repeated verbatim by at least one Black Atlantic writer, William Wells Brown,

in his *Rising Son; or, The Antecedents and Advancement of the Colored Race* (Boston: A. G. Brown, 1864), 212.

23. [François] Mazères, *Lettre à M. J.-C.-L. Sismonde de Sismondi sur les nègres, la civilisation de l'Afrique, Christophe et le comte de Limonade* (Paris: Renard, 1815), 40, 41.

24. Bailey, *Palace*, 77.

25. Michel-Rolph Trouillot, *Silencing the Past: Power and the Production of History* (Boston: Beacon Press, 1995), 59, 65.

26. See references to "Sans-Souci" in transcribed letters of the colonist Larchevesque-Thibaud, as reprinted in Gabriel Debien and Charles Braibant, "Documents," *Revue d'histoire des colonies* 41, no. 142 (1954): 115, 118; "À louer ou à affermer," *Supplément aux Affiches américaine. Feuille du Cap-François*, Dec. 23, 1789, 4.

27. See "Nègres marrons," *Affiches américaines*, July 8, 1767, 215; "Esclaves en marronage," *Affiches américaines*, Sept. 9, 1767, 296; "Esclaves en marronnage," *Affiches américaines*, July 29, 1772, 398; "Nègre maron," *Affiches américaines*, March 5, 1774, 109; "Nègres marons," *Affiches américaines*, Nov. 6, 1776, 530; "Liste des nègres épaves . . . ," *Affiches américaines*, Feb. 1, 1777, 59; "Esclaves en maronnage," *Supplément aux Affiches américaines*, April 20, 1779, 2.

28. "État nominatif des contribuables de la ville du Cap-Français, tant pour la contribution de guerre que pour celle communale, pour l'an 11ème," 5 DPPC 50, ANOM; *Almanach royal d'Hayti pour l'année 1814*, 111; *Almanach royal d'Hayti pour l'année 1816*, 105; *Almanach royal d'Hayti pour l'année 1820*, 118.

29. Christophe to Dessalines, Sept. 6, 1805; Christophe to Olivier, Jan. 12, 1805, Christophe Letter Book.

30. "ORDONNANCE DU ROI, Qui élève un Monument à la Liberté et à l'Indépendance, sur la Place d'Armes de la Citadelle HENRY," Aug. 20, 1816; reported in *Gazette royale*, Aug. 26, 1816, 3.

31. Bailey, *Palace*, 81–83; *Almanach royal d'Hayti pour l'année 1814*, 14. In the colonial era, Jean-Baptiste Badaillac was the manager of a plantation in Fort-Dauphin and another in Ouanaminthe. See mention of the "Procès-verbal de mise en possession de Sr. Badaillac," in *Alde: Photographies et manuscrits autographes* (Alde: Maison de Ventes aux Enchères, 2012), 114; and "Avis divers," *Supplément aux Affiches américaines*, Aug. 7, 1773, 5–6.

32. "Royaume d'Hayti. De Sans-Souci, le 18 Juillet," *Gazette royale*, July 19, 1815, 4; J. Cameron Monroe, "New Light from Hayti's Royal Past: Recent Archaeological Excavations at the Palace of Sans-Souci, Milot," *Journal of Haitian Studies* 23, no. 2 (2017): 6.

33. Delorme, *1842 au Cap*, 18–19; Monroe, "New Light," 8. There are two different versions of the Desroches painting, a seemingly earlier version, recently restored in Haiti and held by the Frères de l'Instruction Chrétienne, and the final version on display in this book, auctioned in January 2024 to a private buyer by Sotheby's International. See www.sothebys.com. For biographical information about Desroches, see Renaud Hyppolite, "Si le Cap m'était conté," in *Cap-Haïtien: Excursions dans le temps: Au fil de nos souvenirs (1920–1995)*, ed. Max Manigat (Delmas, Haiti: Samba, 2014), 141. In 1878, Desroches acted as a witness to a marriage and was listed as seventy-four years old at the time. Marriage notation for Pierre-de-Dieu Antoine and Marie-Élisabeth Jean-Baptiste Pierre, June 12, 1878, État civil d'Haiti, AGH.

34. For the inscription, see "Royaume d'Hayti. De Sans-Souci, le 18 juillet," *Gazette royale*, July 19, 1815, 4.

35. "De Sans-Souci, le 3 juin," *Gazette royale*, June 2, 1815, 3–4.

36. "Royaume d'Hayti. De Cap-Henry, le 28 juin 1815, an 12," *Gazette royale,* June 29, 1815, 1–4.
37. Laroche to Pétion, Jan. 25, 1816, in *Collection de pièces relatives,* 80.
38. "Du Cap-Henry, le 17 février 1816," *Gazette royale,* Feb. 8, 1816, 3.
39. Prévost to Vastey, Feb. 29, 1816, reprinted in Vastey, *Communication officielle de trois lettres de Catineau Laroche, ex-colon, agent de Pétion. Imprimées et publiées par ordre du Gouvernement* (Cap-Henry: P. Roux, 1816), n.p.
40. The letters between Pétion and Laroche were partially reprinted in the *Gazette,* and also in Vastey's *Le cri de la conscience* (Cap-Henry: P. Roux, 1815), 45–53. See also "De Cap-Henry, le 7 février 1816," *Gazette royale d'Hayti,* Feb. 8, 1816, 1–3.
41. Vastey, *Communication officielle;* Vastey, *Translation of an Official Communication from the Government of Hayti, dated 29 February 1816* (Bristol: John Evans, 1816); "Du Cap-Henry, le 20 novembre," *Gazette royale d'Hayti,* 3. Rainsford first crossed paths with Christophe during the revolution when the French arrested the British soldier and tried him as a British spy. Christophe oversaw the proceedings at the military tribunal. See Grégory Pierrot and Paul Youngquist, "Introduction" to Marcus Rainsford, *An Historical Account of the Black Empire of Hayti* (Durham, NC: Duke University Press, 2013), xxix.
42. Fontanges and Esmangart to Pétion, Oct. 2, 1816, in *Collection de pièces relatives,* 88–90.
43. Pétion to Fontanges and Esmangart, Oct. 6, 1816, in *Collection de pièces relatives,* 93.
44. Fontanges and Esmangart to Pétion, Oct. 6, 1816, in *Collection de pièces relatives,* 94; "Ordonnance du roi, Louis, par la grâce de Dieu, roi de France et de Navarre," in *Collection de pièces relatives,* 95–96.
45. Pétion to Fontanges, Oct. 8, 1816, in *Collection de pièces relatives,* 97–98; Fontanges and Esmangart to Pétion, Oct. 22, 1816, in *Collection de pièces relatives,* 99–100.
46. Fontanges and Esmangart to Pétion, Nov. 10, 1816, in *Collection de pièces relatives,* 120–28.
47. Examples in Marlene L. Daut, "The 'Alpha and Omega' of Haitian Literature: Baron de Vastey and the U.S. Press," in *Haiti and the Early United States,* ed. Elizabeth Maddock Dillon and Michael Drexler (Philadelphia: University of Pennsylvania Press, 1816), 287–310; see also Cushing, "Article VI," 112. Even after the king's death, Cushing's article on Vastey was very influential and was either referenced or quoted several times in the northern United States. See, for example, "Review of New Books," *Literary Gazette; or Journal of Criticism, Science, and the Arts,* Feb. 17, 1821; "From the Catskill Recorder: Revolutionary Incidents. St. Domingo," *Rhode Island American,* Feb. 13, 1821; "From the Catskill Recorder: Revolutionary Incidents. St. Domingo," *Essex Patriot,* Aug. 18, 1821; see also "Article V," *Analectic Magazine,* 403.
48. Cushing, "Article VI," 124.
49. Christophe and Prévost, *Manifeste du roi;* Julien Prévost, *L'olivier de la paix* (Cap-Henry: P. Roux, 1815), 4, 8.
50. "Lettres du Roi, adressée à Messieurs les Généraux et Magistrats de Partie de l'Ouest et de la Province du Sud, assemblés au Port-au-Prince," June 28, 1818, in *Collection de pièces relatives,* 136–38; "Les Généraux, Magistrats et Chefs de Corps de la République d'Hayti, réunis au Port-au-Prince. Au Général Christophe," July 1, 1818, in *Collection de pièces relatives,* 138–40.

CHAPTER 15: THE AGE OF CHRISTOPHEAN PROSPERITY

1. Reprinted in Vastey, *Réflexions politiques*, 136–37.
2. Vastey, *Réflexions politiques*, 140–41.
3. Vastey, *Communication officielle*, 31.
4. Ruth Paley, "After Somerset: Mansfield, Slavery and the Law in England, 1772–1830," in Norma Landau, ed. *Law, Crime and English Society, 1660–1830* (Cambridge University Press, 2002):165–84.
5. "Strafford Indictment," Middlesex Assizes Register, 1804–19, Manuscript held by Jamaica Archives and Records Department, Feb. 1817, 1A/7/4/3, Pleas of the Crown, Middlesex; Vastey, *Reflexions on the Blacks and Whites, Remarks upon a Letter Addressed by M. Mazeres, a French Ex-Colonist, to J.C.L. Sismonde de Sismondi*, tr. W.H.M.B (London: J. Hatchard, 1817). For Hamilton identified as translator, see Daut, *Baron de Vastey and the Origins of Black Atlantic Humanism*, 73–75.
6. *Postscript to the Royal Gazette*, Feb. 15–22, 1817, 1.
7. *Almanach royal d'Hayti pour l'année 1818*, 1; Limonade to Mr. Joseph Tarn (assistant secretary to the British and Foreign Bible Society), May 18, 1818, BFBS Archives Indexes, Foreign Correspondents "L," BSAX/1/L, 1804–97, Cambridge University Libraries (thanks to Julia Gaffield for sharing this item); Wilberforce to Teignmouth, June 18, 1817, in *The Correspondence of William Wilberforce*, 363–65.
8. Limonade to Clarkson, Nov. 20, 1819, in Griggs and Prator, *Correspondence*, 173–77.
9. Joseph Farington, *The Farington Diary*, ed. James Greig (London: Hutchinson, 1928), 8:46. See also another commission Christophe charged Strafford with, involving duties levied against jams Christophe had sent to England: Christophe to Wilberforce, in *The Correspondence of William Wilberforce*, 362.
10. Limonade to Banks, Feb. 7, 1816, transferred from the Department of Printed Books, BL 44919 Z (also cited in the British Library catalog as Add MS 44919); Christophe wrote directly to Banks on July 29, 1819. See Christophe to Banks, July 29, 1819, BL.A.MS 8100.219, Natural History Museum and Library Archives, London, UK.
11. "Du Cap-Henry, le 20 août," *Gazette royale d'Hayti*, Aug. 21, 1816; "Suite de la fête de Sa Majesté la Reine," *Gazette Royale d'Hayti*, Aug. 22, 1816; "Suite de la fête de S.M. la Reine," *Gazette Royale d'Hayti*, Aug. 24, 1816; "Suite de la fête de S.M. la Reine," *Gazette Royale d'Hayti*, Aug. 26, 1816; Vastey, *Relation de la fête de S.M. la reine d'Hayti, des actes du gouvernement qui ont eu lieu durant cet événement, et de tout ce qui s'est passé à l'occasion de cette fête* (Cap-Henry: P. Roux, 1816); "Haytian Affairs. Translated for the Palladium. Cape Henry (Hayti) Aug. 20," *New-England Palladium*, Oct. 18, 1816, 1; "Translated for the Boston Palladium [sic], Cape Henry (Hayti) Aug. 20," *National Intelligencer*, Oct. 26, 1816, 2; "Haytian Affairs. Translated for the Palladium," *Hampshire Gazette*, Nov. 6, 1816, 2.
12. "Suite de la fête de Sa Majesté la Reine," *Gazette royale*, Aug. 22, 1816, 1.
13. Among the surnames listed for these foreigners is that of "Stafford." Though the name is misspelled in this issue, the next issue (dated Aug. 24) of the *Gazette* removes any lingering doubt, because it correctly lists "Thos Strafford" as being in attendance.
14. "Du 16 août. Grand repas donné au commerce étranger par Sa Grâce Monsei-

gneur le Duc de la Marmelade, gouverneur de la capitale, en son hôtel," *Gazette royale*, Aug. 22, 1816, 3–4.

15. Called a "shako" in English, this is a tall, cylindrical hat usually worn by military officers. Christophe's guards are wearing them in the oil on canvas portrait depicting his death included in this volume.

16. "Suite de la fête de S.M. la Reine," *Gazette royale*, Aug. 24, 1816, 1–3.

17. "Suite de la fête de S.M. la Reine," *Gazette royale*, Aug. 26, 1816, 1–2.

18. "Du Cap-Henry, le 20 août," *Gazette royale*, Aug. 21, 1816, 1–4.

19. "Fête de Sa Majesté la Reine d'Hayti," *Gazette royale*, Aug. 20, 1817, 2.

20. "Royalty," *Niles' Weekly Register*, Nov. 9, 1816, 168. Emphasis in the original; "Sable Royalty," *American Beacon and Commercial Diary* (Norfolk, Va.), Oct. 30, 1816.

21. Dridier and Torchiana, "(Cristoforo) Enrico I. Re di Hayti" (1811), personal collection of Marlene L. Daut; *Serie di vite e ritratti de' famosi personaggi degli ultimi tempi: Opera dedicato a sua eccellenza il Signor Conte Enrico di Belle-garde*, vol. 2 (Milan: Batelli e Fanfani, 1818), n.p.; the image appeared in truncated form with the same printed biography in 1822 in the *Collezione di vite e ritratti di uomini e donne illustri degli ultimi tempi* (Rome: Da' Torchii di Paolo Salviucci e Figlio, 1822), 1:300–307.

22. Erica Moiah James, "Decolonizing Time: Nineteenth-Century Haitian Portraiture and the Critique of Anachronism in Caribbean Art," *Nka: Journal of Contemporary African Art* 44 (2019): 11.

23. "Elegant Museum (for Two Weeks Only) at the Room over West & Abbot's Store, next to Barker's Hotel, Consisting of Forty Wax Figures, as Large as Life," *Concord Gazette*, June 17, 1817.

24. "President Boyer," *Barre Gazette*, April 28, 1843.

25. "Haytian Court Dresses," *Lady's Monthly Museum, or, Polite Repository of Amusement and Instruction; Being an Assemblage of Whatever Can Tend to Please the Fancy, Interest the Mind, or Exalt the Character of the British Fair* (London: Dean and Munday, July 1815), 2:343–44.

26. "Suite de la Fête," Aug. 24, 1816, 4; see also "Christophe, King of Hayti," *Hereford Journal*, Sept. 22, 1819, 4.

27. Christophe mentions the payments for Evans in his letter to the Comte de la Taste, Oct. 6, 1816, ACH-15, Nemours Collection. For Evans as a student of Lawrence, see Moiah James, "Decolonizing Time," 12.

28. Quoted in Michel Philippe Lerebours, *Haiti et ses peintres, de 1804 à 1980: Souffrances & espoirs d'un peuple* (Port-au-Prince: Imprimeur II, 1989), 1:94; *Almanach royal d'Hayti pour l'année 1817*, 154.

29. Lerebours, *Haiti et ses peintres*, 94; Christophe to Wilberforce, Nov. 18, 1816, *The Correspondence of William Wilberforce*, 362. A descendant of Wilberforce's tried to sell his copy of the painting to the Haitian government in the early 1900s, but at too high a price. The historian and statesman Alfred Nemours, minister from Haiti to Paris, then purchased the portrait, now housed in his archive at the University of Puerto-Rico, Río Piedras. See Vaval, "Le Roi d'Haïti Henri Christophe," 8n. Another copy is held by the Musée du Panthéon National Haïtien in Port-au-Prince. For the different copies, see Moiah James, "Decolonizing Time," 12.

30. For Saunders as agent, see Farington, *Farington Diary*, 8:88; for the payment, see Christophe to Comte de la Taste, Oct. 6, 1816, Nemours Collection; for Saunders in Haiti, see "Du cap Henry, le 24 janvier 1816, an 13," *Gazette royale*,

Jan. 25, 1816, 1; "Introduction de la vaccine à Hayti," *Gazette royale,* Feb. 8, 1816, 3–4.

31. Farington, *Farington Diary,* 8:76-77, 80–81.

32. "Du Cap-Henry, le 10 octobre," *Gazette royale,* Oct. 17, 1816, 1; Christophe to the Comte de la Taste, Oct. 6, 1816, Nemours Collection; *Almanach royal d'Hayti pour l'année 1817,* 154; for Gulliver's initials as T.B. and Saunders in Port-de-Paix, see, *Almanach royal d'Hayti pour l'année 1818,* 130.

33. Christophe to Clarkson, Feb. 5, 1816, in Griggs and Prator, *Correspondence,* 91.

34. "Royaume d'Hayti. Proclamation. Le roi aux Haytiens," *Gazette royale d'Hayti,* Jan. 9, 1817, 2–4; "Ordonnance du roi," *Gazette royale d'Hayti,* Dec. 28, 1818, 1–4. See also Vendryes, "Introduction" to Cheesman, *Armorial of Haiti,* 5.

35. For lack of female instructors, see Wilberforce to Christophe, Nov. 27, 1819, 389; and Wilberforce to the "Head of the Haytian Government," Dec. 16, 1820, in *The Correspondence of William Wilberforce,* 394; *Almanach royal d'Hayti pour l'année 1820,* 139–42.

36. "Réflextions de l'éditeur," *Gazette Royale d'Hayti,* March 31, 1818, 2–3; *Almanach royal d'Hayti pour l'année 1820,* 11.

37. A digital version is available at "La Liturgie: The Book of Common Prayer in French for Haiti," accessed April 1, 2024, http://justus.anglican.org; "Memorandum of a Conversation with Pierce [*sic*] Saunders signed J.H.," May 1816, Lambeth Palace Library, The National Library and Archive of the Church of England, FP/1-40, Fulham Papers Colonial: Volume XX, 198–201.

38. Grellet to Allen, Aug. 17, 1816, file box 1 Letters While Visiting Haiti, HC.MC-967, Stephen Grellet Papers, HL.

39. Grellet to My Dear Friends [of London], Oct. 29, 1816; Grellet to Allen, Aug. 17, 1816, Grellet Papers, HL.

40. Christophe to Lord Teignmouth, July 29, 1819, BFBS Archives Indexes, Foreign Correspondents "C," BSAX/1/C, 1804–97. Thanks to Julia Gaffield for sharing this document.

41. Young to Wilberforce, Nov. 24, 1819, Miscellaneous Letters and Papers, Add MS 62551: 1400–1983, BL.

42. Clarkson to Baron Turckheim, March 11, 1820, Clarkson/160, St. John's College Library, Cambridge University.

43. Quoted in Madiou, *Histoire d'Haïti,* 5:431.

44. "État des habitations qui ont été accordées par la Comission de Vente et d'Aliénation des Biens Domaniaux du Royaume, aux personnes qui les ont soumissionnées," *Gazette Royale d'Hayti,* March 31, 1818, 4; on Christophe's efforts to prevent food dependency, see also Comte de Limonade (Julien de Prévost), *Instructions pour les établissemens et la culture des habitations caféyères de la couronne* (Sans-Souci, Haiti: L'Imprimerie Royale, 1818), 4–5; and Hamilton, *Memoir on the Cultivation of Wheat Within the Tropics,* 1–10. For total exports, see "État des bâtimens étrangers entrés dans le Port du Cap Henry depuis le 1er janvier, 1817, jusqu'au 10 août inclusivement," *Gazette Royale d'Hayti,* Aug. 14, 1817, 4n; for Banks's praise and the codes of law, see Daut, *Awakening the Ashes,* 278; and Daut, *Baron de Vastey,* 82–83.

45. Prévost, *Relation,* 104; Christophe to the Royal Prince, Oct. 17, 1813, Clarkson and Christophe Manuscript Correspondence, BL.

46. Christophe to the Royal Prince, Jan. 11, 1814, Clarkson and Christophe Manuscript Correspondence.

47. *Almanach royal d'Hayti pour l'année 1815,* 12.

48. For Christophe's complaints, see Christophe to the Royal Prince, June 15, 1816, Clarkson and Christophe Manuscript Correspondence; *Almanach royal d'Hayti pour l'année 1818*, 12.

49. *Almanach royal d'Hayti pour l'année 1820*, 13.

50. William Wilson, *Le précepteur du Prince-Royal Victor-Henry*, trans. Marie-Thérèse Chenet and Lucienne Zennie (Port-au-Prince: Henri Deschamps, 2020), 57–58.

51. "Saladin," History Network, www.history.com.

52. Prince Eugène to Christophe, Sept. 21, 1816, Documenti di Haiti, BCAM; "Summary: Giacomo Costantino Beltrami's life, the Collections at *Angelo Mai*, Research Directions, and Helpful Links," Biblioteca Civica Angelo Mai, Bergamo, 2000, http://legacy.bibliotecamai.org/cataloghi_inventari/archivi/archivi_collezioni_doc/inventario_beltrami/beltsum/english.html.

53. *Almanach royal d'Hayti pour l'année 1814*, 14; for chevalier, see *Almanach royal pour l'année 1820*, 115; and Christophe to Massicot, Aug. 22, 1819, Documenti di Haiti, BCAM.

54. Christophe to Massicot, April 22, 1819, Documenti di Haiti, BCAM.

55. Christophe to Massicot, March 7, 1813, Documenti di Haiti, BCAM; for the Comte du Borgne, who was ordered to stay in bed, see Christophe to Massicot, July 7, 1813, BCAM; for the painter, see Christophe to Massicot, July 29, 1813, BCAM; for Prince Jean, see Christophe to Massicot, Dec. 22, 1815, BCAM; for the king's goddaughter, see Christophe to Massicot, Aug. 19, 1815, BCAM.

56. For Massicot caring for a foreigner in Gonaïves, see Christophe to Massicot, June 15, 1815, BCAM; for officers, see Christophe to Massicot, Nov. 25, 1813, BCAM; for "new Haitians," see Christophe to Massicot, Feb. 13, 1815, BCAM.

57. Christophe to Massicot, Feb. 13, 1815, BCAM.

58. Christophe to Massicot, Nov. 25, 1813, Documenti di Haiti, BCAM.

59. *Almanach royal d'Hayti pour l'année 1814*, 28, 32; Comtesse d'Ouanaminthe to Madame Athénaïs, June 7, 1814, BCAM; Cheesman, *Armorial of Haiti*, 58; Prévost, *Relation*, 107; *Almanach royal d'Hayti pour l'année 1820*, 35.

60. "De Sans-Souci, le 10 septembre," *Gazette royale*, Sept. 10, 1819, 1–4.

61. Chanlatte, *La partie de chasse du roi*; see also "The Hunting Party of the King," in Daut, Pierrot, and Rohrleitner, *Haitian Revolutionary Fictions*, 203–208.

CHAPTER 16: CRACKS IN KINGLY AUTHORITY

1. For Mrs. Bunel's slaves, see "An Accounting of Madame Bunel's Slaves," Dec. 13, 1803, Arthur C. Bining Collection (#1811), box 4, MSS 695 (Bunel, Joseph), HSP.

2. Gordon S. Brown, *Toussaint's Clause: The Founding Fathers and the Haitian Revolution* (Oxford: University of Mississippi Press, 2005); General Thomas Maitland to Henry Dundas, April 20, 1799, WO 1/71, TNA.

3. For Marie Bunel's full name, see the power of attorney granted to her on behalf of her husband, dated Oct. 11, 1810. Collection 490, Pennsylvania Abolition Society, HSP, and "Marriages in Holy Trinity Church, Philadelphia-1796–1806 (Continued)," *Records of the American Catholic Historical Sociey of Philadelphia* 39.1 (March 1928): 56; for her fortune, see Vastey, *Essai*, 178; for the Bunels, in general, see Philippe Girard, "Trading Races: Joseph and Marie Bunel, a Diplomat and a Merchant in Revolutionary Saint-Domingue and Philadelphia," *Journal of the Early Republic* 30:3 (Fall 2010): 355.

4. For the plantations and return to Haiti, see Grandjean to Marie Bunel, Sept. 18, 1804, HSP; for the hotel, see "Avis Divers," *Supplément aux affiches Americaines*, Sept. 4, 1790, 2; baptismal notation for Antoinette Grandjean, May 2, 1787, État Civil du Cap, ANOM; for the marriage, see "Marriages in Holy Trinity Church"; for the street in Cap, see "État nominatif de la ville du Cap Français," 5 DPPC 50, ANOM.

5. For her family members, see Joseph Bunel to Marie Bunel, Sept. 7, 1804, MSS.695, HSP.

6. Order and receipts from Christophe to Joseph Bunel, Feb. 3, 1802, MSS.695, HSP.

7. Girard, "Trading Races," 368; Leclerc to Decrès, Feb. 15, 1802 in *Lettres de Leclerc*, 91–92. Marguerite AnSalle to Marie Bunel, Aug. 9, 1803, MSS. 695, HSP.

8. Marie Bunel to Rochambeau, Nov. 23, 1803, box 1363, Rochambeau Papers, University of Florida Libraries; Duroc to Marie Bunel, April 18, 1812; note signed Cairou and dated from Philadelphia, Oct. 20, 1812; Grandjean to Joseph Bunel, October 1804, MSS.695, HSP.

9. Christophe to Joseph Bunel, Nov. 6, 1804; Comte de Limonade to Marie Bunel, Aug. 11, 1807, MSS.695, HSP; Marie-Louise to Madame Bunel, June 3, 1809, MS Haiti box 71, folder 1, BPL.

10. Marie-Louise Christophe to Madame Bunel, Sept. 3, 1810, MSS.695, HSP.

11. Christophe to Madame Bunel, June 12, 1810, MSS.695, HSP.

12. Vastey, *Essai*, 178.

13. Vastey, *Essai*, 178, 185, 186.

14. Dumesle, "Miscellannée," *L'observateur*, Dec. 1, 1819, 5; P.-P.-P. Duluc, *De Saint-Domingue, observations sur un article inséré dans le "Constitutionnel," le 31 août 1819* (Paris: Librairie du Mercure de France, 1819), 12.

15. "Ordre général de l'armée. Du jeudi 3 janvier 1811," Jan. 3, 1811, 1–3, Miscellaneous Claims vs. Haiti, folders 1–13, United States National Archives and Records Administration; Madiou, *Histoire d'Haïti*, 4:390–92.

16. Store Guard (*Garde Magasin*), possibly Charles Laverdure (per *Royal Almanach of 1814*), to Madame Bunel, April 18, 1812, HSP; *Almanach royal pour l'année 1814*, 102; see also Girard, "Trading Races," 376. Other Bunel family members appear to have continued to live in Haiti. A Marie-Sainte Bunel gave birth to a daughter in Grand-Goâve in 1830, for example. Birth notation for Marie-Louise Labissonière, June 24, 1830, État Civil d'Haïti, AGH.

17. Madiou, *Histoire d'Haïti*, 5:55–75. Christophe also named another of his ships *L'Athénaïre* after his other daughter. See Madiou, 5:56.

18. Madiou, *Histoire*, 5: 138–39; 154–55. Madiou then claimed that "many years ago," "eye and ear witnesses" told him that Christophe afterward gave a speech where he called for the "extermination" of every "mulatto" in Haiti. A print copy of the alleged speech has never been recovered.

19. Madiou, *Histoire*, 5:222.

20. See the collection of known issues of northern newspapers I have gathered at lagazetteroyale.com.

21. "État d'Hayti. Mandement. Corneille, préfet apostolique de l'État d'Haïti, au clergé et à tous ses fidèles [March 8, 1807]," *Gazette de l'État d'Hayti,* May 28, 1807, 15–16.

22. "État d'Hayti. Un mot, un seul, un dernier mot, de P. Corneille Brelle, préfet apostolique de l'État d'Hayti, au P. J. B. Jh Lemaire, curé, en réponse à son invitation pastoral," *Gazette de l'État d'Hayti,* Dec. 7, 1809, 193–95.

23. "Londres," *Gazette de l'État d'Hayti,* Nov. 23, 1809, 185–86; Ambrogio A. Caiani, "When the Pope Was in Prison," *Yale Books,* June 14, 2021, yalebooks .yale.edu.

24. Christophe to Pope Pius VII, signed by Limonade, June 10, 1814, 399AP/255, ANF.

25. Christophe to Pope Pius VII, signed by Limonade, April 12, 1811, 399AP/255, ANF. For the letter as dispatched to the archbishop of Palermo, see King Henry's letter above. For Peltier's role, see Cabon, *Notes sur l'histoire religieuse,* 103.

26. For the pope ignoring Christophe, see Beaubrun Ardouin, *Études sur l'histoire d'Haïti* (Paris: Chez L'Auteur, 1856), 7:409–10n1. Dessalines also reportedly wrote to Pius VII to "invite his holiness to undertake a voyage to the empire of Hayti," not simply to "celebrate a coronation and nuptials, but to administer to the Emperor Jacques and his Empress Josephine [*sic*] the sacrament of baptism." [Lewis Goldsmith Stewarton], *The Female Revolutionary Plutarch, Containing Biographical, Historical, and Revolutionary Sketches, Characters, and Anecdotes* (London: John Murray, 1806), 1:123.

27. Cabon, *Notes sur l'histoire religieuse,* 76; Christophe to Pope Pius VII, June 10, 1814.

28. "Rapports de l'évêque d'Anagni au cardinal Consalvi," n.d., 399AP/255, ANF. For Consalvi's importance to the pope, see Ambrogio Caiani, "Napoleon and the Church," in *The Cambridge History of the Napoleonic Wars,* vol. 1, ed. Michael Broers and Philip Dwyer (Cambridge, U.K.: Cambridge University Press, 2022), 257. See also "Consalvi," in *Biographie moderne; ou, Dictionnaire biographique,* 489.

29. "Coup d'oeil sur Hayti," as part of "Rapports de l'évêque."

30. Julia Gaffield, "The Racialization of International Law After the Haitian Revolution: The Holy See and National Sovereignty," *American Historical Review* 125, no. 3 (June 2020): 864.

31. "Du Cap-Henry, le 13 août," *Gazette Royale,* Aug. 14, 1817, 1; "Fête de Sa Majesté la Reine d'Hayti," *Gazette Royale,* Aug. 20, 1817, 1; *Almanach royal d'Hayti pour l'année 1817,* 3; *Almanach royal d'Hayti pour l'année 1818,* 2, 3; *Almanach royal d'Hayti pour l'année 1820,* 2.

32. Duluc, *De Saint-Domingue,* 12.

33. Duluc, *De Saint-Domingue,* 7, 11–12.

34. "De Saint-Domingue et de Christophe," *Le constitutionnel,* Aug. 31, 1819, 3.

35. Vastey, *Réflexions politiques,* 4–6.

36. Christophe to Brelle, Oct. 1, 1816, Manuscripts, Archives and Rare Books Division, Schomburg Center for Research in Black Culture, Henri Christophe Collection, New York Public Library Digital Collections, digitalcollections .nypl.org.

37. Christophe to Wilberforce, Nov. 18, 1816, in Robert Isaac Wilberforce and Samuel Wilberforce, eds., *The Correspondence of William Wilberforce, Edited by his Sons . . . in Two Volumes* (London: John Murray, 1840), 360.

38. "Du Cap-Henry, le 11 juillet," *Gazette royale,* July 19, 1819, 1.

39. Ritter, "Observations on the State of Hayti at the Conclusion of Christophe's Reign," Jan. 1, 1825, 23.

40. "Intérieur," *L'abeille haytienne: Journal politique et littéraire,* April 16, 1818, 9.

41. *Le télégraphe,* April 5, 1818, 1; for Pétion's fever, see "Intérieur," *L'abeille haytienne,* April 3, 1818, 4.

42. "Intérieur," *L'abeille haytienne,* April 3, 1818, 3–4.

43. *Le télégraphe,* April 5, 1818, 2–4.
44. "Intérieur," *L'abeille haytienne,* April 3, 1818, 6.
45. "Decret du Sénat, portant la nomination du Général de Division Boyer, à l'office de président d'Hayti," *Le télégraphe,* April 5, 1818, 4.
46. "Intérieur," *L'abeille haytienne,* April 3, 1818, 6–8.
47. Vastey, *Essai,* 386; "Intérieur," *L'abeille haytienne,* April 3, 1818, 4.
48. Vastey, *Essai,* 386–87.
49. Vastey, *Essai,* 386–88.
50. Letter from the king addressed to the generals and magistrates of the western and southern provinces assembled in Port-au-Prince, June 28, 1818, in *Collection de pièces relatives,* 136.
51. "Proclamation. Le roi, aux haytiens, de l'ouest et du sud," in *Collection de pièces relatives,* 133–35.
52. "Réflexions de l'éditeur," *Gazette royale,* March 31, 1818, 3.
53. "Les généraux, magistrats et chefs de corps de la République d'Hayti, réunis au Port-au-Prince, au Genéral Christophe," July 1, 1818, in *Collection de pièces relatives,* 138–39.
54. For the kingdom's response to Dumesle's paper, see "De Sans-Souci, le 25 octobre," *Gazette royale,* Oct. 28, 1819, 1; "Hayti," *Niles' Register,* Oct. 17, 1818, 124.
55. "Nécrologie," *Gazette royale,* Sept. 27, 1818, 1–2; "Le 1er novembre," *Gazette royale,* Nov. 5, 1818, 2.
56. See, for example, an announcement of the land policy in "De Sans Soucy, le 20 août," *Gazette royale,* Aug. 30, 1819, 1; for the land assignments, see "État des habitations qui ont été accordées par la Commission de vente et d'aliénation des biens domaniaux du royaume, aux personnes qui les ont soumissionnées," *Gazette royale,* Aug. 2, 1817, 4; for the schools, see "Du Limbé," *Gazette royale,* Sept. 10, 1819, 4; "Ordonnance du roi: *Sur la nouvelle organisation des finances,*" *Gazette royale,* Nov. 14, 1819, 3.
57. "Du Cap-Henry, le 28 août," *Gazette royale,* Aug. 30, 1819, 3.
58. "Du Cap-Henry, le 11 juillet," *Gazette royale,* July 19, 1819, 2.
59. "*Journaux de Paris, le 5 juillet,*" *Gazette royale,* Sept. 10, 1819, 4.
60. "Nouvelles preuves de la trahison de Pétion. Réflexions sur les moyens à employer pour éteindre la guerre civile sans effusion de Sang," *Gazette Royale,* Nov. 9, 1815, 2; Vastey, *Notes,* 24; see also Vastey, *Essai,* 384.
61. Limonade to Clarkson, Nov. 20, 1819, in *A Correspondence,* 173–77; Clarkson to Turckheim, March 11, 1820, Clarkson/160, St. John's College Library, Cambridge University.

CHAPTER 17: A KING IS GONE, BUT NOT FORGOTTEN

1. Wilson, *Le précepteur,* 66–69; "Port-au-Prince. Détails sur la mort de Christophe," *Le télégraphe,* Oct. 29, 1820, 1–2; Louis, *Marie-Louise d'Haïti,* 37–40.
2. "De Sans-Souci, le 18 juillet," *Gazette royale d'Hayti,* July 19, 1815, 4.
3. "De la chute de Christophe," *Le propagateur haïtien,* Oct. 1, 1822, 1–5.
4. See letter signed the Comte de Jérémie reprinted in Dumesle, "Nouvelles de l'armée expéditionnaire," *L'observateur,* Aug. 1, 1819, 6–7.
5. As the Comte de Jérémie, Goman had command over the second division of the "Province of the South," which comprised two arrondissements, including the parishes of Jérémie, Corail, Abricots, Cap-Dame-Marie, and L'Anse Dénau in the first and L'Anse-á-Veau, Petit-Trou des Baradères, and Miragoâne in the

second. *Almanach royal d'Hayti pour l'année 1817,* 61, 93. For Dumesle, see "Nouvelles de l'armée expéditionnaire," 6.

6. For Pétion's attempts, see Madiou, *Histoire d'Haïti,* 5:195–222; Dumesle, "Intérieur," *L'observateur,* June 1, 1819, 14.
7. Dumesle, "Nouvelles de l'armée expéditionnaire," 5.
8. Dumesle, "Intérieur," *L'observateur,* Nov. 1, 1819, 17.
9. Dumesle, "Intérieur," *L'observateur,* Dec. 1, 1819, 14.
10. "De la chute de Christophe," Oct. 1, 1822, 1–5; Camille Large, "Goman et l'insurrection de la Grand'Anse" (1939), in *Portraits et itinéraires,* ed. Michel Soukar (Port-au-Prince: Parténaire Principal, 2014), 22–31.
11. Quoted in "Défection et suicide de Christophe," *L'abeille haytienne,* June 15–Oct. 31, 1820, 73; "De la chute de Christophe," Oct. 1, 1822, 4.
12. "De la chute de Christophe," Oct. 1, 1822, 1–5; for Goman's rank, see Prévost, *Relation,* 70.
13. Prévost, *Relation,* 8–9.
14. "De la chute de Christophe," Oct. 1, 1822, 8.
15. "De la chute de Christophe," Oct. 1, 1822, 5; Boyer to Popham, n.d., ABP-1, Nemours Collection.
16. "De la chute de Christophe," Oct. 1, 1822, 7–9.
17. "Défection et suicide de Christophe," 75–76; "De la chute de Christophe," Oct. 1, 1822, 9.
18. "De la chute de Christophe," Oct. 1, 1822, 9.
19. Stewart to Clarkson, Dec. 8, 1820, Clarkson and Christophe Manuscript Correspondence; see also reprint in Griggs and Prator, *Correspondence,* 222.
20. Christophe to Comte de la Taste, July 6, 1820, ACH-21, Nemours Collection.
21. William Wilson to Sir Christopher Wilson, Oct. 1, 1820, Clarkson and Christophe Manuscript Correspondence.
22. William Wilson to Sir Christopher Wilson, Dec. 5, 1820, Clarkson and Christophe Manuscript Correspondence; see also reprint in Griggs and Prator, *Correspondence,* 22.
23. For his attachment to the prince, see William Wilson to Sir Christopher Wilson, Dec. 5, 1820, Clarkson and Christophe Manuscript Correspondence; for informing Clarkson, see Wilson to Clarkson, Nov. 4, 1820, Clarkson and Christophe Manuscript Correspondence; for Richard pillaging the palace, see Cabon, *Notes sur l'histoire religieuse,* 135.
24. Wilson to Clarkson, Dec. 5, 1820, in Griggs and Prator, *Correspondence,* 213–19. Another physician, Jabez Sheen Birt, who worked in the kingdom, also left an account later published by *Littel's Living Age.* See [Jabez Sheen Birt], "From the MS. Journal of one of his Physicians. The Last Hours of Christophe," *Littel's Living Age,* March 29, 1856, 799–804. For Birt identified as author, see Daut, *Baron de Vastey,* 56n32.
25. "De la chute de Christophe," Oct. 1, 1822, 10–11.
26. *Le propagateur haïtien,* Sept. 1, 1823, 6–7.
27. "Suite de l'article intitulé de la chute de Christophe," *Le propagateur haïtien,* July 1, 1823, 11–12; Wilson, *Le précepteur,* 65.
28. For 7:30, see "Mort du tyran et fin de la tyrannie," *Le télégraphe,* Oct. 22, 1820, 3; for 10:30, see Wilson to Clarkson, Dec. 5, 1820, in Griggs and Prator, *Correspondence,* 217–18; and Birt, "The Last Days of Christophe," 801.
29. Louis, *Marie-Louise d'Haïti,* 40.
30. Wilson, *Le précepteur,* 69; see also Wilson to Clarkson, Dec. 5, 1820, 217–18.

31. Wilson to Clarkson, Dec. 5, 1820, 218–19; "Mort du tyran et fin de la tyrannie," 1–2; Louis, *Marie-Louise d'Haïti,* 41.
32. Boyer, "Ordre du jour," reprinted in *Le télégraphe,* Oct. 22, 1820, 3; "Proclamation. Au peuple et à l'armée de L'Artibonite et du nord de Jean-Pierre Boyer, président d'Haïti," Oct. 16, 1820, reprinted in *Le télégraphe,* Oct. 29, 1820, 2–3; Boyer, "Proclamation. Aux Haytiens," Oct. 26, 1820, reprinted in *Le télégraphe,* Nov. 5, 1820, 3.
33. Johan Albrekt Abraham de Frese, unpublished manuscript, quoted in Thomasson, "Sweden and Haiti," 19.
34. Wilson to Clarkson, Dec. 5, 1820, Clarkson and Christophe Manuscript Correspondence; see also reprint in Griggs and Prator, *Correspondence,* 213–19.
35. Christophe allegedly had several illegitimate children whom he did not recognize. However, most Christophe chroniclers, following Leconte (who does not offer a chain of recitation), claim that Christophe had one daughter out of wedlock whom he did recognize named Blésine (or Blézine) Georges. This daughter is usually said to have wed a member of the Christophean nobility, Nord Alexis, who held the title chevalier of the royal and military order of Saint Henry. Their son, Pierre-Nord Alexis, went on to become president of Haiti from 1902 to 1908, before political opponents forced him into exile in Jamaica, where he died on May 1, 1910, at the age of ninety. At the time of President Alexis's death, the Anglophone press reported *not* that the deceased's mother had been Christophe's daughter, however, but that she was either the former king's, or, alternatively, Dessalines's "goddaughter." Leconte, *Henri Christophe,* 276; Cheesman, *Armorial,* 30; for the goddaughter claims, see, respectively, "The Tyrant Dead: Nord Alexis of Hayti Dead, Cruel Ruller [*sic*] Dies in Exile—Ninety Years Old," *Washington Bee,* May 14, 1910, 1; "Gen. Nord Alexis of Hayti Dead: Famous Negro Leader and An Ex-President," *Baltimore American,* May 2, 1910, 9.
36. Wilson to Mrs. Clarkson, Nov. 12, 1821, Clarkson and Christophe Manuscript Correspondence; see also reprint in Griggs and Prator, *Correspondence,* 233–36.
37. Stewart to Clarkson, Dec. 8, 1820, Clarkson and Christophe Manuscript Correspondence.
38. Wilson to Mrs. Clarkson, Nov. 12, 1821.
39. Wilson to Mrs. Clarkson, Jan. 30, 1822, Clarkson and Christophe Manuscript Correspondence.
40. See "Suite de la lettre du Général Prévost, à ses compatriotes de la partie de l'est d'Hayti," *La Concorde: Journal historique, politique et littéraire,* June 9, 1822, 89–91.
41. *Le télégraphe,* July 17, 1825, 4. A copy of the *Ordonnance* of the French king, Charles X, is reprinted on page 5 of the same issue. For Chanlatte's death, see death notation on October 13, 1828, État Civil de Port-au-Prince, AGH.
42. Louis, *Marie-Louise d'Haïti,* 39.
43. "Détails sur la mort de Christophe," *Le télégraphe,* Oct. 29, 1820, 2. There is also a facsimile engraving of the same painting, in black and white, but missing the portrait of the king in the background, along with a photo of the pistol owned by Christophe, reproduced in Wilson, *Le précepteur,* 67. Another iteration of the image appears with the caption "D'après une gravure populaire de l'époque," in Gabriel Hanotaux et al., *Histoire des colonies françaises et de l'expansion de la France dans le monde: L'Amérique* (Paris: Plon, 1929), 1:548.
44. Jean-Pierre Boyer, "Proclamation. Au peuple et à l'armée," *Le télégraphe,* Aug. 25, 1822, 2.

45. "Mort du tyran et fin de la tyrannie," 2–3.
46. Jean-Pierre Boyer, "Ordre du jour," *Le télégraphe,* Oct. 17, 1820, 3.
47. Boyer to Clarkson, July 30, 1821, Clarkson and Christophe Manuscript Correspondence.
48. Boyer, "Proclamation aux Haytiens," *Le télégraphe,* Nov. 2, 1820, 3.
49. Quoted in Louis, *Marie-Louise d'Haïti,* 43; see also Hénock Trouillot, "La République d'Haïti entre la francophonie et l'américanisme (19è siècle et du début du 20è)," *Revista de historia de América,* no. 80 (July–Dec. 1975): 87–145.
50. Marie Louise Christophe to Boyer, reprinted in *Le télégraphe,* Sept. 23, 1821, 4; for Marie-Louise's grandson, see Catherine Clarkson to Wilson, Feb. 22, 1842, Clarkson/175, St. John's College Library, Cambridge University.
51. J. C. Imbert, Guerrier, N. Segretier, and C. Hérard aîné, "Décret qui accorde une pension viagère à la veuve Jean-Jacques Dessalines," Aug. 21, 1843, HD-1C19, Nemours Collection; Lanier, "Claire Heureuse," 17.
52. [Stewarton], *Female Revolutionary Plutarch,* 133–34.
53. Baron de Vastey to Clarkson, November 1819, in Griggs and Prator, *Correspondence,* 181–82; For the name of Vastey's wife, see Quevilly, *Le Baron de Vastey,* 275; for Daut, see marriage notation for Pierre Deaux and Célestine Dessalines, April 10, 1817, État civil du Cap-Haïtien, AGH.
54. "Acte de décès de la veuve de Toussaint Louverture," reprinted in Alfred Nemours, *Histoire de la famille et de la descendance de Toussaint-Louverture, Avec des documents inédits et les portraits des descendants de Toussaint-Louverture jusqu'à nos jours* (Port-au-Prince: Imprimerie de l'État, 1941), 240.
55. "Extrait des jugements rendus par la Commission militaire, séant au Cap-Haytien," *La Concorde,* May 20, 1821, 5–6.
56. "Suite du voyage à Milot et à la Ferrière," *La Concorde,* June 10, 1821, 18–19.
57. "Memorandum of Information Received 24th August 1826 from Lieutenant Mr. H. Grary [?] Who Was in Saint Domingo in 1819-& in 1822," FO 35/1, f. 182 (1826), TNA.
58. "Suite du voyage à Milot et à la Ferrière," *La Concorde,* June 10, 1821, 18–19.

CHAPTER 18: KINGDOM OF THE NEXT WORLD

1. Quoted in "Madame Christophe," *The New Monthly Magazine and Literary Journal. Part 1. Original Papers* (London: Henry Colburn, 1828), 484.
2. *Journal du Gard,* Dec. 23, 1820, 400.
3. "National Policy," *Morning Chronicle,* Dec. 11, 1820.
4. "Revolution in St. Domingo," *Times,* Dec. 26, 1820, 2. *The Times* had earlier printed in English translation Boyer's proclamation of October 16, 1820, announcing the death of Christophe and the reunification of the north and south under his own rule. See, "Hayti," *Times,* Dec. 19, 1820, 2.
5. "From our Correspondent," *Commercial Advertiser,* May 7, 1818, 2; for the story's refutation, see *The Repertory,* May 12, 1818, 4.
6. "Important from Port-au-Prince," *The American,* Nov. 4, 1820, 2. The same article appeared over the next month in more than two dozen U.S. newspapers, including *The Boston Daily Advertiser, The New-England Palladium, Maine Intelligencer,* and *Edwardsville Spectator.*
7. "Hayti," *New-York Columbian,* Nov. 6, 1820, 2. See also "Extract from a Letter by the Weymouth, Dated Port-au-Prince, Oct. 10," *New-York Columbian,* Nov. 6, 1820, 3.
8. "The Late Queen of Hayti (Madame Christophe)," *Times,* Oct. 16, 1821, 2;

"Christophe Family. María-Luisa, Améthiste and Athenaïre. Haiti. Widow and Daughters of King Henri Christophe (1767–1820)," *Latin Americans in London: A Select List of Prominent Latin Americans in London, c. 1800–1996,* ed. Pam Decho and Claire Diamond (London: Institute of Latin American Studies, 1998); Nicole Willson, "A Black Queen in Georgian Britain," *History Today,* June 2022, 59–60.

9. "Mrs. Wilberforce calls her husband by that pretty diminutive 'Willy.' You must have heard her. D.W." Footnote from original letter.

10. Dorothy Wordsworth to Mrs. Clarkson, Oct. 24, [1822], in Daut, Pierrot, and Rohrleitner, *Haitian Revolutionary Fictions,* 916–17.

11. Quoted in Cora Kaplan, "Black Heroes/White Writers: Toussaint L'Ouverture and the Literary Imagination," *History Workshop Journal* 46 (1998): 45–46.

12. The grandson was Alessandro Ferdinando Eugenio (Alexandre Ferdinand Eugène), whom Marie-Louise listed as her universal heir in her will. Catherine Clarkson to William Wilson, Feb. 22, 1842, Clarkson/175, St. John's College Library, Cambridge University; "Will of Maria Luisa Christophe."

13. Jacqueline Bacon, "'A Revolution Unexampled in the History of Man': The Haitian Revolution in *Freedom's Journal,* 1827–1829," in *African Americans and the Haitian Revolution: Selected Essays and Historical Documents,* ed. Jacqueline Bacon and Maurice Jackson (New York: Routledge, 2010), 90.

14. For the first publication of the rumor, see "We Have Another Fact to State," *Athenian,* May 11, 1827, 3.

15. "From the Boston Columbian Centinel. Madame Christophe," *Freedom's Journal,* May 11, 1827.

16. Reprinted in "Madame Christophe," *Freedom's Journal,* July 4, 1828, 1; this article originated in the British *New Monthly Magazine and Literary Journal* under the title "Madame Christophe," on January 1, 1828. See pp. 481–85.

17. "Madame Christophe," *New Monthly Magazine and Literary Journal,* 481–85.

18. François-René de Chateaubriand, *Oeuvres complètes de Chateaubriand, annotées par Saint-Beuve, de l'Académie française, Mémoires d'Outre-Tombe,* vol. 6 (Paris: Garnier Frères, 1904), 151–52.

19. See the obituary for "Francesca Améthisse [*sic*]": "Italia, Granducato di Toscana Pisa 27. Ottobre. Necrologia," *Supplemento alla Gazzetta di Firenze,* Nov. 5, 1831; LeGrace Benson, "A Queen in Diaspora: The Sorrowful Exile of Queen Marie-Louise Christophe (1778, Ouanaminth [*sic*], Haiti–March 11, 1851, Pisa, Italy)," *Journal of Haitian Studies* 20, no. 2 (2014): 90–101; Alessandro Panajia, *Da Haïti al bel teatro dell'Arno pisano, L'amara vicenda umana di Marie-Louise Christophe Coidavid, regina di Haïti, in collaborazione e con traduzione in francese di Miriam Franchina* (Pisa: Edizioni ETS, 2023), 46–49.

20. "Account of Marie-Louise Christophe in Pisa by Sir Robert Inglis (October 20, 1840)," Fanm Rebèl, www.fanmrebel.com.

21. Letter reproduced in Pierre-Eugène de Lespinasse, *Gens d'autrefois . . . Vieux souvenirs,* vol. 1 (Paris: Éditions de la Revue Mondiale, 1926), 55; see also Panajia, *Da Haïti,* 50–52.

22. For Black women as victims of European scientific observation, see Robin Mitchell, *Vénus Noire: Black Women and Colonial Fantasies in Nineteenth-Century France* (Athens: University of Georgia Press, 2020), introduction and chapter 2.

23. Panajia, *Da Haïti,* 45, 51–52; "Will of Maria Luisa Christophe."

24. Miriam Franchina, "Revolutionary Royalty: Remembering Queen Marie-Louise of Haiti in Pisa," *Age of Revolutions* blog, Aug. 7, 2023.

25. "Madame Christophe (from the New Monthly Magazine)," *London and Paris Observer*, May 18, 1828, 312–15; "Madame Christophe (from a Late English Paper)," *Rhode-Island American and Providence Gazette*, July 1, 1828; "Di Maria Teresa, ex-regina d'Haïti. Aneddoto di storia contemporanea. Estratto dalla Rivista Britannica, marzo 1828," *Giornale di scienze, letteratura ed arti per la Sicilia* 23–24 (1828): 195–206; "Madama Cristoforo (relazione d'un inglese)," *L'eco: Giornale di scienze, lettere, arti, commercio e teatri*, June 4, 1828, 265–67; "Madame Christophe, ex-reine d'Haïti," *Revue britannique*, April 1828, 331–42; on the French version, see Grégory Pierrot, ed., *Toussaint Louverture et après: Anthologie* (Paris: L'Harmattan, 2022), xviii.

26. *Times*, May 16, 1828, 4.

27. "Sales by Auction," *Times*, Jan. 28, 1822, 4; "Sales by Auction," *Times*, Jan. 30, 1822, 4.

28. Thanks to the efforts of Nicole Willson, a commemorative plaque has been affixed to the exterior of Marie-Louise and her daughters' former residence in London on Weymouth. See "London Blue Plaque Unveiling for Marie-Louise Christophe," at *Fanm Rebèl*, April 30, 2024, www.fanmrebel.

29. "Sales by Auction," *Times*, Sept. 24, 1824, 4. See also Nicole Willson, "A Haitian Queen," 57.

30. "Prince Christophe, Brother of Late King of Haiti, Seeks Assistance," CO 318/135, TNA. For the bank deposits, see Willson, "A Haitian Queen," 57.

31. Louis Alexandre Henri Christophe to Lord Glenelg, July 8, 1838, CO 318/135, TNA.

32. Louis Alexandre Henri Christophe (Memorial seeking property of his late brother King Christophe of Haiti), CO 318/129, TNA; L. A. H. Christophe to Glenelg, July 30, 1838, CO 318/135, TNA.

33. "June 3rd. Mr. L. A. H. Christophe," CO 318/315, TNA.

34. "Prince Christophe, Brother of Late King of Haiti, Seeks Assistance."

35. Comte de Limonade to Baron de Dupuy, Aug. 1, 1817, reprinted in *Gazette Royale d'Hayti*, Oct. 10, 1817, 1–2.

36. "We Find in the London Times the Following Report of a Curious Scene in the Police Court," *National Anti-slavery Standard*, Nov. 30, 1848, 108.

37. Letter reprinted in Lespinasse, *Gens d'autrefois*, 78–82.

38. Pierre-Jean de Béranger, "La mort du Roi Christophe, notice présentée par la noblesse d'Haïti aux trois grands alliées"; document signed by Baron Édouard Mounier, Jan. 12, 1821; report from Baron Édouard Mounier, Oct. 23, 1821; 234AP/1-2, ANF.

39. Clint Bruce, ed. and trans., *Afro-Creole Poetry in French from Louisiana's Radical Civil War–Era Newspapers* (New Orleans: Historic New Orleans Collection, 2020), 17.

40. In French, *Lettre au roi sur l'indépendance de la République d'Haïti et l'abolition de l'esclavage dans les colonies françaises*. "Brochure saisi à Paris," Préfecture de l'Oise, April 16, 1821; see also censorship documented from the prefectures of the departments of Vax, April 30, 1821; Nièvre, May 4, 1821; Gers, April 27, 1821; Bordeaux, April 20, 1821, etc. F/7/4333, ANF.

41. Ministère de l'Intérieur, Direction Générale de l'Administration départementale et de la Police, Libraire, *Lettre au roi sur l'indépendance de la République d'Haïti et sur l'abolition de l'esclavage dans les colonies françaises, par Civique de Gastine. Paris, Chez Renaudière*, April 4, 1821, F/7/4333, ANF.

42. "Intérieur. Obsèques de feu Civique de Gastines," *Le télégraphe*, June 16, 1822, 1.

43. Daut, Pierrot, and Rohrleitner, "J. H. Amherst," in *Haitian Revolutionary Fictions*, 65–67; "Royal Coburg Theatre," *Morning Chronicle*, Feb. 8, 1821; "The Mirror of Fashion," *Morning Chronicle*, July 13, 1821; "Coburg Theatre," *Times*, Feb. 10, 1821, 3; "Royal Coburg Theatre," *Times*, May 1, 1821, 3; "Royal Coburg Theatre," *Times*, Oct. 20, 1829, 2; "Royal Coburg Theatre," *Times*, March 2, 1831, 3.

44. Daut, *Tropics of Haiti*, 261n8.

45. "Books Published This Day," *Times*, Feb. 16, 1821, 4.

46. Marriage notation for Marie-Jeanne and Jacques Coidavi [*sic*], État-civil du Cap-Français, Oct. 30, 1778, ANOM. For Zulica as popularized, exotic name, see Julia V. Douthwaite, *Exotic Women: Literary Heroines and Cultural Strategies in Ancien Régime France* (Philadelphia: University of Pennsylvania Press, 1992), 164–70.

47. [Jean-Baptiste] Roman, "La mort de Christophe, tragédie," *Le propagateur haïtien*, Sept. 15, 1823, 17–18.

48. "Le prince d'éventail," *Le courrier*, Sept. 27, 1842, 1–2.

49. Schoelcher, *Colonies étrangères et Haïti*, 2:242.

50. Schoelcher, *Colonies étrangères et Haïti*, 2:154.

51. Limonade to Clarkson, Nov. 20, 1819, in Griggs and Prator, *Correspondence*, 175.

EPILOGUE: THE GREATEST HEIST IN HISTORY

1. "Circulaire. Jean-Pierre Boyer, président d'Haïti, aux commandants d'arrondissement," *Le télégraphe*, Oct. 9, 1824, 1.

2. "Recognition of the Independence of the Republic of Hayti by the French Government," *American Monitor* (London: 1824–1825): 2:276–77; "Haïti reconnue indépendante," *Le télégraphe*, July 17, 1825, 1–2.

3. "Ordonnance de Sa Majesté le roi de France," *Le télégraphe*, July 17, 1825, 5.

4. "Circulaire. Jean-Pierre Boyer, président d'Haïti, aux commandants d'arrondissement," 1.

5. "Proclamation au peuple et à l'armée," *Le télégraphe*, July 17, 1825, 5.

6. Vastey, *Réflexions sur une lettre de Mazères*, 90.

7. Nicolas-Vigor Renaudière, "The Haitian Canto: Homage to His Majesty, Charles X, on the Occasion of the Emancipation of Haiti," trans. Marlene L. Daut et al., in Daut, Pierrot, and Rohrleitner, *Haitian Revolutionary Fictions*, 878–79; see also, in the same volume, poems by Joseph Joachim Victor Chauvet, "Haiti, Lyrical Song," 232–36, and the anonymous "Ode to His Majesty Charles X on the Emancipation of Saint-Domingue," 43–46.

8. "Intérieur," *Le télégraphe*, Nov. 13, 1825, 2–3. See insert for Signet and Develly images.

9. Chauvet, "Haiti, Lyrical Song."

10. There are numerous ads for "maroon negroes" stamped Chanlatte, Chanlat, Chanlate, or some variation thereof, in the *Affiches américaines*. See, for example, "Nègres marons," *Affiches américaines*, May 26, 1778, 162; and perhaps most notably on October 5, 1782, an ad described group marronage from the Chanlatte plantation in Montrouis when the month before "five maroons" tried to escape by canoe. "Esclaves en marronage," *Supplément aux Affiches américaines*, Oct. 5, 1782, 4. For Chanlatte's family history, see Grégory Pierrot, "Juste Chanlatte: A Haitian Life," *Journal of Haitian Studies* 25, no.1 (Spring 2019): 39–65; for a discussion of the common phenomenon of group marron-

age, see Crystal Nicole Eddins, *Rituals, Runaways, and the Haitian Revolution: Collective Actions in the African Diaspora* (Cambridge, U.K.: Cambridge University Press, 2022).

11. Chanlatte, *À mes concitoyens*, 6.

12. Chanlatte, *Le cri de la nature*, 5.

13. Chanlatte, "Les vingt premiers jours du mois d'octobre 1820 an 17: Est-ce un rêve?," *Le télégraphe*, Nov. 5, 1820, 4; Chanlatte, *Henry Christophe*. See also Pierrot, "Juste Chanlatte."

14. "Le Général Chanlatte a chanté les suivans," *Le propagateur haïtien*, Jan. 15, 1826, 7–8.

15. Désiré Dalloz et al., *Consultation de MM. Dalloz, Hennequin, Dupin jeunes et autres jurisconsultes pour les anciens colons de Saint-Domingue* (Paris: Imprimerie de Vve Agasse, 1829), 19, 60–61.

16. Dumesle, *Voyage*, 340 note o.

17. Ministère de la Marine et des Colonies; Cabinet du Ministre (Très Secrete), Paris, April 17, 1825, AP/156/I/20, ANF.

18. Boyer acknowledged this in his letter to Popham, n.d., ABP-1, Nemours Collection.

19. Rapports d'informateurs, folder 2, document 224, n.d., 234AP/1-2, ANF.

20. "France and Hayti," *Niles' Register*, Oct. 9, 1824, 85.

21. Dorvelas Dorval, *Pièces officielles relatives aux négociations du gouvernement français avec le gouvernement haïtien, pour traiter de la formalité de la reconnaissance de l'indépendance d'Haïti* (Port-au-Prince: Imprimerie du Gouvernement, 1824), 83–84; see also Liliana Obregón, "Empire, Racial Capitalism, and International Law: The Case of Manumitted Haiti and the Recognition Debt," *Leiden Journal of International Law* 31 (2018): 597–609.

22. "Recognition of the Independence of the Republic of Hayti by the French Government," *The American Monitor* (London, 1825), 268; see also Gaffield, "Racialization of International Law After the Haitian Revolution."

23. Dalloz et al., *Consultation*, 26–27.

24. "Recognition of the Independence of the Republic of Hayti by the French Government," 270; *Times*, Aug. 5, 1825, 2.

25. "Proclamation au peuple et à l'armée," *Le télégraphe*, July 17, 1825.

26. "Traités entre Hayti & La France: Au nom de la Très Sainte et Indivisible Trinité," *L'union, recueil commercial et littéraire*, Feb. 15, 1838, 1–2; A.M., *Emprunt d'Haïti* (Paris: Imprimerie de Sétier, 1831), 2.

27. *New Hampshire Sentinel*, Feb. 15, 1838; "Latest from England," *New Bedford Mercury*, Feb. 2, 1838; "Important from Hayti," *Pennsylvania Freeman*, March 15, 1838; for the unpopularity of the indemnity, see "Hayti and France," *Zion's Watchman*, April 7, 1838, 56.

28. "Recognition of the Independence of the Republic of Hayti by the French Government," 268.

29. "Jean-Pierre Boyer, President of Hayti, *To the Haytiens!*," reprinted and translated in *Augusta Chronicle*, April 19, 1826.

30. Anténor Firmin, *M. Roosevelt, président des États-Unis et la République d'Haïti* (Paris: F. Pichon and Durand-Auzias, 1905), 325.

31. Schoelcher, *Colonies étrangères et Haïti*, 2:276; see also Daut, *Awakening the Ashes*, 268.

32. Anthony Phillips, "Haiti, France, and the Independence Debt of 1825," canada-haiti.ca.

33. Thomas Laline, " 'Au minimum, la France devrait rembourser plus de 28 mil-

liards de dollars américains à Haïti aujourd'hui,' soutient le célèbre économiste français Thomas Piketty," *Le nouvelliste,* Jan. 20, 2020, www.lenouvelliste.com.

34. Catherine Porter et al., "Haiti 'Ransom' Project," *New York Times,* Nov. 16, 2022, www.nytimes.com.

35. Demesvar Delorme, *La misère au sein des richesses: réflexions diverses sur Haïti* (Paris: E. Dentu, 1873), 8–9.

36. Delorme, *1842 au Cap,* 22.

37. Quoted in Joachim, "L'indemnité coloniale de Saint-Domingue et la question des rapatriés," 362.

38. "Haiti: Aristide's Call for Reparations from France Unlikely to Die," Inter Press Service News Agency, March 12, 2004, www.ipsnews.net; Robinson Geffrard, "Nicolas Sarkozy et ses promesses," *Le nouvelliste,* Feb. 17, 2010, www.lenouvelliste.com; Frank James, "France's Sarkozy Tells Haitians They 'Are Not Alone,' " NPR, Feb. 17, 2010, www.npr.org.

39. Kim Oosterlinck et al., "A Debt of Dishonor," *Boston University Law Review* 102 (2022): 1250n5, www.bu.edu.

40. Peter Hallward, letters in response to Paul Farmer's "Who Removed Aristide from Power?," *London Review of Books,* May 6, 2004, www.lrb.co.uk.

41. Porter et al., "Haiti 'Ransom' Project."

42. Nicolas Rossier and Cathryn Atkinson, "Aristide on Haiti's Earthquake, Cholera, the Election, Reparation, and Exile," Rabble.ca, Nov. 13, 2010.

43. Stéphanie Trouillard, "Hollande's Vow to Settle 'Debt' to Haiti Sparks Confusion," France 24, May 12, 2015, www.france24.com.

44. Phillips, "Haiti, France, and the Independence Debt of 1825," 1; Jacqueline Charles, "Aristide Pushes for Restitution from France," *Miami Herald,* Dec. 18, 2003; "Hollande Promises to Pay 'Moral Debt' to Former Colony," *Guardian,* May 12, 2015, www.theguardian.com.

45. "05 July Poverty Rates in France," Break Poverty Foundation, breakpoverty.com.

46. Henri Martin, "La consommation des ménages dans la France d'outre-mer: Quelles disparités avec la métropole?," *Études caribéennes* 37–38 (Aug.–Dec. 2017), journals.openedition.org.

47. "IFRC Country Acceleration Plan 2019—Haiti," Feb. 28, 2019, Relief Web, reliefweb.int.

48. "Poverty," Global Security, www.globalsecurity.org.

49. Hyeyoon (Alyssa) Choi, "How Colonial-Era Debt Helped Shape Haiti's Poverty and Political Unrest," ABC News, July 21, 2021, abcnews.go.com.

50. "United States," *Morning Chronicle,* June 15, 1842.

51. Delorme, *1842 au Cap,* 33.

52. Delorme, *1842 au Cap,* 33–34.

53. Charlotte Hughes, "Drama on Haiti's Citadel: Country's Stirring Past Made Real for Tourists by Orator M. Louis Mercier," *New York Times,* March 30, 1941; Henry Louis Gates Jr., *Black in Latin America* (New York: New York University Press, 2011), 169.

INDEX

ILLUSTRATION CREDITS

Thomas Jeffreys, Geographer to the King, "Carte de d'isle de la Grenade, cédée à la Grande Bretagne par le dernier traité de paix/Grenada Divided into Its Parishes, Surveyed by Order of His Excellency Governor Scott," February 1775. David Rumsey Historical Map Collection.

Pierre Ozanne and Nicolas, "Siège de Savannah, fait par les troupes du roi aux ordres de Monsieur le Comte d'Estaing, vice amiral de France en septembre et octobre 1779" (Siege of Savannah, undertaken by the king's troops upon the orders of the Comte d'Estaing, vice admiral of France in September and October 1779), Bibliothèque Nationale de France.

Jean-Antoine Pierron, "Carte géographique, statistique et historique de Haity. Hayti ou Ile St. Domingue. Dressée d'apres la carte du Chevalier Lapie par Pierron. Gravé par B. Beaupré, rue de Vaugirard, No. 81, à Paris," 1825. David Rumsey Historical Map Collection.

The Haitian Monument on Franklin Square, Savannah, Georgia. Author's photograph, December 2021.

Battle of Savannah Monument in Franklin Square, Savannah, Georgia. Author's photograph, December 2021.

René Phelipeau, "Plan de la ville du Cap François et de ses environs dans l'isle de St. Domingue," 1786, Bibliothèque Nationale de France.

"Carte topographique de la région du Cap-Français et du Fort-Dauphin, au nord-est de la colonie française ou St. Domingue," 1760, Bibliothèque Nationale de France.

"Plan des habitations de la citoyenne Suzanne, épouse de Toussaint Louverture, général en chef de l'armée de Saint-Domingue," July 1799, 10 DPPC 149, ANOM.

"Façade du côté de la Place d'Armes, de la maison de Christophe," February 1802, 10 DPPC 98, ANOM.

"Plan du rez de chaussé et de premier étage de la maison de Christophe, sise Place d'Armes et rue d'Égalité, le numéro 312," February 1802, 10 DPPC 98, ANOM.

"Bail à ferme à la maison no. 326," December 31, 1794, 10 DPPC 138, ANOM.

Handwritten and personally signed letter from Henry Christophe to "Citizen Magistrate of Port-au-Prince," December 4, 1793, Fondo Campori della Biblioteca Estense, Modena, Italy.

Letter from Henry Christophe, Chef de Brigade, Military Commander and Inspector, to Commissioner Julien Raimond, August 12, 1797, 10 DPPC 92, ANOM.

Henry Christophe, General in Chief of the Haitian Army, to His Majesty, the Emperor, July 13, 1806, box 1, folder 2, Haiti Collection, CHS.

Joseph S. Warin, "Plan de la ville du Cap Français sur lequel sont marqués en teinte noire les ravages du premier incendie, et en rouge les islets, parties d'islets, édifices, etc. qui existent encore le 21 juin 1793," ca. 1793, Bibliothèque Nationale de France.

Vincent, "Plan de l'état actuel de la ville du Cap servant à indiquer les progrès de ses reconstructions," 1800, Bibliothèque Nationale de France.

Vincent, "Plan de l'état actuel de la ville du Cap servant à indiquer les progrès de ses reconstructions," 1800, Bibliothèque Nationale de France.

"Christophe: Incendiaire de la ville du Cap dont il était commandant en chef," ca. 1802, Bibliothèque Nationale de France.

Coat of Arms of King Henry Christophe, MS J.P. 177, fol. 1r., College of Arms, London. Reproduced by permission of the Kings, Heralds, and Pursuivants of Arms.

The Citadelle in Milot, Haiti. Rotorhead 30A Productions, Shutterstock Photo ID: 1296175855.

Citadelle Laferrière (Henry), northern Haiti. Author's photograph, October 2021.

Citadelle Laferrière (Henry), northern Haiti. Author's photograph, October 2021.

Citadelle Laferrière (Henry), northern Haiti. Author's photograph, October 2021.

Direction générale des travaux publics, "Citadelle Henri Christophe, Plan No. 6," Acervos Documentales de Puerto Rico y el Caribe, University of Puerto Rico–Río Piedras, ca. 20th century.

Numa Desroches, *Vue du palais d'Henry Christophe à Sans-Souci* (View of the palace of Henry Christophe in Sans-Souci), ca. 1816–18. Photograph courtesy of Sotheby's, Inc.© 2024.

Bust of Unknown Woman/Goddess or Muse, Palais de Sans-Souci, Milot, Haiti. Author's photograph, October 2021.

Original antique broadside print by Torchiana and Dridier depicting Haitian king Henry Christophe, ca. 1813. Author's personal collection.

Les enfants du Roi Henry Christophe, portrait de Jacques Victor-Henry, Prince Royal d'Hayti, et ses soeurs, Améthyste-Henry et Anne Athénaïs (The children of King Henry Christophe, portrait of Jacques Victor-Henry, the royal prince of Haiti, and his sisters, Améthyste-Henry and Anne Athénaïs), 24 x 20, oil on canvas, ca. 1811–20. Collection Musée du Panthéon National Haïtien, Port-au-Prince, Haiti.

Richard Evans (1784–1871), *Prince Victor Henry, Prince Royal of Haiti,* Acervos Documentales de Puerto Rico y el Caribe, University of Puerto Rico–Río Piedras, 1816.

Richard Evans (1784–1871), *His Majesty Henry Christophe, King of Haiti,* Acervos Documentales de Puerto Rico y el Caribe, University of Puerto Rico–Río Piedras, 1816.

Unknown author, *Portrait of the Death of Henry Christophe, King of Haiti,* ca. 19th century. Private collection and by courtesy of LeGrace Benson.

"Mort de Christophe (D'après une gravure populaire de l'époque)," in Gabriel Hanotaux and Alfred Martineau, *Histoire des colonies françaises et de l'expansion de la France dans le monde* (Paris: Librairie Plon, 1929), 1:548.

Photograph of the headstone over the tomb of the Christophe women, San Donnino Chapel, Pisa, Italy. Author's photograph, April 2022.

William West, Sketches, Drawn After J. H. Amherst's *Death of Christophe,* 1824. British Museum, London.

Photograph of the ruins of Sans-Souci palace, Milot, Haiti. Author's photograph, October 2021.

"Le 11 juillet 1825, L'ordonnance de S.M. Charles X, qui reconnait l'indépendance d'Haïti est reçu par le Président Boyer, aux acclamations de toutes les classes d'habitans de l'isle" (On July 11, 1825, the ordinance of His Majesty Charles X, recognizing the independence of Haiti, was received by President Boyer, to the acclamations of all classes of inhabitants of the island), 1825, Bibliothèque Nationale de France, QG-3-FOL.

"S.M. Charles X, le Bien-Aimé, reconnaissant l'indépendance de St. Domingue" (His Majesty, Charles X, the Beloved, recognizing the independence of St. Domingue), 1825, Bibliothèque Nationale de France, Cabinet des Estampes.

Eugène-Ferdinand Buttura (1812–1852), "Cap Français. Saint Domingue," Acervos Documentales de Puerto Rico y el Caribe, University of Puerto Rico–Río Piedras.

"Portrait of Toussaint L'Ouverture," Schomburg Center for Research in Black Culture, Photographs and Prints Division, New York Public Library Digital Collections. 1830–39.

"Jean-Jacques Dessalines, fondateur de l'indépendance d'Haïti" (Jean-Jacques Dessalines, founder of the independence of Haiti), Schomburg Center for Research in

Black Culture, Jean Blackwell Hutson Research and Reference Division, New York Public Library Digital Collections. 1888.

S. G. Goodrich, "Christophe Crowned King of Haiti," in *A Pictorial History of America; Embracing Both the Northern and Southern Portions of the New World, Illustrated with More Than Three Hundred Engravings* (Hartford: House & Brown, 1848).

"Pétion, président d'Haïti (1807–1818)," Schomburg Center for Research in Black Culture, Jean Blackwell Hutson Research and Reference Division, New York Public Library Digital Collections, 1888.

René Périn, *L'incendie du Cap; ou, Le règne de Toussaint-Louverture, où l'on développe le caractère de ce chef de révoltés, sa conduite atroce depuis qu'il s'est arrogé le pouvoir, la bassesse de tous ses agens, la férocité de Christophe, un de ses plus fermes soutiens, les malheurs qui sont venus fondre sur le Cap, la marche de l'armée française, et ses succès sous les ordres du capitaine général Leclerc* (The burning of Cap; or, the reign of Toussaint-Louverture, in which the character of this rebel leader is developed, his atrocious conduct since he assumed power, the baseness of all his agents, the ferocity of Christophe, one of his strongest supporters, the misfortunes that befell Cap, the march of the French army, and its successes under the command of Captain General Leclerc) (Paris: Chez Marchand, 1802).

Anonymous, *Débarquement de la flotte française à Saint-Domingue, faisant suite aux révolutions de cette île; révolte des nègres: événemens déplorables de la guerre desastreuse qui suivit le débarquement; second incendie du Cap par les noirs; massacre et destruction presque générale de l'armée et des colons; avec un précis historique de l'érection de cette île en Royaume d'Haïti* (The landing of the French fleet in Saint-Domingue, subsequent to the revolutions on that island; revolt of the Negroes: deplorable events of the disastrous war that followed the landing; second burning of Cap by the blacks; massacre and almost general destruction of the army and the colonists; with a detailed history of the transformation of this island into the Kingdom of Haiti) (Paris: Tiger, 1816). Bibliothèque Nationale de France, 8-LK12-559.

A NOTE ABOUT THE AUTHOR

Marlene L. Daut is professor of French and African Diaspora Studies at Yale University. She teaches courses in anglophone, francophone Caribbean, African American, and French colonial literary and historical studies. She has written for *The New Yorker, The New York Times, The Nation, Essence,* and *Harper's Bazaar.* She lives with her family in New Haven, Connecticut.

A NOTE ON THE TYPE

The text of this book was set in Sabon, a typeface designed by Jan Tschichold (1902–1974), the well-known German typographer. Based loosely on the original designs by Claude Garamond (ca. 1480–1561), Sabon is unique in that it was explicitly designed for hot-metal composition on both the Monotype and Linotype machines as well as for filmsetting. Designed in 1966 in Frankfurt, Sabon was named for the famous Lyons punch cutter Jacques Sabon, who is thought to have brought some of Garamond's matrices to Frankfurt.

Composed by North Market Street Graphics,
Lancaster, Pennsylvania

Printed and bound by Lakeside Book Company,
Harrisonburg, Virginia

Designed by Michael Collica